STUTTERING

A Second Symposium

Under the advisory editorship of J. JEFFERY AUER

STUTTERING

A Second Symposium

Jon Eisenson, Editor

Scottish Rite Institute for Childhood Aphasia
San Francisco State University

Harper & Row, Publishers

New York, Evanston, San Francisco, London

Sponsoring Editor: *Michael E. Brown*
Project Editor: *Alice M. Solomon*
Designer: *Frances Torbert Tilley*
Production Supervisor: *Francis X. Giordano*

Library of Congress Cataloging in Publication Data
Eisenson, Jon, 1907–   ed.
    Stuttering: a second symposium.

    Includes index.
    1. Stuttering. I. Title. [DNLM: 1. Stuttering.
WM475   S937]
RC424.E35   1975   616.8′554   75-19478
ISBN 0-06-041882-6

Contents

Foreword

In the introduction to *Stuttering: A Symposium* (1958), Wendell Johnson compared the problems of stuttering and the search for its cause to the parable of the blind men and the elephant. Each investigator, working without the benefit of total vision, "saw" (perceived) the nature of the animal according to the part of the elephant's anatomy he happened to grasp. It may well be that, despite the passing of the years since the first symposium was published, we have not moved much closer to deciding the nature of the beast. But we do know appreciably more about its behavior and peculiar habits. To avoid the dangers of extending the analogy, today we have fewer clinicians concerned with the etiology of stuttering and proportionately more concerned with the modification of the behavior identified as stuttering.

The change in attitude and emphasis may be associated with a larger movement among therapists who deal with human behavior problems to get away from the medical model and move toward another model, not always specifically or clearly identified, that might be more positively therapeutic for the client. The medical model presumably tries, by "orthodox" medical means, to deal with illness by arriving at a diagnosis of the underlying pathology (possible cause) before prescribing for the symptoms. Most speech (language) pathologists, despite the name of the profession they are identified with, are today less concerned with possible cause than they are with amelioration of symptoms, if not of cure. Most, but not all! There are still a few, of whom the editor is one, who hold to the belief that if we can discover the cause we will be in a better position to prescribe or administer therapy than if we deal with symptom modification and give up the search for the cause. This position does not argue against doing whatever we can for stutterers in terms of modifying the specific symptoms of stuttering as well as the associated behaviors that may generate from individual stutterers' reactions to their stutterings. The proponents of this position may also accept the proposition that initiating causes may be different from maintaining causes, that what keeps stuttering going may be different in dynamics from what may have been responsible for its onset.

Stuttering: A Second Symposium contains three essays by contributors to the first symposium who have modified and updated their points of view in terms of new evidence pertaining to their original positions. These contributors are Oliver Bloodstein, Joseph Sheehan, and Jon Eisenson. Charles Van Riper, also one of the original authors, chose to write on a subject different than that of his first essay; the present essay does not deal with theory or the specifics of therapy, but with the role of the stutterer's clinician. The new contributors are Gene Brutten, Roger Ingham, and George Shames. The reader may note a similarity among the authors in point of view as to the treatment of stuttering behavior. The editor recognized this similarity but felt that the individual emphases vary enough that this symposium would be enhanced in value and scholarly significance by their inclusion.

If we were to categorize the contributions as to theoretic beliefs regarding the cause or causes of stuttering, three positions would emerge. The first is that stuttering is a learned form of behavior which has its onset in early childhood and often continues into the adolescent and adult years. The therapeutic implication of this position is that *what has been learned can be unlearned and replaced by individually and culturally more acceptable behavior.* A second and related position is that stuttering is a manifestation of an approach-avoidance conflict. Therapeutically, stuttering is best treated by dealing with the individual and the nature and causes of his personal roles and conflicts that involve speaking conducive to stuttering. A third position is that stuttering is associated with essential organic (central nervous system) differences, a least during the years when language is acquired and possibly into adult life. Although we are not likely to be able to rid the individual of his "slightly" deviant nervous system, we can help him deal with the forces and manifestations of his organic makeup.

The "directive" to each contributor was to write an essay that presents his point of view about problems and issues involved in stuttering. Each contributor was encouraged to say what he has to say his own way, with a minimum of restraint in regard to format. The result of the directive is this symposium. We hope that it will be as well received as the first symposium. We regret that all of the contributors to the first symposium are no longer with us to be invited to write essays for the present effort.

Therefore, *Stuttering: A Second Symposium* is dedicated to the memory of Doctors I. Peter Glauber, Wendell Johnson, and Robert West. Somehow we feel that what they had to say has not been ignored in the present writing. Sincerely, we wish they could have spoken for themselves.

Jon Eisenson

Stuttering as Tension and Fragmentation

Oliver Bloodstein, Ph.D.

Professor of Speech, Brooklyn College; member of the doctoral faculty, City University of New York. Fellow, American Speech and Hearing Association. Author of *A Handbook on Stuttering*. Contributor to professional journals including the *Journal of Speech and Hearing Disorders,* the *Journal of Speech and Hearing Research,* the *Journal of Communication Disorders,* and the *British Journal of Disorders of Communication.*

Introduction

The view to be presented in this chapter may be summed up by saying that stuttering is a struggle reaction which reflects the speaker's moment of doubt about his ability to say a word or other element of speech and has its origin mainly in early experiences of speech failure or histories of speech pressure. The act of stuttering is caused essentially by something the stutterer wrongly thinks is so. It is not to be treated in most cases as a neurosis, a deficiency in skill, or even primarily as an undesirable habit; rather, it is to be treated in the same ways we might use to change the distorted human behavior we attribute to dogma, superstition, prejudice, or assumptions that are contrary to fact.

This is not the first such theory of stuttering. The essential idea of anticipatory struggle goes back a long way into the history of thought about the disorder. Like most of its predecessors, however, the anticipatory struggle theory we will develop here has distinguishing features of its own. They may be stated as follows:

1. Stuttering consists, in essence, of tensions and fragmentations in speech.
2. In behavioral terms, it may be described as a response to stimuli representative of past speech failure.
3. The ultimate origins of stuttering are to be found in tensions and fragmentations in the speech of most normal young children. What is called stuttering in early childhood differs from these tensions and fragmentations chiefly in degree (the continuity hypothesis).
4. Virtually any persistent form of communicative failure or difficulty may serve as a provocation to increased tension and fragmentation in a child's speech.
5. Such provocations tend to operate most powerfully in the presence of environmental speech pressures.

I. THE MOMENT OF STUTTERING

An adequate theory of stuttering must explain both the moment of stuttering and the origin, or etiology, of the disorder. These are two quite different things. In the first case we are asking why a stutterer, having spoken normally for so many seconds, minutes, or longer, suddenly repeats, prolongs, or blocks on a sound again. What is our conceptual model of this isolated event with reference to which we may explain its immediate cause? In the second case we are asking how the stutterer acquired his disorder—the conditions under which he first began to stutter weeks, months, or years before. We will begin this chapter by considering the moment of stuttering.

In general terms, the hypothesis that we will elaborate is that stutterers exert themselves in their speech attempts in varied and unusual ways on the assumption that this is what they must do to carry their attempts out successfully. They behave as though they have acquired a belief in the difficulty of speech, or of specific speech segments, and appear to struggle against an imagined obstacle in the process of articulation. An especially good way to frame this concept of the moment of stuttering is to say that it is a reaction of tension or fragmentation resulting from the threat of failure in the performance of an automatic, serially ordered activity.

Tension and Fragmentation
in Speech

What, precisely, is a stuttering block? I believe there is a fairly simple answer to this question that makes virtually the whole range of integral features of stuttering intelligible. Speech is a motor skill. When performed by human subjects, almost any motor skill has a peculiar sort of vulnerability. If the persons who perform the activity believe it important to carry it off well (e.g., if there is a critical audience), any serious reason they have to doubt they can do so may interfere with their performance. One form this interference takes is muscle tension. As they try too hard they may become too tense, or tense in the wrong muscles, or in the wrong way. Another is fragmentation. They may take the activity apart and do it piece by piece. In particular, they are likely to carry out a small bit of the beginning of the activity by itself and may reproduce this fragment repeatedly as long as the whole thing seems too difficult to do all at once.

Tension

The element of tension is evident in stuttering regardless of what form the symptoms take. It is especially conspicuous during stutterers' prolongations of sound and in their percussive articulatory attacks and explosive transitions; but it is also to be seen during repetitions and silent stoppages. It is, in fact, probably impossible to stutter in any way at all without excessive muscular tension in some form—that is, with the articulators relaxed. Conversely, if stutterers want to throw themselves into a block deliberately—to initiate the experience of the real thing as opposed to an imitation—about the only way they seem to be able to is to bear down on the first sound of the word with excessive articulatory effort (see Bloodstein and Shogan, 1972). Significantly, tension is one of the first things stutterers usually talk about when asked to tell what it feels like to have a block. They most often localize the tension in the mouth or jaw or in the chest or diaphragm. Persons professionally trained in the physiology of speech who also happen to be stutterers have occasionally contributed illuminating introspections into this aspect of stuttering. A good one is the following:

> . . . the stutterer perceives the heightened tonus of the articulatory
> closures and constrictions as though an impediment or obstacle were
> present in the speaking channel. This misperception . . . is due to the
> perceptual magnification of the hypertensed constrictions and overfirm
> closures. The illusory impediment may be felt at any place along the
> airway—in the larynx, in the velar or hard palate areas, at the lips, at
> any place where constriction or closure may occur. It is experienced as
> a cleaving or sticking together of the lips, or of the tongue or the mouth
> surfaces, or of the ventricular and true vocal folds. It is felt also as a
> stoppage, as a barrier, which interrupts and blocks ongoing movements
> of the articulatory structures. (Freund, 1966, pp. 98–99)

Stuttering, then, may be considered to be in large part something people do when they become unusually tense about the way they talk. The stutterer's misfortune is that talking is one of those things one can do well only without trying. Talking is not unique in this respect. "Loosen up—you're too tense" is advice we have heard innumerable times when we were performing an activity poorly because we were trying too hard. In most cases the problem was merely too little experience. But suppose that the habit of trying too hard when performing the activity became chronic and was complicated in time by hardened self-concepts, a history of frustration, anticipations of failure, and finally by anxiety. It is not hard to imagine that what began as a slight motor awkwardness might become magnified by degrees until it resembled something akin to developed stuttering behavior.

Fragmentation

Like tension, fragmentation is present to some degree in essentially all stuttering behavior. It is not a matter of repetitions alone. When stutterers prolong a sound or attack it with effort, they also tend to break its natural transition into the next sound. They isolate their targets, as it were, as they strike at them. Furthermore, the isolation may be as critical a reason for their speech difficulty as the tension. Van Riper (1954, p. 429) put this well when he pointed out that, in the stutterer's expectation of difficulty on a threatening sound, he tends to prepare himself to say the sound as a fixed articulatory position rather than as a normal movement leading into the rest of the word.

It is the repetitions, however, that become so clearly understandable as examples of fragmentation. Why should anyone repeat a sound he has already said adequately, perhaps several times? The answer may be found in the observation that such behavior almost always occurs on the first sound of the word, or at least on the first sound of a stressed and conspicuous part of the word. The repetition may therefore be viewed as the stutterer's successive fragmentation of this word, or word-part, in response to a feeling of helplessness to say the whole thing all at once. It is no wonder that the repetition of the last sound of a word is all but unheard of in stuttering.[1] Stuttering is above all a difficulty in "getting started," as various writers have pointed out and countless stutterers have testified. This is hardly anywhere as evident as in the stutterer's repetitions of the beginnings of words. In these cases he seems obsessed by the difficulty of articulating the word in its entirety. Instead of saying it spontaneously and automatically, he seems to concentrate his attention on initiating it—like a golfer rehearsing the first part of his swing or a dart-thrower rehearsing the beginning of his throw.

Sociomotor disorders

When we describe stuttering as a reaction of tension and fragmentation, we are saying something about speech. We are implying that it is an activity peculiarly liable to failure and that considerable importance tends to be attached to doing it well. This is obviously so. Speech is a skilled, automatic, serially patterned activity that requires a very high order of motor planning (cf. Frick, 1965). It is also subject to rigid cultural standards and unmercifully exposed to social scrutiny. Although speech is outstanding in this respect, it is not unique. Playing a musical instrument in public has some of the same attributes. To some degree, so does writing. It is instructive that reactions which resemble stuttering have often been noted in both of these activities. An especially common example is provided by the professional musician who has excellent command of his instrument except when faced with an audience. Johnson (1932, p. 41) cites a case of piano stuttering and Van Riper (1952) of trumpet stuttering; violin stuttering has been mentioned by various writers.

One of the most intriguing of such disorders seems to occur in the manual communication of the deaf. Silverman and Silverman (1971) sent letters to 78 teachers at residential schools for the deaf asking whether they had ever observed any disintegration of fluency in manual communication comparable to stuttering. Of the 33 who responded, 25 said they could understand manual communication and, of these, 13 reported they had observed the phenomenon. It was said to consist of "repetitions of signs, repetitions of initial letters in fingerspelling, 'involuntary' interjections of 'extra movements' in fingerspelling, and hesitations in fingerspelling" (p. 46).

Stuttering is not the only disorder of its kind. Rather, it appears to be the most prominent member of a family of disturbances in those motor skills that are practiced before other persons or have some type of social implication. The more complex and highly programmed the skill and the more pronounced its social aspects, the greater its potential for disruption by tensions and fragmentations. Stuttering may be termed a "sociomotor" disorder.

Stuttering as a Response to Stimuli Representative of Past Speech Difficulty

A verifiable statement of the anticipatory struggle hypothesis

The anticipatory struggle hypothesis may be stated in various ways. So far we have defined stuttering as a reaction of tension and fragmentation in speech, and this way of expressing our conception of the behavior will do better than any other for most purposes. If such a description suggests any explanation of stuttering, however, it is only because it implies the operation of certain expectations or beliefs on the part of stutterers about speech or about themselves as speakers. Unfortunately, cognitive processes of this kind do not lend themselves readily to experimental investigation. This means that, if we are to verify the anticipatory struggle hypothesis in the laboratory, we must find a way to state it in behavioral terms. This is not so difficult to do. In effect, Wendell Johnson formulated such a statement in the 1930s in carrying out, with his students and associates at the University of Iowa, some of the earliest research on the moment of stuttering. Two of those studies are of exceptional interest from this point of view.

The consistency effect. As is well known, some fundamental scientific discoveries are difficult to make mainly because they are so simple that it takes unusual vision to see their implications. The consistency effect (Johnson and Knott, 1937) was such a discovery. The question was simplicity itself: If stutterers read a passage aloud several times in succession, will they tend to stutter on different words or on the same words from reading to reading? The answer makes a considerable difference, as we see the moment we give the question some thought. If stutterers blocked on different words in successive readings, and other aspects of the situation had remained constant, we would speculate that stuttering is either a random kind of behavior or a symptom of some type of internal process that operates independently of the outside environment. If it occurs on the same words, on the other hand, it is apparently a learned response to stimuli of some sort in the reading material. Some basic issues are evidently involved.

Johnson and Knott found a strong tendency for stuttering to occur on the same words from reading to reading. In the second reading, for example, 73 percent of the stuttered words were words that had been stuttered in the first reading. Even as late as the tenth reading, 61 percent of the stuttering still occurred on words that had been stuttered in the first. They concluded that stuttering was not a haphazard phenomenon, but a response to identifiable stimuli.

The consistency is far from perfect, of course. It is intriguing to dwell on the meaning of the observation that to some extent a subject will tend to stutter on new words from reading to reading in such a situation. At present we can only speculate about this. But the significance of the consistency effect itself appears unmistakable. It is the outstanding evidence that stuttering is, in principle, a predictable response to stimuli and, at least in large part, a learned form of behavior.

Adjacency. The consistency effect led Johnson to a second finding. He reasoned that if the words on which a subject had stuttered as he read a passage were covered up, so that he had to skip over them in reading the passage a second time, most of his stuttering should be eliminated. Of course, some stuttering would remain, since consistency is not perfect. But suppose his new stuttered words were now covered up, and this process were repeated successively. Would his stuttering eventually disappear? Would he run out of stimuli for stuttering? Johnson and Millsapps (1937) tried this. Their subjects read a passage three times, after which all stuttered words were blotted out. Then they read the remaining words three times. Again the stuttered words were blotted out, and once more the remaining words were read three times.

In the course of this procedure the stuttering was reduced radically, and for some of the milder subjects it was completely eliminated. But in the majority of cases new stutterings continued to spring up, even after the second removal of stuttered words. Many of the new stutterings even occurred consistently on the same words in successive readings. It was clear that stuttering did not take place only as a fixed response to certain words or phonetic sequences. What, then, were the stimuli for the stutterings that remained? Examining the data, Johnson and Millsapps made an unexpected discovery. Many of the stutterings had occurred on words immediately adjacent to the pencil markings by which previously stuttered words had been covered up. Of such adjacent words, 23 percent were stuttered. Of the words not adjacent to pencil markings, less than 5 percent were stuttered. Johnson and Millsapps concluded that the markings themselves were the stimuli for many of the remaining stutterings and that this was so because the markings had served as cues "representative of past stuttering."

A great deal is implied by this statement. Johnson and Millsapps were asserting that the blacked-out words had served to remind the subjects of some difficulty they had had in a previous reading of the passage. They were also suggesting that such a reminder is enough to precipitate, in some manner, a new instance of stuttering. If this is a fact, it is hardly a self-evident one. From a naive point of view, this is the last response that might be expected; one might think the stutterer would talk better as a result of a reminder of this sort. Clearly, to say that stuttering is a response to cues representative of past stuttering is to voice a special and particular viewpoint about the nature of the disorder. It should not be difficult to see that it is essentially an alternative formulation of the anticipatory struggle hypothesis. If stuttering is brought about by the threat of difficulty or failure in speech, what is the observable stimulus for it? In the most general terms, it is anything that "represents" or in some way evokes the experience of former difficulty or failure. Time and time again the anticipatory struggle hypothesis has been expressed in the form of the observation that a stutterer may have difficulty with his speech because of the trouble he remembers having had before with the same word, listener, or situation (or one like it). The adjacency effect affords a model of this observation that can be tested at will in the laboratory. When Johnson and Millsapps described stuttering as a response to stimuli representative of past stuttering, they therefore fashioned a statement of the anticipatory struggle hypothesis that has the outstanding advantage of relatively easy verifiability.

Why the use of the term "representative"? Why not use "associated with" or some other term from the vocabulary of conditioning in what is essentially a behavioral definition of stuttering? In actuality, Johnson and Millsapps probably chose their words carefully. It is significant that, when the adjacency effect is examined closely, it turns out to be difficult to explain in terms of simple laboratory models of conditioning. Suppose that a given word in a reading passage is a stimulus for stuttering. The object now is to condition the stuttering to a different stimulus, namely, heavy pencil markings drawn through words. The usual conditioning scheme would require that the blot appear in close association with the original stimulus word and that the subject stutter on that word. With a few repetitions of this, the blot might then acquire the power to instigate stuttering on words not previously stuttered. Nothing like this happens in the adjacency experiment. In the first place, the blot is not associated with the stimulus word in the usual way because it obliterates it. Even more important, however, is the fact that the required stuttering can no longer take place on the stimulus word once the blot covers it.

The adjacency effect is intelligible either in cognitive terms (i.e., in terms of what the subject knows or surmises about the relationship between the blackout cues and his previous stuttering) or in terms of some more complex conditioning paradigm than will ordinarily do for animal learning experiments. This is perhaps what might have been expected. As far as we know, the behavior we have been calling sociomotor tension and fragmentation is a peculiarly human type of morbidity.

What is the stimulus for stuttering?

We may sum up one of the major accomplishments of this early research of Johnson and his co-workers by saying that in effect they succeeded in framing the anticipatory struggle hypothesis in behavioral terms. They did this by formulating a general statement about the nature of the discriminative, or cue, stimuli that govern stuttering. Their work clearly suggested that the way to verify the anticipatory struggle hypothesis experimentally was to study the relationship of stuttering to certain types of cue stimuli.

Some of my students and I have done a number of studies of the stimulus for stuttering from this point of view as part of a program of research on stuttering at Brooklyn College. The results we have gathered at this writing tend, I think, to shed some useful light on the nature of this stimulus.

The power of blackout cues.   Looked at closely, the adjacency effect exhibits some remarkable and puzzling features. A stutterer reads a passage several times. Then he is given a new copy of the passage without any explanation of why some of the words have been blacked out. He is told only that he is to skip over the blotted words. Yet, if Johnson and Millsapps were right, he will proceed to react to some of the blots as mementos that he has been stuttering and is apt to stutter again. A person could hardly be blamed, perhaps, for wondering if the adjacency phenomenon does not have some other explanation. Furthermore, it is not difficult to think of reasons why any words blacked out at random in a reading passage might produce adjacent stutterings. Stuttering is more likely to occur on the first word of a sentence or even of a list of words; perhaps the blot simply creates a new psychological beginning. The blot is also likely to make the next word harder to predict from the context, and we know that there tends to be more stuttering on words of low predictability. The more we considered it, the more plausible appeared the hypothesis that even random blots would show an adjacency effect.

We were wrong. When we put it to the test (Rappaport and Bloodstein, 1971) the results we got were actually not quite like any we had anticipated. We had each of our subjects read under two conditions: One was the usual adjacency condition in which the words blotted out were those the subject had just stuttered in several previous readings; the other was exactly the same except that the blotted words were chosen entirely at random. Since all the testing of a given subject was done on a single occasion, we gave the two conditions to half the subjects in one order and to the other half in the other order. We did this as a routine procedure, little realizing that we were manipulating a critical variable in the experiment.

The effect of the random blots proved to depend on the order of the conditions. For those subjects who received them first, the random blots showed essentially no tendency to produce adjacent stutterings. For those subjects who received the random blots second, however, the result was a definite adjacency effect. The answer we had obtained was a surprising vindication of Johnson and Millsapps. In themselves, blackout cues had no effect. But once they had been related to previously stuttered words, not only did they cause an adjacency effect in the same passage, but they even had the power to produce adjacent stutterings when placed at random over different words in new reading material.

We were left with little doubt about the meaning of the adjacency effect. Adjacency seemed to offer convincing evidence that stuttering might occur as a response to stimuli evocative of past stuttering. This seemed to go a considerable way toward verification of the anticipatory struggle hypothesis. It also provided a way to approach a perplexing problem that the hypothesis poses in connection with the phenomenon of anticipation.

Adjacency in the absence of ability to predict stuttering.   The anticipatory struggle hypothesis has often been expressed by saying that stuttering is caused by the anticipation of stuttering. Certainly, it would seem that some form of anticipation of some kind of speech failure must be involved if the hypothesis is correct. Furthermore, many stutterers report that most of their blocks are preceded by a vivid feeling of expectancy and that, by and large, the more they anticipate stuttering the more they seem to do it. It is little wonder that some of the earliest studies Johnson and his co-workers carried out on the moment of stuttering were concerned with anticipation. Since they could not observe anticipations directly, they chose instead to verify whether stutterers could accurately predict the occurrence of their blocks. During oral reading, subjects were instructed to indicate by a hand signal whenever they thought they were about to stutter on the next word. Their accuracy proved to be quite high. In general, they were able to predict the occurrence of over 90 percent of their stutterings and tended to improve with practice (e.g., see Knott, Johnson, and Webster, 1937).

There were some exceptions, however. Furthermore, this research was done with adult subjects. It ignored the fact that the acute sense of impending stuttering which may be termed "expectancy" is a feature of the more advanced forms of the disorder. Many children who stutter do not verbalize any feelings of expectancy (Bloodstein, 1960a). Many of them are also unable to predict the occurrence of their blocks (Silverman and Williams, 1972). Does this mean that their stuttering cannot possibly be an anticipatory struggle reaction? The question is obviously crucial for the theory we are developing. It should also be clear that, following our random blots experiment, we had a fairly good way of trying to answer the question. As a follow-up of that study, we therefore began to investigate the adjacency effect in stuttering children (Avari and Bloodstein, 1974).

Our subjects were 12 stutterers of elementary-school age. We first tested their ability to predict the occurrence of their stutterings during oral reading. Six of them could not signal any of their blocks in advance. Of the remaining 6, one anticipated all of his blocks but the others were able to anticipate, at most, a third. Then, using a different passage, we tested the subjects for the adjacency effect. Adjacency was observed in every case. It was comparable in amount to that of adult stutterers, and it was no less evident in the subjects who had anticipated none of their blocks than in those who had been able to predict the occurrence of some of them.

In short, a stutterer may have little skill at predicting the words on which he will block and yet give every evidence of stuttering in response to cues related to previous difficulty. This means that we must be very careful about how we define anticipation in relation to stuttering. If we say that people stutter because of the things they do when reminded that they are stutterers or have stuttered in the past, we necessarily imply that they stutter because, in some sense of the term, they "anticipate" having trouble with their speech. On this basis we may speculate that stuttering is essentially always an anticipatory struggle reaction. But this is not to say that all stutterers must experience a feeling of expectancy before all of their blocks or that they must be capable of predicting the occurrence of all or any of their stutterings. As we will see, anticipation has many possible meanings.

Are the stimuli largely individual or group factors? We have been giving an account of a research program on the stimulus for stuttering for which our broad hypothesis was that stimuli related to past failure or difficulty play a central role in stuttering behavior. On the level of clinical experience, considerable support for this hypothesis comes from stutterers' personal accounts of how words or sounds first became difficult for them to say. Van Riper (1972, pp. 269, 270) has provided some good examples showing that these words or sounds seem to be ones the stutterer remembers (1) because of having experienced severe frustration or penalty when saying them or (2) because he accumulated many stuttering memories through frequent use of those words or sounds under stress (e.g., his own name).

These clinical observations are, of course, impossible to confirm by means of experimental study. The best we can hope for in the laboratory is verification of some of their implications. Some indirect evidence of this kind was provided in early research by Johnson and Brown (1935) on the speech sounds that give stutterers difficulty. They found that stutterers tended to block far more on some sounds than others, but that these difficult sounds varied markedly from case to case. Except for a tendency for consonants to give more trouble than vowels, this and later research has shown that no one sound is clearly harder for stutterers as a group than any other. This has the very important implication that the reason certain sounds become especially difficult for the stutterer has to do not so much with anything about the sounds themselves, but more with his personal experiences with those sounds.

In brief, the phonetic factor in stuttering is largely an individual factor. Presumably, however, there are many other stimuli in the speech sequence besides the phonetic ones to which stutterers respond when they block. Can our conclusions about the phonetic stimuli be generalized to all cues for stuttering in the speech sequence? Is the individual factor stronger than the group factor for all the stimuli? At first glance, the answer would seem to be no. Certainly, the other contextual stimuli for stuttering that we know about are factors that apply to stutterers as a group. Most stutterers as a group block more often on content words than on function words; they have particular trouble on the initial words of sentences; they are more likely to stutter the longer the word, the less frequently it occurs in the language, and the harder it is to predict from the preceding context.[2] On the other hand, our knowledge of the power of these stimuli has been very inexact. If any belief exists that group factors such as these largely determine whether a given word will be stuttered, it has been mere assumption. As we will soon see, when we tried to check this assumption by research of our own, the results showed that it is probably far from true.

Consistency exceeds congruity. We must return once more to the meaning of the consistency effect. We said that it shows stuttering to be, in part, a response to stimuli. Suppose we now raise the question, What stimuli? Exactly what are the features of the reading material that make subjects block over and over again at certain places as they read a passage successively? We would have to answer this by referring to everything that past research has shown us about the kinds of words that stutterers are especially prone to block on in connected reading. That is, we could enumerate such features of the word as its initial sound, grammatical function, length, position in the sentence, frequency of usage in the language, and predictability. These are essentially the only factors we know of that determine whether a word will be stuttered.

Yet it is easy to see something lacking in the use of so many group factors to explain the consistency effect. By definition, group factors are factors that would not serve to explain individual differences among subjects in the distribution of their stutterings. But the consistency we observe in stuttering is the consistency of a subject with himself, not with others. What if stutterers are not consistent with each other with respect to the words on which they block in reading the same passage? That is, what if each stutterer blocks consistently on a somewhat different set of words? That would seem to say that the controlling stimuli, whose power is so clearly shown in the consistency effect, are chiefly individual factors—not the group factors with which research has so far been concerned.

We thought it would be valuable to explore these questions by comparing the consistency of stutterers with the congruity from subject to subject in the loci, or distribution, of their stutterings (Hendel and Bloodstein, 1973). For this, a measure of intersubject congruity was needed. We patterned it on the percentage of consistency. The congruity of a given subject, A, with another subject, B, was defined as the percent of A's stuttered words that were also stuttered by B in reading the same passage. Given a group of subjects who had all read the same passage, we could compute each subject's congruity with every other subject. Each subject's average congruity with the other subjects could then be compared with his percentage of consistency in two readings of the passage. We gave our rationale for this comparison as follows:

> If a group of subjects tend to have high consistency scores in repeated readings of a given passage, we may infer that their stuttering has been strongly influenced by certain variables in the reading material. If, at the same time, these subjects differ among themselves considerably with respect to the words of the passage on which stuttering occurs, it argues that these controlling variables are highly specific to each individual case. If, on the other hand, the distribution of the stutterings was very much alike from subject to subject, whatever factors were responsible for this would also account for the high self-consistency from reading to reading. We are concerned, then, with the relative magnitude of certain comparable measures of consistency and intersubject congruity in the loci of stutterings.[3]

The study was carried out with 17 stutterers. In every case the subject's consistency in repeated readings of the passage was found to be greater than his mean congruity with other subjects, in most cases by a wide margin. On the average, only 18 percent of a subject's stuttered words were also stuttered by another subject (congruity). By contrast, 48 percent of the average subject's stuttered words had been stuttered by the same subject in a previous reading (consistency). We had found out that most of the factors known to influence the loci of stutterings in the speech sequence play only a relatively small part. The loci are determined in larger measure by factors that differ from stutterer to stutterer.

It appears that what we know about such factors as word length, sentence position, grammatical function, the relative difficulty of consonants and vowels, and the like would help us very little in predicting stuttering. At best, they seem to represent only some very broad generalizations about the kinds of stimuli by which stuttering is governed. If we are ever to be able to predict accurately the words on which a given subject will stutter, it will have to be to a large extent with reference to stimuli that operate for him alone. Precisely what such individual factors might be is a question still to be answered. There is hardly any question that words and sounds which are highly specific to each case weigh heavily in the control of stutterings. In principle, any number of other features of speech might become cues for some stutterers and not others.

At any rate, the fact that the stimuli—whatever they are—are chiefly individual in nature points in a rather obvious way to the influence of a stutterer's personal history of experiences with those stimuli. For the most part, there is little inherent in the stimuli as such that gives them the power to elicit stuttering. This seems to fit well with the hypothesis that almost any attribute of the communicative process or ambience that serves as a stimulus for stuttering does so ultimately because of past experiences of frequent, severe, or severely penalized speech difficulty.

The cues are stable.   In every inference we draw about the stimuli for stuttering from studies of the consistency effect, there is one proviso: We are assuming that the stutterer's response in the consistency experiment is a valid analogue of his behavior outside the laboratory. When we observe him blocking at much the same places in repeated readings of a passage, we infer that this is due to stimuli to which he has learned to respond with stuttering some time before. We therefore tacitly assume that he would have responded to the same stimuli yesterday and will tomorrow or next week. There are good reasons why such an assumption might be questioned.

We have not considered an alternative explanation of the consistency effect: It might be that the subject tends to block on words on which he has stuttered in a previous reading simply because he remembers having just blocked on those words. Even if stuttering were not a relatively stable response to stimuli in the stutterer's ordinary daily experience, the consistency effect might still arise as a transitory laboratory phenomenon.

It became clear, then, that we could not be sure of the meaning of many of our findings until we had removed this doubt about the meaning of the consistency effect. To do that, we had to find out to what extent the effect depended on the subject's memory of stuttering in the initial reading. The best practical approach seemed to be to try to interfere with this memory. A series of three experiments were done for this purpose.

First we tested the effect of interposing oral reading of extraneous material between the first and second readings of a passage (Seidel, Weinstein, and Bloodstein, 1973). There was no effect. The subjects' mean consistency scores were almost exactly the same as in consecutive readings of a passage.

Next we tried interposing a time interval of two weeks between readings (Seidel, Weinstein, and Bloodstein, 1973). Some decrease in consistency was observable, but it was ambiguous since it was not statistically significant. The principal finding was that most of the consistency the same subjects had shown in consecutive readings was still clearly present.

The two experiments, then, essentially answered our question. If memory of stutterings in a previous experimental reading was a factor in the consistency effect, it was apparently not the major one. But there was still the nonsignificant observed drop in the consistency effect to ponder. Was it due to the two-week interval or merely to chance? We repeated the experiment, this time with an interval of four weeks (Stefankiewicz and Bloodstein, 1974). The essential observations were the same. A group of subjects with a mean percentage of consistency of 63 in two consecutive readings still had a significant mean consistency of 49 percent when a four-week interval was interposed between readings. This time the decrease proved to be significant.

These studies produced two main findings. The critical one was that subjects who stutter when reading a passage will show a substantial tendency to stutter on the same words when reading the passage again even as long as four weeks afterward. There can hardly be any further doubt that stuttering in oral reading is a response to contextual stimuli that maintain their power over periods of time in a relatively stable way. The possibility that a subject's memory of stuttering in the initial reading also contributes to the consistency effect is by no means ruled out. But the effect of such memory, if any, appears to be outweighed by the effect of the more general and lasting kind of memory of stuttering in relation to certain features of speech during past weeks, months, or years.

The other finding was that the consistency effect does begin to decay perceptibly in time—certainly in four weeks, probably in two weeks, and perhaps even after much shorter intervals. This may be a measure of the degree to which the cue-stimuli that evoke stuttering for a given individual are subject to change as a result of new stuttering experiences. Or it may mean that memories of stuttering in the initial reading do contribute to the consistency effect as usually measured. Until more work is done with both longer and shorter time intervals, it will be difficult to be sure of the explanation.

Further Evidence
for the Anticipatory Struggle Hypothesis

We have reviewed some findings from a program of research designed to test a central assumption of the anticipatory struggle hypothesis about the stimulus for stuttering. It is improbable that any conceptual model of the moment of stuttering will ever be verified directly by a crucial experiment like the one that showed that yellow fever is transmitted by the *Aëdes aegypti* mosquito. More likely, it will be "proved" by the explanations it can provide for a broad array of stuttering phenomena. I have attempted comprehensive surveys of these phenomena in relation to the anticipatory struggle hypothesis elsewhere (Bloodstein, 1972; 1975, chap. 5). Here we will limit ourselves to a number of examples related to one broad question: Under what conditions does stuttering occur?

As far as possible we will make use of objective research findings in the discussion that follows. Some of our observations, however, will be essentially clinical in nature. These are to be accepted with the reservations that are appropriate in the case of such data, but also with an appreciation of the peril involved in ignoring them. As with other human problems of comparable complexity, one's understanding of stuttering ripens slowly with experience; the laboratory investigator who has not worked with many stutterers clinically labors under a severe handicap.

Social stress or complexity

As a sociomotor disorder stuttering occurs primarily in social situations and, other things being equal, becomes intensified when stutterers feel socially ill at ease, tense, insecure, or uncomfortable or when they need approval, feel inferior, or expect to be rejected. Writers have commented on these aspects of stuttering in clinical observations far too numerous to cite. It is also clearly evident in reports of stutterers themselves on the conditions under which their speech difficulty varies (Bloodstein, 1950a, 1950b). The exaggerated speech consciousness that seems to lie at the root of stuttering is a pernicious form of self-consciousness, and what is called self-consciousness is, of course, in reality an abnormal consciousness of others. When stuttering is increased by fear, stress, or penalty, it is primarily by social fear, social stress, and social penalty.

The social factor has been investigated experimentally through research on the effect an audience has on stuttering. In a classic study, Porter (1939) showed that the frequency of stuttering increased with audiences of one, two, four, and eight listeners. Further studies have served, in general, to confirm this (Hahn, 1940; Shulman, 1955; Dixon, 1955; Siegel and Haugen, 1964). Conversely, when the stutterer is alone the frequency of stuttering has been found experimentally to be very low in most cases (Steer and Johnson, 1936; Porter, 1939; Hahn, 1940; Šváb, Gross, and Langová, 1972). Some stuttering often remains in this situation, but this is not particularly surprising. Even if the "audience" is only the stutterer himself, it is neither completely absent nor totally uncritical.

Difficulty of the motor plan

As we have already emphasized, sociomotor disorders tend to occur in automatic, serially ordered kinds of behavior. Whether the activity affected is speaking or playing the violin, it stands to reason that the more complex and demanding the motor plan by which a complex act is organized, the greater the threat of failure and the more likely the occurrence of tension and fragmentation. This certainly seems to be true in stuttering.

We know, on the basis of experimental evidence, the following facts: (1) There tends to be more stuttering on long, polysyllabic words than on short ones. (2) Other things being equal, words that occur relatively infrequently in the language and are unfamiliar give the stutterer more trouble, by and large, than do more common words. (3) Connected speech is stuttered more often than speech produced word by word, as in reading a word list. (4) Easiest of all is speech uttered syllable by syllable. (5) Talking rapidly is apt to be one of the most difficult speaking tasks for the stutterer, and talking slowly one of the easiest.[4]

In brief, the greater the challenge to a speaker's ability to perform speech as an automatic, serially ordered activity, the greater the likelihood of stuttering. This is true, moreover, even though stutterers as a group show no lack of gross motor skill in nonspeech movements of the articulators[5] and even though there appears to be no sequential speech act, no matter how difficult, that the most severe stutterer cannot produce fluently at times. In other words, stuttering is not simply a breakdown of speech organs overtaxed by complicated serial patterns of motor activity. It is only when stutterers are overly impressed by the demands that the speech act is about to make on their motor-planning ability that it seems to become too much for them.

The adaptation effect.   The fact that stuttering is influenced by the ease or difficulty of the motor plan, or pattern, of speech seems to afford an answer to a puzzling question: What is the meaning of the adaptation effect in stuttering? It is well known, as a result of many dozens of research reports, that the frequency of stuttering tends to decrease in the course of successive oral readings of the same material. The stuttering declines from reading to reading at a decreasing rate, begins to reach a minimum in just a few readings, and amounts at its lowest point to roughly 50 percent of the initial stuttering in the average case. Under ordinary conditions the decrease is only temporary; the stuttering returns to its former level if the passage is not read aloud for a few hours. This is, in brief, the nature of the adaptation effect.

There are, of course, scores of other conditions under which stuttering is reduced even more radically. The reason adaptation has received so much attention is perhaps chiefly an accident of history and need not concern us here. It is enough to say that an extraordinary amount of research effort has been expended in the attempt to explain this phenomenon and to reconcile it with one or another theory of stuttering.

Any attempt to understand the adaptation effect must begin logically by recognizing that there can only be adaptation *to* something; the term "adaptation" is meaningless unless we specify what that something is. With this in mind, we can see that an important step was taken quite early when investigators raised the question whether the decrease in stuttering occurred only when the reading passage remained constant. Donohue (1955) and others gave stutterers continually changing material to read. A decrease in stuttering did occur, but it was relatively small. This clearly meant that in the usual adaptation experiment some of the reduction in stuttering was due to adaptation to the experimental situation as a whole; but most of it was adaptation to the reading of a given passage.

What was the reason for the adaptation to the passage? This question evoked many different answers. For example, it was suggested that the stuttering is extinguished by repeated occurrence without reinforcement. Adaptation was also said to be due to a reduction of anxiety caused by the repeated stuttering itself or the subject's discovery that its consequences were not as bad as he had expected. A number of workers compared adaptation to the decrease in the strength of a learned response in the course of repeated evocations of the response through the influence of "reactive inhibition." Adaptation has also been attributed to a reduction in meaningfulness of the material through repeated reading, as well as to increased automatization of the stutterer's vocal and articulatory sets as he continues to reread the passage.[6]

As we examine these hypotheses we note that they embody essentially two different notions about what the stutterer adapts to. Some—by far the majority—imply that he adapts in some way to repeated stuttering; others suggest that he adapts to repeated reading as such. Which is it? To obtain the answer we need to see what happens when the stutterer rehearses the passsage repeatedly without stuttering on it. We attempted such a study using unison reading to keep stuttering to a minimum (Frank and Bloodstein, 1971). Each subject read a passage five times in unison with one experimenter; the sixth time he read alone. On another occasion the same subjects read a comparable passage six times independently, as in an ordinary adaptation series. We found that, in the sixth reading of the unison condition, the average amount of stuttering stood at almost precisely the same point as it did in the sixth reading of the ordinary adaptation series. In other words, the repeated readings reduced stuttering to the same extent regardless of how much stuttering was encountered in the process. It was evidently repeated reading, not repeated stuttering, to which the subject was adapting.

In short, the effect of this experiment was to narrow down the plausible explanations of the adaptation effect to those which imply that it is due to rehearsal of the reading material. But rehearsal itself may be subdivided. For example, does repeated silent reading of the material have any effect? The answer is no, as several studies have shown (Peins, 1961; Robbins, 1971; Brenner, Perkins, and Soderberg, 1972). We may also ask whether rehearsal with silent articulatory movements tends to reduce stuttering. At the date of this writing, two out of three studies indicate that it does (see Wischner, 1947; Robbins, 1971; Brenner, Perkins, and Soderberg, 1972).

Our best guess is that the adaptation effect is due to active rehearsal, either silently or aloud, of the motor patterns of speech. If this is so, it is explained with particular aptness by our assumption that stuttering blocks are related in part to the speaker's anticipations about the difficulty of the motor plan. We have already suggested that the reason stutterers tend to have less difficulty when talking slowly or syllable by syllable is that they are more confident of the serial patterning. But there is another way speakers can make the motor plan less formidable: by rehearsing it. We have all experienced this when we repeated an unfamiliar word aloud or silently articulated it to ourselves until its pronunciation became easy and automatic. For this reason we rehearse oral reading beforehand when we want it to go smoothly before an audience. That the rehearsal actually accomplishes this end has been demonstrated in every study of the effect of repeated reading on the disfluency of normal speakers (e.g., Silverman, 1970a, 1970b).

In essence the stutterer appears to adapt because, in speech that has been rehearsed, there is less of that suggestion of difficulty to which he is so apt to fall prey. But what of the normal speaker? What is the mechanism by which rehearsal ensures fewer errors and hesitancies in any person's speech? It is obvious that, as in any learning, some type of memory is involved. If memory of the motor plan for speech is analogous to other types of memory, we may speculate that when a speaker utters a new combination of sounds, words, or phrases, its motor plan is momentarily held in some type of short-term memory storage. If the plan is rehearsed soon afterward, it may be assumed to pass into a memory store where it is retained for more extended periods—long enough for oral reading to benefit from the rehearsing the reader did hours before. Still more rehearsal evidently consolidates the motor plan in long-term memory, as is clear from all of the words in our vocabularies and the many familiar word combinations we can say fluently many months or years after the last rehearsal.[7]

All of this fits in well with some of the phenomena of stuttering adaptation. For example, adaptation may be arrested by a distracting stimulus such as a sudden loud noise (Wischner, 1947; Wingate, 1972). This may be compared to the interference effects that have been found in short-term memory for sensory information such as verbal items; that is, it is possible that such a stimulus disrupts the short-term memory of motor plans for speech and prevents their transmission to longer-term storage.

In addition, there is the phenomenon of spontaneous recovery, already mentioned. In experiments on adaptation it has been repeatedly shown that stuttering returns to its original level some hours after the last reading of a passage. This, too, is made intelligible by a rehearsal hypothesis: The stutterer apparently reacts to the gradual decay of the motor plan in memory storage when no further rehearsal takes place. It is a matter of common experience that our practice of an oral reading selection is generally effective only on the occasion for which we prepared the selection. This does seem to raise a further question, however. In principle, we should be able to fix the memory of motor speech plans in long-term storage indefinitely by giving the plans enough rehearsal. Could we defeat spontaneous recovery of stuttering by a sufficient number of adaptation trials? But we hardly need to ask this question. We are talking about nothing more or less than certain kinds of memorized material. Stutterers tend to have less difficulty when they recite by heart the Pledge of Allegiance, poems, nursery rhymes, prayers, or other continually rehearsed material, even when the last oral rehearsal took place months or even, in some cases, years earlier.

Self-concept as a stutterer

One of the most powerful and most subtle factors in stuttering is the person's self-concept as a stutterer, or the extent to which the person is conscious of or attentive to his speech, his stuttering, or his role as a speaker or a stutterer. (See Joseph G. Sheehan's chapter in this *Symposium*.) This factor manifests itself in many ways; but unfortunately few of these are easily investigated experimentally, and attempts to do so are peculiarly liable to the distortions that may result from clumsy laboratory analogues of clinical observations. We will consider a few examples of a sort that should be familiar to almost every speech clinician.

Stuttering is a relatively commonplace disorder, and it is not unusual for a speech clinician to discover that the stranger sitting next to him on the plane to Walla Walla is a stutterer. The circumstances under which he finds this out are sometimes rather significant, however. In some cases a half hour or so of conversation may go by without a trace of any difficulty whatever until he happens to let fall a remark that reveals his occupation. Precisely at that moment the stranger may begin to stutter and continue to do so through the remainder of the conversation.

As this suggests, many stutterers seem to talk normally a good part of the time essentially because they forget they are stutterers. Speech clinicians are well equipped for stirring up their memories. If this is the case, we might expect to find evidence of it in the speech clinic—and we do. Walking across my college campus, I have sometimes been surprised to pass a student deeply absorbed in fluent and spontaneous conversation and to recognize him as a stutterer who rarely says a sentence without difficulty in the clinic. For such people the speech clinic is above all a place where their self-concepts as defective speakers dominate their consciousness. Of course, this is not necessarily typical. In many cases stutterers' self-concepts as speakers dog them almost everywhere; and stutterers' perceptions of the speech clinic as a place to feel understood, accepted, and safe from the threat of punishment for stuttering may so far outweigh other factors in the situation that they tend to talk more fluently than usual.

A counselor, interviewing a stuttering high school girl about her attitude toward drugs, told the author that she blocked in answering every question until the counselor unexpectedly asked her, "Your sister died of an overdose, didn't she?" She paused, evidently shaken, and asked with perfect fluency, "How did you know that?" The familiar observation that stutterers often talk normally when carried away by surprise, emotion, or the like demonstrates what happens when they become oblivious to their speech, as the following examples also suggest. A college student reported that if he were suddenly called on in class while absorbed in taking notes, he would often respond fluently until it dawned on him that he was not stuttering and then he would begin to block. Another student said he could often talk normally in ordinary conversation provided he had his mind on what he was talking about and could forget he was a stutterer. He said, "Last night after going to a play I can't remember stuttering all the way from the play until I got back to the dorm and saw Dr. [Wendell] Johnson's book on the desk."

Finally, there is a peculiar feature of stuttering behavior that has received scant attention in the literature, though we observe it continually in day-to-day contacts with stutterers. It is that stutterers ars especially likely to have difficulty when repeating something the listener has failed to hear. There are few occasions on which we can so reliably predict that the stutterer will block as when we have said to him, "Excuse me—what did you say?" He will often stutter in response to this, even if he has been having little other difficulty. This observation, at first somewhat puzzling, seems to illustrate rather well the self-concept factor. The key to this effect appears to be the well-known fact that the acoustic code of language is highly redundant; that is, the listener tends to be able to perceive the speaker's message correctly even when quite a few elements are missing, a fact we make good use of under the unreliable conditions of everyday listening. Moreover, it is to be assumed that we all learn from experience the extent to which this is so. So, when the listener signals, "I didn't hear what you said," he is in effect saying, "Don't rely on me to synthesize your message by supplying the missing parts. You didn't give me enough to work with." This is as much as to say, "Pay some more attention to your speech"; and it is calculated to heighten the stutterer's consciousness of his role as a speaker.

To sum up, there are various conditions under which stuttering comes and goes as the stutterer's flawed self-image as a speaker is blurred or sharpened. For this reason he may often talk fluently when the listener can predict what he is about to say, or when he finds himself in new surroundings, or when talking to a stranger who is not expecting him to stutter, or when he alters his speech pattern even in the most subtle manner. As a result, stuttering often seems to be ruled by the most ephemeral conditions of the stutterer's attention, perception, or cognition. There is hardly a word on which he struggles, no matter how severely, that he can't often say easily a moment later, and the difference that makes for stuttering or fluency sometimes seems finer than a razor's edge. For this reason the wall that separates the stutterer from being a normal speaker almost always gives the impression of being the thinnest of partitions. Conversely, when he talks fluently the chance that he might stutter almost always seems ominously present.

Anxiety, Anticipation, and the Moment of Stuttering

Anxiety does not play a central role

The anticipatory struggle hypothesis has been stated in many ways, by no means all equally meaningful or consistent with what we know about stuttering. One of the least satisfactory, except in a strictly qualified sense, is the maxim that stuttering is due to anxiety about speech or stuttering. It is undeniable that anxiety can be a potent force in stuttering. But careful observation reveals so much evidence that blocks may occur in the absence of anxiety in any of its ordinary meanings that we must be skeptical about the part it should play in a comprehensive understanding of the disorder.

Six operational definitions of anxiety

To begin with, the term "anxiety" may be defined in so many ways that the question of how or whether it is related to stuttering is essentially meaningless except to the extent that we specify what definition we are using. First and foremost, anxiety is a certain kind of personal and private feeling. This is primary. If it were not for such a feeling the question of how to define anxiety would never arise at all. Unfortunately, like other private sensory experiences, it is not amenable to scientific study. Consequently, we study in its place other things we suppose to be related to it. We can distinguish at least six different tests that have been used for the purpose or with the effect of investigating the relationship of stuttering to anxiety. We will consider, in the following discussion, what each of them has disclosed.

1. Autonomic arousal. A favorite recourse of investigators of anxiety is some measure of autonomic arousal. A number of the earliest studies of stuttering were concerned with such measures.[8] They produced quite a bit of evidence of changes in heart rate, blood distribution, reflexes, breathing patterns, and the like before and during speech. These were certainly signs of excitement and exertion, and it is not difficult to interpret some of them as indications that the subjects were experiencing anxiety. This was comfortably in accord with a persistent notion that blocks were due to anxiety, and it is only hindsight that allows us to see clearly that the presence of anxiety in association with stuttering was far from proof that one was causing the other.

The development of instrumentation of advanced design has made it possible to pursue more refined approaches to this issue, and a number of studies have failed to support some old assumptions. For example, Gray and Brutten (1965) found that palmar sweat measures of autonomic arousal did not vary consistently with frequency of stuttering during the course of adaptation. Similarly, Adams and Moore (1972) observed that auditory masking with white noise reduced stuttering but had no effect on palmar sweating. Using a different technique, Gray and Williams (1969) measured pupil diameter just prior to stuttering blocks and could find no evidence of any significant pupillary dilation.

Some investigations, on the other hand, have shown a relationship between frequency of stuttering and level of autonomic response. Examples are the palmar sweat study of Brutten (1963) and the galvanic skin response studies of Berlinsky (1955) and Kline (1959). In the aggregate, the findings so far suggest that increased autonomic arousal is a frequent concomitant of stuttering reactions in adult subjects, but by no means a necessary one.

2. The effect of tranquilization. It is well established that tranquilizing drugs tend to be highly effective in decreasing anxiety. We can therefore use the administration of such drugs as a convenient operational definition of reduction in anxiety and ask whether this serves to reduce stuttering. A series of studies of the use of tranquilizers in stuttering therapy has provided a somewhat equivocal answer.[9] The drugs certainly produce some benefit in many cases. On the whole, they seem to work better than placebos. But we look in vain for evidence of a very sharp drop in stuttering to match the radical elimination of anxiety that tranquilizers tend to bring about. A number of writers report a greater tendency for the blocks to become less effortful than to decrease in frequency.

We would have to draw the same conclusion we drew from the physiological data: There seems to be some evidence here of a link between stuttering and anxiety, but it is weak and inconsistent. Considerable stuttering may apparently occur in the tranquilized state.

3. The effect of desensitization. Another method that has been used successfully to alleviate anxiety is reciprocal inhibition (or systematic desensitization), the deconditioning procedure devised by Joseph Wolpe. It has also been used with stutterers with the aim of eliminating speech-related anxieties. The effects on stuttering have been variable. Good results have been reported, but not in all cases.[10] Of particular interest is a study by Gray and England (1972), who used independent measures of electrical skin conductance to check on how well their procedures worked to reduce anxiety. In the course of six months of therapy there were decreases in both anxiety, as so measured, and stuttering. The authors emphasized, however, that while anxiety was generally diminished, the gains in speech fluency were relatively small and did not seem to take place concomitantly with the reductions in anxiety. They interpreted their results to show a lack of corespondence between stuttering and anxiety.

4. The effect of punishment. Anxiety can be defined operationally as an effect of punishment, and so it is reasonable to ask whether punishment for stuttering tends to result in more stuttering. As we saw earlier, there is plenty of clinical evidence to suggest that, on the whole, stuttering tends to increase in situations in which there are severe social penalties for stuttering. But stutterers have been observed to talk quite fluently in such situations too.

Ostensibly, it might seem that the best answer to our question is to be found in laboratory experiments designed to study the effects of punishment on stuttering. A rather large number of such studies have been done, with the unexpected result that stuttering tends to decrease markedly rather than increase.[11] At first glance this finding may seem not merely to qualify the assumption that stuttering increases as anxiety goes up, but to flatly contradict it. This impression fades as we look more closely, however. The procedure in these studies has been to present the subject with a presumably aversive stimulus following, as quickly as possible, each stuttering block. The stimuli, which have all worked about equally well, have included electric shock, loud noise, delayed auditory feedback, time-out from speaking, cues representing the loss of small amounts of money, or verbal stimuli such as "wrong" or "no." For the most part, such "punishments," administered under laboratory conditions, hardly seem calculated to stir up any emotion clearly identifiable as anxiety by most definitions of the term. This is underscored by the finding that even such stimuli as the words "right" or "tree" are effective in reducing stuttering (Cooper, Cady, and Robbins, 1970). There is a variable of considerable force operating in these experiments, and the question of what it is requires an answer. It does not appear to be anxiety. These studies were not, of course, designed for studying the effect of anxiety as such, and we can only conclude that research for this purpose must take some different form.

5. Speech avoidance behavior. It is reasonable to define anxiety in terms of avoidance reactions. From this point of view, our daily clinical reports of the stutterer's avoided words and speech situations are more than enough to document the power of anticipated stuttering to produce anxiety. This, of course, tells us little about the extent to which such anxiety results in stuttering. There does, however, seem to be one revealing fact to be learned from clinical observation of avoidance behavior: A considerable amount of stuttering may be done by individuals who seldom try to avoid words or speech situations or to show any other overt signs of anxiety about speaking. This is true of some adults, but it is especially true of large numbers of stuttering children of all ages.

The question of how children feel about their stuttering is difficult and complex, and it is hardly possible to say something about it without oversimplifying it. We can no longer put complete credence in the old notion of a "primary" stage in the development of stuttering in which children are serenely ignorant of any difficulty with their speech. Speech avoidance reactions are to be observed in some cases at every stage in the development of stuttering and sometimes take severe forms at a very early age.[12] As exaggerated as some old concepts were, however, there was a core of valid observation in them. Children do not often exhibit the chronic and persistent avoidance behavior that is common in adolescents and adults. Children's avoidances, like their other emotional reactions to stuttering, are likely to be occasional or at least intermittent; in some, they seem all but nonexistent. This is true not only of those whose speech interruptions are mild, "simple," and easily confused with so-called normal disfluency. Indeed, we find children of all ages who often struggle very hard when they speak, yet seem to have little need to conceal it and seldom let an opportunity to talk go by without exploiting it to the limit. In short, children are capable of acute anxiety about stuttering, as defined by avoidance of speech, but many of them—and some adults as well—seem capable of considerable stuttering with little or no anxiety, so defined.

6. *Verbal self-report.* There may be no more valid test of the presence of a subjective state than the report of the person who says he has it. From this standpoint, it is urgent to find out what we can about anxiety from stutterers themselves. The majority of stutterers who are mature enough to give articulate accounts of the introspective side of stuttering verbalize plenty of anxiety, of course. Furthermore, so many of them perceive it as the most important factor in bringing their stuttering about that it would be difficult to dismiss this perception out of hand. Most of these persons are adults whose stuttering is in its fully developed form. Even among adults, however, there are reports that run counter to the general rule. For example, some individuals insist that they rarely experience any fear of stuttering, though they may sometimes block severely. Among the rest, moreover, there are some who report occasions on which they stutter without fear: for example, when they are alone or in the speech clinic, where, as we have seen, some stutterers have unusual speech difficulty despite the fact that they feel particularly free from anxiety.

It is also worth noting an observation often made by those of us for whom the reduction of anxiety about speech has constituted an important part of the effort to eliminate stuttering clinically: Although some stutterers tell us, after months of confronting their feared words, listeners, and situations, that they feel very little of their old apprehension, they may sometimes continue to stutter substantially as before until special measures are taken to help them modify their speech behavior.

Do tensions and fragmentations require anxiety?

We have formulated in six different ways the question of how stuttering is related to anxiety about stuttering, and we have gotten essentially the same answer. Such a relationship exists, but it is varying, qualified, and inconsistent; in many instances stuttering may evidently occur when there is little anxiety about speech, stuttering, or anything else. This answer has some important implications for the outlook on stuttering we are developing in this chapter. It means that if stuttering is an anticipatory struggle reaction, it is not primarily by virtue of the role that is played by anxiety in any of the usual meanings of that term. Anxiety has loomed so large in modern anticipatory struggle theories that such a statement may seem to border on the paradoxical. But there are any number of ways to formulate the anticipatory struggle hypothesis without reference to anxiety.

In this chapter I have suggested that stuttering is a response of tension and fragmentation in speech which has developed as a result of past experiences of speech failure. Tensions and fragmentations are based, in the final analysis, on beliefs the speaker holds about the difficulty of speech. Such beliefs may be held with varying degrees of anxiety or with no anxiety of any consequence at all. For example, if the stutterer is convinced that "February" is a difficult word to say, he may resolutely tense his muscles of articulation, detach the first sound from the rest of the word, and attack it with might and main for no other reason than that he is convinced that these are the things he must do in order to say the word. Anyone who assumes that such events must necessarily involve excessive autonomic arousal may well be looking at them from a highly subjective point of view. Although they often do involve such arousal, their ultimate sources are to be described most appropriately in terms of certain convictions, preconceptions, or expectations the stutterer entertains about speech or certain speech elements.

As a result of social penalties, most stutterers do eventually become persistently anxious about stuttering, of course, and when that happens their stuttering often seems to vary as a function of their anxiety. But this may occur simply because greater fear of stuttering means more anticipation of stuttering, heightened attention to speech, and a consequent raking up of all those irrational assumptions and curious personal dogmas that seem to form the basis of stuttering. At the same time, alleviating stutterers' anxiety states by drugs or anything else may often have little effect on their speech behavior because it leaves them still possessed of everything they know about speech that isn't so.

Anticipation: A word with many meanings

The underlying cognitive basis of stuttering is hard to fathom by scientific means. We move somewhat in the right direction, however, when we relate stuttering to anticipation rather than to anxiety. Although we have ruled out anxiety as a necessary condition for stuttering, this is not the same as ruling out anticipation. A hypothesis about the moment of stuttering that has been stated quite often is that stuttering is caused by anticipation. To what extent is this statement true? The answer, in our opinion, is that the hypothesis is valid provided we are careful about how we formulate it. The results of past research, discussed earlier, must serve to put us on our guard about the question of anticipation. It is a complex one because the term "anticipation" may be used in the context of stuttering with various meanings. A quick glance at some of the distinctions we may make will give us some immediate indication of the problem.

In terms of content, anticipation may refer to a sense of impending stuttering so vivid that it includes premonitions of the very form and duration of a block; or it may simply denote a vague preconception that some speech activity lying directly ahead will be unusually taxing. It may occur with varying degrees of conviction. It may be so colored by emotion that its presence is easily demonstrated by measures of autonomic arousal; on the other hand, it may consist of an essentially objective judgment that a word soon to be attempted will require special care if it is to be said without stuttering. It may precede stuttering by intervals of varying duration. It may be located anywhere in consciousness from its center to its extreme periphery.

It is evident that the question of whether stuttering is caused by anticipation is ambiguous as stated. There are several clear and unambiguous questions we may substitute for it. But they are somewhat different questions, and they do not lead to the same answer. We will discuss six such questions.

1. Prediction of stuttering. There is, first of all, the question of whether essentially all stutterers can accurately predict the occurrence of all of their stutterings. We have touched on this question before, and unequivocally the answer is no. Ability to predict stuttering is generally greater in adults than in children. In adulthood it often becomes very high, especially in relatively severe cases of stuttering; but there are many exceptions, and accuracy is almost never total in any case.

This ability corresponds roughly to what is often called expectancy, a kind of anticipation older and more severe stutterers tend to report, and which they describe as a keen awareness that a stuttering block is imminent on a specific word. Generally speaking, such expectancy is an advanced development. If the ability to predict stuttering were the only form in which we could observe anticipation in relation to stuttering, we would have to conclude that stuttering could occur in the absence of anticipation.

2. *Autonomic arousal prior to the block.* Some workers have sought to define anticipation in terms of increased autonomic activity occurring just prior to stuttering. This implies the use of the physiological measures we have already discussed as indicators of anxiety. Such measures have rarely been applied with specific attention to the period immediately preceding a block, however, except in some early research surveyed by Van Riper (1936). A notable exception is the study by Gray and Williams (1969), already cited, in which no evidence could be found of any unusual pupil dilation just before the initiation of stuttered words.

Such studies, of course, are really concerned with the question of how much autonomic arousal is present during anticipation. We have little reason to assume, however, that anticipation cannot occur without the kinds of physiological changes that are normally associated with anxiety.

3. *Neuromuscular activity preceding the block.* A different type of physiological correlate of anticipation may be afforded by electromyographic (EMG) measures. Van Riper (1954, pp. 429–443) has described certain muscular preparatory sets in which stutterers tend to place their speech organs in anticipation of stuttering. Little objective research has been done on this aspect of anticipation. Bar, Singer, and Feldman (1969), however, have described the use of electromyography with a stutterer to show that expectancy was associated with increased subvocal laryngeal muscle activity. A broad application of the EMG technique may be useful in the further study of muscular activity anticipatory of stuttering.

4. *Effect of a time interval preceding speech.* Anticipation may be defined in a particularly satisfactory way by a procedure used in a study by Goss (1952). Goss had adult stutterers look at stimulus words for varying intervals of time while they waited for a signal to say the words. As the waiting interval increased from 2 to 10 seconds, the likelihood of stuttering progressively increased. (Stuttering also increased for intervals shorter than 2 seconds, presumably as a different kind of pressure came into play.)

This is analogous to the familiar observation that the longer stutterers have to wait their turn to recite in class or answer "here" or "present" during roll call, the more certain they are to stutter. Forte and Schlesinger (1972) studied this effect systematically with children in a natural classroom situation. On a series of occasions, each of 20 stutterers, aged 8 to 15 years, took turns reading aloud with 5 other pupils chosen from the stutterer's class. On every occasion each child read once, in an ordinal position determined by the seating arrangement. The effect of seating position on stuttering corresponded closely to the findings of Goss. The stuttering declined from the first to the second position, but rose progressively from the second to the sixth.

Evidence of this kind bears in the most fundamental way on the question of how stuttering and anticipation are related. The mere association of the two is, of course, no indication that one causes the other, and the view is sometimes expressed that anticipation is simply the stutterer's awareness of the stimuli to which his blocks have been conditioned. As far as it goes this is true, of course. But the fact that the probability of stuttering on a word is related to the length of time the stutterer waits for the signal to say it seems a clear indication that there is more to anticipation than that. In at least the sense defined by the Goss experiment, stuttering is functionally dependent on anticipation. Furthermore, the work of Forte and Schlesinger suggests that such a dependent relationship is to be found in children as well as adults.

5. Implications of the role of cues.   Earlier in this chapter we discussed stuttering as a response to stimuli representative of past speech difficulty. We suggested that this was the most rigorous form in which we could state the anticipatory struggle hypothesis and reviewed evidence in support of it. At this point we may note that such a statement, by implication, defines a relationship between stuttering and a certain type of anticipation. If a word-stimulus representative of past failure has the power to produce a stuttering block, then presumably it is because it evokes an expectation on the stutterer's part that he will have difficulty on it again. In this sense of the term, anticipation is essentially always at work in stuttering if our hypothesis about the controlling stimuli for stuttering is correct.

In this context it is possible to suggest an answer to a persistent question about the anticipatory responses inferred to underlie stuttering: Are they necessarily highly conscious? Awareness is often described as having various levels. Can we learn to respond to stimuli anticipatory of certain events without being highly aware of the process? The evidence of conditioning is that we can and do. A discriminative stimulus, for example, is often said to "signal" the availability of reinforcement or the imminence of punishment. In other words, we have learned to anticipate reinforcement or punishment in response to the stimulus. Yet we do not need to recognize the role of the stimulus, or even be aware of its presence, in order to respond effectively to it. Similarly, it may be assumed that stutterers are able to respond without awareness to cues that signal the imminence of speech failure. If so, it is hardly any wonder that not all stutterers can predict the occurrence of all of their blocks.

6. Expectation of speech difficulty in a general sense. There is a final sense of the term anticipation in which it plays a broad and vital role in stuttering. When we relate stuttering to anticipation, we usually think specifically about anticipation of stuttering. There is evidence, however, that underlying the disorder more deeply than the expectation of stuttering is an anticipation of speech difficulty or failure of a very general kind: a tendency to evaluate certain segments of the message as difficult to encode in exactly the same sense that a normal speaker may spot certain serial patterns of speech in advance as difficult, laborious, or challenging.

We have touched before on the difficulty of the motor plan as a factor in stuttering. A case in point is the well-documented observation that, other things being equal, there is generally more stuttering on long, polysyllabic words than on short ones. In bringing this up again in relation to anticipation, it is necessary to point out an easily disregarded fact. Research has shown that, with very few exceptions, stuttering occurs on the first sound of the word; so when the stutterer reacts to the length of a word by stuttering, in the vast majority of instances the block is on the initial sound.[13] The implications should be carefully pondered. It is easily overlooked that a stutterer who blocks on the first sound of a word because it is long and polysyllabic cannot possibly be reacting in any simple and immediate way to its difficulty or complexity, but only to some type of preliminary evaluation of its difficulty or complexity; that is, unless we are to believe that the block is caused by an event that has not yet happened, we are forced to conclude that it is due to anticipation of the event. There are, in fact, few clearer illustrations of the role of anticipation in stuttering.

It is anticipation with a somewhat new meaning, though this meaning was implicit in some of the earliest statements of the anticipatory struggle hypothesis that attributed stuttering to speech "doubt," or to the speaker's belief in the difficulty of speech. We may speculate that in this highly generalized form anticipation is essentially always in the background when stuttering takes place. Pervasive, frequently on a low level of consciousness, and present at every stage in the development of stuttering, it may be surmised to be the germinal form from which those more specific expectancies so common in the most advanced phase of the disorder gradually develop. It is perhaps in this sense that stuttering may be described as an anticipatory reaction with the greatest generality.

Stuttering is a response to cues representative of past difficulty, not necessarily past stuttering. Only such a statement is broad enough to define stuttering in its earliest as well as its most advanced forms. Even the youngest child may have a rudimentary sense of impending speech difficulty that is not a premonition that he will stutter, but merely a diffuse perception that a speech element will be hard to say.

II. ETIOLOGY

We have devoted quite a few pages to a single question: What is the nature of the moment of stuttering? We now come to the second question that a theory of stuttering must answer: How does the problem develop? In the light of everything we have said about stuttering up to this point, this amounts to asking how a child originally acquires his belief in the difficulty of speech. In this section we will develop some hypotheses about the manner in which such beliefs grow out of early experiences of speech failure.

The Brooklyn Group: A Clinical Study
of the Etiology of Stuttering

At the Brooklyn College Speech and Hearing Center in the years from 1950 to 1955, I conducted what amounted to a clinical investigation of the early histories of young stutterers. Most of the information collected on all such children and their parents who came to me for diagnostic evaluation was recorded in a uniform manner that later permitted examination of the data in a relatively systematic way. During this period I saw, in addition to many older stutterers, 108 stuttering children from 2 to 6 years of age. These children, constituting what we will refer to as the Brooklyn group, included 90 boys and 18 girls. The length of time that had elapsed between the time the speech difficulty was first noticed by the parents and the occasion on which the child was initially seen at the center ranged from three weeks to approximately four years, eight months.

During the gathering of this body of clinical data I was under the influence of Wendell Johnson's well-known theory that stuttering is caused by unrealistic demands for fluency imposed by anxious or perfectionistic adults who evaluate a child's normal speech hesitancies as stuttering. When I sifted the data in search of their meaning, there did seem to be frequent evidence of parental pressures. In addition, however, there was an unexpected variety of experiences of speech failure, histories of speech frustration, and chronic difficulties of communication that appeared to have coincided with the development of stuttering.

The evidence seemed to be that virtually any imaginable source of a child's conviction that speech is difficult and requires effort or care may lead to struggle reactions or, as we have referred to them in this chapter, tensions and fragmentations in speech. It is this view of the etiology of stuttering that we will develop here, based chiefly on the 108 cases of the Brooklyn group and supplemented freely by later clinical observations on children of all ages seen at the center.

For purposes of discussion, it is convenient to divide the factors that may contribute to tense and fragmented speech into two broad categories: (1) Some appear to serve as immediate provocations for stuttering. They consist, for the most part, of speech difficulties or failures that become a recurring or dominant feature of a child's experience. (2) The others are factors that create a general atmosphere of communicative pressure in which a child may become especially vulnerable to provocations for stuttering.

The provocations

Delayed speech. Fully one-third of the children in the Brooklyn group were described by their parents as "late talkers"; they were said to have persisted for a relatively long time in "baby talk" or were "difficult to understand before they began to stutter." By and large, the Brooklyn cases corroborated past research findings of speech retardation among stutterers (see Bloodstein, 1975, pp. 175–176).

What do we mean by delayed speech? Children are known to differ considerably in their rates of language development, and normalcy permits a wide range of variation. Strictly speaking, few of the stutterers referred to by their parents as late talkers were probably far outside what would ordinarily be considered normal limits. The typical child begins to say his first words by the time he is about a year old and to speak in simple sentences by about age 2. With a few exceptions, all that could be said in deprecation of the speech development of the stutterers in the Brooklyn group is that they were somewhat slower than average; many of them had not said their first words until age $1\frac{1}{2}$ or 2 and their first sentences until $2\frac{1}{2}$ or 3.

In several cases, moreover, what the parent referred to as late talking turned out to be, on further questioning, merely average or actually superior speech development by any reasonable standards. One boy who had been a source of anxiety to his parents for a time because they considered his speech development retarded had acquired sentences at *$1\frac{1}{4}$ years of age.* In another case the mother of a girl only 2 years and 10 months of age worried about the child's inability to pronounce sounds that normal children sometimes do not learn until age 6 or so. In cases of this kind the parents' report of their child's slowness in speech seemed to be essentially an ominous reflection of their own unrealistically high standards.

That many of these children had actually made somewhat slow progress in developing speech and language skills, however, is hardly to be doubted. Frequently, other people besides the parent had evidently regarded the child as delayed in speech or defective in articulation. That is, relatives or neighbors had commented, playmates had teased, or strangers had had great difficulty in understanding. In some cases there was a history of delayed speech in other members of the family. In many cases the late persistence of infantile errors of articulation was observed in the clinical interview and served as partial corroboration of the parent's report of delayed onset of speech. Furthermore, there were a few instances in which the child had been examined earlier— many months before stuttering was first noticed—because of failure to speak at the expected time or because of infantile articulation. For example, one boy was brought to the center at age 3 because he was saying only a few single words. When he was seen again at age 5, language was fully developed, but he was conspicuously repeating and prolonging many of his sounds and exhibited a few typical associated mannerisms.

It is reasonable to assume that the child who falls behind in language development may find communication something of a struggle at times, especially if he is subjected to parental attempts to hurry his speech development. In such cases, the suggestion that speech requires laborious preparations and special effort may become powerfully established. We should take stock of precisely what it means to be a little behind in speech development in our society. It is a society that is extraordinarily conscious of speech, as almost any speech therapist can testify. If we accepted for remedial work all children whose parents thought they needed it, speech clinics would be overrun by essentially normal children whose basic problem is that they do not speak as well as the child next door. It is not difficult, then, to imagine the social pressures to which parents are exposed when their children are seriously delayed in speech. The humiliating remarks of neighbors, the helpfully meant confidences of friends and relatives, and the "cruelty" of other children are often hard to endure. The harassed parents tend to harass the child, and the youngster is apt to find his backward speech a focus of intense concern.

Defective articulation. Five children in the Brooklyn group were said to have begun to stutter while attending the center for help with their articulation, an interesting and significant observation that is matched by many similar reports of speech clinicians elsewhere. Ordinary defects of articulation appear to constitute the most common single provocation to stuttering. An unusually large number of stuttering children appear to have them. Evidence for this has come from a series of studies and seems indisputable (see Bloodstein, 1975, pp. 178, 179).

Parents often assume that a lisp or infantile *r* is due to carelessness, a "lazy" tongue, or excessively rapid rate, and the child may be urged to "slow down" or "be careful" about the way he speaks. Such children may in time become essentially fearful of speaking. When they are brought to the speech clinic, the examiner's invitations to converse may draw forth no more than a whispered word or two, and all of the parents' bribery and commands may not be enough to make them speak at all. In general, this is the reaction of children who have been coached, corrected, and criticized so often that they go about virtually in a continual state of stage fright. It is not difficult to understand why some of these children so profoundly doubt their ability to get their words out acceptably that they begin to buffet and beat their way through speech.

This appears to be, on the whole, the most plausible explanation for the large number of young stutterers in the Brooklyn group who could not "speak clearly" or "make themselves understood" before their stuttering was first noticed. In these cases the parents frequently reported that the child had been made upset, impatient, or resentful by their attempts to improve his articulation. A number of parents commented specifically that stuttering had first been observed soon after the child had begun to exhibit these reactions. One girl of 5 years, originally a late talker, had been exposed to the combined efforts of her mother, her sister, and a neighbor to help her overcome her "baby talk." When seen at the Speech and Hearing Center because she was having trouble "getting her words out," she was badly frightened and refused to speak. Significantly, she stuttered only on those sounds that she misarticulated, according to the mother. A similar observation was made by another parent. The child had acquired his first words late, at age 3. Some time afterward the mother noticed that he was not "forming his sounds right," particularly the *l* and the *g*. Directing him to watch her mouth as she said them, she devoted herself to the task of teaching him these two sounds. She first regarded him as a stutterer when, at age 5, he was observed to repeat the sounds *l* and *g* frequently at the beginnings of words. By the time he appeared at the center about five months later, the boy was repeating and prolonging a good many other sounds as well and had acquired the habit of releasing himself from blocks by means of a rapid expulsion of breath.

It is interesting to notice how often the mention of transient stuttering crops up in the case histories of children who are brought for examination only because of articulatory difficulties. The mother of one such 5-year-old boy reported that she had noticed him stuttering after the speech teacher at his school began to devote 15 minutes of her lunch hour to helping him with his articulation. Another child of 4 with severely defective articulation was found to stutter as well, but almost entirely on words beginning with *s*. It developed that the mother had been giving him "lessons" on how to say the sound. During the initial interview, the child often approached *s*-words with extreme caution even when he did not stutter on them. In a third case the mother described how the child, whom she had never heard to stutter, on one occasion suddenly began to force grotesquely on the word "ship" when she tried to help him articulate it properly. A fourth case was a boy brought for examination because of articulatory substitutions, not stuttering, whose mother remarked at the close of the interview, "Every now and then he suddenly exhausts all his breath when he speaks. What is that?"

A final case in point was Daniel, a 5-year-old boy who was brought to the center because of his markedly infantile articulation. In the initial interview the mother complained that he was "stubborn" and refused to practice his sounds at home. Later in the interview she said that the father, who regularly helped Daniel with his sounds, tended to be very insistent, raising his voice and becoming impatient when the boy did not succeed. In addition to the articulatory difficulty of concern to the parents, Daniel also showed a tendency to block on words with simple, hard attacks. Shown a picture of a baby, he avoided naming it by pretending not to recognize it. Asked whether it was a baby or a man, he answered, "A man." The mother had noticed Daniel's blocking for three or four weeks prior to the interview and said it was often accompanied by a rigid posture of his body. She did not appear to have thought about it as stuttering.

Oral-reading experiences in the classroom. If the words with which the stutterer has difficulty may sometimes provide a clue to the etiology of stuttering, it will be worthwhile to record an interesting observation made on somewhat older stuttering children. When these children stuttered in oral reading, they almost invariably blocked on the unfamiliar or "hard" word, of whose identity or pronunciation they were evidently uncertain. Many a 9- or 10-year-old who read "Arthur, the Young Rat" aloud during the initial clinical interview stuttered on little besides "zealous," "flightly," and "shirker." Furthermore, it has been instructive to see how, on occasion, a child's efforts to "sound out" the strange word apparently turned into a stuttering block. The importance of this is most readily seen in relation to certain other observations. First, in some cases stuttering is initially observed in the classroom during the early grades. Second, some stutterers block only in oral reading. We occasionally discover adults who speak fluently and spontaneously in vital interpersonal relationships, yet since early elementary-school days have had a troublesome stutter when reading aloud. Third, the very fact that the majority of stutterers have some difficulty in oral reading—even though, as usually performed, it differs sharply from the normal pattern of communicative speech to which stuttering is otherwise almost wholly confined—appears to reflect the stutterer's experiences in the classroom and is perhaps additional evidence that such experiences may be enough to precipitate the disorder in some cases.

These facts serve to call to our attention that delayed speech and immature articulation are not the only sources from which children may, under certain conditions, receive the persistent impression that talking involves the overcoming of obstacles. The danger probably exists in any situation in which a child is repeatedly expected to speak in a manner somehow beyond his depth, in which he continually makes mistakes, and in which the consequences of an error are—from his point of view—grave and dreadful. For some children the oral-reading situation as it is to be found in certain classrooms fulfills these requirements exceptionally well. Some of these children may have reading problems per se. Others may merely have somewhat poor verbal ability or limited skill at pronunciation, which the oral-reading situation serves to make conspicuous. Even among adults, we occasionally see cases in which stuttering exists together with a gross verbal poverty and articulatory ineptness and appears to be related to a lifelong sense of inadequacy at pronouncing somewhat long and difficult words.

In still other cases the essential factor appears to be the interaction of a timid, withdrawing child and a severe, impatient teacher. One child in the Brooklyn group was reported by his mother to have begun to stutter in his classroom in the second grade. He was a sensitive and insecure child who was so terrorized by his teacher's scoldings that he would often come home in tears. In itself, this might have mattered little. It also developed, however, that in the oral-reading situation the teacher insisted on speed and laid down the remarkable rule that there was to be no pausing except at periods.

Cluttering. Abnormalities of speaking rate or phrasing are probably still another source of difficulty. Of particular importance is cluttering, a familiar type of rapid, indistinct, staccato utterance whose cause does not appear to be reliably known, although it is evidently quite common in children. Weiss (1964) believed that stuttering symptoms frequently appear as the result of the child's efforts to overcome a tendency to clutter. It is perhaps significant that one of the most common complaints with which children of practically all ages are brought to a speech clinic is that they "talk too fast and swallow their words." This is a potential source of serious concern to parents. There was definite evidence that it contributed to stuttering in some cases in the Brooklyn group. One girl of 7 was observed to force and repeat at age 5½, but prior to that she "had always been a rapid speaker" and had been urged continually to speak more slowly. A boy of 6 "began by just jumbling up and talking very fast before he actually stuttered," according to his mother. In still another case a first-grade teacher noticed that the child "spoke too fast" and began to remind her systematically to talk slowly. The mother did this at home as well, on the advice of the teacher. Six months later this girl appeared at the center exhibiting rapid sound repetitions with gasping and frequent retrials. Rapid, cluttered speech was also observed during the interview.

The same combination of symptoms may sometimes be seen in adults. What experienced speech clinician has not seen individuals who seem to both stutter and clutter? A noteworthy case of this kind was a college student, aged 18, who reported that he had been stuttering for only two years when he came for help. As far back as he could remember he had spoken very rapidly. As he grew older his family nagged him about his rapid speech with mounting intensity. "They didn't let me alone," he said. As an adolescent he finally made diligent attempts to talk slowly, but these proved of little use. Then he began to have great blocks that contracted his face and hunched his body. During the course of his therapy it was found that the rapid, staccato utterance had persisted. His clinician observed it even during occasional periods of complete freedom from stuttering of several days' duration.

Other provocations. Delayed language development, ordinary defects of articulation and pronunciation, reading difficulties, and cluttering are not the only provocations to stuttering. Clinical experience discloses examples of many more. Although the following cases are relatively rare, they all exemplify the same principle: Virtually anything at all that is calculated to shake children's faith in their ability to speak may bring with it an appreciable danger that persistent forms of stuttering will result.

Sometimes such provocations are to be found in the disturbances of speech and language of those who are classified as aphasic, brain injured, cerebral palsied, or mentally deficient. Peacher (1945) mentions a brain-injured patient who "developed stuttering as a secondary manifestation in his attempts to obviate a very evident motor dysphasia"

(p. 159). Other instances in which stuttering appeared as an aftermath of transient aphasic disturbances are cited by Eisenson (1947). In this connection one recalls with new interest familiar accounts of stuttering observed after a severe blow on the head followed by temporary loss of speech. One example was a 19-year-old stutterer seen at the Brooklyn College Speech and Hearing Center who also had severe difficulty in reading and spelling. He reported that all of his difficulties, including the stuttering, dated from the age of 9, when he suffered a brain concussion with loss of consciousness after falling from a tree. Upon his return to school after the injury, his grades immediately began to drop. He attended a vocational high school and at the time of his examination was a skilled cabinetmaker, although his reading abil:ty was approximately at the third-grade level. His speech problem was a severe stutter accompanied by characteristic symptoms of tongue protrusion, clicking of the teeth, and speaking on residual air.

I saw another adult stutterer who was not concerned about his stuttering as much as his inability to pronounce unfamiliar words. Although his silent reading comprehension was adequate, he was almost completely lacking in the ability to determine the pronunciation of a word by reading it. A pharmacist by profession, he had great difficulty with technical words. He could recognize the name of a pharmaceutical by memorizing the way it looked in print, but was unable to identify it if he heard it pronounced and could not pronounce it when he saw it. His written speech was on a grade-school level. He had gotten through college by relying on the notes of his friends and by having someone correct his papers and themes for spelling, grammar, and composition.

Mutism may represent another provocation to stuttering. Almost every speech therapist is familiar with reports of the onset of stuttering following a period of speechlessness after a severe shock. For example, one child in the Brooklyn group witnessed a bad automobile accident at age 3. When his mother found him two hours later, he was apparently making an unsuccessful attempt to say "mama." Despite her frightened efforts to help him, or perhaps in part because of them, the boy stopped talking completely for three weeks. When his speech came back, it came with strenuous hard contacts and rapid sound repetitions.

Assuming the authenticity of such accounts, and it is certainly hard to doubt it in all cases, why do episodes of this kind sometimes terminate in stuttering? At least part of the answer may be that, for some children, the experience is enough to leave them in some genuine doubt about their capacity for speech.

I have received occasional accounts of the appearance of stuttering in conjunction with postadenoidectomy speech difficulty. One child had his tonsils and adenoids removed at age 3. Prior to the operation his speech had been immature and difficult to understand. Afterward he became all but unintelligible, and it was painful for him to speak. About five or six days after surgery, his stuttering was noticed for the first time.

There are almost certainly many more circumstances than we have enumerated that may serve to infect children with the conviction that speech is an arduous process. Some of them are probably subtle and obscure. I have seen any number of cases in which provocations in the form of unusual past speech failures were hard to identify in the child's history and quite possibly did not exist. Even when they do, we can be sure that such factors are rarely enough to produce stuttering by themselves. Otherwise we should expect all children with articulatory problems to become stutterers. There was evidence in the Brooklyn case material that, generally speaking, another necessary condition for the establishment of stuttering is the existence of some source of environmental pressure that ultimately results in the child's exaggerated conscience about speech.

Sources of speech pressure

Parental perfectionism or overconcern. Few characteristics of stuttering have so frequently been commented on as the tendency of the disorder to be associated with environmental pressures on children to live up to high standards of behavior. Evidence of this comes to us in three forms. First, stuttering abounds everywhere among those people who are most competitive in their social organization and who train their children most strictly in the observance of complex codes of behavior. Second, in our own culture stuttering appears to have its highest incidence in segments of the population that are socioeconomically the most upward-moving. Third, there is a tendency for parents of stutterers as a group to be more exacting than average in their child-training policies.[14] They are often described as dominating, overprotective, anxious, or obsessively perfectionistic. Whatever its most precise description in a specific case, the point about the parental environment is that it tends to favor the imposition of excessively high standards of speech and their acquisition by the child. It is conceivable that even the most articulate child who is subjected to pressures to exceed his speech or language capabilities may learn to evaluate his speech attempts as failures and acquire that assumption of basic inadequacy in speaking which appears to us to underlie the tendency to stutter.

In the majority of cases in the Brooklyn group, the parental environment seemed to live up to its reputation for being exacting or overanxious. Such a description is a matter of degree, of course, and is difficult to offer if on a rigorously objective basis. If we keep these things in mind, it may not be too misleading to say that in about two-thirds of the cases the evidence seemed incontrovertible.

In many cases the parents would have been best described as perfectionistic. There was evidence of strict, demanding, nagging parental discipline, with the imposition of many restrictions in the home and heavy pressures to live up to adult standards of conduct. A few mothers voluntarily described themselves as perfectionists. Some gave accounts of plainly coercive feeding, weaning, and toilet training. One mother began attempts to toilet train her child when he was 4 months old. Others, with apparent pride, gave accounts of rigid prescriptions with regard to cleanliness, manners, obedience, and the performance of various aspects of the daily routine. "I would like him to be perfect," was one mother's comment. Frequently, these parental reactions could be observed directly in the interview situation. One 7-year-old was reminded so often to sit up straight, take her hand away from her mouth, and say "yes" instead of "yeah" that it was actually somewhat difficult to converse with her.

Frequently, the chief source of pressure seemed to be an adult other than the mother—for example, an aunt living in the home who exercised stern discipline or an overly meticulous housekeeper who cared for the child while the mother worked. In one case, at least, it was almost certainly the father, a talented and perfectionistic musician; the child was recalled to have asked him on one occasion, "Daddy, why is it everything I do is wrong?"

In many cases excessive protectiveness would have been a more suitable description of the dominant parental attitude than perfectionism. Mothers often spoke freely of themselves as overprotective. Their great anxiety and concern frequently seemed to have to do with much more than just the child's speech. Many boys and girls in the Brooklyn group were generally hovered over and worried about, and their food, rest, and other aspects of their health and development were watched with overwhelming intensity. One boy of $5\frac{1}{2}$ years had only recently been allowed to play out of his mother's sight. Another, aged 6 years and 11 months, enjoyed being fed while he watched television. A child whose mother had died when he was an infant was cared for by a grandmother and two aunts. The grandmother remarked, "We feel so sorry for him that we do things for him we don't need to."

In corroboration of this finding, a large number of the children were relatively dependent and immature in behavior. In one-third of the cases there were reports of unnecessary demands for help with dressing, washing, and feeding or other evidence of social immaturity. During the clinical interview, it was not unusual for a child of 6 to refuse to leave his mother or for a child of 4 to attempt to toy with papers on the examiner's desk or to insist on taking home the crayons with which he had been allowed to play.

The overprotective parents overlapped somewhat as a group with those who tended to be obsessively perfectionistic. As an illustration, one mother explained her son's social immaturity by saying that she was rarely satisfied with the way he "did things" and was consequently inclined to help him too much. It is possible that the most severe effects on children were often those produced by a dominating type of protectiveness or extremely anxious high expectations, because this kind of environment would appear to undermine the children's capacity to fulfill its unrealistic demands at the same time that it pushes and prods them to outdo themselves. An instructive example was the case of a 4-year-old boy who was separated from his mother only with difficulty during the interview. She explained that he clung to her continually and confessed that she had "overprotected him at one time." The boy, however, was expected to "fight his own battles and not come crying," and his father had taken the practical step of teaching him to fight with boxing gloves. The same child was determined to learn to read and write, a fact that his mother attributed with misgiving to her pride in his precocious ability to read and spell a few words.

Another outstanding example was provided by the case of Steven, a 14-year-old boy seen at the center. The focus of the problem was apparently a protective, overanxious, and demanding father. On one occasion Steven's friends refused to let him play with them, saying that if he played his father would be there to help him run with the ball. Steven's 21-year-old sister had never been allowed to go anywhere alone. Along with this overprotectiveness, the father had always expected both children to live up to very high standards, especially with regard to schoolwork and intellectual achievement. Steven thought of himself as stupid, according to the mother, because he had continually been called stupid by his father. The mother tried to help by repeating that he was "lazy, not stupid."

An instructive illustration of the manner in which high standards of speech may be related to a broader pattern of parental anxieties was provided by the mother of a 4-year-old stutterer. By her own admission her handling of the boy was inconsistent and vacillating. She confessed intense feelings of anxiety about the child and inadequacy as a parent, and there were many family problems about which she had already been advised to seek psychological guidance. She was tortured by her son's habit of creeping on the furniture and other normally disorderly behavior, and she was concerned not only about his stuttering but also about his slight lisp. One of her more significant comments was, "Since my childhood I liked people to speak well. If a girl had grammatical errors or anything like that in her speech I didn't want her as a friend. My great fear was that my child wouldn't talk well."

While the majority of stutterers do not appear to come from markedly unwholesome home environments, some of the cases described serve to emphasize the important point that some conditions often associated with stuttering are also conducive to severe adjustment difficulties. As was to be expected, many of these children seemed to have such difficulties. Not only did they frequently exhibit somewhat compulsive or dependent tendencies, but about one-third were feeding problems; about one-fifth were enuretic; and about one-third had exaggerated fears or night terrors or were chronic worriers. Most of these problems, of course, are fairly common among children. So is a certain amount of overconcern among parents. Of even greater moment, however, is the fact that some stutterers in the Brooklyn group did not seem to have any such traits or symptoms, and some of the parents were not anxious or demanding at all. Many of the parents made positive impressions of substance, warmth, and understanding. Their children, furthermore, often gave the appearance of being friendly, spontaneous, and self-possessed, in addition to being free of so-called "nervous" symptoms.

It is quite consistent with our assumptions about the etiology of stuttering that this should be so. The stuttering of these children probably was not caused directly by neurotic family backgrounds any more than it was caused by maleness, which characterized so large a proportion of them. Perfectionism and protective overconcern are to be found in any number of families in which all of the children are normal speakers. Such features of the home environment appear to contribute to the development of stuttering only when they serve as a source of unusual pressures on speech. Furthermore, they are by no means the only source of such pressures.

The personality of the child. Just as important, in many cases, as the pressures imposed on the child by a parent are the demands he makes on himself as a result of such traits as excessive need for approval, perfectionism, sensitivity, or anxiety. Neither these nor any other traits of personality are necessarily associated with stuttering. They appear often enough, however, to suggest that they are among the factors that may facilitate its development.

The youngsters in the Brooklyn group were often described as "good" children. Many of them appeared to be unusually meticulous and to have exceptionally high goals. One boy of 6 reacted to the request that he copy a circle by saying "I can't make it as round as that." In building a tower of blocks, he used extreme care to make the corners of each block coincide with those of the one beneath, and in making several folds in a piece of paper he took pains to see that the edges met accurately. His mother described him as very clean and well behaved, and an assistant in whose charge he was placed during part of the interview remarked about his extraordinary politeness. The compulsive orderliness shown by this boy was to some degree a feature of about one-fourth of the case histories of the group. As typical examples, one child before going to bed at night needed to have his shoes in a special place, the room and closet doors closed, and the chairs placed just so; another child became upset if the arrangement of his toys was disturbed in the slightest or if he was accidentally wet or dirtied.

In the records of somewhat older stutterers, this type of report is less common, but in their place there is frequent mention of meticulosity, high aspirations, and strong desires to excel. A 10-year-old girl was said to be capable of destroying 10 or 15 sheets of paper in doing her homework. A boy of the same age often arose at 6:00 A.M. to study. Another boy, aged 9, was said to be a "perfectionist" about his schoolwork. It was recalled that as a small child he would cry when dirty and that he was completely toilet trained at 8 months. The parent was generally at a loss to explain the child's need for perfection. "We never expect it of him," was a frequent comment.

Such children are, of course, peculiarly disposed to see their small mistakes as large failings. They are also unusually easy prey to the praise or disapproval they receive from their social environment. So are anxious, sensitive children. An example, representative of quite a few, was Jeffrey, aged 6, an only child who cried when separated from his mother during the initial interview. He had a history of occasional night terrors and frequent bed-wetting and was described as tense, fearful, and emotional. On entering kindergarten he had objected that it was too noisy. Soon afterward he was said to have begun to stutter and to react to his stuttering by asking, "When am I going to stop doing this?" His teacher's comment was that he was shy and liked everything to be "just so." She said about his stuttering, "When he doesn't know a word he starts that."

Another instructive lesson was provided by Roy, a 6-year-old stutterer who had a normal-speaking identical twin brother. When I asked the mother in what other ways the two children differed besides their speech, her answer was, "Roy is more sensitive and less aggressive."

Demanding speech models. Children, as is well known, unconsciously try to emulate the behavior of adults or older children with whom they identify. For this reason, there may be some speech pressure stemming simply from the fact that a child's parents or older siblings are in the habit of talking unusually rapidly, fluently, or with a vocabulary that abounds in polysyllabic words. There is even more pressure when one of the child's models is gifted with beautiful or effective speech that is an object of family pride. I have often been struck by a father, frequently a minister, rabbi, teacher, or lawyer, whose articulateness is in blunt contrast to the speech of the boy he brings for examination. Even if exceptionally good speech was never asked of this boy, either expressly or by virtue of certain values he encountered in the home, one can be reasonably sure that he inflicted on himself all of the consequences of such demands merely in the natural process of competing with his father. In one memorable case, the father described himself somewhat mysteriously as a "public speaker."

Excessive approval of the child's speech. Paradoxically, there may even be some danger when speech becomes a focus of attention because it is extraordinarily good. There are perhaps rather significant implications when parents wistfully report that the child "was an extremely early talker," "spoke beautifully before he stuttered," or "at the age of 1 knew 20 nursery rhymes." Such comments may offer a clue to a situation in which the speech process came to be invested with the hobbling threat of failure because the child's good speech was so intensely valued.

One child, before he was first heard to stutter at age 3, was a rapid, fluent, and voluble speaker who enjoyed standing in front of his home and regaling passersby with such badinage as, "Hey! How you? How your mother? How your father?" One day while on a walk with his mother they met an acquaintance of hers to whom the boy promptly said, "Hi lady, you a nice lady, I like you, lady," and much more, rapidly, to the same effect. The lady was so astonished, and made so prolonged an uproar about the boy's speech that, according to the mother, he stopped talking for four or five days and immediately stuttered severely when he did begin to speak again.

Other sources of speech pressure. There are no doubt many other reasons why children come to have an abnormal need for approval of their speech. One boy in the Brooklyn group was obliged to live up to standards set by a fraternal twin brother who was said to have overshadowed him from the start in various aspects of development, including language. Another case was that of a boy whose parents had accepted with difficulty the knowledge that he was slightly retarded mentally and tended to make a great fuss about all of his intellectual and verbal achievements. A factor that was given considerable emphasis by Johnson was a climate of anxiety about speech that prevails in some families in which cases of stuttering have been common. In such families a belief that stuttering is hereditary and the children are apt to stutter may sensitize a parent to the way the child talks (see Johnson et al., 1967, pp. 262–266). Finally, as some of our illustrations have suggested, the kind of atmosphere that hangs over the oral recitation situation in some classrooms may provide yet another instance in which children are continuously subjected to excessive demands for skill at speaking.

Summary remarks

The findings of the Brooklyn study seem to imply that stuttering is a child's conscientious effort to speak acceptably despite his conviction that he cannot do so. It germinates readily in an environment that is in some manner critical or anxious about speech and is frequently related to certain provocations in the form of inferior language skill, articulatory substitutions, pronunciation errors, or any other difficulties that may leave a child in doubt as to his basic ability to communicate properly. We may call stuttering a severe form of speech consciousness. It serves to remind us that, as a natural consequence of its deep social implications, speech is far more vulnerable as an object of fear and self-consciousness than other modes of human behavior.

If the processes by which children learn their verbal skills are hazardous from the point of view of stuttering, this seems to be especially true in surroundings where standards are high and pressures severe. In themselves, the speech defects and language deficiencies that frequently seem to precipitate stuttering are slight by almost any reasonable objective criterion. What stuttering seems to reflect, in the final analysis, is a society that promotes intense competition for status and prestige and capriciously accepts the most trivial refinements of speech as valid symbols of their attainment.

The Continuity Hypothesis

It is now well known that normal young children tend to have a considerable amount of disfluency in their speech. If we are to understand the etiology of stuttering fully, one of the critical questions we must answer is whether stuttering is related in any way to such disfluency and, if so, how. If such a relationship exists, we must choose between two points of view about its nature. One is Wendell Johnson's view that stuttering is the child's effort to avoid normal disfluency. A more recent concept, and one that is in better accord with the theory of stuttering we have developed in this chapter, is the continuity hypothesis.

It regards what is generally called stuttering in young children as a more extreme *degree* of certain specific types of normal disfluency.

Difficulties in distinguishing early stutterings from normal disfluencies

It was Johnson, in the late 1930s, who was first struck by the surprising observation that it is difficult to distinguish between some young stutterers and some nonstutterers by listening to the way they speak: not because stuttering children do not hesitate and repeat, but because normal speaking children do too, often in the same way and sometimes to the same or a greater degree. Ultimately, Johnson and his associates (1959, chap. 8) backed this up with a considerable body of research evidence. They recorded the spontaneous speech of a large number of children who had been classified, by their parents and others, as stutterers and nonstutterers and analyzed the disfluencies of both groups according to eight categories of disfluency. With respect to most of these categories, there was little difference between the groups in frequency of disfluency. The stutterers did exceed the nostutterers in the average frequency of several of them, especially sound and syllable repetitions, word repetitions, and prolonged sounds. From this standpoint, it might seem that disfluencies of these types are characteristic of stutterers. Unfortunately, it is not that simple because, as Johnson pointed out, there was considerable overlap between the two groups in the distribution of these disfluency types. We may take as an example the case of sound and syllable repetitions, in which the average difference between the two groups was widest. Even in this category about 20 percent of the male "nonstutterers" had more disfluency than 20 percent of the male "stutterers." The data for females were comparable. Moreover, the great majority of nonstutterers, about 75 percent of the boys and about 90 percent of the girls, exhibited some amount of sound and syllable repetition in the course of producing an average speech sample of 500 words (Johnson and associates, 1959, p. 217).

Even more interesting were the findings relating to tension. The tape recordings were not analyzed from this point of view, but the parents of children in both groups were asked about the extent to which they had observed signs of tension in the children's speech. Much more tension was reported by the parents of stutterers; but 14 percent of the fathers and 6 percent of the mothers of the nonstutterers also said they were observing tension in their children's disfluencies at the time of the interview, despite the fact that no child in the group had at any time been considered a stutterer. At least two of these children were evidently closing or blinking their eyes. Furthermore, a number of nonstutterers were said to be aware of their speech interruptions or to show signs of surprise, bewilderment, or irritation when they occurred (Johnson and associates, 1959, p. 146, and Appendix A, pp. 79, 80, 104).[15]

The remarkable conclusion to which all of this leads is that as yet we have no way of defining or describing stuttering objectively that would serve in all cases to differentiate a "stuttering" child in an unequivocal way from a child who speaks normally. We would, of course, have little difficulty in distinguishing stuttering children from others *as groups* on the basis of a difference in average occurrence of certain symptoms. But this fact may be of little help when we try to determine from a sample of speech whether a given child brought to us for a diagnostic evaluation is a stutterer or not.

If we wish, we may gloss over this difficulty by supposing that the majority of children could probably be classified as either stutterers or nonstutterers with statistical reliability by groups of listeners. Although this may be true, however, it has little relevance to either the practical clinical problem posed by certain individual children or the broad question of how stuttering and normal disfluency are related. The *majority* of children might also be classified by judges as fat or thin, or as tall or short, with poor reliability only for a relatively small number of individuals midway on the continuum of weight or height. Yet we recognize that these are actually continuous variables, and when we characterize a child as thin, short, delayed in speech development, or poorly adjusted emotionally, we do so with the tacit understanding that in each case we are dichotomizing a continuum at a convenient point in an arbitrary way. Generally speaking, we have not recognized this in the case of stuttering, however. We have usually tended to assume that there is a natural distinction between children who stutter and those who speak normally. Even though we have now learned that there are syllable repetitions, prolongations, and occasionally even signs of effort or tension in the speech of a large proportion of ordinary young children, we have generally continued to operate on the assumption that there must be some way to tell if a child was a "stutterer" or a "nonstutterer"—if only we could find it. This is a conceptual holdover from the days, not long ago, when the distinction seemed obvious because it was not yet widely recognized that most normal young children are markedly disfluent.

Normal disfluencies as anticipatory struggle reactions

In essence, the hypothesis I am proposing is that the reason stuttering and nonstuttering children seem to overlap so widely with respect to the types and frequencies of their disfluencies is that anticipatory struggle behavior is not confined exclusively to children who come to be called "stutterers." Many of the pressures and provocations that appear capable of generating anticipatory struggle reactions are, to some degree, essentially commonplace features of the ordinary child's daily experience. To some extent, then, it is only to be expected that most ordinary children will exhibit mild degrees of tension and fragmentation in their speech from time to time. I do not mean to imply that all normal disfluencies are to be seen in this light. I am simply suggesting that, among the disfluencies of most normal young children, there are certain types that have a potential for developing into identifiable episodes of stuttering if the pressures and provocations that produce them become relatively intense or chronic. Among such types are sound, syllable and word repetitions, prolongations, and signs of effort or tension in the articulation of sounds. If these are stutterings when they occur in the speech of one child, there seems little reason to call them anything else when they appear in the speech of another child. From this point of view the continuity hypothesis might be stated by saying that most young children stutter. Some do it more than others, and a few do it so severely and persistently that parents and others begin—gradually in most cases—to perceive that the child has a defect of speech.

When I suggest that a normal child may have anticipatory struggle reactions I mean not only that on occasion he does some of the things as he talks that children called "stutterers" do, but that he does them for similar reasons. To be sure, these reasons are hard to characterize with much precision. A 3-year-old's cognitions, and his verbal repertoire for symbolizing them, are different from an adult's, and the nature of such a child's perception that speech is difficult or involves the threat of failure or trouble is necessarily obscure. It is self-evident, however, that even ordinary, typical children frequently have speech experiences which they may perceive in some manner as failures or frustrations; furthermore, it does not seem beyond belief that such children occasionally respond to stimuli evocative of such experiences with some mild tension and fragmentation in speech.

There is, of course, an immediate practical application of all this that relates to any young child in our clinical experience who might tend to leave us in doubt about whether we should classify him as a stutterer or a normal speaker. It implies that any attempt to make such a "diagnosis" is a futile and meaningless exercise. We can describe his tensions and fragmentations, count them, compare them with norms, find out under what conditions they occur, determine how much of a problem they are for the child or anyone else, and make a judgment about whether he should be getting some help from us because of them. But we cannot tell whether he is or is not a "stutterer."

The continuity versus the either-or point of view

At a quick glance the continuity hypothesis may seem to some readers to be hard to distinguish from the diagnosogenic concept of Wendell Johnson. The hypothesis owes a great debt to Johnson's work, which led directly to it, but Johnson's theory of the relationship between stuttering and normal disfluency was in the most fundamental sense an either-or theory. It put extraordinary emphasis on the need to make a clear distinction between the two. It held that any similarity between them existed only in the minds of certain parents who sometimes mistook normal disfluency in their children for stuttering, with perilous consequences.

For a time Johnson believed that children might be called "stutterers" rather than "disfluent normal speakers" if their interruptions were marked by effort, tension, or strain; if they regarded themselves as stutterers; and if others regarded them as stutterers. This proved unsatisfactory when his own later research disclosed evidence that there were tensions in the speech of some children whom no one had ever regarded as stutterers. When Johnson and his associates (1959, chap. 8) collected their massive body of data on children's speech, its ultimate meaning turned out to be that there was no observation or measurement that could be made on a child's disfluency—whether on frequency of occurrence, average "extent" (number per instance) of repetitions, type of disfluency, or anything else—that would serve to show in any categorical way that he was stuttering rather than talking normally on a given occasion. Johnson summed this up by saying that there were "no 'natural' lines of demarcation between 'normal' and 'abnormal' degrees of nonfluency" (Johnson and associates, 1959, p. 205). This was as close to the continuity hypothesis as he came. The simple and obvious conclusion might have been that "stuttering" and "normal" disfluency differed from each other only in degree. Johnson never took that final step. Instead, he reasoned that if stuttering could not be operationally differentiated from normal disfluency by any feature of a child's speech, then it could not be defined as a feature of a child's speech at all. Accordingly, he drew a distinction between disfluency—of any kind or degree—and stuttering. Disfluency was a feature of speech. Stuttering was defined as a *problem* that under certain circumstances arose for a *listener* (Johnson and associates, 1959, p. 219 and chap. 10).

It is not hard to see that Johnson's thinking took such an unusual turn because of one basic fact: He could not or did not choose to free himself from the notion that something could only be either stuttering or normal. The reason for this was only partly that this was the old and firmly rooted common sense. Perhaps to an even greater degree it was due to Johnson's fascination with the simple and appealing theory that stuttering began as a child's efforts to avoid normal disfluency. It is exceedingly difficult to find any middle ground between the avoidance of something and the thing being avoided. The diagnosogenic theory is sometimes ambiguously referred to as the theory that stuttering "grows out of" or "develops from" normal disfluency. In actuality, the diagnosogenic theory pits stuttering against normal disfluency in the most blunt way and leaves little room for a continuity between them in any dimensional sense.

Parallels in the distribution of "stutterings" and "normal" disfluencies

The principal evidence that there appears to be no operationally meaningful way to differentiate the disfluencies of early stuttering from those of normal speech comes from observations of the frequency, form, or severity of the disfluencies. Speech interruptions have still other observable features, however. For example, they have a pattern of distribution in the speech sequence (i.e., they are more likely to occur at certain loci than at others) and they vary in frequency under different conditions. Is there some kind of natural distinction between "normal" and "abnormal" disfluency that can be defined with reference to such information? As yet, the work that has been done on children from this point of view is comparatively meager, and it has suffered somewhat from a tendency to lump together all of the various types of normal disfluency indiscriminately, including some that are probably not tensions and fragmentations at all in the sense in which we have been using these terms. Despite this, however, such information as we have seems to contain an appreciable amount of support for the concept of continuity.

The consistency effect, which has been noted in the case of very young stutterers, has been found in the distribution of disfluencies in preschool nonstutterers as well (Wynia, 1964; Bloodstein, Alper, and Zisk, 1965). The loci of their disfluencies with respect to the various grammatical parts of speech are also remarkably similar (Bloodstein and Gantwerk, 1967; Helmreich and Bloodstein, 1973). For preschool children, the record beyond this point is blank at this writing. It is of interest, however, that even in children of elementary-school age, both stutterings and normal disfluencies exhibit the consistency and adaptation effects and are influenced in similar ways by word length, sentence position, grammatical function, and phonetic factors (Williams, Silverman, and Kools, 1968, 1969a, 1968b; Neelley and Timmons, 1967). In fact, these parallels extend to adults, as further work by Silverman and Williams and others has shown; but it should come as no surprise that there may also be some qualitative differences between stutterers and nonstutterers by adulthood.[16]

These studies have been concerned almost exclusively with the distribution of disfluencies. The possibility that "stuttering" and "nonstuttering" groups of preschool children might be clearly differentiated by the conditions under which their disfluencies vary in frequency has so far not been directly investigated, but there are indications that this question will come under increasing study (see E.-M. Silverman, 1973).

The prevalence of transient stuttering in young children

Another observation that seems to accord in a simple and natural way with the continuity hypothesis is the unusual number of transient episodes (i.e., of a few months or less) of stuttering during the early childhood years. These appear to be so numerous, so brief, and often so mild, that we are hard put to find the line that separates them from variations in the severity of "normal" disfluency. Investigators of the speech behavior of normal 2–5-year-olds (Ilg, Learned, and Lockwood, 1949; Métraux, 1950) have often had to talk of the frequent "stuttering" of "normal" children, a use of terms that anticipates the continuity hypothesis. Glasner and Rosenthal (1957) questioned the parents of 996 children entering the first grade in Ann Arundel County, Maryland, and found that 15.4 percent of them gave accounts of stuttering in their children. Somewhat less than half of this percentage were said to be still stuttering. Transient cases of stuttering in young children have also been reported by Andrews and Harris (1964, p. 30). Perhaps the outstanding interest of such reports from the point of view of our hypothesis is the possibility they suggest that many more cases go undetected in such surveys because they are of too brief duration to be memorable to parents or to be observed by investigators. Nearly anyone whose professional work relates in some way to the speech of young children has heard occasional reports of stuttering lasting for only a few days.

We have been discussing the phenomenon of transient stuttering in early childhood without asking of what, precisely, it consists. Descriptions are scarce, but there is little indication that early transient stuttering differs from more persistent forms of early stuttering. This is to say that it appears highly varied in form. While some reports suggest that it is predominantly simple and repetitive, it is anything but that in many cases. The best evidence for this comes from a somewhat unexpected source. Transient stuttering does not often reach the speech clinic, but I have had considerable personal experience with it through students, former students, and professional colleagues who have consulted me about what proved to be brief outbreaks of stuttering in their own children. In some cases the difficulty was marked by severe effort and strain and by reactions of frustration. Most of the parents who described such behavior to me were at pains to emphasize that it was "not normal nonfluency." They were afraid I would assume that they had misdiagnosed normal disfluency as stuttering. I did not, of course, not because this would have been incorrect, but because the question of whether they had or not is in a basic sense unanswerable. They believed their children's speech behavior could not be normal because it involved tension and struggle. One might just as well have insisted that it could not be abnormal because such transient episodes are essentially commonplace among ordinary children and very soon pass without a trace. In the context of the continuity hypothesis, of course, the question disappears. It is only a quibble about the use of terms.

"Onset" as a dubious concept

If most young children have rudimentary anticipatory struggle reactions in their speech, it follows that the so-called onset of stuttering is hardly more than a convenient fiction. Strictly speaking, there can be no onset of stuttering in the sense in which it has usually been conceived. There can be a moment when a child's gradually increasing tensions and fragmentations first strike a parent as abnormal or a day on which certain provocations cause an abrupt intensification of them, and for certain practical purposes it may be useful to refer to such an occurrence as the "onset" of the child's stuttering. But there can rarely be a specifiable date on the calendar on which a child begins to stutter after having spoken without any stuttering before. This is a curious implication of the continuity hypothesis, but it is also a very useful one. It yields a solution to an important problem that has probably arisen for almost anyone who has tried to think systematically about the etiology of stuttering since about 1942.

Since about that date, the year of Johnson's first publication on his diagnosogenic theory, we have had a situation in the field of speech pathology in which a fairly large number of young children whose parents claimed they were stuttering could have received markedly conflicting clinical diagnoses on the basis of identical observations of their speech. Such children have been called "stutterers"—sometimes "primary stutterers"—by some and "normal speakers" by others. Now, if we take it for granted that stuttering has an "onset" at some identifiable moment, it is also common sense that it has certain "initial," "beginning," or "incipient" symptoms. Furthermore, if we wish to do research on the onset of stuttering it is unavoidable that we ask questions about these initial symptoms. Under what conditions do they occur? What are they like? At what loci do they appear in the speech sequence? Do they show the consistency effect? How does the child react to them? Do they ever involve effort or tension? The questions are endless, but without exception they are futile. How can we ask anything about the initial symptoms of stuttering unless we first define what we mean by initial stuttering? But in order to define it, we must assume the answers to some of the most important questions we are asking. From this circularity there is no way out, since no observations can be made to determine whether a definition is "correct"—it is only a matter of convenience.

When our thinking is blocked by a logical dilemma of this sort, it is usually a sign that there is an error somewhere in our assumptions. It seems apparent where that error has been. The "initial" symptoms, or "onset," of stuttering are not things that anyone has ever directly heard or seen. In the most basic sense they are concepts, not facts. Moreover, they are concepts that seem to conceal a fundamental misapprehension about the way in which stuttering and normal disfluency are related. The onset of stuttering is a figment of the either-or dogma. Johnson could talk readily about it. In the context of the continuity hypothesis, we cannot. We can ask questions about the speech interruptions of young children. We can, if we wish, confine these questions to certain specific types of disfluency. If we think it is interesting to do so, we can ask such questions about children who have just recently been regarded by their parents as stutterers. But we cannot ask any questions about children at the "onset" of stuttering or about children who are "beginning" or have just "begun" to stutter.

III. TREATMENT

When stuttering persists into later childhood and adulthood, the problem as a whole tends to change and develop in various ways and presents itself in different forms requiring essentially different methods of treatment. The process of change is, of course, continuous, and it probably varies considerably from individual to individual. I have found it convenient to think of the treatment of stuttering in terms of four general phases of development. These represent four clinical pictures that should be familiar to almost every experienced speech clinician. Since they differ in the characteristic age levels at which they appear, we may infer that they represent successive stages in a process of development that is typical for stutterers. The process, however, evidently proceeds rapidly for some and slowly for others, since the age ranges at which we observe these patterns tend to overlap very widely. In addition, as many stutterers are to be found "between" these four descriptions as "at" them. A few may seem to fit nowhere in this scheme. If so, it is the scheme that is at fault, not the stutterer. A detailed description of the identifying characteristics of these phases has appeared in an earlier publication (Bloodstein, 1960a, 1960b, 1961).

Phase 1

Age range: approximately 2 to 6 years.

Description.   The speech difficulty usually tends to come and go in the form of episodes of varying duration and frequency. The children stutter chiefly when excited or when they have a lot to say. Essentially any of the symptoms of stuttering may be present. Contrary to a once commonly held assumption, there may be strenuous blocks and associated, or "secondary," features; these do not belong exclusively to advanced forms of stuttering. In many cases, however, a conspicuous aspect of the pattern is a frank, relatively simple repetition of whole words, syllables, and sounds.

The speech repetition appears to occur with striking regularity at the beginning of sentences, clauses, noun phrases, verb phrases, or other syntactic units. While essentially all parts of speech are stuttered, there is an unusual tendency to stutter on function words, especially conjunctions and pronouns. In short, these children are often heard to begin their sentences or clauses by saying "I-I-I," "He-He-He," "But-But-But," "So-So-So," or the like. In general, they seem to be doing what a child might be expected to do if he were fragmenting whole syntactic structures rather than words.

Typically, these children do not avoid speech and may give at least the outward appearance of being unconcerned about their stuttering most of the time. Many of them, however, from time to time express emotional reactions of frustration on becoming blocked in their efforts to speak. They may cry, hit themselves on the mouth, or ask, "Why can't I talk?" Despite this, they give little evidence of having formed any distinct self-concepts as stutterers or defective speakers.

They should not be confused with Phase 2 stutterers, some of whom enter that phase as early as age 4.

Goals and rationale.   Although Phase 1 stuttering has many of the essential characteristics of anticipatory struggle behavior at any stage of development, it is a rudimentary problem, indistinguishable from the minor eruptions of increased disfluency that are apparently common in early childhood as transient phenomena. The main goal of therapy is therefore the prevention of more advanced forms of stuttering. To this end we must at all costs prevent the child from developing a self-concept as a defective speaker. This means that our main concern must be with the child's reputation as a speaker in his family environment. Parent counseling must therefore be the major therapeutic approach.

Ideally, every parent should be enrolled in the speech clinic for an indefinite period of counseling. In practice, however, much briefer contacts are often justified. In the first place, parents frequently come merely for advice or reassurance, and the clinician will sense that they are unprepared for extended clinical contacts. Moreover, extended therapy is not always necessary. The stuttering frequently tends to disappear after a single clinical interview. This is particularly true of very young children who have been stuttering for a short time. (Needless to say, many of these problems would probably has resolved themselves just as quickly had there been no interview at all.) In such cases, more prolonged counseling may be held in reserve for use if needed.

Removing environmental pressures

Among the most important of the factors that threaten to turn Phase 1 stuttering into a chronic disorder are pressures imposed on the child in ways discussed earlier in this chapter. These arise in the majority of cases from the child's home environment. The removal of pressures may be divided into a number of somewhat different aspects for purposes of discussion.

Any effort to change some of the parent's behavior must start with the removal of guilt about the child's stuttering. The mother who brings her stuttering youngster to the clinic is likely to have a crushing sense that she herself was somehow implicated in the development of his speech difficulty. "What did I do wrong?" is a question that, in one form or another, she may ask as anxiously as "Will he outgrow it?" While she, and the father as well, must be helped to accept a sizable share of responsibility for the child's speech improvement, there is hardly a more effective way of intensifying her anxieties than to corroborate her suspicion that his stuttering resulted from abnormalities in her relationship with him. On the other hand, our confidence in her basic adequacy as a parent will leave her better able to accept suggestions for specific changes in her behavior. We may not be able to tell her with conviction that she had nothing to do with her child's stuttering. But we can, in our opinion, truthfully tell her that stuttering seems to be brought about by a combination of many factors or conditions and that stuttering children appear to be found in every conceivable type of

family environment, not excluding some which seem in many ways unusually wholesome and favorable.

We must insist on the removal of all speech pressures. This is perhaps
the central concern of therapy, toward which everything else is in some
way directed. The parents must put a stop to any tendency they may
have to correct the child's articulation, pronunciation, or choice of
words, his speaking rate, or any other real or imagined flaw in
his communication and in particular, of course, his stuttering. A somewhat special question this may raise is what to do about the youngster
with definite infantile errors of articulation when the parents are deeply
concerned about these. Perhaps the best way of making certain that
they do not agitate the child about these errors is to accept him for
articulatory therapy. If we do, however, the remedial operation should
be regarded as a rather delicate one. Pains must be taken to see that
the acquisition of new articulatory habits never becomes a struggle.
This means we should limit ourselves with unusual strictness to auditory
stimulation in teaching the new sounds, avoiding any technique that
draws attention to movements or positions of the articulators. Furthermore,
attempts to transfer the sounds to conversation should be deferred with
more than ordinary care until there is not the slightest doubt about
the child's ability to use them easily in connected speech.

In many cases there will be no speech difficulty other than stuttering.
Furthermore, even when some other speech difficulty originally served
as a provocation to stuttering, the parents' anxieties will usually have
concentrated themselves long since upon the struggle behavior itself.
Consequently, removal of speech pressures is in most cases essentially
a matter of eliminating parental reactions to the child's stuttering. It
is not enough to merely advise parents to ignore the stuttering or avoid
bringing it to the child's attention. We must be sure they fully understand
all of the ways they may be telling their child to "stop that awful stuttering." Many parents do not appear to be aware that they do this when
they praise the child for speaking fluently, promise him a bicycle for
his birthday if he stops stuttering, finish a difficult word for him, or
stop what they are doing to look at him when he becomes blocked.
Some parents do not even seem to realize that they do this when they
tell the child to speak more slowly, stop and start over again, or think
before he speaks.

Moreover, it is not enough to tell the parents that they must not
do any of these things. Few parents can probably hide their feelings
from the child for long if they are profoundly distressed, and every
effort should be made to reduce their anxiety about the stuttering. There
are at least three things that can be done to decrease the parents' anxieties.
First, they must be given a certain amount of basic information about

stuttering. They must know that the disorder appears in many stages and that their own child's speech difficulty represents a very rudimentary form, different in symptomatology and far removed in development from stuttering in an advanced state. They may be told that, in this rudimentary form, stuttering affects a great many normal children for brief periods. We may not tell them, of course, that their child will certainly outgrow his stuttering, although we know how fervently they want to hear this; but we may tell them that any young child who stutters has an excellent chance of outgrowing it to begin with and that their child's chances will be vastly improved if the problem is handled wisely at home.

Second, it is a good plan in most cases to give the parents something positive and concrete to do for the child that will allow them to feel they are actively helping him overcome his difficulty. Some useful practices that parents may institute at home will be described shortly. Here it may be said that a certain part of the benefit of these probably lies in their effect on the parents. We must bear in mind that a mother who is overwrought about her child's stuttering may find it very disquieting to be told that, beyond doing her best to make no issue of it, there is nothing for her to do but wait and hope.

Third, parents should be advised to come back at intervals if there continues to be no improvement in the child's speech. Each time they return we may review the advisability of beginning a program of clinical therapy with the child himself or of arranging to see the parents regularly for a period of intensive guidance. One of the chief purposes of the advice to bring the child for reexamination, however, is to let the parents know that we are willing to assume a definite share of the responsibility for the child's improvement. They should never be permitted to feel they are being left to face their difficulties entirely alone.

When necessary, the parents should be helped to understand in what respects they might be less restrictive and demanding in their attitudes toward the child's behavior as a whole. As we have seen, the pressures that are imposed upon a child's speech are often found in a setting of generally high standards or overconcern. Parents may tend to be overly critical of the child's developing physical and intellectual abilities; expect too much in such matters as cleanliness, manners, and obedience; or attempt excessive regulation of the child's eating, sleeping, and play habits. If the parents are able to be less anxious or perfectionistic about the child's general behavior, this may help to make them more easygoing about his speech. The advice to relieve the child of accumulated pressures occasionally appears to have exceptionally practical results. We must be careful, however, to apply this advice with discrimination. Some parents of stutterers are, if anything, too weak and indecisive in their exercise of discipline and parental control. Because children need to feel safe and cared for, there must be a degree of firmness in the manner in which they are handled and an imposition of certain demands and limits. It is not parental strictness in itself that warrants our concern, but the kind of strictness that insists on essentially adult qualities of responsibility, consideration, foresight, or judgment or in various ways puts a premium on social maturity or intelligence beyond the child's capacity.

In a certain number of cases psychotherapy may offer the only practical hope of reducing parental pressures. While parental pressures are always to some degree complex in their motivation, there are some cases in which they seem to arise to an unusual extent from neurotic anxieties or compulsiveness, from the mother's abnormal need to keep the child dependent on her, from guilt about feelings of rejection, or from the desire to use the child's achievements for the sake of the parent's personal prestige. In such cases there may be little to be gained by suggesting changes in the parents' behavior until there have been far-reaching changes in the parent-child relationship.

Reinforcing the child's anticipation of fluency

It is probably necessary for a child to harbor a sense of inadequacy in speech for a long period of time before he becomes a confirmed stutterer. In the meantime, anything designed to give him a feeling that he can speak without frustrating interruptions would appear to be a very worthwhile preventive measure.

Experiencing success. One method that seems excellently calculated to strengthen anticipation of fluency is to see that the child experiences daily successful, pleasant, and rewarding speech with a minimum of stuttering. This may be done effectively by the parents themselves. Most stuttering youngsters are capable of a vast amount of fluent talking. Not only do they tend to have frequent periods during which they do not stutter, but, like older stutterers, even when their difficulty is at its most severe they can often recite simple rhymes; speak rhythmically, in a whisper or in unison with someone else; echo another person's utterance; speak to their dolls or pets; talk for a puppet, or assume a role in a play without stuttering. By setting aside a half hour or so each day for dramatizing familiar stories, reciting poetry, playing simple word games, or capitalizing on the child's fluent speech in any other entertaining and interesting way, a parent with sufficient motivation and some guidance should be able to develop a constructive program for immunizing the child against the harmful effects of his stuttering experiences by proving to him over and over again that he is basically able to talk without stuttering. While these procedures may be used in a speech clinic, they appear to be best carried out at home, where it is somewhat easier to avoid the implication that they are intended as remedial measures.

Eliminating conditions that create disfluency. A second means of systematically fighting off the suggestion that speech is barbed with difficulties is to decrease in every way possible the occasions that precipitate the child's most severe stuttering. Some of the ways in which the parents may be able to do this are avoiding situations that are charged with excitement for the child, being more responsive when he tries to gain their attention, seeing to it that he needs to compete as little as possible with others in the family for the opportunity to speak, and requiring him to speak as little as possible under conditions of conflict or emotion. Each individual child requires a special study of the conditions under which his stuttering occurs. In some cases, these conditions will not permit clear-cut identification or will not be readily amenable to change. In many cases, however, the stuttering may come and go in waves of severity, and the most conspicuous difficulty may be confined to certain "bad" days. If so, the parent should be prepared at such times with some absorbing occupations that the child may pursue for the most part alone or which necessitate a minimum of speaking.

Phase 2

Age range: about 4 to adulthood. Phase 2 is most usual in children of elementary-school age.

Description. The difficulty in most cases no longer comes and goes, but has become relatively chronic. The distinctive Phase 1 repetitions of whole words, including many pronouns and conjunctions, has disappeared or markedly diminished. Stuttering is no longer confined to the first word of a sentence, clause, or phrase. The child now appears to be fragmenting words rather than syntactic structures.

Most important of all, the child has developed a self-concept as a defective speaker. His use of the words "stutter" or "stuttering" is usually the best evidence of this, but a 6-year-old expressed it clearly by saying, "There's a little voice in me that goes uh-uh-uh. I can't help it. It's hard for me. It's easy for other people but not for me." (By contrast, one 4-year-old's complaint, "I can't say goodnight to my daddy," expressing only a reaction to the immediate experience of being blocked, is more typical of the verbal reactions of Phase 1.)

Despite their knowledge that they are "stutterers," the children are generally not bothered by that knowledge and still tend to talk freely except on occasion. The report of the parents or, in some cases, the children themselves is that they stutter chiefly when excited or when they try to talk too fast. In this and other respects, the stuttering problem is in a relatively rudimentary form.

Among children of elementary-school age, Phase 2 stutterers are to be carefully distinguished from Phase 3 and 4 stutterers, who are also frequently found in the primary grades and require essentially different methods of treatment.

Goals and rationale. The central objective is very clear. We must combat the child's self-concept as a speech defective by every means possible while it is still newly formed. Finding the best method of achieving this, however, presents some unusual problems.

In the literature in speech pathology, Phase 2 stuttering has scarcely ever been identified as a distinct entity, and a climate of opinion about its treatment has not yet developed in the field. When clinicians largely trained to deal with either "primary" or "secondary" stuttering have encountered Phase 2 stuttering in remedial speech classrooms in the public schools, they have generally been unprepared for it. This has given rise to a widespread impression that the stutterer from about 7 to 12 years is difficult to treat. If so, perhaps this is partly because such an attitude on the part of a clinician is difficult for a stuttering child to overcome. If we want to deal effectively with the Phase 2 stutterer, we must begin by discarding this assumption. Probably at no stage in the development of stuttering, except Phase 1, is the child's speech so likely to suffer from the expectations of others that he will fail to talk well, or so likely to improve because others think he will do better.

In point of fact, there appear to be some very good reasons to believe that, potentially, Phase 2 stuttering is among the easiest of speech disorders to treat. In the first place, there is much that should lead us to assume that this would be so. In many respects, the difficulty is still in a rudimentary stage of development. The child is usually still quite young and malleable. The stuttering has generally not been of long duration. Also, we have unquestionable evidence that throughout the age range at which Phase 2 stuttering is most prevalent, children recover from stuttering at a very high rate spontaneously (Andrews and Harris, 1964; Sheehan and Martyn, 1966; Dickson, 1971; Cooper, 1972).

In the second place, a considerable body of clinical evidence suggests that with these cases, to a far greater extent than with others, almost anything works. The earlier literature on stuttering contains many anecdotes about stuttering schoolchildren who were helped to overcome their speech difficulties by teachers without special training who used such measures as breathing exercises or articulatory drills. A story repeated many times is about the stutterer who entered the school debate tournament or declamation contest under the coaching of a concerned teacher and stopped stuttering in the process of winning it. It is a believable story when we consider the effect such an experience is calculated to have on a child's self-concept as a speaker.

Furthermore, it has been my personal impression, based on experience in a metropolitan area densely populated by speech clinicians with somewhat varied backgrounds of training, that in the treatment of Phase 2 stuttering the greatest successes often tend to be achieved by those who have enthusiastically taught children to chew air while speaking, to do breathing exercises, to practice talking in time to rhythms, or to use other devices that sophisticated clinicians have regarded for years as ineffectual. Generally speaking, it is the clinician who is highly sophisticated by the standards that have become widely accepted in the United States who has been most likely to feel defeated by this type of stuttering problem.

The lesson that recovery at this stage is often easy also tends to be borne out by reports of effective self-help that we receive from time to time. Since one of the most typical comments of Phase 2 stutterers in clinical interviews is that they stutter when they talk too fast, it is perhaps not surprising that they often report as well that they can prevent stuttering by talking slowly. In fact, in the case of some individuals in this phase, this sometimes has an anomalous effect that we almost never encounter in later phases. We occasionally find stutterers who feel they do better as long as they "think" about their speech and worse when they forget about it, for example, at home or with their close friends.

This capability for exercising a certain amount of choice in the matter of stuttering may not be an uncommon feature of Phase 2 stuttering. A number of children in my experience demonstrated this capacity in the clinic. One 8-year-old girl was a Phase 2 stutterer who was said to have been stuttering for three years. Although her stuttering as described by her mother was apparently severe, none of it was to be heard during the interview, though she spoke freely and spontaneously. She had abruptly stopped stuttering two days before, immediately on being told that she was to be taken to the Speech and Hearing Center. The mother explained that the child virulently resented the prospect of speech therapy as an interference with her play.

Methods.[17]   In summary form, a clinical program aimed at the self-concept of the Phase 2 stutterer and designed with attention to the peculiar problems and opportunities he tends to present might reasonably consist of the following:

1. Parent counseling
2. General speech improvement designed to establish a self-image as an effective speaker
3. General personal development
4. Subtle and appropriate use of suggestion

To succeed, therapy in this phase must avoid any minute attention to symptoms that might produce anxiety. It must also deal with Phase 2 stutterers' characteristic lack of any deep feeling of need to work on their speech difficulty. In addition to parent counseling along the lines suggested for Phase 1, at least two approaches suggest themselves; both meet the two requirements and at the same time appear to deal with the problem of defective speaker self-image that seems to be fundamental to stuttering behavior. One is an intensive program of general speech improvement aimed at superior levels of achievement in all aspects of communication with the exception of fluency. Such a program should be designed to provide stimulating and challenging training— appropriate to the child's age level—in voice and diction, conversation, oral interpretation, public speaking, and other communication skills. It does not seem farfetched to assume that, at this early stage, a powerful feeling of success as a speaker carefully cultivated in this way might be enough to counteract the feelings of failure on which the child's stuttering appears in large part to be based. In principle, this might be useful therapy for even the most advanced stutterer; but it would appear to be most easily applied before the stutterer has acquired severe and persistent fears of speaking.

A second approach, which is related to the first, is to increase the child's sense of personal worth by every means possible: helping him to develop new interests, abilities, and assets; minimizing old liabilities; and enhancing his prestige in the eyes of his friends and classmates. Measures of this type are calculated to strengthen the stutterer's feeling of adequacy as a person and thereby make him less prone to anticipate speech failure or to feel an excessive need for speech approval. References to this aspect of therapy are to be found in writings by Johnson and Van Riper.

Still another means of treatment that is worth considering for Phase 2 is suggestion in certain appropriate forms. For the most part, suggestion has been applied, throughout its long history of use, in advanced cases of stuttering. It appears to fail too often with such cases, primarily because of the advanced stutterer's strongly rooted fear of stuttering. The suggestion-inspired expectation of fluency that so often brings temporary relief tends to disintegrate as it comes into conflict with the powerful expectations of stuttering that are bound to arise sooner or later as long as the old fear of the consequences of stuttering persists. It might reasonably be argued, however, that inasmuch as there is so little fear of the consequences of stuttering in Phase 2, the effects of suggestion might be more durable. The observation that so many different expedients seem to work in this phase tends to bear this out. It should also be considered that if suggestion should fail at this stage, there is at least little risk of the emotional upheaval and severe relapse often suffered as an aftermath by the more advanced stutterer whose hopes have been raised so high by the temporary recovery. Suggestion does not, of course, necessarily mean hypnosis. In fact, it is probably used most effectively with stutterers when applied indirectly, in the form of a method or technique in which the stutterer has a strong belief. From this point of view, suggestion need mean little more than a visible attitude of optimism on the part of the speech clinician in conjunction with such remedial measures as have already been discussed.

The use of suggestion with Phase 2 stutterers is recommended here as an expedient that deserves to be subjected to clinical testing unprejudiced by the knowledge of its past failures with later phases of stuttering. It should always be borne in mind that it is through the acceptance of certain suggestions that children acquire the beliefs which appear to underlie stuttering and that by the same token it is always a form of suggestion, broadly speaking, to which recovery from stuttering is to be attributed. There appears to be little difference, as far as some of the basic forces at work are concerned, between learning from a parent that one is doing poorly and may do worse and learning from a speech clinician that one is doing well and will almost certainly do better.

To this we must add a postscript. At the date of this writing considerable clinical experimentation is being done with conditioning therapies for stutterers—particularly with various applications of operant conditioning. It is still too early to foresee the future of these methods clearly; but we would guess that if they prove to be of value, it will be above all because of their usefulness with Phase 2 stutterers. The reasons may no doubt be readily surmised. One of the most important is that while it seems urgent to work with stutterers directly in this phase, we must often contend with children who seem hardly more than politely pleased at the prospect of not stuttering any more. Operant conditioning has an inherent appropriateness from this point of view because, by its very nature, it places no special reliance on the children's desire to talk more fluently as a source of reinforcement for changes in their behavior.

Phase 3

Age range: approximately 8 years to adulthood. Phase 3 is seen most often in adolescents.

Description. Stutterers now tend to report that they stutter most in certain "difficult" situations—for example, oral recitation at school, asking for items in stores, or asking strangers for directions. Usually, they have begun to consider certain words or sounds to be difficult and to use occasional word substitutions and circumlocutions when they encounter them. The first distinct expectancies of stuttering are likely to appear. On the other hand, they still talk freely and willingly under most conditions, even in situations they consider difficult. Their emotional reactions to stuttering are likely to come only at occasional moments of stress and even then tend to consist only of exasperation, anger at themselves, or frustration, rather than fear or embarrassment.

Briefly stated, they exhibit early forms of almost all of the important features of fully developed stuttering—with the exception of persistent fear and avoidance of speech. In the school environment we soon recognize the Phase 3 stutterer as the familiar boy or girl who seems to have an advanced form of stuttering problem, yet continually volunteers to recite in class and may be communicative and gregarious, even to the point of being "popular."

We must be careful to distinguish this phase of the problem from Phase 4, since Phase 4 stutterers are also found in the adolescent years in fairly large numbers.

Goals and rationale. Some of the approaches that are suitable for Phase 2 may still be of value at this stage and should be seriously considered as elements of the treatment program. By this time, however, the underlying self-concepts and convictions—in essence, the superstitions about speech—have become so firmly established that it may be futile to try to eliminate the stuttering by a direct attack on its cause. On the other hand, the stutterer is now generally mature enough so that we can reasonably attempt a different kind of direct approach that is usually not possible earlier: namely, modification of the stuttering behavior in essentially the same way we do in Phase 4. Although Phase 3 stutterers are not socially handicapped by their speech difficulty, they typically recognize it as a problem, have given serious thought to the future, and are ready to cooperate in a program of remediation "if it will help" them. It therefore becomes realistic to apply some of the best methods that have been developed for the treatment of stuttering in its most advanced form.

The only qualification that we must make—in the most emphatic terms—is that we are not concerned in this phase in any systematic way with the reduction of anxiety about stuttering. Like Phase 2, the type of problem that we see in Phase 3 has rarely been described in the literature. Public-school speech clinicians, identifying it as "secondary" stuttering on the basis of its advanced features, have sometimes refused to believe that these youngsters did not have deep anxieties and have spent fruitless hours teaching them to maintain an objective attitude about their stuttering. At best, this is a waste of time. At worst, it contains a negative suggestion that may do some harm.

In substance, we are advocating the use at this level of those techniques of Phase 4 therapy that have to do with symptom modification. Since we will deal with them in the next section, there is no need to describe them here. It is only necessary to point out that the clinician who applies them to Phase 3 must be prepared to adapt them so they make sense to children who may be as young as 8 or 9. This has been done admirably by D. E. Williams (1971).

In outline form, the major aspects of a clinicial program for most Phase 3 stutterers might consist of the following, with perhaps considerable emphasis on the last item:

1.   General speech improvement
2.   Personal development
3.   Symptom modification

Phase 4

Age range: approximately 10 years to adulthood. Phase 4 is typical of adult stutterers.

Description. The principal diagnostic features are chronic fear and embarrassment, evidenced by habitual avoidance of various speech situations. There are usually numerous indications of emotional reaction to stuttering. Words and sounds are feared. Expectancies tend to be frequent and colored by anxiety. There is elaborate and constant use of word substitutions and many other stratagems for avoiding blocks. Sensitivity develops to real or imagined listener reactions. Stuttering is avoided even as a subject for conversation. In a word, stuttering has now become a significant personal handicap. This is the classic case of developed stuttering as it has been depicted since journal articles, monographs, and textbooks have dealt with the subject.

Among adults, we must be careful to distinguish Phase 4 stutterers from others because some stutterers reach adulthood without having progressed beyond Phase 3 or even Phase 2.

Goals of treatment. Clinical theory and practice of the past few decades have produced a detailed program of procedures and techniques for the treatment of what we have described as Phase 4 stuttering; the program originated for the most part in the work of Johnson, Bryngelson, and Van Riper and was further developed by their students. The approach consists of systematically planned observations and experiences directed toward essentially two major objectives:

1. Reduction of anxiety about stuttering
2. Modification of the stuttering behavior

Reducing anxiety about stuttering

Earlier in this chapter, we pointed out that stuttering is probably not related to anxiety in so simple a way as to make it possible to eliminate it merely by eliminating the anxiety. Nevertheless, there are several good reasons for which anxiety reduction, as far as this is possible, must be a major goal when we work with Phase 4 stutterers. First, it is an end in itself because the anxiety is usually the most handicapping aspect of the problem. Second, excessive anxiety about stuttering will tend to prevent them from working on other aspects of the program designed to help them modify their stuttering behavior. Finally, while reducing anxiety probably offers no total solution to the problem, in varying and unpredictable degrees it does often result in a decrease in stuttering; this is probably because, as was pointed out earlier, less fear of stuttering often means fewer occasions to expect it and less of the unusual attention to speech that appears to cause moments of stuttering.

A number of different approaches may be taken to reduce anxiety. Before we discuss them, however, we must offer an urgent word of caution: We should never imagine it possible for stutterers to rid themselves of all fear of stuttering, and we should avoid filling them with feelings of guilt about the apprehensions they will inevitably have as long as they stutter. Our clinical zeal must not be allowed to override our empathic understanding of the stutterer's problem. We live in a society that is peculiarly forbidding in its attitude toward what it considers to be incompetence at speech. There probably would be far fewer stutterers if this were not the case. Fortunately, it is not necessary to remove every trace of fear in order to achieve our objectives. Our immediate goal is mainly to overcome the worst panic reactions and reduce the fear as much as reasonably possible.

Bringing the problem out into the open. This aspect of treatment appears to hold the key to all others, in the sense that little further progress can usually be achieved if stutterers are unable to carry it through successfully. If they cannot admit frankly to others that they stutter, it is a significant indication that they are basically unable to accept the fact. Self-acceptance, in turn, is a most vital part of any type of personal adjustment. Until stutterers are able to accept their speech problem unemotionally in the privacy of their own self-evaluations, everything else must be subordinated to that goal.

This work may be broken down into several somewhat distinct aspects.

1. *Stutterers must freely admit their problem to associates who may not be aware of it.* Most stutterers intensely desire to be regarded as normal speakers. So zealously may they dedicate themselves to this end that some of their closest associates may be among those who do not know they stutter. By standing constant guard over their speech, stutterers have been known to conceal their difficulty from wife, husband, or children for many years. It is not at all unusual to find that it has been kept from coming to the attention of casual acquaintances or even fiancées. Sometimes, it is true, these persons turn out to have known all along. But the result, as far as the stutterer is concerned, is the same. The threat of exposure is a constant source of anxiety. Furthermore, sooner or later the pretense is almost bound to crumble in a cloud of mortification in spite of every trick to avoid stuttering that the stutterer knows.

2. *They should cultivate the ability to discuss their stuttering casually and objectively with others.* Most of the time the listener is well aware of the speaker's stuttering, but even when it is most obvious they may both adopt an attitude of profound obtuseness, acting as though there were nothing extraordinary at all about the stutterer's struggles to speak. The situation becomes tense and unnatural for both. This is the essence of the problem that stutterers may have in social adjustment. In many respects it is like the problem any handicapped person may have in establishing normal social relationships. If handicapped people are sometimes rejected socially, it is partly because they stir in us an uneasy feeling of inadequacy. We are not certain exactly how to treat them, and we feel especially obliged to weigh beforehand what we say to them. This is by no means true of all such individuals, however. Sometimes we encounter a handicapped person who appears to inspire others with a desire to know him better, and whose associates seem genuinely oblivious to his handicap. In such cases we usually find a person who in one manner or another conveys the information that it would not hurt or embarrass him if someone were to broach the subject of his clubfoot, spastic paralysis, or artificial limb. It is this knowledge that

stutterers must somehow convey about their speech handicap. The surest, most direct way is to bring up the subject themselves from time to time as the occasion calls for it so that it may be talked about, disposed of, and forgotten.

Most stutterers who have protected this sensitive area for many years find difficulty in exposing it in this way until they have had some practice at it. Some of this practice may be obtained under the direct supervision of the clinician. Many stutterers will gain what amounts substantially to their first experience at talking about their problem when they speak before an audience of other stutterers in the speech clinic. Later, it may be possible for the clinician to accompany the stutterer while he initiates conversations with strangers on the pretext of making a survey of public reaction to stuttering or opinion about its cause and treatment. If the therapy is conducted in a school setting, an effective method is to arrange for stutterers to visit several classes in small groups for the purpose of giving brief talks about stuttering. Some topics they might plan to touch on are: "how it feels to have a block," "how listeners react to my stuttering," "tricks I have used to avoid stuttering," "conditions under which I can talk fluently," or "memorable experiences as a stutterer." Under the spur of questions from the audience, they will find to their surprise that the subject of their stuttering is practically inexhaustible. Other experiences will need to be obtained through "assignments" to discuss their remedial work or to bring up the subject of their stuttering with relatives and friends.

If possible, stutterers should collect a repertoire of amusing anecdotes about their stuttering or even stuttering jokes and acquire the ability to tell them skillfully and with enjoyment. Many stutterers, including some who learn to become quite objective about their speech, seem basically unable to see any humor in it—a failing for which they may perhaps be pardoned. Nevertheless, there is probably no more reliable way of establishing a reputation as a stutterer who is not easily embarrassed about his speech than by developing a sense of humor about it.

3. *They should learn to announce that they stutter on entering particularly difficult and feared speaking situations.* One college student began her first oral presentation in an introductory speech course by saying, "We've been asked to talk about something on which we're experts. I'm going to talk about stuttering. I've been doing it for about 17 years, and I think I'm an expert at it." She had little further anxiety in this class. The point is that once stutterers establish a general understanding that they may have trouble with their speech, there is no longer any need to dread the awful hush of shocked surprise which is the great terror of such a situation. In many cases stutterers would be happy enough to make such an announcement as a means of making a situation

of this kind more tolerable, but need to be shown how. If they can do it in a whimsical or good-humored way, so much the better. But even the slightly acid statement, "I stutter. I don't have any apologies to make for it, but it may take me a while to get started sometimes," goes a long way to win the stutterer respect and acceptance.

4. *When they encounter exceptional difficulty in speaking, they should be prepared to make an appropriate remark that will help them to "pass it off" lightly.* "There will be a slight delay in transmission due to technical operating difficulties" or "We will have a brief intermission between words" are examples that have been tested successfully. One of a stutterer's most troublesome fears may be that in a formal social situation, before an audience, or on some other crucial occasion, he may suffer the humiliation of becoming so completely blocked he is unable to go on. A stutterer may rarely or never have had such an experience, but the possibility may be enough to make every word a crisis in such a situation. Once armed with a weapon against this extremity, though he may never need to use it, the knowledge that he has it may be all he needs to face these situations in relative security.

Learning that normal speakers are not perfectly fluent. Like most other people, most stutterers have little conception that disfluency is a constant feature of normal speech until they have paid special attention to it. Learning how disfluent most normal speakers are may help them be more tolerant of some of the interruption in their own speech.

Wendell Johnson used to make this point in a compelling way in his lectures. In our society, he said, we tend to label everyone and then proceed to react to the labels. These labels are often two-valued and represent negative and positive evaluations (stupid-smart, ugly-beautiful, unpopular-popular, etc.). In a similar way, stutterers tend to assume that humanity is divided into stutterers and perfectly fluent speakers. They tend to believe, in other words, that the only alternative to stuttering is to speak perfectly. Because they want so badly not to stutter, they place a very high value on perfect fluency. They become perfectionists about fluency. These unrealistically high standards tend to maintain the tensions and anxieties that perpetuate their stuttering. Essentially, they are defining normal speech in a way that makes it almost impossible for them to attain it.

By far the best way for stutterers to learn about normal disfluency is by observing it. For example, it is a good idea for a stutterer to pretend that a normal speaker—perhaps one of his teachers—is a stutterer and to make a tally mark on a scrap of paper for every block he hears in the teacher's speech during a 10-minute period. The number of stutterings he records is likely to astonish him. By making such observations on a moderate-size sample of normal speakers, he will soon learn that, as with respect to most other abilities and personal attributes, ordinary people are distributed along a continuum with respect to fluency of speech. A small number at one end of the continuum seem to have very few, perhaps almost no, hesitations or interruptions; a few at the other end hardly ever seem to say a whole sentence fluently; most normal speakers form a large bulge on the continuum between these two extremes.

Having absorbed this lesson, the stutterer may be ready for another surprising discovery. He will probably tend to assume that stutterers like himself all occupy a small segment at the extreme disfluent end of the continuum labeled "for stutterers only." If his sampling of the disfluencies of normal speakers has not been too narrow and if his own stuttering is not too severe, or if the speech of other stutterers is available for comparison, it may be possible to show him that there are some stutterers who are more fluent, at least by count of numbers of disfluencies, than some normal speakers. In some measure, it appears that the extent to which a speaker talks abnormally or has a speech defect depends on how he reacts to his disfluency or allows himself to be handicapped by it. Some stutterers have severe problems but rarely block. Some normal speakers are hardly conscious of having any speech difficulty at all despite the fact that they rarely say more than a few words at a time without interruption.

Naturally, the gaining of such insights by stutterers is not likely to be immediately reflected in noticeably better speech. But if it does no more than temporarily reinforce them to the point at which they feel encouraged to go on to more difficult things, it will in the long run have made a significant contribution to their improvement.

Evaluating listener reactions realistically.   Whatever the punishing consequences of stuttering, they practically always have something to do, ultimately, with a listener; that is, they have something to do with the manner in which a listener reacts or is believed to react to the stuttering, the attitudes he seems to adopt, and the inferences he draws or seems to draw about the speaker. If stuttering is punishing it is because it is punishing to be laughed at, pitied, or thought a fool. Surprising as it may seem, this punishment may often be reduced markedly without changing the behavior at all. One of the best opportunities for modifying the consequences of stuttering as they appear to stutterers is found in the disparity that tends to exist between the listener's attitude and what it is imagined to be. It is difficult for many stutterers, sensitized by past experience to unfavorable reactions, to avoid exaggerating them and observing them even where they do not happen to be. Careful study of listener reactions by stutterers with the help of their clinicians will frequently do a great deal to keep these tendencies at a minimum.

Johnson pointed out that one of the outstanding things to be learned from such observations is the distinction between descriptions of and inferences about listener reactions. When a stutterer says, "He looks down when I start to talk to him," this is a description. Its accuracy can be checked independently by another observer, and there are means by which one can determine how often listeners behave in accordance with such a description. On the other hand, "He becomes embarrassed when I speak to him" or "He feels sorry for me" or "He gets annoyed" are inferences. Too frequently stutterers behave as though such inferences were descriptions. That is, they do not appear to feel any need to test their assumptions. They seem to regard them as simple facts. The peculiar viciousness of this identification is that it permits sutterers to go on indefinitely believing that their listeners are "amused," "impatient," "embarrassed," "shocked," or practically anything else. Once acquired, there is no means of checking and rejecting such inferences that stutterers are likely to stumble on by themselves. Such inferences can be made to fit almost any listener, any facial expression, any behavior, any circumstance. Stutterers must be taught, therefore, to distinguish clearly between inferences and descriptions. They should next be trained to reserve their inferences about their listeners' reactions and to make statements about them that are essentially descriptive: to learn to say, in other words, that listeners look away, smile, frown, attempt to help with difficult words, or the like. Such assertions can be verified objectively, and stutterers should then be given every opportunity to find out by observation how frequently their listeners actually do these things. Experiences of this kind are calculated to make stutterers question a good many of their assumptions.

Another way to teach stutterers to be more cautious about the inferences they draw is to give them the chance to compare the inferences with those of other observers. An effective method, when working with a group of stutterers, is to arrange for a nonstutterer to be interviewed for several minutes by one member of the group while the others jot down their interpretations of the listener's reactions. As a rule, such interpretations will show little agreement.

In the foregoing discussion, we have been concerned solely with stutterers' exaggerations and misconceptions of their listeners' reactions. When all is said and done, however, we cannot deny that listeners occasionally do interrupt stutterers, attempt to hurry them, or give other evidence of reacting strongly to stuttering; this is a fact we are obliged to help stutterers face. Malreactions should be discussed objectively as troublesome but wholly expected occurrences, and they should be examined above all from the point of view of the possible reasons for them. Once stutterers begin to ask exactly why occasional listeners appear to find it so difficult to tolerate their hesitations, they may decide it is the listeners who are in need of help. This is an extremely liberating realization, but one that does not come naturally to the average stutterer. Although he may condemn the listener bitterly for his malreactions, they correspond so closely to his own unfavorable appraisals of himself that he is usually all too ready to assume that he himself is the only one who has any problem.

Improving social and emotional adjustment. It will be difficult for the stutterer to reduce his fear of stuttering if he is an unusually anxious, inadequate, insecure person. For this reason stuttering therapy does not exclude broader forms of personal guidance when necessary. The immediate question that must be answered in the case of each stutterer is whether his emotional difficulties warrant the specialized attention of a trained psychotherapist. The decision to refer a stutterer for such help must be made with care and in itself requires a basic knowledge of personality problems. On the one hand, it is dangerously negligent to allow a clinically neurotic person to trail his anxieties, depressions, hysterias, or compulsions ineffectually to one speech therapy session after the next without making such a referral. On the other hand, too many referrals for psychotherapy reveal a degree of naiveté about emotional disorders and perhaps a certain amount of panic on the part of speech clinicians faced with somewhat difficult cases. It must always be kept in mind that personal problems are universal and that most people have the capacity to cope with them without assistance. There are certain emotional storms that are characteristic of various temporary stages of maturity or common life situations; few are more violent than those surrounding the acceptance of adult roles in adolescence and young adulthood—the period during which stuttering in its developed form is so frequently treated.

If there are any emotional problems with which speech clinicians can often be of direct help, it is with problems of social adjustment that are due in large measure to the stuttering itself. While every reduction in the fear of stuttering will tend to result in a capacity for more active social participation, the reverse is also true. The more adequate individuals feel in social relationships, the less reason they have to fear stuttering. For this reason no effort should be spared in helping stutterers acquire new social assets and find opportunities for capitalizing on them. Clinicians should do everything possible to see that stutterers know how to conduct themselves in all of the common social situations and have no reason to feel ashamed of their personal appearance. I recall one 12-year-old girl whose ability to face and handle her stuttering problem underwent a substantial improvement after her clinician taught her how to dress, wear her hair, and lower herself into a chair in a graceful and feminine manner. Other stutterers have been helped similarly by suggestions that they learn to dance or see a doctor about a problem of excessive weight.

Overcoming avoidance.   Precisely because of their fear of stuttering, stutterers tend to make their difficulty more handicapping than it needs to be. A stutterer may do so by declining responsibilities requiring speech; by avoiding social situations; by speaking as little as possible in situations he cannot avoid; and, when he must speak, by resorting to word substitutions and circumlocutions that distort his meaning and to devices that hamper his speech and intensify his blocks. The more handicapping he makes his stuttering, furthermore, the more threatening and fearful it becomes and so the more he avoids it in all ways possible. This process can be reversed. One of the primary concerns of therapy is to develop in stutterers a conscience that prevents them from avoiding stuttering. This is not always as difficult as it might appear. The typical stutterer is rather easily convinced that he should not cringe before the world in an attitude of apology merely because he stutters. From there it is not far to fostering in him a sense of pride in his ability to get along without avoidances. Many stutterers before very long reach a point at which they derive a feeling of achievement from every feared speaking situation entered voluntarily, every feared word attempted, and every block they have with a minimum of embarrassment, struggle, and associated mannerisms for avoiding stuttering. One immediate consequence of this is that they talk more, do more, and show a rapid general improvement in their capacity for constructive relationships with others. This is often one of the earliest substantial results of therapy.

There are, generally speaking, two useful methods for working on the elimination of avoidances. One is to take aim directly at the stutterers' most difficult and feared speaking situations, especially those they meet frequently in the normal course of their activities. It is here that the most important, sometimes essentially the only, features of their problem are concentrated. These situations will differ from case to case. Typical examples are the classroom, the telephone, and various social situations. In the individual case these may usually be narrowed down to a particular classroom, to telephone conversations with certain people, or, perhaps, to a weekly club meeting that is mined from beginning to end with the threat of stuttering. These may be marked off as the arenas in which a stutterer will face his stuttering and overcome his avoidances, and in some cases it may be desirable to conduct the therapy as a whole almost entirely on the basis of its relationship to these particular situations.

The second way to help stutterers cope with their avoidance tendencies is to arrange for them to have stuttering experiences far in excess of those demanded by their ordinary daily routines. For this purpose stutterers may stop people in the street to ask them for directions, price articles in stores, ring people's doorbells to inquire whether so-and-so lives there, or seek out any of a hundred other possible speaking situations. Not only the number but also the character of these situations can often be prearranged to advantage. It is possible to contrive situations that are especially efficient as clinical exercises because they contain the concentrated venom of certain stuttering experiences. For example, the stutterer may plan 10 situations in which he will begin a sentence with "what," "why," "when," or "where" because these words are obstacles that he usually avoids by means of circumlocution. Or he may make three telephone calls in the course of which he stops in the middle of a sentence and remains silent until the other person hangs up, because this is exactly the eventuality he dreads most when he speaks on the telephone. Furthermore, because it would be difficult to do anything more antipodal to avoiding stuttering than performing it deliberately, it may be helpful for him to learn to block on purpose in some of his situations. Such "stuttering" should, of course, be carried out in the spirit of a test of his ability to assume an objective attitude toward his speech interruptions and should, therefore, consist of simple repetitions or prolongations with a minimum of hurry or tension.

When Phase 4 stutterers begin to confront their feared situations, words, and listeners, they are meeting their problem head-on in the most direct way. They have reached the core of therapy. Some lasting and significant amelioration of the problem is within reach. At the same time, progress in some cases may become difficult and slow at this stage. Experienced clinicians will therefore have laid the groundwork for this stage of therapy beforehand very carefully through work on the aspects of the treatment program we have already covered. This will go a long way to help. In addition, we must be prepared to use every possible means of making situational work less threatening. Situations should be systematically graded in difficulty. There is inestimable value in group work, with the opportunity it affords for making use of group morale. An excellent source of help that should not be neglected is the repeated role playing of difficult situations before they are attempted outside the clinic. Finally, we may help prepare stutterers for feared situations by using imagery in the procedure known as "reciprocal inhibition," or "systematic desensitization" (see the chapter by Brutten in this *Symposium*). The extent to which reciprocal inhibition in itself can produce lasting benefit for stutterers is a question that only the future can decide. In the meantime, however, nothing is to be lost by reducing anxiety, even if the effect is temporary, if it will make it possible for stutterers to enter some of the situations they have been in the habit of avoiding and to learn from direct experience that those situations are not so difficult or fearful.

Whatever methods are used to eliminate avoidances and teach stutterers that stuttering is not so fearful, the projects or assignments they undertake should be specific, clearly defined, and capable of evaluation in terms of relative success or failure; this rule applies to other phases of stuttering therapy as well. In addition, it is of the utmost importance to keep in mind two related principles having broad application to the planning and evaluation of stutterers' work in outside situations. The first is never to assume, simply because we have told stutterers clearly and repeatedly what we believe they must do and why, that they have an adequate understanding of what we mean. The second is never to assume, once we have listened to stutterers' accounts of the experiences they have had, the observations they have made, and the things they have accomplished or failed to accomplish, that we have a rough idea of what they were talking about. Anyone who ignores these precepts will almost certainly receive some jarring surprises before learning to demonstrate to the stutterer as well as possible what he would like him to do and to observe the stutterer as much as possible while he does it. Stuttering therapy cannot be confined comfortably to an office. The clinician who tries to do so will soon discover that such therapy tends to become vague, abstract, and fundamentally out of touch with the realities of the stutterer's problem.

Modifying the stuttering behavior

Despite the importance of anxiety reduction, the principal aim of stuttering therapy in Phase 4 is not to enable stutterers to "learn to live with it," but to help them overcome it. As soon as they have begun to develop some ability to look at their problem calmly and objectively, they can take the first steps toward the ultimate goal of eliminating the stuttering or reducing it as much as possible.

How far is it possible to go in eliminating stuttering in Phase 4? We hear conflicting views about the prognosis of developed stuttering that range all the way from the expression "Once a stutterer, always a stutterer" to claims of complete "cures" of many stutterers by some workers. The truth, as far as can be surmised from a critical survey of a broad array of clinical observations, seems to lie somewhere in between (see Van Riper, 1973, chap. 7). Essentially complete and stable recoveries take place in Phase 4 as in other phases, but the recovery is probably a good deal more likely to be complete in those Phase 4 stutterers who have not yet reached adulthood. Even adults sometimes seem to overcome stuttering literally without a trace, but this does not appear to be the usual outcome of treatment. More often, the most successful clinical efforts to eliminate stuttering tend to leave a residue of occasional mild hesitancies that seem to be somewhat in excess of most normal disfluency in adults. With these hesitancies also tends to remain a faint vestige of the old self-concept as a stutterer and remnants of its ancillary attitudes, assumptions, and expectancies.

We can only speculate about why it is so difficult to eliminate stuttering in adulthood completely. If the conception of stuttering we have developed in this chapter is valid, stuttering can be said to be the fault of the speaker's system of personal values. If he forgot that he was a stutterer and simply went ahead on the assumption that he would have no difficulty, he would speak quite normally; if he doesn't do that, it is because he is suffering from some essentially irrational evaluations. The values that underlie stuttering are apt to begin as childhood values, and so long as they remain childhood values, there is a likelihood they will be discarded in due course along with a belief in the bogie man. Once they become part of the value system of an adult, however, they tend to be as hard to get rid of as Aunt Hilda's aversion to polyandry or Cousin Stanley's habit of voting Democrat. They can be eliminated, but this may require either slow personal development over a span of years or an experience so profoundly altering that it is tantamount to being born anew.

In any event, this stubborn resistance of adult Phase 4 stuttering to total eradication is curious rather than important from a practical point of view. The lingering traces that tend to remain after effective treatment are at worst a minor annoyance rather than a problem or handicap. Essentially, the modification of Phase 4 stuttering is in most cases a feasible undertaking.

How, then, should we approach this goal, and with what rationale? My views on the modification of stuttering are based on the fundamental premise of the Iowa school of stuttering therapy: The central problem of treatment is not the difficulty of bringing about fluency, but the high probability of relapse; few quick cures are likely to be durable; and, in general, the most reliable way to achieve a lasting reduction of stuttering is to do it slowly and gradually through a process that enlists stutterers' comprehension of what they do when they stutter, why they do it, and how and why they are capable of altering their behavior. It is this kind of approach to symptom modification that will be described here.

Reducing the tensions. As we saw earlier in this chapter, tension is one of the two basic aspects of stuttering to which virtually all of its complex symptomatology may be reduced. It is a very large part of what stutterers feel when they block, and it is directly responsible for a great deal that observers see and hear. Eliminate the tensions and we all but eliminate the stuttering.

In attempting to change any kind of stuttering behavior, we must begin by helping stutterers make thorough analyses of what they are to change. Such symptom analysis plays a significant role in therapy from more than one point of view. To begin with, Phase 4 stutterers tend to be quite vague about the nature of their struggle behavior. Although usually all too aware of their "stuttering," they tend to perform it so emotionally, hurriedly, and automatically that it may be hard for them to say even in general terms what they are doing when they stutter. How can we expect them to stop doing something, or to do less of it, when they are essentially in the dark about what that something is? If they know they are pressing their lips together hard when they say certain sounds, there is a realistic possibility that they may eventually learn to talk without doing this; but there is hardly any way for anybody to stop "stuttering."

Symptom analysis, then, may help give stutterers a sense of the basic alterability of their stuttering which is of the utmost importance for the outcome of therapy. From this standpoint, however, it is not enough for stutterers simply to be able to describe the features of their stuttering. As Johnson, D. E. Williams, and others have pointed out, stutterers must also be able to see their stutterings as things they do rather than things that simply happen to them. This is crucial. Clinicians who are steeped in theory may easily take it for granted that stuttering is behavior much like any other. But to stutterers, it is not likely to feel that way at all. When they block they tend to feel as though their speech apparatus has been momentarily stricken by paralysis or has acquired a will of its own. This cannot be overemphasized. The average Phase 4 stutterer is baffled by his stuttering. One of the most disagreeable things about it is that he can't explain why it "happens." This is precisely the value of classifying stuttering symptoms as tensions or fragmentations rather than as blocks, repetitions, or the like. It is urgent that we select a system of classification that will make the behaviors intelligible. The most effective way to teach stutterers that stuttering is something they do is to give them convincing reasons for believing it.

In helping stutterers analyze their tensions, we must start by conveying to them the basic concept of the vocal apparatus as an airway, or speech tube, that extends from the lips to the glottis. Stutterers must learn to see that they prevent themselves from speaking by pinching off the tube at various points in different ways: by means of bilabial, labiodental, linguadental, lingua-alveolar, linguavelar, or glottal constrictions. Depending largely on the sound he is attempting, the constriction may be total, resulting in a complete stoppage or an explosive block, or it may permit some continuous escape of air, resulting in a prolongation of sound. In some cases severe tension may even result in a rapid repetition if muscles go into clonic spasm.

This will all seem exceedingly simple to anyone who has gotten a passing grade in introductory phonetics, but it is far from self-evident to the typical stutterer. To gain his point of view, we must recall the time when the elementary facts of phonetics came to us as a succession of surprising revelations. It is hardly any wonder that stutterers tend to be at a loss to describe what they do when they stutter. They are without the most rudimentary information they need to do so. We must not neglect to give it to them.

Symptom analysis should begin as early as any other aspect of the clinical program. In fact, it has its own contribution to make to the development of an objective attitude. Much of the actual modification of stuttering in speech situations outside the clinic will have to wait until the stutterer's fears have diminished somewhat; but the first attempts at it in practice sessions under the clinician's guidance may begin as soon as the symptom analysis has been done.

Once the stutterer has localized the places in the vocal tract where he habitually exerts too much tension, he may practice stuttering with less of it. As he blocks on a word he tries to do so without effort. He does not fight or struggle. Understanding and feeling that he is pressing his lips together, battering his tongue against his palate, or closing his glottis tightly, he deliberately tries to relax these contacts as he stutters and to perform the block simply, softly, and lightly without hurry or strain. J. D. Williams puts it well in his advice to stutterers:

> Do *not* change your usual rate of speaking unless you really speak
> too fast to be understood (very few people do). Leave your nonstuttered
> speech alone. But when you start to tense up and stutter, *at that instant*
> shift into slow motion. Don't give up your speech effort, but try to do
> everything easily, gently and slowly. Relax and let go; keep your lips,
> tongue and jaw moving without jamming. Don't panic. Take all the time
> you need; keep things moving slowly. Keep your confidence and don't
> buckle. Keep going forward slowly but positively. Totally resist any feeling
> of hurry or pressure. Let 'em wait. At some critical point in time (a
> second or less, two seconds, ten seconds or more) you will suddenly
> know you're over the hump. You'll feel your tension drain away as your
> confidence surges back. Simply finish that word and keep talking along
> at normal speed until you tense up for another bout of stuttering. Then
> you instantly shift into slow motion again.[18]

In essence, the stutterer must learn to unclench his tongue as he unclenches his fist. The problem, once he is no longer confused and distracted by fear, is one of becoming able to identify immediately the muscular state of each of various parts of the oral apparatus. If he finds this difficult, it may be helpful to make use of the well-known principle of Jacobson's progressive relaxation. Jacobson's method is one by means of which a person may be trained to localize and voluntarily dissipate minute amounts of tension in each of his skeletal muscle groups in turn, and to do this progressively until he is in a state of relatively complete relaxation (see Jacobson, 1938). For the purpose of stuttering therapy, it is probably not necessary or desirable to teach the stutterer how to relax the limbs or torso, except perhaps as a brief demonstration of the principle to be learned. What is required is simply that the stutterer learn to relax that rigid stance of the tongue, jaw, and lips with which he readies himself for supposedly difficult words or sounds. Jacobson's basic technique of producing the tension purposely in varying degrees and studying the associated muscle sensations seems excellently suited to this purpose. It is possible to study all of the various articulatory contacts in this manner. In some cases, it may be enough to focus attention on one or two points of contact that represent the stutterer's major sites of difficulty.

It should be emphasized that we do not encourage stutterers to *talk* in a relaxed manner or in any other unaccustomed way, but only to *stutter* in a relaxed manner. It is also important to keep in mind that our immediate aim is not fluency, even if the stutterer can momentarily achieve it, but only a pattern of stuttering that is milder, simpler, less conspicuous, and less impeding to speech. For the time being, his most pressing need is to know how to manage his speech difficulties when he has them and to learn to handle speaking situations as a stutterer. It will be some time before he gradually develops the assurance to shoulder the responsibility of being a normal or near-normal speaker.

Reducing fragmentation. Stuttering turns two faces to the imagined difficulty of speech. One is the contorted face of effort; fragmentation is the other. Fragmentation expresses all of the stutterer's hesitancy, his feeling of helplessness to go on in the expectation of difficulty too great to cope with.

The problem of identifying fragmentations is quite different from that of analyzing tensions. It is not a matter of localizing proprioceptive cues. The chief difficulty results instead from the fact that fragmentation pervades the stutterer's speech in forms that are often subtle. The easy assumption that tension expresses itself in blocks or prolongations while fragmentation takes the form of repetition is not sufficiently accurate, though it has a crude sort of validity. For one thing, there is a certain kind of rapid, tremorlike repetition of sound, as we have already seen, that probably does not primarily reflect fragmentation at all, but extreme tension of muscles. Even more important, however, is the need to recognize that fragmentation goes beyond repetition. Stutterers need to learn that it is present in their abnormal pauses, their jerky rhythm or phrasing, and their habit of saying sounds, syllables, or words in isolation. In fact, whenever normal movement stops in speech there is fragmentation. For this reason, most examples of tension are examples of fragmentation too, just as tension is involved in most fragmentations. The two are not readily separated. They are two aspects rather than two types of stuttering. At most, we can distinguish forms of stuttering in which one or the other aspect is especially conspicuous.

When stutterers thoroughly understand the meaning of fragmentation and have carefully studied the typical examples of it in their own speech, they are ready to make the first attempts to eliminate it. The key to this is to restore normal movement to speech. In a deliberate, unhurried way, they need to keep their articulators moving as they stutter. Van Riper (1954, p. 429) expresses this by saying that stutterers must prepare themselves to say a feared sound as a movement leading into the succeeding sound, rather than as a fixed articulatory position. D. E. Williams advises stutterers not to hold back, but to keep moving ahead into speech.

The type of Phase 4 stutterer whose speech difficulty is dominated by fragmentation and consists chiefly of repetitions may find it very difficult to keep moving forward with a "come what may" attitude as long as he still has some fear. A good plan for him may be to start by slowing down his repetitions, performing them with less hurry and tension, and learning to exercise greater control over them by doing them in a more "voluntary," deliberate way. In a later stage of therapy he can then turn his attention to making integrated, forward-moving, undelayed attempts on whole words.

Some further considerations. In addition to the essential tensions and fragmentations, there are usually some associated features of stuttering. For the most part, these consist either of extraneous movements or of interjected speech fragments. Many Phase 4 stutterers exhibit comparatively few of such secondary symptoms, while in some they may represent a very large part of the abnormality. These need to be identified too, and, like the integral symptoms, they also require the kind of analysis that does not merely describe them but also makes them intelligible to the stutterer. He is scarcely likely to know that he closes his eyes when he stutters, much less why, or that it is behavior that he himself performs and can therefore stop. For this purpose, Van Riper's classification of associated features as symptoms of avoidance, postponement, starting, and release (in his more recent writing, avoidance, postponement, timing, and escape) is well suited (see Van Riper, 1973, chap. 12).

Ordinarily, the elimination of secondary symptoms may be incorporated without difficulty in the work stutterers do to modify their integral symptoms. As we help them perfect a way of stuttering that is simple, effortless, and forward moving, they will learn to strip the block of its complicated extraneous features. Most of the postponements, starters, and release devices, in fact, are themselves elaborate kinds of tension and fragmentation; some are not always clearly separable from the essential stuttering reactions except in a somewhat abstract way. Sometimes, however, a secondary reaction or mannerism may need some special attention because it is unusually conspicuous or resistant to the stutterer's efforts to eradicate it. In such cases teaching him to stutter without the head jerk or the interjection of "you see" may generally be accomplished in any of the ways in which we go about changing other speech habits.

This does not exclude the techniques of operant conditioning in the hands of those who have been trained to use them effectively. The same applies to many other aspects of stuttering therapy. At this writing I would be extremely reluctant to suggest for Phase 4 many of the methods of quickly inducing fluency that have been advanced as operant-conditioning therapies. Most of them clearly violate the fundamental premise for stuttering therapy stated at the outset of this discussion of the modification of stuttering. Used with skill and sophistication, however, the technology of operant conditioning might be applied in dozens of ways in the kind of program for gradual elimination of stuttering behavior that we have outlined here.

Finally, it must be pointed out that this account of therapy has dealt with only some fundamental procedures. Unusually refined methods have been developed for modifying stuttering in programs similar in basic orientation to the one we have described briefly. Of outstanding importance are Van Riper's techniques of cancellation, pullout, and preparatory set. Explanations of these and other practical techniques are found in his discussion of his own inventive approaches to stuttering therapy (Van Riper, 1973, chaps. 8–13).

The Clinician-Stutterer Relationship

Any attempt to help a stutterer with his speech involves a relationship between two people. This relationship may either be left to chance or deliberately molded to conform to a specific conception of what it should be like. Too often it is merely allowed to develop as it will. Depending on the individual or the occasion, the clinician may assume the role of a teacher who demands the stutterer's work when due; a priest who hears his confessions, encourages, and guides him; a big brother who fights his battles for him; a parent who is emotionally involved in his successes and failures; or a friend with whom he exchanges confidences and good-natured abuse. In the author's opinion there is one kind of relationship that is far more suitable for stuttering therapy than any other: That is what might appropriately be termed a "clinical relationship." While it is difficult to give this term an exact meaning, we may understand it to refer in a general way to relationships of the type existing in a successfully maintained psychotherapeutic situation between patient and therapist. Psychotherapeutic relationships vary, but most of them appear to have certain significant features in common. There are perhaps few descriptions of the clinical relationship so directly applicable to remedial work with stutterers as that found in Rogers's account of "nondirective," or "client-centered," psychotherapy, and it is on his depiction of it that this discussion is based (see Rogers, 1942, 1951).

Our behavior toward the stutterer in the clinical situation and the relationship that we establish with him should be governed by at least four basic principles.

1. *All good therapy is based on a belief in the individual's innate capacity for emotional growth.* This is far from a euphonious banality. A good many of the mistakes made by inexperienced speech clinicians appear to stem from the assumption that the stutterer is essentially a blank and that it is the clinician's responsibility to direct in minute detail the entire program of speech rehabilitation. One of the greatest rewards of experience is the sense of detachment made possible by the knowledge that the stutterer, if given time, can usually be counted on to exercise in his own behalf all of the human qualities of initiative, motivation, resourcefulness, and potentiality for improvement and that he, not the clinician, is the leading actor in the scene. It is this knowledge, moreover, that makes feasible one of the most satisfactory methods of conducting stuttering therapy: working intensively on a few carefully chosen situations that represent the stutterer's special problem at the moment. If he can once enjoy a sense of accomplishment and success— say in the classroom or at a club meeting—whether it is in the matter of alluding casually to his stuttering, volunteering to speak, using feared words, effectively altering some of his stuttering behavior, or doing anything else that helps him to handle the situation adequately or gain a feeling of acceptance as a stutterer, we need have little fear that he will fail to seek a repetition of his triumph in other difficult situations.

The converse of this is to try to prepare the stutterer deliberately for every fearful contingency, an attempt that is impossible and aims at so much that it makes direct contact with almost nothing.

2. *To be effective, therapy must be conducted in a permissive atmosphere.* In the first place, it is obviously desirable for the stutterer to be able to express all of his feelings about his problem and his reactions in the course of therapy, no matter how embarrassing, shocking, or ridiculous they may seem to him. For this reason the clinician must receive everything the stutterer tells him in a manner that indicates his complete and uncritical acceptance. But permissiveness should not stop here. The stutterer must be made to understand that there is nothing in the course of clinical work that he will be required to do in the sense that he is required to do class assignments or schoolwork. This is especially important when therapy is administered in a school setting, where the clinic is something to which one is assigned and the clinician gives every appearance of being a teacher. This rule, though perhaps contrary to a certain amount of practice, is of the utmost importance if the advantages of a clinical relationship are to be gained.

What of the assignments that we "give" the stutterer? It follows from what we have said that these should be assignments the stutterer is willing and eager to carry out and that, as far as possible, they should represent his own choice, based on a thorough knowledge of the courses of action open to him. In particular, the wise clinician will learn to take advantage in one form or another of every suggestion that comes from the stutterer himself, even when he knows that by certain criteria other ways of proceeding would be preferable.

3. *Therapy should stress the clarification of attitudes and feelings of the person being helped, in preference to persuasion, reasoning, advice, or reassurance.* It is quite true that in treating stuttering the therapist must communicate a large amount of sheer information. But a point is frequently reached in the clinical session at which further explanation is merely a somewhat impulsive response to the stutterer's objections, fears, resistance, or other emotional reactions. At this point sound therapeutic principles demand that the clinician do less talking and the stutterer more. *Much of the time the clinician will find that his most valuable articles of equipment are the phrases "What do you mean?" "Give me an example," or "Tell me more about that."* There are several reasons for the great usefulness of these phrases. First, there are many occasions when the only alternative to using them is to argue with the stutterer, a practice that may be said categorically to have little place in stuttering therapy. Second, the clinician who asks for further explanation will often find to his astonishment that he actually had not understood what the stutterer was trying to say. Third, what the stutterer

usually needs more than anything else on such occasions is the opportunity to clarify his own feelings. The clinician must learn that when, after a substantial period of therapy, the stutterer asks with emotion, "Do you think I should tell my girl friend I stutter?" the chances are that he is not really asking to be told the answer. He is probably saying, "I'm all confused. I can't make up my mind to do it. I have to talk this over." And the best reply that the clinician can make is, "Tell me some of the things that run through your mind when you think about it."

4. *Good therapy is "client centered."* That is, it is based on the individual's own values, not the therapist's. It is concerned with the individual's problems as he himself sees them, not with the problems a therapist thinks he ought to have. This means, among other things, that the stutterer is the only one qualified to judge whether, when, and for how long his stuttering warrants clinical attention and the only one qualified to point out the specific aspects of his problem for which he needs help. From this point of view, it is exceptionally important for the speech therapist to listen carefully to the manner in which the stutterer describes his difficulties. If the only problem of any real concern to him is that he stutters when reading aloud at school, it is poor therapy to seize on his speech when he makes introductions because the therapist has observed that he stutters "badly" in this situation. The issue can perhaps be made particularly clear by referring to a somewhat different type of choice that arises in clinical work when the stutterer has an additional speech deviation, for example, an articulatory defect. Shall we attempt to help him with it? It is surprising how cogently arguments can be advanced on both sides without regard for virtually the only relevant question: Does the stutterer want this assistance? If he does not, then pressing it on him constitutes an unwarranted attempt to burden him with a problem that is more suitably to be regarded as ours than his. If he does, it is questionable whose problem we solve by withholding such help. On the same principle, if a stutterer wants therapy we should never decline to help him on the grounds that his stuttering is too slight. It is not the business of a speech therapist to determine, in spite of the stutterer's opinion to the contrary, that he does not have a problem.

Handling resistance to therapy

By far the most frequent test of our ability to apply these principles is provided by the phenomenon of resistance. At the outset of his clinical practice, the speech clinician is likely to be somewhat baffled and dismayed when the stutterer delays, makes excuses, or refuses to comply with suggestions. Yet such behavior is exactly what we should expect when we ask the stutterer to do so many things he has been trying so hard for so long not to do. It is not the fact of resistance that should concern us but the form the resistance takes.

Admission of fear. The most common and least serious form of resistance is an open admission of fear. It is a healthy reaction to therapy that generally occurs when the "assignments" become somewhat difficult and threatening. This simple, acute form of resistance in most cases simply calls for patience on the part of the clinician and an accepting attitude toward the stutterer's feelings while it runs its course. As we pointed out earlier, considerable help may be given him by the proper planning of therapy. In the final analysis, however, the stutterer whose clinical progress is impeded by acute fear is like a person standing for the first time on the high diving board. No one can make his decision for him, but if he must dive, then sooner or later he will. Or, if the reasons are not sufficiently compelling, he will not, and if this is his decision he should not be privately regarded as though he were beneath contempt. It is not for any clinician say that avoidance and conceal-ment, whatever their drawbacks, may not be the best possible adjustment for a given stutterer *at a particular time.*

Rationalization. A second form of resistance more difficult to deal with is characterized by rationalization. Too insecure in his own self-esteem to appreciate how helpless and afraid he is, the stutterer comes to believe that there are other reasons for his failure to pursue an active program of clinical work. For example, he may feel that he does not have the time, that he does not approve of the method, or that his stuttering does not actually "bother him that much." What are we to do about assertions of this sort? The answer is that, although we will certainly wish to ask the stutterer to explain these reasons more fully, there is nothing for us to do but appear to accept them at face value. In the first place, rationalization is a self-protective device. We cannot and dare not try to remove it by storm. Perhaps the most direct approach permissible is to introduce the subject of rationalization as a topic for group discussion in the hope that certain group members will be helped to gain insight into their own rationalizations more rapidly when they are ready to do so.

In the second place, we cannot be so sure that the stutterer's reason for not participating more fully in therapy is wholly a rationalization. If we simply ask him to "tell us more," we may discover that what seemed to be resistance was chiefly an inability to budget his time efficiently or a lack of information. Nor do we know at once how tightly the stutterer is prepared to cling to his rationalizations, if this is what they are. We may find that the process of explaining his assertions to us was all that he needed in order to recognize them as rationalizations.

On the other hand, we may be strengthened in our suspicion that we are confronted with an organized defense against the threatening aspects of speech therapy. If so, we must keep in mind that the situation is far from hopeless if we are not insistent on definite signs of recovery by the second Wednesday in May. Clinical experience shows that in time, either as we succeed in reducing the stutterer's fear somewhat or as he becomes more mature and adequate as a person, his defense may become less urgently needed and he may gradually find more time to work on his problem or see more sense in the clinical procedures.

Intellectualization. The third form of resistance consists of the behavior often referred to as "intellectualization." This is usually the most difficult of all to overcome, partly because it appears in the guise of acceptance. The intellectualizer, frequently an intelligent and articulate person, may quickly absorb an abstract understanding of stuttering therapy and compliantly verbalize many of the attitudes expected of him. But his glibness proves to be no more than an effective evasion of active clinical work. It is his obvious pleasure to prolong the clinical hour in talk. The greater part of his friendly chatter may be related more or less directly to his speech difficulty, and much of it may consist superficially of the most hang-head self-excoriation. But the intellectualizer feels nothing: This is the essence of his problem. The stutterer who begins therapy in a mood of angry intransigence rarely presents any serious difficulty. In most cases all that is necessary is to put an accepting face on his hostility and wait for the hurricane to blow itself out in a rain of lachrymose emotion; his very spontaneity of feeling offers the most favorable forecast of the future. But the agreeable countenance of intellectualization is not sun, rain, wind, frost, or fog. Incapable of frank and unambiguous emotion, the intellectualizing person is often somewhat repressed, overcontrolled, and peculiarly resistive to change.

These are the essential patterns of resistance that stutterers for the most part exhibit. It cannot be denied that they may occasionally offer obstacles so great that for the time being failure, or what appears to be failure, must be accepted as unavoidable. The stutterer's anxiety may be too great, or perhaps there are more complicated and neurotic reasons for his resistance.

It is necessary, however, to add an extremely important word about failure. As a word for the outcome of speech therapy, "failure" suffers from the same vagueness and is subject to the same extensive qualifications as the word "cure." It is quite true that stutterers sometimes fall short by measurable degrees of certain more or less clearly definable therapy goals. But these are our own goals, the ones we have chosen for the stutterer. We must always keep in view the familiar clinical phenomenon of the stutterer who, having kicked and fought his resistive way through a period of therapy and having appeared to gain essentially nothing from the experience, returns months or years later, a remarkably changed person, to tell us of his gratitude for all we did for him. Whenever we hastily assume that therapy has been a "failure," we do not consider the arbitrary, personal nature of the criteria we use to make such a judgment; nor do we take into account the enormous capacity for change, maturation, and adjustment that nearly all human beings appear to demonstrate when given sufficient time.

Notes

1. Examples of repetitions of the last sound of a word have occasionally been reported, however; for example, see Van Thal (1957). In the only case of this kind I have ever seen, the frequent repetition of the final sound appeared to be a device for postponing the attempt on the next word.
2. For general reviews of the research on the factors influencing the loci, or distribution, of stuttering in the speech sequence, see Beech and Fransella (1968), pp. 129–136; Van Riper (1971), pp. 185–189; and Bloodstein (1975), pp. 206–214.
3. This excerpt is from Hendel and Bloodstein (1973), p. 38. Courtesy of the North-Holland Publishing Co.
4. For detailed documentation of these statements, see Bloodstein (1972).
5. This statement is based on evidence from a series of studies by various workers on the oral musculatures of stutterers; see Bloodstein (1975), pp. 134–136.
6. For more detailed explanation and attribution of these theories of adaptation, see Bloodstein (1975), pp. 236–243.
7. For a discussion of the hypothetical roles of short-term, intermediate-term, and long-term human memory traces, see Wickelgren (1970).
8. See Van Riper (1971), p. 174, and Bloodstein (1975), p. 13, for reviews of findings on measures of autonomic arousal.
9. For reviews of studies on the use of tranquilizers, see Burr and Mullendore (1960); Kent (1963); and Van Riper (1973), pp. 160–165.
10. See reviews of the effect of desensitization by Ingham and Andrews (1971), and Van Riper (1973), pp. 54–56.
11. Siegel (1970) has provided a detailed survey of research on the effect of punishment.
12. For documentation of these and other remarks on avoidance behavior based on a clinical study of stuttering children, see Bloodstein (1960a, 1960b, 1961).
13. For direct evidence of this finding, see the study of the effect of word length by Wingate (1967); he explicitly reported that all of the blocks recorded in his experiment were on the initial sounds of words.
14. Essential documentation for these statements is summarized in Bloodstein (1975), pp. 92–101, 182–188.

15. E.-M. Silverman (1972a, 1972b) has gathered additional data on 4-year-old normal-speaking children showing that, among their most frequently appearing types of disfluency on some occasions, are those often considered typical of stutterers. These are repetitions of syllables and one-syllable words and what Silverman refers to as "dysrhythmic phonations" (breaks, prolongations, and signs of effort and tension within words).

16. One qualitative difference between stutterers and nonstutterers was reported by Deutsch (1972), who could find no evidence of the adjacency effect in the disfluencies of adult normal speakers.

17. The suggestions regarding the treatment of stuttering in Phase 2 have been adapted, with minor changes, from a previous publication (Bloodstein, 1961).

18. This excerpt is from J. D. Williams, "What You Can Do About Your Stuttering," in *To the Stutterer* (Memphis, Tenn.: Speech Foundation of America, undated), p. 60.

References

Adams, M. R., and Moore, W. H., Jr. (1972) The effects of auditory masking on the anxiety level, frequency of disfluency, and selected vocal characteristics of stutterers. *Journal of Speech and Hearing Research*, 15, 572–578.

Andrews, G., and Harris, M. (1964) *The syndrome of stuttering*. London: Heinemann.

Avari, D. N., and Bloodstein, O. (1974) Adjacency and prediction in school-age stutterers, *Journal of Speech and Hearing Research*, 17, 33–40.

Bar, A., Singer, J., and Feldman, R. G. (1969) Subvocal muscle activity during stuttering and fluent speech: A comparison. *Journal of South African Logopedic Society*, 16, 9–14.

Beech, H. R., and Fransella, F. (1968) *Research and experiment in stuttering*. Elmsford, N.Y.: Pergamon.

Berlinsky, S. L. (1955) A comparison of stutterers and nonstutterers in four conditions of induced anxiety. *Speech Monographs*, 22, 197. Abstract.

Bloodstein, O. (1950a) Hypothetical conditions under which stuttering is reduced or absent. *Journal of Speech and Hearing Disorders*, 15, 142–153.

Bloodstein, O. (1950b) A rating scale study of conditions under which stuttering is reduced or absent. *Journal of Speech and Hearing Disorders*, 15, 29–36.

Bloodstein, O. (1960a) The development of stuttering: I. Changes in nine basic features. *Journal of Speech and Hearing Disorders*, 25, 219–237.

Bloodstein, O. (1960b) The development of stuttering: II. Developmental phases. *Journal of Speech and Hearing Disorders*, 25, 366–376.

Bloodstein, O. (1961) The development of stuttering: III. Theoretical and clinical implications. *Journal of Speech and Hearing Disorders*, 26, 67–82.

Bloodstein, O. (1975) *A handbook on stuttering*, rev. ed., Chicago: National Easter Seal Society for Crippled Children and Adults.

Bloodstein, O. (1972) The anticipatory struggle hypothesis: Implications of research on the variability of stuttering. *Journal of Speech and Hearing Research*, 15, 487–499.

Bloodstein, O., Alper, J., and Zisk, P. K. (1965) Stuttering as an outgrowth of normal disfluency. In D. A. Barbara, ed., *New directions in stuttering*. Springfield, Ill.: C. C Thomas.

Bloodstein, O., and Gantwerk, B. F. (1967) Grammatical function in relation to stuttering in young children. *Journal of Speech and Hearing Research*, 10, 786–789.

Bloodstein, O., and Shogan, R. L. (1972) Some clinical notes on forced stuttering. *Journal of Speech and Hearing Disorders*, 37, 177–186.

Brenner, N. C., Perkins, W. H., and Soderberg, G. A. (1972) The effect of rehearsal on frequency of stuttering. *Journal of Speech and Hearing Research*, 15, 483–486.

Brutten, E. J. (1963) Palmar sweat investigation of disfluency and expectancy adaptation. *Journal of Speech and Hearing Research*, 6, 40–48.

Burr, H. G., and Mullendore, J. M. (1960) Recent investigations on tranquilizers and stuttering. *Journal of Speech and Hearing Disorders*, 25, 33–37.

Cooper, E. B. (1972) Recovery from stuttering in a junior and senior high school population. *Journal of Speech and Hearing Research*, 15, 632–638.

Cooper, E. B., Cady, B. B., and Robbins, C. J. (1970) The effect of the verbal stimulus words *wrong*, *right*, and *tree* on the disfluency rates of stutterers and nonstutterers. *Journal of Speech and Hearing Research*, 13, 239–244.

Deutsch, S. E. (1972) *The adjacency effect in the distribution of disfluencies in normal speakers* M.S. thesis, Brooklyn College.

Dickson, S. (1971) Incipient stuttering and spontaneous remission of stuttered speech. *Journal of Communication Disorders*, 4, 99–110.

Dixon, C. C. (1955) Stuttering adaptation in relation to assumed level of anxiety. In W. Johnson, ed., *Stuttering in children and adults*. Minneapolis: University of Minnesota Press.

Donohue, I. R. (1955) Stuttering adaptation during three hours of continuous oral reading. In W. Johnson, ed., *Stuttering in children and adults*. Minneapolis: University of Minnesota Press.

Eisenson, J. (1947) Aphasics: Observations and tentative conclusions. *Journal of Speech Disorders*, 12, 290–292.

Forte, M., and Schlesinger, I. M. (1972) Stuttering as a function of time of expectation. *Journal of Communication Disorders*, 5, 347–358.

Frank, A., and Bloodstein, O. (1971) Frequency of stuttering following repeated unison readings. *Journal of Speech and Hearing Research*, 14, 519–524.

Freund, H. (1966) *Psychopathology and the problems of stuttering*. Springfield, Ill.: C. C Thomas.

Frick, J. V. (1965) *Evaluation of motor planning techniques for the treatment of stuttering*. Report on Grant No. 32-48-0720-5003, U.S. Office of Education.

Glasner, P. J., and Rosenthal, D. (1957) Parental diagnosis of stuttering in young children. *Journal of Speech and Hearing Disorders*, 22, 288–295.

Goss, A. E. (1952) Stuttering behavior and anxiety theory: I. Stuttering behavior and anxiety as a function of the duration of stimulus words. *Journal of Abnormal Social Psychology*, 47, 38–50.

Gray, B. B. and Brutten, E. J. (1965) The relationship between anxiety, fatigue and spontaneous recovery in stuttering. *Behavior Research and Therapy, Ther.*, 2, 251–259.

Gray, B. B., and England, G. (1972) Some effects of anxiety deconditioning upon stuttering frequency. *Journal of Speech and Hearing Research*, 15, 114–122.

Gray, K. C., and Williams, D. E. (1969) Anticipation and stuttering: A pupillographic study. *Journal of Speech and Hearing Research*, 12, 833–839.

Hahn, E. F. (1940) A study of the relationship between the social complexity of the oral reading situation and the severity of stuttering. *Journal of Speech Disorders*, 5, 5–14.

Helmreich, H. G., and Bloodstein, O. (1973) The grammatical factor in childhood disfluency in relation to the continuity hypothesis. *Journal of Speech and Hearing Research*, 16, 731–738.

Hendel, D., and Bloodstein, O. (1973) Consistency in relation to inter-subject congruity in the loci of stutterings. *Journal of Communication Disorders*, 6, 37–43.

Ilg, F., Learned, J., and Lockwood, A. (1949) The three-and-a-half-year old. *Journal of Genetic Psychology*, 75, 21–31.

Ingham, R. J., and Andrews, G. (1971) The relation between anxiety reduction and treatment. *Journal of Communication Disorders*, 4, 289–301.

Jacobson, E. (1938) *Progressive relaxation*. Chicago: University of Chicago Press.

Johnson, W. (1932) *The Influence of stuttering on the personality. University of Iowa Studies in Child Welfare*, vol. 5, no. 5.

Johnson, W. et al. (1967) *Speech handicapped school children*, 3rd ed. New York: Harper & Row.

Johnson, W., and associates (1959) *The onset of stuttering*. Minneapolis: University of Minnesota Press.

Johnson, W., and Brown, S. F. (1935) Stuttering in relation to various speech sounds. *Quarterly Journal of Speech*, 21, 481–496.

Johnson, W., and Knott, J. R. (1937) Studies in the psychology of stuttering: I. The distribution of moments of stuttering in successive readings of the same material. *Journal of Speech Disorders*, 2, 17–19.

Johnson, W., and Millsapps, L. S. (1937) Studies in the psychology of stuttering: VI. The role of cues representative of stuttering moments during oral reading. *Journal of Speech Disorders*, 2, 101–104.

Kent, L. R. (1963) The use of tranquilizers in the treatment of stuttering. *Journal of Speech and Hearing Disorders*, 28, 288–294.

Kline, D. F. (1959) An experimental study of the frequency of stuttering in relation to certain goal-activity drives in basic human behavior. *Speech Monographs*, 26, 137. Abstract.

Knott, J. R., Johnson, W., and Webster, M. J. (1937) Studies in the psychology of stuttering: II. A quantitative evaluation of expectation of stuttering in relation to the occurrence of stuttering. *Journal of Speech Disorders*, 2, 20–22.

Métraux, R. W. (1950) Speech profiles of the preschool child 18 to 54 months. *Journal of Speech and Hearing Disorders*, 15, 37–53.

Neelley, J. N., and Timmons, R. J. (1967) Adaptation and consistency in the disfluent speech behavior of young stutterers and nonstutterers. *Journal of Speech and Hearing Research,* 10, 250–256.

Peacher, W. G. (1945) Speech disorders in World War II. *Journal of Speech Disorders,* 10, 155–161.

Peins, M. (1961) Adaptation effect and spontaneous recovery in stuttering expectancy. *Journal of Speech and Hearing Research,* 4, 91–99.

Porter, H. v. K. (1939) Studies in the psychology of stuttering: XIV. Stuttering phenomena in relation to size and personnel of audience. *Journal of Speech Disorders,* 4, 323–333.

Rappaport, B., and Bloodstein, O. (1971) The role of random blackout cues in the distribution of moments of stuttering. *Journal of Speech and Hearing Research,* 14, 874–879.

Robbins, M. G. (1971) The effect of varying conditions of rehearsal on the frequency of stuttering. Ph.D. dissertation, City University of New York.

Rogers, C. R. (1942) *Counseling and psychotherapy.* Boston: Houghton Mifflin.

Rogers, C. R. (1951) *Client centered therapy.* Boston: Houghton Mifflin.

Seidel, A., Weinstein, R. B., and Bloodstein, O. (1973) The effect of interposed conditions on the consistency of stuttering. *Journal of Speech and Hearing Research,* 16, 62–66.

Sheehan, J. G., and Martyn, M. M. (1966) Spontaneous recovery from stuttering. *Journal of Speech and Hearing Research,* 9, 121–135.

Shulman, E. (1955) Factors influencing the variability of stuttering. In W. Johnson, ed., *Stuttering in children and adults.* Minneapolis: University of Minnesota Press.

Siegel, G. M. (1970) Punishment, stuttering, and disfluency. *Journal of Speech and Hearing Research,* 13, 677–714.

Siegel, G. M., and Haugen, D. (1964) Audience size and variations in stuttering behavior. *Journal of Speech and Hearing Research,* 7, 381–388.

Silverman, E.-M. (1972a) Generality of disfluency data collected from preschoolers. *Journal of Speech and Hearing Research,* 15, 84–92.

Silverman, E.-M. (1972b) Preschoolers' speech disfluency: Single syllable word repetition. *Perceptual and Motor Skills,* 35, 1002.

Silverman, E.-M. (1973) The influence of preschoolers' speech usage on their disfluency frequency. *Journal of Speech and Hearing Research,* 16, 474–481.

Silverman, F. H. (1970a) Course of nonstutterers' disfluency adaptation during 15 consecutive oral readings of the same material. *Journal of Speech and Hearing Research,* 13, 382–386.

Silverman, F. H. (1970b) A note on the degree of adaptation by stutterers and nonstutterers during oral reading. *Journal of Speech and Hearing Research,* 13, 173–177.

Silverman, F. H., and Silverman, E.-M. (1972) Stutter-like behavior in the manual communication of the deaf. *Perceptual and Motor Skills,* 33, 45–46.

Silverman, F. H., and Williams, D. E. (1972) Prediction of stuttering by school-age stutterers. *Journal of Speech and Hearing Research,* 15, 189–193.

Steer, M. D., and Johnson, W. (1936) An objective study of the relationship between psychological factors and the severity of stuttering. *Journal of Abnormal Social Psychology*, 31, 36–46.

Stefankiewicz, S. P., and Bloodstein, O. (1974) The effect of a four-week interval on the consistency of stuttering. *Journal of Speech and Hearing Research*, 17, 141–145.

Šváb, L., Gross, J., and Langová, J. (1972) Stuttering and social isolation: Effect of social isolation with different levels of monitoring on stuttering frequency (a pilot study). *Journal of Nervous and Mental Disease*, 155, 1–5.

Van Riper, C. (1936) Study of the thoracic breathing of stutterers during expectancy and occurrence of stuttering spasm. *Journal of Speech Disorders*, 1, 61–72.

Van Riper, C. (1952) Report of stuttering on a musical instrument. *Journal of Speech and Hearing Disorders*, 17, 433–434.

Van Riper, C. (1954) *Speech correction: Principles and methods*, 3rd ed. Englewood Cliffs, N.J.: Prentice-Hall.

Van Riper, C. (1971) *The nature of stuttering*. Englewood Cliffs, N.J.: Prentice-Hall.

Van Riper, C. (1972) *Speech correction: Principles and methods*, 5th ed. Englewood Cliffs, N.J.: Prentice-Hall.

Van Riper, C. (1973) *The treatment of stuttering*. Englewood Cliffs, N.J.: Prentice-Hall.

Van Thal, J. H. (1957) Observations on unusual behavior by stammerers. *Folia Phoniatrica*, 9, 42–44.

Weiss, D. A. (1964) *Cluttering*. Englewood Cliffs, N.J.: Prentice-Hall.

Wickelgren, W. A. (1970) Multitrace strength theory. In D. A. Norman, ed., *Models of human memory*. New York: Academic.

Williams, D. E. (1971) Stuttering therapy for children. In L. E. Travis, ed., *Handbook of speech pathology and audiology*. New York: Appleton-Century-Crofts.

Williams, D. E., Silverman, F. H., and Kools, J. A. (1968) Disfluency behavior of elementary-school stutterers and nonstutterers: The adaptation effect. *Journal of Speech and Hearing Research*, 11, 622–630.

Williams, D. E., Silverman, F. H., and Kools, J. A. (1969a) Disfluency behavior of elementary-school stutterers and nonstutterers: The consistency effect. *Journal of Speech and Hearing Research*, 12, 301–307.

Williams, D. E., Silverman, F. H., and Kools, J. A. (1969b) Disfluency behavior of elementary-school stutterers and nonstutterers: Loci of instances of disfluency. *Journal of Speech and Hearing Research*, 12, 308–318.

Wingate, M. E. (1967) Stuttering and word length. *Journal of Speech and Hearing Research*, 10, 146–152.

Wingate, M. E. (1972) Deferring the adaptation effect. *Journal of Speech and Hearing Research*, 15, 547–550.

Wischner, G. J. (1947) *Stuttering behavior and learning: A program of research*. Ph.D. dissertation, University of Iowa.

Wynia, B. L. (1964) *The consistency effect in the speech repetitions of normal speaking young children*. M.S. thesis, Pennsylvania State University.

Conflict Theory and Avoidance-Reduction Therapy

Joseph G. Sheehan, Ph.D.

Professor of Psychology, University of California, Los Angeles. Consultant in Clinical Psychology, Veterans Administration. Diplomate in Clinical Psychology, American Board of Professional Psychology. Fellow of the American Psychological Association and the American Speech and Hearing Association. Consulting Editor, *Journal of Communication Disorders, Journal of Fluency Disorders.* Author of *Stuttering: Research and Therapy.* Contributing author of *Psychopathology, A Source Book; Stuttering, A Symposium; Stuttering, Significant Theories and Therapies; Readings on the Exceptional Child; Speech Therapy; Stuttering and the Conditioning Therapies; Learning Theory and Stuttering Therapy: Conditioning in Stuttering Therapy.* Contributor to professional journals including the *Journal of Abnormal Psychology,* the *Journal of Communication Disorders,* and the *Journal of Speech and Hearing Disorders.*

Introduction

Seldom are the probable origins of a disorder so clearly portrayed as in the case of the problem called "stuttering." We observe a blocking, a hesitancy, an indeterminate stoppage in the forward flow of speech. Or we find grimaces, postponements of halfhearted attempts, accessory vocalization on "I" or "well" or "and," long silent pauses, splitting of sounds, fixations of articulatory postures, evident fear of trying the word, fluent asides, giving up, pretending to think, pretending to give up, backing up—all amid a galaxy of other apparently ineffectual instrumental behaviors. The push-pull, the tug-of-war, the holding back in the midst of going ahead, the to-be-or-not-to-be: All these telltale signs of conflict are visible and audible in the disorder.

The stutterer scans constantly ahead to see whether he dares to proceed, becoming a gambler with his self-esteem on the line. Though he tries, he finds it hard to put up a front, for most people a social necessity. He is robbed of the dignity of hiding his feelings about himself, for they burst through to block his speech at the most crucial and frustrating moments.

By far one of the more important statements we can make about the disorder is that the majority of stutterers are able to speak most of their words fluently. Fluency is a fair-weather friend that deserts the stutterer when he needs it most: to say some *thing* important to some *one* important. His speech is the tire that appears to be flat on only one side, but the condition means that he can't count on getting there.

Another striking feature is that the person who stutters has his greatest difficulty in presenting *himself* through the act of speaking. All speech is an important avenue of social presentation of the self. In the stutterer, the role of self is illustrated dramatically: Many stutterers can shift roles into "someone else," by assuming accents or taking a part in a play. For the duration of that special role, they may be quite fluent. Some have even become professional actors, enjoying stage fluency in roles that enabled them to hide behind a make-believe character. Yet before and after entering into that false role, they blocked severely when speaking as themselves.

Marilyn Monroe was a stutterer, among her other problems of identity and self-expression. So were Jack Paar and Gary Moore before the repeated experience of public self-presentation enabled them to gain self-assurance before audiences.

One of our most fascinating cases was a professional actor who was able to run children's puppet shows, taking the part of each different character fluently in turn. Only when he began to study the Stanislavsky method, emphasizing acting from the self, did he lose his stage fluency and his television acting job. As further evidence for stuttering as a disorder of the social presentation of the self, we may cite an experiment we have demonstrated consistently in educational films and television appearances.[1]

In the experiment, two stutterers read separately and block severely when speaking as individuals; then they read the same passage together, as a duet, and do so with fluency and ease. The effect is not due to repetition of material (adaptation), for they can continue indefinitely, reading new material with fluency, so long as they *stay in unison.* We knew two stutterers who became good friends and tried to help each other out by speaking chorally in difficult moments, like two drunks leaning against one another so they could stagger down the street.

Singing is another example of a special and probably unreliable route to temporary fluency. Though it is commonly observed that stutterers can always sing without stuttering, we recall vividly our personal experience, in Van Riper's clinic, of blocking severely on the second word of "Auld Lang Syne." The line went, "Should uh . . . au . . . au . . . uh . . . uh . . . auld!" Everyone was a little more auld by the time we finally got that word out. Clinically, we have also observed that singing is no guarantee of fluency, though most benefit from the special features inherent in the behavior of singing. A most successful country-western television personality, Mel Tillis, sings with great fluency and commercial success. In conversation, he still avoids and still stutters. But he is open enough to make his audience comfortable, and he tells a story with a great sense of timing.

All of the foregoing dramatizes vividly the role aspect of stuttering. We hold that stuttering is a false-role disorder, a flaw in the social presentation of the self, and that stuttering is based on a role conflict. Equally and as part of this analysis, our basic theory of stuttering is

---

[1] The "Mike Douglas Show," "Dinah's Place," and "Life with Linkletter," among others. See also *The Iceberg of Stuttering,* a 55-minute film available from the UCLA Media Center.

that most of the observed abnormality is learned behavior best understood and best treated as a double approach-avoidance conflict.

In this chapter, we explore the problem of stuttering by means of
several applicable models and comparisons. Many involve different levels
of analysis and do not compete with or contradict one another. Among
the theoretical models are conflict theory; role theory; homeostasis and
physiological feedback systems; principles of serial learning; drive-reduction learning theory; contiguity theory; classical conditioning; instrumental conditioning; the projective hypothesis; the primacy of conflicts;
psychoanalytic theory; role therapy; psychotherapy through action; reinforcement and behavior modification principles; finally and most inclu-
sively, avoidance-reduction therapy.

The theory and viewpoint presented here entail principally their own
level of analysis. For example, avoidance-reduction principles underlying
the therapy may combine psychotherapy and more direct behavioral
modification in varying degrees. This chapter is not designed to exclude
other possible approaches to the complex problem of stuttering or to
deny the possible validity of future theories or therapies. The chapter
does essay an integration of knowledge from disciplines whose scientific
base appear most directly applicable to the reduction of the mysteries
of the problem called "stuttering."

Definition of stuttering

So difficult is the problem of defining stuttering that we have reserved
it for this separate presentation. Ironically, it is necessary to know quite
a bit about the problem before the definitional difficulties are compre-
hended. It is of course simple to rehash a dictionary sort of definition,
but experts have encountered great disagreement even at this seemingly
elementary level. One reason is that stuttering is a relative term, like
adjustment, abnormality, or neurosis, whose definition depends on a
social and cultural context that varies from one place to another in
the world and erodes with the shifting sands of time and semantic usage.

The same problem is encountered in defining what is "abnormal"
or deviant behavior generally. If a youth wearing today's male hair styles
had suddenly appeared in the 1930s or 1940s, he would have been
quickly judged to be either a transvestite or a homosexual. But then,
so might Buffalo Bill, Jesus Christ, or Sir Walter Raleigh. The point
is that what is assumed to be normal in one time and place may be
viewed very differently in another context. A traitor is one whose cause
has not won the day; if it has, he becomes a patriot. Those who George
III regarded as traitors we refer to as the "Founding Fathers." The definition of normality hinges on who has the floor at the moment.

We believe that the definition of stuttering may be best accomplished by specifying the categories under which persons may be considered to be stutterers. As the literature of speech pathology reveals all too clearly, it is impossible to set precise limits on all the behaviors that might at some point in time, to some experts, be defined as stuttering behavior. Some people who regard themselves as stutterers are more visibly fluent than others who fumble all over the place but never entertain such a thought. It is much easier to enumerate examples of what might be considered stuttering behavior than it is to offer a precise definition of stuttering, though it has been tried plenty of times (see, for example, Wingate's "standard definition of stuttering," 1964).

The problem is complicated by the circumstance that nearly normal speakers may be said to "stutter" at times or to show behavior that might be considered by some listeners as stuttering. In emphasizing the evaluational aspect of what is to be called "stuttering," Johnson (1961) concluded that "stuttering is a statement about a listener." When different observers judge moments of stuttering, there is always considerable variation in the amount of agreement among them. Even when the interjudge reliabilities are relatively high, as in successive totals of repeated readings of the same material, there may be disagreement as to which word was "stuttered." One of the reasons for this is that, as we previously reported, stutterers frequently spend considerable time stuttering trying to say words they have already uttered successfully (Sheehan, 1946, 1974). "Going back for a running start" is partly responsible. The starting phrase is usually spoken fluently, though it may be repeated in rising attempt to approach the speaking of the feared word. In the occasional instance when even the starting phrase of a word becomes a point of blocking, the judgment of what word was stuttered becomes ensnarled to a considerable degree. In repeating previously spoken phrases for a running start, we have personally had the experience (fortunately not common) of actually getting stuck at a point farther back in the sentence! How is this to be counted—as two instances of stuttering or as four? No wonder judges sometimes disagree!

Normal speech, or at least the speech of speakers considered normal, contains numerous hesitations, fumblings, "uhs," word repetitions, short-phrase repetitions, and crutch phrases (OK, you know, well). Wendell Johnson (1946) originally called these behaviors *nonfluencies*. Later, at the suggestion of Robert West, he renamed them *disfluencies* (Johnson et al., 1961).

Stutterers frequently use pet phrases as "fluent asides" to gain time or to reassure themselves that they can still vocalize. Their stalling tactics permit a fear-reducing rehearsal.

Because normal speakers do use crutches, it is sometimes argued that the stutterer's crutches are of little importance. However, the timing devices and elaborate filibustering behaviors of stutterers comprise a substantial portion of their handicap. To be a negotiable crutch, the act must be something that normal speakers plausibly do. Anything that only stutterers do would not be a crutch but a giveaway, a revelation of the stutterer role the person strives strenuously to conceal.

In developing his semantogenic theory of stuttering, Johnson (1946) stressed the importance of the listener in determining what constitutes instances of stuttering. He stated that "stuttering begins not in the child's tongue but in the parent's ear." If of course there were no list of disagreements as to what constitutes stuttering, it would be relatively simple to define the disorder in terms of a list of behaviors characteristic only of stutterers. Some behaviors, such as syllable repetition, grimaces, forcing, and jerky speech attempts, appear to be more or less distinctive of stuttering, at least in its advanced stages. Yet we constantly encounter individuals who consider themselves stutterers and have anxiety about possible stuttering, though they sound more fluent than some members of the clinic staff.

Stuttering viewed as handicap differs from stuttering merely viewed as behavior. Villarreal (1950) distinguished between stuttering as defect and stuttering as handicap, two aspects of stuttering therapy analogous to the distinction we are making here. The defect side of stuttering refers to the speech behavior, whereas the handicap aspect refers to the constellation of feelings and attitudes. There is an interesting parallel here between classical and instrumental conditioning. While the stuttering pattern appears to be instrumentally conditioned, the stutterer's feelings and emotional problems are for the most part classically conditioned. In therapy research we have frequently found it necessary to rate improvement on the instrumental or behavioral side, separate from the psychotherapeutic or attitudinal side (Sheehan, 1954a).

We have put aside the definition of *stuttering per se* as impossibly inferential. Instead, the definitional problem in stuttering is best approached by defining the criteria by which one is judged to be a stutterer, rather than by trying to offer a generic definition. If we define who is a stutterer, then we make a beginning toward understanding the problem as it exists for those who have it. Three distinguishing categories emerge: speech behavior, speech anxiety, and perception of self. Here is our own standard definition:

> A stutterer may be defined as a person who shows, to a degree that sets him off from the rest of the population, any one or more of the following groups of symptoms: (1) blockings, stickings, grimaces, forcings, repetitions, prolongations, or other rhythm breaks or interruptions in the forward flow of speech; (2) fear or anticipation of blockings, fear of inability to speak, or related symptoms prior to words or to speaking

situations; (3) a self-concept which includes a picture of himself as a stutterer, a stammerer, speech blocker, or a person lacking normal speech fluency. (Sheehan, 1958a, p. 123)

A stutterer is one who fails to say the word on time. Or if he does get the word out on schedule, he accompanies the utterance with a telltale grimace or timing movement. Or he drawls and chants to utter his words, usually at the behest of a voice trainer or an operant conditioner. A few are stutterers only to themselves, going through agonies of anticipation of stuttering blocks they may once have had, but never currently experience. We call the last groups implicit stutterers, and some are more fluent outwardly than normal-speaking members of our clinic staff.

The more typical stutterer, who fails to get the word out on time, is found performing a mysterious variety of tricks and crutches "to get the word out." The instrumental behaviors that stutterers go through while apparently struggling to get a word out are often pathetically irrelevant to the act of speaking. The very irrelevance of the stutterer's efforts to speak probably provides a principal source of audience bewilderment and irritation. As we showed in a phonetic analysis long ago, on almost one-half of stuttering blocks in adults there is some form of phonetic irrelevancy, or stuttering, on the wrong sound. We also noted that "stutterers are frequently found attempting to say words and sounds they have already spoken successfully" (Sheehan, 1946, 1974, pp. 193, 211). Similar observations have been offered by Van Riper (1971, 1973) and Wingate (1966). Van Riper has long made it a feature of his therapy to point out to the stutterer the lack of logical relationship between his spasm-pattern and the proper movements necessary for the speaking of the word.

The iceberg of stuttering

The handicap of stuttering is traditionally defined in terms of the blockings, repetitions, mouth posturings, and grimaces that the stutterer goes through in trying to utter a word; but it is much more than that. A stutterer is one who does not know where his next word is coming from. Moreover, he doesn't know when the next situation will arise in which he will need that word. Even his fluency may give him little more than a feeling of thin ice. The to-be-or-not-to-be, to-speak-or-not-to-speak is always with the stutterer, and from this gnawing, pervasive uncertainty springs the major portion of his handicap. The symptoms we see make up only the top of the iceberg: Far greater, and more dangerous and destructive, are those that lie underneath.

The more the stutterer tries to spare his listener by covering up, the larger this unseen handicap becomes. He goes through anguished rehearsal of many a speaking crisis that never comes. Because he never knows with certainty just what the next situation will bring, he becomes a gambler with his self-esteem as the stake. He may be racked with self-doubt and anxiety even during apparently fluent moments. Even the listener seldom experiences the relief which the occasional fluent moments might bring, because he also knows that at any time the awkward blockings may return.

The listener, as well as the stutterer, is caught in a conflict. What should he do when the stutterer is struggling? Should he watch the debacle or avert his gaze? Should he help the stutterer with a painfully obvious word or let him flounder? Should he give some friendly recognition to the difficulty, or help the stutterer pretend it isn't there? Knowing little about the disorder, he gets his cue from the stutterer himself. Through the interplay of perceptions, the listener concludes that stuttering must be something shameful and joins the stutterer in pretending that nothing is out of the ordinary. By engaging in a false role, the stutterer draws his listener into an equally false role. In the manifest experience of his conflict between going ahead and holding back, the stutterer inadvertently places the listener in a conflict as well.

The blockings seem to come in waves, and those waves hit hardest when both the content and the listener are significant, as in making a request of an authority figure. Yet it is not always so, and the stutterer can sometimes surprise himself and everyone by speaking fluently in a crisis. Such breaks are seldom really lucky for the stutterer; people may grow more intolerant, saying, "Well, that shows he can talk if he really wants to." And that same fluency may be experienced by the stutterer less as relief than as a future role-expectation.

When the stutterer is on the crest of a fluency wave, he may set up a role expectation that facilitates his downward slide toward the trough. The basketball team that is trying to keep a victory string going may feel more pressure than one that isn't.

Development of stuttering

Speech is not only learned, but is a skilled act. A child of three obviously has far less experience in performing this act under a variety of interpersonal conditions. He is expressing himself, presenting himself socially for the first time in his young life, and he is doing it through the precise execution of an intricate sequence of timing movements.

In several respects, the young speaker is like the new field-goal kicker on a college football team. He must also execute a precise sequence of serial responses with skill and aplomb. First, those on his side must protect his opportunity. Second, external time pressure from the opposition reduces his chances for success. Third, self-imposed time pressure foreshortens the sequence and aborts the effort. Fourth, just one early failure in a crucial situation may readily disrupt future performance. Fifth, such "choking up" is far more common in rookies.

The young child is a rookie on the field of conversational competition. He needs opportunity and protection. Vulnerable to outside pressure, he may easily learn to pressure himself. His self-esteem eroded, he may "choke up"—a fascinating phrase that dramatizes the role of the speech apparatus in emotional expression.

When the pressure is gone, back out in the playroom that is the practice field of speech learning, the child's easy flow of mostly fluent sequential movement resumes. If he drops the ball momentarily, he picks it up again easily. No choking up here. The automatized aspect of speech may be strengthened through prolonged practice and success in acquiring the comfortable speaker role.

Speech is learned through a sequence of movements. The law of economy of movement dictates that excess response be dropped in the interest of efficiency. Especially pertinent here is an excellent discussion of serial learning found in Hilgard and Marquis (1940).

We are not neurologically perfect beings. All of us are disfluent at times, with a range of disfluency that might be represented like this:

Highly Fluent ———————————————— Highly Disfluent

Those on the right side of this continuum obviously run a much greater risk of experiencing some kind of audience reaction, especially in a taut or impermissive setting. Even a disfluent child will not suffer from his neurological imperfections provided he does not develop avoidance reactions toward them. Such reactions and evaluations have been extensively studied by Johnson (1955; Johnson et al, 1967), whose semantogenic theory suggests that stuttering becomes a problem only after the listener evaluation and as a result of it.

Development of conflict theory

Observations of various kinds of conflicts operating in the stutterer have been made by various authorities, all the way back to the German writer Wyneken (1868), who considered the stutterer a *sprachzweifler*, a "speech-doubter." The stutterer was like one seized with uncertainty at the moment of attempting a leap, therefore unable to make the leap with necessary aplomb.

Johnson and Knott (1936) described stuttering in terms of a configuration that involved a conflict between the communicative impulse and the impulse to inhibit expected stuttering. Related observations on conflict have been reviewed by the author as part of earlier publications of the approach-avoidance conflict theory of stuttering (Sheehan, 1951, 1953a, 1958a).

Wide divergence has appeared among various writers as to the nature of the conflict and its relation to the stuttering. For some it has been a conflict over gratification of instincts; for others, a conscious interference with an automatic process; for still others, a rivalry between cortical hemispheres.

Few who have ever observed a stutterer closely will dispute the essential accuracy of Wyneken's observation. Yet until recently very little systematic attention had been given to the role of conflict in stuttering. And no one seemed ready to build a theory based solidly on conflict as an essential explanation for the disorder or to relate treatment to such a theory. The six main theories of stuttering listed by Van Riper in the first and second editions of his text (1939, 1947), made no mention of conflict theory. Systematic models for conflict behavior had appeared in the psychology literature (Lewin, 1935; Miller, 1944), but the literature on stuttering reflected no such developments. As a student at the University of Michigan, I recall my surge of excitement at discovering how well Miller's conflict models fitted both the primary and the secondary behaviors of stuttering. The systematic interpretation of stuttering as conflict behavior comprised about one-half of my doctoral dissertation, submitted in August 1949, under the title, "The Experimental Modification of Stuttering Through Nonreinforcement." It was published without revision in the *Journal of Abnormal and Social Psychology* (Sheehan, 1951). In May, 1950, I first presented the theory of stuttering as an approach-avoidance conflict to the Western Psychological Association convention in Santa Barbara. The abstract included these words:

> Stuttering is a resultant of approach-avoidance conflict, of opposed
> urges to speak and to hold back from speaking. The "holding back" may
> be due either to learned avoidances or to unconscious motives; the approach-
> avoidance formulation fits both. A recent experiment is cited in which the
> author was able to reduce stuttering through the reinforcement of approach
> responses (Sheehan, 1950a).

The present writing concerns largely an expansion and revision of a theory of stuttering as an approach-avoidance conflict in terms of conflicting urges to speak and to hold back from speaking. The theory seeks to integrate advances in clinical psychology and learning theory into a systematic theory of stuttering and to relate treatment procedures logically to a systematic theory.

Stuttering as an Approach-Avoidance Conflict: Basic Statement

In terms of its simplest aspects, what we have to account for in stuttering is a momentary blocking. Almost mysteriously the stutterer is stuck on a word, and then, for reasons just as baffling, he is able to continue. An explanation of stuttering must account for these twin features of the stutterer's behavior.

Most theories of stuttering have focused on the hesitancy, on what produces the blocking. But from the standpoint of systematic theory as well as therapy, it is just as important to explain termination of the block as the block itself. We raised this question during the course of our first systematic investigation of stuttering (Sheehan, 1946). We asked, "What seems to determine the moment of release, the moment at which the stutterer can finally say the word?" (p. 69).

Two questions then become essential in the explanation of the stutterer's behavior: (1) What makes him stop? (2) What enables him to continue? In response to these twin questions, two central hypotheses may be stated:

1. The conflict hypothesis. The stutterer stops whenever conflicting approach and avoidance tendencies reach an equilibrium.
2. The fear-reduction hypothesis. The occurrence of stuttering reduces the fear that elicited it, so that *during* the block there is sufficient reduction in fear-motivated avoidance to resolve the conflict, permitting release of the blocked word.

The discussion that follows will take up each of these in turn.

The conflict hypothesis

If stuttering occurs whenever approach and avoidance tendencies reach an equilibrium, we should be able to analyze the process in terms of the relative strengths of the gradients of each. Miller (1944) and Dollard and Miller (1950) provided an excellent theoretical model for such an analysis (Figure 1).

For the stutterer, the speaking of a difficult word involves a goal, that of communication; but it also involves a fear, that of an inability to communicate. The stutterer thus has a "feared goal" in Miller's sense. Conflicting tendencies in the stutterer to approach and to avoid are represented by solid and broken lines respectively. From the fact that the fear-motivated avoidance gradient is steeper than the reward-motivated approach gradient, it can be seen that an organism put in an approach-avoidance conflict situation will *go partway and then stop* or oscillate in the zone where the gradients cross. This is exactly the

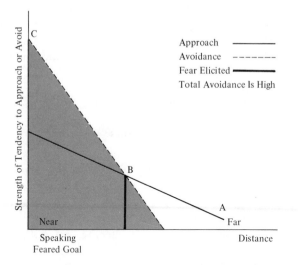

Figure 1. Stuttering as a result of conflicting tendencies to approach and to avoid the act of speaking (single approach-avoidance conflict), when total avoidance tendency is high. Since the avoidance gradient is always steeper than the approach gradient, the intersection at point B is in this case relatively far from the goal, and momentary fear, or "fear elicited," is moderate.

behavior the stutterer shows when attempting a feared word or when entering a feared situation. He says "K-K-K-Katy" or blocks silently after having begun the word. He freezes at the instant of picking up the phone or halts on the threshold of a strange office.

If this formulation is essentially correct, we are in a position to answer the first question. The stutterer stops after advancing partway because he is in a conflict situation, and the moment of his stopping is determined by the relative strengths of approach and avoidance gradients. Stuttering behavior itself has a hesitant character because it is the result of a conflict. Such an interpretation of stuttering accords well with Freud's classic view of the nature of neurotic conflict:

> . . . neurotic symptoms . . . are the result of a conflict. The two
> powers which have entered into opposition meet together again in the
> symptom and become reconciled by means of the *compromise* contained
> in the symptom-formation. (Freud, 1943, p. 313)

In the compromise, that is, the symptom of stuttering, the conflict is neatly externalized.

In the light of the conflict model, we hold that the famous "primary symptoms" of stuttering, those of repetition and prolongation, result from the vacillation and fixation that occurs at the point where the gradients cross. The primary symptoms of stuttering are strikingly parallel in form to the primary behaviors found in approach-avoidance conflict experiments. It is worth noting that even normal speakers placed in a conflict situation will sometimes show some of the same oscillation and fixation that reflect the clash of approach and avoidance forces in stuttering.

So-called secondary symptoms in stuttering may be viewed as the result of instrumental conditioning, first of escape and second of avoidance. The stuttering pattern consists for the most part of instrumental acts that are phonetically irrelevant; yet they must have a reinforcement history of sporadically successful release of the difficult word. Moreover, stutterers are often found stuttering on words and sounds they have already spoken successfully (Sheehan, 1946). The stuttering pattern is not an isolated single response, but an example of a serially learned response. Stuttering also involves, in its own special way, the learning of a skill, just as speaking involves the learning of a skill. What happens to a skilled sequential act when great punishment suddenly looms as the penalty for failure? Elsewhere (Sheehan, 1950, 1970a) we compared the stutterer to a man walking a plank. Placed flat on the floor, he could do it easily; but if the plank is placed across a chasm, he would try so desperately to avoid falling off that he might be much more likely to do so. Efforts to avoid error in such situations tend to increase rather than decrease the undesired behavior. Efforts to avoid a consequence can sometimes bring it about. The stutterer is a terrified walker on the plank of speech performance.

In *Dr. Jekyll and Mr. Hyde*, Robert Louis Stevenson wrote that in every human personality two forces struggle for supremacy. Every stutterer struggles to go forward against his own Hyde, the part of him he feels compelled to hide. The choice by Stevenson of the name Hyde was of course poetically symbolic; it is fascinating that the tendency of the stutterer to hide his stuttering from public view is probably the central perpetuating factor.

Earlier we quoted Freud on the nature of neurotic conflict. We believe that the disorder of stuttering is dramatically illustrative of neurotic maladaptive learning. Neuroses are learned behaviors; they do not spring full blown out of an unfathomable psychic well. The instrumental behaviors that make up the bulk of the stuttering pattern are acquired through periodic and differential reinforcement. In the choice of instrumental acts with which to cope, the stutterer is constantly exercising choice. And choices are always reflective of the dynamics of the chooser.

Even though Freud never developed a theory of stuttering, he did recognize that the disorder has aspects of conflict. Writing in *The Psychopathology of Everyday Life*, he observed:

This leads on to those speech-disturbances which cannot any longer be described as slips of the tongue because what they affect is not the individual word but the rhythm and execution of a whole speech: disturbances like, for instance, stammering and stuttering caused by embarrassment. But here too, as in the former cases, it is a question of an internal conflict, which is betrayed to us by the disturbance in speech. (Freud, 1965, pp. 100–101)

In an effort to keep the exposition of the conflict model as simple as possible, we have thus far considered only a single approach-avoidance model for stuttering. However, the model that comprehensively illuminates the problem of stuttering—as well as many other problems—is double approach-avoidance conflict.

In his "Experimental Studies of Conflict" (1944), Miller listed four basic kinds: (1) approach-approach conflict, (2) avoidance-avoidance conflict, (3) single approach-avoidance conflict, and (4) double approach-avoidance conflict. Of the four, by far the most significant in human problems is double approach-avoidance conflict. We have all been confronted with two alternatives, each of which contained both positive and negative features. Going ahead on any course of action is difficult, for once the decision is reached, the alternative course becomes more attractive.

In our discussion of stuttering as simple approach-avoidance conflict, speaking has been the approach response; not speaking has been the avoidance response. But at times there are approach and avoidance tendencies to the act of speaking as well as to the act of not speaking. This involves some additional assumptions and a further analysis, in terms of Miller's double approach-avoidance conflict (Figure 2), which may account better for certain instances of stuttering.

The conflict on speaking is as follows: There is an approach tendency for speaking, since it is socially demanded. But since speaking entails the danger of stuttering, there is an avoidance tendency based on the fear elicited by this danger. This is the type of conflict that Johnson and Knott (1936) held responsible for stuttering.

The conflict on not speaking is as follows: There is an approach tendency for not speaking, because silence becomes an attractive alternative to the danger situation of speaking. But this alternative is also to be feared.

In a situation that calls for speech, not speaking or not being able to speak in itself involves a threat. Many stutterers show a *fear of silence,* and any dead stop in their communication spurs panicky efforts to release the block. Many of the irrelevant and apparently unintelligent symptoms of the stutterer can be understood as a filibustering, a measure taken against the fear of silence.

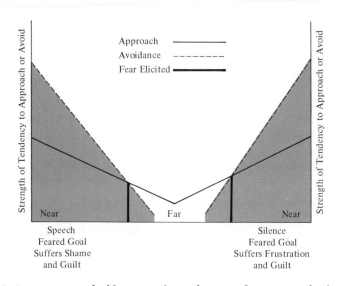

Figure 2. Stuttering as a double approach-avoidance conflict, as a result of conflicting urges toward speech and toward silence. Movement toward either feared goal elicits more momentary fear, which increases until the goal (speech or silence) is reached and is then reduced, reinforcing the instrumental response series preceding attainment of the goal. Guilt follows either choice. Goal attainment of either silence or the speaking of a word resolves the conflict only momentarily, for as the need to speak returns, the conflict recurs.

Consequently, there is an avoidance tendency for not speaking as well as an approach tendency for not speaking. Movement toward either feared goal elicits more fear, so that the net approach tendency will be greater toward the more distant goal. As this is approached (e.g., as the stutterer gets closer to or further from the speech attempt), the alternative goal becomes more distant, hence less dangerous and more attractive. The stutterer will then turn and approach the other goal until it becomes too feared. Dollard and Miller's prediction for this type of situation is "one of stable equilibrium like that of the pendulum" (1950, pp. 366–367). Such behavior toward feared words and situations is characteristic of the stutterer.

The paradoxical increase in "fear elicited" as lowered avoidance permits a closer approach to the feared goal is equally true of simple approach-avoidance conflict.

The conflict between speech and silence

Double approach-avoidance conflict is at the heart of the stuttering problem. This kind of conflict includes both avoidance-avoidance and simple approach-avoidance conflict. For a stutterer, both speech and silence have positive and negative features.

The conflict in stuttering is not simply between speaking versus inhibiting expected stuttering. In the double approach-avoidance conflict situation, there is both a conflict between speaking and not speaking and between being silent or not being silent. The avoidance does not come primarily from the fear of stuttering as such but from the competition between the alternative possibilities of speech and silence, with the stuttering a result of this conflict.

Guilt can become attached to speaking, to silence, and to stuttering. Caught as he is in double approach-avoidance conflict, the stutterer is caught between two choices, each of which threatens the bitter along with the sweet. He can speak, thus achieving his aim of communication, but at a cost of the shame and guilt he has learned to attach to his stuttering. Or he can remain silent, abandon communication, and suffer the frustration and guilt that such a retreat carries with it. These choices are depicted in Figure 3, showing stuttering as a double approach-avoidance conflict. So the stutterer has a choice between shame or frustration, and guilt has become attached to either choice.

Speaking holds the promise of communication but the threat of stuttering; silence eliminates temporarily the threat involved in speaking, but at a cost of abandonment of communication and consequent frustration. Many stutterers show a *fear of silence* and filibuster furiously in

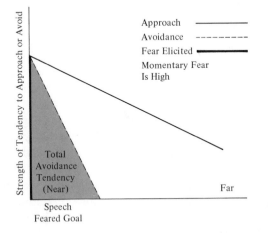

Figure 3. With a reduction of the avoidance gradient and an increase in the strength of the approach drive, the feared goal of speaking is reached. Momentary fear as represented by a vertical line dropped from point B, the intersection of the gradients, is high just before the speaking of the feared word, or entrance into the feared situation.

their speech to keep any pause from becoming dangerously long. Since most stuttering occurs initially, silence plus the necessity to begin becomes a conditioned cue for the painful experiences of fear and stuttering.

Why should silence come to be feared? In terms of conditioning theory, there is good reason. As studies by Brown (1945) have shown, and as nearly all stutterers have found from experience, stuttering occurs most frequently on initial sounds and on the first word of the sentence. Silences seem to freeze the stutterer, and he has trouble breaking the ice.

Since moments of silence precede moments of stuttering with the regularity of Pavlov's bell, it is not surprising that silence as such becomes a cue for the arousal of anxiety. Many stutterers show such a dread of silence that they adopt filibustering behaviors into their stuttering patterns.

There is yet another reason, on a different level of analysis, why the stutterer should fear displaying silence. To be mute, in dreams, is a symbol of death; the dead are often represented this way in bereavement dreams. The use of silence for hostility, in those who dare not express it more openly, has been experienced, at least on the receiving end, by all of us. Catatonics are said to be rigid because they are holding their destructive impulses in check and mute because they have turned their death wishes, originally felt toward others, toward themselves. Periods of silence may arouse guilt in the stutterer because of the hostility implied in the act. Fluent speech itself, as well as stuttering, may equally imply hostility and correspondingly produce guilt.

Basic assumptions of approach-avoidance conflict theory

In this section we review the assumptions underlying the conflict model on which our theory is based. Some early credit concerning this model should go to Lewin (1935, 1951), who analyzed children's behavior in terms of conflicts between driving and restraining forces. He formulated hypotheses about gradients of approach and avoidance in the language of his Gestalt-type, topological psychology. In behavioral language, Miller (1944) and Dollard and Miller (1950) have developed—with much greater thoroughness—a testable model for the analysis of conflict. In preceding sections we have already indicated this model and have illustrated it extensively through our applications of the model to the problem of stuttering. We also noted the four types of conflict posited by Miller (1944).

Dollard and Miller (1950) formally state four assumptions they deem to be essential to their analysis of conflict behavior:

1.   The tendency to approach a goal is stronger the nearer the subject is to it. This will be called the *gradient of approach.*

2. The tendency to avoid a feared stimulus is stronger the nearer the subject is to it. This will be called the *gradient of avoidance.*
3. The strength of avoidance increases more rapidly with nearness than does that of approach. In other words, the gradient of avoidance is *steeper* than that of approach.
4. The strength of the tendencies to approach or avoid varies with the strength of the drive upon which they are based. In other words, an increase in drive raises the *height* of the entire gradient. (pp. 352–353)

In addition to the four assumptions just enumerated, we have found it necessary to specify others. While our self-designation in the role of adding to the Miller and Dollard conflict model may appear presumptuous, we wish to point out that several of our points are implied in their discussion, while the others are logical extensions from the model. Here then, are the extrapolations and additional assumptions necessary for our own adaptation of conflict theory:

5. Momentary fear, or "fear elicited," is a function of the height at which the gradients cross, and varies directly with an ordinate dropped from the point of crossing to the baseline.
6. Anxiety potential is relatively independent of momentary fear, is reflected in the total area under the gradient of avoidance, and varies directly with the height of this gradient.
7. Even though anxiety potential is high, momentary fear will not be experienced unless the approach gradient becomes sufficiently strong to enable some movement toward the feared goal.
8. Once the feared goal is reached, momentary fear associated with approaching that goal is reduced, reinforcing the instrumental act or series of instrumental acts bringing about the termination of the sequence.
9. Reinforced instrumental patterns and classically conditioned responses tend to become habituated. In line with the law of economy of effort, they also tend to become shortened.
10. Reinforced instrumental and conditioned response patterns tend to move up in the response sequence, to become anticipatory.
11. When there are social or other penalties attendant on the manifestation of anxiety-produced responses, their visible expression becomes inhibited in accordance with principles of instrumental avoidance learning (especially passive avoidance) and instrumental escape learning.
12. The inhibition of outward behaviors, by social penalty for their appearance, favors covert rehearsal behaviors. Covert rehearsal behaviors may also have a fear-reducing function.

Another possible assumption, implied but not spelled out by Dollard and Miller, concerns possible curvilinearity of the gradients. The straight line usually depicted in graphic illustrations of approach-avoidance conflict, both Miller's and our own, might not hold in all cases. The number of linear functions in nature is fairly limited. We stay with the straight-line model because it seems parsimonious and because we know of no solid evidence to indicate any other than a linear function.

The conflict model may be viewed in spatial terms, as we have illustrated in the movement of a stutterer toward a feared word or situation. The gradients may also be considered as mathematical relationships.

The assumption that the gradient of avoidance is steeper than the gradient of approach was derived from the earliest work on approach-avoidance conflict, as reported by Lewin (1935, 1951). Lewin developed gradients for approach and for avoidance, in terms of driving and restraining forces, using the concepts of positive and negative valence. He reported observational and experimental studies of children's behavior, in the language of topographical or field psychology. Neal Miller (1944) and Dollard and Miller (1950) approached conflict behavioristically, in terms of Hull's drive-reduction reinforcement theory. Evidence for the steeper slope of the avoidance gradient may be found in reports by J. S. Brown, (1942, 1948), by Miller (1944), and by Dollard and Miller (1950).

Stuttering behavior follows predictions from conflict theory with impressive regularity. For stuttering, especially, the anxiety-motivated avoidance gradient functions as though it is steeper than the competing approach gradient for speaking. Other conflict behaviors, such as going to the dentist, proposing marriage, or diving into icy water, all fit the double approach-avoidance model exactly as predicted. Approach responses are manifested more strongly while the feared goal is at a distance; but as the goal is neared, avoidance tendencies become increasingly more evident, and conflict ensues. Usually, conflict is expressed as fixation or oscillation at the zone in which the gradients cross. Going part-way and then stopping, as would be predicted from a steeper gradient of avoidance, is characteristic not only of stuttering but of decision processes and other conflict behaviors as well.

Time is another significant dimension in the analysis of conflict. As the stutterer moves through the speaking of a feared word, two shifts are occurring at once: (1) an increase in momentary fear as he moves closer to the feared goal and (2) a simultaneous fear reduction due to the occurrence of the stuttering behavior itself. Principally, the fear reduction occurs during the moment of stuttering, in sufficient quantity to permit release of the blocked word. Earlier in the sequence, considerable fear reduction may occur through covert rehearsals of the instrumental stuttering pattern. Even during this rehearsal, there is a simultaneous and counteracting buildup of immediately felt avoidance tendency. Postponement behavior and halfhearted speech attempts may be evident during this period.

Our first formal addition to the conflict model specified that fear elicited at a given moment, or momentary fear, is a direct function of the height at which the gradients cross. When competing approach and avoidance drives are both weak, or when the gradients cross far from the goal, fear will be slight. When drives are strong or when the crossing occurs close to the goal, momentary fear will be strong. Momentary fear will be increased either by (1) an increase in communicatory or approach drive; or (2) by a reduction in the strength of the avoidance gradient. The latter is clinically preferable. In Figure 3 we portrayed the effect of an increase in approach with only moderate decrease in avoidance; momentary fear is high, though the goal is reached. Figure 4 presents the effect of a substantial avoidance reduction.

Since the experience of fear is punishing in itself, approach-avoidance situations tend to punish courage and reward cowardice. At least, until the feared goal is actually reached, this is the situation. Once the goal is reached, tension and anxiety associated with the conflict are momentarily reduced. The series of instrumental acts that have brought about the achievement of the feared goal are thereby strengthened, relative to other available response systems.

Since reinforced responses tend to move up in the response hierarchy (Hull, 1943), the instrumental pattern comprising stuttering, as an example, will move up in the timetable of response performance. In the case of stuttering, three things appear to happen at this point: (1) In-

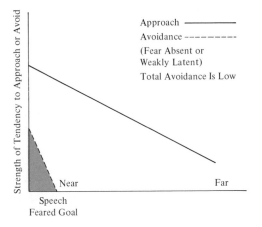

Figure 4. When avoidance strength is greatly reduced, momentary fear is absent or weakly latent. The shaded area represents the total avoidance potential, or "reservoir of fear." Figure 4 portrays what happens with successful avoidance-reduction therapy, or with spontaneous recoveries brought about by decreased avoidance.

strumental acts comprising the stuttering pattern tend to become anticipatory. (2) Classically conditioned autonomic responses associated with anxiety also move up in the response sequence (though perhaps not at the same rate). (3) The response sequences, both classical and instrumental, will become part of a covert preparatory rehearsal, which has the function of reducing fear by streamlining the motoric sequence.

Stutterers frequently report that once they begin on a word, it appears as though the stuttering is something happening to them (Johnson, 1961). Once we have begun to swing the bat or throw the ball, the sequence almost seems to continue itself. At a certain point in the time sequence, the moment of stuttering reaches a kind of momentum. The following passage is enlightening:

> The first incipient responses will produce additional cues with learned connections to further responses in the sequence; and the cues produced by responses nearer the time of reinforcement elicit a still stronger tendency to continue. Similarly drive-producing responses seem to become stronger nearer the point of reinforcement. In this way a sequence of responses seems to pick up something analogous to momentum; it is much easier to stop the sequence before it gets started than after it is well under way. (Dollard and Miller, 1950, p. 358)

A classic experiment by Van Riper (1938) did reveal, however, that stutterers were able to interrupt their blocks when given a preliminary set and prearranged signal to do so. In such circumstances, a response readiness to interrupt becomes part of the preparatory set. In the usual nonexperimental situation, no such set exists, so stutterers continue to feel a compulsion to continue once they have started the sequence.

Levels of conflict

Several points concerning the approach-avoidance conflict model should be made: (1) It relates stuttering to anxiety and avoidant behavior in a systematic, meaningful way. It shows *how* anxiety leads to stuttering. (2) Approach-avoidance theory is a theory for normal speakers as well as stutterers, and for primary stutterers as well as secondary. All groups respond to conflict situations in terms of greater speech hesitancy. The young stutterer showing syllable repetitions and prolongations, in our opinion, is not a victim of dysphemia or neurological block; nor is he merely "nonfluent." He is already showing outward symptoms of approach-avoidance conflict, just as is the clerk asking the boss for a raise, the suitor proposing marriage, and perhaps *you* when you are explaining your driving tactics to the motorcycle cop. (3) Approach-avoidance theory distinguishes two kinds of secondary symptoms, but states that primary and secondary stutterers are victims of the same conflict. We do not offer a physiological or dysphemic explanation for primary stuttering and an educational theory of secondary stuttering. The same conflict theory explains both.

Again, we wish to stress that approach-avoidance theory postulates that primary and secondary symptoms arise from the same source; further, that the symptoms of stuttering arise from the same conflict as the hesitancies of all of us; still further, that approach-avoidance conflict is not confined to speech, and the stutterer's problem finds its counterpart in many kinds of personal problems and neuroses.

When we speak of "approach-avoidance conflict," we are referring to the double kind—not the single kind, which exists nowhere in nature, but only in Miller and Dollard listings of the possible varieties of conflict. All significant social conflicts probably involve some degree of double approach-avoidance conflict. There is sweet and bitter with each choice, and whichever one does, he tends to regret it. The negative features of the alternate choice lose their terrors in the distance. That is one reason why "distance lends enchantment." Socrates was once asked by a young man whether he should marry. "Whichever you do," said the great teacher, "you'll regret it."

Approach-avoidance conflict in stuttering may occur at five fairly distinct levels: *word level*—conflicting urges to approach or to avoid the speaking of the feared word; *situation level*—to enter or not enter a feared situation; *feeling*—to express or inhibit the expression of heavy emotional content; *relationship*—to enter into or to avoid certain kinds of interpersonal relationship; *self-role, or egoprotective*—accepting or rejecting role-expectations, especially those for intellectual achievement. Stuttering has its origins at self and role levels, though the conflict is expressed outwardly at word and situation levels.

Avoidance and the conflict model

The reactions of professional colleagues to a formal theory, such as our presentation of stuttering as a double approach-avoidance conflict, are always useful in revealing the strengths and weaknesses of the theory. In those places where you are wrong, or a proper subject of skepticism, colleagues are energetic in pointing it out. When you are right, they are quick to decide that they really knew about it all the time.

The conflict model on which our theory is based had been available some years before, but nothing had been done to illuminate the problem of stuttering by that means. Lewin (1935, 1951) wrote of approach and avoidance conflict in the late 1930s. Miller published his review of experimental studies of conflict in the J. McV. Hunt volumes in 1944. Later, with Dollard, Miller applied the model to psychotherapy, including some specific problems such as alcoholism (Miller, 1944; Dollard and Miller, 1950).

The theoretical model as derived from Lewin and from Miller included *conflict* as a generic term, as a process. We have employed the same terminology. Thus we speak of stuttering as a double approach-avoidance conflict, and we set up the reduction of avoidance as the basic goal of therapy. A total process called "conflict" is basic to the origin, maintenance, and treatment of the problem called "stuttering." It is an abuse of the conflict model to speak in the plural of "approach-avoidance conflicts," as though they were droll little problems carried by certain stutterers.

The conflict model itself does not really require drive-reduction reinforcement theory as an explanation for the resolution of conflict. Of course, it is necessary to consider the gradients of approach and of avoidance, and of relative shifts in spatial or strength factors that bring about the termination of a particular moment of conflict.

Our first presentation of stuttering as approach-avoidance conflict, in a doctoral dissertation concerned primarily with the modification of reinforcement of stuttering (Sheehan, 1951), was not committed to drive reduction. From our discussion of "termination of the sequence" and our careful avoidance of posited drive reduction in that dissertation, it is clear that the "S-R (stimulus-response) contiguity" position of Guthrie (1935, 1938), and his concepts, had influenced this presentation.[2] At the University of Michigan, we went through a "Guthrie stage" and were especially intrigued by his formulation of an interference theory of extinction. The 1951 study could be easily conceived as an interference procedure for inducing extinction.

Avoidance is the heart and core of stuttering. Avoidance behavior— holding back—is essential for the maintenance of stuttering behavior. Stuttering simply cannot survive a total weakening of avoidance, coupled with a concerted strengthening of approach tendencies. If there is no holding back, there is no stuttering. What distinguishes all stuttering behavior? A holding back. And what happens in situations in which the stutterer doesn't care? He becomes fluent.

What do we mean by "avoidance behaviors"? In our earlier writing (Sheehan, 1951, 1953a, 1958a), it had seemed too obvious to go through the banality of enumeration. Operationally, "avoidance" is merely a name we give to the class of behaviors in which organisms are observed to

---

[2] Guthrie's S-R contiguity position is a formulation in which reinforcement is seen as preserving the bond between stimulus and response. The removal of reinforcement brings about a return to trial-and-error behavior, which interferes with the preservation of the stimulus-response bond and so disrupts the previously learned response. In Guthrie's system, great stress is placed on the termination of a response sequence, a usage we adapted directly to response sequences in stuttering (Sheehan, 1951).

move away from a goal or to remain away in a situation in which the usual behavior is to move closer to the goal.

For example, Mowrer and Viek (1948) demonstrated "fear from a sense of helplessness" by showing that laboratory rats showed more food refusals following shock they could not control compared to their litter mates who were given equal shock but could turn it off. It is hardly operationally reckless to designate the food-refusal behavior as avoidance. In fact, it can be called "food avoidance" as a direct observation, without any inference at all. The most rigorous behaviorists in American psychology have all used avoidance without showing visible perturbation over the occasionally inferential quality of the usage. We will continue to refer to behaviors that involve holding back or retreating from a goal of speaking as avoidance. We introduced the term "holding back" into speech pathology, and it is still our favorite synonym for avoidance behaviors.

Active avoidance behaviors may be operationally defined as instrumental responses that involve movement in a direction opposite a goal, rather than toward it. Passive avoidance behaviors may involve refusal to make any response in the direction of the goal. Although these particular definitions are framed in our own words, the distinction between the two kinds of avoidance may be found in the writings of Solomon (1964). Extensive discussion of avoidance behavior may also be found in such classic conditioning and learning theory sources as Hull (1943, 1952), Hilgard and Marquis (1940), Miller (1944), Mowrer (1947, 1956), Hilgard (1948, 1956), and Dollard and Miller (1950).

There are certain logical relationships among fear, avoidance, and the exacerbation of stuttering that point both to the nature of the disorder and to the direction of behavior toward recovery or continuance. Our studies of spontaneous recovery from stuttering (Sheehan and Martyn, 1966, 1970; Martyn and Sheehan, 1968) have consistently shown a difference between those who recovered and those who did not, in terms of the behavior they had exhibited toward the problem. Those who remained in the category "stutterer" spent their energies on various kinds of avoidance: They just denied that the problem existed, or they sought quick mechanical cures, including hypnosis, breathing exercises, portable noise generators, or modified hearing aids providing delayed auditory feedback. In sharp contrast, those who recovered advised such approaches as these:

1. Talk more.
2. Go ahead anyway.
3. Slow down.
4. Take it easy.
5. Push onward.
6. Don't let stuttering keep you from taking part in life.

In corroboration of our theoretical position, we have discovered that reduction of avoidance and enactment of some kind of approach behavior constitute a common thread running through the recovery process (Sheehan and Martyn, 1970, 1971). Independent investigations by Gregory (1969), Borkman (1974), Dickson (1971), Shearer and Williams (1965), Cooper (1972), and Walle (1975) provide grist for the same conclusion.

The Conflict Hypothesis: Evidence and Implications

If stuttering occurs when competing approach and avoidance tendencies are at a point of equilibrium, it should vary as follows: Stuttering behavior should be increased by (1) a reduction in the approach tendency and (2) an increase in the avoidance tendency. Conversely, stuttering behavior should be decreased by (3) an increase in approach tendency and (4) a decrease in avoidance tendency.

Let us examine the evidence, what there is of it. In general, we have more evidence on the influence of increases and decreases in the avoidance drive. The myriad studies showing the relationship between social penalties of various kinds on stuttering, or involving the effect of such penalties, provide some of our best evidence. Unfortunately, the recent spate of studies purporting to show that stuttering is reduced through contingent punishment suffers from uncontrolled distraction or disruptive stimuli effects. We must depend in part on clinical observation and on consensual validation as part of the evidence.

1. The effect of conflict on disrupting the fluency of children and adults is easily observed. Children tend to be nonfluent, disfluent, or show stuttering-like behavior when speaking under conditions in which they are unsure of themselves, when competing for the floor under interruption threat, or when forced to confess something about which they feel guilty.

2. When there is ambivalence about the message or its reception, speech tends to become hesitant. Marriage proposals, asking the boss for a raise, and talking to a traffic cop are all fairly obvious examples, as we have noted (Sheehan, 1953a, 1958a).

3. People in authority, those who have the capacity to withhold reward or inflict punishment of various sorts, have been shown to elicit more stuttering (Sheehan, Hadley, and Gould, 1967), and adaptation to them is more difficult. This result is depicted graphically in Figure 5.

4. A self-esteem threat precipitates more difficulty for those who are already categorized as stutterers. Bardrick and Sheehan (1958) showed that stutterers had much more frequent stuttering when forced to read material derogatory to stutterers as a group.

5. For whatever our clinical experience is worth, we have been im-

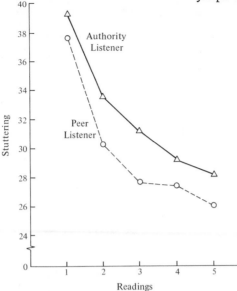

Figure 5. Mean frequency of stuttering to authority listeners (Ph.D.'s introduced by title) and to peer listeners (fellow students introduced by nickname) over five successive readings of two 200-word passages. Authority listeners elicited a higher frequency of stuttering and a slower course of adaptation (P = .05). (From J. G. Sheehan, R. Hadley, and E. Gould, "Impact of Authority on Stuttering." *Journal of Abnormal Psychology*, vol. 72, no. 3, 1967, p. 291. Copyright © 1967 by the American Psychological Association. Reprinted by permission.)

pressed with the extent to which stuttering in children may be alleviated or eliminated when the parents are successfully prevailed upon to reduce their system of demands and increase expressions of support.

6. Penalty, which may reasonably be assumed to increase avoidance tendencies in a stutterer, has been shown by repeated study to have the predominant effect of increasing the frequency of stuttering. Some of the studies are those by Van Riper (1937a), Eisenson and Horowitz (1945),[3] Frick (1951), Frederick (1955), and Sheehan, Hadley, and Gould (1967).

---

[3] The study by Eisenson and Horowitz found that more difficulty is experienced with material that is meaningful than with material that is not. Greater penalty would presumably attach to stuttering that interfered with the communication of meaningful material. Bardrick and Sheehan (1958) reported least stuttering when reading numbers, where penalty for stuttering may reasonably assumed to be minimal. Difficulty in communication with authority figures, as in the Sheehan, Hadley, and Gould (1967) experiment, involves a situation with far greater potential for social penalty than communication with casually introduced peers. In his comprehensive survey of conditions under which stuttering is reduced or absent, Bloodstein (1969) noted reduced penalty along with distraction. Even that may be considered to involve a reduction in penalty for stuttering, since the social and role-demand characteristics of the situation are altered.

Disagreeing with our conclusions regarding these studies, Siegel (1970) has attempted to make a case for punishment when administered contingently. The joker in his argument is this: "contingent" or immediately presented consequences inevitably produce artifacts built on stimulus novelty or on situation disruption. Contingently applied stimuli, or randomly applied stimuli, tend to reduce stuttering behavior, whether or not they have been assumed to be "punishment."

We may not properly conclude that contingent punishment reduces stuttering; we may conclude only that alteration of the stimulus pattern tends to alter the frequency of stuttering behavior. Most often, the result is reduced frequency; occasionally, stimulus alterations increase frequency. For example, increases are effected by bringing more people into the room (Porter, 1939), by increasing communicative responsibility (Eisenson and Wells, 1942), introducing self-esteem threat (Bardrick and Sheehan, 1958), speaking to authority figures (Sheehan, Hadley, and Gould, 1967), interrupting without explanation (Gould and Sheehan, 1967), threatening to shock for each stuttered word (Van Riper, 1937a), and a host of other conditions ably reviewed by Van Riper (1973). Decreases have been reported with just about every study in which some form of stimulus novelty was introduced. For example, Cooper, Cady and Robbins (1968) found that the word "tree," when applied contingently, was just as effective as either "right" or "wrong." It was not the quality of the stimulus but the fact of its application. Similarly, Biggs and Sheehan (1969) found that random presentation of a masking tone was just as effective in reducing stuttering frequency as was contingent presentation.

The logical relationship between social penalty and stuttering is largely undisputed. Aside from the spurious drop in stuttering frequency brought about by stimulus novelty or situational disruption, increased social penalty brings about increased stuttering. The relationship between social penalty and stuttering is strongly supportive of our conflict hypothesis, that is, that stuttering behavior occurs when competing tendencies toward speech and toward silence, or toward approach and avoidance, come into equilibrium.

The Fear-Reduction Hypothesis: Evidence and Implications

The conflict hypothesis held that stuttering occurs whenever competing approach tendencies (toward speech) and avoidance tendencies (toward silence) reach an equilibrium. As a sequel, we propose the fear-reduction hypothesis, which holds that the occurrence of stuttering behavior reduces the fear that elicited the behavior. Were it not for some such process, once the strength of approach and avoidance drives reached an equilibrium, the conflict would never be resolved. When the conflict moment is resolved, it must be brought about through either (1) an increase in approach behavior or (2) a decrease in avoidance tendency. Although we have pointed to some examples of the first, as in sudden fluency produced by anger or the motivating properties of an unaccustomed role, we consider the second far more likely.

For some reason, the stutterer appears to be in a better position to speak a difficult word after he has gone through his instrumental stuttering pattern, even though all of the instrumental acts involved are functionally unrelated to the act of speaking. The sheer irrelevance, the phonetic irrelevance of stuttering behavior, is one of its most fascinating features. Moreover, subvocal rehearsal, or "stuttering under one's breath" first, appears to have fear-reducing properties for some stutterers. Postponement symptoms, such as have been described by Van Riper (1937b, 1937c, 1938, 1971, 1972, 1973), appear to illustrate the fear-reducing effect of such rehearsal. The stutterer reports that he feels he can't possibly say the word at the moment, but if he waits awhile, he will be able to say it. What happens during the waiting? What has he done to change the situation? Surely, simple passage of a few seconds' time doesn't alter the balance of forces in conflict. What does?

We reason as follows: The trick or crutch, the instrumental act, the stutterer employs immediately before the moment of release (the moment when he can say the word) is reinforced by the completion of the communicative act involved in the speaking of the word.

Speaking the feared word is a goal for the stutterer, and whatever he does that immediately precedes the successful production of the word becomes an instrumental act leading to reinforcement. By the principle of the goal gradient (Hull, 1943, 1952), all instrumental responses preceding the response successful in producing the word are also reinforced, depending on their proximity to the successful response. Since the same instrumental response (such as eye blink, head jerk, mouth opening, body movement) is not consistently successful in bringing about the moment of release, different tricks are tried by the stutterer in a modified trial-and-error learning situation. As his desperation mounts, he may pick them in a sequence of increasing listener repugnance.

We believe that the sporadic nature of the stutterer's tricks are induced by intermittent reinforcement. The resistance of responses in the stuttering pattern to extinction stems from the same partial reinforcement. The sporadic success of the stutterer's tricks and crutches appears to be based on shifting patterns of stimulus novelty. It is well established that novel stimuli of all kinds reduce stuttering behavior instantaneously, if only temporarily. We discuss the phenomenon extensively in this chapter. Seeing a new movie, hearing a new song, or reading a new book all involve patterns of stimulus novelty. Once experienced, they lose the reinforcing properties inherent in their stimulus novelty, and time must elapse before they reacquire any reinforcing properties. Figuratively speaking, every novel response has its refractory period. When enough instrumental acts bringing stimulus novelty are worked into the stutterer's repertoires, he can begin to recycle some of the old ones.

Meanwhile there is some drift in the nature of the instrumental response, for parts of that response have been differentially reinforced. Heraclitus and Wendell Johnson (1946) both told us that no man steps into the same river twice. Neither does the river have the same man step into it twice, because the man is just as subject to constant change as the river. The next time a stutterer uses a crutch, an instrumental act for which he has been reinforced in the past, both the proprioceptive feedback and the muscle movements are likely to have drifted a bit. Stutterers sharpen their skills and hone down their stuttering patterns, just as all speakers do with their speaking mannerisms.

The choice of trick or crutch is necessarily idiosyncratically representative of the dynamics of the stutterer. The stutterer's pattern is projective of his personality, just as his responses to inkblots might be. The stutterer's pattern is his Rorschach. He chooses the tactic initially, and the choice reflects important things about him. He may choose, as one stutterer did, to use a forbidden four-letter word as a starter. With instrumental reinforcement and habituation, he was soon muttering the crutch under his breath, sometimes out loud. The stutterer who displays a poker face and long silent postponement has chosen a defense different from the stutterer who bobs his head and jerks out the word with a grimace. Only the early stages of this process need to involve projective choice. Once there is sufficient instrumental reinforcement, the condensation-of-serial-reactions principle converts the motor pattern of stuttering into a skilled act. It functions on automatic control in response to distinctive cues, just as speaking normally does.

We do not posit that the stutterer is constantly exercising conscious choice. He may occasionally, however, in an effort to introduce sufficient novelty into his stimulus environment to achieve a false and temporary fluency.

Of course, both classical and instrumental conditioning are involved in stuttering. In a paper delivered to the Western Psychological Association (Bardrick and Sheehan, 1956), we once tried to relate psychotherapy and stuttering therapy to Mowrer's two-factor theory. We were about to extend our interpretation of stuttering in terms of Mowrer's original two-factor theory when he pulled the rug from under us by revising it (Mowrer, 1947, 1956). We liked the division into "conditioning" and "problem-solving" better than the revised classification into "drive-incremental" and "drive-decremental" learning. Interestingly, Brutten and Shoemaker (1967), who more completely and systematically applied Mowrer's two-factor theory to stuttering, seem to have preferred the original version as well.

The research evidence bearing on our conflict theory of stuttering has been extensively summarized previously and need not be repeated here in its entirety. A few studies along our own research odyssey, however, bear particular mention. In a study of masseter-tension patterns before, during, and after the moment of stuttering. Sheehan and Voas (1954) found that a buildup of tension occurred as the stutterer moved through the block. Since a tension buildup would be expected as the feared goal is approached, a prediction from the conflict model was upheld. The Sheehan and Voas (1957) comparison of negative practice with other voluntary stuttering methods demonstrated quicker adaptation with syllable repetition (bounce) and prolongation (slide). Although rehearsal of the motor plan is an important factor in any adaptation design, as has been indicated by Bloodstein (1972), Van Riper (1971, 1973), and others, another factor that appeared to be operating was the reduction of avoidance through practice of the feared behavior. Sheehan and Voas concluded that the slide and bounce were superior because they brought about contingent reinforcement of an instrumental approach response, while the traditional Dunlap negative practice method (Dunlap, 1932) of imitating the secondary stuttering pattern involved contingent strengthening of avoidant behaviors.

Another study (Sheehan, Cortese, and Hadley, 1962), using graphic portrayals of before, during, and after the moment of stuttering, produced judgments of reduced tension on about one-half of the *after* portrayals. In this respect, the study confirmed a cycle of events reported by Wischner (1952). However, other factors—dejection, shame, and guilt—appeared concurrently, so that tension reduction after the block was not judged to be a period of unalloyed joy. Guilt, in particular, was highly prevalent in the moment after stuttering.

A recent study by Dabul and Perkins (1973) might be cited as partially supportive of our fear-reduction hypothesis. Their results indicated that stuttering can reduce stress-induced systolic blood pressure. The lowered systolic blood pressure was unrelated to effort exerted in speech, but was a function of frequency of stuttering within the person. The result appears to indicate an anxiety-binding function of the overt manifestation of stuttering behavior. The occurrence of stuttering appears to reduce a physiological response associated with fear and stress.

Our conflict theory rests most directly upon the conflict hypothesis.

We are as sure as we can be of anything that it is sound. The fear-reduction hypothesis is a forced addition, occupying a secondary role. We framed it in a necessary effort to explain how the momentary conflict is resolved in order to account for the obvious fact that once stuck. the stutterer does not remain stuck forever.

The validity of the conflict hypothesis does not depend on the validity of the fear-reduction hypothesis. The latter is just one means of accounting for the momentary conflict resolution. Possibly there are alternative explanations that would be compatible with the conflict hypothesis. Some future hypothesis might account for the resolution of the conflict, for the fact that the stutterer does not remain stuck indefinitely once he has begun to block on a word. Our personal hypothesis-programmer has thus far been unable to come up with a better explanation than the fear-reducing effect of the behavior in which the stutterer engages from the beginning of the block to the moment of release. Possibly future theorists or researchers will come up with a better explanation of how the conflict moment is resolved. The interpretation of stuttering as conflict behavior might thereby be strengthened.

Momentary fear versus total avoidance potential (anxiety)

In earlier publications of the approach-avoidance conflict theory of stuttering, we have used the terms "fear" and "anxiety" as they are commonly used, more or less interchangeably. For example, Miller and Dollard make no sharp distinction, nor do psychoanalytic writers in general. However, many ambiguities have resulted.

In this paper and henceforth, we propose a distinction between fear and anxiety as related to stuttering. First, the term "fear" will be limited to "fear elicited," as referring to momentary or effective fear, depending on the height of the intersection of the gradients of approach and avoidance. Miller and Dollard consistently used the term "fear elicited" in this manner.

Second, the term "anxiety" will be used to refer to the total potential for avoidance, that is, all the shaded area under the gradient of avoidance. In an earlier writing we called this the "reservoir of fear" (Sheehan, 1953a).

The distinction is exactly parallel to that between kinetic and potential energy, with fear as the kinetic and anxiety as the potential. With less precision, the usage also corresponds to the traditional clinical distinction, with fear referring to specific objects and anxiety reserved for more generalized, free-floating forebodings. Thus we speak of the anxiety-derived gradient of avoidance, while we speak of the amount of fear experienced by the stutterer at a given moment in space and time.

Some of the paradoxical nature of the stuttering problem may be clarified through this distinction. When a stutterer avoids a situation early enough, he experiences little fear. But a stutterer with an equal amount of anxiety-motivated avoidance tendency may approach much closer to the "feared goal" of speaking. He is doing more of what we want him to do in therapy, but he is experiencing much more fear than the one who runs away when he first hears the distant sounds of battle.

From the foregoing distinction, it should be clear that fear depends on where the person is on the gradients, independent of the slope and height of the gradients. In contrast, anxiety depends on the total area under the gradient of avoidance—on the height and, theoretically, on the slope. But since the slope of the avoidance gradient is believed to be a constant, only the height determines the total area. The distinction between the terms *"fear"* and *"anxiety"* in relation to conflict theory may be clarified by reference to Figure 4.

Stuttering and homeostasis reversal

Stuttering is a notably paradoxical disorder, and the persistence of stuttering appears to go counter to such venerated principles as the law of effect and the homeostasis of organismic functioning. In *Nature and Man's Fate*, (1959) Garrett Hardin presents an account of body temperature control in relation to homeostasis that inspires us to draw a parallel to the problem of stuttering. Ordinarily, organisms react to disturbance in such a way as to minimize or reduce the effects of that disturbance. The case of the stutterer who reacts to stuttering and dysfluency with increased maladaptive struggle appears to go against the principle of homeostasis, as we have noted elsewhere (Sheehan, Cortese, and Hadley, 1962).

Within a reasonably narrow range, Hardin points out, the body reacts homeostatically to correct any deviation up or down in temperature. Thus when we have a fever, the body sweats more; when we are cold, we stop sweating and become dry. All of this fits the principle of homeostasis: The human organism reacts to a disturbance in such a way as to minimize the effects of that disturbance and restore previous equilibrium. This response is referred to in homeostatic terms as "negative feedback" (Hardin, 1959).

But this principle operates only within relatively minor stresses on the system. If the limits of negative-feedback reactivity are exceeded in either direction, a reversal of homeostasis, known as "positive feedback" begins. When the body temperature rises to something like 107 degrees, with some individual variation, a "vicious circle" is established: "Increased temperature causes the chemical reactions of metabolism to go faster, which increases the temperature, which increases the chemical reactions further, which . . ." and so on (Hardin, 1959, p. 51). When we become so cold that our body temperature falls approximately 10 degrees below normal, there is a runaway process in the opposite direction. Hardin concludes, "In general, self-maintaining systems (like life) are self-adjusting only within limits. To keep them going, we must see to it that they are held within the limits in which negative feedback is operative."

To carry the parallel further, let us assume that within a normal range of stumbling speech and fluency failure, or in the absence of any event that changes one's conception of himself as a speaker, negative feedback prevails; that is, we react to the disturbance in such a way as to minimize it. As in the negative-feedback regulation of temperature through perspiring or closing off the pores, there are more or less definite limits, subject to some degree of individual variation. When the outer limits of fluency failure are experienced, the person may begin to force or struggle automatically, as he might while pushing a door that unexpectedly became stuck. And if he ran into enough doors that stuck, he might begin to view the task of opening a door differently. Doors are now a special obstacle. One must take pains, forcing repeatedly or prolongedly. If that still doesn't work, force harder. Try it again. And watch out next time.

Homeostasis reversal, or positive feedback sets in in relation to fluency failure when the process just discussed gets under way. Efforts to prevent a consequence can sometimes bring it about. We have used the plank-walking analogy (Sheehan, 1950, 1970). Anyone can easily walk across a 2-by-4-inch plank placed across the floor. But if it were placed between two tall buildings, or across a chasm, one would be in danger of falling off from the very effort engaged in trying to prevent it.

The antihomeostatic effects of positive feedback are readily explainable with reference to the double approach-avoidance conflict model. For a stutterer who has once gotten into the vicious circle of positive feedback, increased efforts to keep from falling off the fluency plank only increase avoidance behavior, associated conflict, and resultant stuttering.

In sports something akin happens when an athlete "chokes up" in a big game. When skilled acts of motor performance are involved, motivation needs to be within limits. An optimal level of arousal is called for. A considerable body of research with the Taylor Manifest Anxiety Scale supports the conclusion that performance is best with a moderate amount of anxiety motivation, rather than with very low or very high anxiety. Klopfer (personal communication) used to make a distinction between "constructive anxiety" and "destructive anxiety" with reference to Rorschach performance.

Stuttering and the ring of punishment

Somewhat parallel to the observations we have just made on stuttering and antihomeostatic feedback, we may cite a contribution by Worell (1965) in terms of what he calls "the ring of punishment." Worell concludes that punished behaviors that are surrounded by other punished behaviors become in time relatively inaccessible, that is, repressed. It is fairly obvious that stuttering behavior is founded on punishment, with instrumental escape learning leading to instrumental avoidance behavior.

There is preponderant evidence that increased social penalty leads to increased frequency of stuttering. Studies that report "contingent punishment" as being effective in reducing stuttering behavior, for the duration of the experiment at least, have capitalized on the novel stimulus effect of contingent presentation.

When immediate distractions are not present, and when there is an evident social penalty, stuttering frequency increases for most stutterers. For example: more stuttering and more difficult adaptation to authority figures (Sheehan, Hadley, and Gould, 1967); and increased frequency with shock threat (Van Riper, 1937a; Frick, 1951), shock administered (Frick, 1951; Frederick, 1955), increased communicative responsibility (Eisenson and Wells, 1942), increased meaningfulness of the material (Eisenson and Horowitz, 1945), self-esteem threat (Bardrick and Sheehan, 1958), more persons in the audience (Porter, 1939), interruption and unexplained imposition of silence (Gould and Sheehan, 1967), increased information load (Sitzman, 1968), increased role commitment to fluency (Sheehan, 1975), and many others. Except for distraction effects, it does not take any wizardry to observe that stuttering generally varies in direct proportion to the amount of social penalty placed upon its appearance. That is the experience of the stutterer and the experience of just about every experimenter who did not fall victim to the contingent reinforcement of the experimenter through distraction (e.g., see Sheehan, 1970a, chap. 8; 1970b).

Diversity in the manifestation of the behavior is characteristic of stuttering. There are seeming exceptions to the social-penalty effect, such as a stutterer's rising to an occasion and speaking with unaccustomed fluency; but these are usually interpretable through the intervention of other forces. A special role may be involved, or there may be an increase in the communicatory drive. The special role may bring reduced avoidance tendency because not the self, but a disguised self, is being presented. Increase in drive to speak may entail some additional fear en route, but the goal of speaking the feared word may be more readily reached. We have earlier pointed to the effect of anger or sudden stress in producing a spectacular fluency through the heightening of the entire gradient for approach (Sheehan, 1953a, 1958a).

The ring-of-punishment model is illuminating in the manner in which instrumental behaviors acquired through punishment pile up on one another. They also help us understand why, during therapy, old mannerisms the person reports he has not used for years sometimes make their appearance in the stuttering pattern. Since they are instrumental acts that have been ringed by punishing consequences, they have been suppressed. The tendency of stutterers to conceal their stuttering pattern from themselves, to cut off the feedback, may also relate to the ring-of-punishment concept. When the feedback is restored through self-observation and effective monitoring during therapy, the ring of previously inaccessible behaviors begins to unravel, like a knot within a knot.

Anxiety and punishment

In the traditional language of conditioning and learning, "punishment" is defined in terms of the characteristics or properties of the stimulus. Hull (1943), for example, defined a set of "noxious stimuli," which by inference to included certain social stimuli as well as the more biological, tissue-destroying, noxious stimuli. Defining punishment is not without its difficulties when this traditional approach is used. But then, definitional controversies have swirled similarly around many other venerable terms in the conditioning literature: learning, reinforcement, law of effect, etc.

Some operant conditioners, of a more radically operational bent, have attempted to solve the definitional difficulties in a very special way. Reinforcers are defined by their effects. Thus any stimulus is a reinforcer if it increases the probability of an operant response. Positive reinforcers, when added to a situation, strengthen the probability of an operant response. Negative reinforcers are stimuli that, when removed from a situation, strengthen the probability of an operant response. As Skinner defines it, punishment is different from negative reinforcement. It is an experimental arrangement, opposite from reinforcement, but not necessarily opposite in its effects (Skinner, 1953; Hilgard, 1967).

We believe that considerable confusion has been introduced into the stuttering literature, by many operant conditioners, by using "punishment" as a synonym for improvement. When delayed auditory feedback (DAF) or noise is introduced into the situation, and the stuttering frequency subsequently drops, they assume that the stimulus must have constituted "punishment." A scientific stance would require some independent definition of the punisher, other than the fact that its introduction into the environment resulted in a reduction of stuttering frequency. When "punishment" equals "improvement," then of course punishment works. We have criticized this usage in earlier writings (Sheehan, 1970a, 1970b). When punishment is inferred from any behavior reduction following the introduction of a stimulus, then "punishment" has a meaning that is both circular and absurd.

Van Riper (1973) has pointed out that, under this definition of punishment, even positive reward for stuttering could be considered as punishment. He reported an informal experiment in which he arranged for a pretty girl clinician to kiss the stutterer every time he stuttered. By the operant definition, this would have constituted "punishment" because its introduction into the stimulus environment was followed by a drop in the previous baseline of stuttering frequency. So the pretty girl's kiss was "punishing"? The absurdity requires practically no reduction.

The relation between punishment and anxiety is conceptually clear (Hessell, 1971). Freud long ago defined anxiety as the anticipation of punishment, a psychological definition no more recent figure has been able to improve upon. The operant conditioners like to sneer at the construct of anxiety, as we have already noted. When you key in on the application of punishment as a way of life, it's nice to pretend at the same time that there's no consequence such as anxiety: One of the many criticisms leveled against the deliberate use of punishment is that fear or anxiety responses inevitably increase. As Hilgard (1948, 1956) has pointed out, the use of punishment in learning situations leads to highly undesirable by-products. For example, there may be an interference with the extinction of maladaptive responses. In accordance with the old (1908) Yerkes-Dodson hypothesis, there may be a breakdown in the discriminability of instrumental acts under increased motivation. High drive in itself may interfere with performance, and punishment tends to produce elevated drive states. Solomon and Brush (1956) described the "partial irreversibility" of punishment-based learning. Skinner (1953) concluded that punishment is in the long run an ineffective instrument for the control of behavior:

> The effect of punishment was a temporary suppression of the behavior, not a reduction in the total number of responses. Even under severe and prolonged punishment, the rate of responding will rise when punishment has been discontinued, and although under these circumstances it is not easy to show that all the responses originally available will appear, it has been found that after a given time the rate of responding is no lower than if no punishment had taken place. (pp. 183–184)

The father of operant conditioning did not advocate the widespread use of punishment; as the preceding passage illustrates, he specifically called attention to its undesirable properties.

A famous figure in history who wrote eloquently of the punishment and guilt associated with stuttering was St. Augustine. Here is part of his road to sainthood:

> O God, my God, great was the misery and great the deception that
> I met with when it was impressed upon me that, to behave properly
> as a boy, I must obey my teachers. This was all that I might succeed
> in this world and excel in these arts of speech which would serve to
> bring honor among men and to gain deceitful riches. Hence I was sent
> to school to acquire learning, the utility of which, wretched child that
> I was, I did not know. Yet if I was slow at learning, I was beaten.
> This method was praised by our forebears, many of whom had passed
> through this life before us and had laid out the hard paths that we
> were forced to follow. Thus were both toil and sorrow multiplied for
> the sons of Adam.
>
> We discovered, Lord, that certain men prayed to you and we learned
> from them, and imagined you, as far as we could, as some sort of mighty
> one who could hear us and help us, even though not appearing before
> our senses. While still a boy, I began to pray to you, my help and
> my refuge, and in praying to you I broke the knots that tied my tongue.
> A little one, but with no little feeling, I prayed to you that I would
> not be beaten at school. When you did not hear me and it was "not
> to be reputed folly in me"—my punishments, which were then a huge
> and heavy evil to me, were laughed at by older men, and even by my
> own parents who wished no harm to befall me.
>
> Where was I in that sixteenth year of my body's age, and how long
> was I exiled from the joys of your house? Then it was that the madness
> of lust, licensed by human shamelessness but forbidden by your laws,
> took me completely under its scepter, and I clutched it with both hands.
> My parents took no care to save me by marriage from plunging into
> ruin. Their only care was that I should learn to make the finest orations
> and become a persuasive speaker. (Ryan, 1960, p. 67)

The use of punishment has its enthusiastic advocates. An example may be found in a recent case report by Berecz (1973), who advocates "precision punishment" leading to "cognitive arousal." His attitude toward precision in the scientific tradition of operationalism is revealed in his statement, "Cognitive arousal refers to the active imagining or arousing of cognitions within any sensory modality or blend of modalities" (p. 257).

We are reminded of the story of the kindhearted mule trainer who started his training procedure by picking up a two-by-four and giving the animal a hefty wallop on the rump. When the owner protested that the mule trainer had advertised himself as kindhearted, the trainer replied, "Oh, I'm *very* kindhearted. But first I've got to *get his attention.*"

Some behavior therapists argue that many of the things a permissive clinician does may be incidentally punishing in some respects. True enough. But because some punishment may be incidental in human interaction, does it therefore follow that punishment should be set up as a way of life? Even if our therapy already has punishment in it, why add more? If contingent punishment were in any way effective in reducing stuttering behavior, every case would be cured in childhood. The failure of the stutterer to communicate smoothly and effectively provides constant frustration and punishment that could not be more contingent. Contingent punishment is inherent in the experience of stuttering.

Wingate (1959) concluded that stuttering was reduced by "calling attention" to it. His procedure involved punishment by a break in the communication process (the stutterer had to repeat the stuttered word until spoken once fluently), or by signaling the stutterer that he had just stuttered. As with so many other studies purporting to show the effects of punishment, his results may be parsimoniously attributable to something else. Pausing, in itself, changes the stimulus situation sufficiently to introduce distraction or novel stimulus effects. When the pause is combined with the motoric activity involved in receiving the signal, a double artifact has been introduced.

In an ambitious and extensive reexamination of the literature on stuttering and punishment, Seigel (1970) attempted to make a positive case for the effectiveness of "contingent" punishment as opposed to more generalized threat of penalty. As we have noted, many behavior therapists use the term "penalty" for general or nonspecific punishments and reserve the use of the word "punishment" for contingently applied penalties. Siegel concluded that punishment was effective in reducing stuttering behavior in experiments in which it was contingently applied, and he arrived at fairly optimistic conclusions regarding the future use of punishment in suppressing stuttering behavior.

The flaw in the application of "contingent" punishment is that there is a built-in artifact. Any disruptive or novel stimulus introduced into the experimental environment will be likely to reduce stuttering, contingent or not. Operant experiments tend to have few subjects and even fewer controls. It is necessary to separate the effects of contingent application of any kind of stimulus that may be said to be novel, disruptive, or distractive, from whatever general effects the random or noncontingent introduction of the stimulus may have. The effect of contingent punishment has not yet been separated from the contingent application of anything—or for that matter, from the noncontingent application of anything.

When a control has been used on stimuli that were alleged to produce a contingent effect, the results have been in support of the proposition that stimulus application per se, rather than anything contingent, had been the effective agent. For example, Biggs and Sheehan (1969) introduced a control condition into a replication of the widely reprinted experiment of Flanagan, Goldiamond, and Azrin (1958). Whether the supposedly aversive stimulus (a 105 dB noise blast) was applied randomly, or contingently on stuttering, or contingently on fluency, made no difference. In the case of the control used by Biggs and Sheehan but not by Flanagan et al., the random application of the tone had just as much effect in reducing stuttering as did the contingent application. Moreover, the subjects in the Biggs and Sheehan study rated the experience of stuttering as more unpleasant than the noise.

A clever experiment by Cooper, Cady, and Robbins (1970) illustrates the distracting effect of "punishment" with equal clarity. They found that the positive, negative, and neutral words ("right," "wrong," and "tree") presented contingently, all led to a reduction in the frequency of stuttering. The authors suggested that the three verbal stimuli may have had the effect of calling attention to stuttering. They cited the study by Wingate (1959) that simply calling attention to stuttering reduced its frequency.

Operant conditioning and DAF approaches

Academic and clinical fields move through cycles, with emerging fads carrying new terms based on slight variations of old substance. The bottles look new, but the wine is so old as to have spoiled long ago. Yet newcomers pick them eagerly off the shelf.

In a partial review of behavioral approaches to stuttering, Ingham and Andrews (1973) observed, "The recent upsurge of interest in the use of rhythmic stimulation techniques is usually traced to Van Dantzig, who described 'syllable-tapping' therapy in 1940" (p. 411). Their next reference was to Meyer and Mair (1963), who by then had "provided promising preliminary data on the use of a hearing aid style of electronic metronome."

The Van Dantzig (1940) report on syllable-tapping was the first article I summarized and evaluated for Van Riper's seminar at Western Michigan University. Van Dantzig's offering was considered retrogressive. Tapping out the title and author's name with fluent ticktock rhythm, I acted out the absurdity of the method. To me syllable-tapping was an old story that had no happy ending. I had tried it in junior high and high school, using an ordinary lead pencil. Vividly I recalled my embarrassment when I pressed too hard and the pencil lead flew high in the air, to everyone's amusement but mine. After that I tapped for awhile on the eraser side, then gave it up completely, so I thought.

But finger-tapping remained a part of my instrumental stuttering pattern for many ensuing years.

It's hard to see how Meyer and Mair found the metronome so promising in 1963, when I had found it so unpromising in 1936. Then in high school, I was taking a few piano lessons from a nun for 35 cents an hour. Even at those prices the facilities included a metronome, with which I practiced at various speeds until I could talk as mechanically as Tik-Tok of Oz. Unsurprisingly, no enhancement of my social self-presentation resulted. Even in the 1930s, the number of situations in which one would be willing to Tik-Tok was sharply limited. Like the townspeople in the old Jewish story of the ragged peddler, when given a choice I preferred an old handicap to a new one.

Because stuttering is blatantly a disturbance in the rhythm and forward cadence of speaking, instantly amenable to artificially induced variations in tempo, it was perhaps inevitable that treatises on rhythmic therapy should occupy a large chunk of the literature, historic as well as contemporary. No excitement greeted the Van Dantzig paper in 1940; it was a large dud. It was the behavior therapists and the operant conditioners who exhumed the corpse with great acclaim in the 1970s. But interest in the rhythmical treatment of stuttering goes back far earlier than Van Dantzig. For example, Wyneken (1868) systematically advocated its use. From earliest times in America, patents were obtained on devices to improve the stutterer's rhythm (Katz, personal comm).

Therapies such as masking, DAF, metronome-timing, syllable-tapping, shadowing, and the like all share a common fallacy: They assume that the stutterer must be taught how to speak fluently, or be helped to speak fluently, and that the artificial fluency thus achieved can be stretched indefinitely to cover all future occasions, even those formerly eliciting anxiety, avoidance, and blocking. The fallacies are numerous: (1) It is not necessary to use artificial devices to have the stutterer experience fluency; he does speak fluently on most words anyway. (2) No satisfactory evidence has ever been presented to show that experience in speaking fluently results in response generalization with respect to fluency. In fact, there is reason for believing the opposite. Elsewhere we have argued that the cyclic variation of stuttering frequency might be explained by conceiving stuttering to be a cluster of fear-reducing responses. The occurrence of stuttering appears to reduce the fear that elicited the behavior. Fluency may bring about a role expectation for a higher level of fluency than the person may be capable of maintaining over the long run.

The stutterer who uses crutches with temporary success at the beginning of a speaking situation is like a tourist who has learned two or three French phrases to perfection. When he meets a Parisan, he tries them out, and gets in return a rapid volley of French that he can barely comprehend, let alone respond to. The stutterer who uses false fluency equally sets up a role expectation on which he cannot deliver. Like the tourist, his pretense becomes painfully obvious; he is worse off than if he had never assumed the false mantle of fluent speaker in the first place. A pose detected is far worse than no pose at all.

Time pressure as a factor in stuttering

A basic feature of stuttering behavior is that the stutterer is under time pressure to a great extent. He comes to learn to dread pauses, and the room settles around him with awful stillness when he begins to speak. The stutterer's block always seems longer than it really is, both to the stutterer and to his listeners. An experiment in which stutterers estimated the length of blocks against the actual blocks showed that they estimated significantly longer times (Ringel and Minifie, 1966).

It is suggested that time pressure is a basic variable in stuttering, that it is through time pressure that the effect of interpersonal relations in stuttering is mediated. It is also through time pressure that anxiety and guilt and conflicts of all kinds come to play a part. When the stutterer feels in a subordinate or inferior role, or when he is speaking to an authority figure, he is likely to feel he isn't really worthy of taking the other person's time. Many stutterers feel apologetic and guilty about their stuttering because of this seeming imposition. Many of the devices of stutterers are adopted to speed up the speech attempt and to shorten the block; these conspicuously have a self-defeating purpose. For a stutterer, "haste makes waste" is all too true. Unsystematic awareness of the role of time factors in stuttering has been shown by the older school of speech therapists, and even by neighbors and friends who are always urging the stutterer to slow down, to take it easy, to take his time. However ineffective these are as therapeutic measures, they do reflect a probably accurate perception of the stutterer as a person who is hurrying himself to an unnecessary extent. Stutterers learn to overtrigger the speech attempt, to startle, to become gun-shy of speech itself.

Many stutterers show a *fear of silence,* and any momentary pause or cessation of sound of their own speech brings on reactions approaching panic. Perhaps because most stuttering occurs on initial syllables and the stutterer has more trouble when he starts, he learns to dread the necessity for starting. He learns to dread any period of silence in his own speech, to fear it, and to become quite intolerant of it.

For a stutterer, silence is followed with the regularity of Pavlov's bell by a punishment: the experience of stuttering. In this way, the stutterer becomes conditioned to avoid silence in his speech. A great many of the stutterer's symptoms can be understood as filibustering, as measures taken to prevent the occurrence of silence. The stutterer puts himself under such extreme time pressure because he has learned that silence is dangerous. Stuttering itself is a compromise between speech and silence, a result of conflicting urges to speak and not to speak. Any organisms in double approach-avoidance conflict are characteristically pulled one way and then the other and are likely to attempt responses to competing cues. Similarly, many stutterers try to respond simultaneously to every cue in the situation.

Stutterers feel far more guilty over delaying their listeners than the realities of the situation require. It is a common experience among speech pathologists to have stutterers report being unable to carry out speech assignments because they didn't want to take the person's time. Now, most stuttering blocks are not over two or three seconds' duration (Sheehan, 1946; 1974). The actual time the listener is made to wait is really very small, yet with a dominant or important figure or with more people in the room, guilt and resultant time pressure multiply. The more total time, in blocking-seconds, that the stutterer piles up on people, the guiltier he feels about his speech.

How can we deal with this pressure therapeutically? Time pressure is so basic in stuttering that enumeration of nearly every therapeutic goal would be required to deal with the problem. But reduction of the stutterer's guilt generally, especially that over taking other people's time, is certainly of basic importance.

Time pressure, then, is an important variable in stuttering and perhaps in all interpersonal interaction. As such, it is worthy of systematic investigation. Yet previous research has left this important area virtually untouched.

Objective and subjective time pressure

We may distinguish between *objective* and *subjective* time pressure. The source of objective time pressure is the listener; the source of subjective time pressure is the speaker.

Objective time pressure is probably the historical source of much of the stutterer's difficulty. When people are impatient or intolerant listeners, or tell the child to hurry up and say what he has to say, or otherwise provide a situation that calls for immediate speech response at the cost of some penalty, then an objective time pressure situation exists. Both child and adult stutterers seem especially vulnerable to being hurried by their listeners, as in an evident threat of interruption, for example, saying good-bye to someone who is walking away.

A probable factor in the difficulty so many stutterers report on the telephone is that there is a built-in objective time pressure to vocalize. If the listener has answered the phone and hears nothing in response, he is likely to become quickly irritated, to demand who is calling, etc. We know of one stutterer whose heavy breathing patterns led female listeners to conclude that they were receiving obscene phone calls!

Though objective time pressure is important in stuttering, especially in early avoidance conditioning, it is not the principal time pressure to which the stutterer is subject.

The most important time pressure is that which the stutterer imposes on himself. Just as the guilty flee where no man pursueth, the stutterer sprints verbally whether the situation calls for it or not. A strongly conditioned, self-imposed time-pressure set appears to be operating within the stutterer as he struggles to speak. It is probably significant that Aristotle thought that the stutterer's problem was that he thought faster than he spoke. So many others have had the same thought that it is practically a cultural cliché, as well as a tired pronouncement that every stutterer has heard all his life. If you have grown up with the constant refrain of "slow down, take a deep breath, relax," such suggestions are merely tolerated and experienced as social penalities. Yet both Aristotle and the neighbor have observed something for which there is behavioral evidence, that is, that the person who stutters hurries himself to an unnecessary extent. We investigated the possibilities of a self-imposed time-pressure set in stuttering by means of a word association task in a doctoral study at the University of California, Los Angeles (Stunden, 1965). The results indicated that stutterers do tend to operate as though they had a self-imposed time-pressure set.

One of the central findings of the Sheehan-Martyn (1966, 1968, 1970) studies on recovery, also corroborated in studies by others, was that some stutterers frequently offered as their advice to other stutterers to "slow down and go ahead anyway." Many rhythmical and distraction devices, such as the metronome or delayed speech feedback, have the effect of slowing the stutterer's rate of utterance. Although we reject those devices for reasons stated earlier, we have recognized in our therapeutic procedures that stutterers do tend to rush themselves (Sheehan, 1970a, 1970b).

We believe that it is the stutterer's *rate of response* rather than his rate of speech that he needs to change. A panicky overeagerness to respond quickly to every little pressure in the situation is frequently observed among severe stutterers. We do not ask stutterers directly to slow down. He has heard this advice all his life, and he rightfully rejects it. Slowing down as a positive ritual usually involves artificiality, with scant carry-over to everyday speech. No stutterer wants to sound like a zombie—not even a fluent zombie.

We prefer to work on time pressure via monitoring. When the stutterer is enabled to observe vividly the extent to which he applies time pressure to himself, then he may engage in both a new look and a new choice. As with the basic process of monitoring, once the stutterer becomes vividly conscious of his maladaptive behaviors, he begins to drop them out automatically, to resume his more adaptive and natural way of speaking.

A voluntary stuttering method that has been found to facilitate adaptation and improvement is a voluntary prolongation of the initial sounds of the words which we have called the "slide" (Sheehan and Voas, 1957). Used principally on nonfeared words, the slide appears to have several important properties. One of these involves a shift on the part of the stutterer to a set in which he is more willing to pace himself with deliberate speed instead of the usual frenzy. When voluntary stuttering works in reducing fear and blocks, it appears to do so partly through creating a greater willingness on the part of the stutterer to take the listener's time. Not too much of it, but enough so that he doesn't have to speak under the disorganizing impact of self-imposed time pressure.

Predisposition to stuttering

Certain features of the disorder of stuttering, as we know it today, call for continued consideration of the possibility that some unknown factor of predisposition exists. At least, the possibility cannot entirely be discounted. Here are some of the reasons:

1. The distribution of stuttering throughout the world is on a fairly uniform basis of incidence. Such universality of the disorder is alone suggestive of some kind of underlying constitutional factor.

2. Variations in the incidence of stuttering across widely differing cultures are not as great as one might be led to expect from the cultural divergences themselves. The incidence and prevalence remain relatively constant. For example, see Aron (1960, 1962) on stuttering among the Bantu of South Africa; Eisenson (1966) on stuttering in the kibbutzim of Israel; Lemert (1953, 1962, 1970) on stuttering among the Kwakiutl and among Pacific and Polynesian groups; Murray (1958) on stuttering among Japanese; Stewart (1959) on stuttering among North American Plains Indians. Lemert's (1970) critical review and summary of cultural factors in stuttering is especially pertinent; so is Van Riper's (1971, 1973).

3. Stuttering runs in families, to the extent that about one-fourth of all cases report one or more stutterers in the immediate family. We are currently publishing a critique and review of the evidence (Sheehan and Costley, in press). While familial incidence leaves three-fourths of the cases unaccounted for, it is still too consistent a finding to ignore (Andrews and Harris, 1964; Sheehan and Martyn, 1970).

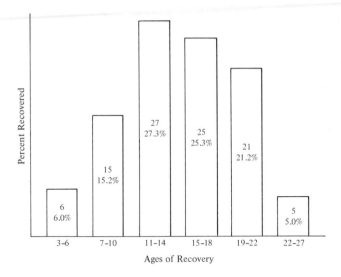

Figure 6. Ages at which spontaneous recoveries (permanent remissions) occur, based on data from 5,138 University of California students, of whom 147 had at some time been definitely categorized as stutterers.

4. In regard to the sex ratio, four or five times as many males as females become stutterers. While role expectations for males probably tend to be more exacting, it is difficult to account for such a huge discrepancy on any other basis than some kind of predisposing factor connected with maleness. Males have a more hazardous intrauterine life, and many more miscarriages result from male conceptions. Just the slightly later rate of maturation of the male child does not appear sufficient to account for the sex ratio in stuttering, though both may result from some common factor. The predominance of maleness in stuttering is paralleled by a similar predominance in many other disorders (e.g., autism and learning disorders).

5. The age of onset in stuttering is consistently related to certain stages in the developmental sequence. Most notably, the "period of resonance," or high readiness in language learning, noted by Lenneberg (1966, 1967a, 1967b) is also the period during which stuttering develops and flourishes. At the end of this stage, as Figure 6 depicts, spontaneous remissions or recoveries begin to occur to a significant degree (Sheehan and Martyn, in press).

Against this background that suggests some kind of predisposing factor in at least some cases of the disorder, we must point out some cautions and counterarguments.

1. Every effort to hypothesize and isolate a physiological difference between stutterers and nonstutterers has ended in failure upon replica-

tion of the study. Such efforts have been reviewed by Ainsworth (1971), Perkins (1970), and earlier by Hill (1944a, 1944b), Johnson et al. (1959), and Johnson et al. (1967). Van Riper's (1971) review led him to a conclusion favoring evidence for what he calls "the organicity of stuttering." Stromstra's 1956 research, long unreplicated, supports Van Riper's conclusions. We remain dubious and unconvinced that the evidence for any particular physiological difference distinguishing stutterers from nonstutterers has been shown to be adequate. Every time a difference is reported, it vanishes under the impact of more rigorous subsequent study (see, for example, Jensen et al., 1975).

2. The more poorly controlled a study is, the more likelihood of reporting a positive physiological difference.

3. More physiological studies deserve replication—a recommendation we have developed elsewhere (Sheehan, 1970a, chap. 8).

4. Some years ago, Wendell Johnson et al. (1967) issued a set of challenges for any physiological theory of stuttering. He asked theorists how the physiological condition might explain much of what might be called the "social psychology" of stuttering. So far as we know, no physiological theorist has ever tried to meet the challenge.

Our previous reluctance to recognize the possible predisposing factors in stuttering stemmed partly from disillusionment with the cerebral-dominance theory that dominated early physiological approaches to stuttering. As studies of aphasia have shown, laterality is clearly related to speech and brain function. Early reports by Bryngelson (1939) and others indicated a significant relationship between stuttering and sidedness. The Orton-Travis theory of cerebral dominance held that it was better to be strongly committed to either left- or right-side preference. Language and speech disorders such as stuttering were thought to be more likely in a twilight zone of ambilaterality. On the basis of the theory of cerebral dominance, stutterers at Iowa in the 1930s wore plaster casts on the nonpreferred hand to reduce bimanual activities and so, presumably, to strengthen the margin of the dominant gradient. In Van Riper's clinic in 1939–1940, we had to forsake such two-handed activities as typing and piano playing. We also practiced jaw bite and panting to a rhythm pattern, and simultaneous talking-and-writing, to reduce our dysphemia and enhance our diadochokinesis. "Go West, young man,"[4] was the order of the day. We were moved to compose the following limerick:

At Wisconsin the principal thesis
Is the stutterer's diadochokinesis

-----

[4] Robert West, a founding father of scientific speech pathology, then at the University of Wisconsin. In his speculations on stuttering, West was strongly inclined toward medical models and terminology.

So please Doctor West
Give us a rest
And break down your words in small pieces.

Cerebral dominance as applied to stuttering was a beautiful theory eventually destroyed by ugly fact. More rigorous later studies, as exemplified by Johnson and King (1942) using the Van Riper (1934, 1935) vertical-board test of laterality, found no evidence of a relationship between sidedness and stuttering. Hill's critical reviews (1944a, 1944b) led him to the same conclusion. Studies of the onset and development of stuttering by Johnson and others produced no difference in laterality between stutterers and controls. In our own samples of University of California students, we found no difference in stated hand preference among active stutterers, recovered stutterers, and normal-speaking controls (Sheehan and Martyn, 1966, 1970).

Because the early evidence on handedness had proved misleading, we came to be suspicious of what we have referred to as "the elusive predisposition concept." However, our same three University of California samples also confirmed both the familial-incidence pattern and the sex ratio found by many previous investigators. These facts, together with the universality of stuttering as reflected in a nearly uniform prevalence throughout the world, point to some type of undiscovered predisposition factor or factors.

In summary, then, there are persisting reasons for retaining the possibility that some kind of physiological predisposition for stuttering exists. We do not seem to progress much toward finding whatever it is. In any case, it might account for only a small segment in the total development of stuttering, even in the one-fourth of cases that appear familial in background. Most important, physiological theories have not led anywhere in terms of treatment. Both Eisenson (1958 and in this *Symposium*) and Van Riper have advanced physiological theories, though they advocate therapy systems based mostly on psychological and learning principles. Our own according of diplomatic recognition to the ever-present possibility of some known predisposing factor doesn't change our therapy a whit. Even if such a factor can later be found, as a result of improved technology, we would suspect that stuttering could still be understood and treated as a double approach-avoidance conflict.

Avoidance-Reduction
Therapy

When stuttering is viewed as a double approach-avoidance conflict, the twin goals of reducing avoidance tendencies and increasing approach tendencies follow logically. Because avoidance-reduction permits the least amount of therapeutically elicited anxiety, we stress that side of the conflict first. It is much easier to go ahead after some of the fear-motivated avoidance has been reduced.

The title of this chapter reflects our conviction that avoidance-reduction is the keystone of the therapeutic arch. Rid a stutterer of every last vestige of avoidance behavior with respect to his role as a speaker, and you will have rid him of his problem. Stuttering is founded on fear and avoidance; they feed upon one another.

In order for the disorder to be maintained, fear-motivated avoidance behaviors must be reinforced at least intermittently. And in the usual situation of the stutterer, the crutches and distractions work part of the time. Responses learned under such intermittent or partial reinforcement are notoriously difficult to extinguish. It is fascinating that stutterers undergoing therapy cling so long to their favorite crutches, and maintain "islands of avoidance" long after they have learned the subversive effects such islands have on their eventual achievement of fluency. There is indeed a phenomenon of resistance among stutterers; figuratively, the neurosis fights for survival. Curiously, much resistance is encountered 80 percent or 90 percent of the way through, probably as a result of anticipatory relaxation or premature closure.

Although others have included in their therapies some exercises in nonavoidance as part of their general armamentarium, it has tended to be an incidental aspect. In Van Riper's (1973) "shotgun approach," it has been one of the pellets, along with many, many others. Similar statements could be made for therapies advocated by Johnson and by Bryngelson and, for that matter, for James Hunt's (1863) therapy.

Just as the basic view of stuttering presented here is that it is a double approach-avoidance conflict, so our basic view of therapy is that total reduction of avoidance behaviors specific to the speaker role must be accomplished. Avoidance-reduction is the major vehicle of therapy. Any concept (such as "control of stuttering," or "suppression of stuttering behaviors") or any procedure (such as the phony "establishment" of fluency via distractive or disruptive stimuli) that entails avoidance tendency is alien to our therapy. We have previously (Sheehan, 1970a,b) and elsewhere in this chapter pointed out the dangers of distractive and disruptive training procedures. Fluency obtained by such means has a short life span. Out, brief candle of operant fluency! Less obvious is the effect of such terms as "control" or "handling your blocks." While they do not provide the illusion of quick fluency, they have no business in a therapy based on avoidance-reduction; they tend to increase the stutterer's already overwhelming tendency to hold back from the moment of speaking.

Often in therapy the stutterer is given conflicting messages. How can he go ahead if at the same time he must "handle his blocks" and control something that isn't there? The control concept has had the counterproductive effect of strengthening the stutterer's feeling that stuttering is some kind of an entity, a thing that just happens, a relentless directive from the fates.

An essential first step in accepting one's role as a stutterer, carried out through observation and monitoring, is that what he calls "his stuttering" consists of his own behavior. Who is doing the doing? He is. Who is making the choices? He is. Who can change what he is doing? He can. Who else? Nobody. To paraphrase Harry Truman, the buck stops with the stutterer himself. He must accept responsibility for making changes, though it is the therapist's responsibility to provide him with a better modus operandi.

In avoidance-reduction therapy, fear is not to be suppressed. Its expression by the stutterer should be encouraged, just as the expression of any feeling is generally desirable. Where feelings are concerned, there are no rights or wrongs. A feeling has a validity of its own, however unfortunate its origin. It deserves the clinician's respect and is to be accepted as is, if the person is to feel accepted and respected. So many stutterers have heard all their lives that they should not have fear that they have come to feel guilt over fear. They learn to pretend not to fear, to keep a stiff upper lip, to whistle through the verbal cemetery.

Although the client's feelings are to be accepted, and the expression of those feelings are to be encouraged, we do not have to be equally neutral with respect to what the person *does* in response to those feelings. That a stutterer feels stark fear and paralyzing avoidance urges is natural enough; if he begins to take initiative and attack feared situations as he should, he will experience vivid increases in momentary fear. What the stutterer does at the point of experiencing vivid fear is most crucial. If he approaches or attacks the feared word in the feared situation, he succeeds. How he sounds at the moment is irrelevant, except as grist for the mill of instrumental pattern analysis. If he caves in to the fear and lapses into a crutch or trick (e.g., fluent aside), he has failed, even though he may have shown enough false fluency to keep an operant conditioner busy counting.

One of the beauties of avoidance-reduction therapy is that, if the person really adheres to the principles of the therapy, he cannot fail. It is not a matter of control, or of expertise in some trick, or stretching artificially created fluently at the price of eternal vigilance. The conflict that is stuttering cannot survive when one side of the conflict is diminished to the vanishing point.

Individuals vary in how well they can respond to the challenge of avoidance-reduction therapy. Those who are absolutely courageous are assured of eventual success. Even the timid may achieve some reduction of anxiety by being more open about acceptance of the stutterer role, with its paradoxical ticket to fluency within reasonable limits.

Avoidance-reduction therapy is an already available solution to the problem of stuttering, because those who really face the problem succeed. On the child level, the direction of therapy toward eliminating those forces that cause the child to hold back or to be uncertain of himself point equally toward a sure and systematic remedy. The problem is that it is so difficult to get adults to be self-accepting and courageous. To prevail upon parents to give up the role demands and pressures that perpetuate the disorder, and probably caused it in the first place, is even more harrowing. However, the rewards for the child's self-assurance are enormous. The problem is to cajole the parents into enough pressure-reduction for an opportunity to observe the occasionally dramatic increase in fluency that results.

Avoidance-reduction therapy
versus avoidance-cultivation therapy

There is a great divide on therapies for stuttering. The older school, from Aristotle onward, aimed at the production of immediate fluency by using various devices to prevent the occurrence of fear or stuttering. Aristotle suggested that the stutterer thought faster than he spoke and that the tongue was too sluggish to keep up. However, along with many other stutterers, I have occasionally spoken faster than I thought. But most speakers seem able to do both without blocking in the process.

The older school has typically employed distraction or disruption devices in an effort to first produce and then extend a fluency acquired through some special means. Fluency can be produced temporarily by hypnosis, confidence-achieving suggestions, and various mechanical devices. So prevalent have been machines for curing stuttering throughout history that an enterprising lawyer who is also a member of the Council of Adult Stutterers in Washington, D.C., catalogued a whole array of patents obtained to cure stuttering (Katz, personal communication). Some older examples are variants of Itard's fork, which distorted the tongue position sufficiently to produce distraction-based fluency for a time. More recent patents have included portable masking and modified hearing aids, now so expensive that the effects are not likely to outlast the schedule of payments. Commercial motives have characterized these "new" devices; some of the same professionals who sell and push them in paid advertisements work the other side of the street by advertising their wondrous cures in scientific journal articles and book chapters.

Direct fluency methods characterize the older therapies. Often it is assumed that the stutterer needs to learn to talk all over again, or that he needs to use some special kind of control system. Or, an attempt is made to suppress the stuttering behavior through punishment for stuttering ("contingent" punishment).

It appears that some stutterers can successfully undertake a voluntary suppression of their stuttering behavior at least for a period of time. At least, they may diminish it. Although the mechanisms involved are unclear, the clinical observations are too frequent to be ignored. Possibly an increase in approach drive during a crisis situation is involved; possibly, some kind of false role accounts for the fluency. But this ability does not appear to be a sound base for permanent recovery. Like all false fluency, it is a fair-weather friend. The techniques of suppression and control desert the stutterer when he needs them most.

We characterize the older school we have just been describing as the Distraction, or Avoidance-Cultivation, method. Fluency produced "experimentally" by distractive or disruptive means, as by masking noise or metronome count, is carefully nurtured in the hope that it may be spread from the special condition that produced it to more general situations throughout life. Great premium is placed on the prevention of moments of stuttering and the avoidance of the near occasions of fear and difficulty. When failure is experienced, the stutterer is to begin again or to go back to an earlier point in the sequence of confidence nurturance.

The avoidance-cultivation school was based on the hope that moments of blocking could be prevented and that moments of fluency could be extended through response generalization. Unfortunately, most of the operant conditioning studies done to date on stuttering follow this older school.

With therapies that aim at the prevention of moments of stuttering, and the stretching of fluency through the cultivation of avoidance of difficult situations, there is never an assurance of a method for meeting future fear and failure. By their very nature, such therapies increase the penalty on stuttering, the avoidance component, and the conflict. That they "work" for awhile at all is probably due to the novel-stimulus effect, or distraction principle. This means that their half-life is far less than the stutterer's full life.

The cultivation of fluency and suppression of stuttering behavior appeals to the worst in the stutterer: his tendency to deny the problem, to cover up, to conceal. And unless the cover-up is complete—in itself a fantastic and unlikely achievement—the stutterer will be worse off. His avoidance tendencies will have been strengthened. If "programs" of such elaborate nature aim at pushing stuttering down under the surface, then the behavior must be shameful indeed.

The school of avoidance-cultivation does not in itself imply quackery; it is just that virtually all of the quacks choose this approach, because it offers quick fluency and impresses the customer.

With a more global, psychotherapy-oriented, or self-discovery oriented approach, the results are slower and, though surer, are far less instantly dramatic. Moreover, there is not the same magic-wand appeal to the therapist. His role is that of helper and sharer in discovery, amply rewarding for a healthy and mature person. However, that role does not have comparable appeal to those "experimenters" who have a need for dramatic, controlling manipulation of others.

The reinforcement of the experimenter

The world abounds with amateur therapists for stutterers. Every stutterer learns that neighbors and even strangers offer advice. So common are the methods suggested that they comprise a major part of the folklore of stuttering. As we have previously indicated, the stutterer is constantly being urged to take a deep breath, to slow down, to relax, to think before he speaks, and so on. The stutterer learns that everybody thinks he knows how to treat the problem, but nobody really does. Therapy comes easy, but therapists aren't to be trusted. Advice is offered for nothing and is worth just that.

Why should a disorder provide such a universally inviting target? From Aristotle (384 B.C), who believed that the stutterer's trouble was that he thought faster than he spoke, through Avicenna (tenth century A.D.), who suggested that the stutterer should take a deep breath, through Perkins (1971) who uses delayed speech feedback, a fantastic array of devices have been offered to make the stutterer quickly fluent. When first tried, any device is likely to work for awhile and then "wear out," or become habituated into the stuttering pattern.

One of the tricky features of undertaking therapy with stutterers is that anything in the way of a technique to bring about immediate fluency is likely to work at least temporarily. Quick fluency is reinforcing to the undiscerning therapist, as well as to the stutterer. Experimenters seeking apparatus to reduce stuttering are prone to the same risk. So long as the experimenter follows an operant approach, defining positive and negative reinforcement in terms of immediate effects, he may easily be misled. What he assumes by the nature of his approach to be positive or negative reinforcers may be merely a reduction of stuttering frequency due to the novelty and artificiality of the stimulus. He can easily be reinforced for functionally irrelevant techniques, just as the naive therapist or the stutterer can. The juxtaposition of novel stimuli with sudden reductions in the frequency of stuttering can make the experimenter every bit as "superstitious" as any of Skinner's pigeons.

The stutterer who has gone through the cycle of false hope and later discouragement has learned to be wary of anything that brings him immediate fluency. He may have feasted on false fluency so much that he comes to view all fluency as false—another problem with which the therapist must cope in the later stages of therapy.

The stutterer's wariness of distraction techniques is often more discerning than the enthusiasms of the operant conditioner. And the stutterer's scepticism is sound. In our studies of the recovery process, in the absence of any therapy at all, we did not find that former stutterers had recovered through distraction methods. Instead, distraction devices characterized those who had continued to stutter—and comprised a substantial portion of the visible handicap.

Avoidance-reduction therapy involves acceptance by the stutterer and by his therapist of the problem that must be faced and conquered. Distraction techniques and avoidance-cultivation therapies involve denial. Mr. Hyde must be kept hidden. By increasing the holding-back behavior, avoidance-cultivation therapies increase the intensity of the conflict and aggravate the problem. Part of the paradox of stuttering is that the person speaks best when he's not trying to keep from stuttering or doesn't care whether he does. He is at his worst when he is trying to hide, or trying to speak perfectly (Sheehan, in press).

The Blarney Stone illusions

The intermittency and apparent unpredictability of stuttering, plus the frequent episodes of comparatively free speech, may be responsible for fostering the many illusions that are part of the folklore. One of the most common is the quick-cure illusion. Since fluency appears so suddenly on a temporary basis, it becomes easy for the stutterer to imagine that by next Tuesday, he may be fluent as a faucet. Hypnosis has a special attraction for many stutterers and their parents, who see the problem vanishing with a magic puff. Even the famous legend of the Blarney Stone is reported to have originated with stuttering, according to one version:

> They say there is a story behind every stone in Ireland, of which probably the best known is that which concerns the stone at Blarney Castle, near Cork. Many years ago, according to the story, a man was cursed with a stutter that no one could cure until a witch hung him by his legs outside the battlements of the castle, telling him to kiss a stone on the outer wall; he did, and he was cured, perhaps as a result of the shock. For a long time thereafter those who sought the gift of eloquence underwent the same perilous ordeal. . . . (Davies, 1972)

The original association of the term "blarney" with eloquence is credited to Elizabeth I, who concluded that the Irish chieftain who ruled the castle was plying her with soft words while maintaining his independence. Legends grow about quick and miraculous cures for stuttering, whether or not a basis exists in historical fact.

Commentary on behavior modification in stuttering

In this section we review some of the attempts at behavioral modification of stuttering, excepting our own, for they are covered throughout the chapter.

Any evaluation undertaken of the role of behavior modification in stuttering is necessarily superimposed upon the structure of basic assumptions as to the nature of the disorder. Moreover, behavior modification covers a wide range of approaches and techniques, from the reciprocal inhibition therapy of Wolpe to the special language and methodology distinctive of operant conditioning. Any technique is first of all a tool, a surgeon's scalpel, whose effective use depends on the skill of the user. It requires no endorsement of the medical model to see that the appropriateness of the intended use necessarily depends on the patient and the kind of problem he presents. Behavior therapists accord some recognition to the latter point when they speak of the "reinforcement history" of the person.

Stuttering is not a simple unitary symptom, but a disorder of great complexity and diversity. No two stutterers make the same faces when they stutter, nor are their emotional and behavioral patterns ever identical. The effects of reward and punishment on stuttering depend on the kinds of learning that have gone on before. Stuttering is not maintained or reinforced by a single, simple cycle of events. And four out of five cases of stuttering are not maintained at all.

The disorder of stuttering is full of paradoxes. Why should anybody have difficulty speaking in this glib world in which so much of what is said is banal and useless? Why should children continue to stutter when the behavior is apparently more punished than rewarded? Why do some stutterers recover spontaneously? Why should anyone stutter most when he is trying hardest to avoid it? Why does one child subjected to pressure begin to stutter while another, equally pressured, does not? Why should stuttering behavior frequently decrease when it is treated with greater permissiveness but increase with social penalty?

We are in basic agreement with the widely held view that stuttering is primarily a set of learned behaviors. Each stutterer possesses, to a greater or lesser degree, both an emotional handicap and a pattern of instrumental behaviors. The stutterer is classically conditioned on an emotional basis and instrumentally conditioned in the learning of his stuttering pattern. These twin aspects of stuttering were indicated in our previous analyses of conflict levels, and correspond to the Hilgard and Marquis (1940) classification of types of learning.

We are equally in agreement with the empirical principle of reinforcement. Behavior is determined by its consequences: This is one form of the principle of determinism, the thesis that behavior is lawful and subject to scientific investigation. Reward or punishment obviously influence behavior, even though we do not always understand the manner in which they work. When a behavior is first rewarded and then punished, or first punished and then rewarded, the pattern of reinforcement becomes much more complex. Stuttering appears not to follow a single, simple reinforcement pattern, and stutterers as individuals vary markedly in their responses to reward and punishment. Clinicians consider this under the heading of the psychodynamics of the person, while behavior therapists cover it with the equally vague term "reinforcement history." There is ample reason for believing that the effect of reward or punishment applied immediately is quite different from long-range consequences that are rewarding or punishing. Simple rewards for fluently spoken words over a short time period, as during an experimental session, may have zero effect on the future probability of stuttering in the very different stimulus conditions of life outside the laboratory.

To make stutterers fluent in a sheltered environment is as meaningless as it is easy. We do it inadvertently all the time. The perceptive clinician soon learns what nearly every stutterer knows: that fluent intervals lead neither to a diminution of fear nor to a solution of the problem.

Too many operant studies have been directed at the spread of fluency, rather than the reduction of anxiety and the modification of the instrumental responses that make up the more visible portion of the stuttering pattern. The history of the treatment of stuttering is largely made up of therapies built upon devices to produce sudden and immediate fluency. Behavior modification therapy can be more effective if we use it for the modification of stuttering through nonreinforcement. The value of this approach is that it takes into account the inevitability of future anxiety and some stuttering-like responses (disfluencies).

Perfect fluency is not obtainable and is a self-defeating goal. We illustrated this in our role-commitment study, a level-of-aspiration-for-fluency situation. Severe stutterers set more ambitious fluency goals than did mild stutterers, just the opposite of what might be expected on the assumption that people behave logically (Sheehan, in press). In an anagram-solving task, Pruett (1968) found severe stutterers to be higher in expectancy of success than either mild stutterers or normal speakers.

It is regrettable that so many therapists and "experimenters" set up fluency as a direct goal for the stutterer. On the basis of everything we know about stuttering behavior, direct pressure toward increased fluency results ultimately in the exacerbation of the problem. Except for the misleading intrusion of novel-stimulus effects, the ultimate effect is felt immediately. We see this illustrated in stutterers who have "worn out" certain tricks or instrumental behaviors, so that they no longer work. We have described this process in learning terms elsewhere (Sheehan, 1946, 1951, 1970a, 1974). So has Van Riper, both earlier and more recently (1937a, 1973). The worn-out tricks remain as phonetically irrelevant instrumental behaviors, maintained through intermittent reinforcement. The stuttering pattern then becomes a sequence or cluster of such responses, whose useless appearance makes no sense unless we consider their vestigial origin, in terms of the reinforcement history of the individual.

As Johnson (1946, 1961), Johnson et al. (1959), and others showed many years ago, most stutterers speak most of their words fluently. Have not the fluently spoken words of stutterers already been subjected to a vast amount of positive reinforcement? For a stutterer, the social consequences of speaking a word fluently are, it could be argued, even more strongly reinforced than in the case of a normal speaker. Can the operant conditioners hope to do better? Can "laboratory" manipulations of masking and delayed side-tone effects really accomplish what a lifetime of positive social reinforcement has failed to accomplish?

We believe that the problem lies elsewhere. Since stuttering has been learned in response to punishment and is perpetuated for most stutterers by anticipations of further punishment (by which we use the shorthand terms "fear" and "anxiety"), stutterer has no need for reinforcement of fluent words. He can be helped to modify, through the use of reinforcement and nonreinforcement, his avoidance reactions. He can be helped to break out of the vicious circle of self-reinforcement. We have methods to rescue the stutterer from the "ring of punishment" described by Worell (1965). Avoidance-reduction calls for courage on the part of the stutterer, together with sensitivity, imagination, and skill on the part of the clinician, but there is nothing very mysterious about the process. And there is nothing very easy about it, either. Shortcuts to immediate fluency invariably lead back to stuttering: This is the history of every case. The ontogeny of the stutterer's experience reflects the phylogeny of the field of stuttering therapy.

The ease of obtaining immediate fluency points up a fallacy common in applications of the operant approach. Since stutterers are already fluent much of the time, the claim to "establishment" of fluency responses is open to question. In the case of a previously noncommunicative, autistic or retarded child, "establishment" may really refer to the acquisition of a new response or a new response cluster. In the case of stuttering, "establishment" of fluency hardly rates as much of an achievement. The crucial issue is the conditions under which the response is "established."

Since stuttering is a response cluster motivated by fear, immediate fluency is a grand illusion. The experienced clinician has learned to guard against too much enthusiasm over bursts of immediate fluency. In the case of avoidance-cultivation therapies, chance episodes of fluency are likely to perpetuate the illusion of "sudden cure by next Tuesday."

We have emphasized that stuttering is a response cluster motivated by fear and conflict. Since the operant approach denies itself the use of constructs, factors such as anxiety tend to be ignored. This seems to lead to the unspoken premise that fluency is good no matter how obtained. But, as already noted, immediate fluency provides an illusion of improvement. Under what conditions can the stutterer maintain fluency? What is he to do when he experiences stress and anxiety, as he inevitably will? What is he to do when he stutters? Unless he has learned to weaken the fear and avoidance responses, reduced his struggle behaviors and dependence on crutches, he will revert all the way back to ground zero.

The crucial question relates to the stimulus condition, both external and internal. Fluency "established" in the sheltered environment of the research room can disintegrate rapidly under the disorganizing impact of anxiety. In therapy we must break up the old, nearly one-to-one, relationship between stuttering and anxiety. The stutterer can profit from learning to stutter without the old anxiety, and from experiencing anxiety without inevitably following it with the responses of his old stuttering pattern. Since the stuttering pattern is not a single response, but a cluster of responses, the reduction of the stuttering-anxiety relationship can be accomplished most effectively by isolating the components of the pattern through monitoring.

But since anxiety is a construct, observable only in terms of its effects, for some operant conditioners it does not exist. They would exile it from science. To remain consistent, they would also have to exile such constructs as contained in atomic theory, for example, $E = mc^2$.

Unless something is done about reducing anxiety or severing its relationship to the responses called stuttering, what are stutterers to do when they experience the cues that set off moments of difficulty? So long as the sequence of

^{s}word$\rightarrow^R$fear

^{s}fear$\rightarrow^R$stuttering

persists, then the fluency the stutterer has already "established" under anxiety-free conditions involving very different cues has no effect whatever on that sequence. And this is the crucial sequence with which the stutterer must deal—not the "experimental establishment" of an S-R connection he has used successfully all his spoken life.

First catch one tiger

The classical and age-old recipe for "tiger stew" begins with these ominous and all-important words: "First catch one tiger. Then prepare as follows: . . ."

In other words, accomplish the main mission first, before expatiating on the ramifications and marvelous consequences if only the major premise were true. Meat before garnishes: First show that there is a tiger and that you can catch him before branching off with marvelous recipes for how to cook him.

You haven't cured a periodic drunk by showing that he can be sober part of the time; he can do that already. You can only claim a cure if you can show that under the stimulus conditions which formerly characterized bouts of drunkenness, he now remains sober and has for a long time. Without follow-up, a reported cure has about as much impact as the midnight conversion of a hungry wino at a rescue mission. But that is about all the follow-up the behavior therapists have been providing. Anecdotes and enthusiastic testimonials abound in behavior modification reports, but hard data on follow-up are missing.

The "first tiger" requires the demonstration that artificial or experimentally induced fluency can be carried over to socially significant situations. The evidence has not been produced. Such evidence should be the starting point of operant research on stuttering, not a belated afterthought accorded weak recognition.

Of course, one may hope. But how hopeful is it really when one must subsist on a diet of strung-out hopes? This is what stutterers have been living with all their lives. They know only too well the folly of expecting too much from "false fluency." They have already tried and worn out distraction devices more sophisticated than those reported by many appliers of operant conditioning.

Just because an operant procedure is under apparent rigorous control does not mean that any ensuing loose assertion by the experimenter is therefore validated. Trivial (though apparently rigorous) procedures become the launching pad for putting into orbit the most lofty and far-out innuendos that behavior therapy is about to cure all sorts of ills and revolutionize society.

Guidelines for judging therapy techniques

In *Stuttering: Research and Therapy* (Sheehan, 1970a), we proposed a set of guidelines for judging therapy techniques, especially those billed as "new therapy methods." We feel they are worth including here. Despite a number of continuing theoretical puzzles, we do know enough about the factors surrounding stuttering to treat the majority of cases successfully. The price is courage on the part of the stutterer and skill on the part of the clinician. Any stutterer who goes thoroughly through the avoidance-reduction therapy presented in this chapter will shed a substantial portion of his handicap. Pioneering studies on the outcome of stuttering therapies, including our own, demonstrate this very clearly (Gregory, 1968, 1969, 1972).

What guidelines are available by which to judge a proposed "new" therapy technique? How is the practicing therapist to evaluate various procedures now appearing in the literature, sometimes under imposing experimental auspices? From our view of stuttering as a multilevel approach-avoidance conflict, as a self-role conflict and a false-role disorder, we propose the following criteria for judging a therapy technique:

1. Does the technique lead to approach or avoidance behavior?
2. Is the technique true to the self or does it represent a false role? Is the technique based on honesty or falsity?
3. Does the technique allow for future fear and fluency failure? Does it provide a means for dealing with the inevitable?
4. Does it call for behavior expression or suppression?
5. Does it call for "control" of something that really isn't there?
6. Does it create a dependence on itself or does it provide eventual freedom?
7. Does it produce fluency directly or indirectly? Does it hinge on the spread of artificially induced fluency?
8. Are the results of the technique lasting and permanent or only temporary? For example, are basic attitudinal changes toward the self and others facilitated?
9. Does the therapy offer the stutterer eventual independence of the therapist?
10. Is the technique systematically related to a comprehensive theory of stuttering and supported with scientific evidence?

Subjected to such scrutiny, many frequently advocated and widely used techniques nominate themselves for the discard pile. Yet stutterers are still exhorted to forget the problem, to relax, to take a deep breath, to take a pill, to get hypnotized, or to walk around with a portable noise generator. Each of these violates nearly all of the listed criteria. For example, speaking with a noise-producing modified hearing aid produces immediate, temporary, and very false fluency. Rather than leading to independence, it fosters dependence on both gadget and therapist.

It is clearly suppressive, calls for vigilance and control, is premised on successful avoidance of stuttering, and is based on the fantastic hope that falsely created fluency can be stretched to cover all occasions.

Avoidance-reduction concepts for stutterers

The following are ideas that can be presented to any adult or adolescent stutterer who has sufficient motivation and courage to tackle avoidance-reduction therapy. They are presented briefly here, but spelled out more thoroughly in *Stuttering* (Sheehan, 1970a). In that work, we called it "role therapy," emphasizing the action-taking aspect; it now seems more generic to call it "avoidance-reduction therapy." The ideas are expressed in the language of direct communication to the stutterer.

1. Your stuttering is a conflict between going ahead and holding back. To improve, you must reduce and finally get rid of the holding back of your habits of hiding and avoidance.
2. Your stuttering is a false-role disorder. You will remain a stutterer so long as you continue to pretend not to be one.
3. Just as you have stuttered most of your life up to now, you will stutter somewhat the rest of your life.
4. You have a choice as to *how* you stutter. You do not have a choice as to *whether* you stutter.
5. What you call your stuttering consists mostly of the tricks, the crutches you use to cover up.
6. Your stuttering is like an iceberg—most of the handicap you keep concealed beneath the surface. If you get more of it up above the surface, you will get rid of it more easily.
7. Your stuttering is *something you do*, not something that happens to you. It is your behavior, not a condition. It is not a defect nor an illness, but a series of mistakes you continue to make: mistakes you can correct with a little self-study and courage.
8. Working on your stuttering, attacking and conquering situations from which you have always retreated, can be fun.
9. Reducing your tricks of avoidance is not a process you need to keep working on forever. You have learned a set of attitudes, feelings, and habits; you can learn a new set.
10. It is far better to stutter openly and honestly than to use a trick, especially if temporarily successful.
11. Your stuttering won't hurt you, and your fluency won't help you.
12. In accepting yourself as a stutterer, you choose the route to becoming a more honest, relaxed speaker.

13. You have a choice in *how* you stutter; you can choose to stutter openly and smoothly.
14. The more you run away from your stuttering, the more you will stutter. The more you are open and courageous, the more you will develop solid fluency.

The "Fourteen Points for Stutterers" just presented have been derived from over 40 years' clinical and research experience with stuttering, including extensive servitude on both sides of the desk. Comparative study of those who recover, as against those who don't, have revealed what we knew long ago from personal experience with stuttering: Distraction and quick-fluency methods are futile. Only quacks promise the two-week cure. Fundamental positive changes of a lasting nature typically take time. Lasting negative effects can be achieved quickly through one-trial punishment learning that carries partial irreversibility. But the stutterer who can accept his stutterer role, who can renounce his false-role behavior and reduce his avoidance, who can develop the courage to "go ahead anyway," is on his way to recovery.

Avoidance-reduction therapy procedures

In this section, we describe briefly our therapy procedures for adults. With due regard for the role of the family in the treatment process, they may be adapted for adolescents and older children (usually 8 and above), who must be worked with directly. However, any stutterer still living with his parents or in the family circle should be treated with regard to the place of the family in the neurosis and in the therapy (Sheehan, 1970a). The stutterer who comes to the clinic on his own is probably best fitted to begin avoidance-reduction therapy. The procedures presented here must be embedded in a set of clinical principles that may be found in the Role Therapy chapter of *Stuttering: Research and Therapy* (Sheehan, 1970a).

We assume that the role assignments presented below are to be carried out in a group setting. The group can be more powerfully therapeutic than even the most skilled individual therapist, though he may provide the yeast for the rising of the group identity. We find it most useful to phrase avoidance-reduction assignments in this chapter just as we present them to beginning stutterers in the clinic.

For information, we give adults and adolescents our *Message to a Stutterer* (Speech Foundation of America, 1972) and encourage them to send for other publications of the Speech Foundation of America. For those who desire more information on our therapeutic procedures and rationale, we also encourage the reading of our own book (Sheehan,

1970a). The advantages of this as a primary reference are twofold: First, it is consistent with what we do; second, the rationale of therapy is more thoroughly spelled out than is possible in the clinic. We do present therapy rationales, as simply and as clearly as we can, in connection with giving out assignments and in connection with group and small group discussions of the stutterer's resulting experience.

Searching out what others have to say on stuttering can be a rewarding source of coffee-break discussion. Some of our favorite authors for this purpose are Bloodstein (1969), Gregory (1968, 1972), Johnson (1961), Van Riper (1971, 1972, 1973), and Williams (1957, 1971). But we do not use these other sources as a starting point for group discussions in the clinic. It is better to start from what members of the group are doing and what their immediate experiences have been.

We shall present one sequence of assignments we have found useful as a core of experiences when starting in the clinic. We have covered in considerable detail the clinical context in which such assignments are to be used and the clinical principles on which they are based (Sheehan, 1954a, 1958a, 1970a). We refer especially to the psychotherapeutic aspect of therapy with stuttering, to primary losses, to secondary gains, to resistances, and to the fact that psychotherapy itself is a kind of avoidance-reduction therapy.

The following are the assignments, in the language in which the stutterers get them. For invaluable suggestions on these assignments we are indebted especially to Vivian M. Sheehan and to Leonard Robin.

1. EYE CONTACT

Interpersonal communication is nearly always facilitated by eye contact, and that between speaker and listener is particularly important. You soon learn that you shape the audience response depending on the attitude you display. If you avert your eyes when you stutter, you increase the shame and the mystery, and you lose touch with your audience. Four points are particularly worth noting:

1. Establish eye contact *before* you begin to speak. Two or three seconds of quiet eye contact can get you off to a better start.
2. Some people will look away no matter how much you try to keep contact. To succeed, it is sufficient that *you* look at them.
3. At first you may find yourself staring people down, but don't worry about it. You can overcorrect a little and then let the pendulum swing back. No stutterer ever had a sustained problem of too much eye contact.
4. Later on you may occasionally look away from your listener, which

is natural. But be sure you don't look down or away just at the moment of stuttering.

Here are some specific assignments we have found helpful. Do these or devise comparable ones for yourself. Learning how to give yourself assignments is like acquiring any skill such as typing or piano playing. Keep your goals practical and specific so that you will have something definite to report. You may find it useful to keep a "stuttering notebook," including in it your assignments and reports of experiences, together with everything you learn about the problem called stuttering.

1. *Write down* the names and eye colors of 10 people to whom you stutter.
2. Using a mirror at home, see if you can keep eye contact with yourself while reading aloud. Notice what you do!
3. *Write down* 25 words on which you stuttered while maintaining eye contact.
4. Use your name with good eye contact to 5 different people.
5. Note something you have done on your own initiative that you did to achieve good eye contact.

2. DISCUSSING STUTTERING

You can begin accepting your role as a stutterer by discussing stuttering with friends and acquaintances. When you reach a point of sharing your stuttering openly with your listener, you will feel much less fear and tension. You should not try harder to be more fluent because you will only be saying, "I am not really a stutterer." When you do this, you merely increase your fear of discovery and fall back into the vicious circle of stuttering more because you try to hide it.

1. Discuss stuttering openly with 6 people of your acquaintance. Ask the following questions:
   a. Have you ever known other stutterers?
   b. How does my stuttering affect you?
   c. What do you think causes stuttering?
   d. What do you think should be done about stuttering?
   Write a short description of their answers.
2. Discuss your stuttering with at least one stranger, asking the same questions as in No. 1.

3a. EXPLORING YOUR STUTTERING

We want to explore your stuttering, and we invite you to do the same. Oddly enough you probably don't know what you do when you "stutter." Because it's unpleasant, you've probably covered it up from yourself as well as others. Let's discover all the crutches you use now. When you have explored your stuttering pattern, you won't have so much fear of the unknown.

1. List as many as you can of the different kinds of crutches you now use to hide your stuttering. A crutch is something a stutterer uses to hide his stuttering while trying to be as fluent as possible. Some of the more common crutches are: eye blink, head jerk, and substitution of one word or phrase for another ("um," "uh," "well").
2. The "Speech-Pattern Checklist" can serve as a guide to help you see what you actually use as crutches.
3. Select 2 of your favorite crutches and write down a total of 10 situations in which you use either of them.

3b. SPEECH-PATTERN CHECKLIST

1. How do I avoid stuttering?
   - ( ) I give up when I have difficulty.
   - ( ) I substitute words.
   - ( ) I change the order of words.
   - ( ) I pretend to think about what I want to say.
   - ( ) I don't talk.
   - ( ) I try to keep talking without pausing to take a breath.
   - ( ) I split words (e.g., break one-syllable words into two syllables).
   - ( ) I begin to speak when someone else is talking.
   - ( ) I use fluent asides.
   - ( )

2. How do I postpone stuttering?
   - ( ) I pause.
   - ( ) I beat around the bush.
   - ( ) I repeat previous words and phrases (running start).
   - ( ) I introduce unnecessary sounds.
   - ( ) I use fluent asides.
   - ( ) I pretend not to hear.
   - ( ) I start over and over until I have a jumble of unintelligible words and sounds.
   - ( )

3. What "starters" do I use?
   - ( ) I introduce unnecessary words, sounds or phrases ("well," "um," "uh," "you know," etc.)
   - ( ) I use some stereotyped movement.
     - ( ) Shift body.
     - ( ) Jerk head.
     - ( ) Clear throat.
     - ( ) Swallow.
     - ( ) Blink eyes.

( )   Tap foot.
( )   Yawn.
( )   Snap finger.
( )   Finger pressure.
( )   Move hand.
( )   Move foot.
( )   Lick my lips.
( )   Click my tongue.
( )   Stick out my tongue.
( )   I giggle.
( )   I change pitch.
( )

4. LEARNING THE LANGUAGE
OF RESPONSIBILITY

Your stuttering is not something that happens to you, but something that you do. See if you can observe and describe your stuttering in language which recognizes that you have a part in it, that it is your own behavior. You are doing the doing. You have responsibility and you have choice. First you must assume responsibility for your doing the stuttering before you can make a choice on what you can do with your stuttering pattern.

1.   Write down five times that you catch yourself not using the language of responsibility, such as, "My eyes blinked" or "The words got stuck in my mouth."
2.   Find two examples—one of responsible language and the other of nonresponsible language—in the newspaper for our "Stuttering Scrapbook."
3.   Formulate, carry out, and write down an eye-contact assignment for yourself.

5. MONITORING

Your first job is to observe what you do continuously, a process we call "monitoring." If you really monitor well, you will begin to drop many of your crutches automatically. You can make faster progress by alert monitoring than by consciously trying to prevent your crutches.

We do not ask you to consciously drop your crutches, only to become curious about those crutches and aware of what you do when you stutter. We want you to monitor, to become aware of what you do to interfere with your natural capacity for fluency.

In order to learn the process of monitoring, begin by observing just one crutch you know you use as follows: FIRST CRUTCH _____.

1. In two situations (one on the telephone with a mirror propped up in front of you, the other of your own choice), each day for two days, watch yourself and note how you use this particular crutch. Note the words and the things you do before, during, and after. Note how many times you use the same crutch, etc.

   SECOND CRUTCH _____.

2. Repeat with a second crutch the next two days using two other situations.

3. On the fourth day, you are ready to try monitoring your speech in a larger sense of just noting what you do when you stutter: to experience the movement of stuttering by seeing, hearing, and feeling. See how many different crutches you can catch yourself using.

   This time, on the fifth and sixth days, go into two situations (as above) but see if you can observe exactly the series of things you do when you stutter. It is not enough to answer the question, "What did you just do?" by saying "I stuttered." You should note operationally exactly what you did: for example, closed your eyes, stuck out your tongue, inhaled, interrupted the stuttering, snapped your fingers, and so on.

6. INITIATIVE AND FEAR-SEEKING

You will progress much farther and speak more easily if you keep seeking out feared words and situations instead of just letting them happen to you. The "initiative set" is incompatible with the "avoidance set" for each new speaking situation. In stuttering therapy you never stand still. Unless you are pushing back the frontiers of fear and difficulty, you are lapsing into retreat.

If you find yourself even tempted to avoid a situation, it means your attitude is slipping and you have lost initiative. Never postpone a challenge presented by the premonition of fear. Carry with you a set to go into any situation in which you anticipate difficulty. Your readiness in itself will make things easier in the long run.

Seek out one situation each day for the specific purpose of working on your speech. Select a time period in a familiar situation, a new situation, or some situation you would ordinarily avoid and monitor or keep eye contact in these situations. Write down a fairly complete description of each of these situations. Answer the following questions: To whom? What about? What did you do? How did you feel afterward?

7a. COUNTING SUCCESSES AND FAILURES

Before you began this therapy, you probably thought that any fluency was a success and any stuttering was a failure. But now all that is changed. A block is not a failure; neither is a fear a failure. It is only as you experience both that you can learn to respond more adequately. In the new approach, covering up or using a crutch is a failure even if the most immediate effect is that you sound more fluent. And stuttering openly and more easily counts as a success that can increase your security and eventually your ease of speaking.

Work from the "Successes in Open Stuttering" list and see how many successes you can get each day. Note the failures in passing, but focus on expanding your number of successes each day. Write down on the checklist which successes you accomplished. Collect a minimum of _____ each day.

7b. SUCCESSES IN OPEN STUTTERING

Count it as a *failure* if you:

1. substitute
2. look away during a block
3. use a starter
4. stop halfway through the block
5. do not have sound in the block (preformation)
6. back up and start over
7. ruin an open stuttering assignment with fluency immediately afterward
8. cover up your stuttering successfully
9. stall a long time before entering a situation
10. try to talk fluently at any cost
11. show embarrassment that puts your audience ill at ease
12. perform an assignment halfheartedly
13. respond quickly and automatically to every little pressure in the situation
14. give yourself the benefit of the doubt
15. use a crutch to get the word out

Count it as a *success* if you:

1. establish eye contact *before* beginning to speak
2. monitor well—that is, observe exactly *how* you stutter
3. stutter, but bring the sound in immediately
4. stutter forward
5. stutter with good eye contact
6. go out of the way to enter a situation especially for your speech (initiative)
7. put the hardest word first in the sentence
8. complete any feared word you start
9. choose feared words instead of "easy" words
10. mention your stuttering casually without shame

7c. COUNTING SUCCESSES

	Establish eye contact before speaking	Enter situations to work on speech	Complete any feared word	Mention your stuttering	Keep good eye contact throughout stuttering	Use feared words instead of easy words	Others
Thurs.							
Fri.							
Sat.							
Sun.							
Mon.							
Tues.							
Wed.							

8. EXPOSING THE ICEBERG

Get as much of your stuttering above the surface as you can. After studying the iceberg diagram (illustrated below), draw your own "iceberg of shame and guilt" in three different situations each day for four days.

The Iceberg of Stuttering:

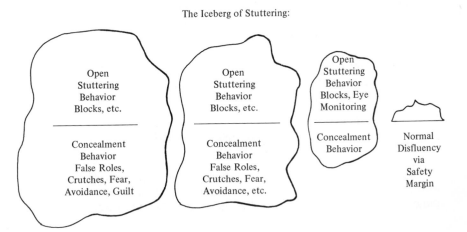

Work from the "Successes in Open Stuttering" list and draw an iceberg for each day according to whether you do more on the open side (second list) or on the hidden side (first list).

9. STUTTERING OPENLY AND EASILY

Make your stuttering a public event. Let your listener know exactly the kind of trouble you are having through an open display of your stuttering.

To do a really good job of stuttering openly, or forward, you should be open in your stuttering blocks; that is, you should stutter so that your listener can see your blocks clearly enough to describe them, and your stuttering blocks should begin to release themselves. Do not struggle, jerk, or force; just keep stuttering openly.

Collect 10 words on which you managed to get sound into your speech attempt immediately. In order to get 10, you will have to try many more than that.

The key to success in this assignment is a willingness to let the other person know that you are having some difficulty in getting the word out. You will be able to get the sound in simultaneously with the speech attempt if you are willing to have a block equivalent to the amount of fear on the word. If you try to shorten the block or to flip out the word with no stuttering at all, you will fail in the assignment. You must be willing to stutter long enough on a word to learn how to do it openly and well.

10. RESISTING TIME PRESSURE

Record instances of how you react to time pressure, and create several such situations for yourself. How much of the pressure you felt was due to the other person's behavior and how much was your own internalized time-pressure set? Note words and situations in which you hurry yourself when there is no need for it.

1. Collect five situations in which you feel time pressure put on you and are able to resist it. It does not count if your listener waits patiently for you to stutter. Telephone operators, postal clerks, bus drivers, and the like do an outstanding job of creating time pressure.
2. Collect five more situations in which you put time pressure on yourself. Note at least five words on which you hurried yourself. One of the most frequently hurried words is "Hello" on the telephone.

11. PAUSING AND PHRASING:
USE OF SILENCE

Breathing, one of the most conditionable of responses, is notoriously associated with fear states. Lapsing into silence is a natural defensive biological reaction all the way up and down the phyletic scale.

Part of your built-in time-pressure system as the stutterer is that you never pause for breath except in the "dead stops" before feared words. You need to learn to phrase normally so that you do not begin speech on residual air. Much of your problem of forcing results from your failure to pause, with initiation of long sentences on residual air, and almost inevitable hanging up even *before* your first feared word. At that point you may be long out of breath, but your intolerance of silence is such that you dare not pause. If you do, you may feel obligated to go back for a running start on the phrase, and you may actually get stuck at an earlier point. No wonder that your speech may seem hopelessly entangled in a thicket of ever-breathing phrasing changes!

1. Engage in two conversations each day for the sole purpose of working on your pausing and phrasing.
    a. First listen attentively to your own use of pauses and how long you try to make your phrases, in order to monitor.
    b. Then speak 5 consecutive sentences in which you
        (1) prewrite the sentence, planning short phrases and long pauses;
        (2) deliver the sentence as you have premarked it.
2. Since you probably have a habit of phrasing too long and pausing too short, you may not succeed at first; you may have to try 15 or more sentences in order to get 5 consecutive sentences that you do well.

12. REDUCING STRUGGLE

You struggle because you try to avoid and conceal and deny your stuttering. This is a principal source of your muscle tension. Monitor closely and observe carefully five blocks each day. After each ask yourself, "Why did I force so much? What was I trying to cover up?" It is much better to ask yourself, "Why force?" than it is to tell yourself to relax, for that only becomes a source of more tension. Though it is folly to try to relax as a means of avoiding stuttering, it is a perfectly good idea to explore how relaxedly you can stutter, provided you are open about it.

Each day see how relaxedly you can stutter on 15 words. Write down the words and rate then as to how well you succeeded. Use the scale:

	TENSION		
WORD	low		high
1.		1 2 3 4 5	

13. VOLUNTARY STUTTERING

The principle of negative practice stated that you can eliminate bad habits by practicing them consciously. Research has shown that the most effective form of voluntary stuttering is a smooth syllable prolongation, or "slide," on *nonfeared* words. You should slide or stutter voluntarily, principally on nonfeared words. You may also find it useful to slide as an alternative method of stuttering on feared words. However, initially you should confine your voluntary stuttering to nonfeared words.

Criteria for Good Voluntary Stuttering

1. Voluntary stuttering should be done with good eye contact.
2. Voluntary stuttering should be used on words that you *do not* fear.
3. To stutter voluntarily, you prolong the first sound of the word (not the vowels in the middle).
4. Voluntary stuttering uses a shift or movement, not a positing.
5. Good voluntary stuttering is unhurried.
6. Voluntary stuttering is varied in length from word to word.
7. When you are using voluntary stuttering in a situation, do not speak fluently immediately afterward.
8. Voluntary stuttering is done with a smooth release.

Assignment

1. Underline nonfeared words in a newspaper article and practice stuttering voluntarily out loud in front of a mirror following the criteria above. You should do this five minutes each day.
2. Prewrite two sentences each day, underlining the words in the sentence on which you will voluntarily stutter; then use these sentences in practice with some person you can ask to listen to you.

14. VOLUNTARY STUTTERING

One means of satisfying the fear of stuttering is to stutter voluntarily, that is, stuttering on nonfeared words in all kinds of situations. Stuttering voluntarily is an operational way of being open. This has the effect of helping you reduce the pressure that you feel when you try to avoid stuttering, and of enabling you to handle your speech more effectively in a speaking situation.

1. Stutter voluntarily to some words at home three times each day. Write down the words. Choose easy sounds to begin with, such as *"m, s, l."*
2. In three other situations each day, stutter voluntarily at least twice. Don't be alarmed if you experience some fear, tighten up, and begin to stutter in your old way. This is a common experience when beginning voluntary stuttering. Just keep on stuttering voluntarily until you can finish the word comfortably without jerking.

15. EXERCISING CHOICE

Remember, you are going to stutter. You have a reservoir of fear that at this time can only be dissipated by stuttering. Right now you have a choice about how you stutter. You may stutter more, but do it more easily by stuttering on words voluntarily when you ordinarily could say them fluently. This is one way to begin to change your way of responding to fear, and eventually it will help you lose your fear of stuttering.

This is one way to be more open in and about your stuttering. It will help you to go ahead without trying to avoid stuttering—for it is not a crutch, but a new and easier way to stutter.

1. With the first person that you talk to every morning, stutter voluntarily on the first nonfeared words that you say.
2. In five other speaking situations each day, stutter voluntarily on at least 10 nonfeared words.
3. At least once each day in a school or work situation, stutter voluntarily to someone you know well.
4. Since you're going to stutter anyway, see if you can respond to the signal of fear by stuttering easily. Keep trying this until you can do it successfully at least twice.

16. SAFETY MARGIN
AND TOLERANCE FOR DISFLUENCY

Most of you have spent a good deal of your speaking life trying to put your best foot forward, trying to speak better than you really can. You have spent years straining to talk as fluently as possible. As a result, you feel more tension, anxiety, and pressure. The result is more stuttering and less fluency. This is just another kind of vicious circle.

The basic idea of safety margin is to show the other person at all times more stuttering and less perfect speech than you really can deliver. Instead of straining to be perfect in your speech, or covering up any bad features, don't let your listener hear how good your speech can be. In doing this, you will "oversatisfy" the fear and build for fluency later on. While stuttering openly, you will have the security that comes from knowing you can speak better at any time. This is your "margin of safety."

Stuttering voluntarily is one way of building a margin of safety. You build a margin of safety by stuttering more than you have to. Oversatisfy the fear or do a little more stuttering, voluntarily or otherwise, than you would have to do in each situation. Then you do not have to strain to be as fluent as possible. Oversatisfying your fear and developing an acceptance of your natural disfluencies and bobbles will help you develop your "safety margin." As a healthy by-product of safety margin, you'll become much more fluent.

A. Keep in two columns situations in which you have oversatisfied or undersatisfied the fear. This is called a +margin or a —margin.

List the situations: for example, "Phone call to Bill Thursday Night"

+margin	—margin
1.	1.
2.	2.
3.	3.
4.	4.
5.	5.
6.	6.
7.	7.
8.	8.
9.	9.
10.	10.

B. In 10 situations each day voluntarily stutter at least three times to oversatisfy the fear. Keep a counter with you and count the number of times you voluntarily stutter while in the situation. Note whether you feel more at ease in the situation.

Rowing across the lake: The nonprogress illusion

One of the frequent problems encountered in avoidance-reduction therapy, or any therapy which recognizes the reality that fundamental changes take time, is that the person cannot readily see progress while he is in the midst of making it. Moreover, he cannot easily picture a time when he will no longer have to be "working on his speech."

The aim of avoidance-reduction therapy is not an eternal vigilance as a price for fluency; rather, the therapy aims to bring about a sufficient shrinkage of the anxiety and avoidance potential so that an effortless forward flow of speech results. Fluency comes as a by-product of the total reduction of avoidance behaviors. So does "relaxation." One should not have to keep trying to "control" something—especially when no something was there in the first place. If the stutterer is still trying to "control his stuttering," or "handle his blocks," then he has been working on a suppressive therapy, not an expressive one.

Working in therapy can be like rowing across a lake: As you leave the shore, you can see it recede from view, and you know you're getting somewhere. At the other end, when you finally near the opposite side, you can again discern definite progress, for each stroke is rewarded by a successively larger visible surge toward the final goal. But in the middle, in the longest part of the haul, you have to keep pulling on the oars over and over and over and over, without visible encouragement from either shore.

We have a clinical responsibility to point out this illusion of nonprogress, and to help the stutterer realize that he can eventually work himself out from under the need to row any longer. Personally, I never work on my speech; though with my past history of severe stuttering, I maintain a set toward attacking rather than retreating from any signal that a situation may be difficult. As with any public speaker or lecturer, I attend to my own process of speech communication and monitor my own interactions with my audience. When a stutterer reaches the point where he can work on his speech rather than just his stuttering, he has reached an operationally identifiable milestone of progress.

Improving general speaking skills: Making up for lost time

The stutterer who has recovered in adolescent or adult life, either in the clinic or by his own efforts, will have missed years of normal opportunity to sharpen general speaking skills. We know that it takes business executives and teachers, for example, years to become confident and accomplished speakers, even though they have never had a speech handicap. The recovered stutterer must make up for years, possibly, of lost opportunity to develop confident speaking skills.

In the later stages of therapy, after a stutterer has achieved a sufficient measure of fluency as a by-product of avoidance-reduction, we sometimes embark upon a crash program to help the newly recovered stutterer catch up on general speaking skills.

Aside from the obvious fact of lack of opportunity to practice and develop speaking skills in a normal fashion, there are often direct residues of the old stuttering pattern even during fluent moments. For example, I had learned a monotone and a poker voice, so had to work on stress, phrasing, pausing, and suitable inflection with appropriate emphasis. Fortunately, in the venture of sharpening up the speaker role, the principle of the will-to-health seems to be on the side of success. Once the fear, tension, and instrumental acts of avoidance and escape are reduced, there is a healthy shift toward a more normal balance and equilibrium in the speaking pattern. Monitoring, or close observation of maladaptive speaking habits, becomes appropriate, just as in the earlier monitoring for crutches.

Working on the general speaking pattern doesn't have to be just an afterthought. In many stutterers, the stuttering pattern itself is intertwined with poor speaking mannerisms: for example, the stutterer who never pauses to take a breath, who phrases all wrong, who pauses only before feared words instead of at the end of phrases or sentences.

To summarize some of the foregoing points:

1. Monitoring can be expanded to the speaking pattern, not just the stuttering pattern.

2. Many stutterers need extra help, during ending phases of therapy, in direct work on more adaptive speaking habits.
3. We do a stutterer a major disservice if we drop him out of therapy the moment he achieves a satisfactory degree of fluency. He must be helped toward a more effective pattern, unless he managed previously to develop one despite his stuttering handicap.
4. We are often asked about the value of public speaking courses for stutterers. While we would not plunge a new client into such courses, they may have a place in the closing phases of therapy.
5. Toastmaster's Clubs have been found useful for many stutterers.
6. Stutterers' clubs may be helpful, provided the group is motivated toward meeting the public instead of providing a mutual refuge and sanctuary from the world of normal speakers. Borkman (1974) concluded from her study of stuttering clubs that those which survived and were most valued by their membership were those oriented toward openness and the reduction of avoidance. Walle (1975), in his work with the Council of Adult Stutterers at Catholic University in Washington, D.C., has operated on a similar premise.
7. The stutterer should keep "initiative" in speaking at every opportunity. To catch up for lost time in developing speaking skills, he needs to increase his talking time substantially.

The surfacing of role deprivation during recovery

One of the features of the recovery stages in stuttering is that the stutterer gets to try out roles that his speaking handicap had formerly prevented. Frequently, "new" problems emerge during these periods. For example, one stutterer who had been so severe that the could not speak to girls became much too pushy in asking for dates. He simply had not learned what constituted encouragement and what did not, so that experience in role perception in this type in possible dating relationships was lacking. For a time he became a Mr. Magoo, so far as the opposite sex was concerned. The problem stemmed from previous role deprivation, not really "new" but merely brought to the surface by the new system of interactions that the attainment of relative fluency had brought about.

One of my teaching assistants, a very pretty girl, became quite frightened of one of our male stutterers who kept asking her for dates and passing her passionate notes. His attentions were all the more unwelcome and alarming because she had first tried to discourage him tactfully and gently. But he persisted, seemingly because he failed to get the message that she wanted nothing to do with him. Perhaps he would have been deficient in role perception anyway, even had he never stuttered. Our recent comparison of stutterers and normal speakers on role perception showed no differences (Sheehan and Lyon, 1974). In each group, there are some who are interpersonally insensitive. The socially clumsy stutterer we just described had perhaps acquired some of his myopia from role modeling, for his mother had struck us as insensitive. But at least in part, he seemed to be a victim of his lack of opportunity to go through a more normal trial-and-error in meeting the opposite sex during his adolescent years. Only after he was able to speak more fluently did his role skill deficiency reveal itself.

Integration in a new role: Adjustment to fluency

The handicap of stuttering involves a severe primary loss—that of the ability to communicate effectively via speech. The stutterer cannot say what he wants to say when he wants to say it. Moreover, he can't count on being able to respond at all to most elementary questions: his name, his work, where he lives, and so on. The primary loss is a huge one. Given an opportunity, most stutterers would cheerfully trade their blocked speaking for more normal and fluent speech.

The adult who has enacted the stutterer role for most of his life, even though he has been forced by fear and conflict, often finds that he cannot make the exchange so readily. Like any handicap that interferes with normal participation in certain kinds of competitive striving, stuttering can come to serve a defensive function. It can also arise in the first place as a neurotic defense. The stutterer role can become ingrained into the self-concept, even though the role is a hated one. A special kind of self-role conflict surfaces when the stutterer progresses to the point where he is speaking more fluently than is consistent with his self-concept. Sudden resistance, self-sabotage, and all sorts of related problems may emerge. The stutterer may feel, "I shouldn't be talking this well." Similar resistances to the role changes involved in improvement may be noted in psychotherapy with emotional problems, and in speech therapy with other communicative handicaps.

Since stuttering keeps its possessor out of many kinds of dangerous competition, the stutterer may have been led to believe that if only he did not stutter, there could be no limit to the greatness of his accomplishments. The Demosthenes legend fosters such an illusion. We are reminded of the case of the fellow who felt that he wasn't popular because he stuttered. When he got over it, he discovered that his friends didn't like him anyway.

There are two ways to be disappointed in life. One way is never to get the things you wish for; the other way is to get them. With the attainment of relative fluency and ease in the speaker role, the stutterer gains a strength. But in the exercise of that newfound strength, he discovers and exposes other weaknesses. His stuttering can no longer be a peg upon which to hang all his shortcomings. The defensive function, whatever there was in his particular case, is lost. He has attained parity with normal speakers, but at a price of new competition with them. The cold hard world is still the cold hard world, even after you've conquered your stuttering.

When he finally achieves a fair degree of fluency, the stutterer seems to experience reactions in two stages. First is a feeling of strangeness that he should be talking so well, a feeling almost of guilt over fluency—possibly a recathexis of some of the old guilt attached to stuttering. Unless measures are taken through psychotherapy to deal with these feelings, relapse may occur at this point, just when the stutterer appears to have found relief at last.

A second stage in the stutterer's adjustment to his fluency may involve, surprisingly, reactions of disappointment. Some painful adjustments in self-concept take place. No longer can the stutterer maintain his rationalizations of the tremendous strides he would make if only the stuttering did not hold him back.

Once he has attained fluency, the stutterer and his newfound free speech do not automatically live happily ever after, and clinical experience shows that many problems can result from fluency. Two of our cases illustrate this point. One was the cure that almost produced a divorce: A previously meek accountant used his new gift of tongue to lash back at his dominating wife, and the storms that followed almost broke up their marriage. The other case was a 15-year-old whose parents were shocked by the by-products of his sudden improvement. He went through a period of being a thoroughly revolting adolescent, and not until they were willing to accept him in a new role did the behavior problem diminish.

Because such events are not rare, continuation of therapy well beyond the first attainment of fluency is usually advisable. When fluency is reached, therapy should not terminate, but should merely enter a new final phase. Only after he has adjusted to his fluency, and to the problems resulting from his own improvement, is the stutterer ready to handle a more normal role in society.

Avoidance-Reduction Therapy for Children

Improving the demand-support ratio

That a child should falter or hesitate or block in the forward flow of his speech, when others seem so glibly fluent, has long been a mystery. One of the most stable facts concerning the disorder of stuttering has been the age of onset: typically, between 2 and 7. Whatever lies in the background of the genesis of this problem, it must make itself felt at these early ages.

In a stuttering child we see a particular kind of conflict externalized. He wants to go ahead and express himself, while at the same time he holds back! Why isn't he fluent like everyone else? Why doesn't he go forward easily? And why is his trouble greater when speaking upward to adult authority, upward on the status gap?

As an expression of what the child feels towad himself and others, stuttering does not arise out of a vacuum. There's a reason for it. It doesn't just happen. Like charity, psychopathology begins at home. Members of the family are necessarily members of the problem. The child who has begun to stutter is a statement about his parents. And they are quite correct in regarding that statement as unflattering, as a reflection on their performance in the parental role. A psychiatrist once defined the family as "a tyranny run by its sickest member." Waller (1938) pointed out long ago that the neurotic is splendidly equipped for battle in family interaction and frequently dominates the more normal spouse. And when a neurotically motivated parent stays at the command post, the children may begin to suffer the consequences.

We believe that in the literature of communication disorders, too much attention has been directed toward the speech-labeling behavior of the parents and far too little to their interpersonal behavior toward their child.

A most crucial factor appears to be what we have termed the "Demand-Support Ratio" (Sheehan, 1970a). We ask, first, what are the demands on this child? What is expected of him, exacted from him? What is he required to do? Second, what support is given him to meet the demands? We believe the Demand-Support Ratio to be a critical factor not only in the emergence of stuttering in children, but in all human interaction. For example, husband-wife, employer-employee, coach-player, and patient-therapist relationships may all be examined in the light of the demand system and the relative support provided.

A child who has begun to stutter is probably a child who has had too many demands placed upon him while receiving too little support. In every sense he is his parents' symptom.

Another stable fact on stuttering is the repeated finding of a four-to-one or five-to-one ratio of males to females (Johnson et al., 1959; Andrews and Harris, 1964; Gregory, 1972; Sheehan and Martyn, 1970; Van Riper, 1971, 1972). We offer as one partial explanation of the sex ratio in stuttering that a male child usually tends to get a little less support, while more is expected of him. For example, he is supposed to be braver, tougher, not cry so much, be more self-sufficient, manly, and so on.

Other factors may also operate, such as differences in rate of maturation, but they produce differences in the same direction as the difference in the Demand-Support Ratio.

With a very young child—3, 4, 5 or 6, and even 7 or 8 in some cases—it's probably better not to work with the child directly except as a last resort. This recommendation poses special problems for public school clinicians, because the school system often doesn't provide opportunities and incentives for working with parents.

As captives in the therapy, often as resentful captives, the parents are typically defensive and difficult to budge. Too often the system as set up assumes that the problem resides inside the child and that if the child is treated, supplemented by a "parent conference" or two, that is sufficient. But parents who have put on the magnitude of pressures that create stuttering are not so easily convinced of the folly of their ways, nor so easily dissuaded from continuing to pursue them.

Speech therapists are often seen as unmarried schoolteachers who do not really know as much as the parents know about raising children. Parents tend to assume they really know about bringing up children, showing remarkable ability to isolate themselves from the fact that they produced a problem as well as a child. Naturally enough, most parents want to believe that the problem is just within the child. They hate to recognize their own role in producing and maintaining his stuttering.

In the Rogerian tradition, we assume a will to health on the part of clients, including children who stutter. Given a chance, they will tend to get better. But the same may not be true for parents. The producers of psychopathology must have some need for the end product, if we are to stay with the psychological principle that all behavior is maintained by its consequences.

Sometimes, if you can reach even one parent, the increased support from that parent can lighten the load. The stuttering child is overburdened. Just lifting one or two or three of the burdens—the demands—will enable him to carry the load fluently.

Occasionally, the teacher becomes an important part of the child's burden. In the early grades, the child is likely to be totally at the mercy of the classroom teacher to whom he is assigned. The first teacher is particularly important; this is called the "primacy effect" in the literature on impression formation and in the literature on learning. Some parents fail to support their child when he has trouble with a teacher. They assume it must be the child's fault, and they throw the combined weight of their authority against him. The child needs to feel that someone important is on his side.

I remember well that about 25 years ago, while serving as an assistant to Wendell Johnson at the University of Iowa, I actually thought he had a parent-blaming complex. He seemed unduly tough on parents, going so far in one instance as to make the dastardly suggestion that parents should treat their own children as thoughtfully and courteously as they would a guest in their house. These days, when dealing with persistently pressuring parental behaviors, I recall that naive student reaction with both amusement and an appreciation of poetic justice.

There was also Johnson's marvelously supportive, accepting, and tolerant behavior toward his then adolescent son, who was busy testing the limits of swearing disrespect for his father whenever his graduate students would gather at their home. "If that helps Nicky feel better about himself," he would say in his warmly patient way, "that's fine with me." That same loved and respected son grew up to be not only a eloquent speaker, but a brilliant lawyer, legal-staff aide to a Supreme Court justice, head of the Maritime Commission, and forceful member of the Federal Communications Commission. Wendell Johnson's proudest moment was said to be when he was introduced to President Lyndon Johnson as "Nicky Johnson's father." That the loved and accepted son came to love, respect, and revere his father could be attested by anyone who heard Commissioner Nicholas Johnson's moving speech in reminiscence of his father at the 1970 meetings of the American Speech and Hearing Association in New York.

Putting pressures on a child is like crossing a railroad crossing without looking. Most of the time, you can get away with it; but sometimes you get caught. The parents of stutterers are those who got caught. Other parents may have been just as pressuring, but either they had a more resilient child or they produced other problems that were less embarrassingly visible than stuttering.

Parents typically show little insight into the effects of their demands on the child, or the pervasiveness of those effects. Providing the parents a clinical opportunity to see the effects of their pressures, and to see the startlingly beneficial effects of a reduction of the pressures, must rank as a fundamental goal in the counseling of the stutterogenic parent.

Parental counseling may be one time when the language of nonresponsibility may be used to good effect. Instead of charging the parents with their full measure of guilt, it is better to give them observational assignments or to let them see a sample of their interactions with the child on videotape. We observe ourselves far more objectively and effectively during videotape playback than we do during our ongoing behavior. In the Psychology Department of the University of California, Los Angeles, we have frequently used videotape feedback in this manner.

Unfortunately, it cannot always be assumed that parents love and accept their child and are willing to change their ways in order to help. Our experience dictates that this is an unworkably naive assumption. Presumably the parent is truly motivated to get rid of the problem behavior, insofar as stuttering is embarrassing and annoying. But that the parents love the child sufficiently to take stock of their ways, and change as the situation requires, is a clinical assumption that simply and unhappily does not hold in far too many cases. Unless the clinician can gauge the parents' motivation and willingness to change, he can easily lose the case and the possible opportunity to help the child.

The crucial pressures are not in relation to speech per se but to achievement pressure, especially intellectual-achievement pressure. And when young children between 2 and 7 demonstrate intellectual achievement, they do so principally through the speaking process. The act of speaking is thus set up perfectly to become a vehicle of neurotic defense. If the child stutters, then he cannot be expected to compete in the way he otherwise would. We have seen 4-year-olds who could perform impressive intellectual feats, though they blocked throughout the performance.

For those who rather naively object that such young children would be unaware or unresponsive to the parental demand system at 2, 3, or 5, we recall the story about an incessantly pressuring mother. She is pushing a stroller through the park with another toddler in hand and is stopped by another woman who exclaims, "What beautiful children! How old are they?" The mother replies, "The *doctor* is four and the *lawyer* is two." Maybe the sins of the parents aren't always visited upon the child, but their unfulfilled ambitions are.

The biggest problem in counseling parents of stuttering children is not what they have done to the child that brought on the stuttering— though that is necessarily considerable! It is what they insistently do after they are seen in the clinic, in terms of continued demands and disciplinary measures, despite the most valiant efforts of the clinician. With the development of the symptom of stuttering, the child has tried to send the parents a meassage. Somehow parents don't get the message or, if they do, they ignore its implications for changes in their own behavior.

The parental control and demand system tends to be centered around (1) the child's eating habits, (2) way he keeps his room, (3) what he wears, (4) haircuts, (5) cleanliness, (6) not too much noise, and (7) music lessons.

Defensiveness, bluffing, and incorrigibility are three chief characteristics we have encountered in parents of young stutterers. Often they are disguised by a superficial layer of guilt or a thin veneer of concern for the welfare of the child.

Some of the statements of parents are so revealing as to be self-indicting. The mother of a 4-year-old child said, "The trouble with Jimmy is that he doesn't take life seriously enough." If you think of the context out of which that comes, it makes you shudder a bit.

We recall another case: the parents who, in response to clinical recommendations, began to increase manifestations of love and support, desist from interruptions, and cut down on excess household rules, such as heavy emphasis on the child's keeping his room clean and orderly. In response to this favorable change in the Demand-Support Ratio, the child's stuttering subsided. Months later, the parents wanted to know when they could go back to treating their child "normally" again!

To take a third case: the mother of an 11-year-old girl who responded to an assignment to bring back some evidence that she was reducing her compulsive regimen of pressuring the girl to keep her room neat and spotless. Apparently feeling she was making a great concession, the mother wrote, "Let her clean her room when it needs it."

The fourth case calls for presentation in somewhat greater detail. It concerns a 16-year-old boy who began to show fairly good response to a direct, avoidance-reduction approach. He wanted to begin dating girls, a normal, healthy, and desirable response that the parents frustrated in two chief ways. First, they kept him in a male-only parochial school he hated, instead of the public school where his friends were, which he strongly wanted to attend. Second, they were niggardly about letting him use the family car, using this rare privilege as a control weapon. He had to beg earnestly before permission was begrudgingly granted, always with more strings than a kite factory.

Even after numerous conferences with parents to get them to relent from manipulative tactics, they took the following incredible action:

Before going out for an evening of pleasure, they assigned him to baby-sit for his younger sisters. At 14 and 13 respectively, they were old enough to take baby-sitting jobs, let alone merely baby-sit themselves. Enjoined by his parents from leaving the house, the boy interrupted his boring and frustrating evening by going across the street to visit a friend for 15 minutes. During this time, to his added misfortune, the parents came home early. Casting aside all the previous clinical appeals to reduce pressure and punishment, they issued an on-the-spot ultimatum: He could not drive the car again *for six months*. The father then drove him to his next therapy appointment, complaining about the inconvenience of the drive, which the father brought upon himself with his stupidly punitive tactics.

Speaking to the therapist, the boy hung his head in shame, saying "I-I-I-I g . . . g . . . g . . . goofed I-I-I r . . . r . . . really g . . . g . . . g . . . uh, goofed." His blocked speech on this shameful occasion reflected a regressive rollback to his original level of stuttering when he first began therapy. When the clinician pointed out to the parents that the boy was afraid of them, the father said proudly that he wanted it that way, for boys should respect their elders. Asked by the clinician for a commutation of the boy's six-month sentence of car-lessness to one week, or two at worst, and for a shift to a public school where he didn't have to say "sir" to all his teachers and where he might even talk to girls, the father exploded, "Ridiculous! Not a chance!" and pulled the boy out of therapy as a punishment to both boy and therapist.

What is a clinician to do in the face of such blatant incorrigibility on the part of parents? Here was a boy who was responding quite well to therapy, so far as his own actions were concerned. But speech depends on morale, and these parents were constantly demoralizing in their effects. Not even a motivated and courageous stutterer can succeed while being emotionally sabotaged and held down at home. Perhaps this is one of the reasons that the years 19–22 are significant years in the frequency of recovery from stuttering (Sheehan and Martyn, 1966, 1970). They are years of growing independence in decision-making, of significant role change in being one's own person. So long as this boy's parents manipulated and controlled him by arbitrary and prolonged punishment, his prospects for recovery are best summed up in his father's words: "Ridiculous! Not a chance!"

Ironically, the parent blamed most by the child, or against whom he expresses the most negative feeling, is often not the real culprit. The mechanism of identification with the aggressor operates to cause the child to join with his own worst enemy against the parent who is really more loving and supportive. The rejecting parent is often the more sought, and it is unsafe to cross him. But the better parent may be opposed more openly, with the impunity conferred by loving accep-tance. Later in therapy with the family, the deeper currents of feeling turn out to run opposite to those superficial but more detectable ripples.

So, we have found that the parent who is obviously getting the blame is often the more loving. He or she is more willing to accept responsibility and is so appalled by the spouse's rejection of their child that he or she wants to cover up. However, it does not have to be rejection. Just pressure—achievement pressure—is sufficient. Many ap-parently concerned and loving parents are also pressuring parents.

Pressures at school may act as precipitants. In our studies of the recovery process, sometimes the first vivid situation was at school. But we found that stuttering has its origins at home, not at school. The child stutterer is likely to be in the grip of the forces that led to his stutering in the first place.

With more advanced and mature children, it is sometimes possible to go through a series of steps similar to those in adult therapy. Even then we must cope with home and environmental pressures, or the defensive function of stuttering will reassert itself and relapse will occur. When stuttering serves as a defensive attempt to cope with a difficult situation, a purely symptomatic or behavioral approach will not be sufficient.

In situations where parents seem unwilling to change their ways, sometimes a visit to an adult stutterers' group will have a sobering effect. From behind the observation mirror, we may say something like this: "See that fellow over there with a grotesque grimaces? Unless you stop picking at your son and help him to feel more secure about himself, he's going to grow up to be like that." In other instances, techniques for the study of family interaction may be of help.

Direct work should not be undertaken until we see how the child responds to a removal of pressures. Our field has built a myth that the so-called "secondary" stutterer is likely to remain in the vicious circle forever unless assisted by therapy. For us, one of the most revealing findings of the Sheehan and Martyn studies on recovery is that so many of those who show struggle, avoidance, use tricks, have definite awareness, and use the word "stuttering" as applied to what they're doing, have a good chance of recovering unless the parents or the wrong kind of therapy gets in the way (Sheehan and Martyn, 1966, 1970; Martyn and Sheehan, 1968). Studies by Cooper (1972), Dickson (1971), and others have corroborated these findings and have presented additional data on recovery.

What if the parent is totally rejecting of our best clinical efforts to get him to take the pressures off? We fear that the cause is likely to be lost when that happens, but sometimes we try direct therapy with the child anyway. The therapy is a simplified and miniaturized version of what we do for the adult. Some of the important differences to be considered between child and adult therapy are these:

1. The child is brought.
2. The child doesn't feel the problem as his.
3. The child has fewer intellectual, conceptual resources.
4. The child often has a more fragile self-esteem, is more dependent upon peers, and is more other-directed.
5. Most important of all, the child doesn't have much to say about the things that go on in his life. He is always the victim of the decision process, never the decision-maker.
6. Primary and originating factors are more important, mechanical aspects of therapy less important.

However, we may sometimes suggest the following to the older or more mature child: (1) Everybody stutters or stumbles on words sometimes. (2) Most people just stumble along comfortably. (3) He has gotten himself into a habit of struggling against the possibility of stumbling in speech. (4) Most of those who stumble like this get over it by themselves. (5) If he accepts the idea that he will stick or stumble on a word occasionally, then he won't struggle so much against doing it. (6) If he is going to stick or stumble on a word anyway, he might as well do it smoothly and easily. (7) Talking is basically easy, and the more we do it the better we get at it. (8) It is better to go ahead anyway and say what you want to say. (9) It is not wise to substitute words or duck out of situations, such as reciting in class.

In *Stuttering: Research and Therapy* (Sheehan, 1970a), we proposed an assignment for parents as a starting point in the parental counseling process. They are asked to observe and write down, systematically, an analysis of five situations during the week when their child was most fluent and five situations in which he had the most difficulty. Some of the questions to be covered are:

1. To whom was he speaking?
2. What was he trying to say?
3. What form did his stuttering take? Note exactly.
4. What did he do in response to the difficulty he appeared to be having?
5. How did others react to his stuttering?
6. How did he react to their reactions?
7. What pressures appeared to be in the situation?

Since the frequency of stuttering when speaking to a parent figure is a rough index to the character of the interpersonal relationship, then leads for therapy are provided. The parent who fluffs off on the assignment may be providing some of the most important data of all.

In our studies of the process of "spontaneous recovery" from stuttering, we observed that some change in home environment was a significant factor in initiating the recovery process. The most obvious form of this finding was in our first report (Sheehan and Martyn, 1966), that the years 19–22 are significantly related to recovery. These are also the years of burgeoning independence and freedom from the steady tyranny of parental role expectation. Recoveries that had taken place during earlier years seem to have begun following some substantive change in the parental environment: such things as separation, divorce, bereavement, or a shift to or from a grandparent or other relative. Although we were able to obtain only the barest description of the home atmosphere in the recovery interview, we did find that tension in the home appeared to be a factor in both the onset and perpetuation of stuttering. Wingate (1964b) made a similar observation.

As is so often the case with the problem called stuttering, we experience some dissonance between our clinical observations and convictions, as against what more or less objective published studies show. According to our experience, parents of stutterers often attempt to sabotage clinical efforts to help the child. Although they may be outwardly cooperative and may even profess great burdens of guilt, they frequently persist adamantly in their rules for and demands on the child. It seems to be difficult for them to see the contribution to the child's problem of their own behavior, particularly of their rules and the demands imposed by the rules. Sometimes a relatively slight relaxation of the parent demand system, or an increase in support and positive regard, brings a substantial increase in fluency. A central problem is getting parents to change their own behavior enough to experience this positive result. Another central problem is to keep the parents from spoiling their success by reverting back to their old ways.

It is puzzling that comparison studies of parents of stutterers do not show more substantial differences from the parents of normal speaking children. An implication of our own theory, as well as that of Johnson (1946, 1961), is that the parents of stutterers might be expected to be more rigid, demanding, and perfectionistic. In other words, they should show more characteristics of the more obsessive-compulsive personality. However, available measures such as MMPI profiles[5] do not reveal systematic differences. A possible reason is that control-group parents are also pressuring, but may produce various problems other than stuttering.

Moreover, there is no reason to suppose that a parent would have to be neurotic to produce a neurosis in a child. We have studied parents who were clinically quite normal, although not very lovable, and who were quite rejecting and demanding toward certain of their own children.

It is also possible that the parental behaviors we keep observing clinically as important in stuttering are not adequately tapped by existing psychological tests such as the MMPI. We once undertook such research using PARI, the Parent Attitude Research Inventory, as developed by Bell and Vogel. We found the data difficult to come by because of parental apathy, and the preliminary results were equivocal. Kintsler (1961) tried to detect a possible factor to covert rather than overt parental rejection and claimed that mothers of stutterers showed more of the covert kind. We also have the evidence from Goldman (1967) that the sex ratio in stuttering in black stutterers in Tennessee depended on

---

[5] The Minnesota Multiphasic Personality Inventory, an empirically derived paper-and-pencil test revealing similarities between the subject's response patterns and those of diagnosed clinical groups. Validity scales are included as a check on faking, comprehension of items, and test-taking attitude. Summaries of MMPI and other personality comparisons of stutterers and their parents with normative groups may be found in Sheehan (1970a), Chapter 3.

whether a matriarchal or patriarchal pattern existed in the family. Johnson et al. (1959) also concluded from his extensive studies that the parents of stutterers tend to be somewhat more perfectionistic. Such studies are supportive evidence for the proposition that certain kinds of parental behaviors do affect the incidence of stuttering. In comparison studies, Moncur (1951, 1952, 1955) found that more mothers of stutterers gave responses indicative of parental domination, and that stuttering children more often display symptoms of maladjustment.

Since stuttering runs in families, it is not uncommon to find parents who themselves have stuttered and who have been in the lucky 80 percent who recover spontaneously without treatment (Sheehan and Martyn, 1970). On a priori grounds, one might suppose that this would be an ideal situation, for the parent who has had the problem of stuttering should be in a good position to empathize. With rare exceptions, we have found the opposite to be true. The stuttering, or ex-stuttering, parent tends to be the most intolerant of all, sometimes because he hasn't completely solved his own problem and is threatened by its appearance in his child, and sometimes because of the "I did it—I got over it—why can't he?" reaction. Sometimes also, one parent uses the stuttering child as a whipping boy, as a surrogate for the administration of disciplinary control that cannot be maintained over the spouse.

As we pointed out earlier in this chapter, there is a great divide on therapy for stuttering. There are those therapies that teach avoidance of stuttering wherever possible, try to reinforce fluency, and offer special techniques or programs aimed at the immediate suppression of stuttering. The stutterers who continue as stutterers usually try to avoid stuttering as much as possible and, for a while at least, get ecstatically happy whenever they encounter a burst of fluency. They ride the roller coaster of cyclic variation with eternal optimism. In this school of treatment we find "modern" operant conditioners who program the stutterer successfully for laboratory fluency, report this grand accomplishment in journals with triumph and pride, and then throw in almost as an afterthought the pious hope that someday they might find a way to stretch this sheltered fluency into real life. Figuratively speaking, they program the stutterer to walk a tightrope placed flat on the ground. Since the response is thereby "established," all the stutterer has to do is duplicate the feat when the tightrope is high up in the air. This is called the "transfer" phase. Keeping on keeping on is called "maintenance."

Young stutterers do not have to be "reinforced" for speaking fluently. The inherent rewards of free speech compared to that which is halting or grimacing contain more social reinforcement than any contrived experimental program. Until operant conditioners and others have really demonstrated that they can stretch laboratory fluency into real life, until they stop pretending there is no such thing as anxiety, and until they give stutterers tools for dealing with future fear, they will continue to help themselves more than they ever help the stutterers. We in the clinics will continue to get the backwash of those supposedly cured through mechanical crutches. Just playing games, as some speech therapists are reported to do, may be less destructive to a child's self-sufficiency than a modified hearing aid that will multiply with his stuttering to make him feel even more different.

By now it is probably obvious that we do not favor direct-fluency methods. Instead, we advocate an indirect fluency method, in which fluency comes as a by-product of the ultimate reduction of all avoidance, whatever the source. Among the salient points of this therapy, which we have described in publications on the approach-avoidance conflict theory of stuttering, are the following: role acceptance of ourselves as stutterers; openness in discussing stuttering; exploring what we do as we stutter; the monitoring of tricks and crutches; learning the language of responsibility; accepting stuttering as something we do, not as something that just happens as a result of fate; exploration of different styles of stuttering; learning to stutter without a key trick; learning to stutter more openly, more vocally; learning to stutter in a smooth, forward-flowing style; experiencing and overcoming the fear of silence; learning pausing and phrasing in normal patterns, rather than just dead stops before feared words; learning to recognize and desist from self-imposed time pressure; developing immunity to audience reactions that are impatient, hostile, or cloying; and learning to become one's own stuttering clinician (Sheehan, 1970a).

The older child stutterer for whom direct work is appropriate may pick from the smorgasboard of what we offer to find some dishes that are to his own liking and suited to his own needs. For example, just being supported in establishing eye contact before speaking, or getting the idea that he may stutter a little at times but does not have to struggle to speak, or learning how to stutter a little more openly and smoothly: Any of these things may strike a responsive chord in a child stutterer, and may enable him to go ahead more comfortably. Stuttering comfortably—smoothly and comfortably—is a simple idea that many young stutterers have found to be intriguing and appealing and even daring. When we get more of the stuttering iceberg above the surface, we begin to help it melt away.

Therapeutic approaches for children: Conclusions

Since this section has ranged widely in scope, we present some conclusions. With a stuttering child, members of the family are always members of the problem. Where possible, leave the child alone and treat the parents. Of crucial importance is the demand-support ratio, which may be explored through observational assignments for the parents.

The entire system of parental demands, not just those on speech, should be discovered, and the demands reduced. Support should be increased by letting the child make his own decisions a few times, for example, on what to eat, when to play, or when to go to bed. Parental bluffing and incorrigibility show up frequently during this process. Parents must be enabled to see the contribution of their pressure system to the disfluency of their child. It is useful to treat a child stutterer indirectly for a sustained period in any case. The fact that a child calls stuttering by its name doesn't mean that he's hopelessly enmeshed.

Whether a child should receive direct therapy depends not only on his age and maturity; it is also a clinical decision calling for sensitivity and judgment on the part of the therapist. When it is judged appropriate to work with a child directly, it is best to respond very permissively to his disfluencies, or his stutterings. Help him feel that talking is easy and that he should not have to struggle. Show him, if appropriate, that he has a choice in how he stutters, and that he can do it smoothly and openly. Give him the idea that he will probably continue to stutter for awhile, but that he can do it more easily. Reward him for openness and courage, not for achieved fluency. And when he does improve, keep on counseling with the parents to see that they do not put the pressures back on and start the whole cycle over again.

Summary

1. Stuttering is viewed as a double approach-avoidance conflict, having its origins in the role uncertainties of the child.

2. As a role conflict and an approach-avoidance conflict, stuttering behavior is a result of opposed urges to speak and to hold back from speaking.

3. In the double conflict, there are competing tendencies for approach and avoidance toward speaking, as well as approach and avoidance toward silence. The stutterer fears silence, as well as speech.

4. Principal hypotheses concerning stuttering behavior spring from two fundamental questions: (a) What produces blocking? (b) What determines release?

5. The conflict hypothesis: The stutterer blocks or stops whenever conflicting approach and avoidance tendencies reach an equilibrium.

6. The fear-reduction hypothesis: The occurrence of stuttering reduces the fear that elicits it sufficiently to permit release of the blocked

word, resolving the conflict momentarily and enabling the stutterer to continue.

7. The fixations and oscillations found in organisms caught in approach-avoidance conflict situations are strikingly similar to repetition and prolongation, often called the primary symptoms of stuttering.

8. Secondary stuttering behaviors appear chiefly to be instrumental response clusters adopted in a compensatory effort to go forward in the face of avoidance tendency or to reach the goal by a roundabout route. The stuttering pattern is reinforced as serial behavior, moves forward in the response sequence, and becomes overlearned, like a skilled act. In this manner, stuttering behaviors are periodically reinforced, and anxiety is "bound" within them. Stuttering is perpetuated by instrumental escape and avoidance behaviors, but tends to disappear when approach behaviors are strengthened.

9. In 80 percent of the cases in which it begins, stuttering is not perpetuated, but disappears without treatment by the time the person reaches college, provided he has faced the problem.

10. Five fairly distinct levels of conflict emerge: *word level*—conflicting urges to approach or to avoid the speaking of the feared word; *situation level*—to enter or not enter a feared situation; *feeling*—to express or inhibit the expression of heavy emotional content; *relationship*—to enter into or to avoid certain kinds of interpersonal relationship; *self-role, or ego-protective*—accepting or rejecting role-expectations, especially those for intellectual achievement. Stuttering has its origins at self and role levels, though the conflict is expressed outwardly at word and situation levels.

11. Principal ingredients in the psychology of stuttering include the following: self-esteem threat, excessive role demand, intellectual-achievement pressure, shame, guilt, anxiety about oneself, fear of failure in speaking, self-imposed time pressure, authority threat, compulsion to continue speaking once started, use of fluent asides and other false-role behaviors, maintaining flimsy pretense with the listener that nothing is out of the ordinary, frustration over primary loss of ability to communicate, occasional use of stuttering behavior as a power operation against the listener, and the ego-defensive function of the handicap in keeping the possesssor out of demanding role expectations.

12. Stuttering is not a unitary disorder, but a role-specific behavior that can be carried by individuals with widely differing personality dynamics. Possible subtypes of stutterers may be obscured by the group comparisons necessitated by statistical control.

13. Although no specific factor has ever been reliably isolated, the possibility remains that physiological or genetic predisposing factors may lie in the background of stuttering. However, it must be a factor that vanishes or ceases before adulthood in 80 percent of the cases. Though

scientifically unsatisfactory, this conclusion is made inevitable by certain persistent census-type facts: (a) universality of occurrence, (b) universal age of onset across cultures, (c) significant tendency toward spontaneous recovery or remission at puberty, (d) 25 percent familial incidence, and (3) overwhelming predominance of maleness (four- or five-to-one).

14. Despite possible predisposing factors, nearly all of what is visibly and audibly observed as stuttering behavior is learned—both by emotional (classical) conditioning and by instrumental, or motoric, conditioning. Just as speech is principally a learned skill, so is stuttering.

15. Stuttering may be considered as an example of homeostasis reversal, of antihomeostatic (positive) feedback.

16. Therapies may be divided into two classes: (a) distraction, or avoidance-cultivation, and (b) avoidance-reduction. The first was rejected, for distraction therapies have the adverse effect of increasing the avoidance tendency responsible for the stutterer's conflict, while offering him no means of coping with future apprehension and relapse.

17. Stuttering makes its first appearance in childhood, at a time when the child is speaking upward to adult authority, upward on the status dimension. A status-gap hypothesis specifies that stuttering varies with the twin factors of speaker self-esteem or status compared to listener authority or status.

18. With young children, members of the family are members of the problem and must be worked with to alter the demand-support ratio in the direction of reduced demands and increased support.

19. With adolescents, it is often necessary to combine the family therapy used with children with an adaptation of adult avoidance-reduction therapy.

20. With adults, the basic goal of therapy is the total reduction of avoidance, including all tendencies to hide, conceal, use tricks or crutches, or deny the stutterer role. Paradoxically, role acceptance as a stutterer eliminates much of the false-role behavior that comprises stuttering, and leads toward more normal speech.

21. When stuttering is viewed as an approach-avoidance conflict, total avoidance-reduction is the basic and essential goal. Avoidance-reduction therapy for stuttering involves a role-taking therapy, a psychotherapy through action. Since psychotherapy and avoidance-reduction therapy both seek to reduce "holding-back" behavior, they are compatible, both in theory and in operation.

References

Ainsworth, S. (1971) Methods for integrating theories of stuttering. In L. E. Travis, ed., *Handbook of Speech Pathology and Audiology*. 2nd ed. New York: Appleton-Century-Crofts.

Andrews, G., and Harris, M. (1964) *The Syndrome of Stuttering.* London: Heinemann Medical Books.

Aron, M. L. (1960) Some general aspects concerning stuttering which indicate fields of research. *Journal of the South African Logopedic Society*, 6, 3–7.

Aron, M. L. (1962) Nature and incidence of stuttering among a Bantu group of school-going children. *Journal of Speech and Hearing Disorders*, 27, 116–128.

Bardrick, R. A., and Sheehan, J. G. (1956) Psychotherapy and speech therapy in terms of two-factor learning theory. Paper read to Western Psychological Association. *American Psychologist*, 11, 477.

Bardrick, R. A., and Sheehan, J. G. (1958) Emotional loading as a source of conflict in stuttering. Experiment reported in J. Eisenson, *Stuttering: A symposium*, pp. 138–140. New York: Harper & Row.

Berecz, J. M. (1973) The treatment of stuttering through precision punishment and cognitive arousal. *Journal of Speech and Hearing Disorders*, 38, 256–267.

Biggs, B. E., and Sheehan, J. G. (1969) Punishment or distraction? Operant stuttering revisited. *Journal of Abnormal Psychology*, 74, 256–262.

Bloodstein, O. (1969) *A handbook on stuttering.* Chicago: National Easter Seal Society for Crippled Children and Adults.

Bloodstein, O. (1972) The anticipatory struggle hypothesis: Implications of research on the variability of stuttering. *Journal of Speech and Hearing Research*, 15, 487–500.

Borkman, T. (1974) Personal communication.

Brown, J. S. (1942) The generalization of approach responses as a function of stimulus intensity and strength of motivation. *Journal of Comparative and Physiological Psychology*, 33, 209–226.

Brown, J. S. (1948) Gradients of approach and avoidance responses and their relation to level of motivation. *Journal of Comparative and Physiological Psychology*, 41, 450–465.

Brown, S. F. (1945) The loci of stutterings in the speech sequence. *Journal of Speech Disorders*, 10, 181–192.

Brutten, E. J., and Shoemaker, D. J. (1971) A two-factor learning theory of stuttering. In L. E. Travis, ed., *Handbook of Speech Pathology and Audiology*, Second edition. New York: Appleton.

Brutten, E. J., and Shoemaker, D. J. (1967) *The modification of stuttering.* Englewood Cliffs, N.J.: Prentice-Hall.

Bryngelson, B. (1939) A study of laterality of stutterers and normal speakers. *Journal of Speech Disorders*, 4, 231–234.

Cooper, E. B. (1972) Recovery from stuttering in a junior and senior high school population. *Journal of Speech and Hearing Research*, 15, 632–638.

Cooper, E. B., Cady, B. B., and Robbins, C. J. (1970) The effect of the verbal stimulus words *wrong, right,* and *tree* on the disfluency rates of stutterers and nonstutterers. *Journal of Speech and Hearing Research*, 13, 239–244.

Dabul, B., and Perkins, W. H. (1973) The effects of stuttering on systolic blood pressure. *Journal of Speech and Hearing Research*, 16, 586–591.

Dalali, I. D., and Sheehan, J. G. (1974) Stuttering and assertion training. *Journal of Communication Disorders*, 7, 97–111.

Davies, D. A. C. (1972) *Ireland—this beautiful world.* Tokyo: Kodansha International, Ltd.

Dickson, S. (1971) Incipient stuttering and spontaneous remission of stuttered speech. *Journal of Communication Disorders*, 4, 99–110.

Dollard, J., and Miller, N. E. (1950) *Personality and psychotherapy.* New York: McGraw-Hill.

Dunlap, K. (1932) *Habits? Their making and unmaking.* New York: Liveright.

Eisenson, J. (1958) A preservative theory of stuttering. In J. Eisenson, ed., *Stuttering: A symposium.* New York: Harper & Row.

Eisenson, J. (1966) Observation of the incidence of stuttering in a special culture. *Asha* (Journal of the American Speech and Hearing Association), 8, 391–394.

Eisenson, J., and Horowitz, E. (1945) The influence of propositionality on stuttering. *Journal of Speech Disorders*, 10, 193–197.

Eisenson, J., and Wells, C. (1942) A study of the influence of communicative responsibility in a choral speech situation for stutterers. *Journal of Speech Disorders*, 7, 259–262.

Fenichel, O. (1945). *The psychoanalytic theory of neurosis.* New York: Norton.

Flanagan, B., Goldiamond, I., and Azrin, N. (1958) Operant stuttering: The control of stuttering behavior through response-contingent consequences. *Journal of Experimental Analysis of Behavior*, 1, 173–177.

Frank, A., and Bloodstein, O. (1971) Frequency of stuttering following repeated unison readings. *Journal of Speech and Hearing Research*, 14, 519–524.

Fransella, F. (1972) *Personal change and reconstruction: Research on a treatment of stuttering.* London: Academic Press.

Frederick, C. J., III. (1955) An investigation of learning theory and reinforcement as related to stuttering behavior. Ph.D. dissertation, University of California, Los Angeles.

Freud, S. (1943) *A general introduction to psychoanalysis.* New York: Garden City Books.

Freud, S. (1965) *The psychopathology of everyday life* (translated by Alan Tyson). New York: Norton.

Frick, J. V. (1951) An exploratory study of the effect of punishment (electric shock) upon stuttering behavior. Ph.D. dissertation, State University of Iowa.

Goldman, R. (1967) Cultural influences on the sex ratio in the incidence of stuttering. *American Anthropologist*, 69, 78–81.

Gould, E., and Sheehan, J. G. (1967) Effect of silence on stuttering. *Journal of Abnormal Psychology*, 72, 441–445.

Gray, B., and England, G., eds. (1969) Stuttering and the conditioning therapies. Monterey, Calif.: Monterey Institute for Speech and Hearing.

Gregory, H. H. (1969) *An assessment of the results of stuttering therapy.* Final report, Research and Demonstration Project 1725-S, Social and Rehabilitation Service, U.S. Department of Health, Education, and Welfare.

Gregory, H. H. (1972) *Stuttering: Differential evaluation and therapy.* Indianapolis: Bobbs-Merrill.

Gregory, H. H., ed. (1968) *Learning theory and stuttering therapy.* Evanston, Ill.: Northwestern University Press.

Guthrie, E. R. (1935) The psychology of learning. New York: Harper & Row.

Guthrie, E. R. (1938) The psychology of human conflict. New York: Harper & Row.

Hardin, G. (1959) *Nature and man's fate.* New York: Holt, Rinehart & Winston.

Haroldson, S. K., Martin, R. R., and Starr, C. C. (1968) Timeout as a punishment for stuttering. *Journal of Speech and Hearing Research,* 11, 560–566.

Hessell, W. F. (1971) Anxiety level in relation to time delay and stuttering during self-formulated speech. Ph.D. dissertation, University of California, Los Angeles.

Hilgard, E. R. (1948, 1956, 1967) *Theories of learning.* New York: Appleton.

Hilgard, E. R., and Marquis, D. G. (1940) *Conditioning and learning.* New York: Appleton.

Hill, H. E. (1944a) Stuttering. I. A critical review and evaluation of biochemical investigations. *Journal of Speech Disorders,* 9, 245–261.

Hill, H. E. (1944b) Stuttering. II. A review and integration of physiological data. *Journal of Speech Disorders,* 9, 289–324.

Hull, C. L. (1943) *Principles of behavior.* New York: Appleton.

Hull, C. L. (1952) *A behavior system.* New York: Appleton.

Hunt, J. (1863) *Stammering and stuttering, their nature and treatment.* London: Longmans, Green.

Ingham, R., and Andrews, J. G. (1973) Behavior therapy and stuttering: A review. *Journal of Speech and Hearing Disorders,* 38, 405–441.

Jensen, P. J., Sheehan, J. G., Williams, W. N., and LaPointe, L. L. (1975) Oral sensory-perceptual integrity of stutterers. Folia Phoniatrica (in press).

Johnson, W. (1946) People in Quandaries: The semantics of personal adjustment. New York: Harper & Row.

Johnson, W. (1961) *Stuttering and what you can do about it.* Minneapolis: University of Minnesota Press.

Johnson, W., et al. (1959) *The onset of stuttering: Research findings and implications.* Minneapolis: University of Minnesota Press.

Johnson, W., et al. (1961) Studies of speech disfluency and rate of stutterers and non-stutterers. *Journal of Speech and Hearing Disorders,* Monograph Supplement No. 7, 1–62.

Johnson, W., Brown, F., Curtis, J., Edney, C., and Keaster, J. (1967) *Speech handicapped school children,* 3rd ed. New York: Harper & Row.

Johnson, W., and King, A. (1942) An angle board and hand usage study of stutterers and nonstutterers. *Journal of Experimental Psychology,* 31, 293–311.

Johnson, W., and Knott, J. R. (1936) The moment of stuttering. *Journal of Genetic Psychology,* 48, 475–480.

Johnson, W., ed., assisted by Leutenegger, R. R. (1955) *Stuttering in children and adults: Thirty years of research at the University of Iowa.* Minneapolis: University of Minnesota Press.

Katz, M. (1970) Personal communication.

Kennedy, R. F. (1974) *Times to remember.* New York: Doubleday.

Kintsler, D. B. (1961) Covert and overt maternal rejection in stuttering. *Journal of Speech and Hearing Disorders,* 26, 145–155.

Klopfer, B. (1970) Personal communication.

Knepflar, K. J. (1965) *A comparative study of fluency in the parents of stutterers and nonstutterers.* Ph.D. dissertation, University of California, Los Angeles.

Lemert, E. M. (1953) Some Indians who stutter. *Journal of Speech and Hearing Disorders,* 18, 168–174.

Lemert, E. M. (1962) Stuttering and social structure in two Pacific societies. *Journal of Speech and Hearing Disorders,* 27, 3–10.

Lemert, E. M. (1970) Sociological perspective. In J. G. Sheehan, ed., *Stuttering: Research and therapy.* New York: Harper & Row.

Lenneberg, E. H. (1966) Speech development: Its anatomical and physiological concomitants. In E. C. Carterette, ed., *Brain function: Speech, language, and communication.* Los Angeles: University of California Press.

Lenneberg, E. H. (1967a) The biological foundations of language. *Hospital Practice,* December, 59–67.

Lenneberg, E. H. (1967b) *Biological foundations of language.* New York: Wiley.

Lewin, K. (1935) *Dynamic theory of personality.* New York: McGraw-Hill.

Lewin, K. (1951) *Field theory in social science.* New York: Harper & Row.

Luper, H. L. (1956) Consistency of stuttering in relation to the goal gradient hypothesis. *Journal of Speech and Hearing Disorders,* 21, 336–342.

MacKay, D. G. (1969) To speak with an accent: Effects of nasal distortion on stuttering under delayed auditory feedback. *Perception and Psychophysics,* 5, 183–188.

Martin, R. R. (1968) The experimental manipulation of stuttering behaviors. In H. Sloane, Jr., and B. MacAulay, eds., *Operant procedures in remedial speech and language training.* Boston: Houghton Mifflin.

Martin, R. R., and Siegel, G. M. (1966a) The effects of response contingent shock on stuttering. *Journal of Speech and Hearing Research,* 9, 340–352.

Martin, R. R., and Siegel, G. M. (1966b) The effects of simultaneously punishing stuttering and rewarding fluency. *Journal of Speech and Hearing Research,* 9, 466–475.

Martin, R. R., and Siegel, G. M. (1969) The effects of a neutral stimulus (buzzer) on motor responses and disfluencies in normal speakers. *Journal of Speech and Hearing Research,* 12, 179–184.

Martyn, M. M., and Sheehan, J. G. (1968) Onset of stuttering and recovery. *Behaviour Research and Therapy,* 6, 295–307.

Martyn, M. M., Sheehan, J. G., and Slutz, K. (1969) Incidence of stuttering and other speech disorders among the retarded. *American Journal of Mental Deficiency,* 74, 206–211.

May, A. A. (1968) A study of the presence of normal speaking disfluency in stutterers with high and low listenability ratings. Ph.D. dissertation, University of California, Los Angeles.

Meyer, V., and Mair, J. M. M. (1963) A new technique to control stammering: A preliminary report. *Behaviour Research and Therapy*, 1, 251–254.

Miller, N. E. (1944) Experimental studies of conflict. In J. McV. Hunt, ed., *Personality and the behavior disorders*, New York: Ronald.

Modigliani, A. (1971) Embarrassment, facework, and eye contact: Testing a theory of embarrassment. *Journal of Personality and Social Psychology*, 17, 15–24.

Moncur, J. P. (1951) Environmental factors differentiating stuttering children from nonstuttering children. *Speech Monographs*, 18, 312–325.

Moncur, J. P. (1952) Parental domination in stuttering. *Journal of Speech and Hearing Disorders*, 17, 155–165.

Moncur, J. P. (1955) Symptoms of maladjustment differentiating young stutterers from nonstutterers. *Child Development*, 26, 91–96.

Mowrer, O. H. (1947) On the dual nature of learning—a reinterpretation of "conditioning" and "problem-solving." Harvard Educational Review, 17, 102–148.

Mowrer, O. H. (1956) Two-factor learning theory reconsidered, with special reference to secondary reinforcement and the concept of habit. *Psychological Review*, 63, 114–128.

Mowrer, O. H., and Viek, P. (1948) An experimental analogue of fear from a sense of helplessness. *Journal of Abnormal and Social Psychology*, 43, 193–200.

Murray, F. P. (1958) Observations on therapy for stuttering in Japan. *Journal of Speech and Hearing Disorders*, 23, 243–249.

Mysak, E. D. (1960) Servo theory and stuttering. *Journal of Speech and Hearing Disorders*, 25, 188–195.

Mysak, E. D. (1966) *Speech pathology and feedback theory*. Springfield, Ill.: Charles Thomas.

Patty, J., and Quarrington, B. (1974) The effects of reward on types of stuttering. *Journal of Communication Disorders*, 7, 65–77.

Perkins, W. H. (1970) Physiological studies. In J. G. Sheehan, *Stuttering: research and therapy*. New York: Harper & Row.

Perkins, W. H. (1971) *Speech pathology: an applied behavioral science*. St. Louis: Mosby.

Porter, H. V. K. (1939) Studies in the psychology of stuttering: Stuttering phenomena related to size and personnel of audience. *Journal of Speech Disorders*, 4, 323–333.

Prins, D. (1970) Improvement and regression in stutterers following short-term intensive therapy. *Journal of Speech and Hearing Disorders*, 35, 123–134.

Prins, D. (1972) Personality, stuttering severity, and age. *Journal of Speech and Hearing Research*, 15, 148–154.

Pruett, H. L. (1968) Persistence and level of aspiration in stutterers. Ph.D. dissertation, University of California, Los Angeles.

Ringel, R. L., and Minifie, F. D. (1966) Protensity estimates of stutterers and non-stutterers. *Journal of Speech and Hearing Research*, 9, 289–296.

Robinson, F. B. (1964) *An introduction to stuttering*. Englewood Cliffs, N.J.: Prentice-Hall.

Ryan, J. K. (1960) Translation. *The confessions of St. Augustine*. New York: Image.

Ryan, B. P. (1971) Operant procedures applied to stuttering therapy for children. *Journal of Speech and Hearing Disorders*, 36, 264–280.

Ryan, B. P., and Van Virk, B. (1974) The establishment, transfer, and maintenance of fluent speech in 50 stutterers using delayed auditory feedback and operant procedures. *Journal of Speech and Hearing Disorders*, 39, 3–10.

Sarbin, T. R. (1943) The concept of role-taking. *Sociometry*, 6, 273–285.

Sarbin, T. R. (1964) Role theoretical interpretation of psychological change. In P. Worchel and D. Byrne, eds., *Personality change*. New York: Wiley.

Sarbin, T. R., and Allen, V. L. (1968) Role theory. In G. L. Lindzey and E. Aronson, eds., *Handbook of social psychology*, 2nd ed. Reading, Mass.: Addison-Wesley.

Shearer, W. M., and Williams, J. D. (1965) Self-recovery from stuttering. *Journal of Speech and Hearing Disorders*, 30, 288–290.

Sheehan, J. G. (1946) *A study of the phenomena of stuttering*. M.A. thesis, University of Michigan.

Sheehan, J. G. (1950a) A theory of stuttering as approach-avoidance conflict. Paper read to Western Psychological Association. *American Psychologist*, 5, 469.

Sheehan, J. G. (1950b) The fight to speak. "University Explorer" broadcast, University of California, Berkeley. Columbia Broadcasting System.

Sheehan, J. G. (1951) The modification of stuttering through nonreinforcement. *Journal of Abnormal and Social Psychology*, 46, 51–63.

Sheehan, J. G. (1953a) Theory and treatment of stuttering as an approach-avoidance conflict. *Journal of Psychology*, 36, 27–49.

Sheehan, J. G. (1953b) Rorschach changes during psychotherapy in relation to personality of the therapist. *American Psychologist*, 8, 434–435.

Sheehan, J. G. (1954a) An integration of psychotherapy and speech therapy through a conflict theory of stuttering. *Journal of Speech and Hearing Disorders*, 19, 474–482.

Sheehan, J. G. (1954b) Rorschach prognosis in psychotherapy and speech therapy. *Journal of Speech and Hearing Disorders*, 19, 217–219.

Sheehan, J. G. (1956) Stuttering in terms of conflict and reinforcement. In E. Hahn, ed., *Stuttering: Significant theories and therapies*, 2nd ed. Stanford, Calif.: Stanford University Press.

Sheehan, J. G. (1957) The marital status of psychoanalysis and learning theory. *American Psychologist*, 12, 277–278.

Sheehan, J. G. (1958a) Conflict theory of stuttering. In J. Eisenson, ed., *Stuttering: A symposium*. New York: Harper & Row.

Sheehan, J. G. (1958b) Projective studies of stuttering. *Journal of Speech and Hearing Disorders*, 23, 18–25.

Sheehan, J. G. (1964a) Stuttering as approach-avoidance conflict. In C. R. Reed, I. E. Alexander, and S. S. Tomkins, eds., *Psychopathology: A source book*. Reissued, Science ed., Wiley Paperbacks, 303–325.

Sheehan, J. G. (1968a) Stuttering as a self-role conflict. In H. H. Gregory, ed., *Learning theory and stuttering therapy*. Evanston, Ill.: Northwestern University Press.

Sheehan, J. G. (1968b) *The iceberg of stuttering*. Educational film, 55 minutes. Produced by station ACF, University of California, Los Angeles.

Sheehan, J. G. (1969a) Cyclic variation in stuttering: Comment on Taylor and Taylor's "Test of predictions from the conflict hypothesis of stuttering." *Journal of Abnormal Psychology*, 74, 452–453.

Sheehan, J. G. (1969b) The role of role in stuttering. In B. Gray and G. England, eds., *Stuttering and the conditioning therapies*. Monterey, Calif.: Monterey Institute for Speech and Hearing.

Sheehan, J. G. (1970a) *Stuttering: Research and therapy*. New York: Harper & Row.

Sheehan, J. G. (1972) Reflections on the behavioral modification of stuttering. In C. W. Starkweather, ed., *Conditioning in stuttering therapy*. Memphis: Speech Foundation of America, 123–136.

Sheehan, J. G. (1972) A new venture into the nonreinforcement of stuttering. In E. P. Trapp and P. Himelstein, eds., *Readings on the exceptional child*. New York: Appleton.

Sheehan, J. G. (1974) Stuttering behavior: A phonetic analysis. *Journal of Communication Disorders*, 7, 193–212.

Sheehan, J. G. (1975) The effect of role commitment on stuttering. *Journal of Abnormal Psychology*, 83. (In press.)

Sheehan, J. G., et al. (1964b) Characteristics and qualifications of the clinical supervisor. In *Seminar on Programs of Training for Speech Pathologists and Audiologists*. Washington, D.C.: American Speech and Hearing Association.

Sheehan, J. G., Cortese, P. A., and Hadley, R. G. (1962) Guilt, shame, and tension in graphic projections of stuttering. *Journal of Speech and Hearing Disorders*, 27, 129–139.

Sheehan, J. G., and Costley, M. S. (1975) A reevaluation of the role of heredity in stuttering. *Journal of Speech and Hearing Disorders*, 40, in press.

Sheehan, J. G., Hadley, R. G., and Gould, E. (1967) Impact of authority on stuttering. *Journal of Abnormal Psychology*, 72, 290–293.

Sheehan, J. G., and Lyon, M. (1974) Role perception in stuttering. *Journal of Communication Disorders*, 7, 113–125.

Sheehan, J. G., and Martyn, M. M. (1966) Spontaneous recovery from stuttering. *Journal of Speech and Hearing Research*, 9, 121–135.

Sheehan, J. G., and Martyn, M. M. (1967) Methodology in studies of recovering from stuttering. *Journal of Speech and Hearing Research*, 10, 396–400.

Sheehan, J. G., and Martyn, M. M. (1970) Stuttering and its disappearance. *Journal of Speech and Hearing Research*, 13, 279–289. Reprinted in E. P.

Trapp and P. Himelstein, *Readings on the exceptional child.* New York: Appleton, 1972.

Sheehan, J. G., and Martyn, M. M. (1971) Therapy as seen by stutterers. *Journal of Speech and Hearing Research,* 14, 445–446.

Sheehan, J. G., and Martyn, M. M., (1975) Patterns of recovery from stuttering. *Journal of Communication Disorders* (in press).

Sheehan, J. G., Martyn, M. M., and Kilburn, K. L. (1968) Speech disorders in retardation. *American Journal of Mental Deficiency,* 73, 251–256.

Sheehan, J. G., and Voas, R. B. (1954) Tension patterns during stuttering in relation to conflict, anxiety-binding, and reinforcement. *Speech Monographs,* 21, 272–279.

Sheehan, J. G., and Voas, R. B. (1957) Stuttering as conflict: A comparison of therapy techniques involving approach and avoidance. *Journal of Speech and Hearing Disorders,* 22, 714–723.

Sheehan, J. G., and Zelen, S. L. (1955) Level of aspiration in stutterers and non-stutterers. *Journal of Abnormal and Social Psychology,* 51, 84–86.

Sherrad, C. A. (1975) Stuttering as "false alarm" responding. *Perception and Psychophysics* (in press).

Siegel, G. M. (1970) Punishment, stuttering, and disfluency. *Journal of Speech and Hearing Research,* 13, 677–714.

Silverman, F. H., and Williams, D. E. (1971) The adaptation effect for six types of speech disfluency. *Journal of Speech and Hearing Research,* 14, 525–530.

Sitzman, R. B. (1968) *Stuttering as a function of word predictability.* Ph.D. dissertation, University of California, Los Angeles.

Skinner, B. F. (1953) *Science and human behavior.* New York: Macmillan.

Solomon, R. L. (1964) Punishment. *American Psychologist,* 19, 239–253.

Solomon, R. L., and Brush, E. S. (1956) Experimentally derived conceptions of anxiety and aversion. In M. R. Jones, ed., *Nebraska symposium on motivation.* Lincoln: University of Nebraska Press.

Speech Foundation of America (1972) *To the stutterer* Memphis, Tenn.: Fraser.

Speech Foundation of America (1964) *Stuttering: Treatment of the young stutterer in the schools.* Memphis, Tenn.: Fraser.

Stewart, J. L. (1959) Problem of stuttering in certain North American Indian societies. *Journal of Speech and Hearing Disorders,* supplement, 6, 1–87.

Stromsta, C. P. (1956) A methodology related to the determination of the phase angle of bone-conducted speech sound energy of stutterers and non-stutterers. *Dissertation Abstracts,* 16, 1738–1739.

Stromsta, C. P. (1959) Experimental blockage of phonation by distorted sidetone. *Journal of Speech and Hearing Research,* 2, 286–301.

Stunden, A. A. (1965) The effects of time pressure as a variable in the verbal behavior of stutterers. *Dissertation Abstracts,* 26, 1784–1785.

Šváb, L., Gross, J., and Langová, J. (1972) Stuttering and social isolation: Effect of social isolation with different levels of monitoring on stuttering frequency: A pilot study. *Journal of Nervous and Mental Disease,* 155, 1–5.

Van Riper, C. (1936) A study of the thoracic breathing of stutterers during expectancy and occurrence of stuttering spasms. *Journal of Speech Disorders*, 1.

Van Riper, C. (1937a) The effects of penalty upon frequency of stuttering spasms. *Journal of General Psychology*, 50.

Van Riper, C. (1937b) Effect of devices for minimizing stuttering on the creation of symptoms. *Journal of Abnormal Social Psychology*, 32, 185–192.

Van Riper, C. (1937c) The growth of the stuttering spasm. *Quarterly Journal of Speech*, 23, 70–73.

Van Riper, C. (1938) A study of the stutterer's ability to interrupt the stuttering spasm. *Journal of Speech Disorders*, 3, 117–119.

Van Riper, C. (1947) *Speech correction: Principles and methods*, 2nd ed. Englewood Cliffs, N.J.: Prentice-Hall.

Van Riper, C. (1971) *The nature of stuttering*. Englewood Cliffs, N.J.: Prentice-Hall.

Van Riper, C. (1972) *Speech correction*, 5th ed. Englewood Cliffs, N.J.: Prentice-Hall.

Van Riper, C. (1973) *The treatment of stuttering*. Englewood Cliffs, N.J.: Prentice-Hall.

Villarreal, J. J. (1950) Two aspects of stuttering therapy. *Journal of Speech and Hearing Disorders*, 15, 215–220.

Walle, E. L. (1975). Personal communication.

Waller, W. (1938) *The family: A dynamic interpretation*. New York: Holt, Rinehart & Winston.

Williams, D. E. (1957) A point of view about stuttering. *Journal of Speech and Hearing Disorders*, 22, 390–397.

Williams, D. E. (1971) Stuttering therapy for children. In L. E. Travis, ed., *Handbook of speech pathology and audiology*. New York: Appleton.

Williams, J. D., and Martin, R. B. (1974) Immediate versus delayed consequences of stuttering responses. *Journal of Speech and Hearing Research*, 17, 569–575.

Wingate, M. E. (1959) Calling attention to stuttering. *Journal of Speech and Hearing Research*, 2, 326–335.

Wingate, M. E. (1964a) A standard definition of stuttering. *Journal of Speech and Hearing Disorders*, 29, 484–489.

Wingate, M. E. (1964b) Recovery from stuttering. *Journal of Speech and Hearing Disorders*, 29, 312–321.

Wingate, M. E. (1966) Stuttering adaptation and learning. I. The relevance of adaptation studies to stuttering as learned behavior. *Journal of Speech and Hearing Disorders*, 31, 148–156.

Wingate, M. E. (1970) Effect on stuttering of changes in audition. *Journal of Speech and Hearing Research*, 13, 861–873.

Wischner, G. J. (1952) Anxiety-reduction as reinforcement in maladaptive behavior: Evidence in stutterers' representations of the moment of difficulty. *Journal of Abnormal Psychology*, 47, 566–571.

Wischner, G. J., Brown, S., Sheehan, J. G., and West, R. (1959) The problem of stuttering and problems of rate and fluency. In W. Johnson, ed.,

Research needs in speech pathology and audiology, *Journal of Speech and Hearing Disorders,* monograph supplement, 5, 26–30.

Worell, L. (1965) The ring of punishment. *Journal of Abnormal Psychology,* 70, 201–209.

Wyneken, C. (1868) Ueber das stottern und dessen heilung [Concerning stuttering and its cure]. *Zeitschrift fur Rationelle Medizin,* 31, 1–29.

Yerkes, R. M. and Dodson, J. D. (1908) The relation of strength of stimulus to rapidity of habit-formation. *Journal of Comparative Neurology and Psychology,* 18, 459–482.

Zelen, S. L., Sheehan, J. G., and Bugental, J. (1954) Self-perceptions in stuttering. *Journal of Clinical Psychology,* 10, 70–72.

III

Stuttering: Topography, Assessment, and Behavior-Change Strategies

Gene J. Brutten, Ph.D.

Research Professor of Speech Pathology, Professor of Psychology, Southern Illinois University; Former Fulbright Professor, University of Utrecht, Holland. Fellow of the American Speech and Hearing Association. Coauthor (with Donald J. Shoemaker) of *The Modification of Stuttering;* contributor to professional journals and handbooks.

W hat stuttering is and what can be done to bring about its modification are inexorably tied together. What the therapist can do depends on the particular behaviors involved. But even those clinicians who are behaviorally oriented have often neglected to specify the responses they seek to modify. Instead, all too often, they have directed their attention to moments of stuttering.

Moments indicate only that some undefined event has occurred at some particular instant, which in some way is judged to be stuttering. The behavioral characteristics of stuttering moments are not specified. They are not made explicit even though the component behaviors are neither constant from instant to instant nor from speaker to speaker.

The Stuttering Moment:
A Behavioral Analysis

Undefined moments have become the basic clinical and experimental unit because of a lack of agreement about what constitutes the behaviors called "stuttering." It is no easy matter to discriminate the behavioral characteristics of stuttering and to distinguish them from those of normal speech and from other forms of fluency failure. The use of moments made it possible to temporarily skirt these essential distinctions. Moments are so molar—relate to units so large—that stuttering behaviors were thought likely to be caught in the net even though they were not specified. But moments masked more than they revealed. Their behavioral elements were never fully described. Furthermore, the reliance on moments diverted attention from behavioral specifications fundamental to the definition of stuttering and from the differential assessments that behavior therapists find basic to modification (Mischel, 1968; Kanfer and Phillips, 1970; Brutten, 1973).

Other difficulties have derived from the concept of stuttering moments. One of the more insidious ones is the tendency to view them as a response compound rather than as a mixture of behaviors. Moments have come to be treated as if their separate behaviors are fused together into a constant entity. Not even the early and dramatic finding that different moments are composed of only a few of the same behavioral components seemed to affect a change. The presence of specific and changing behavioral elements within each moment received little attention even though the tools for a more precise molecular analysis were available. Johnson and his students (1959, 1961) had specified operations by which at least eight forms of dysfluency could be discriminated. Moreover, molecular analysis had an early beginning in the work of Barr (1940), who explored the behaviors present during stuttering moments. Similarly, in 1946, Sheehan quantitatively analyzed the audible behaviors that stutterers display. Barr's research led her to stress that what was theoretically and clinically important was a specific understanding about stutterings. For this reason, she studied "the events observable during those discrete moments of behavior which are regarded as examples of stuttering" (p. 277). Sheehan (1973) also pointed out that the elements of the moment were significant for differential diagnostic and therapeutic decisions. He contended that a need exists for determining which behaviors constitute stuttering so that normal speakers could be differentiated from the stutterer. His research led him to suggest that stutterers and nonstutterers could be distinguished by the different dysfluency types they display. Further, he called for discrimination between repetitions and prolongations, behaviors common to those who stutter, and the responses that they "employed as instrumental acts to satisfy fear and bring about termination of the block."

Despite the enlightened call for more precision, the use of the molar moment prevailed. Only recently has there been a concerted effort at molecular analysis. The molecular search for the behaviors that differentially define stuttering and dictate clinical strategies was not undertaken in an organized fashion until long after the initial probings of Barr and Sheehan. It arose again because of the two-factor theory of stuttering and associated behaviors and the factorial implications of the distinction between classical and instrumental conditioning (Bloodstein and Brutten, 1966; Brutten and Shoemaker, 1967; Brutten, 1970).

Two-factor theory, a framework based on differences in learning categories, gave renewed impetus to behavioral specification in studies of stuttering. The theory was tested initially in a study by Webster and Brutten (1972). In this cinematic analysis of the molar moment, four different behaviors displayed by a single subject were minutely followed during repeated oral readings of the same passage. Part-word repetition, repetitions that were predominantly of a single syllable, interjections of sounds that were not an integral part of the words spoken, and eye blinks were inspected separately and independently. From this molecular analysis it became apparent that all of these elements did not follow the same course and that molar moments did not equally represent all of the behavioral components. The part-word and single-syllable repetitions did not correlate significantly with either interjections or eye blinks, and the direction taken by the summated molar moments was often different from that of a particular behavior. Molar moments turned out to be a mixture of behaviors whose elements were often dissimilar from each other and from the totality. Thus, molecular analysis revealed that the molar moments were not a unique compound and that to deal in moments was to do an injustice to the separate behavioral components.

Similar findings were uncovered by Sakata and Adams (1972), who also studied the frequency and course of individual behaviors. It was their purpose to test what they saw as a discrepancy between the contention that the stuttering moment is a functional unit and the Brutten-Shoemaker (1969, 1971) contention that the molar moment is a concept that obscures significant behavioral differences. Although the behavioral repertoire of their subjects differed somewhat from those in the previous study, they also found that the moment of stuttering is not a compound. Each subject's behaviors decreased somewhat during the repeated oral readings of the same material, but they did not change to the same extent or in the same way. For example, interjections showed a marked absolute decrease, yet some of the other behaviors varied very little. Clearly, moments of stuttering did not adequately reflect the distinctive patterns of the separate behaviors. The correlational matrix varied from a $+.925$ for part- and whole-word repetitions to a nonsignificant $+.375$ for phrase repetitions and interjections. Moreover, many of the measured behaviors differed significantly from each other in their rate of adaptation. The experiment substantiated the Webster and Brutten findings. The investigators agreed that there were substantial disparities among the behaviors which are a part of the molar moment and that a real need to discriminate among them through a more analytic approach exists.

Zenner (1971) also made a molecular analysis of stuttering moments. His stutterers exhibited various "primary" and "secondary" behaviors. Each of the verbal and nonverbal behaviors studied were ones that would traditionally be seen as integral aspects of stuttering moments. Yet, they did not generally behave like moments of stuttering. Only 12 of the 71 behaviors displayed by the individual speakers correlated significantly with moments, and these did not do so consistently. The co-varying behaviors tended to differ from subject to subject. In addition, some of the significant co-relationships were inverse; the course taken by stuttering moments was on occasion opposite from that taken by a particular behavior. These data led Zenner to make an insistent call for the separate analysis of behaviors and the abandonment of molar measurement.

The evidence that stuttering moments are mixtures of different be-haviors which act in differing ways is certainly not limited to studies which require the massed repetitive readings of constant material. The same findings are observed whether the subject reads aloud continuously changing contextual material or speaks extemporaneously. This is exem-plified in Figure 1, which graphically displays the frequency and course of 9 different behaviors during 30 minutes of continuous oral reading. Though the general trend is decremental, the trial-by-trial occurrence of each of the behaviors is clearly individualistic. The frequencies of this stutterer's behaviors are observably different, and moments are anything but compounds whose constituents had been fused together into a new substance. Similar findings were also made apparent by the extensive research of Prins and Lohr (1968, 1972). In one portion of their larger study on the behavioral components of stuttered speech, they recorded audible and visible aspects of stuttering moments. These measurements were made while the subjects repeatedly read aloud the same passage

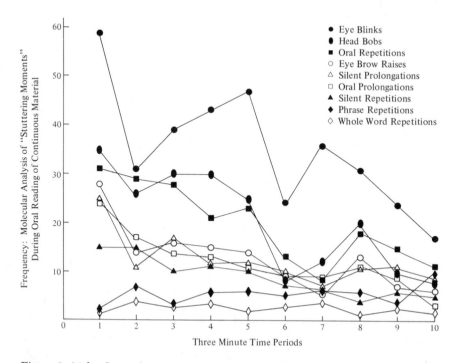

Figure 1. Molecular analysis of the behavioral elements of an individual's stuttering moments during oral reading of continuous material (after Schweizer, 1975).

and while they spoke extemporaneously. In both of these speech circumstances, it was evident that the moments encompassed combinations of various and changing behaviors. The moment of stuttering was not a unitary phenomenon in either of the speech settings. Consequently, Prins and Lohr (1968) concluded that a real need exists for a multidimensional description that would take into consideration the "several relatively independent audible-visual factors of stuttering."

Stuttering and associated behaviors: Factoring the molar moment

The inadequacy of stuttering moments need not be belabored. The molar moment is neither behaviorally descriptive nor consistently representative of its ever-changing components. Zenner (1971) has pointed out that many of the measured elements of the behavioral mixture evidenced at fixed moments in time showed a nonsignificant covariation. Sakata and Adams (1972) have pointed out that only certain of the behaviors correlated significantly. This finding was consonant with those of both the Webster and Brutten (1972) and the Prins and Lohr (1968) studies. But probably nowhere is the independence of certain aspects of stuttering moments more evident than in the study conducted by Oelschlaeger (1971). One aspect of her study involved an analysis of phoneme repetitions, interjections, and word rate by means of multiple linear regression. This analysis revealed that the correlations between these three particular behaviors were generally negligible. No one of these behaviors could serve adequately as a predictor variable for any other one. For example, information about the occurrence of part-word repetitions did not allow one to predict successfully the occurrence of interjections. This was not surprising since the intercorrelations were $-.028$, $+.179$, $-.151$, and $+.008$ for the two individual subjects studied in two separate experiments. It was apparent that "behaviors traditionally regarded as stuttering operate independently of one another, thus precluding the prediction of one from the other. This evidence lends further support to the contention that the use of the molar definition of stuttering is inappropriate" (Oelschlaeger, 1971, p. 106).

To be sure, there is a general lack of covariance between specific behaviors and the molar moment. But not all of the behaviors displayed by individuals who stutter failed to correlate significantly. The first indication that this was indeed the case came from the Webster and Brutten study (1972). Though part-word repetitions and interjections did not correlate significantly, two significant and disparate clusters became apparent among the four behaviors they studied. As the correlational matrix shown in Table 1 points up, part-word repetitions and repetitions of single-syllable words correlated significantly. So too did eye blinks and interjections. None of the other combinations co-varied, however.

TABLE 1
SPEARMAN RANK CORRELATIONS AMONG MOLECULAR ELEMENTS
OF AN INDIVIDUAL'S MOLAR MOMENTS OF STUTTERING

Behaviors	Correlation
whole- and part-word repetitions	+ .800*
whole-word repetitions and interjections	+ .558
whole-word repetitions and eye blinks	+ .286
part-word repetitions and interjections	+ .215
part-word repetitions and eye blinks	− .200
interjections and eye blinks	+ .843*

* Significant at 0.05 level.

These data deserve careful consideration, especially since prior to the beginning of the experiment the subject defined part-word repetition as an involuntary behavior and eye-blinking as a voluntary adjustment.[1] He did not comment about either of the other two behaviors; he seemed unaware of their occurrence. Nevertheless, the repetitions of single-syllable words were counted because they, like the reportedly involuntary part-word repetitions, have been considered phenotypic of stuttering. The unreported interjections were also followed because, like the voluntary eye blinks, these behaviors have been seen as secondary to stuttering. It is of more than passing interest that the behaviors thought to define stuttering correlated significantly with each other. So, too, did those considered to be secondary behaviors. Even more impressive was the fact that the stuttering behaviors did not correlate significantly with the secondary ones. Two different classes of behaviors seemed to have been factored from this subject's moments. These findings are consistent with those of Oelschlaeger (1971), who also found that phoneme repetitions and interjections did not correlate significantly, and with the data of Sakata and Adams (1972), whose study revealed a significant correlation between part- and whole-word repetitions but the absence of one between these repetitions and interjections.

The neat separation of behaviors into two categories has not been supported by all molecular research. Interjections and phrase repetitions, behaviors considered to be secondary to stuttering, did not correlate significantly according to Sakata and Adams. Zenner (1971) also found that the behaviors he defined as secondary did not necessarily correlate.

[1] On two separate occasions prior to this experiment, the subject described the behaviors that he viewed as component parts of his "stuttering." On these occasions, he consistently specified those behaviors that he felt were involuntary and those which he used as purposive adjustments.

However, most of his subjects evidenced a statistically significant relationship between part- and whole-word repetition. This co-relationship might have been even more consistently apparent if the definition of whole-word repetitions did not include both unisyllabic and multisyllabic words. Nevertheless, it does seem clear that the presence of one form of behavior does not *necessarily* indicate the presence or absence of still another form. It is not necessary, in other words, for individuals who stutter to display both repetitions and prolongations of a phoneme or to exhibit them simultaneously. In the same vein, interjections and eye blinks do not occur among all stutterers, and they need not correlate positively with each other and negatively with phonemic repetition and prolongation. In brief, the behavioral repertoires of stutterers show individual differences, and the behavioral patterns evidenced by a single stutterer are not entirely predictable.

Although the data have illustrated more than a trend for certain behaviors to correlate positively, others to co-vary negatively, and still others to show no necessary concordance, it is apparent that individual differences exist. To place the behaviors of stutterers in a proper perspective, both their independence and co-relationship need to be recognized. It was this fact that led Prins and Lohr (1968) to observe the audiovisual behaviors of 19 stutterers. Since they were concerned with differential behavioral assessment as a guideline for choosing therapeutic procedures, they explored the presence or absence of commonalities among the different behaviors by factor analysis. By this means the behaviors that had an underlying commonality clustered together, or loaded, on the same factor; it was possible to get a more fundamental look at the co-relationship between molecular aspects of a speaker's performance than is likely with simple correlational procedures like those used in the studies just reviewed.

Ten factors were computed from the extemporaneous speech data and these showed that whole-word repetitions, phrase repetitions, revisions, incomplete phrases, and broken words loaded on the first factor, along with part-word repetitions and prolongations. However, the first five behaviors loaded negatively on factor one, while part-word repetitions and prolongations loaded positively. This suggested that two behavioral clusters existed. This was made even more apparent when maximizing procedures were used to clarify distinctions. When behaviors were assigned to the factors where their loading was the highest, phrase repetition, interjection, and prolongation loaded on the same factor, the first two positively and the third negatively (−0.80). Data like these led Prins and Lohr to compare all of their relevant findings with the two-factor behavioral separations predicted by Brutten and Shoemaker (1967, 1971). Their two-factor theory proposes that involuntary repetitions and prolongations of simple and compound phonemes are the result of classically conditioned negative emotion and that these behaviors are fundamentally different from voluntary adjustive responses like revisions, phrase repetitions, and interjections. The two-factor behavioral distinctions were supported. As Prins and Lohr pointed out, 7 of the 10 factors were consonant with the predictions. On this basis they stated that "Brutten and Shoemaker's hypothesis concerning two basically different behavioral components in stuttering is supported by the factor analysis data. The factors show a definite separation pattern" (Prins and Lohr, 1972, p. 69).

Two-Factor
Behavior Theory

In one form or another, two-factor views about learning have been present for well over half a century. They have persisted because it is apparent that organisms learn as a result of two quite different conditioning procedures. This fact has been recognized by nomenclature that distinguishes between Type I and II learning, respondent and operant conditioning, and learning that is either problem-making or problem-solving. Commonly, the two conditioning categories are referred to as "classical" and "instrumental." Classical conditioning procedurally involves the contingent relationship between two stimuli, whereas instrumental conditioning is a function of stimulation that is response contingent. In one case, that is, the stimulation is consequent upon some aspect of the stimulus situation and in the other it is a consequence of the response made. These procedural differences are clear even if the process or processes that underlie the conditioning of the two classes of events have not been fully determined.

Classical conditioning

Classical conditioning, as we have already stated, procedurally depends on the relationship between two stimuli, one most properly called a "*conditional* stimulus" (C.S.) and the other an "*unconditional* stimulus" (Uc.S.).[2] The Uc.S. has the name it does because it unconditionally evokes behavior that is called an "unconditional response" (Uc.R.). This

---

[2] These stimuli and the responses associated with them have frequently been referred to as "conditioned" and "unconditioned." These terms may be used interchangably with "conditional" and "unconditional," though the latter two words are a truer reflection of Pavlov's intentions.

is a basic response to the stimulus, one that is not dependent on learning. An Uc.S. is inherently capable of calling forth behavior.[3]

C.S.'s do not unconditionally evoke a particular response; in this sense they are "neutral" stimuli. The organism may evidence an orienting reaction when a C.S. is present, but little more will usually occur. If, however, an Uc.S. is made *contingent* upon a C.S., the relatively neutral stimulus ultimately becomes capable of evoking a different behavior. In other words, in order for the C.S. to evoke a response that it did not previously elicit, it must be contingently paired with an Uc.S. Its evoking potential is conditional upon this contingency. A conditional response (C.R.) will not be called forth by the C.S. if this stimulus and the Uc.S. have been randomly paired (Rescorla, 1967). Mere association between the stimuli is not sufficient. The learning that leads to a C.R. is dependent on some scheduled arrangement between the C.S. and Uc.S., such that when one of these stimulus events occurs, the other is likely to follow. The classic example of these scheduled S-S (stimulus-stimulus) arrangements are the Pavlovian ones in which Uc.S.'s like shock or food, are made contingent upon an originally neutral C.S., like a tone or light. Pavlov's dogs soon learned to respond to these C.S.'s as they did to the primary Uc.S.'s. They yelped, jumped, withdrew a paw, or salivated and chewed the air when the once neutral stimuli appeared. They had learned about their environment; they seemingly knew that the C.S.'s signified the probable occurrence of a negative or positive consequence. Through experience they learned about the contingent relationships between the stimuli—when one was present, the other was likely to follow—and they responded. The C.S. had become informing; it served as a signal of forthcoming environmental events.

Informing signals are by no means limited to the laboratory environment, and expectancy is not the response province of lower organisms. Humans also learn about specific aspects of their stimulus world as a result of S-S contingencies that are positive or negative. They come to expect food when there is activity in the kitchen or the clock strikes six. "It's dinner time" is an expression that attests to the temporal expectations that result from classical conditioning. They may even find themselves salivating as these stimulus signals of food increase in number or intensity. Similarly, they learn to anticipate negative stimulation. C.S's may be changed from neutral to negative as a result of unconditional stimulation that is noxious. Organisms may learn, that is, to "respect" or possibly even to respond with negative emotion to specific stimuli.

---

[3] Higher-order stimuli may also *serve* as unconditional stimuli, but their ability to evoke a response is dependent on learning. Since this ability to evoke a response is truly conditional and not inherent, it can be unlearned.

The sound of screeching brakes, the rattle of a snake, or the phrase "watch out" are signals of contingent events that are negative.

C.S.'s are most often signals of forthcoming stimulus events. They generally serve to provide meaningful information. But C.S.'s may occasionally be misinforming. When this happens the C.R.'s are likely to be inappropriate. Classically conditioned positive or negative emotion, for example, may result from a chance-created "contingency" between a C.S. and a Uc.S. The anticipation of a consequence when the conditional stimulus is present is thus superstitious since the assumed S-S relationship is accidental. A scheduled contingency does not exist in the real world, but a stimulus relationship is nonetheless anticipated. The antecedent stimulus is a misinforming signal, and the emotional response is inappropriate. A conditional emotional response (CER) may not be appropriate for still another reason. The environmental circumstances have changed since conditioning occurred. Therefore, the C.S. is not currently informing. It does not give a true indication of the stimulus consequence to come. But there may not be an opportunity for this discrepancy to be noted. If an instrumental response is quickly made, as when a fear-evoking C.S. leads to avoidance, the observation that a negative consequence no longer follows cannot be made (Levis, 1966). As a result, the learned S-S relationship is not modified, and the CER is inappropriately maintained (Solomon, Kamin, and Wynne, 1953).

Instrumental conditioning

Learning is not limited to the classical conditioning that results from stimulus-contingent stimulation, and behaving is not confined to involuntary conditional responses like evoked emotional reactions. Other contingencies produce learning, and organisms employ a broad range of voluntary adjustments. Learning also takes place when *certain* responses are contingently stimulated. The frequency of these responses will change in a way that is adjustive to environmental consequences. Generally, response-contingent stimulation that is positive will increase their frequency and negative consequences will suppress them. Organisms are informed by the consequences of their actions, and they adjust. They learn to make those responses that are instrumental in bringing about positive stimulation. They learn to avoid making those responses to stimuli that lead to negative consequences or to a reduction in positive ones. They escape from stimulus circumstances they find aversive. They voluntarily behave in ways that are environmentally adjustive. People will, for example, wear their hair in a way that leads to compliments, slow down their car when a sign indicates consequences that should be avoided, or escape from an intolerable work situation.

Instrumental adjustments that have been learned because they were useful may not be currently adaptive. Circumstances may be avoided that are not presently dangerous or approached because the consequences have been positive. These anachronistic responses are not easily modified. They often have a long and complex history of contingent stimulation. As we have seen, reinforcement for C.E.R.-motivated avoidances can reduce reality testing and impede change. Although the situation is no longer noxious, the organism runs from it *as if* it were. Moreover, adjustments can continue to occur on the basis of a very thinned schedule of reinforcement. They may continue or even be enhanced by negative stimulation. Also, adjustive behaviors may be superstitiously conditioned by reinforcement that seems contingent. Reinforcing stimuli may accidently be associated with a response in a way that approximates a contingent relationship. Behavioral adjustments, like carrying a rabbit's foot, can be maintained by the superstitious belief that the response led to reinforcement. Consequently, the modification of maladaptive responses is not always achieved easily.

The interaction between classical and instrumental conditioning

It is clear that organisms make behavioral adjustments. People, for example, purposively change their speech, their words, and their dress in keeping with the information derived from consequent stimulation. These response-contingent consequences do not occur in an environmental void. The stimulation is also contingent upon the complex stimulus situations in which the responses take place (Kimble, 1961). Thus, instrumental and classical conditioning often occur at the same time. As a result of this overlapped conditioning we learn to behave in specific ways in different situations, with different people, and at different times. Organisms learn to discriminate among the stimulus circumstances in which particular ways of behaving are reinforced or punished. They are motivated, that is, to behave in ways that are organismically utilitarian.

Some knowledge about the environment comes from its reactions to voluntary adjustive responses. Discrimination results from the contingent reactions to responding; but situational stimulation also creates discrimination that relates to the environment. Clearly, much is learned about the environment from stimulus-contingent stimulation that is totally unrelated to the responses that are being made. We can learn to fear rattlesnakes or guns without ever having handled them. Through response-independent classical conditioning, people learn about such varied stimuli as listeners, speech situations, and words.

Conditioning is the process by which organisms learn about their environment. Whether the informing stimulation is stimulus-dependent or response-dependent, or both, we learn that a particular consequence is likely in a particular setting. As a result, emotional responses are conditioned and, instrumental responding is motivated. Because of the experiences we have in certain settings or with certain people, we react with the positive or negative emotional responses that motivate approach or avoidance adjustments.

Although adjustive responses are usually instrumental in bringing about reinforcement, they are not always successful. Sometimes the organism may not be able to respond in a way that leads to positive stimulation or that permits avoidance of negative consequences. The consequent stimulation may be independent of the response or the response repertoire may not be adequate for the circumstance. When this happens, conditioned negative emotion is heightened and behavioral disorganization may result. The organism's activities become disjointed and disrupted. There are cognitive, physiological, and motor disturbances. Difficulty or failure is anticipated and sympathetic responses flood the autonomic nervous system, interfering with fluent motor performance (Mowrer and Viek, 1948; Broadhurst, 1957; Schmeck and Bruning, 1968). This is not an event that occurs only among lower animals. Heightened negative emotion interferes also with the adequacy of human performance (Grinker and Spiegel, 1945; Kasl and Mahl, 1965). More than gross instrumental acts, such as maze-running or bar-pressing, are interfered with by classically conditioned emotion. As Skinner (1957), among others, has pointed out, this interference is basic to various forms of disorganization—including those he identified as stutterings.

We have had a necessarily limited look at the training procedures that result in classical and instrumental conditioning and their relationship to the involuntary and voluntary responding that organisms display. Clearly, these forms of conditioning and their interactions account for much human behavior. For example, there is nothing unique about responding emotionally or in ways that are means to certain ends. All people at one time or another have been emotionally aroused by environmental stimuli and have attempted to adjust to these circumstances. We have been pleased and frightened. We have been attracted toward and have run from various stimulus circumstances. The same is true of individuals who stutter. They behave in ways that are fundamentally similar to the ways we all do. All humans display emotional and adjustive responses, and disorganization is not unique to stutterers.

Classical conditioning: Fluency and fluency failure

The words used and the situations in which conversation takes place are some of the significant C.S.'s associated with speaking. In and of themselves these stimuli are neutral; there is nothing inherently pleasant or noxious about them. Their relative neutrality can be changed by experience, however. These and other speech-associated stimuli can be conditioned by consequent events in ways that are either positive or negative. Typically, positive consequences become contingent upon speech stimuli and upon the stimuli associated with the act of speaking. Parents talk to their children as they feed them, bathe them, or change the circumstances that discomfort them. Ordinarily, speech sounds that have positive stimulation contingently associated with them surround children. Speech sounds, the speaker, and the speech environment generally become C.S. positive. For example, children repeatedly hear words like eat or good and then receive the Uc.S. of food. At different ages and points in time, speech continues to be contingently stimulated in ways that are positive. Negative stimulation is present on occasion but, in general, speech-associated stimuli are followed by positive consequences. As a result, the stimuli associated with speech and the act of speaking become pleasant signs. Ordinarily, speech-associated stimuli evoke positive emotional responses, speech is motivated, and the positive consequences of communication lead to further positive classical conditioning. This positive emotional response to speech-associated stimuli promotes fluent motor production. It is no wonder, then, that most speakers are fluent and that their speech signal is *normally*—that is, predominantly—fluent. Fluency typifies speech. Fluency failures occur rarely (Johnson, 1961; Brutten and Shoemaker, 1967).

Fluency is the normal state, and fluency failure indicates unusual motor performance. Whether or not the failures are clinically significant, they do not characterize speech. The sporadic fluency failures that we all show at one time or another *are* disturbances. Fluency failures may result, for example, from the organismic stress of momentary fatigue, excitement, medication, or alcohol. But the fact that stress of this and other kinds can disturb everyone's speech at one time or another does *not* mean that people are *normally* dysfluent or that dysfluency is normal.

Though fluency failure is not normally evidenced, its occurrence may be inconsequential. Sporadic fluency failures associated with an unexpected occurrence, a strange word, a particularly novel event, or an overly generous bartender are neither clinically significant nor of concern to listeners. These sporadic disturbances are unheard, overlooked, or joked about. But fluency failures that are consistent, for whatever reason, are not subject to such cavalier responses from either lay listeners or pathologists. There is something quite different about listener reactions to fluency failures that characterize the speech signal or that occur consistently in circumstances which are atypical for such behavior. Then both professionals and lay listeners view the behavior as different from normal.

Fluency failures are known to be associated with disorders as varied as schizophrenia, apraxia, and alcoholism. Failures, therefore, can be clinical signs of specific organic and emotional conditions. Moreover, they occur with a certain circumscribed consistency that distinguishes organic conditions which are central or peripheral from those which are a result of negative emotional conditioning. The locus of fluency failures may be limited to multisyllabic words as a result of neuromuscular difficulties or to words that contain specific sounds that evoke negative emotional responses. They may occur on complex words no matter what the speech circumstances or only in particular situations or with certain people.

Our present concern is with fluency failures that are created by the negative emotional conditioning of words and situations. Words or their component parts and speaking situations or aspects thereof are not positively conditioned for all speakers. For some individuals certain elements of speech and speaking become C.S.'s that signal negative consequences. Their mere presence evokes heightened sympathetic activity, the cognitive anticipation of speech difficulty, or both. To an extent that exceeds chance, such objectively nondangerous stimuli as the sound of a ringing phone, the sight of a specific word, or the presence of a particular listener consistently evoke negative emotion. The exact conditioning history that had led these relatively neutral stimuli to evoke emotional responses may never be fully known, even for a particular person. The specific experiences involved are undoubtedly individualistic. But whether the emotional conditioning is a result of the generally negative environment in which speech occurs, the negative stimulation of specific speech stimuli, or response-contingent negative stimulation, it seems clear that certain individuals learn to react emotionally to speech-associated stimuli and are dysfluent in their presence. Negative emotional responses to speech-associated stimuli interfere with the voluntary motor adjustments necessary for fluent speech.

The presence of emotional conditioning is deducible from the stutterers' self-reports of the words and situations that lead to felt concern and from the anticipation of speech difficulty. These data have been reviewed (Bloodstein in this *Symposium* and Wischner, 1947) and need not be fully restated. Nevertheless, some of the data that are relevant to negative stimulation and classical conditioning, the stimulus evocation of negative emotional responses, and the relationships between conditioned emotion and speech disorganization need to be discussed. They are basic to the first factor of two-factor theory.

Negative stimulation, conditioning, and fluency failure

Much of the available information about the effect of a negative-stimulus setting on the fluency of speech has come from naturalistic observation and self-reports. Experimental studies have been few in number because of a real concern that negative emotional conditioning may have a lasting and deleterious effect. In recent years, however, studies using negative stimuli have begun to appear. They generally confirm negative stimuli as a cause of speech disorganization.

In studies of the effect of a noxious environment on speech fluency, negative unconditional stimulation that is contingent on the general speech situation or some particular aspect of it is often used. The stimulation is presented no matter what response the speaker makes. The stimulation is response independent; it is not contingent on specific behavior. The negative stimulation is stimulus contingent in the training manner that is typical of classical conditioning. The effect of introducing negative stimulation into a speech situation becomes apparent in reports of research by Brookshire (1969), Meyer (1972), and Stassi (1961). One part of the first of these studies involved the presentation of 95-decibel bursts of white noise during the middle, or "conditioning," segment of three consecutive oral-reading periods. Negative stimulation was not present during either the preceding (base-rate) or the following (extinction) periods. This was Brookshire's method for rechecking the data from previous research which indicated that the delivery of negative stimuli into a speaking situation "evidently causes some disorganization of speech" (p. 126). This effect was confirmed; the repetitions of normal speakers were significantly increased by negative stimuli that were not response contingent. Fluency failure was, that is, a function of noxious situational stimulation.

The second illustration (Meyer, 1972) of the effect of situationally contingent negative stimulation also involved the use of noise. In this study, the researcher used a continuous, changing, and complex sound stimulus that had previously been determined to be negative. The introduction of this stimulus into a speech environment increased the frequency of measured repetitions. The normal-speaking subjects in the noise group displayed significantly more repetitions of simple and compound phonemes than did the individuals in the nonstimulation group.

Another aspect of Meyer's study involved the presentation of response-independent shock. Repetitions increased, but not significantly so. However, shock and the continuous noise together resulted in significantly more repetition than did noise alone. These data not only led to the conclusion that phoneme repetitions are a function of environmental noxiousness, but that, as negativity increases—as it did when both negative stimuli were present—the disorganization of fluency intensifies concurrently. Meyer went on to suggest that the conditions that increase the fluency failures of normal adults may well be like those which are present at the onset of stuttering.

Stassi (1961) also introduced a negative stimulus into a speech environment. "Wrong," a higher-order negative stimulus, was delivered in a preprogrammed way that made the speech situation more or less noxious. In one condition it was presented all the time. In the other conditions it was delivered 66, 33, and 0 percent of the time. In all of the conditions it was delivered in a way that was response independent. Positive stimulation was delivered also; its frequency was reciprocal to the number of wrongs presented. Thus, the degree of negativity in the stimulus situation was a net result of negative and positive stimulation, neither of which was dependent on the kind of speech response made. The important point is that the scaled degree of observed dysfluency increased as a function of the net situational negativity. There was significantly more judged dysfluency when the negative stimulation was continuously present than when it was not present or minimally present. As a result, Stassi suggested that the understanding and development of stuttering may well be associated with the persistence of negative stimulation in a way that is similar to a "learned-anxiety reaction" (p. 361).

The studies on the effect of a negative environment make it clear that speech can be disorganized by negative stimulation. The introduction of a negative stimulus into speaking environments increased fluency failure, and these failures were increased as a function of the negativity of the stimulation. However, these studies gave no evidence of conditioning. To be sure, negative stimulation was contingent upon the stimulus situation and classical conditioning may well have taken place, but learning was not tested. No effort was made to determine if the stimulus situation was now consistently associated with more fluency failure than it was before being contingently paired with negative stimulation.

Hill's (1954) study is pertinent to any consideration of the effect of classically conditioned negative stimuli on speech. This pre-post investigation involved a comparison between the judged degree of fluency failure evidenced before and after the negative conditioning of stimulus lights that were part of the speech situation. More specifically, the 30 nonstuttering subjects of this experiment first spoke self-composed sentences for a block of six trials in the presence of experimentally neutral lights. Then, for another block of six trials, these colored lights were contingently paired with shock. Though these conditioning trials were few in number, their effect was marked. Speech in each of the three test blocks that followed the pairing of the lights with shock was statistically more dysfluent than it was in the prior control period. As Hill pointed out, the lights after the pairing became a threat of penalty—a sign of danger—which led to disorganized speech that was "quite indistinguishable from what is generally termed stuttering" (p. 302).

Savoye (1959), spurred on by Hill's findings, also studied the effect of negative C.S.'s on the amount of dysfluency. To the extent that fluency failures might be created by these circumstances, she saw such investigations as an inroad into the analysis of the conditions that are antecedent to stuttering. In her study, both the experimental and control groups of nonstuttering subjects were given a 10-second tone after each one minute and 50 seconds of a one-hour oral-reading period. For the experimental group alone, the offset of this tone was followed by an electric shock. This shock, whose level was higher than that which each of the subjects defined as very annoying, was thus contingent upon the tone removal rather than any particular response. Savoye analyzed fluency failures displayed in the 10-second time periods that preceded, were concurrent with, and immediately followed the presentation of the tone. She also analyzed the dysfluency exhibited in the 10-second time period that fell midway between the occurrence of two successive tone presentations. This period was one that, for the experimental group, was temporally furthest from the unconditional stimulation. During each of these time periods, except the midway one, there was significantly more fluency failure in the experimental group than in the control group. Moreover, although there were no significant differences in the frequency of dysfluency evidenced by the control group during the four 10-second intervals, there were statistically reliable differences in the experimental group. The period just before the tone presentation and the period when the tone was on were both characterized by increased fluency failures. Both time and tone became C.S.'s that were signs of negative consequences, and each was associated with a heightened disruption of fluency. As Savoye pointed out, dysfluency appears to be functionally related to the presence of "anticipation."

The C.S.'s that are indicative of negative consequences need not be discrete events, such as lights or tones. Stimuli that are conditionable include speech situations as well as the specific elements that make them up. The discrete stimuli used in studies like those undertaken by Hill (1954) and Stassi (1961) make it evident that the words speakers use and the individuals with whom they talk can become negatively conditioned. These findings help clarify the data which show that the photograph of a feared listener, the presence of a symbol of past word difficulty, or a very general sign of previous speech failure can serve to increase the likelihood of dysfluency (Berwick, 1955; Brutten and Gray, 1961; and Johnson, Larson, and Knott, 1937). But still larger and more complex settings can also serve as C.S.'s. Negative speech environments, like those studied by Brookshire (1969), Meyer (1972), and Stassi (1961) can also be conditioned. Indeed, negative speaking environments—speech circumstances that have come to be noxious—appear to be one possible setting for the onset of stuttering.

Stuttering is most likely to begin during childhood. Although the onset is not limited to these years, the beginnings of stuttering occur more frequently among the young. It seems plausible to relate this observation to the fact that youngsters are less capable than adults of resisting environmental stress and changing negative environmental circumstances. Children are in a relatively vulnerable position. Moreover, unlike adults, children have not had the benefit of years of adequate and successful speech experience. The child is learning how to use a new tool. Speech is not well habituated, and the interference created by emotional responding reflects this fact. Since the normally fluent speech of adults can become disorganized by negative stimuli, it is not surprising that the speech of children is even more susceptible to breakdown. Moreover, an even greater range of negative stimuli may serve as the basis for disruptive emotional conditioning. Negative stimuli that are less intense than those that have been shown to disorganize the normal fluency of adults can create fluency failures among children. Indeed, even minimal excitement or its anticipation may increase the fluency failures of some children.

Conditional stimuli and emotional responding

We have seen that the presence of negative stimuli can disrupt normally fluent speech. Shocks, white noise bursts, and a complex mixture of sound all have been shown to increase fluency failures. We have seen, also, that stimuli contingently followed by negative stimulation become classically conditioned. They become conditional signs of negative stimulation. The presence of these C.S.'s then serve to reduce speech fluency. In other words, stimuli that have not previously affected fluency come to disorganize it as a result of S-S conditioning.

The fact that certain stimuli are associated with disorganized fluency is not in question. Fluency failure has long been known to vary with negative states or conditions. The disorganization of fluency varies with stimulus circumstances. But why? For what reason may the rate of fluency fall when, for example, the speaker faces an audience, a notable person, or a stranger? None of these listeners are objectively dangerous. The answer seems to be that these stimuli have come to elicit negative emotion, a response class that interferes with motor performance. Speech is a fine motor act and one that can be disorganized by circumstances that are stressful, anxiety provoking, frustrating, shameful—that is, by events that evoke emotion. This effect is not limited to speech performance. The fluency of various motor acts may become disorganized as a result of negative emotion. Negative events have disrupted the performance of musicians, finger spellers, ball players, and laboratory animals (Liddell, 1944; Roman, 1959; Silverman and Silverman, 1971).

The term "emotion" does not exist apart from the behaviors it describes. Emotion, positive or negative, is a conceptual shorthand that must ultimately refer to specific ways of responding. Responses viewed as indicative of emotion may, however, be described at quite different behavioral levels. Cognitive, physiological, and motor responses have all been used as measures of emotional behaving, and each has been indexed by different instruments. It is clinically important to realize, then, that the term "emotion" encompasses many responses to stimulus states and that these responses are measurable. In brief, emotion is not an empty construct.

Cognitive Measures
of Emotion

A classic definition of "anxiety" refers to anticipation of difficulty (Freud, 1936). This emotional response relates, then, to an expectation of negative stimulation. Anticipation is evoked by certain people, places, or events—stimuli that have become signs of consequent negative stimulation.

For most people, the stimuli that are associated with speech are not cues of impending difficulty. A speech situation, the people that one speaks with, and the particular words or sounds used are not C.S.'s that have a history of unconditional consequences which are negative. For most, the conditioning experiences are positive and the opportunity to speak, interact, and communicate is pleasant. Although this is generally true also for the individual who stutters, it is not always so. Stutterers, unlike nonstutterers, do have some *consistent* anticipation of speech difficulty. They are anxious about specific speech situations or certain of the sounds and words they use when speaking (Shumak, 1955; Skalbeck, 1957; Martin and Haroldson, 1967). To a greater or lesser extent, individuals who stutter react phobically to speech-associated stimuli that are objectively nondangerous. They may anticipate difficulty on the phone, sweat over its ring, and avoid its use. Emotion-motivated avoidance may even lead them away from reinforcement. Anticipation of difficulty with a sound or word has led to the purchase of a train ticket that goes to a stop beyond the appropriate city or to the refusal of a marriage proposal. The city and surnames were considered fearfully difficult to say. These negative emotional responses are not inconstant. The speech-associated stimuli that evoke the anticipation of difficulty are not fleeting elicitors of emotional responding. Conditioning has taken place; the individual has learned about the stimuli in the speech environment, and certain of them often give him pause—*when* wondering.

However, negative anticipation that reduces fluency and disorganizes normally fluent speech does not characterize the stutterer's reaction to all speech-associated stimuli. The average stutterer is predominantly fluent, and many speech stimuli have a neutral or positive valence. The repetitions and prolongations of stuttering generally occur with relative infrequence, and most speech-associated stimuli elicit no concern. It would be a disservice, then, to refer clinically to the individual who stutters on certain words and in specific situations as a "stutterer" if the use of this term at all suggested ever-present negative emotion and all-encompassing speech disruption. The disorganizing anticipation of difficulty needs to be individually particularized. Due recognition must be given to the fact that positive or negative anticipation depends to a great measure on an individual speaker's experiences. We need to recognize also that the anticipation of difficulty does not develop at any particular developmental stage or phase. Negative anticipation, the awareness that speech will be difficult, may be apparent among stutterers of any age. It is evidenced by statements as general as "I don't speak right" or as specific as "I have trouble on words that begin with s and m." These different levels of awareness are not a function of growth; they are reflective of experience. It is not useful, that is, to suggest that the anticipation of difficulty occurs late in the development of stuttering (Bloodstein, 1960; Van Riper, 1963). Neither the presence of anticipated speech difficulty nor the occurrence of stuttering behaviors is developmental. Both are a function of an experience history rather than of a disorder's inherent course.

The view that stuttering is a developmental disorder has been strongly criticized (Brutten, 1970; Brutten and Shoemaker, 1971) and is being abandoned (Van Riper, 1971). Attempts to chart the developmental course of stuttering grew out of a medical, or disease, model, one that describes the orderly stages through which a disorder courses. But the behaviors of those who stutter do not fit adequately into generalized stages or phases. The behavioral reality is that individual stutterers respond in ways that are dependent on *their* experience history; the presence of behaviors do not necessarily follow a predetermined path. The proposed developmental stages are not descriptive of individual stutterers. An individual stutterer may well begin at any phase, miss a stage, or display an intertwined mass of behaviors that cannot be developmentally separated. Clearly, the behavioral model of stuttering is more descriptive. It recognizes that learning histories are individual and that the occurrence of behaviors is dependent on individualized experiences.

Physiological Measures of Emotion

There is no doubt that the anticipation of difficulty is more likely to be clearly and specifically *reported* by older individuals. A young child is not often sophisticated enough to point up more than the rather general anticipation that speech is difficult. Despite this fact, word and situational fears have been displayed by individuals of all ages.

Emotional responses have been made apparent by other than self-report procedures. Physiological measures, ones that do not depend on either a speaker's full awareness of specific C.S.'s or an ability to report anticipation, have often been used to index speech-associated negative emotion. To be sure, physiological measurement also has limitations. The organism's response lag, the delay created by the measuring instrument, and the contamination created by body movements can interfere with the assessment of emotional responding. Such classic measures of emotion as sweating, heart rate, and muscular tension can be affected by movements like those associated with speech. They can be seriously hampered also by such voluntary adjustments as arm-swinging, head-turning, and jaw-clenching (Williams, 1955). It is no wonder then that physiological changes observed *during* the speech of stutterers have been seen as confounded (Hill, 1944).

Emotional responding to speech-associated conditional stimuli can be ascertained, however. It can be culled from the physiological responses that occur just prior to speaking and from reactions to speech stimuli when speech is not required. This was illustrated by an early investigation in which heart rate during the silent periods prior to speech showed a greater acceleration for stutterers than nonstutterers (Travis et al., 1936). Over the years similar differences were uncovered by a number of other researchers (Fletcher, 1914; Moore, 1959), and this was suggestive of a relationship between negative emotion and stuttering.

Changes in respiration are also considered indicative of emotional responding. It is not surprising, then, that the duration of the inspiration-expiration ratio and a number of breathing irregularities tend to differentiate those words on which stuttering is anticipated from those on which it is not. These physiological changes occur even before the cognitive expectation of stuttering or nonstuttering is signaled. As Van Riper (1936) has pointed out, words on which speech difficulty has been anticipated can be distinguished from word stimuli that have not been feared by the breathing pattern that "existed immediately subsequent to the exposure of the word" (p. 69). Apparently, words are C.S.'s that affect the patterns of breathing vital to speech production.

The anticipation of difficulty is not limited to words or their integral components. Speech situations may also cause concern. Robbins (1919), who did a plethysmographic investigation of "shock" stimuli and stuttering, found that their presence limited blood flow. Imagining different speech situations that were the scenes of previous failures had the same effect. Blood flow decreased markedly, even though speech was not called for. Merely the visualization of speaking in a setting that the subjects found to be negative brought about vasoconstriction that was like that found when shocking stimuli were presented. As Robbins put it, "fear of stammering with no attempt at speaking produces vasoconstriction in the periphery as it does during actual stammering" (p. 321).

More recent investigations of the physiological effects of anticipation are worthy of consideration. One of these is something like the eye-movement studies of years past (Jasper and Murray, 1932; Moser, 1938). These early studies showed that prolonged fixation and unusual eye movements occurred during the speech of those who stuttered. The current study, one just completed by Brutten, Janssen, and Fisher, involved the silent and oral reading of a connected passage. The subjects were asked, just *prior* to the silent reading, to view a long list of individual words and to underline those on which they anticipated speech difficulty. This list contained all of the words that subsequently were in the connected experimental passage and many more words that were not. Then, the subject was locked into equipment that made it possible to trace the saccadic movements of the eye during silent reading (Macworth, 1958; Norton and Stark, 1971).

This eye-marking system employed two cameras, one that videotaped the reading material as it moved down a monitor and one that taped the light reflecting off the fovea. These two were synchronized by a mixer and filmed. The film was then scored, frame by frame, to determine the location of the fovea and its movements during the silent reading. As a result it was possible to determine if there was any relationship between previously determined anticipation, eye movements during silent reading, and fluency failures during a subsequent oral reading. Analysis of the eye movements during the silent reading revealed that significantly more fixations occurred on those words where speech difficulty was anticipated than on those where fluent production was expected. Fixations were significantly more prevalent, also, on those words that were later stuttered. Moreover, most of the eye fixation occurred on those words where difficulty was anticipated and dysfluency was observed. The fewest were found where difficulty was not expected and did not occur. The presence of word anticipation was demonstrated also through the reversals of the fovea to previously viewed words of the silently read passage. The number of frames involved in fixation was significantly greater not only on those words where difficulty was anticipated but also on those to which the eye reverted. Although the signaled anticipation prior to the silent reading did not assure the presence or absence of reversals by the fovea, fixation was significantly more prevalent when word difficulty was anticipated and reversals observed than when they were not.

Another interesting study involving physiological measurement of negative emotion and its relationship to fluency and fluency failure was conducted by Zimmerman and Knott (1973). They examined the anticipatory responses of stutterers and nonstutterers to word stimuli just prior to speech. Their investigation was based on the repeated finding that a preparatory cortical reaction, or contingent negative variation (CNV), is observable when two stimuli are presented in a sequential order and a particular response is to be made contingent upon the second of these.[4] Forty different and individually presented words served as the first of the paired stimuli. After 1500 milliseconds, the second stimulus, a light flash, was presented as a signal that the word shown was to be spoken immediately. The nonstutterers showed a CNV during the period between the occurrence of the first and second stimulus. So too, did the stutterers, but only on those words that were not stuttered when the time came for them to be spoken. In contrast, there was no shift in the potential on *any* of the words that were subsequently stuttered. The absence of the CNV indicated that there was a negative emotional response during the anticipatory period which preceded only those words which were stuttered. Clearly, the presence or absence of stuttering was predictable in terms of the emotional response to word cues.

The relationship between negative emotion and frequency of stuttering has been highlighted also by the biofeedback research of Treon, Tamayo, and Stendley (1972). Within certain limits they were able to train individuals who stutter to self-regulate the amplitude of their emotional responding. Then, the frequency of their fluency failures was studied under negative (sweat) levels that were low or high. Stuttering moments were counted during each of these separate periods and during initial and final three-minute segments when there was no self-regulation. An average of 2.4, 3.0, and 3.6 moments occurred in the low-amplitude, unregulated, and high-amplitude periods, respectively. The frequency of stuttering moments was significantly greater when negative emotion was high than when it was low. The difference existed even though the self-regulation was not completely successful and the desired amplitudes were not always attained. For this reason, the investigators separated the periods into those where the low and high levels of palmar sweat emotion were achieved at least three-fourths of the time. When this was done an even more marked frequency distinction became apparent. An average of 1.7 moments was displayed during the low-level

---

[4] A slow surface negative potential, or CNV, appears when the second stimulus in the S-S pair serves as the signal to respond. The amplitude of this anticipatory reaction is known to be *diminished* by stress. The greater the negative emotional reaction is, the smaller the CNV will be (Low and Swift, 1971; Knott and Irwin, 1973).

periods, while 4.1 instances of stuttering occurred during the high-level periods. These data further confirmed the tested hypothesis that there is a functional relationship between the physiological excitation that is a correlate of "tension/anxiety feelings" and stuttering.

Valyo (1971) also used a measure of palmar sweating to study emotional responding, but he did not count fluency failures. Instead, he compared the skin potential response (SPR), amplitude, and wave form of his stuttering and nonstuttering subjects in various nonspeech, prespeech, and speaking circumstances. The stutterers displayed more diphasic and positive wave forms, behaviors considered indicative of moderate-to-high arousal, than did the nonstutterers. Valyo concluded that the "stutterers and non-stutterers could be differentiated by the amplitude parameter of SPR since stutterers, in general, maintained a higher degree of autonomic arousal than did non-stutterers" (p. 1904). Though in the period just before the onset of speech both groups displayed an increase in sweating, the stutterers reacted to a greater extent than did normally fluent speakers.

This anticipatory tendency is more clearly reflected in the research of Ickes and Pierce (1973). Following up on the work of Robbins (1919), which has been described, they made plethysmographic measures of blood volume in the periods before, during, and after the speaking of 50 individual words. Each of these words and a green light were simultaneously presented for 30 seconds. The offset of the light signaled the stuttering and nonstuttering subjects of this experiment that they were to speak the displayed word within 4 seconds. Following the completed production of the word, there was a 30-second recovery period, once again, before the light and another word were presented. During *each* of these three periods, there was significantly more vasoconstriction when the stutterers spoke words dysfluently. There was no significant difference in these segments when both of the subject groups later spoke the words fluently. In the anticipatory segments some reduced blood volume was evidenced among stutterers, even as fluently spoken words were approached. The blood volume of nonstutterers never decreased during this same anticipatory period. But in neither of these cases was there a significant change in vasoconstriction. The *only* statistically significant change was that displayed by stutterers as they approached the time when they were to speak those words on which they eventually stuttered. These data, like those we have reviewed, support the contention that negative emotional responding precedes the occurrence of "stuttering moments." So, too, did the increase in blood volume that followed in the recovery period. This increase led the authors to conclude that emotion is causal to stuttering and is not merely an aftereffect of the disturbance of fluency.

Motor Measures
of Emotion

The disintegration of normally fluent speech performance has repeatedly been used as a sign of negative emotion by those involved with problem areas other than stuttering. Those concerned with the diagnosis of psychological problems have noted the circumstances associated with disarrayed speech and have used fluency failures as evidence of a negative emotional state (Grinker and Spiegel, 1945). Mahl (1956, 1959, 1961), for example, stressed that disturbances of speech are often more indicative of a current emotional state than is the content of a patient's comments. His research studies have indicated that, aside from adjustive interjections like "ah," "uh," and "uhm," speech disturbances increase as a function of negative emotion. He found that fluency failures were significantly higher during those portions of clinical interviews characterized by conflict and during experimentally devised circumstances where palmar sweating also revealed a heightened negative emotional state than they were in less negative circumstances. On the basis of data like these, Mahl moved from content to nonlexical assessment of negative emotion. As he pointed out, "it is well known that anxiety has a disruptive effect on finely coordinated behavior, and speech is an instance of finely coordinated behavior par excellence" (Mahl, 1959, p. 179). This point has been made also by Shames and Sherrick (1963), who viewed dysfluencies as evidence of the demanding nature of the speech situation. They indicated that the repetitions of normal children are most likely in circumstances which are noxious or deprivational. The presence of repetitions, unlike self-editing interjections, was functionally related to these negative states.

Negative stimuli also increase the fluency failures exhibited by stutterers. Stutterings increase with word and situational stimuli that are thought to be noxious and have been associated with past speech failure (Johnson and Millsapps, 1937; Berwick, 1955; Dixon, 1965). The frequency of measured stuttering varies, for example, with the kind of listener, with the perception of listeners as easy or difficult, with the size of the listening audience, with the speaker's previous experiences in speech situations, and with words or sounds according to their expected difficulty. Findings such as these make it evident that the disruption of fluent motor production is a dependent function of negative emotion. So, too, do the data from speech-specific questionnaires. They indicate that the frequency of reported stuttering correlates significantly with scaled emotional reactions to speech stimuli (Shumak, 1955; Brutten and Shoemaker, 1974).

It should be made clear, however, that negative emotion may disrupt several forms of motor performance. Disruption is not limited to speech acts or to those individuals called "stutterers." The study by Adams and Dietz (1965) exemplifies this fact. They investigated the speed with which stutterers and nonstutterers responded to stimulus words considered positive, negative, or neutral. A comparison of the latency of their written associative responses revealed that both groups reacted similarly; both stutterers and nonstutterers took longer to respond to negative than to neutral stimuli. However, the stutterers' latency to negative words was significantly greater. On this basis the investigators concluded that, while emotion interferes with the performance of *all* individuals, its effect on the performance of those who stutter is more pronounced. These findings were consistent with those on associative latency reviewed by Adams (1969), who saw the slowed response time as evidence of the behavioral disorganization created by emotion-evoking stimuli. King (1961) also saw the finding that stutterers were significantly slower on motor tasks as an indication that negative emotion hinders performance. On each of four alternating activity tasks, they responded more slowly than did nonstutterers. Since there was no evidence that the stutterers were generally more perseverative in a way that suggested organicity, King contended that the differences were probably the result of the emotional state created by the test situation. Indeed, few current theorists would argue that stuttering is directly linked to organic impairment. The fact is that "despite some rather fundamental differences, there appears to be a consensus that stuttering develops initially in environmental conditions that are marked by some measure of stress and emotionality" (Siegel, 1968, p. 49).

Instrumental conditioning and adjustive responding

All individuals attempt to cope with their environment by making adjustive responses. Stutterers are no different. They make voluntary adjustments to improve their conditions. They seek to attain positive stimulation. They try to avoid or escape stimuli they find noxious or aversive. These responses are reinforced if they are *instrumental* in increasing positive emotion or reducing negative emotion.

There is no question that stutterers generally avoid words and situations they find noxious or escape from the aversive consequences which often follow stuttered speech behaviors. Although not all stutterers manifest speech-associated adjustive responses, behavioral accommodation is often dramatically obvious. Frequently, avoidance and escape responses are more numerous and striking than the repetitions and prolongations that characterize stuttering. Although these adjustive responses do not define stuttering, they often constitute a clinically significant aspect of the speaker's communication problem. They command clinical attention, especially since not all of the adjustive mannerisms that stutterers use turn out to be consistently or currently adaptive. They may also be so unusual that they lead to additional negation. Their number and the fact that their use varies from moment to moment indicate that they are not continually reinforced. They may seem to be of help at one time, but may fail at others. But partial reinforcement maintains these responses. Indeed, adjustive responses that are occasionally reinforced are in some ways more strongly fixed than are those which are always instrumental in reducing negative or increasing positive emotion (Notterman, Shoenfeld, and Bersh, 1952; Freides, 1957; Kimble, 1961). Hope springs eternal and one never knows when an adjustment will be reinforced again. It is little wonder, then, that the instrumental elements of stuttering moments evidence a lack of momentary consistency (Webster, 1968; Oelschlaeger, 1971). Even when the same instrumental behaviors are repeated, their relative position in the moment is not predictable. A particular instrumental response may be found anywhere in the behavioral sequence (Luper, 1954).

The instrumental adjustments of stutterers and their voluntary as well as purposive nature is a matter of record. So, too, is the range of these responses. Respiratory, phonatory, articulatory, and resonatory processes are often involved. But instrumentals are not limited to the "speaking system." Voluntary responses of innumerable kinds are used to avoid or escape negation. The most common of these instrumental responses have been compiled in behavior checklists so that therapists can quickly determine the presence of these readily modifiable responses (Shumak, 1955; Brutten, 1973).

Research has shown that not all of the behaviors in a stuttering moment are modified by the same tactics (Webster, 1968; Starkweather, 1970; Janssen and Brutten, 1973), a finding consistent with the factorial distinctions already pointed out. It is apparent also that molar moments are generally composed of stuttering behaviors and instrumental adjustments. Therefore, the gross behavior change reported when molar moments of stuttering are stimulated is of little clinical use. The reports permit no determination of which of the many and varying behaviors underwent modification. The fact that a particular aspect of the molar mixture was subject to modification by contingent stimulation may even be masked by the absence of change in or by an increase in other momentary behaviors. Zenner and Webster's (1972) study made this clear. They contingently stimulated molar stuttering with "wrong" during the fifth of 10 continuous oral-reading trials. The 4 trials that preceded this experimental segment and the 5 that followed served as controls against which change attributable to contingent stimulation could be measured. The frequency of molar moments and the molecular components of these moments were charted relative to the number of words read during each trial. Though the relative frequency of the moments remained essentially unchanged, averaging approximately 14.5 percent and 15.6 percent in the preceding and following control periods and 15 percent during the experimental segment, there were observable changes in certain specific behaviors. Pharyngeal clicks decreased, but nasal emissions and nonintegral sound interjections increased. In contrast, part-word repetitions remained fundamentally unaltered. The instrumental elements responded in ways that were different from those of a stuttering behavior, and, as a result, the researchers were led to "seriously question" studies involving the contingent stimulation of molar moments.

Whether or not a behavior is an instrumental response need not be evaluated from the molecular analysis of molar moments. This determination can be made directly by observing if behavior change results from response-contingent stimulation. Instrumentals are manipulated by consequences. Behaviors that are modified by contingent stimulation can be distinguished from those that have not been changed or do not respond as instrumental adjustments do. Martin, Brookshire, and Siegel (1964) conducted one of the first studies to explore the effect of punishment on specific elements of stuttering moments. Their study was designed to determine whether particular behaviors could be suppressed by response-contingent negative stimulation (shock) without contraindicating side effects. Toward this end they first punished their subject's nose-wrinkling, which essentially reduced to zero, and then the repeated interjection of a nonintegral sound (ah-ah-ah), which was also suppressed. Initially, the suppression of nose-wrinkling and interjecting was not associated with a change in the number of words spoken. Ultimately, however, the word rate dropped to a level that approached zero whenever shocks could be made contingent upon the target behaviors. The reduced word rate was instrumental in avoiding punishment. Other contraindicating changes also occurred. As a result of the continued punishment of nose-wrinkling and interjecting, there was an eightfold increase in the number of prolongations. This increase was notable not only because it was maintained for a number of sessions, but also because it was associated with a marked decrease in verbal output. The researchers concluded that "the use of punishment as a response depressant, particularly in the re-introduction after some extinction, results in some undesirable side-effects or competing behaviors" (p. 9). This conclusion was justified since prolongations increased and word rate decreased. But just as important is the recognition that all of the behaviors measured other than prolongations decreased. Prolongations reacted in a way that was different.

In 1966 Martin and Siegel reported some of the findings just discussed. They also described the effect that contingent shock had on the tongue protrusions of another subject. Protrusions averaged about 12 for each 2-minute segment over a 40-minute pre-experimental session. This approximate average, demonstrated again during the first 8 minutes of a session that was conducted four days later, reduced to zero with the introduction of response-contingent shock. Removal of the shock brought a progressive increase in tongue protrusions. Clearly, tongue protrusions were under the control of their negative consequences. The same sort of behavioral control was reported for another of this subject's responses. His *s* prolongation was also reduced by contingent shock.[5] This behavior also returned to about its initial level when the contingent stimulation was removed.

Quist and Martin (1967) also investigated the effect of contingent negative stimulation on the specifically defined behaviors of two of their three subjects. For one subject, the results are unclear since all forms of repetition or prolongation were contingently stimulated by the delivery of "wrong." However, for the second subject the target behavior was an interjected "uh," and for the third it was the interjection of a prolonged *n* that was not an integral part of the words spoken. Both of these behaviors diminished as a result of punishment. The number of "uhs" decreased more than 85 percent, even though the number of words spoken did not reportedly vary in a systematic way. The interjected nasal sound reduced from an initial base-rate of 26, for each 2-minute period, to an average of about 16. On withdrawal of the contingent negative stimulus, the interjections displayed by both of these subjects raised to approximately their initial base-rate level. It would seem clear, then, that interjections are manipulable by their consequences. The interjected "uh" and *n* in this study, the "ah" in the Martin, Brookshire, and Siegel investigation, and what may be the interjected *s* prolongation in the study by Martin and Siegel reflect on the manipulability of this response class.

Brutten and Shoemaker (1967, 1971) have postulated that interjections and responses like nose-wrinklings and tongue protrusions are voluntary adjustments which are instrumental in the attainment of negative or positive reinforcement. Brutten and Shoemaker contrast these adjustive responses with involuntary behaviors, like some forms of repeti-

---

[5] The contingently stimulated *s* prolongation was not described. Thus, it may have been an interjected and nonintegral aspect of the word spoken or one that occurred only on *s* words. Nonpurposive prolongations of sounds that are an integral part of the words spoken do not appear to be suppressed by response-contingent negative stimulation (Brutten and Shoemaker, 1972; Janssen and Brutten, 1973). Nonintegral prolongations are probably best viewed as interjections and instrumental adjustments. They have been reduced by punishment (Quist, 1966).

tions and prolongations. It is their contention that these nonadjustive behaviors are not instrumental responses. If this distinction is meaningful, instrumental adjustments and involuntary behaviors should respond differently to consequences. This premise led Webster, and then a number of other researchers, to stimulate contingently various behaviors whose particular topography was specified and whose voluntary adjustive or involuntary nature was pre-experimentally explored. Webster (1966) previously had found that during oral reading the course of a "secondary" adjustment did not correlate with that of a "primary" stuttering behavior. In contrast, he had found that the adjustive response (interjection) and a behavior defined by his subject as voluntary (eyelid closure) correlated significantly with each other. However, neither one of these responses correlated significantly with the subject-defined involuntary behavior or with the primary behavior. These data helped give direction to Webster's (1968) investigation of the effect of punishment. The study involved those behaviors that his two subjects defined as voluntary adjustments and those they considered noninstrumental and involuntary. The first subject indicated that he voluntarily turned his head completely to the side when he anticipated or was having speech difficulty. He declared that his part-word repetitions were involuntary. The second subject studied also stated that part-word repetitions were involuntary rather than adjustive. He indicated, however, that he used a movement of the head and jaw as a purposive coping response.

The modifiability of voluntary adjustments is apparent in Figure 2, which graphically illustrates the significant suppression of head turns. Head turns, the reportedly voluntary adjustment, behaved as instrumental responses do; they were decreased by a negative consequence. The second subject's voluntary movements also decreased. There were

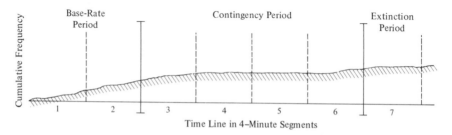

Figure 2. Cumulative record of a subject's voluntary head turns during 28 minutes of oral reading. Negative stimulation was presented as a consequence of head-turning during the contingency period. No stimulation was given during either the base-rate or extinction periods (after Webster, 1968).

significantly fewer movements of the head and jaw in the experimental period than during the initial segment of the base-rate period. This change was not attributable to the contingent negative stimulus "wrong," however, since the head-jaw movements reduced from 13 during the first 4-minute segment of the base-rate period to zero during the second segment. Response manipulation by the independent variable could thus not be illustrated during the experimental period. Nevertheless, the change in frequency is notable.

Contingent negative stimulation did not suppress the involuntary part-word repetitions of either of the two subjects. As Figure 3 makes apparent, the first of these subjects showed an initial *increase* in part-word repetitions as a result of punishment; but this statistically significant change was temporary. The second subject's frequency of part-word repetitions was not significantly modified during any of the 4-minute segments of the 16-minute period. Clearly, part-word repetitions did not behave like an instrumental adjustment. For neither of these two subjects was their frequency suppressed by response-contingent negative stimulation.

Webster's findings do not stand alone; they have had repeated support from the data of studies that used various negative consequences. Starkweather (1970), for example, employed contingent shock at a level predetermined as painful in the low-intensity condition and as nearly intolerable in the high-intensity group. In both conditions shock was contingent upon repetitions of sounds and syllables, behaviors that each of the four subjects studied defined as involuntary. These reportedly noninstrumental repetitions were not suppressed by either the relatively low-

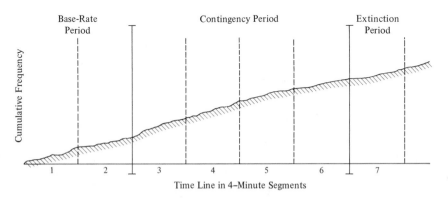

Figure 3. Cumulative record of a subject's involuntary repetitions during oral reading. Negative stimulation was consequent upon repetitions during the contingency period only (after Webster, 1968).

or high-intensity stimulation. Their frequency was similar to that displayed during the stimulation-free base-rate period. Moreover, when the contingent shock was removed there was a *decrease* in the measured repetitions. An increase would have been anticipated if the shock stimulus suppressed the target behavior. The findings were essentially the same when the low- and high-intensity conditions were combined. The contingent delivery of shock regardless of intensity also failed to demonstrate the manipulability of part-word repetitions.

Oelschlaeger (1973) questioned the generalizability of the findings that repetitions of single and compound phonemes were not manipulable by their consequences. Since all of the data were based on contingent stimulation that was negative, she chose to employ a consequence that was positive. Awards of money, which on an a priori basis had been shown to be a positive stimulus for each of her subjects, were made contingent on part-word repetitions. There was no significant behavioral manipulation by reinforcement for *any* of the four subjects studied. Indeed, the presentation of response-contingent positive stimulation was not associated with even descriptive evidence of an increase in repetitions. If anything, there was a general decrease; but this change seemed unrelated to the presence or absence of the positive stimulus.

The evidence that not all behaviors displayed by individuals who stutter are manipulable by consequent stimulation is not limited to just particular repetitions. Prolongations of word-integral phonemes, another behavior considered phenotypic of stuttering, also appears to be non-manipulable. This became evident in the recent study of Janssen and Brutten (1973), who employed shock as intense as the four subjects were willing to withstand. This stimulus, which the subjects reported to be very strongly negative, was made contingent upon oral prolongations during the experimental segment. Negative stimulation was not presented during either the base-rate or extinction periods. For *none* of the subjects were oral prolongations suppressed by the introduction of shock. This is consistent with the previous findings of Brutten and Shoemaker (1972), who reported that the contingent delivery of "wrong" did not reduce the frequency of this behavior. Janssen and Brutten found that, for three of the subjects, the frequency of oral prolongations was not significantly different from that shown during the base-rate period. The lack of statistically significant change in oral prolongations is evidenced in Figure 4, which also displays the course of this subject's other behaviors. The fourth subject, whose behaviors are illustrated in Figure 5, showed a significant increase in oral prolongations when shock was introduced following a base-rate period. This change is not clearly attributable to the negative stimulus, however, because it was maintained even when the shock was no longer present. Nevertheless, the dramatic *increase* in this and most of the other behaviors is noteworthy.

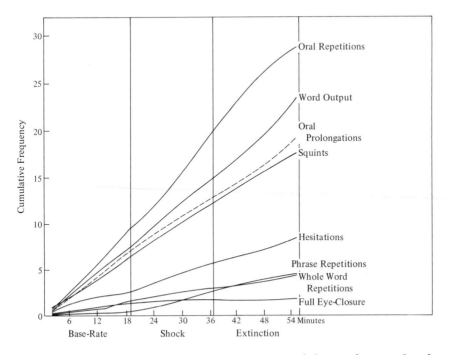

Figure 4. Cumulative frequencies of a stutterer's separate behaviors during oral reading. Intense shock was contingent upon oral prolongations during the second 18-minute period. (After Janssen and Brutten, 1973).

The data reviewed point up that some of the speech and speech-associated behaviors displayed by stutterers are modifiable by contingent stimulation. The instrumental nature of these particular responses is clear from the behavior change associated with the presence and absence of particular consequences. Interestingly, the behaviors modified by consequent stimulation are those that stutterers have reported as voluntary and adjustive responses and which theorists have viewed as secondary or accessory to stuttering (Van Riper, 1963; Wingate, 1964). The consonance between performance, verbal report, and theoretical posture is significant. It suggests that there is reality to the view that adjustive behaviors form a unique category. Certainly, they factor out in ways that are different from repetitions and prolongations. Repetition and prolongation of a phoneme, behaviors reported to be involuntary and judged to be *the* elements that define stuttering, have not been manipulated by contingent stimulation. These behaviors represent another category, one that factors out in a way that is distinct from the loadings evidenced by instrumental responses. We have, that is, two categories to contend with when we go about viewing the myriad behaviors that

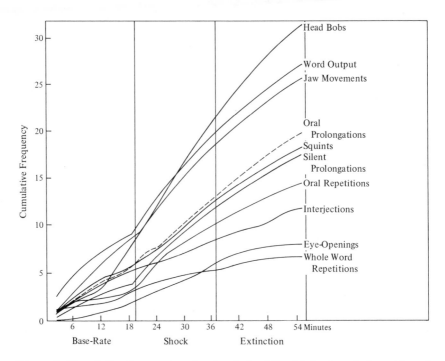

Figure 5. Cumulative frequencies of molecularly defined behaviors during oral reading. Shock followed oral prolongations throughout the middle period. Punishment was not delivered in either the base-rate or extinction periods (after Janssen and Brutten, 1973).

traditionally have been seen as a single "moment of stuttering." The categories are representative of separate factor-one (involuntary) or factor-two (voluntary) behaviors, and each must be assessed separately.

Behavior Assessment

Two-factor assessment has the purpose of teasing out the separate behaviors to be modified in ways that are differentially suggestive of particular therapy procedures. It serves as a means for distinguishing between specific negative emotional and adjustive responses. This separation of behaviors into categories of responding has clinical utility because it serves to highlight both the general strategy of therapy and the specific tactics of behavior change.

Behavior therapy is no longer limited to a few procedures routinely used. There are an ever-increasing number of therapeutic strategies and a widening range of tactics that are currently available to the clinician for bringing about significant behavior change. These approaches are now being tailored to the specific behaviors being modified and to the particular way they were conditioned. Therapists have become increasingly strident in their call for recognition of the importance of behavioral specificity and history in determining the overall strategies and particular tactics to be used with a specific client (Eysenck, 1960; Ullman and Krasner, 1965; Wolpe, 1969).

A careful assessment is necessary if the direction that therapy takes is to be unambiguous and if the tactics are to be efficiently related to the specific behaviors displayed in particular stimulus settings. If the clinician is to prepare an adequate and flexible blueprint of therapy for an individual who stutters, it is imperative that the cue stimuli which elicit emotional responding and the discriminative stimuli which are associated with particular adjustive attempts be determined. It is most likely that both factor-one and factor-two stimulus-response relationships will be displayed. Therefore, the behaviors in both categories need to be assessed for the adequate planning of therapy. Clearly, the specific responses within these categories require clarification so that a therapist may identify appropriate behavior-change procedures. The Behavior Assessment Battery (BAB) was developed to meet these clinical needs. The BAB utilizes autonomic, self-report, and performance measures to sample both emotional and adjustive responding. Thus, physiological, cognitive, and motor elements of the presenting complaint are studied in ways that have a direct bearing on clinical decision-making.

Behavioral assessment battery: Speech-specific emotional responding

Negative emotional responses to speech situations and to the words used in speaking are assessed by palmar-sweat, situational-checklist, and expectancy procedures.

Palmar sweating as a measure of the sympathetic reaction of the autonomic system to specific stimuli dates back many centuries and covers a wealth of pure and applied investigations (Mowrer, 1953; Kuno, 1956; Brutten, 1959). The origin of this approach to the measurement of negative emotion was the naturalistic observation of the co-relationship between *localized* sweating and stress. This concomitance is reflected in folk language that cross-culturally makes reference to those stimulus events that are "no sweat" and those in which one "sweats it out." Measurement procedures were developed, and these attested to the validity of the folk observation. The development of various approaches for determining the extent of emotional—that is, nonthermal—sweating has continued through the years. The Sudorimeter is one of the measurement systems that was developed and is the one used in the BAB.[6] Through

----

[6] The Sudorimeter is manufactured by the C. H. Stoelting Company, Chicago, Illinois.

chemical means the Sudorimeter determines the discrete amount of sweat that accumulates on the palmar side of a finger during a fixed test period. The sweat, in solution with applied chemicals, produces an ink fingerprint when it is brought into carefully determined contact with specially treated film. The reaction is immediate, and the darkness of the print reflects the amount of sweating in a way that is photometrically quantified.

Negative emotional responses to speech-associated stimuli are determined only after three successive prints are taken in a nonspeech setting. The third of these prints provides the basal sweat level. This basal level is compared with the emotional response to an extemporaneous and then to an oral-reading speech situation. Speech is called forth first by the instruction to describe a picture and then by asking that particular graded material be read aloud.[7] The speech setting remains the same. Only the chance to change words is varied. Words on which difficulty is anticipated can be simply and covertly altered during extemporaneous speech. Word changes are unlikely and obvious during oral reading. Feared words can be easily avoided during extemporaneous speech, and so the emotional response is primarily to the speech situation. In contrast, word fear is of singular importance during oral reading. This is all the more true because the oral reading follows extemporaneous speaking. The oral reading occurs in a setting that is not new. The repeated situational experience lessens the emotional response to the speech setting and points up the reaction to words. These test manipulations thus make it possible to assess the negative emotional reponses to a speech situation and to specific words. Moreover, both of these responses can be compared with the negative emotion elicited when speech is not called for.

The introduction of two different speech situations following three silent periods does not significantly affect most people. The need to speak does not alter the amount of emotional sweating. Speech offers no concern, and the repeated experience leads to a continued adaptation to the test situation. For those to whom speech stimuli are negative, however, there is a notable reversal in the Palmar Sweat Index (PSI). Negative emotion increases with the call to speak or to say certain unavoidable words. Sweating is measurably above the basal level. Occasionally, the PSI will even match or exceed the sweat response to the start

---

[7] Card 12 of the Thematic Apperception Test (Murray, 1943) is generally used as the stimulus picture. For youngsters, a different picture and instruction ("tell me about it") are available. The selection of "reading" material depends on ability and varies from sentence-ordered pictures, to a list of words in primary type, to word lists and passages graded up to adult levels. A number of forms of these materials are available for retesting purposes.

of the assessment. Such a sweat reaction represents a considerable emotional display since the BAB occurs in a nonpermissive setting. The
individual is told of being under test for the purpose of behavioral
exploration. As a result, the first print is generally the darkest one; the
initial emotional response to being tested is usually the most intense.

Procedures besides the PSI are used to cross-check whether some
speech situations and/or words are associated with negative emotion.
The Speech Situation Checklist (SSC) is one of the means for evaluating
any initial evidence that these stimulus classes, or one of them, induces
negative emotion. In addition, this checklist serves to specify some of
the particular environmental circumstances that currently elicit negative
emotion. It does so by offering 51 real-life speech circumstances for
scaled evaluation. The speech circumstances are quite varied. Moreover,
in some of the situations the words used are the speaker's choice, whereas
in the others word substitutions are not feasible. In any event it provides
a means for reporting those speech-associated stimuli that *currently* elicit
negative emotion.[8]

The SSC is an internally consistent measure and one whose total
score reflects the magnitude of the emotional reaction to different speech
stimuli. Moreover, varimax factor analysis has revealed that the SSC
taps different classes of word and situational events. The first of the
factorial clusters points up circumstances where the necessary words
are relatively unchangeable. Buying a ticket to a specific place, telling
a cab driver one's destination, and making an appointment are examples
of the items that load highly on this factor. Distinctly different events
load strongly on the second factor. This factor relates specifically to
interpersonal speech situations that are stressful. It represents life situations in which one is trying to get across a point of view, arguing,
apologizing, and being criticized.

Clearly, the word-specific stimuli to negative emotion revealed by
the items that load heavily on factor one are different from the situational
ones of the second factor. But these are not the only word and situational
aspects factored from the SSC. Factor three predominantly represents
naming activities. Being asked to give your name, giving your name,
introducing oneself, and making introductions are items that load highly
on the third factor. So, too, do reading aloud an unchangeable passage
and saying a sound or word that has in the past been troublesome.
The fourth factor is still different, for it points up items concerned with
the listening audience and their reactions. This factor brings together

---

[8] Speech disorganization in these same situations is also checked by the described
self-report procedure. As a result the SSC makes it possible to assess the presence
or absence of a correlation between reported negative emotion and fluency failures.

speech situations in which one gives a prepared speech, is speaking before a group, talks after being teased about speech, or asks the teacher a question.

The first four factors revealed by the varimax rotation are indicative of speech circumstances where there is heightened negative emotion. In contrast, the fifth of the five factors made evident by the rotations brings together those circumstances that tend to elicit little negative emotion, situations where the speaker is talking with a young child, an animal, or a close friend or is "high." Stutterers have traditionally reported that these circumstances provide little stress.

It should be apparent from the above analysis that the SSC provides the clinician with information about various kinds of situational and word stimuli which currently elicit felt negative emotion. The words and the specific sounds that cue-off this response are still more precisely examined by yet another test segment of BAB, one in which the client silently views speech material and signals anticipated "difficulty." More specifically, the individual being assessed points out those words or sounds on which he anticipates difficulty if he were then and there to speak them aloud.[9] On three separate but immediately repeated occasions, the client looks at a new copy of the same passage and makes these judgments. In this way, the consistent locus of word concern can be particularized to an extent that even exceeds that made possible by the responses to the SSC. To be sure, the checklist report that speech difficulty is specific to one's name or to the purchase of certain specific items permits further exploration of the words and phonemes involved. If saying one's name (Mark) and purchasing a ticket (to Boston) evoke negative emotion, it is possible to determine if the response is limited or encompasses various words that begin with these phonemes.[10] But such determinations can be still more finely assessed through expectancy responses to specific words. The consistent locus of concern made evident by silent expectancy readings will, for example, point up whether words beginning with m and b frequently evoke negative emotion. Furthermore, other sounds that are consistent stimuli for foreboding will also be iden-

---

[9] The stimulus materials employed vary according to reading ability. They range from sequentially ordered pictures that represent specific words, to word lists, to sentence-ordered words, to passages. The anticipation of difficulty is signaled by pointing to the pictures or by underlining the words or sounds that evoke concern. These materials are matched to those used during the oral reading when, as previously described, a palmar sweat print is taken.

[10] The initial phoneme is of prime concern since it is almost without exception the one that is spoken dysfluently if the word is stuttered (Johnson and Brown, 1935; Hahn, 1942).

tified by this procedure. Particular information of this kind is not directly tapped by the more general items of the checklist, although it is likely to be suggested by responses to those that are word-specific.

As we have seen, word-induced negative emotion is reassessed by BAB procedures that overlap and increase in specificity. The behavioral analysis progresses from its general indication, possibly first made evident by the palmar sweat response to the oral reading of a fixed passage, to the emotional reactions elicited by the word-specific items of the SSC, and then finally to the signaled expectation of concern about particular words or even specific sounds.

A similar progression from general to specific occurs in the evaluation of emotional responding that is predominantly situational. The first assessment of situationally induced negative emotion involves palmar sweat measurement during an extemporaneous speech circumstance where the words used are unrestricted. The next test of situational concern involves the SSC, whose items frequently explore circumstances that are totally unrelated to specific words or sounds. The evaluation of situational concern is narrowed still further by interview procedures that follow up on the self-report responses to the SSC. This procedure, which is also used to check on the word concerns revealed by BAB tests, serves to expand on the information brought to attention by PSI and SSC measurements.

Behavior assessment battery: Speech-specific adjustive responding

The assessment battery explores more than emotional responses. Its procedures also sample the instrumental adjustments that speakers often use as they seek to avoid or escape negatively charged speech situations or words. The Behavior Check List (BCL) provides the person being assessed with a list of 97 different behaviors, most of which stutterers have used as voluntary adjustments. The BCL now being used asks only two things of the person being assessed. First, he must indicate which, if any, of the 97 behaviors listed are those he *currently* displays either when preparing to speak or when speaking. Second, he must indicate which, if any, of these selected behaviors are used purposively as aids to speech. Those presently thought to be a means of avoiding or escaping difficulties associated with speaking are, in other words, separated from the individual's larger behavioral display. The voluntary nature of the reportedly purposive adjustments is then tested. The individual is instructed to omit one or another of each of these behaviors during short periods of extemporaneous speech and oral reading. The volitional nature of the separate behaviors becomes apparent if their occurrence is markedly reduced or eliminated. Voluntary responses are manipulable by stimulus-contingent instructions; stutterers can limit the frequency of voluntary adjustments if they are asked to do so (Oelschlaeger, 1971). Clinical experience has confirmed these experimental findings and has made instructions a viable procedure for cross-checking the validity of the behavioral distinctions that are part of BCL.

Typically, fewer behaviors are checked on the BCL than are observed by the clinician. Perhaps habituation masks awareness or perhaps the consideration of these responses is negative and to be avoided. For whatever reason, the assessor needs to determine if there are behaviors displayed other than those that are reported. Toward this end, the BCL serves as a means for the clinician to record the behaviors observed during the extemporaneous speech and oral-reading portions of the assessment. Then the unreported behaviors are also tested to see if they too are modifiable by instructions. The clinician names first one and then another of these behaviors. This is often enough to produce recognition and evaluation of their voluntary or involuntary nature. Occasionally, however, a behavior is not recognized. It may even be unrecognized after it has been verbally described. The behavioral topography needs clarification. Therefore, depending on its form, the individual behavior is brought to the speaker's attention visually or acoustically. Only after the speaker can accurately identify the behavior is the instruction given that it be omitted from speech. Only after clear discrimination of the behavior is it feasible to assess its voluntary manipulability.

Other than antecedent instructions are used to check behaviors that may be adjustive responses. Response-contingent but nonnegative consequences are also used to determine a behavior's manipulability. A nonnegative *informing* stimulus is made contingent upon a particular behavior to determine if its frequency is notably reduced by this consequence of its occurrence. The word "now," a light, or a pencil tap exemplifies the stimuli that have been made contingent upon a response such as an arm swing, a head turn, or a leg movement. Sometimes, moreover, the use of a response-contingent stimulus is joined to stimulus-contingent intructions. The speaker is instructed that a particular behavior is to be omitted and that, if it does occur, attention will be called to its presence. The consequent stimulation is thus an immediate reminder of the antecedent instructions. Together, these informing stimuli have a powerful manipulative effect on adjustive responses.

Differential assessment

Experience with the BAB and with the speakers assessed has made it clear that significant behavioral differences exist among those who seek help. Not all dysfluent speakers, by any means, manifest either speech-associated negative emotion or situational and word fears that correlate with the occurrence of fluency failures. Not all dysfluent speakers are concerned about their speech, and not all who are concerned about speaking show speech disruptions. Fluency failures can have other than conditioned emotion as their antecedent, and speech concern rather than fluency failures may be the appropriate therapeutic target.

Clearly, there are diverse emotional reactions to speech. There are also various forms of fluency failure. These differences significantly alter the strategies and tactics of behavior therapy. They are critical to therapy. It is a disservice to wantonly lump together all dysfluents because they evidence grossly similar fluency failures. There are notable differences in the topographies of fluency failures, and these reflect differences in antecedents that should be used to guide the choice of therapy procedures. The suggestion that stuttering is the watershed fed by various rivers is perhaps a harmless analogy (Van Riper, 1963). But it is not harmless if it is taken as an indication that distinctions among dysfluents are unnecessary and serve no therapeutic purpose. The absence of differential assessment promotes routinized therapy; the same procedures are pressed into use for all dysfluents since note is not taken of the real differences in causative antecedents, behavioral topographies, conditioning categories, and reinforcement histories.

The BAB reflects not only the long present recognition that fluency failure can result from various functional states or organic conditions (Goda, 1961; St. Onge, 1963; Van Riper, 1963; Jones, 1966), but it also reflects the more recent realization that the success of behavior therapy rests on knowledge about the responses to be changed (Goldfried and Pomeranz, 1968). As Kanfer and Phillips (1970) have pointed out, "in order to apply a behavioral model comprehensively to the entire treatment process . . . the behavior therapist needs systematic methods to collect information to appraise the patients' difficulties and to reach decisions concerning the most appropriate treatment" (p. 496). This viewpoint has begun to affect therapists concerned with the modification of speech behaviors. Among those factors that verify the growing awareness of the import of assessment to speech therapy are the insistence on molecular specifications of the behaviors to be modified (Webster, 1968); the call for recognition that the effect of contingent stimulation depends on, in part, the nature of the environment into which consequences are introduced (Meyer, 1972); the urging that care be exercised so that behavioral technology does not become so routinized that the therapist ignores differences among the responses to be modified; and the highlighting of the relationship between response type and behavior-change procedures. Here Oelschlaeger's (1973) statement is pertinent:

"Differential behavioral analysis appears to be a necessary antecedent to . . . specific therapeutic procedures" (p. 73).

One important aspect of behavior analysis relating to the targets of therapy concerns negative emotional responses that are not tied to speech stimuli. As we have seen, a number of the assessment procedures of the BAB are used to determine if negative emotion is elicited by speech-specific situations or by words. Other battery procedures, however, are designed to sample emotional responses to stimuli unrelated to speech or speaking. A modified version of Geer's Fear Survey Schedule II (FSS) explores fear responses to a wide range of nonspeech stimuli.[11] Geer (1965) constructed the FSS so that fear refers to "a negative emotional response evoked by a relatively specific stimulus" (p. 45). This 51-item checklist samples fear reactions to such varied stimuli as cars, heights, darkness, mice, crowds, and tests. Factor analysis of this checklist by Bernstein and Allen (1969) shows that the items cluster together in ways which suggest that the FSS taps fear responses to live organisms, death and illness, social interaction, and social evaluation. The FSS, then, provides for assessment of the negative emotional responses to particular environmental circumstances that are not primarily specific to speech.

The knowledge provided by the modified FSS, as well as that gained from some of the other BAB procedures, helps make obvious an individual's particular emotional concerns. The test data serve to make clear the presence of fear responses and their specific nature in a way that often calls attention to differential behavioral distinctions. The dysfluent speaker who is not emotional about the nonspeech environment is distinguished from one who is. The individuals whose concerns are not speech-associated are behaviorally differentiated from those whose negative emotional responses are specific to words or speech situations. These and other differences are clinically meaningful; their importance does not relate to diagnostic naming or class counts. It is not for nosological or actuarial reasons, but for significant therapeutic purposes that differential assessment is undertaken. Information of the kind provided by the various BAB measures clarifies the responses that are the targets of therapy and influences the choice of therapeutic tactics.

The determination of therapeutic targets is of no little import. For this reason, the BAB employs overlapping evaluations. Nonspeech emotional responses, for example, are sampled not only by the self-report fear schedule, but also by physiological responses. As we have noted,

---

[11] The SIU modification involves a change from a seven- to a five-point scale to make this test procedure consistent with that used in the SSC, another of the checklists that is an integral part of the BAB.

the first three palmar sweat prints are taken in a setting where the client is aware that speech will not be required. The third of these palmar prints serves as the basal level against which to compare the emotional response to speech circumstances. The PSI from the first print, on the other hand, is compared with the total score on the FSS. Both the initial physiological response and the self-report data, then, are used to determine whether nonspeech stimuli evoke marked emotional responses. Typically, the FSS total score and the initial PSI provide a consistent indication of emotional responses evoked by nonspeech stimuli.[12] However, each of these test procedures adds a different dimension to the assessment of emotional responding. The FSS is particularly useful in determining specific stimuli that elicit emotion. The repeated PSI measurements are helpful because they index an individual's adaptability to a constant situation. The measurements point up how readily the individual being assessed adapts to a stressful setting.

The FSS and PSI scores provide a complementary impression of the extent to which nonspeech stimuli evoke emotional responses. Widespread emotional responses to situations explored by the fear schedule and considerable palmar sweating that does not show change with repeated experience in a silent-test situation provide clinical evidence that the client should be referred for psychological assessment. Such decisions depend on normative data, the responses of special groups to these tests, and the evidence that the FSS and PSI procedures are clinically useful. At this time it is not appropriate to review this evidence. However, it should be noted that Bernstein and Allen's (1969) study of the FSS provides a mean total score for unselected individuals.[13] Their sample responded to the FSS items much like Geer's (1965) normative subjects did. Norms for some selected groups of subjects are also available. Shoemaker and Brutten's recently compiled data, which come from stutterers responding to a five-point scale, show a mean total score of 108.08 and a standard deviation of 38.40. Responses to the test items made evident both the generally heightened level of negative emotion and the degree of concern that having to speak elicits; only death

---

[12] At times there is a notable discrepancy between the FSS total and the initial PSI. This discrepancy generally reflects the fact that the cognitive and physiological aspects of "the problem" are different. The self-perceived difficulties are significantly different from those reported by the autonomic nervous system. This information is helpful in determining the therapeutic targets and the tactics that are appropriate.

[13] A mean total score of 98.64 (standard deviation of 38.47) resulted from the seven-point scale used. The mean total of 81.81 and 108.47 for males and females, respectively, was quite similar to the 75.78 and 100.16 displayed by Geer's subjects. These means have been adjusted for use in the BAB. The SIU modification of the FSS employs a five-point rather than a seven-point scale. The adjusted mean total score is 70.45 rather than 98.64.

of a loved one evoked a greater emotional response than did speaking before a group. Otherwise, individuals who stutter responded in a nondistinctive fashion. Factor analysis showed no notable difference in the clustering of responses. Like unselected subjects, individuals who stutter responded in ways that factored into death and illness, social evaluation and interaction, live organisms and water, injury, and classical phobias.[14]

The PSI has a long history of clinical use (Brutten, 1959). Most frequently the index has served to reflect emotional change evoked by the introduction of a particular stimulus event (Bixenstein, 1955; Bode and Brutten, 1963). In the assessment battery, for example, the measurement of the emotional response to extemporaneous speech and oral reading follows a nonverbal basal sequence. Mowrer (1953) has pointed out that palmar sweating reacts very sensitively to significant stimulus changes. For this reason, he considers it ideal for state measurement. It has value, in other words, not as an index of "personality"—assumed to be a stable trait—but as a reflection of emotional responding to specific and changing scenes. Its clinical utility as a state measure has been attested to repeatedly (Light, 1951; Ellsworth and Clark, 1957; Paul, 1964).

Notable differences in the way individuals behave become clear from various segments of the assessment procedures. Emotional responding is but one area where distinctive features are considered. Just as negative emotion may or may not be a correlate of dysfluent speech, fluency failures may or may not occur consistently on specific words. Consistency is clinically significant; so, too, is inconsistency. The determination that fluency failures are consistently specific to words (words of a certain kind or composition) or are dispersed in a chance way is meaningful because it is reflective of antecedent conditions. In the BAB the loci of dysfluency are evaluated for consistency on the basis of the five repeated oral readings of the same passage that follow the extemporaneous speaking task.[15]

Consistency is not the behavioral province of only those who stutter (Brutten and O'Brecht, 1965; Neelley and Timmons, 1967). Various individuals display some degree of consistent dysfluency. But young stutterers display significantly more consistency than comparable nonstutterers, and adult stutterers display an average consistency of 65–70 per-

---

[14] The fourth factor, injury, reflected the preponderance of males in the sample of stutterers. Rubin, Katkin, and Weiss (1968), in their factor analysis of Geer's normative data, showed that this response clustering was evidenced by males though not by females.

[15] Palmar sweat measurements are made on the first, third, and fifth of these oral readings. The first of these is made to see the negative emotional response to fixed material, whereas the others reflect on the emotional adjustment that results from repeated experience with the same passage.

cent (Johnson and Inness, 1939). As a result, consistency can be used discriminatively. As Johnson has pointed out, "stuttering does not occur haphazardly or in a random or chance fashion, but as a response to identifiable stimuli" (Johnson et al., 1967, p. 210). The non-random distribution of one speaker's fluency failure is illustrated in Table 2, which summarizes a segment of a BAB data sheet. This speaker's dysfluencies clustered at certain words, ones which reportedly began with a feared sound. The consistency with which certain words were repeated or prolonged are strikingly evidenced by the cumulative data. By the fifth oral reading most words spoken dysfluently were those that had previously offered difficulty.

Consistency does not always predominate. Some speakers display fluency failures that are primarily neoteric, or newly evidenced. The loci of fluency failures are new rather than consistent. Dysfluency occurs on words that had previously been spoken in a fluent manner. Table 3 illustrates the presence of another speaker's failures that have quite different loci from reading to reading. Dysfluency is present, but its occurrence is not specific to certain word stimuli. Moreover, this individual's failures did not vary with situational events. Relatively few fluency failures occurred, and their topography was not clinically significant. Therapy decisions were consonant with these data. Behavior-change procedures were directed at the evaluation of dysfluencies as nonsignificant rather than the decrease in their frequency.

Neotericity, the measure of inconsistent dysfluency, does not necessarily suggest the absence of clinical significance. Similarly, the presence of consistency does not necessarily indicate that the fluency failures

TABLE 2

FLUENCY FAILURES DURING REPEATED ORAL READINGS
OF A BAB SPEECH PASSAGE

Reading	Frequency	Consistency	Cumulative Consistency	Neotericity	Cumulative Neotericity
1	80				
2	98	71		27	
3	114	88	91	26	23
4	116	95	103	21	13
5	110	92	105	18	5
Recovery Period: Interspersed Activities					
6	109	89	107	20	2

TABLE 3
FLUENCY FAILURES DURING REPEATED ORAL READINGS
OF A BAB SPEECH PASSAGE

Reading	Frequency	Consistency	Cumulative Consistency	Neotericity	Cumulative Neotericity
1	7				
2	5	2		3	
3	6	0	1	6	5
4	4	1	0	3	4
5	5	0	1	5	4
Recovery Period: Interspersed Activities					
6	5	1	1	4	4

characterize stuttering. The fact that stuttering behaviors are consistent to words or situations does not mean that other forms of dysfluencies born of different antecedents do not also display consistency. This is exemplified by a recently seen client whose fluency failures were consistent though specific to multisyllabic words about which there was no concern. Word or sound fears were not present, and speech was as dysfluent in one situation as in another. Moreover, the failures generally occurred on other than the initial sound. Though the client had a general feeling that speech performance was below par, there was no specific concern about speech situations or words. Behavioral observations like these are clinically meaningful. Fluency failures, even consistent ones, are not necessarily indicative of stuttering. The repetitions and prolongations of stuttering are consistent, but consistency alone does not denote stuttering. The research of Deal and Darley (1972), for example, has shown that repetitions and prolongations of sounds are major error types among patients with apraxia of speech. Moreover, approximately 13.5 percent of the apraxics' failures were of a kind grossly like and often confused with stuttering. These failures were not neoteric: "The errors were not scattered randomly throughout the reading material but tended to occur in a somewhat predictable fashion" (p. 644). However, their occurrence was predominantly a function of word length, and neither instructions designed to vary expectancy nor masking noise delivered so as to reduce auditory feedback had a significant effect on their frequency. Thus, these failures behaved in a manner that was discriminably different from stutterings. The frequency of stuttering moments has been repeatedly manipulated by these very same variables (Johnson and Sinn, 1937; Shane, 1963).

Caplan (1972) too, has focused attention on differential assessment and the "stuttering-like" speech of those who have a pathology of the central nervous system. When she compared the behavioral patterns of dysphasic patients with those that are classic to stuttering, various differences became apparent. For the dysphasic, interjections were the most frequent form of dysfluency; function words were associated with failures to a greater extent than were content, or lexical, words, and the frequency of dysfluency increased rather than adapted during repeated readings of the same oral material. These are remarkable findings for they are diametrically opposed to those that have come from individuals who stutter.

Caplan, like Deal and Darley, discovered that the observed dysfluencies were primarily dependent on word length.[16] This finding suggested neurological influences on motor coordination rather than conditioned emotion or other causative antecedents. Deal and Darley similarly suggested that the errors they observed were essentially a function of a motor disorder. They saw disordered motor programming and not situational variables as being at the root of the failures evidenced. Yet, as Caplan has pointed out, even professional listeners reacted to the taped speech samples of the dysphasic subjects in terms of stuttering. The mere sound of dysfluency occasioned a diagnosis, one that was markedly incorrect. As a result, she reemphasized the need expressed by St. Onge (1963) that "symptoms" be divided into separate syndromes as an aid to diagnosis and therapy planning.

Not only apraxics and dysphasics manifest stuttering-like behaviors. Various organic conditions affect speech in ways that may be grossly similar to stuttering. Meningitis, Down's Syndrome, Parkinson's disease, syphilis, and Wilson's disease are but some of the conditions that may result in a failure of fluency (Goda, 1961; Preus, 1973). So, too, may drugs and alcohol intoxication. But the behavioral topographies differ with differences in the antecedent conditions. This was made clear by Sobell and Sobell (1972), who were particularly interested in the specific types of speech failure created by different degrees of intoxication. Their counts, based on Johnson's dysfluency categories, revealed that not all forms of fluency failure increased as a result of alcohol. Three different kinds of interjections were significantly affected. So, too, were word

---

[16] Word length and grammatical factors are partially independent properties. Thus, though longer words were more apt to be spoken dysfluently by dysphasics than were shorter words, it is understandable that function words (i.e., prepositions, pronouns, conjunctions) evidenced more fluency failures than did the generally longer content, or lexical, words.

omissions, revisions, and broken words. But repetitions—sound, word, and phrase repetitions—were among the error types that *did not* increase. These failures actually decreased somewhat. The Sobells pointed out that on the basis of their data it was possible to describe "a profile of alcohol-induced dysfluent speech of alcoholics" (Sobell and Sobell, 1972, p. 865). As a result of this behavioral profile, alcoholics can now be distinguished from those whose dysfluency has another antecedent. Alcohol, which is a central-nervous-system depressant (Bennett, 1966), interferes with normal fluency in a distinctive fashion, one that is behaviorally apparent under molecular examination.

We have been considering the loci, form, and antecedents of the fluency failures displayed during the five oral readings that are a part of the BAB. These oral trials are followed by three expectancy readings of a different, though matched, passage. Three times the individual under test silently reads a different copy of the same material and underlines those words on which he anticipates difficulty. Following this he reads the passage aloud. This makes it possible to determine if there is any relationship between expected difficulty and observed failure. This relationship is cross-checked and expanded by comparing the characteristics of the words that elicit anticipation and the ones that were spoken dysfluently during the previous five oral readings. In this way, the presence or absence of word fears are determined and analyzed with respect to the occurrence of fluency failures. The absence of word anticipation may suggest no more than that situations rather than words are the emotion-evoking stimuli. But the presence of considerable dysfluency in the absence of both word anticipation and specific situational fears indicates the need to look toward other antecedents, ones quite different from negative emotion specific to speech. Such was the case for the individual whose expectancy scores appear in Table 4. Fluency failures

TABLE 4

ANTICIPATED AND OBSERVED FLUENCY FAILURES DURING THREE SILENT AND ONE ORAL READING OF A BAB EXPECTANCY PASSAGE

	Frequency	Consistency	Cumulative Consistency	Neotericity	Cumulative Neotericity
Silent Reading					
1	6				
2	2	1		1	
3	0	0	0	0	0
Oral Reading					
1	53	1	1	52	52

were clearly present, although they were not anticipated. When the expectancy passage was read aloud, the number of dysfluencies approximated that displayed during the previous oral readings. These oral readings showed that the loci of difficulty were predominantly neoteric. The fluency failures were not specific to words initiated by a particular phoneme or to words that were multisyllabic. As a matter of fact, no specific characteristics were discernible. Moreover, there was no evidence from the other BAB procedures that the frequency of failures was sensitive to changes in speech situations. The assessment data, then, pointed neither to speech-specific negative emotion nor to those organic conditions where word consistency is characteristic. In this instance, however, the considerable PSI and the marked responses to the items of the FSS suggested that speech was not the primary problem. Recently, a somewhat similar pattern was manifested by another client. Neither words nor speech situations elicited concern. Dysfluency was evident, but it tended to be inconsistent (neoteric). However, the test procedures indicative of general emotional difficulties were not above average. What became apparent, though, was that speech was slow, slower than it had been, and a general hesitancy about speaking was developing regardless of the situation or words involved. What consistency there was during oral reading occurred on somewhat longer and more complex words. Words containing certain consonant blends seemed to be produced in a "broken" fashion. These were the initial behavioral signs associated with a medical diagnosis of early and progressive cerebellar degeneration.

More typical are expectancy scores like those in Table 5. At least for those individuals whose consistency during oral reading is suggestive of word-specific difficulty and whose responses to the SSC indicate concern about such items as unchangeable passages, specific sounds, and

TABLE 5

ANTICIPATED AND OBSERVED FLUENCY FAILURES DURING THREE
SILENT AND ONE ORAL READING OF A BAB EXPECTANCY PASSAGE

	Frequency	Consistency	Cumulative Consistency	Neotericity	Cumulative Neotericity
Silent Reading					
1	73				
2	77	58		19	
3	68	50	58	18	10
Oral Reading					
1	77	56	64	21	13

names, it is likely that neotericity will be relatively low. Of course, consistent expectancy will not be much in evidence if it is situational stimuli that are the predominant cues for negative emotion. Thus, what needs to be understood is that a complete plan for behavior change does not flow from one test score or one set of scores. The therapy blue-print that the assessment battery provides requires both an understanding of the separate test results and a thorough comprehension of their integrated relationship.

Assessment: An overview with implications for therapy

Any assessment procedure requires experience. The interpretive nuances that come with its continued use are not easily transmitted by the printed page. This is especially true when a battery of integrated tests is involved. The BAB is no exception. Although it is a simple battery to use, it has some evaluative complexities. Perhaps a few illustrations of integrated findings and their relationship to behavior change will be clarifying and will preclude aimless therapy. Perhaps it will give direction to the therapist in determining the responses to be changed and the tactics most likely to bring about modification. Trying to modify "stuttering" rather than specific behaviors is like jousting with windmills. Dealing with all who are called "stutterers" in the exact same way denies the behavioral differences that exist among dysfluent speakers. The assessment procedures sketched in this chapter provide the therapist with a means for gathering individualized information that is specific rather than general. It thus permits the discriminative use of therapeutic tactics that are tailored to the particular needs of individuals.

It is the individual's behavior display and not the diagnostic class that is the focus of therapy. The relationship between the behaviors in evidence and therapy planning becomes clear from sequentially looking at the interfaced data that come from an actual assessment. The summary of data from our most recent assessment appears in Table 6. This unselected client responded markedly to the test situation (PSI of 72) despite the fact that speech was not required. This finding was consistent with the FSS score of 188. It was not, then, the test situation alone that elicited negative emotion. The responses to the FSS items were suggestive of widespread emotional responding. Situational emotion adapted rapidly with repeated experience. Palmar sweating reduced from 78 to 28. It continued to fall even when extemporaneous speech was required. The PSI was 20 when the standard picture was being described. Oral reading, however, brought a relatively sharp reversal of this downward trend. Both the difference between the measured emotional response to these two speaking situations and the fact that it was the reading of fixed material that elicited a notable emotional response were

TABLE 6
BEHAVIOR ASSESSMENT BATTERY: DATA SUMMARY

I. Emotional behaviors

A. Physiological

During Silence
PSI Print 1. 72
PSI Print 2. 28
PSI Print 3. 28

During Speech
PSI Print 4. 20 (extemporaneous)
PSI Print 5. 34 (oral reading)

B. Cognitive

1. FSS: response total of 188 to nonspeech situations. Mean item score of 3.5.
2. SSC: column-one total of 168. Mean emotional response to word and situational stimuli of 3.3.
3. Expected word difficulty

Reading	Freq.	Consistency	Cum. Consis.	Neoter.	Cum. Neoter.
1	12				
2	18	12		6	
3	17	15	16	2	1
Oral	56	13	15	43	41

4. Interview: anticipates difficulty on specific sounds and words and in particular situations. Negative emotional responses to words and their elements predominate, but situational concerns are prevalent.

C. Motor

1. Oral reading

Reading	Freq.	Consistency	Cum. Consis.	Neoter.	Cum. Neoter.
1	52				
2	43	31		12	
3	38	30	38	8	0
4	38	31	33	7	5
5	33	31	31	2	2
6	38	27	34	11	4

2. SSC: column-two total of 178. Mean speech disruption to word and situational stimuli of 3.4. Degree of disruption consistent with emotional-response level reported.
3. Speech behavior: disruptions characterized by oral and silent repetitions and prolongations of *t, d, f, v, s, p,* and *k.*

TABLE 6 (*Continued*)

II. Instrumental behaviors

   A. BCL: 17 voluntary adjustments reported. Word-specific adjustments predominate, but situational manipulations are numerous.

   B. Topography

     1. Observed adjustments include
       a. word change
       b. pitch variation
       c. pauses
       d. hand movements
       e. rate change

     2. Reported adjustments include

       avoidances
       a. word change
       b. lowering of pitch
       c. silent rehearsals
       d. shunning of speech situations
       e. written communication
       f. self-instructed relaxation

       escapes
       a. hand swing
       b. increasing of speech rate
       c. interjected phrases

     3. Contingency management
       a. Stimulus-contingent stimulation: Hand movement, pitch, and rate change were reduced by instructions that these behaviors be omitted.
       b. Response-contingent stimulation: Word changes and pauses were among the behaviors reduced by neutral consequences.
       c. Stimulus- and response-contingent stimulation produced some reduction in all behaviors reported to be voluntary adjustments.
       d. Involuntary behaviors: Prolongations and repetitions were not manipulated by either stimulus- or response-contingent stimulation.

---

clinically significant. The behavioral pattern suggested that word-specific concerns predominated. Moreover, the fact that there was less negative emotion during extemporaneous speech than during oral reading pointed to the possibility of instrumental adjustments, like word changes. Data from both the SSC and from the silent expectancy readings confirmed the presence of word-specific emotion. The checklist total of 168, which was well above the mean score for those who stutter, indicated that the most disturbing speech situations were those where there was a need to use specific words. Enforced use of a previously troublesome sound or word, ordering a specific item, placing a person-to-person call, and buying a ticket to a specific place elicited considerable negative emotion. In contrast, talking in a rap session, arguing with parents, and talking with a salesgirl offered far less difficulty. Moreover, the expectancy readings made it evident that the words on which speech difficulty was anticipated were to a great extent those on which fluency failure occurred. Although there was more dysfluency than the client anticipated, 13 of the observed failures were among the 17 expected, and 15 of the dysfluencies had been anticipated on at least two of the three silent-reading trials.

That the locus of difficulty was to a great extent tied to specific words was made apparent, once more, by the assessment data of the six oral readings. Consistency was marked, and it was maintained throughout the readings. There was a solid core of words on which the failures occurred; neotericity was low. This was so even during the recovery reading following much interspersed activity. Analysis of the loci of both the expected and observed dysfluencies verified that the failures generally occurred on words that began with specific phonemes.

The presenting complaint centered around word fears and these fears were confirmed. However, the average emotional response to the FSS items was 3.3, and the situational items—talking on the telephone, speaking with a stranger, and being interviewed—were said to elicit "much" fear. Failures were underestimated when anticipation was limited to words. Some part of this difference between the expected difficulty and the observed failures was likely to be attributable to situational emotion. But the concern with words did predominate. Even the instrumental responses reported on the BCL were more apt to be word-specific (i.e., silent repetition and omission and substitution of sounds, words, and phrases) and to be used to cope with word fears (i.e., pausing before specific words and word change) than they were likely to be designed to cope with situational emotion. Some were exclusively situational, however, as befits the presence of these concerns. There was complete avoidance of certain speaking situations, refusal to attempt speech in other circumstances, and the use of self-instructed relaxation at other times. However, these instrumental adjustments were fewer in number and in use.

Not all assessments, by any means, show the particular behavioral patterns we have been discussing. Although there is generally evidence of word and situational emotion, there is typically a more even mix than that observed with the client whose responses we have just been discussing. This is clear from the BAB assessments that have been reported previously, even though they illustrate various response patterns (Brutten, 1973; Webster and Brutten, 1974). Among these, for example, is one where nonspeech emotion is limited and there is minimal word-specific emotion, but the arousal created by speaking situations is highly evident.

As we have seen, distinctive patterns suggest different antecedents and loci of difficulty. But therapeutic judgments demand more than general patterns. More significant is whether the conditional stimuli are particular words or specific situations or both. It is necessary to know which particular stimuli cue-off negative emotion, not just their general classification. Similarly, it is not enough to be aware that adjustive responses are employed. For therapy to have a firm practical base, it is necessary to know the particular adjustive responses used to cope with specific situational and word difficulties and the stimulus circumstances that set the occasion for their occurrence. These are the primary facts, the ones that are fundamental to therapeutic decision-making.

Reminders that behavior therapy is still in its infancy and warnings that the clinician should not be limited to one approach to change bears reiteration. We have said that the "therapist should not be bound" to any one procedure, that changes in therapy tactics are to be anticipated, and that behavior modification "will be served by those therapists who advance our knowledge in the efficient means of achieving extinction" (Brutten and Shoemaker, 1967, p. ix). These comments were and still are meaningful. New tactics for modifying behavior are constantly being explored and compared with previous procedures (Friedman, 1966; Bandura, Blanchard, and Ritter, 1969; Morganstern, 1973). The fact that therapists are researching new and different clinical methods highlights the fact that no strategy, program, or tactic has been universally successful. It would be improper to suggest otherwise.

Certainly, with regard to the behavioral mixtures that people have called "stuttering," wisdom demands recognition that a number of tactics are usually necessary. This concept is primary to the overall strategy of two-factor therapy. A tactic designed to modify the negative emotional responses to speaking situations may not be entirely successful. Other compatible tactics, often interactive ones, may be expedient. The behavior therapist concerned with speech, like all such clinicians, needs to expand rather than limit available methods of behavior change. The same posture holds true for the clinical approach to instrumental responding. The various procedures for modifying adjustive responses need not be mutually exclusive. Alford and Ingham (1969), for example, found that neither a syllable-timed approach nor a contingency-management approach brought about as full a change in "stuttering" as did the tandem use of these procedures. More recently, Perkins (1973) asserted that modifying the behaviors of those who stutter involves more than one conceptual approach or one particular tactic. He posited that various behavioral components need to be dealt with and an array of tactics invoked for the attainment and maintenance of normally fluent speech. He found no clinical specific for stuttering. The stock use of a particular tactic or combination of procedures independent of the behaviors involved is questionable. Awareness of the behaviors involved, the tactics available, and the individual's responsivity needs to replace slavish devotion to inflexible clinical procedures.

References

Adams, M. R. (1969) Psychological differences between stutterers and nonstutterers: A review of the experimental literature. *Journal of Communication Disorders,* 2, 163–170.

Adams, M. R., and Dietz, D. A. (1965) A comparison of the reaction times of stutterers and nonstutterers to items on a word association test. *Journal of Speech and Hearing Research,* 8, 195–203.

Alford, J. and Ingham, R. J. (1969) The application of a token reinforcement system to the treatment of stuttering in children. *Journal of Australian College of Speech Therapists,* 19, 53–57.

Bandura, A., Blanchard, E. B., and Ritter, B. (1969) Relative efficacy of desensitization and modeling approaches for inducing behavioral, affective, and attitudinal changes. *Journal of Personality and Social Psychology,* 13, 173–199.

Barr, H. (1940) A quantitative study of the specific phenomena observed in stuttering. *Journal of Speech Disorders,* 5, 277–280.

Bennett, A. E. (1966) The effects of alcoholism on brain function. *Western Medicine,* 7, Supplement 3.

Bernstein, D. A., and Allen, G. G. (1969) Fear Survey Schedule (II): Normative data and factor analysis based upon a large college sample. *Behavior Research and Therapy,* 7, 403–407.

Berwick, N. H. (1955) Stutttering in response to photographs of selected listeners. In W. Johnson and R. R. Leutenegger, eds., *Stuttering in children and adults.* Minneapolis: University of Minnesota Press.

Bixenstein, V. E. (1955) A case study of the use of palmar sweating as a measure of psychological tension. *Journal of Abnormal and Social Psychology,* 50, 138–143.

Bloodstein, O. (1960a) The development of stuttering: I. Changes in nine basic features. *Journal of Speech and Hearing Disorders,* 25, 219–237.

Bloodstein, O. (1960b) The development of stuttering: II. Development phases. *Journal of Speech and Hearing Disorders,* 25, 366–376.

Bloodstein, O. (1969) *A handbook on stuttering.* Chicago: National Easter Seal Society.

Bloodstein, O., and Brutten, G. J. (1966) Stuttering problems. In R. W. Rieber and R. S. Brubaker, eds., *Speech pathology.* Amsterdam: North-Holland Publishing Co.

Bode, D. B., and Brutten, G. J. (1963) A palmar sweat investigation of the effect of audience variation upon stagefright. *Speech Monographs*, 30, 92–96.

Broadhurst, P. L. (1957) Emotionality and the Yerkes-Dodson law. *Journal of Experimental Psychology*, 54, 345–352.

Brookshire, R. (1969) Effects of random and response contingent noise upon disfluencies of normal speakers. *Journal of Speech and Hearing Research*, 12, 126–134.

Brutten, G. J. (1959) Colorimetric measurement of anxiety: A clinical and experimental procedure. *Speech Monographs*, 26, 282–287.

Brutten, G. J. (1970) Two-factor behavior theory and therapy. In *Conditioning in stuttering therapy: Application and limitations*. Memphis, Tenn.: Speech Foundation of America.

Brutten, G. J. (1973) Behavior assessment and the strategy of therapy. In Y. Lebrun and R. Hoops, eds., *Neurolinguistic approaches to stuttering*. The Hague: Mouton and Co.

Brutten, G. J., and Gray, B. B. (1961) Effect of word cue removal on adaptation and adjacency: A clinical paradigm. *Journal of Speech and Hearing Disorders*, 26, 385–389.

Brutten, S. R., and O'Brecht, F. L. (1965) An analysis of the fluency failures of non-stuttering children. Unpublished research report, Southern Illinois University.

Brutten, G. J., and Shoemaker, D. J. (1967) *The modification of stuttering*. Englewood Cliffs, N.J.: Prentice-Hall.

Brutten, G. J., and Shoemaker, D. J. (1969) Stuttering: The disintegration of speech due to conditioned negative emotion. In B. B. Gray and G. England, eds., *Stuttering and the conditioning therapies*. Monterey, Calif.: Monetary Institute for Speech and Hearing.

Brutten, G. J., and Shoemaker, D. J. (1971) A two-factor learning theory of stuttering. In L. E. Travis, ed., *Handbook of speech pathology and audiology*. New York: Appleton.

Brutten, G. J., and Shoemaker, D. J. (1972) Punishment of the oral prolongations of a stutterer. Unpublished manuscript, Southern Illinois University.

Brutten, G. J., and Shoemaker, D. J. (1974) Speech Situation Checklist. Copyright, 1974.

Caplan, L. (1972) An investigation of some aspects of stuttering-like speech in adult dysphasic subjects. *Journal of South Africa Speech and Hearing Association*, 19, 52–66.

Deal, J., and Darley, F. (1972) The influence of linguistic and situational variables on phonemic accuracy in apraxia of speech. *Journal of Speech and Hearing Research*, 15, 639–653.

Dixon, C. C. (1965) Stuttering adaptation in relation to assumed level of anxiety. In W. Johnson and R. R. Leutenegger, eds., *Stuttering in children and adults*. Minneapolis: University of Minnesota Press.

Ellsworth, R. B., and Clark, L. D. (1957) Prediction of the response of chronic schizophrenics to drug therapy: A preliminary report of the relationship between palmar sweat and the behavioral effects of tranquilizing drugs. *Journal of Clinical Psychology*, 13, 59–61.

Eysenck, H. J. (1960) *Behavior therapy and neurosis.* New York: Pergamon.

Fletcher, J. M. (1914) An experimental study of stuttering. *American Journal of Psychology,* 25, 201–255.

Freides, D. (1957) Goal-box cues and pattern of reinforcement. *Journal of Experimental Psychology,* 53, 361–372.

Freud, S. (1936) *The problem of anxiety.* New York: Norton.

Friedman, D. (1966) A new technique for the systematic desensitization of phobic symptoms. *Behavior Research and Therapy,* 4, 139–140.

Geer, J. H. (1965) The development of a scale to measure fear. *Journal of Behavior Rsearch and Therapy,* 3, 45–53.

Goda, S. (1961) Stuttering manifestations following spinal meningitis. *Journal of Speech and Hearing Disorders,* 26, 392–393.

Goldfried, M. R., and Pomeranz, D. M. (1968) Role of assessment in behavior modification. *Psychological Reports,* 23, 75–87.

Grinker, R. R., and Speigel, J. P. (1945) *Men under stress.* Philadelphia: Blakiston.

Hahn, E. F. (1942) A study of the relationship between stuttering occurrences and phonetic factors in oral reading. *Journal of Speech Disorders,* 7, 143–151.

Hill, H. (1944) Stuttering: II. A review and integration of physiological data. *Journal of Speech Disorders,* 9, 289–324.

Hill, H. (1954) An experimental study of disorganization of speech and manual responses in normal subjects. *Journal of Speech and Hearing Disorders,* 19, 295–305.

Ickes, W., and Pierce, S. (1973) The stuttering moment: A plethysmographic study. *Journal of Communication Disorders,* 6, 155–164.

Janssen, P., and Brutten, G. J. (1973) The differential effects of punishment of oral prolongations. In Y. Lebrun and R. Hoops, eds., *Neurolinguistic approaches to stuttering.* The Hague: Mouton and Co.

Jasper, H. H., and Murray, E. (1932) A study of the eye-movements of stutterers during oral reading. *Experimental Psychology,* 15, 528–538.

Johnson, W. (1961) Measurements of oral reading and speaking rate and disfluency of adult male and female stutterers and non-stutterers. *Journal of Speech and Hearing Disorders,* 7, Monograph Supplement, 1–20.

Johnson, W., et al. (1967) *Speech handicapped school children.* New York: Harper & Row.

Johnson, W., and Associates (1959) *The onset of stuttering.* Minneapolis: University of Minnesota Press.

Johnson, W., and Brown, S. F. (1935) Stuttering in relation to various speech sounds. *Quarterly Journal of Speech,* 21, 481–496.

Johnson, W., and Inness, M. (1939) Studies in the psychology of stuttering: XIII. A statistical analysis of the adaptation and consistency effects in relation to stuttering. *Journal of Speech Disorders,* 4, 79–86.

Johnson, W., Larson, R. P., and Knott, J. R. (1937) Studies in the psychology of stuttering: III. Certain objective cues related to the precipitation of the moment of stuttering. *Journal of Speech Disorders,* 2, 23–25.

Johnson, W., and Millsapps, L. S. (1937) Studies in the psychology of stuttering: VI. The role of cues representative of stuttering moments during oral reading. *Journal of Speech Disorders*, 2, 101–104.

Johnson, W., and Sinn, A. (1937) Studies in the psychology of stuttering: V. Frequency of stuttering with expectation of stuttering controlled. *Journal of Speech Disorders*, 2, 98–100.

Jones, R. K. (1966) Observations on stammering after localized cerebral injury. *Journal of Neurology, Neurosurgery, and Psychiatry*, 29, 192–195.

Kanfer, F. H., and Phillips, J. S. (1970) *Learning foundations of behavior therapy*. New York: Wiley.

Kasl, S. V., and Mahl, G. F. (1965) The relationship of disturbances and hesitations in spontaneous speech to anxiety. *Journal of Personality and Social Psychology*, 5, 425–433.

Kimble, G. A. (1961) *Conditioning and learning*. New York: Appleton.

King, P. (1961) Perseveration in stutterers and nonstutterers. *Journal of Speech and Hearing Research*, 4, 346–357.

Knott, J. R., and Irwin, D. A. (1973) Anxiety, stress, and the contingent negative variation. *Archives of General Psychiatry*, 29, 538–541.

Kuno, Y. (1956) *Human perspiration*. Springfield, Ill.: C. C Thomas.

Levis, D. J. (1966) Effects of serial CS presentation and other characteristics of the CS on the conditioned avoidance response. *Psychological Reports*, 18, 755–766.

Liddell, H. S. (1944) Conditioned reflex method and experimental neurosis. In J. McV. Hunt, ed., *Personality and the behavior disorders*. New York: Ronald.

Light, B. H. (1951) Tension changes in patients undergoing psychotherapy. Ph.D. dissertation, University of Illinois.

Low, M. D., and Swift, S. J. (1971) The contingent negative variation and the "resting" D.C. potential of the human brain: Effects of situational anxiety. *Neuropsychologia*, 6, 203–208.

Luper, H. L. (1954) The consistency of selected aspects of behavior in the repetitions of stuttered words. Ph.D. dissertation, Ohio State University.

Mackworth, N. H. (1958) Eye fixations recorded on changing visual scenes by the television eye-marker. *Journal of the Optical Society of America*, 48, 439–445.

Mahl, G. F. (1956) Disturbances and silences in the patient's speech in psychotherapy. *Journal of Abnormal and Social Psychology*, 53, 1–15.

Mahl, G. F. (1959) Measuring the patient's anxiety during interviews from "expressive" aspects of his speech. *Transactions of the New York Academy of Sciences*, 21, 249–257.

Mahl, G. F. (1961) Measures of two expressive aspects of a patient's speech in two psychotherapeutic interviews. In L. A. Gottschalk, ed., *Comparative psycholinguistic analysis of two psychotherapeutic interviews*. New York: International Universities.

Martin, H. H., and Haroldson, S. K. (1967) The relationship between anticipation and consistency of stuttered words. *Journal of Speech and Hearing Research*, 18, 323–327.

Martin, R. R., Brookshire, R., and Siegel, G. M. (1964) The effects of response contingent punishment on various behaviors emitted during a "moment of stuttering." Unpublished manuscript, University of Minnesota.

Martin, R. R., and Siegel, G. M. (1966) The effects of response contingent shock on stuttering. *Journal of Speech and Hearing Research,* 9, 340–352.

Meyer, W. H. (1972) The effects of contingent and noncontingent shock, presented in a neutral and negative environment, on phonemic repetitions of adult normal speakers. Ph.D. dissertation, Southern Illinois University.

Mischel, W. (1968) *Personality and assessment.* New York: Wiley.

Moore, W. E. (1959) A study of the blood chemistry of stutterers under two hypnotic conditions. *Speech Monographs,* 26, 64–68.

Morganstern, K. P. (1973) Implosive therapy and flooding procedures: A critical review. *Psychological Bulletin,* 79, 318–334.

Moser, H. M. (1938) A qualitative analysis of eye-movements during stuttering. *Journal of Speech Disorders,* 3, 131–139.

Mowrer, O. H. (1953) *Psychotherapy: theory and research.* New York: Ronald.

Mowrer, O. H., and Viek, P. (1948) An experimental analogue of fear from a sense of helplessness. *Journal of Abnormal and Social Psychology,* 43, 193–200.

Murray, H. A. (1943) *Thematic Aperception Test manual.* Cambridge, Mass.: Harvard University Press.

Neelley, J. N., and Timmons, R. J. (1967) Adaptation and consistency in the disfluent speech behavior of young stutterers and nonstutterers. *Journal of Speech and Hearing Research,* 10, 250–256.

Norton, D., and Stark, L. (1971) Eye movements and visual perception. *Scientific American,* 244, 34–43.

Notterman, J. M., Shoenfeld, W. N., and Bersh, P. J. (1952) Partial reinforcement and conditioned heart rate response in human subjects. *Science,* 155, 77–79.

Oelschlaeger, M. L. (1971) The effect of instructional stimulation on the freqency of repetitions and interjections of four stutterers. M.S. thesis, Southern Illinois University.

Oelschlaeger, M. L. (1973) The effect of response-contingent positive stimulation on the part-word repetitions of four stutterers. Ph.D. dissertation, Southern Illinois University.

Paul, G. L. (1964) Effect of insight, desensitization, and attention-placebo treatment of anxiety: An approach to outcome research in psychotherapy. Ph.D. dissertation, University of Illinois.

Peins, M. (1961) Consistency effect in stuttering expectancy. *Journal of Speech and Hearing Research,* 4, 397–398.

Perkins, W. (1973) Replacement of stuttering with normal speech: I. Rationale. *Journal of Speech and Hearing Disorders,* 38, 283–294.

Preus, A. (1973) Stuttering in Down's syndrome. In Y. Lebrun and R. Hoops, eds., *Neurolinguistic approaches to stuttering.* The Hague: Mouton and Co.

Prins, T. D., and Lohr, F. E. (1968) A study of the behavioral components of stuttered speech (HEW Research Grant OEG-3-6-062382-1882, Final

Report). Washington, D.C.: Office of Education, Bureau of Research, Department of Health, Education, and Welfare.

Prins, T. D., and Lohr, F. E. (1972) Behavioral dimensions of stuttered speech. *Journal of Speech and Hearing Research*, 15, 61–71.

Quist, R. W. (1966) The effect of response contingent verbal punishment on stuttering. Unpublished thesis, University of Minnesota.

Quist, R., and Martin, R. (1967) The effect of response contingent verbal punishment on stuttering. *Journal of Speech and Hearing Research*, 10, 795–800.

Rescorla, R. (1967) Pavlovian conditioning and its proper control procedures. *Psychological Review*, 74, 71–80.

Robbins, S. D. (1919) A plethysmographic study of shock and stammering. *The American Journal of Physiology*, 48, 285–330.

Roland, B. C. (1972) Eye-movements of stutterers and nonstutterers during silent, oral, and choral reading. *Journal of Perceptual and Motor Skills*, 35, 297–298.

Roman, K. G. (1959) Handwriting and speech. *Logos*, 2, 29–39.

Rubin, B. M., Katkin, E. S., and Weiss, B. W. (1968) Factor analysis of a fear survey schedule. *Journal of Behavior Research and Therapy*, 6, 65–75.

St. Onge, R. K. (1963) The stuttering syndrome. *Journal of Speech and Hearing Research*, 6, 195–197.

Sakata, R., and Adams, M. (1972) Comparisons among various forms of individual stutterers' dysfluency. *Journal of Communication Disorders*, 5, 232–239.

Savoye, A. (1959) The effect of the Skinner-Estes operant conditioning punishment paradigm upon the production of non-fluencies in normal speakers. M.S. thesis, University of Pittsburg.

Schmeck, R. R., and Bruning, J. L. (1968) Task difficulty and frustration effect. *Journal of Experimental Psychology*, 78, 516–520.

Schweizer, R. L. (1975) An investigation of the molecular aspects of the moment of stuttering during adaptation and recovery readings. M.S. research paper, Southern Illinois University.

Shames, G., and Sherrick, C. (1963) A discussion of nonfluency and stuttering as operant behavior. *Journal of Speech and Hearing Disorders*, 28, 3–18.

Shane, M. L. S. (1963) Effect on stuttering of alteration in auditory feedback. In W. Johnson and R. R. Leutenegger, eds., *Stuttering in children and adults*. Minneapolis: University of Minnesota Press.

Sheehan, J. G. (1973) Stuttering behavior: A phonetic analysis. Unpublished manuscript, University of California.

Shumak, I. C. (1955) A speech situation rating sheet for stutterers. In W. Johnson and R. R. Leutenegger, eds., *Stuttering in children and adults*. Minneapolis: University of Minnesota Press.

Siegel, G. M. (1968) Disfluencies, punishment, and stuttering. Unpublished manuscript, University of Minnesota.

Silverman, F., and Silverman, E. M. (1971) Stutter-like behavior in manual communication of the deaf. *Journal of Perceptual and Motor Skills*, 33, 45–46.

Skalbeck, O. M. (1957) The relationship of expectancy of stuttering to certain other designated variables associated with stuttering. *Speech Monographs,* 24, 146, abstract.

Skinner, B. F. (1957) *Verbal behavior.* New York: Appleton.

Sobell, L. C., and Sobell, M. B. (1972) Effects of alcohol on the speech of alcoholics. *Journal of Speech and Hearing Research,* 15, 861–868.

Solomon, R. L., Kamin, L. J., and Wynne, L. C. (1953) Traumatic avoidance learning: The outcomes of several extinction procedures with dogs. *Journal of Abnormal and Social Psychology,* 48, 291–302.

Starkweather, C. (1970) The simple, main, and interactive effects of contingent and noncontingent shock of high and low intensities on stuttering repetitions. Ph.D. dissertation, Southern Illinois University.

Stassi, E. (1961) Disfluency of normal speakers and reinforcement. *Journal of Speech and Hearing Research,* 4, 358–361.

Travis, L. E., Tuttle, W. W., and Cowan, D. W. (1936) A study of the heart rate during stuttering. *Journal of Speech Disorders,* 1, 21–26.

Treon, M., Tamayo, F., and Stendley, S. (1972) The use of GSR biofeedback in the modification of stuttering. *ASHA,* 14, 491, abstract.

Ullman, L. P., and Krasner, L. (1965) *Case studies in behavior modification.* New York: Holt, Rinehart & Winston.

Valyo, R. A., Jr. (1971) Skin potential responses of stutterers and nonstutterers during speech and silence. *Dissertation Abstracts International, B: Sciences and Engineering,* 32, 1904–B.

Van Riper, C. (1936) Study of the thoracic breathing of stutterers during expectancy and occurrence of stuttering spasm. *Journal of Speech Disorders,* 1, 61–72.

Van Riper, C. (1963) *Speech correction: principles and methods.* Englewood Cliffs, N.J.: Prentice-Hall.

Van Riper, C. (1971) *The nature of stuttering.* Englewood Cliffs, N.J.: Prentice-Hall.

Webster, L. M. (1966) An audio-visual exploration of the stuttering moment. M.S. Thesis, Southern Illinois University.

Webster, L. M. (1968) A cinematic analysis of the effects of contingent stimulation on stuttering and associated behaviors. Ph.D. dissertation, Southern Illinois University.

Webster, L. M., and Brutten, G. J. (1972) An audiovisual behavioral analysis of the stuttering moment. *Behavior Therapy,* 3, 555–560.

Webster, L. M., and Brutten, G. J. (1974) The modification of stuttering and associated behaviors. In S. Dickson, ed., *Communication disorders: Remedial principles and practices.* Glenview, Ill.: Scott, Foresman.

Williams, D. E. (1955) Masseter muscle action potentials in stuttered and nonstuttered speech. *Journal of Speech and Hearing Disorders,* 20, 242–261.

Wingate, M. E. (1964) A standard definition of stuttering. *Journal of Speech and Hearing Disorders,* 29, 484–489.

Wischner, G. J. (1947) Stuttering behavior and learning: A program of research. Ph.D. dissertation, University of Iowa.

Wolpe, J. (1969) *The practice of behavior therapy.* Elmsford, N.Y.: Pergamon.

Zenner, A. A. (1971) A molecular analysis of stuttering and associated behaviors during massed oral readings of the same material: The adaptation and consistency of behaviors. Ph.D. dissertation, Syracuse University.

Zenner, A. A., and Webster, L. M. (1972) The molar and molecular effects of contingently stimulating the stuttering moment. Unpublished manuscript.

Zimmerman, G., and Knott, J. R. (1973) Slow potentials of the brain and stuttering. *ASHA,* 15, 451, abstract.

IV

Operant Conditioning and Stuttering

George H. Shames, Ph.D.

Professor of Speech and Psychology at the University of Pittsburgh; Coordinator of the Training Program in Speech Pathology and Audiology at the University of Pittsburgh; Adjunct Professor of Speech at Federal City College, Washington, D.C. Consultant to the Veterans Administration Hospitals in Butler, Pennsylvania and Pittsburgh, Pennsylvania. Fellow of the American Speech and Hearing Association, Member of the American Psychological Association. Contributor to professional journals and books, including the *Journal of Speech and Hearing Disorders, Journal of Speech and Hearing Research, Journal of Communication Disorders, Pediatric Clinics of North America*. Project Director of several research grants from the U.S. Office of Education and Social and Rehabilitation Service of the Department of Health, Education and Welfare. Coauthor of *Operant Conditioning and the Management of Stuttering: A Book for Clinicians* (with Donald Egolf).

A Behavioral Perspective
of Stuttering

For many years stuttering has been characterized as being learned or acquired. Such a statement can have many meanings. For some, such a statement is merely a token acknowledgment that stuttering is not present at birth, but that its acquisition may be related to genetic or bioneurochemical factors which become manifest at a later time. For others, this statement may mean that organic factors can be completely ruled out at any age and that stuttering is explainable on purely functional grounds. Within this more restricted view of stuttering as behavior, there are numerous points of view as to the nature of the events considered to be behavior and how these events relate to one another. There are also differences in the conceptualizations of which events are important to understanding the basic nature of stuttering and how to go about alleviating the problem. Terms such as "discriminative stimuli," "responses," "anxiety," "feelings," "anticipations," "imagery," "inhibition," "conditioning," "desensitizing," "avoidance," "conflict," "tension," "counterconditioning," "counseling," "intellectualizing," "punishing," and "emotionality" have been used in talking about stuttering and its therapy. They are illustrations of the diverse frames of reference that have been perceived as being within a behavioral perspective of stuttering. These frames of reference have little in common with one another either theoretically or procedurally, except for being grouped together under the umbrella term of a "behavioral perspective" of stuttering. The focus of this chapter will be on one particular segment of the much larger behavioral perspective, that of operant conditioning. An overview and critical evaluation that relates operant procedures to various aspects of the total problem of stuttering are presented.

For the most part, our theories of stuttering as an acquired problem have created a relatively unique, if not parochial, field of literature. This literature and the research and clinical strategies stimulated by it have developed essentially separately and independently from the theories and research that have dealt most extensively with learning and behavioral acquisition. One can't help but wonder if our indifference to the fields of learning theory and experimental psychology means that the problem of stuttering must be viewed as something unique and different from other acquired behaviors. Either by accident or by design the content of much of our early literature about stuttering seems to have been insulated from the more broadly based theoretical thinking about other forms of behavior. As such, our transactions relative to stuttering, whether they have involved theory, etiology, or clinical management, have not been conceptualized within the purview of the larger perspective of human learning and behaviorism. We therefore have not been disposed toward understanding this problem within the principles and data of learning and behaviorism. There are, to be sure, notable and significant exceptions to this observation: Wischner's (1950) anxiety-reduction hypothesis, Sheehan's (1958) approach-avoidance conflict theory, Wolpe's (1958) reciprocal inhibition theory, and more recently Brutten and Shoemaker's (1967) two-factor learning theory. Each of these theories is a behavioral view of stuttering; each tries to explain in greater detail, and in concert with a bona fide theory of learning and behavioral acquisition, how stuttering is learned. As a result, a greater sensitivity has developed about the importance of analyzing and verifying those specific processes and events that appear to be pertinent to the problem.

One particular behavioral model for examining the processes of learning that has been applied to the problem of stuttering is that of operant conditioning and the principles of descriptive behaviorism. The history of the application of principles of operant conditioning to stuttering, although relatively short, has been quite varied. One of the basic questions that should be faced is whether that history, as short as it is, has been productive. Assessing productivity is a multidimensional issue. We might examine the significance, scope, and frequency of research. We might scrutinize the effectiveness of clinical strategies emanating from operant conditioning or try to determine whether we have a better understanding of the basic nature of the problem. It is not valid to point to the shortcomings of other behavioral approaches to stuttering as evidence of one's own success. Therefore, comparisons among or across points of view of stuttering appear to be counterproductive. Even if such comparative studies were desirable, they could not be carried out until there was universal agreement on standardized criteria and methods of measurement relative to such studies.

Rather, we should be evaluating each approach on its own merits for being able to deal with the critical substantive issues of the problem of stuttering. For purposes of discussion, we can categorize these substantive issues under four main headings: (1) the onset, development, and maintenance of stuttering, (2) the prevention of stuttering, (3) the clinical management of stuttering (therapy), and (4) the promotion of self-responsibility and carry-over. The task of this chapter, therefore, is to highlight and review the work that has gone on in applying the principles of operant behavior to the problem of stuttering and to comment on the relationship of this work to those four issues. The concluding section will deal in part with existing gaps of information and possible directions and tactics for filling these gaps and improving on the status quo.

The terms of operant conditioning

As will be seen in this chapter, the application of operant conditioning to stuttering has been quite varied. However, underlying all of these diverse applications is a basic behavioral principle, involving the *law of effect* (Thorndike, 1933). Whether we are discussing onset and development, prevention, or therapy, the same set of operant principles is involved. Quite simply stated, operant behavior is that behavior whose frequency is a function of its consequences. On certain occasions, certain responses generate consequences in the environment. If these consequences affect the frequency of the behavior that they follow, we are dealing with operant behavior (Skinner, 1953). The occasions for these responses are antecedent to the response and are referred to as "discriminative stimuli." For example, the sight of a mother entering a room may be the discriminative stimulus for her 3-year-old child to emit the verbal response "uppie" (meaning "pick me up"). It is as though the sight of the mother evoked the child's verbal response. However, the strength of the bond between the child's verbal response of "uppie" and the sight of the mother (discriminative stimulus) that preceded it is a function of the relationship between the response and its consequence. If the mother consistently picks the child up after the response "uppie," it is likely that this response will be in great frequency on other occasions of the child seeing the mother enter the room. Table 1 summarizes the various relationships among the elements of operant conditioning and relates each to a process of behavioral operations and the effects of these operations on response frequency.

Types of reinforcement and contingent events. Positive reinforcement (Rf+) in Table 1 refers to a process wherein the presentation of an event following a response is observed to have the effect of increasing the frequency of the response it follows (i.e., a mother picking up a child may be a positive reinforcer for the child's response "uppie"). The reinforcer is contingent on the response, and the response is contin-

TABLE 1
THE ELEMENTS OF OPERANT CONDITIONING

Antecedent events	Responses	Consequent events	Effects on frequency
General situational stimuli	Target responses to be manipulated	Positive reinforcement (Rf+) Event is presented following a response	Increases frequency of response (R)
Discriminative stimuli ("occasions")		Negative reinforcement (Rf−) Ongoing aversive event is terminated contingent on the response	Increases frequency of R
		Extinction Rf+ is withheld	Decreases frequency of R
		Punishment Aversive event is presented following a response	Decreases frequency of R

gent on the occasion. However, what events or processes maintain the mother's behavior of picking up her child? It may be one of positive reinforcement wherein her picking-up behavior is followed by the child giving her a warm and affectionate hug and kiss. On the other hand, if the child has been loudly repeating her verbal "uppie," "uppie," "uppie," the mother's behavior may be a function of a process of negative reinforcement wherein her picking-up response terminates her child's aversive and loud nagging. This latter relationship of increases in response frequency being contingent on terminating an aversive situation is known as negative reinforcement (Rf−). To continue with the same example: If the mother has conditioned her child to say "uppie" through positive reinforcement by picking her up and now withholds the reinforcing event by not picking her up when she says "uppie," we can say that extinction is taking place (provided of course that we observe an associated decrement in the frequency of the child's response). You cannot extinguish a response that you have not first brought under contingent control. In fact, extinction is a common test of such response-contingent control. Finally, we have a process that has come to be known as "punishment," wherein the consequence that is contingent on the response is aversive and has the effect of reducing the frequency of the response. Therefore, if the mother says no to or shouts at the child who says "uppie," and if we observe that the frequency of this response by the child decreases, we may infer that the process of punishment has taken place.

Although Rf+ and Rf— are related to increased frequencies of responses and extinction and punishment are related to decreased frequencies of responses, the rate at which these increments and decrements occur is a function of the way in which these contingent consequences are scheduled. Consequences can be scheduled to occur, under controlled conditions, every time a target response occurs. This type of schedule is known as "continuous reinforcement," and it is useful if you wish to establish a high frequency of a particular response very quickly. However, a response that is acquired on a continuous schedule has been found to be the least resistant to extinction and, therefore, decreases in frequency the most rapidly when the reinforcer is withheld.

Another way of scheduling contingent events is on some type of intermittent schedule. If the contingent event is scheduled on the basis of the emission of some number of target responses, this is known as a "ratio schedule." For example, it would be possible to schedule an interviewer to say, "Yes, I see," every third time an interviewee says the word "mother" in an effort to increase the frequency of occurrence of that word on an FR-3 (fixed ratio of 3) schedule. It is also possible to schedule the interviewer to emit his response on a variable-ratio schedule (as opposed to a fixed-ratio schedule). This schedule involves providing the contingent consequence in a variable manner on the basis of some average number of responses. For example, on a VR-3 (variable ratio of 3) schedule, the contingent consequence may occur after six responses, then after three responses, two responses, four responses, one response, and two responses. Although it is a variable number of responses, it averages out to every three responses.

In many instances, the contingent event is scheduled on the basis of time rather than number of responses. A schedule based on the passage of time is known as an "interval schedule." Just as with intermittent ratio schedules, intermittent interval schedules can be fixed or variable. A fixed-interval schedule involves having the contingent consequence occur after the first target response occurs following a particular passage of a time interval. For example, on a fixed interval schedule of 3 minutes (FI-3) the contingent consequence is presented after the first target response is emitted following the passage of 3 minutes. The variable interval schedule involves providing the contingency in variable passages of time intervals around an average passage of time. The variable interval schedule, although it may be associated with slower rates of responding, is also the most resistant to extinction. It therefore may be considered the most powerful schedule in terms of sustaining a response over a long period of time after the contingency has been withdrawn (Ferster and Skinner, 1957).

In applying these principles and information about operant conditioning, researchers and clinicians alike have recognized the importance of developing and sharpening their observational skills. Observable events have to be designated as precisely as possible. These designated events include the behavior of the subject (client) as well as the contingent consequence to be employed. The process is one of descriptive operationism in concert with the law of effect so that the effects of each experimental manipulation of a consequence can be related clearly and directly to observable actions by both the subject and the experimenter. In this instance, for the problem of stuttering, certain observable behavioral events emitted by the stutterer can be designated in advance as target responses that will generate, by design, specifically designated consequent responses (by the experimenter, clinician, parents, peers, teachers, etc.). The consequence is contingent on the emission of the target response, which means that it occurs only after (as promptly as possible) the target response has been emitted. To determine whether the contingent consequent event in a clinic situation has any systematic effect on the frequency of the target response, behavior has to be systematically studied, much like an experiment. Such an experimental analysis is profoundly different from after-the-fact analysis of behavioral events. The latter is analytical and infers relationships, while the former is experimental and verifies relationships between events.

Applications to clinical relationships

Clinicians are in a privileged position to provide significant consequences following the stutterer's behavior. They can therefore think of themselves as contingent consequators (i.e., people who provide consequences after a target response). The particular responses they select as targets for change and the nature of the consequent behavior are a function of how they view the problem of stuttering, what events they view as important to the problem, and their own style of relating and being of help to people. For some theoreticians and clinicians, the problem of stuttering consists merely of the motor acts of dysfluent speech; for some, it is the belief system the stutterer holds about himself; for others, it includes the stutterer's social approach-avoidance conflicts; for still others, it includes such constructs as anxiety and manifestations of neurosis. As long as any one or all of these conceptualizations of the problem of stuttering can be translated into something that is manifestly observable and is therefore made publicly available to clinicians or experimenters, these frames of reference can be useful for defining target responses within the operant framework.

The nature of the contingent consequence may also vary with the clinician's conceptualizations of the skills, behaviors, and processes involved. If he feels that warmth, acceptance, support, rapport, and empathy are significant aspects of child management, of adult interpersonal interactions, and more specifically of therapeutic interventions, this thinking will influence the form of the contingent consequent behavior (Ivey, 1971; Carkhuff, 1973). These processes can probably be easily translated into observable clinician behaviors or family behaviors and be made contingently available. In all likelihood they would function as positive reinforcers and would therefore be used to increase the frequency of desirable responses (i.e., verbal output, a particular content theme, affect responses, or speech that is free of stuttering).

On the other hand, stutterers are often encouraged to examine painful historical background, become aware of aversive self-images, recognize the positive payoffs of stuttering, evaluate the negative effects of stuttering on listeners, accept the excuse value of stuttering. The clinician may be interested in using procedures that suppress the frequency of dysfluent speech behavior. If he embraces the idea that there are some behaviors emitted by stutterers that are undersirable and interfere with therapeutic progress, his contingent consequent activity might involve such processes as confrontation, disapproval, forcing stutterers to explain or justify positions, or rejection of stuttering and how stutterers talk about themselves. These events are often thought to be aversive and might well function as mild punishers. Clinicians often attempt to first identify and then decrease the frequency of certain undesirable behaviors such as stuttering, comments connoting helplessness, lack of responsibility, social avoidance, and so on. It would be an interesting exercise to draw up your own contingency table, where you list the desirable and undesirable behaviors of a particular stutterer. Then list what you believe your contingent reactions are to them. You can then test out your accuracy by comparing what you say you do (or want to do) against a tape recording of your actual therapy. Such an exercise would help to determine whether you are really doing what you say you do and also whether the relationships between the stutterer's responses and your contingent reactions are working for or against you and the stutterer. For example, are you reinforcing things you want to decrease and vice versa?

An immediate question that should be raised about providing consequences for target responses is, "Where does one start?" How does a clinician strengthen a desirable response that has not been emitted and is not a part of the stutterer's repertoire? An experimental procedure known as "shaping through successive approximations" (Skinner, 1953) has been developed for dealing with this issue. The clinician observes the stutterer's behavior closely and starts with what the stutterer shows he can do. The clinician then provides contingent consequences as the stutterer gradually emits behavior that gets closer and closer to the final response being sought. It is the clinician's job to break up the final behavioral goal into small progressive steps toward that goal and to consequate each step forward by the stutterer. One way to do this is by providing an example or a model for the stutterer to match and to consequate his goodness of fit to the model. Skill in identifying these microunits of behavior and skill in shaping behavior may be the most important dimensions of planning and carrying out successful programs. They require a thorough awareness of goals, subgoals, response topographies, chains of responses, and a judgment about the stutterer's available repertoire of relevant responses.

This initial phase of observing the stutterer's behavior can serve many functions. It tells the clinician where the stutterer is and what he is doing relative to specific target responses. It provides the clinician with a starting point in terms of frequency information for his reinforcement program. It also provides the clinician a point of reference against which he can compare the effects of his program. These observations may be similar to the experimentalist's procedures for obtaining base-rate frequency data, which are important for demonstrating the effects of an experimental manipulation. If the clinician's observations are comprehensive in terms of sampling different circumstances or occasions for the target response, these observations may also be useful in organizing his program. They can describe the circumstances that vary with the frequency of the target response before the program is initiated. The practical values of base-rate data will be dealt with in greater detail in a later portion of this chapter. It is mentioned here to introduce the value of and need for close observation of behavior until the clinician has obtained what he feels is a representative sample of the frequency of the target response. This brief allusion to observing the occasions for these base-rate emissions of target responses introduces an additional experimental procedure and concept that is of significance in dealing with this problem: the process of *changing stimulus control* (Skinner, 1953). The contingent consequence that may control a response on one particular stimulus occasion may not control the response on other occasions. During therapy, such variations in stimulus control may require the development of tactics designed to transfer that control (i.e., from clinician to mother). This may be a deliberate and structured procedure to ensure that the consequent contingencies of the original circumstance are operating in the new circumstance or it may involve the process known as "stimulus generalization," whereby a newly acquired response is emitted under varying circumstances with no apparent transfer procedures having been used. These last two processes may be associated with what we refer to clinically as "carry-over."

Specific applications to stuttering

An overview of operant conditioning and stuttering reveals a wide range of activities illustrating the diversity of interest of these many endeavors as well as the broad need for basic and applied information. Some endeavors have been purely research projects designed to demonstrate the operant nature of stuttering. Others have been designed to develop operant-based therapy programs. Some projects have considered children, whereas others have considered adults; some have focused on normal speakers, whereas others have focused on stutterers. Also, different kinds of target responses and different kinds of contingent consequences have been considered. We will approach these endeavors in terms of what appears to be their outstanding or distinguishing characteristics.

Probably, from a historical sense, the most significant pioneering work done in this area was in the late 1950s by Flanagan, Goldiamond, and Azrin (1958, 1959). These experimenters did their work in an experimental laboratory from the perspective of experimental psychology. Their projects studied meticulously the effects of various kinds of contingent stimulation on the speech fluency and dysfluency of both stutterers and nonstutterers. They spent significant periods of time developing base-rate information, studying the effects of various forms of contingent stimulation, and, ultimately, demonstrating the operant nature of stuttering and of fluency. Eventually, their work evolved into programs of therapy (Goldiamond, 1965a) having special initial emphasis on the use of delayed auditory feedback (DAF) and negative reinforcement. Their work served as a prototypical model for others, who built on their basic findings to develop additional programs of therapy. The Flanagan et al. work raised a number of questions about the basic nature of stuttering. Flanagan et al. raised doubts about the importance of anxiety as a significant construct of the problem of stuttering and held up for scrutiny some of the time-honored ideas about its onset, development, and therapy.

In the early 1960s Shames and Sherrick (1963) developed a theoretical discussion of the possibilities for exploring the clinical problem of stuttering through the principles of operant behavior. Their approach was more of a heuristic analysis of translating back and forth between the principles of operant behavior and the real-world events associated with stuttering. These events, which were familiar to most speech pathologists, were put in relation to one another in terms of various operant paradigms. A number of hypotheses for study that involved real rather than laboratory forms of events were suggested. It appears that the Flanagan, Goldiamond, and Azrin experimental work and the Shames and Sherrick clinical-operant discussion may have provided an impetus for the large number and types of projects that subsequently developed.

Therapy

A number of the projects had as their ultimate primary goals the development of principles and tactics for therapy; others were of a more general type, having implications for both therapy and the basic nature of stuttering. The projects on therapy fall into five main groups:

1. Rate-control therapies
2. Strengthening coexisting fluency
3. Operant tactics applied to traditional therapies
4. Group therapy
5. Suppression of stuttering

Each of these approaches to operant therapy has been based on some particular aspect of the principles of operant conditioning involving positive reinforcement, negative reinforcement, or punishment. They differ from one another in terms of the form and type of the consequent event employed, the target response that was modified, and the way the paradigm was put into operation (individual interview, group setting, isolated and discrete conditioning trials, etc.).

Rate-control therapies

The thrust of the experimental work by Goldiamond, which was built on by Curlee and Perkins (Curlee and Perkins, 1969; Goldiamond, 1965a; Perkins, 1973b) and by Ryan and his colleagues (Ryan, 1971; Ryan and Van Kirk, 1973), was to develop programs of therapy for both child and adult stutterers. The process involves the instating of a new speech response in stutterers that presumably has no prior history for them, as their stuttering does. The focus is on fluency, not stuttering. The end goal of these therapy programs is speech that is free of stuttering. Stutterers learn to prolong their speech utterances and slow down their rate of syllable emission. This pattern of slowed-down speech is then shaped to normal conversational patterns, and carry-over procedures are then employed. One way that stutterers learn to do this is through the use of a DAF recorder within a negative reinforcement paradigm. Talking under conditions of DAF is considered aversive (Flanagan, Goldiamond, and Azrin, 1958, 1959), and one way to terminate this aversive condition is by slowing down and prolonging each utterance. Intervals of stutter-free speech are established as criteria for gradually reducing the amount of the DAF and for increasing the rate of speaking. For example, in the early Curlee-Perkins (1969) program the stutterer had to speak for two consecutive 15-minute periods without stuttering before going to the next-shortest DAF interval. The stutterer started at an interval of 250 milliseconds and went down to zero delay in 50-millisecond steps (a total of six steps). There was also a criterion of two instances of stuttering in any 5-minute segment of talking for moving backward and increasing the DAF. It was possible to go through this particular DAF negative-reinforcement phase of the therapy program in a minimum of 3 hours. At that point the stutterer was faced with monitoring relatively fluent speech off the DAF paradigm. The therapy and the conditioning paradigm radically changed now that the new speech response had been established. The new therapy problem was to strengthen fluency and arrange for its emission in the real world of the stutterer.

Perkins has recently revised this program so that it now involves shaping rate, fluency, breath-stream management, prosody, and phrasing. Criteria for moving forward and backward in the program are not precisely quantitative and deal with more flexibly stated ranges of experiences than previously. Three specific criteria are mentioned: (1) Recover slow, normal speech (if lost) in one-five phrases. (2) If confidence is lost (in ability to produce slow, normal speech), it should be recovered in one session. (3) If the stutterer feels compelled to try to talk faster, he should be able to talk slower more comfortably within two sessions. If any of these criteria are not met, the stutterer is to go back to a previous goal. Also, the stutterer is given most of the responsibility for managing this phase of the DAF program. Although this looser definition of criteria for moving toward establishing fluent speech may be effective and valid, it may also present problems of judgment and ambiguity for both stutterers and clinicians. These issues of judgment may have been minimal in Perkins's earlier program, where criteria were stated in definite, quantitative terms. However, they may have been too restrictive in scope and effectiveness (Perkins, 1973a, 1973b). Perkins has also changed the nature of his carry-over activities. He no longer advocates a time-out punishment procedure for lapses in fluency. Instead, he has arranged for self-monitoring procedures of rating various dimensions of speech while systematically varying the occasions for this monitoring in terms of people, places, and situations. He also notes the possible need for a psychotherapeutic experience based on the programming of Shames, Egolf, and Rhodes (1969).

The Ryan program (1971), which also employs the DAF and the negative Rf paradigm, involves three phases of therapy: establishment, transfer, and maintenance. Although it has the same end goals as the Curlee-Perkins program, it arranges the DAF portion of the program somewhat differently. The length of the DAF intervals is reduced in 50-millisecond steps from 250- to 0-millisecond delay, with a criterion of 5 minutes of stutter-free speech for progressing forward. However, Ryan's program simultaneously moves the stutterer through a progression of different occasions for speaking while reducing the delay (reading, monologues, conversation, changing situational settings, increasing audience size and changing its composition, and increasing length of utterance). There is a simultaneous home program that is part of the transfer phase. This brings the stutterer's family and friends into the contingency program and changes its locale. Ryan describes the transfer phase generally as involving the clinician and then different audiences in locales progressively remote from the clinic.

Eventually, this transfer phase arrives at the same point as the Curlee-Perkins program. In both, the stutterer learns to slow down and prolong his speech; this pattern is shaped by shortening the DAF (eventually to zero) to normal conversational rate, inflection, and fluency. However at this point in the Ryan program the stutterer has emitted this new fluent speech response under a broader set of stimulus circumstance than in the Perkins program because of the systematic introduction of different occasions while fluency is being shaped under the DAF condition. It should be pointed out here that the DAF negative-reinforcement program is only one way to reach this point in therapy. Instructions and examples for prolonging and slowing down have been used by both Ryan and Perkins; they have been reported as being effective, but perhaps as taking a little longer in shaping a prolonged, slowed-down speech pattern to normal conversational rates (Ryan and Van Kirk, 1973; Perkins, 1973b). This, of course, is a positive reinforcement program wherein the stutterer is reinforced for following an instruction or example. Such instructional programs can be supplemented with the use of a tachistoscope for timing the presentation of a stimulus word. Or they can be supplemented merely by manually presenting reading material for viewing, for prearranged lengths of time, that will provide the stutterer with an external "timing device" for slowing down.

The Curlee-Perkins and Ryan therapy programs then radically depart from one another. Now that the stutterers are off the DAF negative reinforcement program, the task is to maintain the pattern of stutter-free speech. Originally the Curlee-Perkins program employed a time-out punishment procedure based primarily on the work of Haroldson, Martin, and Starr (1968). If the stutterer stuttered or his speech got "sticky" after the DAF phase of therapy, the room in which the stutterer was conversing with the clinician was darkened and the stutterer was to remain silent for 30 seconds. The time-out interval was reduced in 5-second intervals as the stutterer met his no-stuttering criterion at increasingly faster rates while off the DAF machine. This time-out procedure then gave way to one of monitoring fluency in a large number of real-life talking situations, going from least to most difficult. Perkins has now dropped the time-out procedures from his program. He has introduced self-responsibility by the stutterer much earlier (during DAF negative-reinforcement fluency training) and has gone to a self-monitoring of fluency phase with systematic programming of situations.

The Ryan program of transfer and maintenance is based in general on the same principles as Perkins, that is, to extend contingencies and consequences to the stutterer's home and real world. However, the task is approached somewhat differently. Ryan varies the situation, the audience, and the task. He employs monologues, reading, and conversations. He may start with tangible reinforcers but introduces social reinforcers over a period of time. He also requires a monitoring (record keeping) of instances of stuttering (Ryan, 1971). Perkins also requires a monitoring of a number of dimensions of speaking (fluency, rate, breath stream, etc.) through a subjective rating procedure (Perkins, 1973b). The rating scale appears to involve both negative and positive ends of the continuum. While consequences of these ratings are provided by the stutterer in the Perkins program, they are provided by friends and family in the Ryan program. The consequences in the Ryan program are prompt, whereas in the Perkins program they appear to be delayed and logged sometime after the emission of the behavior in question. The Ryan maintenance (carry-over) phase is managed by environmental reinforcement, whereas the Perkins program is one of delayed self-reinforcement.

Shames has been exploring the use of the DAF in a rate-control therapy program whereby the DAF functions for only short periods of time as a rate calibrator. Various rates are associated with different delay intervals. Once the rate is established via a DAF negative reinforcement paradigm, the stutterer is taken off of the DAF program; he is then put on a positive reinforcement program for monitoring the slow rate established with the negative reinforcement program or is put on a punishment program for each instance of stuttering. While establishing his slower rate, the stutterer is asked to talk about different topics that he had previously ranked in order of difficulty to talk about. When he can speak about a topic for 5 minutes without stuttering, at a slow

rate, he progresses to the next topic. The topics are usually a series
in a progressively difficult sequence involving such areas as family, marriage, stuttering, sex, goals and aspirations, religion and ethics, occupation, social activities, politics, weather, and sports. After talking on all
of the topics without stuttering, he goes back on the DAF recorder
to establish a slightly faster rate of talking. This is sometimes initiated
with reading. The stutterer repeats the progression through topics. He
returns to the DAF program for each of six delay intervals (250, 200,
150, 100, 50, 0 milliseconds), repeating the series of topics each time.
The DAF phase calibrates the stutterer to progressively faster rates of
monitored fluency. Within this phase of the program, the stutterer may
be reinforced with approval for specific fluency time intervals or be
mildly punished by recycling a stopwatch to zero each time he stutters.
The stutterer may also employ self-punishment procedures by using
a manual counter to tally each instance of stuttering. When the stutterer
reaches a normal conversational rate of monitored fluency, stimulus control is transferred from the interviewer to different people, to different
talking situations, and to different emotional circumstances. Although
these tactics are in their early exploratory stages, the results with two
stutterers thus far have been most promising as they continue to progress
through the early phases of the program.

With one adult male stutterer, there was an initial base-rate of eight
instances of stuttering per minute. His stuttering was characterized by
much muscular tension, long silences, and rapid, repetitive, silent movements of the articulators. He has used the DAF machine to calibrate
a slow, prolonging pattern of talking and is now completely off of the
machine. His rate of talking at 250-millisecond delay was 35 words
per minute. It is now at 150 words per minute, and he has passed beyond
his criteria of talking without stuttering for 5 minutes on each of 11
topics of conversation at each of the delay intervals through zero delay.
He is now monitoring his fluency in free conversation on a positive
reinforcement paradigm for shaping longer fluency intervals. Stuttering
rate is now down to three instances per hour, both with the interviewer
and with his spouse in the clinic situation, as well as with a number
of individuals at work. The form of his stuttering has also dramatically
changed, from its original tense, overt struggling to a barely perceptible
"stickiness." As a part of monitoring his fluency, he is monitoring his
phrasing, rate, and continued phonation in terms of his awareness of
the motor process of talking and his feelings of comfort and confidence.
On his own, he has begun doing these things in outside difficult situations
and is now keeping a daily log on the numbers and types of speaking
situations he is generating for himself. He has just begun monitoring

his length of utterance by deliberately emitting both short and long utterances. All of this is with speech that is free of stuttering and is designed to strengthen a behavioral repertoire which will sustain his fluency.

With a second stutterer, a 10-year-old boy, the DAF was again used as a rate calibrator. He has just recently started his program, but he has already established stutter-free speech at 250 milliseconds; he started with reading single words, then moved to two-word phrases, then sentences, and is now into conversation. He goes back on the DAF machine for a short time each time he enters the next step of the program (the next-longest response). When he can converse freely for 5 minutes without stuttering, he will go back on the DAF to the next-shorter delay interval. It should be pointed out that these rate-control therapies are programmatic in nature. They try to establish a behavior that might be characterized as controlled or monitored fluency through a series of progressive steps. Therefore, changes in the fluency of the stutterer outside the program, of a nonmonitored type, are neither expected nor pertinent to evaluating the progress of the stutterer on the program or during programmed activities. Although such nonmonitored fluency may be emitted and may be a sequal to progress in the program, it does not preclude the need for strengthening the type of fluency that is being programmatically and progressively shaped.

An interesting question can be raised about the validity of shaping a slowed-down, prolonging pattern of speech to a normal conversational pattern of fluency, when such fluency is already a large part of the repertoire of most stutterers. This is a legitimate and researchable question. It is also a question that brings into focus the contrasting emphases of traditional therapy, which cautions against imposing fluency, and operant therapy, which seeks to establish fluency. Perkins (1973a) has suggested an answer in a brief remark, which could be elaborated and extended. The fluency that is part of the stutterer's repertoire while he still stutters is probably being controlled by a number of consequences which are not a part of the relationship or under the contingent control of the clinician. With such multiple control of coexisting fluency by factors outside the therapeutic context, it may be difficult to transfer any control of that type of fluency which develops in the session to circumstances outside the therapy session. Therefore, it is important to build into the strengthening of fluency in the clinic some contingent consequences that will be effective in maintaining that fluency in the stutterer's outside, nonclinical social contexts. Additionally, shaping a new response toward fluency through either DAF or instructions probably develops in the stutterer a heightened awareness of response topography and the ultimate discriminative components and elements of fluent speaking behavior. This awareness develops a behavioral repertoire for "backup" procedures for fluency failures as well as a recognition of the occasions for providing positive consequences during self-monitoring of fluency. For some stutterers, self-monitored fluency may be the final therapeutic result. For others, monitored fluency may be a prerequisite for unmonitored fluency. It appears that different stutterers may be able to reach different goals, and the difference between monitored and unmonitored fluency may be a way of characterizing this difference.

Strengthening coexisting fluency

Unlike the programs designed to shape a newly instated slowed-down pattern of speech into a more conversationally appropriate rate pattern, programs to strengthen fluency are designed to reinforce already established patterns of fluency that coexist with patterns of dysfluent speech. There have been basically two variations of paradigms designed to strengthen coexisting fluent speech. One approach has involved reinforcement on ratio schedules, whereas the other has involved reinforcement on interval schedules. In the former approach, positive reinforcement is provided for a designated number of fluent responses in an effort to shape longer fluent responses in terms of words, sentences, phrases, thought units, and so on (ratio schedule). Such programs start with very short responses and progress to longer fluent responses.

The fluency-interval approach has involved reinforcement for units of time during which the stutterer is fluent. The first step is to compute the stutterer's basal fluency interval (the average amount of speaking time that the stutterer talks without stuttering). This basal level would be the starting point for reinforcing the stutterer with, for example, approval, smiles, points, or money each time he talks fluently for that amount of time. After the stutterer demonstrates that he can speak fluently at a predesignated time interval (usually starting at his baselevel, or just below it), the fluency time interval is fixed at some advanced level or the time is progressively increased in some pattern which the stutterer demonstrates is appropriate for him (i.e., in 1-, 5-, or 30-second steps, etc.).

Rickard and Mundy (1965) were two of the first to report using a fluency-ratio program as the therapy for a child stutterer (in this case, a 9-year-old). Contingent consequation was provided for fluency only. Rickard and Mundy did not consequate stuttering at all. They shaped the child's speech from short one- and two-word utterances to phrases, paragraphs, and eventually free conversation. Reinforcement was in the form of points as well as approval by the clinician. When the goal of fluent speech in free conversation with the clinician was reached, the stutterer's family was brought in to carry on with reinforcement activities at home. However, a follow-up study revealed that the decrement in dysfluency was partially lost when the contingencies were terminated.

Leach (1969) reported seeing a 12-year-old-boy twice a week for a total of 42 sessions, on a fluency-interval program. Leach used money as a positive reinforcer to maintain conversational output. He paid the youngster two cents a minute for talking during a 30-minute session. In addition, during the last 15 minutes of each session he paid the stutterer an additional penny for each 15-second period of fluent speech. This program did not progressively shape longer fluency intervals or change criteria in terms of longer time intervals for reinforcement during the program. It stayed with the 15-second fluency interval throughout. Leach demonstrated that such a program had a decremental effect on dysfluency. Dysfluencies were eventually reduced to less than one per minute. However, similar to the Rickard and Mundy results, a follow-up study revealed that the child's dysfluency rate increased a short time after the experimental program was terminated.

Shaw and Shrum (1972) reinforced fluency intervals with three children who stuttered, but introduced three procedures that varied from Leach's procedures: (1) They chose individualized fluency intervals for reinforcement based on their analysis of each child's operant-level fluency interval during free conversation. As a result two of the children were reinforced throughout the program for each 10 seconds of fluent speech, while one was reinforced for 5 seconds of fluent speech. (2) Each child chose his preferred form of reinforcement by trading in points (48 marks placed in square spaces—one mark for each criterional fluency interval) for a preferred toy or candy. (3) They combined their contingency program with instructions to ensure that the children knew what was expected of them. As in the Leach study, the fluency interval was not being shaped (lengthened). The effectiveness of the experiment was measured by the number of criterional fluency intervals the children emitted and the associated decrement in dysfluency. Each child demonstrated significant increases in the number of reinforceable fluency intervals emitted. Each child also showed significant decrements in dysfluency, although only one reached a point that was considered fluent speech. There was no attempt at carry-over activities, but follow-up studies showed that all three children maintained marked decrements in their dysfluency rates and demonstrated desirable changes in the severity of the stuttering that remained. In all fairness to these authors, their program was more of a demonstration experiment than therapy and they should not be faulted for not developing a carry-over program. The value of this experiment was in demonstrating the possible clinical application of this approach to therapy.

Shames and some of his students have also explored the effectiveness of reinforcing fluency intervals in short-term clinical practice and seminar projects. In one instance with an adult stutterer, a shaping program was employed during a series of five 45-minute conversational interviews (Kodish and Tucciarone, 1973). Based on an observed average level of a 13-second fluency interval during a noncontingent interview, the stutterer was reinforced for emitting progressively longer fluent utterances during succeeding interviews. He reached a fluency interval of 38 seconds in conditioning session number five. Each time the stutterer reached his criterion three consecutive times, the fluency-interval criterion for reinforcement was increased in small time-steps. The interviewer also verbally disapproved each instance of dysfluency. These stepwise increases ranged from 5 seconds during the first two interviews to 1 second during the last three conditioning sessions. Dysfluencies decreased from 179 during the base-rate session to 32 in the final operant-level session. It is interesting to note that, when the progressive increases in fluency intervals were in 5-second steps, the stutterer was unable to increase his fluency interval beyond 29 seconds. When the time interval was decreased to 1-second steps, he increased his fluency interval to 38 seconds.

What could not be accomplished with one time progression could be accomplished with a less demanding one. This shorter time step also changed the character of the shaping program to one that involved much more success than it had previously. The size of the time step in a program for shaping fluency intervals could be quite critical to its success and may be a highly individualized dimension.

In another seminar project, a response-cost punishment paradigm was used to lengthen an adult stutterer's fluency interval during 10 1-hour clinical interviews (Witzel and Schulman, 1973). Each session was divided into segments involving base-rate monologues by the stutterer, noncontingent conversations between the stutterer and the interviewer, and three 10-minute response-cost conditioning segments. Conditioning started at a 30-second fluency interval. When this could be maintained for 10 minutes, the interval was increased in 15-second steps. In step one, at the end of each 30 seconds of fluency, the stutterer was given one point and asked if he wanted to gamble for double the points that he would be fluent for the next 30 seconds, and so on. Therefore, the stutterer could choose to engage in a double response-cost as he preferred or merely be reinforced with one point for his fluency interval and a response-cost if he stuttered, at one point per stutter. In session five, the criterion for the 30-second fluency interval was reached (in reality this was 10 minutes of fluency). In session eight, the 10-minute criterion for a 45-second fluency interval was reached. In session nine, a 60-second fluency interval criterion of 10 minutes was reached. During all 10 interviews, the stutterer gambled for double points, indicating that he thought he would be fluent during the next time interval, 317 times out of a possible 450 times that he reached a time criterion, or about 70 percent of the time. Of these 317 gambles, he was successful 270 times, or approximately 85 percent of the time. It is interesting that the stutterer was more willing to gamble as the time requirements for fluency responses became greater and after he had experienced success in his earlier and shorter fluency-interval trials. This particular approach to response-cost may be analogous to the real-life gambles and commitments that a stutterer takes and to the importance of prior successful experiences with fluency in developing a commitment to future fluency.

Finally, in this area, Ryan (1971) has reported using some variations of the Rickard and Mundy fluent-utterance approach in combination with a fluency-interval approach. Ryan's program varies in its specific steps in terms of the individual stutterer; but generally he starts the stutterer by reinforcing short utterances and progresses to longer utterances (i.e., carrier phrase plus single word, one sentence, two sentences, etc.). He intermingles this with the reinforcement of short fluency-intervals, such as 30- and 45-second monologues. (Marked decrements in stuttering have been observed to levels of less than 1 percent.) At this point the stutterers are entered into Ryan's transfer and maintenance phases. Unlike the previous projects that dealt with positive reinforcement for fluency, Ryan reports good carry-over and sustained long-term results. The major differences among these projects designed to strengthen fluency in terms of carry-over may well be due to the elaborate and structured transfer and maintenance phases developed by Ryan, which are generally applicable once fluency is established.

Operant tactics applied to traditional therapies

The term "traditional therapies" by no means constitutes a homogeneous grouping of therapy activity. For the most part, it is used to distinguish therapies of earlier vintage from operant-based therapies. However, a number of distinctions can be amplified and detailed further and are pertinent to this discussion. Whereas most of the operant therapies have focused their attention directly to either increasing fluency or decreasing stuttering, the traditional therapies have cautioned against seeking fluency and suppressing stuttering (Van Riper, 1949, 1957, 1973). As a result, the traditional therapies have sought to encourage the expression of stuttering and have encouraged stutterers to accept themselves as stutterers; they have attempted to modify the form of their stuttering and to change their attitudes and belief systems; and they have attempted to consider stuttering as a symptom of something more basic to the person. This all has resulted in giving therapeutic attention to such things as anxiety, stutterers' need to stutter, or the ways in which stuttering has interfered with stutterers' realizing their full potential. Such therapies have usually used the individual interview as the vehicle or have arranged small groups in more or less psychotherapeutic or counseling contexts and have used symptom-management activities and situational desensitization (Van Riper, 1949, 1957, 1973). These are the orientations of most speech pathologists to the management of stuttering. It is therefore not surprising that one particular thrust of applying operant-conditioning principles to stuttering would involve viewing these principles as therapeutic tactics which might improve the processes of traditional therapy. By making these processes more descriptive and operational, and therefore more systematized and understandable, it was hoped to make them more effective.

As various projects are reviewed and reexamined, their objectives also deserve comment. At the time they were conceived, there was a need to dissect the art and practice of the then current therapies into comprehensible principles and processes; to remove the mystery and magic of what went on behind the closed doors of the therapy room; and to improve the batting average of the clinician. But there was also present a skepticism that reflected traditional attitudes about gadgets, fears of temporary distraction devices being mistaken for therapy, the alleged dangers of suppressing stuttering, the supposed dangerous effects of seeking fluency, and the high esteem and faith of much of the current theory about stuttering, if not the effectiveness of the therapy of the day.

For the most part, the view of the value of operant conditioning as a set of principles that could become useful in planning tactics and strategies in traditional therapy was developed and implemented by Shames and his students. In a number of early exploratory studies and thesis and dissertation projects, several different traditional therapies were explored in terms of operant-conditioning procedures.

One such project explored the possibility of applying operant tactics to the Travis theory that stuttering is a function of attempting to inhibit the overt expression of unacceptable feelings (Travis, 1957; Honeygosky, 1966). In this instance, the stutterer was in an unsuccessful symptom management program. It was hypothesized that his persistence in stuttering was due to his inability to express feelings and, more specifically, to be comfortable with expressions of anger. An interview conditioning program was designed to provide the stutterer with occasions for the expression of these feelings. Within an interview context, he was seen for 11 50-minute sessions. Consequences that were contingent on the nature of his verbal responses were provided. The interviewer was programmed to ask 10 key questions during each interview (every 5 minutes) that were designed to provide an occasion for an expression of feeling. If the stutterer expressed his feelings (specifically, the feeling of anger in later sessions), the interviewer verbalized his acceptance, approval, and/or understanding. If no emotional expression was emitted by the stutterer, approval by the interviewer was withheld. In 11 sessions this stutterer went from a base operant level of one emotional expression during the first 20 minutes of Session 1 to significantly higher frequencies throughout. In the final session, he emitted 47 emotional comments. At the time these procedures for conditioning emotional content were started, the stutterer stuttered 213 times in the first 50-minute session, for an average of approximately 4 times per minute. In Session 11, the stuttering frequency was approximately 2 times per minute. Although this was a short-term project, the results were encouraging relative to the possibilities of changing the frequency of the overt expression of feelings; also, it was encouraging that such tactics were associated with a decrement in stuttering.

In another early study of a similar design (C. Johnson, 1966; Shames, 1969), the difficulties that an adult male stutterer was having in making progress in a symptom-management program of therapy were thought to be due to his inability generally to make decisions and establish goals for himself. It was felt that this was a general problem for this person which was interfering with his realizing his full potential and that it was a factor in his unsuccessful therapy. It was hyothesized that the way people behave and act in social contexts may be related to the way they talk about the way they act in these contexts (semantogenic relationship between behavior and the verbal characterization of that behavior). It was decided to try to increase the frequency of emission of statements that define and describe goals and statements which connote independent decision-making. A series of 18, 50-minute interviews on a twice-a-week basis was arranged. The first session was a base operant level session, and the final 17 sessions were conditioning sessions. During the conditioning sessions, the interviewer was programmed to ask 8–10 key questions designed to provide occasions for the stutterer to emit goal-setting and decision-making comments. Any time the stutterer emitted a target response (with or without a question from the interviewer), the interviewer consequated it with a verbal response that indicated acceptance, approval, or understanding ("I see," "I understand," "That's reasonable," etc.). If a target response was not emitted or was inadequate when an occasion for it was provided, the interviewer responded verbally with disapproval or lack of acceptance.

The general results of the project showed that there were significant increases in the frequencies of the goal-setting and decision-making comments over the 17 sessions. There were also significant decrements in various forms of dysfluency. For example, in the base operant session, the stutterer emitted 4 positive target responses and would have been given verbal disapproval 4 times when key questions were asked. In the last 3 conditioning sessions, the stutterer emitted 29, 31, and 32 positive target responses in sessions 15, 16, and 17, respectively. Also, during these final three sessions he received disapproval 4 times, 3 times, and once, respectively. The change in repetition behavior over time was also quite marked, even though no consequences were provided for the emission of repetitions. In the base operant session, the stutterer repeated approximately 12 times per minute; in the final therapy session, his repetition rate was about 2 per minute. As with the previous project, the results were encouraging in that it appeared to be possible to change the frequency of emission of statements containing certain content through verbal contingencies; it was also encouraging that such changes were associated with significant decrements in stuttering.

Based on these two projects, it was felt that a better understanding was developing about the processes of interview-type therapy.

In a third type of exploratory study, two projects dealt with applying operant tactics to the clinical process of modifying the form of stuttering. Both projects used Van Riper's (1957) cancellation–pull-out procedures as a model. In one project (Ryan and Shames, 1966), the stutterers in an 8-step program were asked to identify instances of stuttering, to reiterate stuttered words, to stutter on the words in a prolonging pattern, to pull out of stuttering blocks with a prolonging pattern, and eventually to prolong those words on which stuttering was anticipated. The stutterers did this while reading, in a negative-reinforcement paradigm. Each time the stutterers engaged in the desired behavior, the hand on a timer moved, thereby reducing the amount of time they had to spend in oral reading (thought to be an aversive situation). The stutterers not only learned their tasks, but their frequency of stuttering decreased significantly. There was no carry-over from the reading task, carried out in a soundproof booth, to conversation outside the booth.

In the second project (P. R. Johnson, 1966; Shames, 1969), an adult male stutterer was positively reinforced for learning to modify his stuttering in terms of the Van Riper model of cancellation–pull-out procedures.

This was done during conversation in a series of 26 clinical interviews, each 50 minutes long, on a twice-a-week basis. The stutterer was given instructions and examples of the appropriate behavior. Each time he emitted the appropriate modification response, he was given approval. When he failed to do so, the interviewer indicated his disapproval. As in the previous project, the stutterer learned his tasks and there was a sharp decrement in stuttering frequency. In this project, although stuttering decreased, the total modification program, as conceived, might be considered a failure. The stutterer mastered only the first four steps of an eight-step program during the 26 interviews. During the fifth step of the project, his frequency of stuttering had dropped to zero. In a nine-month follow-up, it was observed that stuttering was practically nonexistent, and on the few occasions that he stuttered outside the clinic he usually reiterated the stuttered word by prolonging the first sound.

There is a problem in these programs in that the occasion for the target response and its consequent reinforcement is an instance of stuttering. If, as occurred in these projects, the frequency of stuttering drops to any significant degree, there is also a reduction in the occasions for reinforcing target responses. Under these circumstances, it is questionable whether the modification response would ever be strongly established in the repertoires of low-frequency stutterers. However, given the encouragements from these small-subject, exploratory projects, Shames and his colleagues developed larger-scale projects dealing with research on therapy for both children and adults.

Shames, Egolf, and Rhodes (1969) applied operant tactics to both the Johnson semantogenic-based approach to therapy for adult stutterers and to a modified form of Van Riper's procedures for changing the form of stuttering.

In the semantic program, an interviewer was programmed to provide approval for certain desirable content and disapproval for undesirable content. In general, the desirable content dealt with overt utterances by the stutterer that described behavior and showed awareness of relationships between stuttering and other events (insight statements), positive affect, negative affect, contemplated action, and completed action. The undesirable content dealt with utterances that reflected helplessness and victimization and with ambiguous, nondescriptive characterizations of speech, such as referring to "it" in connection with stuttering (Williams, 1957). Depending on the content of the utterances observed during a 50-minute monologue and during a 50-minute noncontingent interview with the stutterer (who was instructed to talk about anything he wished), the stutterer was put into one of three content-modification programs: (1) If during the monologue and interview the stutterer emitted a large number of undesirable content responses, he was put into a program that provided disapproval by the interviewer for undesirable responses and approval for desirable responses. (2) If the undesirable content responses were observed to be in very low frequency during the monologue and interview, he was put into a program of positive reinforcement, during which desirable content was the only response that generated a verbal consequence from the interviewer. (3) If the verbal output of the stutterer was very low during the monologue and noncontingent interview, a program was used that provided for "verbal lubricants" from the interviewer at particular times during the interviews to keep the stutterer talking (comments by the interviewer that encouraged him to talk).

The general results of this project revealed that stutterers in each of the programs increased their frequencies of desirable content and decreased their frequencies of undesirable content. In addition, there were associated decreases in the frequency of stuttering, even though contingencies were not directly applied to the emission of stuttering. It was also concluded that the programs which provided both approval and disapproval for desirable and undesirable content, respectively, were more effective than the programs which ignored the undesirable content.

An extension of this study was developed by Rhodes, Shames, and Egolf (1971) to determine the tactical value of "awareness" of the contingencies by the stutterer as a factor in content modification programs of therapy. Eight adult stutterers were put through the content-modification program that provides approval and disapproval for desirable and undesirable content. Four of the stutterers were informed beforehand of the contingencies that would be operating and of the value of the positive target responses in therapy; the other four stutterers were not informed. It was found that the informed group acquired the desirable content more rapidly, but eventually the uninformed group acquired the positive content to the same degree. It was also found that the stuttering frequencies of the uninformed group dropped sharply, even without consequences being provided for stuttering; this decrement in stuttering frequency was not observed in the informed group. It was also determined that the initially uninformed subjects became aware of the contingencies on their own by the time the experimental therapy had terminated. It was generally concluded that experiencing the contingency as a means of becoming aware of it was probably more effective than being instructed beforehand about it. It was also possible that the redundancy of repeated instructions throughout therapy for the informed group actually interfered with their progress (Rubin, 1973).

In an individualized version of this content program, Egolf, Shames, and Blind (1971) and Shames and Egolf (in press) combined it with procedures based on the ideas of Sheehan's approach-avoidance conflict theory. In dealing with a female adult stutterer, three stages of therapy were employed. Stage 1 was designed to increase eye contact by having an interviewer say "Look at me" at each instance of loss of eye contact during a series of 40-minute interviews. After four sessions, when eye contact improved, Stage 2 was initiated, which involved a content-modification program as developed by Shames, Egolf, and Rhodes (1969). Twenty-four sessions were held, during which desirable content increased and stuttering frequency and severity decreased. Although undesirable content decreased, the self-concept of "helplessness" was still very prominent. This residual of undesirable content led to Stage 3, which was based in part on Sheehan's approach-avoidance theory and in part on Johnson's semantic theory of stuttering. The stutterer was given three instructions for outside activities:

1. Talk whenever you want to or have the opportunity to (suggested by Sheehan's approach-avoidance).
2. Keep talking, even if you stutter (suggested by Sheehan's approach-avoidance).
3. When in doubt, see what most other people do in the same situation (suggested by Johnson's idea that it is important to know and tolerate "normal" mistakes and behavior).

The stutterer's subsequent 40-minute interviews focused on how well the stutterer implemented these instructions. The clinician gave verbal approval for statements by the stutterer that showed she was following instructions and verbal disapproval for statements indicating she was not following instructions. There were 15 sessions during Stage 3, during which stuttering frequency and severity decreased and positive content increased. Follow-up studies at six months and one year revealed that she was making significant gains in the social aspects of her life and was actively pursuing important life goals. On the occasion of the second follow-up study, she did not stutter.

The research programs dealing with applying operant tactics to directly modifying the forms of stuttering went through a series of changes and phases, in which different types and numbers of modification responses were tried. Starting with the 8-step program developed by Ryan and Shames (1966), which was originally based on Van Riper's cancellation–pull-out procedures, a 10-step program was studied (Carrier, Shames, and Egolf, 1969). This was shortened to a 4-step modification program that was studied on a broader basis within the context of individual interviews (Shames, Egolf, and Rhodes, 1969). The 4 steps involved the following:

1. A pause following every stuttered word and then reiteration of that word

2. Reiteration of the stuttered word by prolonging the initial sound of the word reiterated
3. Interruption of the stuttering and prolonging the initial sound of a stuttered word
4. Prolonging the first sound of each stuttered word

Approval was given contingent on the stutterer emitting the desired response. If the stutterer failed to emit the desired response, the interviewer interrupted him and repeated the task instructions. In general, the stutterers involved acquired the modification behaviors of the program. However, as in the earlier exploratory studies, there were sharp decrements in stuttering frequency even though the contingencies were designed to reinforce positively the modifications of stuttering and not to suppress stuttering. As the results of these programs designed to modify the form of stuttering are now reexamined, an interpretation different from the original one may explain the reduction in stuttering. It seems possible that what was viewed as a positive-reinforcement paradigm for changing the form of stuttering was in reality a punishment program for the emission of stuttering, resulting in its reduced frequency. When one looks at the consequences of each instance of stuttering in this program, it is found that the stutterer's communicative interaction was interrupted, his social reinforcement was delayed, and his progression through his communicative message was postponed. He also had to deliberately reiterate the stuttered word and change the pattern of its emission. All of these events were contingent consequences of each instance of stuttering and may have been quite aversive to the stutterer.

Follow-up studies of 71 stutterers (Blind, Shames, and Egolf, 1972) who achieved fluency during these experimental programs which modified either the content or the form of the stutterers' response revealed that only a portion of them remained fluent. It appears that those stutterers who sustained their clinical fluency were also those who reported significant changes in their life system (many of which changes were not under their control) and who experienced major changes in their self-perceptions.

The research of this group, on therapy for children who stutter again reflects an application of operant tactics to some of the traditional theories about stuttering and about childhood problems in general. Attention was focused on the verbal interaction patterns that operate between children and parents. A number of writers have emphasized the importance of these interactions in the onset and maintenance of stuttering (Johnson 1955, 1956, 1959; Luper and Mulder, 1965).

In one project (Egolf, Shames, Johnson, and Kasprisin-Burrelli, 1972; Kasprisin-Burrelli, Egolf, and Shames, 1972), a system for analyzing parent-child verbal interactions was developed; it was based in part on the ideas of Ginott (1969). Seventeen categories of positive and 18 categories of negative verbal interactions were employed in a system of therapy designed to change the consequences provided by parents for their children's verbalizations. It was hypothesized that these parental consequences were maintaining their child's stuttering. The experimental therapy was therefore a mirror image of the parent-child interaction. After systematic observations and categorizations of the interactions between each parent and child, a clinician would emit the opposite behavior. For example, if the parent did not listen or attend to the child, the clinician attended closely; if the parent interrupted the child, the clinician would give the child a chance to finish each utterance; if the parent did not respond to the substantive content of the child's utterances but instead emitted a non sequitur, the clinician would respond to the child's content during interviews; if a parent showed verbal aggression, the clinician showed support and acceptance; and if the parent showed acceptance of the stuttering, the clinician would confront and not accept the stuttering but instead would provide instructions for alternative forms of talking. Each therapy session was 40 minutes long. When stuttering frequency was reduced to less than 1 percent in a total session with the clinician, the parent was introduced into the sessions. With the parent present, the clinician still emitted the behaviors he had been emitting to provide a model for the parent. The clinician also shared some of his speaking time with the parent in an effort to transfer stimulus control of the child's fluency from himself to the parent. Nine stutterers ranging in age from 5 to 13 were put through this program. While all of the children showed decreases in stuttering, only six completed the program.

Five of the children were reevaluated by observing them in interactions with their parents and with an interviewer. Two of the children were not stuttering at all with their parents, while another two stuttered less than 1 percent of the time with their parents. The data from these nine parent-child interactions were pooled with data from five additional dyads in an analysis by Kaspirisin-Burrelli, Egolf, and Shames (1972). They found that a control group of parents of nonstutterers emitted more positive statements than parents of stutterers before therapy and that the parents of stutterers emitted more positive statements after therapy than at the beginning. This clinical program was later replicated with 13 stutterers in a public-school setting (Seltzer, Shames, and Egolf, 1971). The results were again very positive: All of the stutterers showed marked decrements in the frequency and severity of their stuttering, and the parents showed changes in the patterns of their verbal interactions.

Group therapy

Up to this point, the discussion of operant conditioning and programs of therapy has emphasized the individual situation of one stutterer with one clinician. However, there have been a small number of projects that have attempted to apply operant methodology to a group situation. These projects were carried out, not for expediency (which has often been the impetus for group therapy), but rather because there are certain kinds of events of therapeutic value that are more easily arranged or can be arranged only within a group situation. The nature of these events will become more clear as we review these projects.

Leith and Uhlemann (1970a, 1970b, 1970c, 1972) have developed an approach to stuttering therapy that they call "the shaping group." It is an extension of the work of Shapiro and Birk (1967), who explored the operant model in group therapy. The purpose of the shaping group is to arrange for a "process designed to modify specific behaviors which interfere with the group member's interpersonal relationships" (Leith and Uhlemann, 1970a,b,c). Respondent behaviors are modified through increasing the individual's awareness of precipitating cues, reducing the individual's sensitivity to these cues, and providing the individual with an alternate form of behavior he can substitute for the offending behavior. Operant behaviors are modified through the use of verbal and nonverbal positive and negative reinforcers and punishers. As behaviors indicate movement toward the alternate form of behavior, they are positively reinforced. Behaviors that do not indicate such movement are negatively reinforced or punished. The stuttering members of the group are instructed in the principles of operant conditioning and given training in providing consequences for one another's behavior. Shapiro and Birk pointed out that the precise timing of consequent action in a group is critical to its effectiveness and therefore this training of the members is of the utmost importance. Each group member establishes his individual behavior-change goals. Stuttering is considered as only one of a number of clusters of behaviors that may be so designated. Group members may help one another in determining these behavior-change goals. All of the members are made familiar with each other's goals, and the group members then become consequators for each other's behaviors.

The process involves giving each member feedback from the group on the impact of one's present behavior on others; the effect of one's behavior on others' responses to him; cues in the environment that precipitate, prolong, or terminate the behavior; and the impact of one's altered behavior on others' responses to him. In addition, the stutterers are desensitized to these cues so that alternate forms of behavior can be strengthened. Leith and Uhlemann (1970a, 1970b) report on nine young adults, four stutterers and five nonstutterers, who went through such a group process involving 50 hours over a period of five months. On a number of measures, all of the subjects showed changes in a desired direction in terms of what was said and what was done in the group sessions. They also showed changes in a group rating measure. However, none of the subjects showed any systematic change in self-concept. The changes in stuttering behavior were not consistent. Judges rated severity of stuttering as reduced in four examples, no change in two, and increased in two. Twelve judgments were made of change in stuttering behavior toward the designated goal. Positive change was detected in nine of these judgments, no change in two, and a negative change in one. In a three-month follow-up, it was found that the changes accrued during the group were sustained. The authors felt that a major factor in the limited effectiveness of their program was the time intervals between group sessions, as well as the influence of the data of one stuttering subject who was experiencing severe personal trauma just prior to the terminal measurements.

Another type of group therapy approach was developed in a series of projects by Andrews (1971), Ingham and Andrews (1971), Andrews and Ingham (1971), and Ingham and Winkler (1972). They attempted to develop major control of stutterers' environments by admitting them as residents in a hospital and putting them in a token economy. At admission, the stutterers gave up their real money, which had no value in this small controlled hospital society. The stutterers were trained in various methods of establishing fluency. Following this, they had to earn tokens for the necessities and luxuries of a three-week stay in the hospital. Each stutterer had a different set of subgoals determined by his base-rate of stuttering and his syllable rate. The base-rate was defined as the average of his three best previous sessions, and therefore it changed as the stutterer made progress. Seven times a day, during a daily 12-hour period, the stutterers held group discussions, during which measurements of stuttering and syllable rate were made. If stutterers reached a criterion of a 10-percent reduction in severity of stuttering, they received tokens, which could be traded in for such things as coffee, cigarettes, dessert, phone calls, and privileges. If stutterers regressed, tokens were taken away.

The authors reported on 39 stutterers who went through this program. All of them showed marked reductions in stuttering. However, follow-up studies raised some questions about some of the original methods used for establishing fluency (syllable timing and negative practice). The authors suggested the possible efficacy of short-term, follow-up, token-system booster experiences. Evidently the three-week intensive experience, on its own, does not consistently result in sustained fluency and should be followed with some additional contingency activity.

Finally, a time-out group was employed in therapy by Egolf, Shames, and Seltzer (1971). Time-out from positive reinforcement is viewed as a form of punishment and is designed to decrease the frequency of the behavior on which it is contingent. Haroldson, Martin, and Starr (1968) demonstrated the application of this procedure with individual stutterers on the assumption that talking was self-reinforcing. They observed a decremental effect on stuttering frequency.

In the Egolf et al. study, 10 male stutterers ranging in age from 22 to 52 met weekly for a 90-minute session. They were highly verbal, and talking within the group appeared to be a very positive experience. When this group appeared to be evolving into more of a social than a therapeutic activity, time-out procedures were introduced. Each subject was told that he could talk until he stuttered, at which point he had to relinquish the floor to another group member. The sessions were designed so that each member had an opportunity to speak. The effects of the group time-out procedure were measured in terms of number of words uttered and number of seconds that elapsed until a subject stuttered. The group met for a period of five weeks.

The results of this project showed that, for the ten subjects, the experimental runs during which time-out contingencies were in effect were markedly different from the control sessions when the contingency was not in effect. The mean fluency time of the first noncontingent session was 20.8 seconds; this increased to a mean of 290.3 seconds of fluency when the time-out was in effect. The mean number of words in the non-time-out session was 33.4 per subject; this increased to a mean of 583.6 words during time-out. Individual subjects varied. The poorest showed changes of a few words and a few seconds, one time in the positive direction and the second time in a negative direction. However, another subject went from 37 words to 897 words and then to 1048 words. Still another subject went from 39 words to 1088 words. Some of the fluency times were 30 times longer during the time-out sessions than during the control sessions.

The authors generally concluded that high-frequency stutterers did not do as well as low-frequency stutterers with the time-out procedures. They also suggested (1) using a fixed talking interval to equate opportunities for talking time and time-out intervals or (2) varying these talking intervals individually in terms of individual base-rates. It was also felt that time-out procedures should be combined with a program for reinforcing fluency in a group.

Suppression of stuttering

The application of punishment procedures to the problem of stuttering is being placed into a separate category of consideration because the projects do not fit into any single category, such as studies of onset, prevention, therapy, or nature of the problem. Projects using punishment procedures have implications for all of those issues. The distinguishing feature of such projects is the use of a paradigm in which aversive stimulation is contingent on stuttering, and the purpose is to suppress the frequency of stuttering. This particular area of endeavor has been controversial and the source of much misunderstanding and problems (Fowler and Wischner, 1969; Fowler, 1971).

Punishment as a method of suppressing behavior has been the subject of a great deal of study since Thorndike's (1933) original statement of his law of effect. Fowler (1971) points out that the original bar-slap study by Skinner (1938) and the experimental work by Estes (1944), involving electric shock, highlighted an effect of punishment that was only temporarily suppressing and that the response was recovered when the punishment contingency was removed. Fowler (1971, p. 537) goes on to point out, "These observations coupled with those relating to the clinical interpretation of punishment as something inevitably disruptive, leading possibly to neurotic outcome (e.g., Maier; Masserman), soon fostered the widespread belief or legend as Solomon (1964) has characterized it—that punishment was ineffective in eliminating behavior, and therefore a procedure to be avoided whenever possible." However, current accounts of punishment, notably by such researchers as Azrin and Holz (1966) and Boe and Church (1967), who are just a few among many, point out that punishment procedures do work in eliminating behaviors and that the suppression effect can be permanent. Fowler (1971) further notes that there is a confusion in the definition of "punishment" wherein the functions and mechanisms of operation of the punishment contingency are not distinguished from the *effect* of producing a suppression. The problem appears to reduce itself to whether punishment is to be defined in terms of the properties of the stimulus (noxious and aversive) or in terms of the suppressive effects of the stimulus, or both. Very often, the aversive properties of a suppressing stimulus have not been demonstrated.

Azrin and Holz (1966) and Church (1969) have demonstrated that suppression of behavior through contingent aversive stimulation is related to (1) the promptness of stimulus presentation, (2) the duration and intensity of the stimulus, (3) the degree to which its introduction stands out, and (4) its frequency and variability of occurrence. There also are data to suggest that the subject's history with punishment as well as the availability of an alternative response that would lead to positive reinforcement heighten the suppressive effects of aversive stimulation (Azrin, Hake, Holz, and Hutchinson, 1965; Azrin and Holz, 1966; Brookshire, 1969; Brookshire and Eveslage, 1969).

Each of these correlates could become major issues for clinical application and deserve study as clinical tactics. The question of the need to demonstrate the escape and avoidance properties of the suppressing stimulus is still unanswered. Siegel (1970, pp. 678–679), in discussing punishment and stuttering, recognizes this definitional problem and offers the Azrin and Holz statement of punishment:

> "Punishment is a reduction of the future probability of a specific response as a result of the immediate delivery of a stimulus for that response.
> There is no reference to the properties of the stimulus, nor to internal states of the subject with reference to the stimulus. The definition has two parts. The first specifies the direction of effect . . . a decrease in behavior. The second part of the definition is more crucial . . . In order for a situation to be formally identified as punishing, the punishing stimulus must be arranged as the explicit consequence of the response under consideration." (Azrin and Holz, 1966, p. 381)

In applying these procedures to stuttering, the controversies become even more heightened. Punishing stuttering behavior flies in the face of stuttering theory, wherein the onset of stuttering has been related to the punishment of normal dysfluency. It is counter to previous research on the effects of noncontingent aversive stimulation on stuttering (Van Riper, 1937; Frick, 1951). It is abrasive to traditional principles of therapy, wherein clinicians are trained to accept and support and to create a nonpunitive climate for change. It is also counter to our cultural value system, which emphasizes the rewarding of desirable behaviors rather than the penalizing of undesirable behaviors.

The original studies by Flanagan, Goldiamond, and Azrin (1958) and, more recently, by Goldiamond (1965a) have demonstrated that when DAF or noise is contingent on stuttering, stuttering decreases. These studies led to a systematic program of research by Siegel and Martin and their colleagues at the University of Minnesota. They attempted to reconcile the Flanagan and Goldiamond findings with traditional views of punishment and stuttering. Siegel (1970) has generally summarized the results of these projects:

> In the earliest experiments, electric shock was made the consequence of each stuttering; later verbal stimuli such as "wrong" were substituted.
> In more recent research, the punishing stimulus has been a "time-out" period of several seconds in which the stutterer is not allowed to continue talking, or a "response-cost" method in which the stutterer loses points or money for each moment of stuttering. Most of the sessions have been conducted in the same experimental facility, with the subject alone in a room, while the experimentor monitors from a control room. In some instances listeners have been added, and the subject has been asked to

speak into a telephone. The specific response selected for modification has varied from a global "moment of stuttering" to a more particular behavior, such as a specific facial grimace or a vocal pattern. In general, and with due regard to differences among subjects, all of the techniques used—shock, verbal stimuli, time-out, response-cost—serve as response depressants when arranged as a consequence of the response. This has been true with impressive consistency in both reading and speaking, whether the response was a particular behavior or simply stuttering . . . For the most part the results have not been permanent, and subjects quickly recovered their stuttering rates when the stimuli were withdrawn . . . or when they left the experimental facility. This is a familiar problem to speech pathologists. At present a major effort is being made to find ways to move the more fluent speech out of the laboratory and into more natural settings. (Pp. 681–682)

Perhaps, because of their implications for preventative programs as well as for onset of stuttering, Siegel and Martin undertook a series of studies on punishment of the dysfluencies of normal speakers. Starting with electric shock, and moving over to the use of verbal punishers, these studies first dealt with dysfluencies during reading and then dysfluencies during spontaneous speech. In general, Siegel and Martin found that random aversive punishment had little effect on dysfluencies, while contingent stimulation reduced the frequencies of dysfluencies; the data for reading and speaking were similar. They also found that those subjects who originally had higher dysfluency rates showed the greatest decrements of dysfluency during the contingent-stimulus sessions. Verbal reinforcers (especially the word "wrong") seemed to be more effective in suppressing behavior than shock. The dysfluencies were not recovered when the contingencies were withdrawn during speech. A combination of instructions not to repeat or interject in addition to the contingency was the most effective paradigm for suppressing dysfluency (Siegel and Martin, 1965a, 1965b, 1966, 1967, 1968; Martin and Siegel, 1966a, 1966b, 1969; Brookshire and Martin, 1967; Quist and Martin, 1967; Martin, 1968).

A "highlighting" hypothesis offered by Siegel (1970) has emerged from these studies; it states that any event which brings dysfluencies to the attention of the speaker will cause their reduction. This particular hypothesis has some support from other quarters. Clinicians and researchers have reported that merely having the stutterer count dysfluencies or identify dysfluencies as they are occurring, having an experimenter say the word "tree" (Cooper, Cady, and Robbins, 1970), sounding a buzzer, or having the clinician say the word the stutterer has just stuttered (Blind, Shames, and Egolf, 1973) appears to be associated with decrements in dysfluency and stuttering. Each of these contingent events may serve an informing function rather than an aversive, punitive function.

The highlighting hypothesis and these clinical reports relate to one aspect of a more general theory of self-reinforcement offered by Kanfer and Karoly (1972). Although Siegel hypothesizes about external consequences, Kanfer and Karoly state that there are three stages to self-reinforcement. First is a monitoring activity, which could be akin to the highlighting activity suggested by Siegel. This is followed by an evaluation of the desirability of the behavior. Finally, the subject consequates himself for the behavior he has emitted. In this instance, we might speculate that the stutterer's attention has been called to his dysfluent behavior through his monitoring. It is evaluated as undesirable, and the stutterer implicitly says "wrong" to himself. This, of course, is a simplistic version of an inferred chain of covert events. The overt events are the contingent event of monitoring and the reduced frequency of dysfluency. One of the important implications of the highlighting hypothesis for clinicians, as well as for parents, is that a stimulus event designed to suppress stuttering or dysfluency does not necessarily have to be aversive in its manifest form.

In addition to the results of those projects, which demonstrated that stuttering and dysfluency could be suppressed through contingent stimulation, there are three suppression studies that should be considered in some detail because of their implications for onset and prevention. Two of these, by Brookshire (1969) and Brookshire and Eveslage (1969), consider the history of the subject with punishment. Brookshire analyzed the effects of response-contingent stimulation (punishment) on dysfluency when it was immediately preceded by the same form of aversive stimulation (noise) on a random schedule. This type of arrangement may well resemble the real-life home situation of young children who develop problems of stuttering. If attempts at aversive control are prominent in a household, they are often on an intermittent basis, operate at the convenience of the parents, and are usually of the same form (shouting, spanking, loss of privileges, etc.). In the Brookshire study, 10 normal speakers received contingent aversive stimulation before the random delivery of aversive stimulation. A second group of 10 normal speakers received contingent aversive stimulation after random delivery of aversive stimulation. The usually observed punishment effect of contingent stimulation, whereby dysfluencies decrease, was not observed when random aversive stimulation of the same form preceded it. The decrement was observed only when contingent stimulation preceded random stimulation. The author concluded that random delivery of an aversive stimulus prior to its use as a punishing stimulus interfered with conditioned suppression of dysfluency.

In a second study, Brookshire and Eveslage (1969) used noise in the random session and the word no in the contingent session. They found that, by using a different form of aversive stmulation, the dysfluencies were reduced. There is a suggestion here that the use of the punishment paradigm to suppress dysfluencies in the natural habitats of children would require careful control over its scheduling and form if it is to be effective. Because of the difficulties that may be encountered in controlling such events in a child's natural surroundings, these results may in fact contraindicate trying to program such a paradigm for home use. It points up the potential difference between a controlled laboratory finding and its viable functions in the real world.

Another study that deserves comment is one by Halvorson (1971), which also demonstrated a dilution of the punishment effect and perhaps also contraindicated its clinical or home use, except under carefully controlled conditions. Halvorson based his study on the hypotheses of Holz and Azrin (1961) and Ayllon and Azrin (1966) that maladaptive behaviors may be maintained by punishing stimuli, if paired with reinforcement. Halvorson hypothesized that if punishment for stuttering is paired with reinforcement for fluency, the punishing stimulus may acquire the ability to signal the availability of the reinforcing stimulus to the stutterer, thus maintaining the apparently maladaptive behaviors.

Three stutterers were put through five conditions of spontaneous speech. Condition 1 was a base-rate segment during which the stutterers merely spoke without contingent stimulation. In Condition 2, a response-cost punishment procedure was employed, whereby the stutterer lost a point on a counter after each instance of stuttering. Stuttering frequency was observed to decrease during this condition. In Condition 3, the stutterer was given 10 points after the emission of the first fluent word, following an instance of stuttering during which he still lost 1 point. Stuttering was observed to increase toward base-rate during this pairing of punishment and reinforcement procedures. In Condition 4, all contingencies were withdrawn and stuttering frequency gradually approximated the stutterer's base-rates. In Condition 5, response-cost punishment was reintroduced. Although stuttering again decreased, it did not immediately decrease for one subject as when originally introduced in Condition 2. This result further suggested that punishment for stuttering may have acquired discriminative attributes, functioning as a cue for reinforcement. We see here the possible operation of a chain of events that may be an analogue of the young, developing stutterer's home environment. It is quite common, as suggested by Siegel (1970) to observe parents first punishing their child and immediately following this with lavish displays of affection. The child may soon learn that one way to generate affection and attention (especially in those circumstances where he is deprived or in competition) is to emit undesirable behavior.

One could also speculate about those events and mechanisms that maintain the parents' behavior. Parents maintain their role of authority, are the source of correction and information, can express their love and affection, confirm their power to control their child, and perpetuate their child's dependency. Each of these could be powerful consequences of parents' behavior that could maintain their behavior in high frequency.

One of the significant implications of this particular piece of research is for prevention. Although we do not currently have enough information from this project for clinical or home application, there is a methodology here that may have some prototypical value for studies in the natural environment of children.

Tentative Interpretations and Future Directions

The material reviewed thus far in this chapter has constituted a highlighting of the history of the application of operant-conditioning principles and tactics to the problem of stuttering. Omissions of certain projects from this review, although perhaps inevitable because of space limitations, in no way reflects their lack of importance. Selections of items and the amount of detail given were to accommodate the need to illustrate certain types of research or clinical activities, rather than to catalogue all of the projects pertaining to a particular area. In some instances emphasis was given to the principles involved rather than the specific form of the tactic or technique. It is recognized that today's interpretation may be tomorrow's obsolescence, as new data and tactics are added.

Let us turn to the specific substantive issues, listed at the beginning of this chapter, that were suggested as dimensions for reacting to the productiveness of the operant activities.

Onset and development

One of the issues was the issue of onset and development. Comment about this issue has to be indirect or based on inference. In general, the studies which were done, not as therapy demonstrations but as demonstrations that stuttering and normal dysfluencies are manipulable in terms of the principles of operant conditioning, can be interpreted relative to this issue. Those projects which demonstrated that stuttering and dysfluency decrease with contingent aversive stimulation through negative reinforcement and highlighting, as well as those projects which demonstrated that fluency could be increased through positive reinforcement, strongly suggest that conditioning processes are probably also active in the onset and development of stuttering. However, the particular form that these conditioning processes may take in the child's natural environment have only been suggested (Shames and Sherrick, 1963; Shames, 1968; Burrelli et al., 1972) and have not been experimentally verified. Unfortunately, the field of stuttering research does not enjoy the luxury of having lower species available for experimental verification. Therefore, the crucial experiments of demonstrating the onset of stuttering in children is ethically out of the question. The approach to this problem remains an analytical and inferential rather than experimental one. For example, as in the Egolf et al. (1972) and Kaspirisin-Burrelli et al. (1972) studies, which focused on verbal interactions with parents, the interaction variables are observed; their effects are assessed; parents of stutterers and nonstutterers are differentiated; and, by reversing the effects of the interaction by a mirror-image approach, we might infer—although not experimentally verify—the nature of the variables involved in onset.

The two studies by Brookshire that demonstrated how an experience of random delivery of the same aversive stimulus, if it precedes contingent aversive stimulation, could dilute (if not reverse) the usual suppressive effect of contingent punishment on dysfluencies, suggest an analogue for the development and maintenance of stuttering. The same suggestion comes from the results of the Halvorson study, in which suppression of stuttering is reversed when the punishment of stuttering is paired with reinforcement for fluency. However, all three of these were studies on adults. The Egolf et al. and the Kaspirisin-Burrelli et al. studies on parent-child interaction also constitute a comment about onset and development of stuttering in that positive verbal interactions were observed more frequently with parents of nonstutterers than with parents of stutterers. However, for a number of reasons, within the framework of an experimental analysis of behavior, the critical experimental research on onset has not been done and probably will have to remain within the purview of analytic rather than experimental research.

Prevention

With regard to the issue of prevention, we are again faced with the possibility of much that could be inferred, but very little in the way of experimental verification. Even if we had preventive procedures, a major question remains as to when to invoke them. When is childhood dysfluency and/or family reactions such that preventive measures should be deliberately employed? What you prevent and how you prevent it is closely related to the information (or lack of it) about which we have confidence relative to onset and development. In order to prevent something, we logically would see to it that its etiological factors are not given the opportunity to become active. Van Riper's (1971) focus on what we should be alert to emphasizes the forms of dysfluent speech behavior emitted by the child. He points out that the presence of syllable repetition, the child's awareness, and the frequency, consistency, and duration of dysfluency are dimensions of the child's speaking behavior that should alert us to the possible need for intervention.

However, Shames and Sherrick (1963), Shames (1968) and Egolf, et al. (1972) have suggested that the circumstances for the child's dysfluency are of equal importance. Those events that precede and follow a child's speech dysfluency give us information about the need for intervention as well as about which particular events should be considered. For example, if dysfluency is emitted on the occasions of editing, self-prompting, word finding, or retaining a listener's attention, we might conclude that preventive measures would be inappropriate. These might be considered normal circumstances for dysfluency. They may decrease in frequency or undergo change in form, but they will remain in some strength throughout life. On the other hand, we might observe that dysfluencies are emitted, for example, on occasions of competition for talking time, during interruptions by listeners, while functioning in an overstimulating environment, while being a partner in poor verbal interactions, when receiving penalties and aggression, when experiencing states of deprivation, or when being hurried. Each of these may be occasions of great stress for a young child, and we might conclude that they are active in maintaining and strengthening the frequencies of dysfluencies that could lead to stuttering.

The Egolf et al. (1972) and the Kaspirisin-Burrelli et al. (1972) studies contain the format for some much needed large-scale studies on prevention. Their data on verbal interactions between parents and children can be interpreted as containing some general and specific prophylactic properties. With their verbal interaction model in mind, it would be possible to identify two large, equivalent groups of preschool children; one group would be given the experience of a positive verbal-interaction program (training parents, etc.), and the other group would go through its natural parent-child interaction activities. Periodic comparisons between the two groups on various measures of dysfluencies and stuttering, as well as on social and emotional behaviors over a three-to-four-year period, during the ages 2–5, could provide information about the prevention of many types of behavioral problems. This kind of experimental data is both needed and ethically valid.

Therapy

By far the largest and most significant contribution from the operant area deals with therapy for stuttering. The programs of therapy that have been explored are consistently successful, up to a point. They have employed positive reinforcement for fluency, negative reinforcement for shaping slow rates to conversational rates, mild verbal punishment of stuttering, positive reinforcement for overt content themes, positive reinforcement for modifying the form of stuttering, and positive reinforcement for changing parent-child verbal interactions. Programs have involved group settings and token economies as well as individual therapy.

It has become clear that there are a number of ways to generate fluency in stutterers within the confines of the clinic, hospital, or school setting. However, there are questions to be asked at this point: Does one of the ways for developing clinical fluency have any advantages over the others to suggest it as a preferred method? Is one way faster to accomplish, more durable, carried over better, and so on? Does the way in which fluency is established lead to a totally integrative program of therapy? Or is establishing fluency merely one isolated paradigm that deals with fluency in an isolated sense and does not necessarily have to coordinate or articulate with paradigms for other responses pertinent to the total problem? To answer these questions, let us speculate about those responses that appear to require attention in a total therapeutic sense. We see from the literature that operant-therapy programs have dealt with the following:

1. Establishing fluent speech
2. Establishing self-responsibility
3. Establishing a "belief system" in the stutterer of being a fluent speaker
4. Establishing self-monitoring behavior of fluency
5. Arranging the occasions for monitoring fluency in real-life situations

A general model for stuttering therapy and a sequence of phases of therapy might be inferred from the preceding list (Shames & Egolf, in press). The greatest amount of attention has been given to the first point, establishing fluent speech. From both the standpoints of research and personal experience, it would appear that a great deal of time is not absolutely necessary for establishing clinical fluency; this no longer appears to be a difficult or time-consuming task. Our clinical logic tells us that the sooner we get through event number one (establishing fluency) to events two through five, where the more difficult aspects of therapy are encountered, the sooner we get to our terminal goal of discontinuing therapy.

Seven major types of operant tactics for establishing fluency have been described in this chapter. They include:

1. Rate control through DAF and negative reinforcement
2. Rate control through instructions and positive reinforcement
3. Reinforcing fluency intervals and fluency responses
4. Suppressing stuttering through contingent punishment and contingent highlighting
5. Consequating desirable and undesirable content themes
6. Reinforcing the modification of the forms of stuttering
7. Consequating desirable and undesirable parent-child verbal interactions

A brief summary of some of the outstanding characteristics of each may illustrate and suggest their relative advantages.

Rate control through DAF and negative reinforcement. On the positive side, this program may take only a short time to establish fluency. It heightens awareness of response topography, which in turn prepares the stutterer for monitoring fluency. It provides rules and criteria for movement in the program, both forward and backward in case of later difficulty. Because of early success, it facilitates motivation and affects positively the attitudes and beliefs of the stutterer about himself as a fluent speaker. It appears to coordinate with a total program of therapy.

On the negative side, it can delay a self-perception of self-responsibility for speech behavior. It can generate overdependence on the mechanical manipulation provided by the DAF, and DAF machines are expensive.

Rate control through instructions and positive reinforcement. The positive aspects of this approach are the same as those listed for the use of the DAF machine. On the negative side, it may take a little longer than the DAF program, but still only a relatively short amount of time.

Reinforcing fluency intervals and fluency responses. This type of program takes longer to establish fluency than the previous programs. It does not necessarily heighten awareness of response topography. It does not appear to involve any explicit behavior relative to monitoring fluency. It can provide rules and criteria for moving forward and backing up in the program by increasing or decreasing time durations or response lengths in the event of stuttering. Its real value may be in coordinating it with a DAF program after fluency has been established in order to maintain fluency.

Suppressing stuttering through contingent punishment and contingent highlighting. It appears to take longer to establish fluency with contingent aversive stimulation procedures than with rate-control tactics. It depends to a great extent on external consequation and, therefore, self-responsibility is delayed. A suppression paradigm does not appear to coordinate well with a total therapeutic program unless later combined with positive reinforcement. There is no programmatic dimension involved in terms of moving forward or backward in a program, except in terms of changing from continuous to intermittent schedules of consequences.

Consequating desirable and undesirable content themes. The content response in and of itself may require change without reference to its effects on dysfluency, and therefore it is a program worthy of consideration. However, it does not appear to be the most efficacious method for establishing fluency. This system of verbal conditioning of specific content requires complex training, and it takes longer to get results. It may have more to do with the stutterer's belief system than his fluency.

Reinforcing the modification of the forms of stuttering. This may be a more complicated system than it appears on the surface. Although positive reinforcement is provided for modifying stuttering, overall this program appears to involve punishment for each instance of stuttering. The positive-reinforcement aspects of the system depend on the occurrences of stuttering as occasions for the target response. The punishment aspects of the program, because the program suppresses stuttering frequency, reduce the opportunity for positive reinforcement. Therefore, stutterers do not usually go through the entire modification program. It may be of value to start with a punishment program and then shift to a positive reinforcement for fluency program when stuttering is reduced.

Consequating desirable and undesirable parent-child verbal interactions. This program gets closest to the real-life forms of events that are going on in the child's world of stuttering. However, as a method for establishing fluency, it may take longer than other programs. It may have more value as a program for maintaining fluency and arranging occasions for monitoring fluency under a number of verbal-interaction circumstances.

From the foregoing, it would appear that the rate-control programs (DAF, negative reinforcement, instructions for slow rates, and shaping to normal rates through positive reinforcement) might be the preferred methods for establishing fluency. They may be short in duration; success is early; motivation is enhanced; they are programmatic in the sense of clearly stated rules and criteria for moving forward and backing up; they are descriptive, operational, and easily learned; and their effects are measurable. They can quickly get the stutterer to the point where the real problems in therapy are, that is, move the stutterer's clinical fluency into his real world. Most of the other methods for instating fluency have some of these positive characteristics, but no other single method for instating fluency has as many positive characteristics.

Some of the contraindications of the other methods of establishing fluency might include the following: Highlighting or contingent aversive stimulation does not necessarily involve any type of programmatic dimension that operationalizes the stutterer's responsibility for maintaining fluency. Contingent aversive stimulation may be useful as an initial technique for reducing stuttering, but if the suppressive effect is to be stabilized it requires that it be combined with some positive-reinforcement program for maintaining fluency. It appears that it does not in and of itself articulate with later needs in therapy.

The same type of comments can be made about programs that attempt to reinforce fluency which coexists with stuttering as a means of reducing stuttering. If the monitoring of fluency can be accepted as an integral part of a total therapeutic program, stutterers will have to develop a heightened awareness of the topography of fluency. This awareness by stutterers of what they do when they speak fluently is not explicitly involved in programs that reinforce fluency intervals (or fluent utterances) or in punishment paradigms. There not only is no arranged mechanism or program for lengthening or shortening fluency intervals (i.e., rules for going forward toward normal fluency or backing up in case of fluency failure), but there is also no awareness of the microaspects of fluency behavior. Stutterers may not have developed repertoires of responses that could be useful in gradually changing their responses. Rules can be established: for example, providing positive reinforcement for two minutes of fluency, then for three minutes of fluency; then, if fluency failure occurs, backing up to two minutes of fluency and so on. However, in a program like this, the stutterer either stutters or is fluent. There is no in-between modeled, instructed, or learned behavior. The variable that is systematically modified is the length of fluency time, and that is what is monitored. There is no specific program for shaping a response through successive approximation or for gradually backing up to a previously reinforced form of behavior.

The content-theme and the verbal-interaction programs appear to have greater application to aspects of stuttering therapy that are involved in carry-over (stimulus generalization, transferring stimulus control over fluency) rather than in the establishment of fluency. Such programs are longer in duration, require, complicated training, are more complex in nature, and are not linearally related or behaviorally related to changes in fluency.

Self-responsibility. "Self-responsibility" warrants some discussion (Shames & Egolf in press) as a class of responses to be learned by the stutterer in therapy. Self-responsibility represents one of our more important ultimate behavioral goals. Operationally, this class of responses refers to a process whereby the stutterer takes over and arranges for the occurrence of those events that previously had been arranged by the therapist. This means that the stutterer arranges the occasions for target responses, emits his target responses on these occasions, and consequates his own responses, as had been formerly done by the clinician.

In both operant and nonoperant therapy, the acquisition of this class of responses by the stutterer usually has been either left to chance or left to the stutterer to learn on his own. When self-responsibility has been the subject of interview discussions, it has usually been reduced to processes of prodding, prompting, and giving nondescriptive instructions. It has typically not been dealt with as a class of responses that could be acquired in therapy through the same process of consequation as other responses to be learned.

Training the stutterer to observe, evaluate, and consequate his responses and to apply the rules of his particular therapeutic paradigm—perhaps even as he is in the process of shaping and instating his initial fluency—may become a powerful and useful therapeutic tool. He can generalize these behaviors to other responses later in therapy and in carry-over. This becomes a most vital response class for the stutterer when he reaches that point in therapy when external controls of his behavior by the therapist are to be replaced by or combined with his own self-evaluations and self-generated contingencies.

In training a stutterer in such self-responsibility behavior, the process is one of shaping through positive reinforcement. Actually, the stutterer learns to emit a response about another of his responses or events. It is designed to increase the frequency of self-evaluation responses and of self-generated consequences in accordance with these evaluations so that, eventually, the therapist becomes expendable. Self-responsibility responses in this therapeutic context do not occur in a vacuum or in isolation; they occur in relation to some other response or event that is to be consequated in some fashion. For example, the simple process of the therapist providing approval each time a stutterer identifies an instance of stuttering (if that has been the predesignated behavioral task) and calibrating the stutterer's judgment to the judgment of the therapist could constitute training in self-responsibility, if the stutterer can later accurately identify stuttering on his own without the judgments of the therapist. Such early training could eventually permit a stutterer to go through a DAF program on his own—recognizing when to go forward in reducing delay intervals, when to back up if he stutters, and how to record and tabulate his progress—with minimal intervention by a therapist.

Perkins (1973b), in his newest operant program, has inserted a significant intermediate step of having the stutterer take over and manage the DAF program on his own. The stutterer is then trained in becoming responsible for instating his own fluency. This tactic may well be a key to the long-term success of therapy. Eventually our goal is to have the stutterer become responsible for himself without our intervention and support. We have talked about self-responsibility clinically for quite some time. Goldiamond (1965) referred to "self-control" procedures in his operant program following dismissal from his clinic setting, but Perkins has behaviorally programmed self-responsibility early into his program. As part of a sequence for developing different types of pertinent responses during therapy, it would seem that this should come early (perhaps earlier for adults than for children) and should certainly precede carry-over activities (Shames and Egolf, in press). Later, such self-responsibility activity would extend to stutterers' monitoring their fluency, almost totally on their own. Such training often involves a continuum of responses, which at first are public, overt statements by the stutterers. Eventually they become covert thoughts and judgments that are inferred on the basis of other types of overt responses. If such self-evaluation responses are firmly established early, they can be employed in relation to any other target behavior that stutterers are to deal with during therapy.

The self-monitoring of fluency is a special class of self-responsibility behavior. Whether self-monitoring of fluency is a necessary precursor of nonmonitored fluency is not known. Some stutterers have been observed to go from stuttered speech to stutter-free speech without such monitoring. However, such monitoring does appear to be a built-in phase of some operant therapies (rate control) and therefore justifies discussion.

A self-monitoring technology has developed in contexts outside of the area of stuttering, and some serious tactical questions have emerged from this research that appear to have direct application to therapy for stuttering (Shames and Egolf, in press). The behaviors that have been studied cover a broad range of human problems. They include such behaviors as relaxation (Tasto and Hinkle, 1973); homosexuality (Rehm and Rozensky, 1973); alcohol consumption (Sobell and Sobell, 1973); smoking (Rozensky, 1973); insomnia (Bootzin, 1972); disruptive classroom behaviors (Bolstad and Johnson, 1972); recurrent stealing and eyebrow plucking (Epstein and Peterson, 1973); self-mutilation (Ernst, 1973); inflammatory scratching (Watson, Tharp, and Krisberg, 1972); weight change (Quick, 1972; Mahoney, 1973); and self-concept (Rehm and Marston, 1968).

Attention has focused on the tactics of self-monitoring. Basically, the question reduces itself to whether reliance on external controls is more or less effective than reliance on self-controls. The experimental research has systematically varied certain conditions of self-control and external control as both separate and combined processes to determine their effects on certain target behaviors. The ultimate hope of these studies is to determine how best to help clients become more active participants in the therapeutic process and, eventually, independent of the interventions of their therapists.

Kanfer and Phillips (1966) described a process termed "instigation therapy," whereby the therapist as teacher helps a client plan a program of therapy and then supervises the client as he carries out the program in his own environment. Such therapy is based on the assumption that people can control their own behavior in accordance with the same behavioral principles that underlie their control of the behavior of other people. As such, an active mechanism of self-reinforcement is implied. The invocation of the concept of self-reinforcement becomes useful in explaining the maintenance of behavior in the absence of observable external reinforcers.

Much of the early research was designed to demonstrate the process of self-reinforcement by operationalizing and externalizing it. Kanfer and Marston (1963), Marston (1964, 1965), and Kanfer (1967) demonstrated the parallels between external and self-reinforcement procedures, especially in the effects of different schedules of reinforcement.

Homme (1965) coined the term "coverant" to characterize those private events referred to as thinking and imagining that people might use in self-reinforcement operations. He states that such private activity operates according to the same behavioral principles as public events.

The kinds of questions that have received consideration which appear to have application to the problem of stuttering address themselves to the elements of the operant paradigm as well as to some characteristics of the client.

Kanfer (1970a, 1970b) and Kanfer and Karoly (1972) proposed a model for self-regulation that contains three stages. First, the client attends to his behavior. Such attending behavior denotes monitoring, observing, counting, or getting some type of feedback that he has behaved in a certain way. In the problem of stuttering, this could refer to the observation by stutterers that stuttering has occurred or it could refer to a subclass of behavior that we agree is stuttering, to fluency, to certain specified forms of social behavior (approaching, avoiding), to manifest content of utterances, eye contact, or to any behavior that has been targeted in therapy as pertinent to the problem.

Second, the client evaluates his behavior and judges whether it was desirable and satisfactory or undesirable and unsatisfactory in terms of some predesignated criterion. Again, a judgment about some target behavior is made (e.g., the length of a fluency interval, maintenance of eye contact, the occurrence of a speech repetition).

Third, based on the nature of the evaluation (a judgment as to whether his behavior met the predesignated criterion), the client either reinforces or punishes himself. There are at least two points of view about this process that are of interest to us. One is that self-reinforcement cannot take place without self-monitoring and that self-monitoring automatically triggers all three phases, from monitoring to evaluation to reinforcement. The other point of view is that this is not an automatic process and that self-monitoring does not necessarily lead to reinforcement. This latter interpretation suggests that self-monitoring and self-reinforcement are separate processes involving separate behaviors and that the client must learn to use monitored feedback as a discriminative stimulus for self-reinforcement behavior (Kanfer, 1970a; Mahoney, 1972a; Quick, 1973).

Emerging from these issues is the question of whether it is more effective to monitor desirable or undesirable behavior. Embedded within this question is still another, more basic, question: Is self-invoked positive reinforcement more effective than self-imposed punishment? McFall (1970) demonstrated that one group of smokers who monitored smoking behavior smoked more than a second group, which monitored their resistance to smoking when they wanted to smoke. Mahoney, Moura, and Wade (1973) demonstrated that self-reward was superior to self-punishment. Quick (1973), in an obesity study, did not find any clear-cut differences between groups who monitored their submission to eating forbidden foods as opposed to those who monitored their resistance to eating forbidden foods when made available. Although the data in this literature are not always in the same direction, Mahoney (1972a) feels there is overwhelming evidence to indicate that monitoring desirable behavior which leads to positive reinforcement is far more effective than monitoring undesirable behavior which leads to self-punishment.

The implication for work with stutterers is clearly present and, up to now, has only been the subject of discussion. Should stutterers monitor their fluency or their stuttering? Should they reward or punish themselves? The data regarding smoking and eating behavior suggest that monitoring fluency would be more effective. Aside from the need for data in the context of stuttering therapy, there is also a commonsense clinical logic that may apply. How reasonable or realistic is it to expect stutterers to sustain, on their own, a program of self-punishment? The operant programs for stuttering are faced with the need to get some answers to these questions. The rate-control and fluency-interval therapies lead to monitoring desirable behaviors and positive self-reinforcement. The contingent aversive stimulation programs can lead to self-monitoring of undesirable behavior and self-punishment programs.

The three-stage chain of self-monitoring, evaluation, and self-reinforcement has been extended in research by Bellack, Rozensky, and Schwartz (1973), who investigated the tactic of monitoring before as opposed to after a response is emitted. Such a response is a disclosure of "intent to respond." The data show that monitoring the intent to respond in a designated way is more effective in changing eating behavior than recording the nature of an eating response after it has occurred.

Another tactical question that has been researched is the scheduling of feedback to the client about his progress toward a goal. Is it enough to experience the immediate consequences of individual responses, or does periodic feedback about progress facilitate control of the target behavior? Locke, Cartledge, and Koeppel (1968) state that such feedback is most reinforcing when the information about progress is clear and meaningful. However, Quick (1973) found no differences in weight loss between groups having and groups not having feedback about progress.

Aside from the tactics of self-monitoring, information about subject characteristics and the ways that they have been dimensionalized are also of interest. As might be expected, the more motivated clients do better in self-regulation programs (Kolb, Winter, and Berlew, 1968; McFall, 1970; McFall and Hammen, 1971); those clients who view themselves as being in control of their destinies (Goldiamond, 1965b; Lefcourt, 1966; Rotter, 1966) do better in sustaining behavior when external controls are removed; and those subjects who engage spontaneously in a particular self-regulation tactic do better (Quick, 1973).

Bandura and Perloff (1967) point out that self-evaluation and self-reinforcing patterns may be vicariously learned from parents. This particular finding suggests an additional value of arranging for stutterers to have group therapy experiences.

The ability of persons to perform each of the three elements of self-regulation may be a function of their history of reinforcement (Kiesler, 1966).

Each of these issues has application to the problems of therapy for stutterers. Self-monitoring and self-reinforcement as a process of weaning stutterers from the clinic and of making them more responsible for carryover activities is by no means a simple process, or a process that has absolutely right and wrong tactics. Tactics may be related to the individual characteristics of each stutterer. His motivation, sense of internal control, spontaneous commitment to certain self-regulatory procedures, and history of reinforcement all impinge on decisions regarding the timing, scheduling, and forms of external as well as self-regulated behavior-control activities. As self-responsibility becomes a more refined behavioral process in dealing with stuttering, the Marston (1965) and Kanfer (1967) approaches to these issues appear to provide an appropriate model for scrutiny and possible application.

The stutterer's belief system.   Responses that reflect the belief system of the stutterer have received far more attention from nonoperant therapy than from operant-based therapy. Such responses impinge on pre-carryover as well as the carry-over phases of therapy. For quite some time there was a serious controversy over the issue of when in therapy to consider the attitudes, beliefs, feelings, and self-perceptions of the stutterer. This was an issue within the traditional framework, and it brought into focus some sharp differences between those who emphasized symptom management as opposed to those who emphasized counseling and psychotherapy. One group felt that the stutterer's speech, as behavior, should not be tampered with, if at all, until he had the "right attitude." It was felt that such delays of symptom management were necessary in order to decrease the probability of symptom management tactics being used as ritualistic distraction activities or being perceived as methods for hiding, postponing, and avoiding stuttering. Therefore, the right attitude had to be instilled as a precursor to symptom management. The attitude being referred to here is directly related to the symptom-management activities.

Stutterers were led to believe that they must accept themseves as stutterers. They were encouraged to develop an unchanging, permanent self-concept of themselves as stutterers. Clinicians told them that it was all right to stutter, that they should not feel guilty or ashamed to stutter, should not avoid or hide or suppress stuttering, and that they would always stutter. However, the paradox was that they must try to modify the form of their stuttering so that they and their listeners were more comfortable with it than with their present form of stuttering. Further, some clinicians wanted stutterers to believe that fluency was dangerous. If it did occur during therapy, it may be a first step toward unrealistically seeking stutter-free speech and not tolerating normal dysfluency. These, then, were the beliefs that were vital to the success of later symptom management.

The symptom-management programs associated with these attitudes involved deliberate stuttering, faked stuttering, bounce techniques, prolonging and sliding: almost any kind of controlled stuttering as its goal, just so long as it was viewed as a form of stuttering (Ainsworth, 1953; Bryngelson, 1937, 1953; Johnson 1944; Kopp, 1953; Van Riper, 1953, 1954, 1973).

The other side of the issue proclaimed that the most effective way to change what stutterers believe about themselves as speakers and as persons is through experience. By changing their form of stuttering and providing them with speaking and social experiences with their new form of easier, controlled stuttering, a solid experiential base is established for cognitive and emotional consonance between how they behave and speak and what they believe about how they behave and speak. Therefore, if stutterers first change the form of their stuttering and demonstrate for themselves their ability to control its form, in many speaking situations they will come to believe in themselves as controlled stutterers.

However, whatever the sequence and potency of attitudes and stuttering symptoms are, a belief system that focuses on fluency is excluded; rather, the focus is on stuttering.

A system of beliefs that involves such things as being able to speak without stuttering or perceptions by stutterers of themselves as fluent speakers are more consonant with the goals and behaviors associated with operant approaches to therapy. However, the beliefs of stutterers embrace far more than concepts of fluency. It may be important for stutterers to realize that as fluent speakers, even though fluency is a newly acquired behavior, they will not "stand out" and receive praise from listeners because they are fluent. It may also be important for them to accept the reality of listeners' rejections of stuttering, to recognize the payoff values of stuttering, or believe the reversibility of both speaking behavior and self-concepts.

As a class of responses, the beliefs of stutterers about themselves as speakers have not received a great deal of formal attention within the operant area. Only Shames, Egolf, and Rhodes (1969) and Perkins (1973a) have acknowledged their importance or researched this area from an operant standpoint. Perkins has introduced into his program an explicit awareness by the stutterer of confidence and comfort about the motor aspects of speaking. The Shames et al. content programs, although focusing on overt content themes, appear to relate directly to the stutterers' beliefs about themselves as speakers.

The general lack of attention may be related to the previously discussed issue within the traditional therapy context. Within the operant framework, the consistent experience of speaking fluently and of having listeners react to them as fluent speakers may be all that is necessary for many stutterers to believe they no longer stutter, that they are no longer stutterers, and that they are not considered stutterers by listeners. For others, the experience of fluency is not enough and they may need specific consideration for what they believe about themselves. The memory of stuttering and of being referred to as a "stutterer" may never be forgotten by an adult (however, such forgetting may occur in some instances when therapy is carried on with very young children). But it is possible that the development of new beliefs and self-concepts, in concert with the acquisition of fluent speech, may eventually relegate that memory to the same category of reversibility and temporariness as the memory of a broken leg, a long-term illness, a poor marriage, or a change in careers.

What a person believes about himself and about how he relates to his world and the people around him is a very complicated affair. For the most part it is private, covert, and not held out for public scrutiny. This privacy and resulting lack of availability of a person's beliefs and self-concepts have resulted in a great deal of inference about each individual's self-beliefs. Clinicians have gone to great pains to get stutterers to give even minimal public expression of these personal feelings, to offer some clues about what they believe. Under such circumstances it would be easy to merely apply some overgeneralized, stereotyped belief system to all stutterers, based on a particular dynamic theory about the nature of stuttering or on some experiences we may have had with a few stutterers.

Belief systems are even further complicated because they are most likely based on some mixture of cognition (reasoning and understanding), emotion (feelings and moods), and environmental circumstances. Breaking into a belief system during therapy is not simple. Stutterers will have to want to let the therapists in, if they can. But what can stutterers make available to therapists that minimizes the errors associated with inference? What is observable? Of course there is the stutterer's physical presence, physiological processes, bodily postures (all of the nonverbal behavior presented by the individual) that may reflect his mood or feelings or beliefs. Then there is the verbal behavior of the stutterer— what he says to the therapist, with its manifest and latent content themes. Finally, there are the occasions for these verbal and nonverbal behaviors (i.e., the environmental circumstances in the forms of antecedent events and subsequent, or consequent, events); there are also the relationships among several forms of responses by the stutterer (i.e., overt stuttering and increased heart rate; fluency and stable galvanic skin response, or, GSR). All of these may be important in understanding, communicating about, and changing what stutterers believe about themselves.

Shames, Egolf, and Rhodes (1969), in dealing with stutterers' beliefs, selected only one aspect of this complicated system: the manifest content of utterances emitted during therapy interviews. There was no pretense that the feelings of the stutterer were being manipulated or that his physiological excitement levels were being modified, as in the Gray (1968) studies, whereby GSR was manipulated independently from stuttering in a desensitization framework. In the Shames et al. studies, the manifest content was changed through operant techniques by approving certain desirable content (reflecting such cognitive activity as understanding, behavioral description, approaching talking behavior, etc.) and by disapproving undesirable content (reflecting such cognitive activity as described by Williams, 1957—the "it" in stuttering, helplessness, victimization, and avoidance). This approach to changing a stutterer's speech and what he says out loud about himself deals with the cognitive aspects of his beliefs and is only a first step toward the less accessible aspects of self-concept and self-perceptions involving personal feelings and moods. However, it is felt that, with the recent developments in biofeedback technology in combination with operant technology, this vital area of emotions and feelings will also come in for serious study and, hopefully, clinical application.[1]

Recent research from the fields of experimental psychology and psychosomatic medicine has demonstrated the instrumental control of visceral responses (Kimmel, 1967; Katkin and Murray, 1968; Miller, 1969). Research on visceral responses has covered a broad range of responses on both human and infrahuman subjects. The studies have demonstrated, through biofeedback and operant conditioning techniques the control of such things as systolic blood pressure, heart rate, alpha electroencephalographic (EEG) rhythms, GSR, and neuronal activity. Such visceral modifications have been correlated to various paradigms of positive reinforcement and punishment as well as to specific occasions, such as self-induced thoughts and mental states. Studies by Miller and DiCara (1967); Shapiro and Crider (1967); Miller (1969); Fetz and Smith (1969); Tursky and Shapiro (1969); Shapiro, Tursky, and Schwartz (1970); Nowliss and Kamiya (1970); Schwartz (1970); and Finley (1971), to name only a few, showed that many visceral responses that are often related to states of excitement and emotionalism can be controlled through operant-conditioning techniques. The basic tactic of biofeedback is to provide the subject with some observable event that is an indicator of what is going on internally. For example, certain muscle activity can be represented via an electromyographic (EMG) recorder by the movement of a pointer on a dial; or GSR, heart rate, or blood pressure can be represented by visual feedback of the movement of a pen on a polygraph. The subject is instructed to keep the pen or the pointer within some predesignated range of movement. By attaching external contingent consequences to the regulation of these indicators of internal activity, subjects have been able to slow their heart rate, sustain a stable GSR pattern, and lower their blood pressure. Each of these is thought to be related to emotional excitement levels, which

---

[1] Biofeedback techniques refer to procedures for modifying autonomic responses through instrumental conditioning. Subjects are provided with a signal (visual, auditory, etc.) that indicates an autonomic response by them. Either reinforcing or suppressing contingent consequences are provided to the subject for monitoring the signal to a predesignated criterion.

heretofore had been thought to be relatively inaccessible for instrumental control.

In research closer to the subject of stuttering, Reed and Lingwall (1973) recently reported that in some stutterers a consistent change in GSR activity was observed in association with contingent aversive stimulation (white noise) for instances of stuttering. However, these changes in GSR as a function of punishing and suppressing stuttering were not in the same direction for all of the stutterers in the study. Treon, Tamayo, and Standley, (1972) reported that lowered stuttering rates were associated with self-regulated monitoring of low-amplitude GSR patterns and that higher stuttering rates were associated with self-regulated monitoring of high-amplitude GSR patterns. These two studies, along with the accumulating biofeedback data, point up the possibilities of bringing objective evidence of physiological activity as a reflection of excitement levels and emotionalism to the understanding of the problem of stuttering. In these instances, such physiological data were correlated to stuttering behavior. However, it is obvious that such data can also be correlated to the cognitive aspects of stutterers' belief systems. By obtaining such physiological information, not just in relation to instances of stuttering, but also in relation to the manifest content themes of overt utterances, it would be possible to determine how emotional stutterers may be as they talk about different categories of content during interviews that may impinge on what they believe and perceive about themselves. It would also be possible to provide contingencies for specific content associated with such physiological information in an effort to correlate the cognitive and emotional aspects of the problem (Shames and Egolf, in press).

The interaction of stutterers' belief systems with other aspects of therapy is not clearly understood. On the one hand, it may be related to the success of tactics that take stutterers from monitoring their fluency to talking without monitoring their fluency; (that is, if stutterers learn to believe they are and can be fluent, they eventually may not have to monitor their fluency). But it is also possible that (1) some stutterers do not have to go through a state of monitoring their fluency before talking freely without stuttering or (2) stutterers' belief systems are a separate but valid issue in therapy that does not necessarily relate to the issue of monitored and nonmonitored fluency. As such, the issue of belief systems may deserve separate consideration at some time during therapy and may be only tangentially related to the form of stutterers' speech output.

Carry-over. The final consideration in this chapter deals with issues in carry-over. It seems that much of the discussion thus far has referred to this process, has logically pointed in its direction, or has contained implications for its expedition. By "carry-over," we mean the process whereby those behavioral skills or newly acquired response repertoires that stutterers emit in the presence of their clinicians in a clinic setting are transferred to the everyday, nonclinical situations which stutterers encounter in their lives.

It is clear from the literature that, in many instances, clinic fluency does not carry over into the stutterer's real world. Perkins (1973a) has suggested that about 50 percent of the stutterers maintain clinical fluency outside clinic settings. Ryan and Van Kirk (1973) report higher frequencies, depending on the method employed for establishing fluency. Two-thirds to three-fourths of the stutterers on DAF and length-of-response programs reach the maintenance phase of therapy. Less than one-half of Ryan and Van Kirk's stutterers reach this phase when using time-out or traditional approaches to establishing fluency. However, Ryan and Van Kirk report that they have not observed a single casualty or relapse among stutterers who reach the maintenance phase of therapy. The therapeutic problem of establishing fluency in a clinic setting is not the same as the therapeutic problem of carry-over, and we should not confound the two issues. Very often, in the past, attempts at changing the speech response have been combined with changing stimulus control even before the new response has been established. Ryan and Perkins have tried to separate these two processes. Ryan (1971) refers to processes of establishment, transfer, and maintenance. Perkins (1973b) also separates these issues by first establishing fluency through rate-control procedures and then arranging a systematic series of situational experiences or occasions for monitoring the new speech response.

From the reports in the literature, both of an operant and nonoperant nature, it seems that the most prevalent reason for clinical failure is the lack of systematic programming of carry-over activities for stutterers. Ullmann and Krasner (1965), in their overview of behavior-modification techniques for behavior problems in general, have stated that the focus of therapy is not designed to modify a response per se, but rather is on the response in relation to stimuli. Responses do not occur in a vacuum. For all of us, including those who are stutterers, responses occur in dynamic, social, and emotional contexts of people relating to people. They occur during a number of diverse communicative settings and situations. They occur during calm and during excitement. If the carry-over of behavior acquired during clinical sessions is to be successful, then these diverse occasions for communicating outside the clinic have to be accounted for.

In the operant framework, carry-over can be characterized as a process of transferring stimulus control from inside the clinic and by the clinician to outside the clinic and by the stutterer. The development of self-control (self-consequation) by the stutterer in the clinic setting is the precursor of self-control outside the clinic. The stutterer's responses of self-monitoring, self-evaluation, and self-reinforcement remain the same, either inside or outside the clinic, and have already been discussed. Although such events may vary in form, the process remains constant, even with variations in the occasions for their emission. Therefore, this discussion of carry-over will focus primarily on the various nonclinical occasions for the stutterer's responses.

If therapists are going to formalize their considerations of carry-over and not merely leave carry-over to chance or to stutterers to work out on their own, they are faced with deciding which occasions are important enough to include as a formal part of their therapy. Although there are several ways to approach this type of decision, there is an underlying theme common to all of them. This theme is that successful carry-over is a function of how and to what degree a number of different variables relates to stutterers' emissions of their modified behavior. If the stutterer is now talking relatively fluently, or with some form of controlled stuttering with his clinician in a clinic setting, what happens to this behavior when the real world is faced? It is not enough to exhibit a behavioral repertoire in the highly protective, socially remote, and relatively calm atmosphere of the clinic. How do we go about identifying those variables that may influence stutterers' ability to sustain their newly acquired and desirable behavior?

One source of information is the stutterer's history. From his pre-therapy history of stuttering and fluency, it may be possible to identify those conditions and circumstances during which a stutterer was fluent and when he stuttered. For carry-over tactics, this would mean confronting the stutterer's history, and possibly arranging for some gradual immersion in certain aspects of that history, to test out his new response repertoire.

Another source of information might be the pretherapy base-rate data that were gathered. If such data covered a broadly based sample of a number of different stimulus conditions, a number of circumstances for relative fluency and stuttering could be identified. This approach to identifying pertinent variables for consideration in carry-over activities could serve a double function of providing information around which therapy can be organized. It could make the transition from clinical to nonclinical settings less abrupt.

Still a third source of information is direct observation or analysis of the stutterer in his current everyday routine. By accompanying the stutterer, wiring him with a tape recorder, or listening to his verbal reports, we can identify his normal everyday communication routine and relate these circumstances to his new response repertoire. Finally, there is the research and clinical literature on those variables that affect the frequency of stuttering.

All of these sources of information are available and can be productively utilized in implementing carry-over. From them emerge classes, or categories, of occasions that could be made part of a "carry-over" program. Those specific occasions that have received the most attention and are viable for systematic carry-over tactics include the following:

1. Size of the audience
2. Specific people
3. Different talking situations [telephone, shopping, giving information, etc., as listed in Trotter and Bergmann's (1957) Level of Situational Difficulty Scale]
4. Competition for talking time (being interrupted)
5. Communicative time pressures (being hurried)
6. Topics of conversation (home, occupation, sex, goals, etc.)
7. Emotional excitement (anger, fear, happiness, depression, etc.)
8. Length of utterances
9. Linguistic functions (asking questions, justifying comments, negation, criticizing, etc.)
10. Interpersonal role
11. Aversive stimulation
12. States of deprivation

These 12 circumstances, although not an exhaustive catalogue, describe many of the stimulus conditions that have been observed to affect the frequency of stuttering in various stutterers. It is reasonable to assume that they would affect the ability to monitor, evaluate, and self-reinforce newly acquired fluency. For carry-over, the tactics in general would be to arrange a progression of experiences, within each category of circumstance, beginning with those associated with the lowest frequency of stuttering and progressing to those associated with the highest frequency of stuttering (on the assumption that it would be easier to monitor fluency under conditions of least stuttering and more difficult under conditions associated with most stuttering). Such an arrangement is suggestive of a hierarchy of stimulus conditions based, not on anxiety, but on observations of stuttering behavior or observations on ability to monitor new target behavior (Shames and Egolf, in press).

Each of the circumstances listed can be approached through discussion, role playing, acting out, or realistic encounters outside the clinic to provide the stutterer with experiences with his target behavior under varying degrees and types of stimulus occasions.

Which of these occasions, as well as others, that might be systematically introduced into the therapy program depends on the individual stutterer and the kinds of relationships which have been observed between each of these circumstances and his ability to emit and monitor his target behavior. It is quite conceivable that only one or two of these occasions may be factors in carry-over for some stutterers. Such judgments and therapeutic programming should be decided individually. However, standardized methods for probing the significance of these variables for all stutterers would appear to be a necessary clinical endeavor; such an endeavor would perhaps be of greater functional importance than the time-honored case history and adaptation tests that are so frequently done during diagnostic evaluations.

It should be pointed out that the underlying assumption of these tactics might be held up for examination. I am referring to the hierarchical arrangement suggested for transferring stimulus control within each category. For example, it might not be necessary to increase audience size gradually, or to increase verbal-response length in small steps, or talk to "easy" people before talking to "hard" people. Instead, it might be possible to learn to emit the target response under the most difficult stimulus circumstances, without going through the graduated hierarchy. This is an important and researchable issue that has practical implications for the tactics of carry-over. The answers to such questions do not invalidate the need for the stutterer to learn to monitor his target behavior in a number of different classes of occasions, but they may invalidate a hierarchal approach to such activities.

From the operant literature, only Ryan (1971) and Perkins (1973b) have given significant, systematic attention to some of these factors in therapy, and it may be that their higher success rates with stutterers could be attributed to this facet of their programs.

In addition to systematically varying the occasions, as a means of implementing carry-over, the scheduling of external reinforcement and its ultimate replacement by self-reinforcement procedures may also be important factors.

It is known from both animal and human research that different types of schedules of reinforcement affect both the acquisition and extinction of responses. By definition, "extinction" means withdrawing reinforcement. This is also in part the implication of the clinical process termed "carry-over." Therefore, schedule effects become important for carry-over.

Responses that are acquired through continuous reinforcement have the fastest acquisition rate, but they also have the fastest extinction rate when reinforcement is withdrawn. On the other hand, the same response that is acquired on a variable-interval schedule will have a slower acquisition rate and also a slower extinction rate. It would appear that these data about scheduling effects have a direct bearing on the clinical problem of carry-over. There has been no clinical research as yet to determine scheduling effects on carry-over of clinical fluency or of any target behavior acquired in the clinic. It seems reasonable to assume that these scheduling effects would apply. As a factor in clinical tactics, it would appear that continuous reinforcement, early in therapy, would facilitate establishing some target behavior more rapidly than other schedules. Such an experience in therapy could have very desirable effects on the motivations of the stutterer and could enhance his commitment to therapy. However, it would also seem that such a schedule should be gradually replaced by an intermittent schedule to enhance the carry-over phase of therapy.

It was suggested earlier that external consequences should ultimately be replaced by self-reinforcement procedures. This does not imply a process of extinction whereby reinforcement is withheld, but rather, changing the source of reinforcement. This is also a part of the carry-over process of becoming less dependent on the clinician for consequences and more responsible for one's own behavior. The timing of this replacement during therapy and how it is scheduled could be critical to carry-over. The literature has suggested that some persons may be more dependent on external controls and may never function adequately relative to target behavior without such control. Research that applies Rotter's (1966) internal-external locus of control concepts to the problem of stuttering has yet to be done. Therefore, without any research evidence we can only comment on this as an unresolved issue that needs to be studied rather than suggest a particular and specific clinical tactic.

In one follow-up study of 20 stutterers, Blind, Shames, and Egolf (1972) found that those stutterers who maintained their clinical fluency after leaving the clinic reported significant changes in their life systems. Some of these significant life changes were under their control, while others were not. The fluent speakers reported such events as marriage, birth of a baby, divorce, change in occupation, death in the immediate family, and the achievement of important educational and personal goals. These findings were interpreted as an indication that the stutterers, with their newly acquired fluency, were in a better position to take advantage of some of these significant changes in their lives and were better able to cope with the stresses presented by some of these changes. Such findings suggest that it would be efficacious to encourage conversations and discussions during therapy interviews about such issues. Stutterers may need help to correlate their changes in speaking behavior to their total life system as a readiness for coping. They may need to learn how to generate significant and desirable events that give more meaning to their fluency in the nonclinical world. Such content during therapy interviews could help stutterers get into actions that result in arranging for positive reinforcement in society and help them experience fluency as part of a larger, more integrated human response system.

Conclusions

The most prominent characteristic of operant conditioning is that its interpretations and tactics are based on experimental research data. With regard to stuttering, a number of laboratory analogues of therapy have been developed from experimental studies; in like manner, a number of experimental therapies have resulted in more broadly conceived research projects. As a result, the functional relationships between research and clinical application have been strengthened. The principles and tactics of the experimenter have become models for the transactions of the clinician. Therapists from diverse frames of reference have begun to examine their procedures in greater detail, evaluate their tactics more closely, systematize their thinking, and become more goal oriented. These are healthy consequences of the operant approaches to stuttering whether or not one embraces operant conditioning as their therapeutic vehicle.

Azrin (1972), in an address to the International Symposium on Behavior Modification, stated that we are entering a new era in behavior modification. He comments that it is no longer necessary to demonstrate, from a research standpoint, the validity of applying the principles of operant conditioning to human subjects. We should now be concerned with solving the problems of individual human beings. Rather than generating control tests to illustrate the validity of an operant technique on groups of subjects, we should be focusing on how to solve a particular individual's problem.

We may be gradually approaching this state of affairs with the problem of stuttering, but we certainly have not yet arrived. The implication of Azrin's statement requires that we avail ourselves of a great deal of information about the principles and tactics which are important to clinically resolving each stutterer's problems. For us, this cannot be a call to halt research. Certainly there is still much that is left unanswered. We still need a great deal of evidence to resolve the many issues referred to in this chapter. Although the data are promising enough to apply these principles and tactics while the research goes on, we have not reached a point with stutterers where it is possible to sit back and rest easily. A 50 percent success rate may be better than before, but it still leaves much to be desired. Why the success rate has not been higher is one of the questions to be pursued with further clinical research. Each individual clinical application to each stutterer could easily constitute a part of that research effort if comparable data and measurement systems could be agreed on.

The heterogeneity of operant-based work on stuttering is obvious. Not only have different target responses and different contingent consequences been studied, but the way that stuttering has been measured has also varied. The measurement of stuttering constitutes a large-scale problem in itself. Some researchers tally the number of dysfluencies emitted per minute; others tally the number of words stuttered per minute; others tally the number of words stuttered of the number of words uttered. There are problems in each of these methods. One method does not account for all of the instances of stuttering, while the other does not account for variations in verbal output. Perhaps the best compromise to this problem is a method presented by Wheelden and Rosenberg (1973), who measured both talking time and dysfluency time and computed dysfluency as a percentage of actual talking time. There are, of course, questions of relative reliability among these methods of measuring stuttering. There are some who question whether it is even valid to consider what we hear as the stuttering event. They think of stuttering as a chain of events involving a larger unit of time and responses than the acoustic event to which we might apply contingencies. When the earlier occurring elements of this chain are made observable (during respiration, phonation, etc.), perhaps the target behavior can be consequated long before it becomes an audible event. These kinds of basic issues are perhaps illustrations of the need to develop a more programmatic approach to operant projects in stuttering. There are a number of questions being addressed in different research centers that may well relate to one another.

We can no longer afford to ignore the information already available to us from our sibling fields of investigation. The data that are accumulating regarding instigation and self-regulatory therapies, the biofeedback technology, and the issues of carry-over as they relate to scheduling effects and changing stimulus control have direct application to our work and should be systematically explored in relation to stuttering. Answers to these problems can be found only when we can ask the right kinds of questions about our work. The operant approach has provided a way of asking questions.

Whatever our theoretical and clinical inclinations may be regarding stuttering, our responsibilities in part are to discern those questions and answers in all frames of reference that may be self-serving. Such commentary functions merely to perpetuate the status quo for its own sake. Our interests are in those questions and answers that relate directly to the significant issues involved in the prevention and management of the stuttering problem. Clinical tactics and strategies that are based on clearly stated principles, that have been verified through experimental analysis, and that are supported by replicated data appear to be the most cautious, the most rigorous, and the most disciplined way to achieve such goals.

References

Ainsworth, S. (1953) Secondary stuttering and its treatment. In C. Van Riper, ed., *Speech therapy: A book of readings.* New York: Prentice-Hall.

Andrews, G. (1971) Editorial: Token reinforcement systems. *Australian and New Zealand Journal of Psychiatry,* 5, 135–136.

Andrews, G., and Ingham, R. J. (1971) Stuttering: Considerations in the evaluation of treatment. *British Journal of Disorders of Communication,* 6, 129–138.

Ayllon, T., and Azrin, N. H. (1966) Punishment as a discriminative stimulus to conditioned reinforcer with humans. *Journal of Experimental Analysis and Behavior,* 9, 411–419.

Azrin, N. (1972) New community based reinforcement procedures for alcoholism, marital counseling and job finding. *International Symposium on Behavior Modification.* Bloomington, Minnesota.

Azrin, N. H., Hake, D. F., Holz, W. C., and Hutchinson, R. R. (1965) Motivational aspects of escape from punishment. *Journal of the Experimental Analysis of Behavior,* 8, 31–44.

Azrin, N. H., and Holz, W. C. (1966) Punishment. In W. K. Honig, ed., *Operant behavior.* New York: Appleton.

Bandura, A., and Perloff, B. (1967) Relative efficacy of self-monitored and externally imposed reinforcement systems. *Journal of Personality and Social Psychology,* 7, 111–176.

Bellack, A., Rozensky, R., and Schwartz, J. (1973) Self monitoring as an adjunct to a behavioral weight reduction program. Paper presented to American Psychological Association Convention.

Blind, J., Shames, G. H., and Egolf, D. B. (1972) Critical factors for the carryover of fluency in stutterers. Paper presented at American Speech and Hearing Association Convention.

Blind, J., Shames, G. H., and Egolf, D. B. (1973) The use of verbal punishment as an experimental program of therapy for adult stutterers. Paper presented at American Speech and Hearing Association Convention.

Boe, E. E., and Church, R. M. (1967) Permanent effects of punishment during extinction. *Journal of Comparative and Physiological Psychology,* 63, 486–492.

Bolstad, O. D., and Johnson, S. M. (1972) Self regulations in the modification of disruptive classroom behavior. *Journal of Applied Behavioral Analysis,* 5, 443–454.

Bootzin, R. R. (1972) Stimulus control treatment for insomnia. Paper presented at American Psychological Association Convention.

Brookshire, R. H. (1969) Effects of random and response contingent noise upon disfluencies of normal speakers. *Journal of Speech and Hearing Research,* 12, 126–134.

Brookshire, R., and Eveslage, R. (1969) Verbal punishment of disfluency following augmentation of random delivery of aversive stimuli. *Journal of Speech and Hearing Research,* 12, 383–388.

Brookshire, R. H., and Martin, R. R. (1967) The differential effects of three verbal punishers on the disfluencies of normal speakers. *Journal of Speech and Hearing Research,* 10, 496–505.

Brutten, G. J. (1975) Stuttering: Topography, assessment, and behavior-change strategies. In J. Eisenson, ed., this *Symposium.*

Brutten, E. J., and Shoemaker, D. J. (1976) The modification of stuttering. Englewood Cliffs, N.J.: Prentice-Hall.

Bryngelson, B. (1937) Psychological problems in stuttering. *Mental Hygiene,* 21, 631–639.

Bryngelson, B. (1953) Voluntary stuttering. In C. Van Riper, ed., *Speech therapy: A book of readings.* New York: Prentice-Hall.

Carkhuff, R. R. (1973) The art of helping. Amherst, Mass.: Human Resource Development Press.

Carrier, J., Shames, G. H., and Egolf, D. (1969) The design and application of an experimental therapy program for stutterers. Paper presented at American Speech and Hearing Association Convention.

Church, R. M. (1969) Response suppression in B. A. Campbell and R. M. Church, eds., *Punishment and aversive behavior.* New York: Appleton.

Cooper, E. B., Cady, B. B., and Robbins, C. J. (1970) The effect of the verbal stimulus words *wrong, right* and *tree* on the disfluency rates of stutterers and non-stutterers. *Journal of Speech and Hearing Research,* 13, 239–244.

Curlee, R. F., and Perkins, W. H. (1969) Conversational rate control therapy for stuttering. *Journal of Speech and Hearing Disorders,* 34, 245–250.

Egolf, D. B., Shames, G. H., and Blind, J. J. (1971) The combined use of operant procedures and theoretical concepts in the treatment of an adult female stutterer. *Journal of Speech and Hearing Disorders,* 36, 414–421.

Egolf, D. B., Shames, G. H., Johnson, P. R., and Kasprisin-Burrelli, A. (1972) The use of parent-child interaction patterns in therapy for young stutterers. *Journal of Speech and Hearing Disorders,* 51, 222–232.

Egolf, D. B., Shames, G. H., and Seltzer, H. (1971) The effects of time-out on the fluency of stutterers in group therapy. *Journal of Communication Disorders,* 4, 111–118.

Epstein, L. H., and Peterson, G. L. (1973) The control of undesired behavior by self imposed contingencies. *Behavior Therapy,* 4, 91–95.

Ernst, F. A. (1973) Self recording and counter conditioning of a self mutilative compulsion, *Behavior Therapy,* 4, 144–146.

Estes, W. K. (1944) An experimental study of punishment. *Psychological Monographs,* 57, No. 3, 1–40.

Ferster, C. B., and Skinner, B. F. (1957) Schedules of Reinforcement. New York: Appleton, 1957.

Fetz, E. E., and Smith, O. A. (1969) Operant conditioning of precentral cortical cell activity in awake monkeys. Federation of American Societies for Experimental Biology, Federation Proceedings, 28, 521.

Finley, W. W. (1970) Effects of feedback on the control of cardiac rate. *Journal of Psychology*, 77, pp. 43–54.

Flanagan, B., Goldiamond, I., and Azrin, N. H. (1958) Operant stuttering: The control of stuttering behavior through response contingent consequences. *Journal of Experimental Analysis Behavior*, 1, 173–177.

Flanagan, B., Goldiamond, I., and Azrin, N. H. (1959) In-statement of stuttering in normally fluent individuals through operant procedures. *Science*, 130, 979–981.

Fowler, H. (1971) Suppression and facilitations by response contingent shock. Chapter 9 in R. Church, ed., *Aversive conditioning and learning*. New York: Academic Press, Inc., 1971.

Fowler, H., and Wischner, G. (1969) The varied functions of punishment in discriminative learning. Chapter 12 in B. Campbell and R. M. Church, eds., *Punishment and aversive behavior*. New York: Appleton.

Frick, J. A. (1951) An exploratory study of the effect of punishment (electric shock) upon stuttering. Ph.D. dissertation, State University of Iowa.

Ginott, H. (1969) Between parent and child. New York: Avon.

Goldiamond, I. (1965a) Stuttering and fluency as manipulable operant response classes. In L. Krasner and L. P. Ullman, eds., *Research in Behavior Modification*. New York: Holt, Rinehart & Winston.

Goldiamond, I. (1965b) Self-control procedures in personal behavior. *Psychological Reports*, 17, 851–868.

Gray, B. B. (1968) Some effects of anxiety deconditioning upon stuttering behavior. Final Report, Project No. RD-2021-S, Social and Rehabilitation Service, Department of Health, Education, and Welfare.

Halvorson, J. (1971) The effects on stuttering frequency of pairing punishment (response cost) with reinforcement. *Journal of Speech and Hearing Research*, 14, 356–364.

Haroldson, S. K., Martin, R., and Starr, C. (1968) Time-out as a punishment for stuttering. *Journal of Speech and Hearing Research*, 11, 560–566.

Holz, W., and Azrin, N. H. (1961) Discriminative properties of punishment. *Journal of Experimental Analysis of Behavior*, 4, 225–232.

Homme, L. E. (1965) Perspectus in psychology: XXIV. Control of coverants, the operants of the mind. *Psychology Record*, 15, 501–511.

Honeygosky, R. (1966) The conditioning of verbal expressions of anger. Unpublished research project, University of Pittsburgh.

Ingham, R. J., and Andrews, G. (1971) Stuttering: The quality of fluency after treatment. *Journal of Communication Disorders*, 4, 279–288.

Ingham, R. J., and Winkler, R. (1972) A comparison of the effectiveness of four treatment techniques. *Journal of Communication Disorders*, 5, 91–117.

Ivey, A. (1971) Microcounseling innovations in interviewing training. Springfield, Ill.: C. C Thomas.

Johnson, C. (1966) Verbal conditioning of a stutterer in a therapeutic context. Unpublished M.S. thesis, University of Pittsburgh.

Johnson, P. R. (1966) The use of operant conditioning techniques with a traditional method of stuttering therapy. Unpublished M.S. thesis, University of Pittsburgh.

Johnson, W. (1944) The Indians have no word for it: Stuttering in adults. *Quarterly Journal of Speech*, 30, 456–465.

Johnson, W. (1955) Stuttering in children and adults. Minneapolis: University of Minnesota Press.

Johnson, W. (1956) Perceptual and evaluative factors in stuttering. *Folia Phoniatrica*, 8, 211–233.

Johnson, W. (1959) *The onset of stuttering*. Minneapolis: University of Minnesota Press.

Kanfer, F. (1967) Self-regulation: Research, issues and speculations. Paper presented at the Ninth Annual Institute for Research in Clinical Psychology, University of Kansas.

Kanfer, F. (1970a) Maintenance of behavior by self generated stimuli and reinforcement. Paper presented at the Conference on the Psychology of Private Events, Morgantown, West Virginia.

Kanfer, F. (1970b) Self-monitoring: Methodological limitations and clinical applications. *Journal of Consulting and Clinical Psychology*, 35, 148–152.

Kanfer, F., and Karoly, P. (1972) Self control: A behavioristic excursion into the lion's den. *Behavior Therapy*, 3, 398–416.

Kanfer, F., and Marston, A. (1963) Conditioning of self-reinforcing responses: An analogue to self confidence training. *Psychological Reports*, 13, 63–70.

Kanfer, F., and Phillips, J. (1966) Behavior therapy: A panacea for all ills or a passing fancy? *Archives of General Psychiatry*, 15, 114–128.

Kasprisin-Burrelli, A., Egolf, D. B., and Shames, G. H. (1972) A comparison of parental verbal behavior with stuttering and nonstuttering children. *Journal of Communication Disorders*, 5, 335–346.

Katkin, E. S., and Murray, E. N. (1968) Instrumental conditioning of autonomically mediated behavior: Theoretical and methodological issues. *Psychological Bulletin*, 70, 52–68.

Kiesler, P. J. (1966) Some myths of psychotherapy research and the search for a paradigm. *Psychological Bulletin*, 65, 110–136.

Kimmel, H. D. (1967) Instrumental conditioning of autonomically mediated behavior. *Psychological Bulletin*, 67, 337–345.

Kodish, M., and Tucciarone, M. (1973) Increasing the average fluency interval: An individualized operant conditioning therapy program. Unpublished research, University of Pittsburgh.

Kolb, D., Winter, S., and Berlew, D. (1968) Self-directed change: Two studies. *Journal of Applied Behavior Science*, 4, 453–471.

Kopp, G. (1953) On curing stuttering. In C. Van Riper, ed., *Speech therapy: A book of readings*. New York: Prentice-Hall.

Leach, E. (1969) Stuttering: Clinical application of response contingent procedures. In B. Gray and E. England, eds., *Stuttering and the conditioning therapies*. Monterey, Calif.: Monterey Institute for Speech and Hearing.

Lefcourt, H. (1966) Internal vs. external control of reinforcement: A review. *Psychological Bulletin*, 65, 206–220.

Leith, W. R., and Uhlemann, M. R. (1970a) The shaping group: Theory, organization and function. Scientific Exhibit, American Speech and Hearing Association Convention.

Leith, W. R., and Uhlemann, M. R. (1970b) The treatment of stuttering by the shaping group. Paper presented at American Speech and Hearing Association Convention.

Leith, W. R., and Uhlemann, M. R. (1970c) The shaping group approach to stuttering: A clinical investigation. Scientific Exhibit at American Speech and Hearing Association Convention.

Leith, W. R., and Uhlemann, M. R. (1972) The shaping group approach to stuttering. *Comparative Group Studies*, 3, 175–199.

Locke, S., Cartledge, N., and Koeppel, J. (1968) Motivational effect of knowledge of results: A goal setting phenomenon? *Psychological Bulletin*, 70, 474–485.

Luper, H., and Mulder, R. (1965) *Stuttering: Therapy for children*. Englewood Cliffs, N.J.: Prentice-Hall.

McFall, R. (1970) Effects of self monitoring on normal smoking behavior. *Journal of Consulting and Clinical Psychology*, 35, 135–142.

McFall, R., and Hammen, C. (1971) Motivation, structure and self monitoring: Role of nonspecific factors in smoking reduction. *Journal of Consulting and Clinical Psychology*, 37, 80–86.

Mahoney, M. J. (1972a) Self control strategies in weight loss. Paper presented at the Sixth Annual Meeting of the Association for the Advancement of Behavior Therapy, New York.

Mahoney, M. (1972b) Research issues in self management. *Behavior Therapy*, 3, 145–163.

Mahoney, M. J. (1972) *Self reward and self monitoring techniques for weight control*, Ph.D. Dissertation, Stanford University.

Mahoney, M. J., Moura, N. G. M., and Wade, T. C. (1973) The relative efficacy of self reward, self punishment and self monitoring techniques for weight loss. *Journal of Consulting and Clinical Psychology* (in press).

Marston, A. (1964) Variables in extinction following acquisition with vicarious reinforcement. *Journal of Experimental Psychology*, 68, 312–351.

Marston, A. (1965) Self reinforcement: The relevance of a concept in analogue research to psychotherapy. *Psychotherapy: Theory, Research and Practice*, 2, 1–5.

Martin, R. R. (1968) The experimental manipulation of stuttering behavior. In H. Sloane, Jr., and D. Barbara MacAulay, eds., *Operant procedures in remedial speech and language training*. Boston: Houghton Mifflin.

Martin, R. R., and Siegel, G. M. (1966a) The effects of response contingent shock on stuttering. *Journal of Speech and Hearing Research*, 9, 340–352.

Martin, R. R., and Siegel, G. M. (1966b) The effects of simultaneously punishing stuttering and rewarding fluency. *Journal of Speech and Hearing Research*, 9, 466–475.

Martin, R. R., and Siegel, G. M. (1969) The effects of a neutral stimulus (buzzer) on motor responses and disfluencies in normal speakers. *Journal of Speech and Hearing Research,* 12, 179–184.

Miller, N., and DiCara, L. (1967) Instrumental learning of heart rate changes in curarized rats: Shaping and specificity to discrimination stimulus. *Journal of Comparative and Physiological Psychology,* 63, 12–19.

Miller, N. E. (1969) Learning of visceral and glandular responses. *Science,* 163, 434–445.

Nowliss, D. P., and Kamiya, J. (1970) Control of EEG alpha rhythm through auditory feedback and the associated mental activity. *Psychophysiological Research,* 6, 476.

Perkins, W. (1973b) Replacement of stuttering with normal speech: II. Clinical Procedures. *Journal of Speech and Hearing Disorders,* 38, 295–303.

Perkins, W. (1973a) Replacement of stuttering with normal speech: I. Rationale. *Journal of Speech and Hearing Disorders,* 38, 283–294.

Quick, E. (1973) Self monitoring and the control of overeating. Ph.D. Dissertation, University of Pittsburgh.

Quist, R. W., and Martin, R. R. (1967) The effect of response contingent verbal punishment on stuttering. *Journal of Speech and Hearing Research,* 10, 795–800.

Reed, C. G., and Lingwall, J. B. (1973) An investigation of the relationship between punishment, GSR's and stuttering. Paper presented at American Speech and Hearing Association Convention, Detroit.

Rehm, L., and Marston, A. R. (1968) Reduction of social anxiety through modification of self reinforcement: An instigation therapy technique. *Journal of Consulting and Clinical Psychology,* 32, 565–574.

Rehm, L. P., and Rozensky, R. H. (1973) Multiple behavior therapy techniques with a homosexual client: A case study. Unpublished research, University of Pittsburgh.

Rhodes, R., Shames, G., and Egolf, D. (1971) "Awareness" in verbal conditioning of language themes during therapy with stutterers. *Journal of Communication Disorders,* 4, 30–39.

Rickard, H., and Mundy, M. (1965) Direct manipulation of stuttering behavior: An experimental clinical approach. In L. Ullman and L. Krasner, eds., *Case studies in behavior modification.* New York: Holt, Rinehart & Winston.

Rotter, J. (1966) Generalized expectancies for internal versus external control of reinforcement. *Psychological Monographs,* 80, 9, 609.

Rozensky, R. H. (1973) The manipulation of temporal placement of self monitoring: A case study of smoking reduction. Unpublished paper.

Rubin, H. (1973) An interpretation of the Rhodes et al. study, "awareness" in verbal conditioning of language themes during therapy with stutterers. Personal Communication.

Ryan, B. (1971) Operant procedures applied to stuttering therapy for children. *Journal of Speech and Hearing Disorders,* 36, 264–280.

Ryan, B., and Shames, G. H. (1966) The construction and evaluation of a program for modifying stuttering behavior employing operant conditioning procedures. Paper presented at American Speech and Hearing Association Convention, Washington, D.C.

Ryan, B. P., and Van Kirk, B. A. (1973) Programmed stuttering therapy for children. Paper presented at American Speech and Hearing Association Convention, Detroit.

Schwartz, G. E. (1970) Cardiac responses to self induced thoughts. *Psychophysiology*, 6, 650.

Seltzer, H., Shames, G. H., and Egolf, D. B. (1971) A laboratory method for stuttering children. Paper presented at American Speech and Hearing Association Convention, Chicago.

Shames, G. H. (1968) Dysfluency and stuttering. *Pediatric Clinics of North America*, 15, 691–704.

Shames, G. H. (1969) Verbal reinforcement during therapy interviews with stutterers. In B. Gray and E. England, eds., *Stuttering and the conditioning therapies*. Monterey, Calif.: Monterey Institute for Speech and Hearing.

Shames, G. H., and Egolf, D. B. (in press) *Operant conditioning and the management of stuttering*. Englewood Cliffs, N.J.: Prentice-Hall.

Shames, G. H., Egolf, D. B., and Rhodes, R. C. (1969) Experimental programs in stuttering therapy. *Journal of Speech and Hearing Disorders*, 34, 30–47.

Shames, G. H., and Sherrick, C. E., Jr. (1963) A discussion of nonfluency and stuttering as operant behavior. *Journal of Speech and Hearing Disorders*, 28, 3–18.

Shapiro, D., and Birk, L. (1967) Group therapy in experimental perspective. *International Journal of Group Psychotherapy*, 17, 211–214.

Shapiro, D., and Crider, A. (1967) Operant electrodermal conditioning under multiple schedules of reinforcement. *Psychophysiology*, 4, 2, 168–175.

Shapiro, D., Tursky, B., and Schwartz, G. E. (1970) Control of blood pressure in man by operant conditioning. *Circulation Research*.

Shaw, C., and Shrum, W. (1972) The effects of response-contingent reward on the connected speech of children who stutter. *Journal of Speech and Hearing Disorders*, 37, 75–88.

Sheehan, J. (1958) Conflict theory of stuttering. In J. Eisenson, ed., *Stuttering: A symposium*. New York: Harper & Row.

Siegel, G. M. (1970) Punishment, stuttering and disfluency. *Journal of Speech and Hearing Research*, 13, 4, 677–714.

Siegel, G. M., and Martin, R. R. (1965a) Experimental modification of disfluency in normal speakers. *Journal of Speech and Hearing Research*, 8, 235–244.

Siegel, G. M., and Martin, R. R. (1965b) Verbal punishment of disfluencies in normal speakers. *Journal of Speech and Hearing Research*, 8, 245–251.

Siegel, G. M., and Martin, R. R. (1966) Punishment of disfluencies in normal speakers. *Journal of Speech and Hearing Research*, 9, 208–218.

Siegel, G. M., and Martin, R. R. (1967) Verbal punishment of disfluencies during spontaneous speech. *Language and Speech*, 10, 244–251.

Siegel, G. M., and Martin, R. R. (1968) The effects of verbal stimuli on disfluencies during spontaneous speech. *Journal of Speech and Hearing Research*, 11, 358–364.

Skinner, B. F. (1938) *The behavior of organisms.* New York: Appleton.

Skinner, B. F. (1953) *Science and human behavior.* New York: MacMillan.

Solomon, R. L. (1964) Punishment. *American Psychologist,* 19, 239–253.

Sobell, L. C., and Sobell, M. B. (1973) A self feedback technique to monitor drinking behavior in alcoholics. *Behavior Research and Therapy,* 11, 237–238.

Tasto, D. L., and Hinkle, J. E. (1973) Muscle relaxation treatment for tension headaches. *Behavior Research and Therapy,* 11, 347–350.

Thorndike, E. (1933) An experimental study of rewards. Teacher's College, Columbia University, New York, 580.

Travis, L. E. (1940) The need for stuttering. *Journal of Speech Disorders,* 5, 193–202.

Travis, L. E. (1957) The unspeakable feelings of people with special reference to stuttering. In L. E. Travis, ed., *Handbook of speech pathology.* New York: Appleton.

Treon, M., Tamayo, F., and Standley, S. M. (1972) The use of GSR biofeedback in the modification of stuttering. Paper presented at the American Speech and Hearing Association Convention.

Trotter, W. D., and Bergmann, M. F. (1957) Stutterers' and nonstutterers' reactions to speech situations. *Journal of Speech and Hearing Disorders,* 22, 40–45.

Tursky, B., and Shapiro, D. (1969) Operant conditioning of systolic blood pressures. *Psychophysiology,* 5, 563–564.

Ullmann, L., and Krasner, L. (1965) *Case Studies in Behavior Modification.* New York: Holt, Rinehart & Winston.

Van Riper, C. (1937) The effect of penalty upon frequency of stuttering spasms. *Pedagogical Seminary and Journal of Genetic Psychology,* 50, 193–195.

Van Riper, C. (1949) To the stutterer as he begins his speech therapy. *Journal of Speech and Hearing Disorders,* 14, 303–306.

Van Riper, C. (1953) Speech therapy: A book of readings. New York: Prentice-Hall.

Van Riper, C. (1954) Speech correction methods and principles, 3rd ed. New York: Prentice-Hall.

Van Riper, C. (1957) Symptomatic therapy for stuttering. In L. E. Travis, ed., *Handbook of speech pathology.* New York: Appleton.

Van Riper, C. (1971) *The nature of stuttering.* Englewood Cliffs, N.J.: Prentice-Hall.

Van Riper, C. (1973) *The treatment of stuttering.* Englewood Cliffs, N.J.: Prentice-Hall.

Watson, D. L., Tharp, R. G., and Krisberg, J. (1972) Case study in self modification: Suppression of inflammatory scratching while awake and asleep. *Journal of Behavior Therapy and Experimental Psychiatry,* 3, 213–215.

Wheelden, J. A., and Rosenberg, P. B. (1973) The effect of haloperidol on stuttering. Presented at American Speech and Hearing Association Convention, Detroit.

Williams, D. (1957) A point of view about stuttering. *Journal of Speech and Hearing Disorders,* 22, 390–397.

Wischner, G. (1950) Stuttering behavior and learning: A preliminary theoretical formulation. *Journal of Speech and Hearing Disorders,* 15, 324–325.

Witzel, M. A., and Schulman, E. (1973) The effect of a response-cost paradigm on the length of a stutterer's fluency interval. Unpublished research, University of Pittsburgh.

Wolpe, J. (1958) Psychotherapy by reciprocal inhibition. Stanford, Calif.: Stanford University Press.

V

Operant Methodology in Stuttering Therapy

Roger J. Ingham, Ph.D.

Head of School of Speech Therapy at the Cumberland College of Health Sciences in Sydney, Australia. Contributor to professional journals including the *Journal of Speech and Hearing Disorders, Journal of Speech and Hearing Research, Journal of Communication Disorders* and the *Journal of Applied Behavior Analysis.* He is an Associate Editor for the *Journal of Fluency Disorders.*

Introduction

The period since publication of the first *Symposium* has seen many developments in stuttering theory, research, and therapy. One major feature among these has been the influence of developments in clinical psychology. This influence has been particularly evident since 1958: The trend has been away from a medically oriented, diagnostic view of problem behaviors and toward a behaviorally oriented and therapy-directed analysis of problem behaviors, based largely on principles and practices found in experimental psychology. Learning theories have been prominent in this trend, particularly in providing a theoretical model to describe the development of abnormal human behavior (e.g., Eysenck, 1960). Similarly, this trend has found its reflection in theories of (and research on) stuttering, particularly within the theories of Brutten and Shoemaker (1967) and Shames and Sherrick (1963) and in research associated with these theories. This trend has also been reflected in other theories (e.g., Jones, 1970). However, its most important feature in clinical psychology has been away from theory construction and toward a pragmatic concern with procedures that modify or remove problem behaviors. This has resulted in a relegation—even dismissal—of the significance of the problem behavior's history and an overriding concern with factors in the subject's contemporary environment that control or maintain the problem behavior (Ullman and Krasner, 1965). Procedures have been developed that are primarily therapeutic and, according to proponents of behavior therapy, only incidentally concerned with theory.

In spite of its cursory concern for theory, the practice of behavior therapy is often dominated by theories of behavior control or change. Foremost among these have been the techniques of behavior change that have derived from the classical and operant conditioning paradigms. Each paradigm has had a substantial impact on the practice of stuttering therapy in recent years. This certainly has been true of the work of the present author and his colleagues. Thus, in view of the major concern with procedures that change but do not necessarily explain the appearance of stuttering behavior, this chapter will be devoted to an overview of our own and other contributions to the intrusion of one paradigm: the operant paradigm.

Yates (1970) argues that the emergence of behavior therapy was not simply part of a gradual development, but a response to a crisis among clinical psychologists. The principal aspects of this crisis were dissatisfaction with a "disease model" of problem behaviors, dissatisfaction with an unfulfilling role, and concern over the lack of systematic evaluation of psychotherapy. In many respects these conditions have resembled the situation among speech clinicians, especially with respect to stuttering. For instance, clinicians are faced with an almost bewildering range of theories of stuttering. Indeed, there must be few disorders that have provoked, and continue to provoke, as much theory building. This has even extended to the point where a methodology has been devised to integrate these theories (Ainsworth, 1971). Meanwhile, the influence of these theories has been such that Wingate (1971) has recently conjectured that speech clinicians have now virtually developed a fear of stuttering: fear that direct treatment of stuttering could result in some form of psychological damage and even fear of using the word "stutter" in the presence of the subject. This is not to deny the relevance of theory building to an understanding of this behavior, but the failure of many of these theories to contribute to the development of viable therapy procedures must surely be tantamount to fiddling while Rome burns. And that Rome is burning is highlighted by Van Riper's (1970) recent summary of the situation:

> . . . the state of stuttering therapy in this country generally is inadequate, largely in the hands of untrained graduate students, superficial and confused in goals and methods. Therapy time is woefully inadequate. Follow-up is almost non-existant. Criteria for evaluating therapeutic progress are unsystematic. Protocols are missing. A few isolated workers are experimenting with therapy, but their accomplishments are seldom written up or available. Most of the research on stuttering has been descriptive and, for therapy, rather sterile. With more than a million and a half victims of the disorder in this country [U.S.A.] alone, some integrated attack on the problem is sorely needed. (pp. 53–54)

Thus it is very understandable that the recent literature on stuttering, in particular, has shown growing interest in procedures that effectively modify stuttering and, by implication, have therapeutic possibilities. Accordingly, it is understandable that procedures developed in clinical psychology for modifying a wide range of problem behaviors and systematically evaluating their contribution to therapy should find a place in the practice of stuttering therapy. But the extent to which their contribution has been positive, or indeed applicable, is currently a source of much concern (see, e.g., Speech Foundation of America, 1970). This issue, insofar as it applies to operant methodology, will be pursued in this chapter along with a description of the author's endeavors to integrate this methodology with stuttering therapy. The chapter will also review other integrations of operant methodology and stuttering therapy.

Operant Methodology and Stuttering Behavior

In describing or defining the distinguishing features of behavior therapy, it is becoming customary to assert that it is not founded on or associated with any particular theory of human behavior or abnormal human behavior. For example, Yates (1970) and Krasner (1971) argue that the main distinguishing characteristic is the application of experimental method within a therapy setting. Nevertheless, the foundation of many therapy procedures embraced by the behavior therapy rubric is often located within the principles, or at least the language of, respondent or operant conditioning. Moreover, reports on the therapy process are often largely concerned with the extent to which these principles, which are readily seen in a controlled laboratory setting, can be transferred to the context of therapy. Thus problem behaviors such as stuttering are viewed as responses, or classes of responses, that are investigated in order to identify stimuli or operations which will modify or control the frequency of appearance of the problem behavior. There has also emerged what Krasner (1971) has described as a "belief system": features regarded by practitioners as necessary to the transfer of these concepts into a therapy setting. The elements of this system, he concludes, are

(a) the statement of concepts so that they can be tested experimentally; (b) the notion of "laboratory" as ranging from the animal mazes or shuttle boxes through basic human learning studies to hospitals, school rooms, homes and the community; (c) research as treatment—and treatment as research; (d) an explicit strategy of therapy; (e) demonstration that the particular environmental manipulation was indeed responsible for producing the specific behavior change . . . ; (f) the goals of the modification procedure are usually determined by an initial functional analysis or assessment of the problem behaviors. In effect, what are the environmental determinants, maintainers, and consequences of current behavior, and what possible alternatives can be developed? (Reprinted, with permission, from "Behavior Therapy" by L. Krasner, *Annual Review of Psychol-*

Within this general belief system there has appeared a growing conviction, though often termed a "hypothesis," that many forms of problem behavior may be regarded as operant behavior (Skinner, 1953). This has proved to be an extremely influential and productive approach within behavior therapy. It is probably fair to say that it has spawned and supports many current journals reporting on behavior therapy. Nevertheless, there is still a large step between demonstrating that a problem behavior can be operant and devising effective therapy procedures, based solely or largely on "operant methodology."

Verbal behavior was one of the first types of human behavior to be examined within the framework of operant methodology. From the first demonstration studies by Greenspoon (1955) that a verbal response class of plural nouns could be modified by response-contingent verbal reinforcement, there emerged an abundance of studies that attempted to transfer similar procedures into psychotherapy. And in view of the ready transfer of developments in psychology to speech pathology, it is somewhat inevitable that a parallel development—demonstration followed by application in a clinical setting—should transpire. Perhaps there is also something to be learned from the trend that has followed these studies. Kanfer (1968) has identified four stages in this trend. It began with *demonstration* studies in which reinforcement was found to influence verbal behavior under certain types of conditions. It was then followed by a *reevaluation* period in which the complexity of the phenomenon was recognized. Then occurred a period of *application* to therapeutic conditions, followed by a period of *expansion* with recognition of the theoretical implications of the phenomenon. It is difficult to determine the stage that has been reached in application of operant methodology to stuttering. It has certainly passed beyond the first three stages and is probably entering the final stage. It is one thesis of this chapter that there is much room for reevaluation of the contribution that operant conditioning has made in application to stuttering therapy.

A definitive feature of operant behavior is that the rate of appearance and/or topography of an identifiable behavior, or class of behavior, can be altered by the arrangement of consequences, or contingencies, on its appearance. The contingency, or stimulus, found to modify the frequency of appearance of a behavior is described as "reinforcing" if frequency of appearance increases, as "punishing" if it decreases. The stimulus may be a negative reinforcer if, when its removal is made contingent on the appearance of a behavior, it results in increasing frequency of appearance of the behavior. A reinforcing stimulus also punishes behavior if its removal, again contingent on the appearance of the behavior, results in a decrease in the behavior's frequency of appearance. Hence, by these experimental analyses of behavior, procedures are identified that will modify or control rate and topography of behavior by altering the behavior's relationship to environmental stimuli. Another feature of some forms of operant behavior is that a behavior which has a low probability of appearance at a given time will change its frequency of occurrence if made contingent on the appearance of a high-probability behavior (Premack, 1959).

Altering the rate of a target response class, which occurs at a faster or slower than desired rate, is usually achieved by the use of response-contingent stimulation. But when the target response is not emitted, a procedure is usually directed toward shaping partial or approximate forms of the response toward the target response. The typical shaping procedure involves scheduled reinforcement of increasingly proximate responses to the target response. Sequences of responses, which as a chain might form the target responses, may be shaped by the procedure: A response class or chain of responses may be systematically increased by reinforcing successive additions to the chain.

An experimental analysis of problem behavior in the context of therapy in order to determine whether the behavior is operant is characterized by a relatively standardized procedure. In general, this involves establishing a base-rate measure of the response the clinician intends to modify. The base response rate of the behavior and its variability over time is determined when there is a stable and nonsystematic trend in response rate. Occasionally this criterion is established statistically, but usually the graphed appearance of the data is used as evidence that an appropriate base-rate has been established. At this point a treatment procedure is introduced that is usually designed to bring the behavior under stimulus control and to modify response rate toward the target behavior. The extent to which the procedure achieves modification of the behavior is determined by comparisons of base-rate, treatment rate, and the rate when treatment conditions are removed or extinguished. The extinction procedure, or return to base-rate conditions, is the final stage in what is termed an "ABA" experimental design. This trademark of operant analysis is used graphically or statistically to demonstrate whether the problem behavior is an operant.

In therapy, of course, the ultimate goal is to be able to withdraw the treatment condition, by one means or another, while the rate or topography of the target behavior remains intact or does not return to base-rate. Thus, the treatment procedure used to demonstrate stimulus control over the behavior need not necessarily have therapy value. Different schedules of reinforcement or punishment procedures may be more suited to this purpose. Alternatively, the choice of a therapy procedure may be governed by constraints in the therapy setting. Hence, the therapist's problem is to select a procedure that results in the subject's achieving the target behavior within therapy *and* in the environment in which the behavior occurs. Removal or addition of an aspect of the environment that is paired with the appearance of the response may also modify response rate. Generally, however, one implicit goal of therapy is to alter response rate within a variety of situations and thereby reduce possible situation control. This manipulation of stimulus control is one method by which the target behavior can be transferred or generalized across situations and over time. Alternatively, the therapist may seek to aid generalization by introducing schedules of reinforcement or punishment. Reviewers of behavior therapy procedures often state that constant reponse-contingent stimulation bears little relationship to the reinforcement or punishment schedules that may control behavior in the real world. For this reason, it is suggested that behavior is more likely to be maintained if it is phased out of treatment conditions by an intermittant schedule of reinforcement or punishment (Ferster and Skinner, 1957). Thus, the aim of the extinction phase in therapy using operant methodology is very different to that which is usual in the laboratory setting.

The recovery of base-rate after cessation of treatment may not be expected with some behaviors. For example, the removal of a treatment that achieves the learning of certain academic skills would not be expected to result in the extinction of those academic skills. With this type of behavior it is usual to establish a new base-rate following removal of the treatment, then reintroduce the treatment and measure the effect of the treatment against this new base-rate. Another alternative is to use multiple base-rate measures and introduce treatments for different target behaviors at different temporal intervals (Baer, Wolf, and Risley, 1968). Nevertheless, the maintenance of therapy-affected changes in behavior with extinction of treatment is the goal of most, if not all, therapy programs and is the point at which their worth is measured.

Another way of determining the appropriateness of operant methodology to therapy for a particular problem behavior is to consider the extent to which the essential features of operant methodology can be applied to that behavior. By this means those aspects of the problem behavior that do, or do not, lend themselves to this procedure can be identified, along with the limitations and problems associated with the use of this procedure in therapy. Honig (1966) has listed the following essential features of operant methodology. These features provide a grid against which the appropriateness of this methodology in stuttering therapy can be evaluated.

1. Intensive study of individual subjects
2. Control of the experimental environment
3. Use of a repetitive response that has little immediate effect upon the environment
4. Effective means of controlling the subject's behavior
5. Continuous observation and recording of behavior
6. Automatic recording and programming

Intensive study of individual subjects

Most stuttering therapy programs are concerned with the study of the individual and his speech behavior. Since therapy is principally directed to evaluating the effect of therapeutic endeavors on the subject's ability to communicate in *his* environment, this condition is not foreign to stuttering therapy. It implies an absence of interest in group performance and is incompatible with procedures that evaluate stutterers as a unitary group. Hence, the efficacy of a therapy is generally evaluated within rather than across subjects. A further implication is that different therapy procedures may be suited to different subjects. Therefore, the matching of treatment and subject may involve constant experimentation.

If a therapy procedure is being evaluated for its efficacy, criteria are established for rejecting or continuing the subject in therapy. Logically, this method of therapy evaluation may also lead to assessments of the viability of a particular type of therapy procedure: If subjects regularly fail to respond to a procedure, its clinical usefulness is questionable.

Control of the experimental environment

Experimental studies with operant procedures are usually conducted over a period in which it is possible to maintain careful control over the subject's environment. Transplanting this condition of close control into a therapy setting involves many problems. If this control condition is met completely, in one sense, it is necessary for the therapist to control every aspect of the environment in which the subject speaks. However, therapy usually occupies a relatively small and possibly atypical portion of the subject's daily "speaking life"; it is rarely designed to monitor or control other periods of the day. It is therefore possible that these periods could be exceedingly important to any changes or sustained benefits of a therapy procedure. Positive or negative changes in frequency of stuttering from one therapy session to the next may be as much a result of changes in the environment as changes affected by or within therapy. One solution to this problem is to extend therapy contact time so that all of the subject's environment is a laboratory.

Findley (1966) described one environment that incorporates this possibility. The subject was housed in a programmed environment containing all facilities necessary for daily living, and all of the subject's behavior occurred in conditions available to experimental manipulation and investigation. While this solution might appear unappealing, it should not be overlooked that medical treatment requiring hospitalization often occurs in circumstances that are not far removed from Findley's programmed environment. Moreover, the features of a potentially programmed environment already occur in some stuttering therapy programs. For example, holiday camp programs (Starbuck, 1971) provide environmental conditions or situations that could be controlled and systematically integrated with therapy.

An excellent example of the use of operant methodology in a therapy setting is the "token economy" program (Ayllon and Azrin, 1965, 1968). Such a program is usually conducted in circumstances where significant features of the environment are subject to continuous control. The classroom behavior of children and the behavior of patients in a psychiatric ward are two settings in which token economy programs have been employed in recent years with considerable success (Kazdin and Bootzin, 1972). One principal factor behind the success or failure of these programs has been the extent to which the "treatment environment" can be adequately controlled (Kazdin, 1972). There does not seem to be any reason why it should not be possible to circumscribe and monitor the environment in which speech behavior occurs. The technical problems involved may be formidable, but they are not insurmountable. The most obvious approach seems to be to have the subject in a highly controlled environment where his speech can be constantly monitored or to attempt to constantly monitor the subject in his own environment.

Use of a repetitive response that has little immediate effect upon the environment

Honig (1966) argues that the ideal response is repetitive and change in its frequency of appearance is not associated with any significant change in the experimental environment. For significant changes may confound effects attributable to any programmed consequences. Ostensibly stuttering behaviors appear eminently suitable in this respect since changes in this behavior seem unlikely to significantly alter the speaker's environment. But this assumption may be very misleading. It is logical to assume, for instance, that reduced stuttering would be associated with alterations in the subject's physical environment. Persons who stutter invariably report that they either avoid engaging in conversations or avoid speaking in certain circumstances. It is not difficult to imagine, therefore, that reduced stuttering could involve more speaking with more people and in a wider range of circumstances. Telephone conversations, rendered impossible because of an inability to even begin vocalizing or be understood, may become possible with changes in stuttering. Benefits that may accrue to subjects with reduced stuttering may also be factors important in associated treatment effects. In Australia, for example, it is well known that certain types of employment are not available to persons who stutter; consequently, a change from the presence to the absence of stuttering might mean the difference between becoming or not becoming a schoolteacher or an army officer. It is not inevitable (or even predictable) that these events will follow from changes in stuttering. They are, nevertheless, potentially effects to be considered in a therapy design.

If a more restricted view of "environment" is considered, associated effects of reduced stuttering on speech behavior may be relevant to therapy using operant methodology. One important concomitant of changes in frequency of stuttering might be alterations in speech rate. A variety of studies have shown high correlations between frequency of stuttering and rate of speaking (e.g., Young, 1961; Sander, 1961; Prins and Lohr, 1972). With reduced stuttering, therefore, it is more probable that a faster rate of utterance will occur, along with substantial increases in average daily talking time (Trotter and Brown, 1958). But if reduced stuttering occurs with reductions in speech rate, therapy effects may be confounded. Johnson and Rosen (1937), for instance, indicated that a reduction in a stutterer's oral-reading speech rate was associated with reduced stuttering. Ingham, Martin, and Kuhl (1974) confirmed that this can also occur during the spontaneous speech of persons who stutter.

Changes in many other aspects of speech behavior have been related to reductions in stuttering, and it could be that these appear with changes in stuttering. Rhythmic speech is frequently used in therapy (Andrews and Harris, 1964; Brady, 1971), and its effect in reducing frequency of stuttering is well documented (Barber, 1940; Brady, 1969; Fransella, 1965). Another unusual speech pattern is prolonged speech, which was initially associated with delayed auditory feedback, or DAF (Goldiamond, 1965); but it is also used without DAF (Watts, 1971). Shouting and singing are also patterns of verbal behavior often associated with reduced stuttering. Perhaps these are extreme and improbable associates of reduced stuttering. But in circumstances where fluency is demanded, as in therapy, aspects of these behaviors may appear and confound therapy effects.

It is difficult to determine exactly what reaction stuttering has on the subject's environment. It has been claimed that it causes a variety of reactions in listeners (Johnson, 1959), which in turn may influence aspects of stuttering behavior. Similarly, there may be myriad changes in an individual's speech behavior that accompany reduced stuttering. Possibly, all this can mean is that there is a need to control for the better-known changes when attributing variations in stuttering behavior to a therapy using operant methodology.

Effective means of controlling the subject's behavior

Some procedures that are frequently reported to control and modify stuttering behavior have already been mentioned. However, for purposes of considering their application to operant methodology, they will be divided into response-contingent stimulation and continuous-stimulation procedures.

Response-contingent stimulation procedures. In recent years considerable interest has been shown in reports describing the effects of response-contingent stimulation on stuttering behavior. They have been provocative at a theoretical level because their findings have challenged long-held beliefs about stuttering behavior, but they have also questioned quite a number of traditional approaches to stuttering therapy.

Experimental applications of response-contingent stimulation to stuttering began with a study by Flanagan, Goldiamond, and Azrin (1958). They reported that when a blast of white noise was either delivered or removed after a moment of stuttering, the frequency of stuttering during oral reading by three adult stutterers decreased and increased accordingly. Since this report, various response-contingent stimuli have been demonstrated to reduce stuttering. These include (DAF) (Goldiamond, 1965), electric shock (Martin and Siegel, 1966a; Daly and Cooper, 1967), recorded verbal stimuli (Martin and Siegel, 1966b; Quist and Martin, 1967; Cooper, Cady, and Robbins, 1970), time out from speaking (Haroldson, Martin, and Starr, 1968; Martin and Haroldson, 1967, 1969; Martin and Berndt, 1970; Egolf, Shames, and Seltzer, 1971; Adams and Popelka, 1971), and response cost (Halvorson, 1971). The use of this procedure has not *always* resulted in reduced stuttering (see Brutten and Shoemaker, 1971). Nevertheless, there is sufficient indication in these studies that the frequency of stuttering may be modified by response-contingent stimulation (Siegel, 1970).

The combination of punishment and reinforcement procedures has also been reported to reduce stuttering. Martin and Siegel (1966b) used the verbal stimulus "not good" after each stutter and "good" after 30 seconds of fluency during oral reading. They reported reductions in stuttering during experimental periods that were sustained for a longer duration than reductions in stuttering following instructions to reduce stuttering. They also found that a wrist strap worn during the experimental period could act as a discriminative stimulus when worn during a period when treatment conditions were removed. Moore and Ritterman (1973) reported a similar finding using a combined response-contingent punishment and reinforcement (monetary) procedure during oral reading.

Ostensibly, a more advantageous procedure for clinical practice is reinforcement of periods of fluency. Ensuring a stimulus delivery immediately after each stutter may pose difficulties greater than those involved in deciding whether a time period or prescribed number of words spoken has been free of stuttering behavior. Leach (1969) reported reductions in mean block rate following monetary reinforcement of 15-second periods of fluent conversation. Shaw and Shrum (1972) successfully modified stuttering during the conversation of children with a similar procedure. Russell, Clark, and Van Sommers (1968) used a flashing light and buzzer as reinforcement for the fluent oral reading of words, phrases, or sentences. They also reported successful use of an intermittent reinforcement schedule. But by continuing to expose the oral-reading stimulus for a period of time after a moment of stutter, they may have inadvertently confounded the effects of reinforcement with punishment.

Russell, Clark, and Van Sommers's (1968) report is typical of many of the previously mentioned reports in that it failed to indicate whether reductions in stuttering had occurred with reduced, similar, or increased speech rate relative to base-rate. This is not necessarily crucial to demonstrating that the reinforced or punished aspect of stuttering behaves as an operant, but it is significant in considering clinical applications of these methods. There is evidence in some studies that reductions in stuttering are not attributable to slow speech (Flanagan, Goldiamond, and Azrin, 1958; Martin and Siegel, 1966a; Martin and Berndt, 1970), but the data from other studies are not as convincing.

Continuous-stimulation procedures. In general, as Martin and Ingham (1973) noted, the role of speech behaviors other than stuttering has received little attention in response-contingent stimulation studies. The significance of rate, prosody, pitch, and vocal intensity may be somewhat tangential in these studies, but those factors take on special relevance in considering the effect of continuous-stimulation procedures on modifying stuttering behaviors. While these procedures are frequently reported to reduce or completely suppress stuttering, they are also reported to be associated with changes in the subject's speech pattern.

Voice-signal masking is one continuous-stimulation procedure frequently reported to reduce stuttering behavior. Kern (1932) provided an early report of this effect, which has subsequently been substantiated in a number of studies (e.g., Shane, 1955; Cherry and Sayers, 1956; Maraist and Hutton, 1957; Ham and Steer, 1967; Burke, 1969). There is a strong suggestion in all of these reports that the effect is positively correlated with increases in the decibel level or amount of voice signal which is masked. Other reports (Cherry and Sayers, 1956; Ham and Steer, 1967) implied that the low-frequency components of the voice signal must be masked in order for stuttering to be reduced. This conclusion was challenged by May and Hackwood (1968) on the questionable basis of finding no significant difference in oral-reading rate during high- and low-pass filtered masking. However, the necessary conditions for masking to reduce stuttering seem much more complex than simply masking aspects of the voice signal.

Sutton and Chase (1961) and Webster and Dorman (1970) found almost equivalent decreases in stuttering frequency when masking occurred continuously, only during vocalization, or only with cessation of vocalization. What, therefore, is the necessary condition in the "masking effect" on stuttering? Wingate (1970) has recently offered one interesting hypothesis. He noted that earlier studies on the effects of masking the speech of normal speakers have reported associated changes in rate and syllable duration (Hanley and Steer, 1949), vocal intensity, and vocal frequency (Black, 1950; Atkinson, 1952). As a result Wingate tentatively concluded that the findings "provide additional grounds for suspecting that the improved fluency of stutterers speaking under auditory masking is occasioned primarily through some modifications of vocal functioning in speaking" (Wingate, 1970, pp. 865–866). Some recent support for this hypothesis is provided by the study of Adams and Moore (1972), who found that increased vocal intensity accompanied decreases in frequency of stuttering during masking conditions.

Related procedures: Shadowing, singing, imposed rhythm, DAF. Wingate (1969, 1970) has also suggested that modified vocal functioning may be integral to the modification effect during continuous-stimulation procedures such as shadowing, singing, rhythm, and DAF. The *shadowing* effect on stuttering has been reported (Johnson and Rosen, 1937; Barber, 1939) to occur when a stutterer speaks in concert with one or more persons who are present or even heard over a telephone (Pattie and Knight, 1944). Cherry and Sayers (1956) also noted reduced stuttering when the subject is accompanied by nonidentical speech sounds. Although no data are available from these studies on other aspects of the subject's speech behavior, Wingate (1969) suggests that observation of shadowing "reveals that the salient feature of the speech is that it has an 'intoning' character. This means that speaking under such circumstances encourages accentuation of a 'melody'" (p. 682). If this is true, it would appear that speech behavior during shadowing shares something in common with *singing*. And since persons who stutter are frequently reported to be free of their disability while singing (Bloodstein, 1950), the aspect of verbal behavior that distinguishes singing from nonsinging verbal behavior may be extremely important to the control of stuttering behavior. Wingate (1969) suggests that "emphasis on vocalization to produce some melody" in the stutterer's speech behavior is the significant variable, a variable which is seemingly shared by two other continuous-stimulation procedures—rhythm and prolonged speech.

Rhythmic stimulation is one of the oldest and most intriguing procedures used to reduce stuttering (see Van Riper, 1970). Johnson and Rosen (1937) reported that it was one of the most effective speech patterns for reducing stuttering during oral reading. Barber (1940) found its effect to be similar regardless of whether the rhythmic stimulus was visible, audible, or tactile. Barber also noted that stuttering frequency was less when the stimulus was delivered at the rate of 92 rather than 184 times per minute and when subjects spoke with the stimulus accompanying each syllable rather than each word. The role of slow speech and syllabised speech in the effects associated with rhythmic stimulation was explored in subsequent studies. Fransella and Beech (1965) found that the rhythm effect was independent of changes in rate of speech: Slowing their subjects' speech was associated with reduced stuttering, but the reductions were not comparable to those found during rhythmic stimulation. This study and a study by Azrin, Jones, and Flye (1968) found arhythmic stimulation to be ineffectual. But Brady (1969) found that when subjects were asked to accompany syllables to a beat in both the rhythmic and arhythmic conditions, there were almost comparable reductions in stuttering. However, as Bloodstein (1972) noted, the difference in Brady's study was that subjects could accompany words rather than syllables to a beat during the arhythmic stimulation condition. It would appear from these studies that syllabised speech, especially when it is spoken in a rhythmic fashion, has some features in common with singing. However, the abrupt onset and offset of vocal flow, which characterizes syllabised speech, seems not to emphasize continuity of vocalization between phonemes. By inference, if Wingate's hypothesis is correct, it might be expected that rhythmic stimulation would be only partially successful in modifying stuttering behavior. Some evidence in support of this inference is contained in a report by Meyer and Comley (1969). They found that 17 out of 48 stutterers were unable to master rhythmic speech.

Another unusual speech pattern is reported to occur when stutterers speak during exposure to delayed auditory feedback (*DAF*) conditions.

In a series of studies that described the use of DAF in an operant-conditioning context, Goldiamond (1965) noted that reduced stuttering occurred during conditions in which DAF was expected to be an aversive stimulus. He concluded that a new speech pattern was learned during these conditions and was controlled by different stimuli from those that controlled the stuttering speech pattern. The new speech pattern was described as "prolonged speech" and was mainly characterized by extension or prolongation of the vowel sound within a word.

Many earlier studies (Naylor, 1953; Nessel, 1958; Lotzman, 1961; Chase, Sutton, and Rapin, 1961) reported improvements in the speech behavior of stutterers, particularly severe stutterers, during DAF conditions. Soderberg (1959) also reported increased syllable duration and pitch associated with decreased frequency of stuttering during DAF intervals. When nonstutterers are exposed to DAF, "artificial stuttering" (Lee, 1951) is said to disrupt their speech. However, as Wingate (1969) noted in reviewing studies using DAF with nonstutterers, there are also changes in vocal function that resemble those reported to occur during masking; these include increased vocal intensity, syllable duration, and phonation time. Since there is some evidence (Neelley, 1961) that observers rate speech disturbance in stutterers and nonstutterers as essentially similar during DAF, there is therefore reason to expect that the changes in vocal function are similar and underlie improved fluency during DAF with stutterers.

While DAF may be important in affecting reduced stuttering, it is likely that it behaves as an aid or corrective agent which helps the stutterer maintain the necessary vocal characteristic of a stutter-free speech pattern. Various types of changes in vocal function may transpire under DAF, but not all may result in reduced stuttering. Goldiamond (1965) noted four possible types of speech-pattern responses to DAF (usually a 250-millisecond delay), but only the prolonged speech pattern was favored as suitable for shaping toward normal speech. Goldiamond (1965) reported, "Our total population of stutterers upon whom the procedures have been utilized thus far in 30. In all 30 cases, at a specified 50 minute period in the program there has emerged a fluent pattern of reading which is well articulated, rapid and devoid of blockages" (p. 156). Subsequently, Goldiamond (1967) suggested that DAF may be redundant in this program since prolonged speech was successfully instated by instruction. Thus, the method of controlling stuttering is the result of certain important changes in vocal behavior that happen to be the by-products of the effects of DAF. Some of these changes have been regarded as identifiable and programmable. Webster (1972a), for example, has described developments in a therapy program that was originally based on DAF procedures. He used "gentle initiation of speech sounds" combined with prolonged vowel sounds in a therapy program that employed an on-line computer to feed back information to the subject on departure from a stored model of this target behavior.

In general, there are a number of response-contingent and continuous-stimulation procedures that are reported to modify the frequency of stuttering. It would seem, however, that their effectiveness may depend on certain alterations in speech behavior. This may mean that these procedures are only partially effective in modifying speech behavior toward a pattern which is incompatible with stuttering behavior. Nevertheless, a range of procedures for the operant methodologist to use in controlling stuttering behavior exists. He would, however, be wise to be aware of the significance of changes in vocal functioning associated with their use—particularly in stuttering therapy, where restoration of normal speech is the ideal goal.

Continuous observation and recording of behavior

In most respects the features of stuttering behavior appear to accord well with Honig's (1966) description of a class of behavior suited to operant methodology: "a simple, readily repeatable response . . . which can be objectively and automatically recorded, which the subject can execute over long periods without fatigue, and which can be performed at a wide range of response rates" (p. 5).

The difficult issue that this requirement poses for stuttering stems from the problems involved in identifying the definitive features. Stuttering is far from "simple" to define and may not necessarily be stuttering behavior if it is "readily repeatable." Moreover, it is questionable to regard stuttering behavior as similar from one occasion to the next, even within the same person. Nevertheless, searching for the definitive features of stuttering behavior creates the same problems as defining any other form of human behavior. Ultimately, the definition can only direct attention to aspects of a part of a person's behavior that observers agree distinguishes it from other behaviors.

Certain types of dysfluencies appear regularly in attempts to isolate the characteristics of stuttering behavior (Young, 1961; Sander, 1963); sound and syllable repetitions, blocks, and prolongations all appear to occur more frequently in the speech of persons who stutter. Wingate (1964) made one valiant attempt to incorporate these linguistic features into a definition. But, as Beech and Fransella (1968) noted, Wingate's definition incorporated so many qualifications that it lacked the essentials of a true definition. Perhaps this was inevitable because the definition used categories of dysfluent verbal behavior that also describe the dysfluencies of nonstutterers. On the positive side, however, it did point to some behaviors that, for the sake of parsimony, have been regarded as constituting a "moment of stuttering" (Johnson, 1955). But what behaviors enable a listener to distinguish dysfluent speech behavior from stuttering?

Van Riper (1971) summarized a range of behaviors that have been regarded as guidelines for distinguishing stuttering from normal dysfluencies (see p. 28). Nevertheless, he concluded that the only "essential feature that distinguishes a stutterer from a person with an articulatory disability is the former individual's apparent inability to perform the motor sequencing of a given sound or syllable or word at the proper moments in time" (p. 19). So, in the absence of a mechanical method of identifying the "proper moments in time" when utterances should occur, we are still forced to seek the definitive features from the judgments of observers. Furthermore, the studies of Martin (1965) and Prins and Lohr (1972) suggest that both audible and visual judgments are necessary in identifying all aspects of a moment of stuttering.

An additional measure of speech behavior, which may be relevant to changes in the topography as well as frequency of stuttering, is the extent to which these moments impede the utterance of a word or syllable. Frequency counts of moments of stuttering may be the same for two individuals, yet the features of one individual's stutter must differ markedly from another's if the time taken to say a word or syllable differs. A measure of the duration of individual moments may give one indication of the difference between two subjects (or differences within a subject). Another method is to measure the time to speak a given number of syllables or words, which gives a less accurate measure of topography but has the advantage to operant methodology of ensuring that changes in stuttering frequency are not simply due to changes in rate of speaking. Thus, rate of utterance and frequency counts of observer-judged moments of stuttering provide measures suitable to operant methodology.

There are, however, many other aspects of speech behavior that have been reported in studies using operant methodology with stuttering behavior. Leach (1969) and Shaw and Shrum (1972) used time periods of fluent speech as a response class. Rickard and Mundy (1965) used fluent oral reading of phrases, sentences, and finally paragraphs as response classes that were reinforced at different levels of improved fluency. Martin and Siegel (1966b) verbally punished a moment of stutter and, concurrently, verbally reinforced 30 seconds of fluent speech. The same researchers also used response-contingent stimulation on different types of stuttering behaviors (Martin and Siegel, 1966a). Fractionation of a moment of stuttering has also been advocated by Webster

(1968) and Brutten (1972) as a method of investigating the differential effects of response-contingent stimulation.

Among the stuttering behaviors a subject may not execute over long periods without fatigue are blocks, which, in some subjects, are of such magnitude that they are virtually mute. This writer has observed one such person who was unable to utter a sound for a period of 16 minutes—a behavior it would be difficult not to regard as fatiguing. Such "moments of stuttering" are relatively rare, and their severity may diminish during periods of continuous speech (Rousey, 1958). Consequently, the time duration of a "moment of stuttering" may not always be readily repeatable and stable for purposes of operant analysis. In the context of therapy, however, it may be exceedingly important to have information on more than frequency counts of "moments of stuttering"; one severe block may be of far more significance to the subject (and listener) than a single repetition of a sound or syllable.

It may also be important to know to what extent changes in the frequency of stuttering are affected by the circumstances in which the behavior is monitored and to what extent the behavior is typical of those circumstances. Ultimately, it is probably incumbent on the therapist to indicate the crucial features of the subject's speech behavior when recorded under specified conditions. These conditions may include the very act of recording, since recordings made with or without the subject's awareness after therapy may produce markedly different data (Ingham, 1975). In turn, this may mean that arrangements also need to be made to observe and record speech behavior before, during, and after therapy in a way that will lend credence to overtly observed and recorded data.

Automatic recording and programming

Perhaps the most unfortunate problem facing an experimenter or therapist concerned with counts of "moments of stuttering" is that no machine has yet replaced the eyes and ears of the human observer. If stuttering could be machine-identified, research and therapy for this behavior would probably have advanced far beyond its present status. Nevertheless, audio and audiovisual recorders make it possible to assess interobserver and intraobserver reliability. Recording technology has also reached the somewhat notorious position where it is also possible to record subjects in a variety of speech situations. It has not as yet reached this position in the video field so much of the recording data is only of an acoustic nature.

The rate of appearance of behavior is fundamental to operant methodology. This may take a variety of forms in evaluating stuttering behavior. The rate of appearance of moments of stuttering, frequency counts of different levels of severity (e.g., the number of repetitions or the duration of blocks), and the frequency of specified periods of fluency have all been reported in studies using operant methodology. The rate of words or syllables spoken within an interval of time is another measure used by some researchers, though its relationship to stuttering behavior is necessarily indirect. Another approach is to assess the percentage of speech behavior occupied by moments of stuttering. Thus, changes in the percentage of syllables or words stuttered express a change in the amount of disruption to speech behavior. In view of the absence of automated methods of identifying moments of stuttering, the consistency and speed with which an observer can identify these moments are crucial in determining whether response-contingent stimulation procedures can be suitably applied in research or therapy. One method of determining the consistency of identifications of stuttering is to measure the percentage of agreement on identified instances within and among assessors (Tuthill, 1946). Within-assessor agreement, or reliability, is obviously the most ideal measure of reliability because it is also a measure of confidence in the procedural data in response-contingent stimulation treatment procedures. Experimental studies in which response-contingent stimulation has been delivered contingent on a moment of stuttering have not usually been concerned with identifying the effect of variations in time between the appearance of the response and the delivery of the stimulus. But Adams and Popelka (1971) found that a stimulus can be delivered one or two words after a stutter without loss of effect of the procedure on the frequency of stuttering. When treatment or therapy procedures use *total* moments of stuttering in a number of words as a dependent variable, the correlation between total scores is used to measure reliability. This type of measure can be made with far more reliability than measures of particular moments of stuttering. Young (1969), for example, found that observers are more likely to agree on assessments of total counts rather than on individual moments of stuttering in prescribed periods of speech.

An aspect of stuttering behavior that could present measurement difficulty is word avoidance. It is frequently argued that some persons who stutter are not identified as stutterers because they carefully manage to avoid words they expect to stutter. Unfortunately this behavior, which has been regarded as a definitive feature of stuttering (Van Riper, 1971), has remained largely unresearched. This is especially problematic for a behavioral approach to stuttering because the reliability with which observers can identify its appearance has yet to be established. Perhaps it is a behavior for which subject rather than observer identification is necessary. In any event, the appearance of this behavior may be important to changes in observed moments of stuttering in some subjects during treatment.

Operant methodology in therapy

In general there are many features of stuttering behavior that make it a very suitable behavior for a therapy procedure using operant methodology; but these features must be weighed against measurement problems and the difficulties inherent in attempting to achieve control over this ubiquitous behavior. Experimental studies using operant methodology have used at least two methods of modifying stuttering behavior that are suitable for incorporation within an "operant therapy." One approach involves the arrangement of stimuli as consequences on the appearance or absence of stuttering, and the second is to alter the motor-linguistic characteristics of the subject's speech pattern. With either approach, it seems that the central problem to be solved in transferring operant methodology to a clinical setting is ensuring sufficient behavior control. On the one hand, measurement and control of all the subject's speaking behavior may be necessary to identify environmental stimuli that control his stuttering or need to be incorporated within a therapy program. On the other hand, almost continuous behavioral control may be needed to guarantee that a new speech pattern has emerged that is stutter free and not partially maintained. The extent to which it is necessary to continuously maintain the new speech pattern is an empirical question, but it is difficult to envisage partial maintenance of the new speech pattern as being sufficient to ensure its constant usage by the subject after therapy. Consequently, in order to fulfill the most stringent requirements of operant methodology, it would appear desirable to devise therapy conditions that permit continuous monitoring and control of environmental stimuli and speech behavior. This level of control might then be programmed to fade out until fluency that is durable over time and across situations is attained.

An alternative and less demanding approach might be to establish control over the subject's speech behavior in specified environmental conditions that are significant in the subject's daily life. The therapy strategy may then be to program treatment of the subject's speech behavior in these specified conditions. If, subsequently, the treatment gains were found to be maintained within the conditions treated, the treatment goal of this therapy strategy could be regarded as fulfilled. However, this treatment goal would probably be less than satisfactory to most speech pathologists if the treatment gains were not maintained in outside conditions. For this reason, some other procedures have been designed to extend therapy control beyond therapy conditions. For example, self-control procedures designed for behavior therapy (Cautela, 1969) are now being increasingly used for this purpose. They have recently been used in stuttering therapy (La Croix, 1973), where their application may be exceedingly appropriate. Technology has also been of some assistance in extending therapy control over a subject's daily life: for example, in the use of hearing-aid-style masking units (Trotter and Leach, 1967), metronomes (Brady, 1971), and DAF units (Goldiamond, 1967). These seem exceedingly useful in extending speech-pattern behaviors, although control over the schedule of their use ultimately rests with the subject rather than the therapist. Telemetry technology (Hoshiko and Holloway, 1968) offers a means of extending behavioral control and of monitoring speech behavior to ascertain the efficacy of these technical procedures. But regardless of which strategy is used to integrate operant methodology and stuttering therapy, both therapy and the therapy evaluation procedure must come to terms with the vagaries of speech behavior and the measurement problems involved in establishing the efficacy of therapy.

Token-Economy Stuttering Therapy: an Approach to Speech-Behavior Control in Stuttering Therapy

The following description of the development and design of a Token-Economy Stuttering Therapy Program may serve to highlight some of the difficulties that need to be solved in using operant methodology in stuttering therapy. This program has developed from a series of group therapy programs in which this author endeavored to explore the therapy benefits of welding speech-pattern and stimulus-control procedures. These programs began with a therapy that combined a speech-pattern procedure with group psychotherapy. It was followed by a series of programs that incorporated a limited application of a stimulus-control procedure (token reinforcement) for prosthetic purposes. Finally, programs were developed in which the stimulus-control procedure was expanded into a token economy designed to achieve conditions permitting sustained control over speech behavior.

In many ways the approach adopted in this program of stuttering therapy shares much in common with the approach adopted by Shames (1969a) and his co-workers. They used a traditional stuttering therapy procedure (initially Van Riper's) and then grafted operant methodology onto the therapy. Their aim has been to formalize the operations constituting the therapy procedure and then systematize their application. Both implicitly and explicitly this operant program was initiated with the assumption that the therapy procedures were beneficial, but likely to be more beneficial if therapist effects and therapy strategies were programmed. Hence, clinicians nominated the desired features in an ideal version of a therapy program, and then steps were taken to program their occurrence. The following program grew from similar origins and developed on a similar path.

Phase 1:
Modification of the Andrews and Harris syllable-timed therapy program

The Andrews and Harris (1964) "syllable-timed (S.T.) speech" program had many features in common with traditional stuttering therapy programs. Foremost among these is that it relied on essentially unprogrammed therapist tactics to assist subjects to learn a method to modify their stuttering behavior. The method in this instance, is a form of rhythmic speech known as S.T. speech, which is first taught by having each syllable spoken to the accompaniment of a metronome beat. When the subject is able to speak without stuttering, he is encouraged to use S.T. speech at all times. Initially this speech pattern is slow, monotone, and decidedly unusual. It is not normal speech. With increases in the speed of speech, the subject is expected to introduce the stress features of normal speech. The present S.T. program was conducted with groups of approximately 10 subjects (adults and children) over two main stages. The first was an intensive period lasting about 10 hours a day for 12 consecutive days. The second stage required subjects to attend the clinic for a 3-hour session each week for about 40 weeks. In both stages, a nondirective group pyschotherapy program (Rogers, 1951) was conducted for approximately an hour a day in the first stage and for the same time in second-stage sessions in order to assist subjects to cope with speech situations. Toward the end of the first stage, subjects were sent on "excursions" to practice their new speech pattern in difficult speech situations.

In operation, the S.T. program suffered from a number of drawbacks. Perhaps the most obvious was that it did not permit the intensive study of individual subjects because subjects were required to fit their progress into the program rather than visa versa. It could be argued that, because it was a group program, this precluded individualized therapy. This does not necessarily follow, however, since individualized schedules of therapy can be arranged to coexist in a group therapy. The most pressing and obvious difficulties centered on the procedures for instating, maintaining, and shaping S.T. speech during the first stage. Initially, S.T. speech often vied with the stuttering speech pattern: Many subjects simply preferred stuttered speech to S.T. speech. At the same time it appeared that the method of instating and maintaining practice in S.T. speech rested largely on therapist judgment and persuasiveness. Indeed, it almost seemed that the only behaviors that subjects consistently performed during their stay in the clinic were conversation, eating, and drinking. However, therapists made intermittent "on-line" ratings of syllables spoken fluently and stuttered, as well as ratings of syllables spoken per minute (SPM), in order to gauge subject progress. In an initial attempt to solve these problems, two procedures that took advantage of these measures were designed for integration within the S.T. program. First, it was hypothesized that the subject's preferred use of stuttered speech over S.T. speech could be reduced if the aversive aspects of the stuttered speech were increased and the use of S.T. speech was reinforced. To achieve this, the intensive stage began with a procedure termed "increased stuttering" (I.S.), and was followed by a "token system" (Ayllon and Azrin, 1965).

I.S. required subjects to practice stuttering on every word spoken. In some respects it resembled "negative practice" (Dunlap, 1932) and "voluntary stuttering" (Van Riper, 1958), but differed from them in that its goal was to maintain rather than decrease stuttering during the initial two days of therapy: Subjects were instructed to stutter on every word while in the clinic. At the end of the two days, each subject was required to have doubled his pretreatment percentage of syllables stuttered (%SS) during group conversation (or 25%SS if subjects stuttered on less than 12½ percent before treatment). The subject was required to meet this criterion in a group conversation session before he was permitted to begin the use of S.T. speech.

The Token System (T.S.) was designed around a 45-minute period of group conversation known as a "rating session." Rating sessions were scheduled on five occasions each day. Only at these times could subjects earn tokens with which they could purchase food, drink, or any other item purchasable during their day in the hospital. Each subject was required to speak a specified number of syllables, and tokens were earned or lost according to the %SS during a rating session. The token reward/penalty schedule was individualized, being related to each subject's pretreatment %SS base-rate. A subject with a 40%SS base-rate earned two tokens for reaching his base-rate in a rating session; he earned four tokens for 36%SS, eight tokens for 32%SS, and so on. He was penalized two tokens for scoring 45%SS, four tokens for 48%SS, and so on. A subject with a 10%SS base-rate earned two tokens for base-rate, four tokens for 9%SS, eight tokens for 8%SS, and so on. He was penalized two tokens for scoring 11%SS, four tokens for 13%SS, and so on. Hence, the larger the %SS base-rate, the greater the change from base-rate that was necessary for the subject to earn tokens. It was assumed that variability in performance was more probable with higher %SS scores. With improvement over rating sessions, the base-rate %SS score was accordingly reduced until it reached 0%SS. At this point the subject's rate of speech was shaped toward a range of 180–220 SPM, which is close to normal utterance rate in the adult population in Australia, where the experiment was conducted (Bernard, 1965).

During a rating session, a subject was signaled by the rating therapist whenever he was observed not to be using S.T. speech: At these times the therapist ceased to rate speech. The Token System was designed to reinforce the use of S.T. speech until complete fluency was attained, then systematically to shape speech rate back to normal while maintaining fluency. Between rating sessions, subjects were urged (but not coerced) to practice in order to aid their performance in rating sessions. Therapists also went with subjects on excursions and surreptitiously recorded the subjects' speech performance. The principal purpose of these modifications was not necessarily directed toward improving the outcome of this therapy program: They were mainly designed to assist in the conduct of therapy by programming subject and therapist behaviors. The Token System has an affinity in this regard with the managerial use of token systems in institutional settings (e.g., Ayllon and Azrin, 1968). Nevertheless there are obviously more gains in using such procedures if, in addition to improving therapy management, they also add to the efficacy of therapy.

In 1968 four therapy programs were conducted with different combinations of the four previously mentioned treatment procedures within the format of the Andrews and Harris program. Within the confines of the 12-day program and with relatively matched groups of adult stutterers, it was found (Ingham, Andrews, and Winkler, 1972) that the combination of the Token System and S.T. speech was probably a short-term therapy program superior to those programs that included I.S. and group psychotherapy. The last two treatments seemed redundant (if speech performance scores were used as guides) when associated with the other treatments. In the nine-month second stage the experimenters sought to determine the benefits of different types of treatment schedules. Instead of weekly 3-hour sessions, some groups of subjects were treated once a month or not at all. Rating sessions were used on these occasions, but with a variation on the token system. Subjects paid a small fee for attendance ($2): This fee was recoverable contingent on performance during a rating session. The results (Andrews and Ingham, 1972b) indicated that the second-stage treatment systems did not improve performance. However, the inclusion of the token system during the first stage of treatment reduced the time necessary for groups to achieve levels of performance comparable to those obtained after both stages of the original Andrews and Harris (1964) program.

One criticism that can be leveled at these studies is the concern with group performances in order to evaluate treatment procedures, rather than identification of individual responses to treatment. It was also a prescribed, noncontingent program of therapy: The duration of therapy treatment conditions was predetermined and not contingent on subject performance. Nevertheless, there were some redeeming features. The purpose in these programs was to modify treatment procedures so more efficient use could be made of prescribed therapy techniques within a prescribed time period. With some reservations, group comparisons suggest that more subjects improved during the initial stage of treatment as a result of adding the Token System. There was also evidence that the different second-stage treatment schedules which were introduced did not benefit subjects treated in Token System conditions during the first stage.

Phase 2:
The integration of a token economy with speech-pattern procedures

Much of the achievement of the Phase 1 program amounted to little more than a shattering awareness of the problems involved in trying to increase the efficacy of the S.T. program. There were many deficiencies in the program. The most obvious of these were that (1) the size of the group limited speech practice, (2) transfer from clinic to nonclinic situations was not fully scheduled or controlled, and (3) a treatment period was used that was prescribed rather than contingent on the speech performance of subjects. Many alternative program designs and procedures could be devised to offset these deficiencies. But the most significant problem area in the program centered on the presumed general efficacy of S.T. speech. The program virtually assumed that subjects would replace their old speech pattern with S.T. speech at all times and would, with continuous usage, acquire fluent and acceptable speech. This assumption was made in spite of an absence of procedures in the program designed to achieve these ends.

As previously noted, both S.T. speech and DAF-instated prolonged speech are "speech patterns" reported to reduce stuttering behavior by replacing a pattern of speech that had previously included stuttering. Yet when these speech patterns are employed, the therapy procedures rarely incorporate controls to ensure that the new speech pattern does actually replace the old speech pattern. Most therapy with these speech patterns is reported to be conducted in a part-time fashion: The subject usually attends a clinic for daily (or less) sessions of perhaps an hour in which he is carefully monitored while using the new behavior (e.g., Brady, 1971; Goldiamond, 1965; Curlee and Perkins, 1969). The subject is usually urged to continue self-monitoring and practicing this speech while away from the clinic. These intervals are not subject to therapist control and, consequently, the old speech pattern may occur in spite of the subject's best intentions. One solution is the use of hearing-aid style devices (e.g., Brady, 1971; Goldiamond, 1967), which the subject wears in order to receive continuously the stimulus conditions of therapy. They provide the subject with a prosthesis designed to maintain the new speech pattern at all times or provide backup assistance in difficult speaking situations. But again, the subject's speech behavior is not monitored to ensure that these goals are fulfilled.

One avenue by which increased monitoring may be achieved is by total rather than partial hospitalization of subjects and by the establishment of procedures to increase surveillance over the subject's speech. If such monitoring is achieved, a token system can be extended so that complete Token-Economy conditions obtain. A program was designed that, ostensibly, would permit token control over all of a subject's speech behavior while instating and shaping either S.T. speech or prolonged speech toward target features of normal speech. The program was also designed so that the target speech behavior could be transferred into various difficult speech situations and subjects could follow up to determine the durability of the behavior.

The Token-Economy Stuttering Therapy Program has been described in a number of places (Ingham and Andrews, 1971c, 1973a; Andrews and Ingham, 1972a; Martin and Ingham, 1973). These reports outline an early experimental version of the program that sought to establish the efficacy of the token system in controlling stuttering behavior. That program encompassed an integration of a DAF/prolonged-speech schedule with the token system, a comparison between S.T.-speech- and prolonged-speech-treated subjects during and after treatment, as well as an attempt to identify some significant variables within the treatment process. Some alterations have been made to this program (Ingham and Andrews, 1973c). These have been designed to increase the level of token control over speech behavior during treatment, more systematically wean subjects from therapy conditions, and evaluate posttreatment performance more appropriately.

In the treatment-process period of an experimental program, four adult stutterers lived together under controlled token-economy conditions for a maximum of three weeks (in all, 10 groups of subjects constituted the experimental program).[1] The treatment process was divided into three stages. In Stage A, the token system used in Phase 1 was instituted for 21 rating sessions. In Stage B, either S.T. speech or DAF/prolonged

---

[1] In the present experimental programs, hospital policy did not permit subjects to be hospitalized for longer than three weeks. This partially determined the duration of Stage C but, in practice, every subject managed to complete his treatment schedule.

speech was amalgamated with the token system. Stage C was entered when a subject achieved the Stage B target behavior of 0%SS within a speech-rate range of 180–220 SPM. The subject then negotiated a ranked series of "difficult" speech situations.

The daily program was scheduled so that treatment conditions were extended over most of the subject's speaking day: nine 45-minute rating sessions were conducted at scheduled intervals from 7:00 A.M. to 10:00 P.M. Each group then recorded a 30-minute group conversation that was used as a "probe measure" condition. Each subject was required to speak a specified number of syllables during a rating session, and two therapists rated each syllable spoken as either fluent or stuttered. As in the earlier described program, at the end of a rating session each subject earned or lost tokens according to the %SS relative to his base-line %SS. When no stuttering was recorded, tokens were earned for increases in speech rate. From Stage B, the efficacy of S.T. or prolonged speech in controlling stuttering was assumed and a punishment schedule was established for periods between rating sessions: Subjects were response-contingently penalized one token for any moment of stutter; also, subjects were penalized one token for any period of five seconds of nonspeaking in the presence of a therapist. Every endeavor was made to have therapists continuously monitor the speech of subjects. During Stage B, this was designed to help subjects constantly use the speech pattern and to limit their speech environments to group members.

All food, drink, and luxuries that subjects required during the program were priced in tokens and could be purchased only with individually colored tokens earned in rating sessions. Subjects agreed to these rules before entering treatment and, in operation, the rules were checked through an audit on income and expenditure before each rating session.

Throughout the treatment process, a series of experiments were conducted to "tease out" the treatment effects of some aspects of the program. When possible these experiments used a within-group *ABAB* design; otherwise comparisons were made between groups. In Stage A, an attempt was made to isolate the efficacy of components of the token system (Ingham and Andrews, 1973a). As described earlier, this system was designed to reward reductions in the response class %SS. It also penalizes increases in this response class. Therefore, three experiments were designed to determine (1) the efficacy of the contingent reward/penalty schedule in reducing the response class, (2) the effect of including the penalty schedule in the token system, and (3) the effect of the size of token rewards. These experiments were conducted during 21 rating sessions of Stage A. In 8 of the 10 groups, an *ABAB* experimental design was used during these rating sessions to conduct the three experiments. In each experimental group a base rate trend of %SS scores was established over eight rating sessions. A treatment condition was then introduced for six rating sessions, removed for four rating sessions, and finally reintroduced for three rating sessions. The results are shown in Figures 1, 2, and 3. In the other two groups unmodified Token System conditions were maintained to form a treatment control; the trend of scores for these groups is shown in Figure 4.

The results show that in the B intervals there was an increase in rate of reduction in %SS scores that was not associated with reductions in SPM scores. The findings led to the conclusions that (1) the response class, %SS, was able to be brought under token control, (2) the addition of the penalty schedule to the reward schedule was found to increase further the rate of reductions in %SS scores, and (3) doubling the number of tokens subjects could earn on the reward schedule also increased the rate of reductions in %SS scores. It should be noted that the trend of scores in these experiments was based on mean group scores and the trend in some individual scores did not change in the hypothesized direction. In the group depicted in Figure 1, 3 of the 12 subjects' trend of scores did not evidence a response to changes in treatment conditions. In Figure 2, 2 of 11, and in Figure 3, 1 of 8 subjects were also nonresponders.

During Stage B 4 of the groups were taught S.T. speech, which was integrated with the Token System according to the procedure followed with earlier, nonhospitalized groups. However, it was combined with between-rating-session, token-penalty conditions. This meant that subjects were obliged to maintain fluency at all times in order to avoid losing tokens. The other 6 groups were treated by modification of the DAF procedure that Curlee and Perkins (1969) used to instate prolonged speech. At each delay level (250, 200, 150, 100, 50, 0 milliseconds) subjects were required to speak a sequence of four stutter-free rating sessions before the delay was reduced. The sequence of four rating sessions involved two sessions in which subjects wore headsets, which carried delayed feedback of voice signal, and two in which they did not wear headsets. Subjects also spoke a specified number of syllables in accordance with the speech rate anticipated at each delay level.

When DAF has been used to instate prolonged speech in the speech behavior of persons who stutter, it has been accompanied by an emphasis on a slow rate of speech. Both Goldiamond (1967) and Curlee and Perkins (1969) suggested that the speech rate of subjects at the 250-millisecond delay level should be approximately 25–35 words per minute. Therefore, because the target speech rate in the Token-Economy program was 180–220 SPM, word-per-minute rates were converted to SPM rates. The range of speech rates for each delay level was then calculated by projection from the 0-to-250-millisecond SPM range. This provided

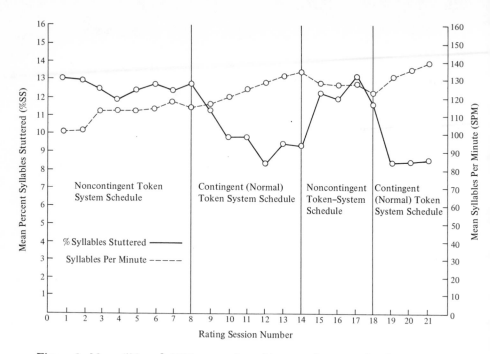

Figure 1. Mean %SS and SPM scores for subjects in Stage A of Token-Economy Stuttering Therapy program during contingent and non-contingent token system conditions (from Ingham and Andrews, 1973a).

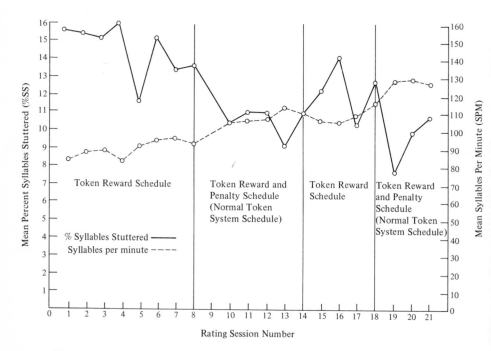

Figure 2. Mean %SS and SPM scores for subjects in Stage A of Token-Economy Stuttering Therapy program during conditions when penalty schedule was removed and added to Token System (from Ingham and Andrews, 1973a).

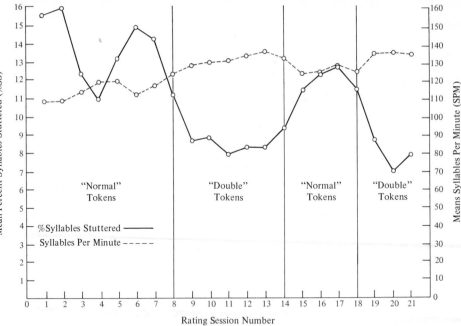

Figure 3. Mean %SS and SPM scores for subjects in Stage A of Token-Economy Stuttering Therapy program during normal and double token reward conditions (from Ingham and Andrews, 1973a).

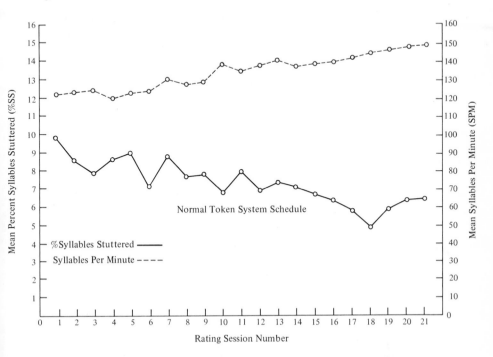

Figure 4. Mean %SS and SPM scores for subjects in Stage A of Token–Economy Stuttering Therapy program (from Ingham and Andrews, 1973a).

the framework for a rate of speech schedule, shown in Table 1, which was integrated with the Token System in order to assist in shaping prolonged speech toward normal fluency.

Table 1 indicates that, at each delay level, subjects were rewarded four tokens for speaking a prescribed number of syllables within a speech-rate range. They were token-penalized for departure from the speech-rate range, as specified in the schedule, and one token for each 0.1%SS stuttering score in a rating session.

As with the S.T. speech group, Stage B began with instructions to subjects on the speech pattern to be adopted. Specifically, they were told to prolong each vowel sound and overlap syllables within and between words with a continuous sound, or "continuous vocalization." They were instructed that this speech pattern would be shaped toward normal speech but that during this shaping program, or throughout Stage B, they were to constantly use the rating-session target speech behavior within and between rating sessions in order to maintain nonstuttered speech. Assessment of a stutter during Stage B was the same as that made during Stage A and C, except that a "prolongation" was not recorded as a stutter until 100-milliseconds delay level was reached. At this level subjects were expected to eliminate effortful prolongation from their speech pattern.

The contribution of the reward/penalty schedule to rate of passage through Stage B of the program for the prolonged-speech group was made by a group comparison procedure. Twelve subjects were rewarded four tokens at each rating session in which they fulfilled the requirements of the rate-of-speech schedule and were stutter free ("contingent re-

TABLE 1

RATE-OF-SPEECH SCHEDULES FOR INTEGRATION OF DAF/PROLONGED
DEPARTURES FROM PRESCRIBED SYLLABLE PER

DAF msec delay	No. of syllables per rating session	Slow SPM tokens penalized						
		−7	−6	−5	−4	−3	−2	−1
250	400			3	6	12	18	24
200	600		6	15	24	33	42	51
150	800	6	18	30	42	54	66	78
100	1000	15	30	45	60	75	90	105
50	1000	24	42	60	78	96	114	132
0	1000	33	54	75	96	117	138	159

ward/penalty group"). Another 11 subjects, matched on %SS and SPM scores, were rewarded four tokens for speaking the syllables required in rating sessions at each delay level ("noncontingent reward/penalty group"). The results (Ingham and Andrews, 1973a) showed that the contingent reward/penalty group passed through Stage B of the program in significantly fewer rating sessions than the noncontingent group. The former group took a mean of 53.4 rating sessions (range 28–79), and the latter a mean of 72.4 rating sessions (range 40–104). From this it was concluded that the schedule increased the rate of passage through the DAF schedule. The virtue of encouraging a rapid passage through the DAF schedule in this duration-determined therapy program was that it increased the amount of time that subjects could spend in Stage C. Nevertheless, in the long term it may benefit subjects to spend more time practicing prolonged speech in the clinic; but if subjects are stuttering, they may take longer to complete Stage B and this may offset the gains of increased practice. Clearly this is an empirical question in need of an answer.

In Stage C an endeavor was made to monitor the performance of subjects as they passed through a hierarchy of increasingly difficult speech situations. Quite obviously the judgment of a "difficult" speech situation is subjective. Some subjects referred to situations that are exceedingly difficult to embrace within a therapy program. Therefore, a four-level hierarchy of speaking situations was established to replace some clinic rating sessions. At the first level, subjects carried a cassette recorder and obtained a 1000-syllable recording of their speech while conversing with an unfamiliar hospital patient. A sequence of two stutter-

SPEECH AND TOKEN SYSTEM. TABLE SHOWS TOKEN PENALTIES FOR MINUTE (SPM) RATE DURING EACH "DELAY" LEVEL
(from Ingham and Andrews, 1973a)

Target SPM range tokens rewarded 4	−1	−2	−3	Fast SPM tokens penalized −4	−5	−6	−7
30–60	66	72	78	84	90	96	104
60–92	101	110	119	128	137	146	155
90–124	136	148	160	172	184	196	208
120–156	171	186	201	216	231	246	261
150–188	206	224	242	260	278	296	314
180–220	241	262	283	304	325	346	367

free recordings, with speech rate at above 180 SPM, entitled subjects to move to the next level. Failure to achieve the target speech behavior on two occasions meant the subject returned to the final level in Stage B. At the next highest level, in Stage C, subjects wore a concealed cassette recorder and conversed with salesmen in a nearby shopping center. The same speech-performance criterion level had to be met before proceeding to the next level. Failure to achieve this meant the subject returned to the previous level. Before beginning the third level, subjects began telephone conversations during intervals between rating sessions. These were 400-syllable conversations that were also rewarded or penalized with tokens. Telephone calls could be made at any time throughout the duration of Stage C, but only to strangers. In the third level of the hierarchy, subjects arranged and were interviewed for a job. This involved telephone calls and conversations with intermediary personnel before the actual interview. Entry to this level was contingent on subjects' attaining complete fluency on a sequence of two of the telephone conversations. For the final level in the hierarchy, a situation that the subjects (all male) agreed was the most difficult was chosen: Each subject had to obtain 500 syllables of conversation with girls on the street in a well-known red-light area of the city. When a subject had obtained a sequence of two recordings stutter free, and above a minimum speech rate at each level in the hierarchy, he completed Stage C.

Experiments on treatment-process variables in phase 2. The program just discussed provoked (and continues to provoke) a number of questions about the effect of the many subject and procedural variables that formed the treatment process. These included the extent to which performance changes in this program were related to changes in experienced, or "state," anxiety (Spielberger, 1966). A sample of eight subjects in the program were asked to rate their "tension state" in each rating session. The results (Ingham and Andrews, 1971b) showed that the mean rating increased slightly throughout the treatment process. It ranged from "I felt tense and definitely not comfortable" to "I felt very tense and very uncomfortable." Insofar as these statements describe state anxiety, there seemed to be no evidence that anxiety reduction was associated with improved speech performance.

Another issue was the extent and form of difference in speech performance resulting from S.T. speech and prolonged speech. There were obviously qualitative differences between these speech patterns, but it was not clear that these differences influenced speech behavior in the latter part of the program. An earlier report by Meyer and Comley (1969) suggested that "speech blockers" experienced special difficulties in acquiring fluent rhythmic speech. While this was not evident in similar subjects during the instatement phase (Stage B) of the token-economy program, there were indications of related effects in the later stages of the program: The low level of stuttering that occurred during this stage was invariably characterized by severe blocks. Furthermore, this appeared to contrast with an impression derived from the Prolonged Speech group: Members seemed to evidence milder moments of stuttering in this phase. Accordingly, data were sought that would resolve the issue (Ingham and Andrews, 1971a). In the first instance, moments of stutter were divided into mild and severe categories: The latter included blocks and prolongations, as these were assumed to be more "effortful" than sound or syllable repetitions. The judiciousness of this division is questionable since multiple sound or syllable repetitions are probably just as effortful. Nevertheless, this category was regarded as more likely to include the milder or less debilitative moments of stutter. Secondly, in pursuit of an answer to the initial question, subjects were selected from the S.T. Speech- and Prolonged-Speech-treated groups. Both groups were matched on %SS before treatment and on the total moments of stutter in the last five rating sessions in Stage C (in this period each subject spoke 10,000 syllables). The percentage of total stutters that were sound or syllable repetitions was calculated before and at the end of treatment. The results summarized in Table 2 indicate that the end-of-treatment "residual" moments of stutter in the prolonged-speech group were almost all characterized by sound or syllable repetitions, but in the S.T.-speech group almost three-quarters of these moments were blocks or prolongations.

TABLE 2

DIFFERENCES BETWEEN SYLLABLE-TIMED AND PROLONGED SPEECH TREATED GROUPS BEFORE AND AFTER TREATMENT ON SOUND OR SYLLABLE REPETITIONS

(from Andrews and Ingham, 1972a)

Treatment variable	Before treatment		End of treatment	
	Mean % syllables stuttered	Sound or syllable repetitions as % of total syllables stuttered	Mean % syllables stuttered	Sound or syllable repetitions as % of total syllables stuttered
Syllable-timed Speech N = 10	13.70	41.50	0.19	37.90
Prolonged Speech N = 10	11.30	40.66	0.14	93.20
t-Test Finding	p = N.S.	p = N.S.	p = N.S.	p < 0.001

In addition to these differences in "quality of stuttering," both groups demonstrated differences in speech rate during the last 15 rating sessions. Although matched on %SS and mean SPM before treatment, there were important differences in the relationship between stuttering and speech rate in both groups at the end of Stage C. Within the last 15 rating sessions, both groups displayed similar mean %SS scores and a similar number of stutter-free rating sessions. But there were marked differences in the speech rate of both groups in rating sessions in which stutters were recorded. The S.T.-speech group was significantly slower than the prolonged-speech group during "fluent" rating sessions: The mean SPM rate in the S.T.-speech group (189.96) was close to the lower end of the target speech rate range (180–220 SPM), while the prolonged-speech group mean (218.55) was near the top of that range. However, in stuttered rating sessions, the S.T.-speech group spoke significantly faster (208.09), and the prolonged-speech group spoke slightly slower (211.90). This finding lent some credence to an impression of differences in speech quality of both groups at the end of treatment: S.T.-speech group seemed restricted in their rate, while moments of stutter appeared merely to impede the flow of speech in the prolonged-speech group.

Another point of concern in the program was the extent to which the speech remained under token control. If fluency was stable only in contingent token-earning sessions during Stage C, its potential durability outside of treatment was poor. One method of determining the durability of speech during treatment was provided by two situations in which token control was not maintained. The first was a probe-measure condition in which subjects made a recording of their speech away from treatment conditions. The second was a series of noncontingent token-earning telephone conversation sessions during Stage C. The 30-minute probe session at the end of each treatment day provided speech-performance data for comparison with similar data from immediately following rating sessions. The trend of mean %SS scores from both situations for all subjects is shown in Figure 5. Only %SS scores are shown because many S.T.-speech group subjects did not have SPM scores recorded during rating sessions. Figure 5 indicates that the falloff in performance when token control was removed was not substantial.

In the telephone conversation task, five groups of subjects followed an *ABAB* experimental schedule: In the *A* sections, subjects were rewarded four tokens on each of four telephone conversations provided they spoke 400 syllables; in the *B* sections, the four calls were made with the addition of a token reward/penalty schedule. The group mean %SS in all four conditions were, respectively, 3.77, 1.95, 2.59, and 0.85. Thus there was a reduction during the contingent-tokens condition (*B*), but the noncontingent-tokens condition (*A*) was not associated with

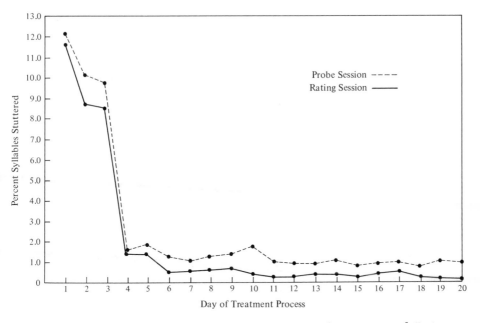

Figure 5. Mean %SS scores for subjects (n = 39) in Probe Sessions and Rating Sessions during Token-Economy Stuttering Therapy program.

complete performance relapse. In fact, the trend of improvement in performance was similar in both conditions.

Winkler (1973) has recently highlighted the pivotal role that token savings play in the effective operation of a token economy. This variable was also significant in this program. Throughout the telephone calls, the trend of token savings was found to be relatively stable. But two groups of subjects were isolated whose savings behavior varied markedly during this period. Five subjects had relatively high savings during the first contingent-token period and low savings during the second contingent-token period. Another group of five subjects had a similar trend of savings except that low savings preceded high savings. Although the relationship between saving levels and contingent-token conditions was fortuitous, rather than a result of experimental manipulation, the trend of scores for both groups (Figures 6 and 7) suggests that high savings may negate token control. In turn this suggests that other instances of poor responsiveness to token control were associated with high savings. As a result, a number of investigations are currently being conducted to seek an optimum token value that will maximize token control. It may be that individualized token values are more likely to achieve this purpose, although this may not be possible because of the problem in determining these values within the short time that subjects are in the hospital.

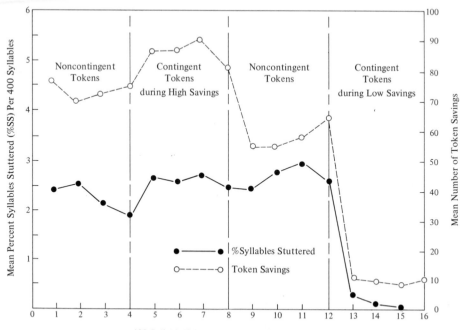

Figure 6. Mean %SS scores and token savings for four subjects who exhibited "high savings" followed by "low savings" during non-contingent and contingent token rewarded telephone conversations. (From Lahey, B., Ed., *The Modification of Language Behavior*, 1974. Courtesy of Charles C Thomas, Publisher, Springfield, Illinois.)

Stage C also included procedures designed to maintain token-control conditions between rating sessions. It was initially anticipated that stuttering could be controlled by simply using response-contingent token penalties. Therefore, base-rate recordings were made of between-rating-session group conversations from five-minute samples. Response-contingent penalties were then introduced: one token for each moment of stuttering during these between-rating-session periods. The results, shown in Figure 8, indicated that subjects reduced stuttering but also ceased talking. After extinguishing this condition, a more demanding condition was introduced: response-contingent token penalties for each moment of stutter *and* five seconds of silence. Figure 8 shows that under these conditions, the number of syllables spoken was reduced, but not to the same extent as in the previous treatment condition. While some subjects resorted to monosyllabic obscenities to avoid being penalized for five seconds of silence, in the main subjects spoke as frequently as during base-rate and extinction conditions.

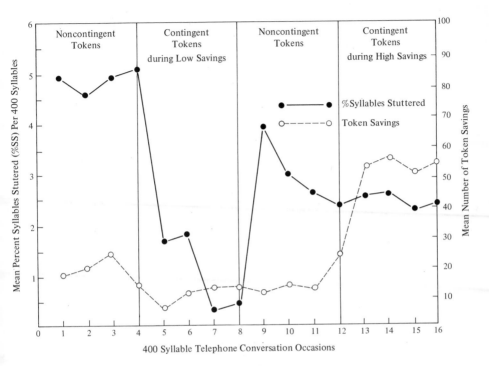

Figure 7. Mean %SS scores and token savings for four subjects who exhibited "low savings" followed by "high savings" during non-contingent and contingent token rewarded telephone conversations. (From Lahey, B., Ed., *The Modification of Language Behavior*, 1974. Courtesy of Charles C Thomas, Publisher, Springfield, Illinois.)

Treatment-outcome evaluation in phase 2. The treatment-outcome evaluation in this experimental program was made by assessing subjects with a battery of personality and speech questionaires, as well as with a group and an individual version of the Iowa Job Task (Johnson, Darley, and Spriestersbach, 1963) on six occasions: six months before treatment, immediately before treatment, immediately after treatment, three months after treatment, six months after treatment, and nine months after treatment. The personality tests were the E.P.I. (Eysenck and Eysenck, 1963), N.S.Q. (Scheier and Cattell, 1961), and I.P.A.T. Self-Analysis Anxiety Scale (Cattell, 1963). The speech questionnaire was the Stutterers' Self-Rating of Reactions to Speech Situations (Johnson, Darley, and Spriesterback, 1963). A three-mode factor analysis was conducted on subject scores and measures on each assessment occasion after a procedure described by Bird (1970). From this analysis four major factors were retrieved, with loadings on measures that suggested the following labels: fluency (factor 1), anxiety (factor 2), depression

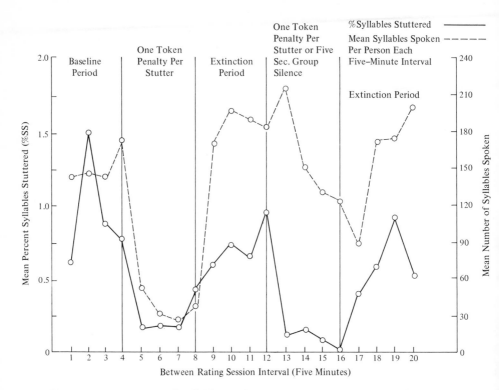

Figure 8. Mean %SS and syllables spoken per person scores during token penalty conditions for stuttering followed by conditions in which penalties were also given for five seconds "silence" in group.

(factor 3), and sensitivity (factor 4). The design of the treatment process did not anticipate changes in personality scores or factors. Nevertheless, if changes do occur in speech behavior, it may follow that this influences patterns of interaction—including those referred to within personality questionnaires.

Factor scores for each subject on each factor and on each occasion revealed the trend shown in Figure 9. Over the six assessment occasions, it is evident that changes in the mean fluency-factor scores were independent of those in the three personality factors. It is arguable whether a group analysis, or even the measures used, could ever identify the variety of subtle changes that may occur in behaviors alluded to by the personality factors. It is only evident that there was no gross common trend associated with changes in the fluency factor. Yet this factor included individual and group Iowa Job Task %SS and rate of speech scores, *as well as* subject self-ratings of avoidance, reaction, and stuttering in situations on the Stutterers' Self-Rating of Reactions to Speech Situations scale. Consequently, there is evidence that self-assessed avoid-

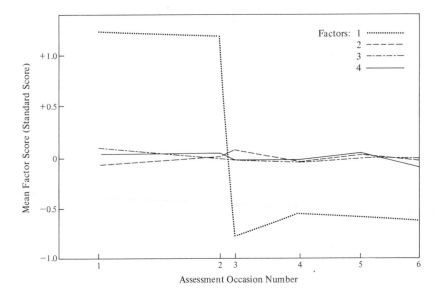

Figure 9. Trend of mean factor scores derived from outcome assessment battery given to subjects (n = 39) on six assessment occasions: Session 1 (six months before treatment); Session 2 (immediately before treatment); Session 3 (immediately after treatment); Session 4 (three months after treatment); Session 5 (six months after treatment); Session 6 (nine months after treatment). (From Andrews and Ingham, 1972a.)

ance of and reactions to situations also changed with treatment. In general, after treatment subjects regarded themselves as coping with situations in a more than adequate fashion.

Of further interest was a post hoc evaluation made to compare the performance of subjects treated by either S.T. speech or prolonged speech. Although this is a dubious procedure, it has the merit of drawing attention to important trends within data. From each treatment group, two groups of 12 subjects were identified who were closely matched on %SS scores on the individual Iowa Job Task immediately before treatment. The means and standard deviations (in parentheses) for both groups are shown in Table 3. There was no significant difference between the %SS in both groups on any occasion. But on each posttreatment occasion (occasions 4, 5, and 6), there was a significantly faster rate of speech in the prolonged-speech group—even though before treatment they spoke at a slower mean rate than the S.T.-speech group. The difference between these two groups was also reflected in fluency-factor scores, which were significantly different—in favor of the prolonged-speech group—on each posttreatment occasion.

Of more relevance to therapy outcome evaluation was the speech

TABLE 3

MEAN AND STANDARD DEVIATIONS % SYLLABLES STUTTERED AND
SYLLABLES SPOKEN PER MINUTE SCORES OF TWO MATCHED GROUPS
(N = 12) ON EACH TREATMENT OUTCOME ASSESSMENT OCCASION

Assessment occasions	Syllable-timed speech group		Prolonged speech group	
	Mean % syllables stuttered	Mean syllables spoken per minute	Mean % syllables stuttered	Mean syllables spoken per minute
1	16.28 (10.83)	103.83 (37.5)	17.61 (10.57)	96.4 (41.5)
2	16.18 (9.26)	102.50 (34.5)	16.65 (8.99)	88.7 (30.5)
3	1.02 (2.81)	202.6 (31.2)	0.00 (0.00)	204.9 (22.8)
4	3.57 (4.12)	179.8 (35.4)	1.37 (3.50)	208.8 (42.1)
5	3.90 (7.12)	180.7 (48.1)	0.67 (1.55)	208.0 (27.8)
6	2.74 (5.27)	180.9 (35.4)	0.55 (1.20)	208.8 (24.1)

performance of all subjects nine months after treatment. Again a comparison between S.T.-speech- and prolonged-speech-treated subjects, which is shown in Table 4, revealed a trend indicating that the latter group gained more from treatment. Nine months after treatment, 9 of the 16 subjects (56.2 percent) in the S.T.-speech group were recorded stutter-free and speaking at above the lowest level of the target speech rate range (180 SPM). In the prolonged-speech group, 15 of 23 subjects (65.2 percent) were in the same category.

TABLE 4

MEAN PERCENT SYLLABLES STUTTERED AND SYLLABLES SPOKEN PER
MINUTE OF ALL SUBJECTS TREATED BY EITHER SYLLABLE-TIMED
SPEECH OR PROLONGED SPEECH ON EACH TREATMENT OUTCOME
ASSESSMENT OCCASION

Assessment occasions	Syllable-timed speech group		Prolonged speech group	
	Mean % syllables stuttered	Mean syllables spoken per minute	Mean % syllables stuttered	Mean syllables spoken per minute
1	13.80	113.7	18.16	93.6
2	13.57	111.6	16.41	91.3
3	0.77	204.4	0.11	206.7
4	3.17	186.5	1.80	204.6
5	2.92	189.7	0.58	208.0
6	2.07	191.7	0.50	204.8

At first glance the therapy outcome results appear encouraging. They suggest that improved fluency was maintained over a nine-month period and that prolonged speech was more beneficial as a therapy agent within the context of the token-economy program, at least for this sample of adult subjects. But this is a very superficial view of the data. In the first place, what has been evaluated is not the extent to which therapy procedures change and maintain fluency, but rather the number of persons who change and maintain changes in fluency as a result of a group of relatively standardized procedures. It is conceivable, for example, that some subjects may have benefited from a more extended or complex therapy schedule. Moreover, it is unlikely that the range of speech situations in Stage C of the program could have embraced the relevant "difficult" speech situations for each subject. Another questionable aspect is the dubious relevance of the methods used to assess the robustness of therapy gains over time and across situations. For instance, although the Iowa Job Task has the merit of being a standard speech situation, it gives no indication of performance in other situations. Furthermore, an assessment procedure in which the subject is aware he is being assessed is loaded with possible discriminative stimuli that could have derived from the therapy program. On the other hand, some decision must be made about what part of the subject's speaking behavior must be sampled, under what conditions, and over what time in order to obtain some confidence in therapy outcome. Another important consideration, particularly in the case of therapy using a new speech pattern, is the extent to which posttherapy speech behavior is similar to normal speech. The type of data measures used to assess therapy outcome in this program gives no indication of the normalcy of speech: %SS and SPM could just as appropriately describe whispering, shouting, or singing.

Phase 3:
Extensions to the design of the token-economy stuttering therapy program

The current adult therapy program (Ingham and Andrews, 1973c) incorporates extensions and modifications derived from the earlier program. These changes stem principally from the difficulty some subjects reported experiencing in maintaining fluency across situations after treatment. The evidence of these difficulties was anecdotal rather than documented, although a covert assessment made on the prolonged-speech group 15 months after treatment revealed more relapse than had been evident on an earlier overt assessment (Andrews and Ingham, 1972b). Notwithstanding this evidence, a combined token-system/prolonged-speech program has been retained; but the duration of procedures for instating, transferring, and maintaining fluency has been increased. In the prolonged-speech instatement phase, the number of rating sessions is increased so that subjects are required to complete six consecutive fluent rating sessions at each delay level. Each rating session in the level must be within the target-speech-rate range for that level.

The transfer stage has been increased in duration and complexity. Subjects are required to pass through different types of speaking situations: (1) speaking to male patients, (2) speaking to female patients, (3) telephoning strangers, (4) speaking with salesmen in shopping centers, (5) speaking with family members at home, (6) speaking with colleagues in place of employment, (7) making a speech before an audience of strangers, and (8) speaking on the telephone in a radio "talk-back" program. Subjects rank these situations into their own hierarchy and are then required to obtain a sequence of three recordings of 1300 stutter-free syllables within the target speech rate. This is 170–210 SPM or slightly slower than in the earlier program. On completing the transfer stage, subjects are discharged from the hospital (and the token system) and begin the maintenance stage.

The maintenance stage is a sequence of decreasingly frequent follow-up contacts. One week after treatment, subjects return to the hospital and complete three different types of rating sessions: a normal rating session, a telephone conversation, and an interview with either a male or a female patient. If the target behavior is achieved in the 1300 syllables in each session, the subject returns two weeks later for the same session. If the same target behavior is achieved, the subject returns four weeks later and, if OK, three months later. If at any time in these four maintenance-stage assessments the subject fails to achieve the target behavior, he returns the following week and begins this "weaning schedule" once more. If no trend of improvement is detected in a sequence of three successive weeks, this schedule is regarded as not beneficial and the subject is discharged from the maintenance stage. Subjects are then assessed at three-month intervals for nine months after total or partial completion of the maintenance stage.

This program represents only a partial step toward a therapy model in which the methodology of operant conditioning can be fully transferred from the laboratory into stuttering therapy. To fulfill this aim, it would seem necessary to have an initial period of total control over speech behavior until fluency is fully instated. Under the same level of control, this new behavior should be transferred into increasingly typical and demanding speech situations. Continuous control over the subject's speech behavior should then be reduced systematically until the subject is able to maintain fluency across all situations. In many respects this program still falls short of this goal. Progress through the program is not fully performance-contingent, as subjects are not able to return to the transfer stage if they fail in the maintenance stage. There is also a rather sharp withdrawal of behavior-control conditions when subjects pass from the transfer to the maintenance stage. Finally, it is not possible to monitor performance across the transfer-stage situations in the maintenance stage. These inconsistencies are unfortunately due to a combination of hospital administration practice and conflict of therapy and employment practices: Adult subjects simply cannot come and go from their jobs according to the demands of a stuttering therapy schedule. Perhaps these problems may not be as great with children because other aspects of their lives are able to be put aside more easily for purposes of therapy. Thus far, it has only been possible to develop a program for adults that approximates these goals. The question that now remains is whether this approximation program is sufficient. Unfortunately, at present this question can only be answered partially because outcome evaluation presents almost as many problems as therapy.

Attributing posttherapy performance gains to therapy, as Paul (1969) has noted, is hazardous: Uncontrolled variables in the follow-up period may contribute as much to follow-up performance as, therapy. For example, it is conceivable that subjects, or those around the subjects, could consolidate gains in a therapy program with a variety of "therapeutic" endeavors. Some groups of subjects from past programs met for this purpose well after their therapy program has ended. It is therefore a moot point as to where to attribute treatment effects for those subjects. A more important consideration is, possibly, the problem of obtaining measures of speech behavior that indicate the subject's typical speech behavior across and within situations. For whatever the problem may be in follow-up evaluation, therapists are concerned mainly about subjects' speech behavior after every therapy condition is removed. One procedure presently being used is assessment at various times, and in various conditions, when subjects are unaware they are being assessed. This is usually done by arranging for "stooges" to interview or telephone subjects at odd intervals after the maintenance stage has ended. These assessments are covertly recorded and provide data unlikely to be affected by variables present during an overt assessment. Arranging such interviews is a tremendously costly and demanding task, particularly when there are many subjects. It is also often impossible to arrange covert interviews in all desirable situations.

One measure of the value of the covert interview was found in an experiment (Ingham, 1975) in which subjects were covertly and overtly assessed by strangers, nonstrangers, and over the telephone three and six months after treatment. This experiment showed that in each covert assessment the nine subjects showed %SS scores which were generally slightly higher than those obtained in overt assessment conditions. Not unexpectedly, SPM scores were very much slower in the covert condition. Perhaps a more significant finding was that six subjects were recorded stutter-free when talking to a stranger in the overt assessment condition three months and six months after treatment. But only one subject was stutter-free when covertly recorded at three months in almost identical conditions (although this increased to four subjects six months after treatment). In other conditions the findings were similar, but with different subjects. In fact only one subject was stutter-free across all situations (covert and overt) at three months and six months after treatment. Therefore, with this more rigorous assessment procedure, the results of the therapy program begin to pale when measured against the demanding goal of complete stutter-free speech over time and across situations.

One possibly confounding variable in outcome evaluation, which is presently being investigated, is the reactive effect of the assessment occasion. Subjects in past programs have often mentioned that when they were aware of a forthcoming evaluation, this signaled a time to increase vigilance over their speech behavior. Therefore, if expected assessment does exert some control over speech behavior, it is possible that this could have occurred throughout the period of overt *and* covert assessments on the previously mentioned group. For this reason the overt- and covert-assessment study is being replicated under conditions when subjects do and do not expect to be assessed. Another important issue is the extent to which measures of fluent speech in outcome evaluation of a speech-pattern therapy program are related to normal fluent speech. One way in which this question can be resolved is by observer judgments of the differences. A study is being made of listener ability to identify recordings of posttherapy speech behavior from recordings of normal speakers.

From the foregoing, the reader can deduce some idea of the issues and problems involved in behaviorally evaluating posttherapy speech behavior. There are many difficult speech situations that subjects report are likely to be associated with increased stuttering. Some can be manufactured (e.g., an argument, talking with a hostile and/or superior speaker); but to ensure they are "difficult" situations requires sampling a variety of the subject's normal and difficult speech situations at varying intervals (and possibly covertly) before and after treatment. The more sampling of speech over time and across the myriad possible speaking situations, the more likely that outcome assessments will be regarded with confidence. At the same time there is a continuing need for research into therapy evaluations so that procedures can be identified that are as necessary to therapy evaluation as, for example, reliability procedures are to evaluating experimental studies.

So far the theme of this chapter has been that procedures can be derived from or integrated with operant methodology to modify stuttering behavior. It also seems possible to extend this methodology so that this modified behavior can be transferred to situations outside the normal therapy setting. The most challenging problems involve the designing of procedures to maintain fluency with removal, or systematic removal, of treatment conditions. There is also a need to design procedures that will adequately verify the effect of these treatments on subjects' speech behavior. The rest of this chapter will be devoted to a consideration of these issues in the procedures and findings of other applications of operant methodology to stuttering therapy.

Alternative Approaches in Stuttering Therapy Using Operant Methodology

In recent years an increasing number of clinicians have published reports on applications of operant methodology in stuttering therapy. Recent reviews of these studies (Martin and Ingham, 1973; Ingham and Andrews, 1973b) have suggested there is much evidence that the procedures used have modified or eliminated stuttering during treatment conditions, but posttreatment data are generally reported poorly. Another feature is that they refer mainly to therapy conducted in conditions that occupy a relatively small period of time in the subject's speaking day. Nevertheless, this does not preclude the possibility that carry-over of therapy gains could eventually extend to all aspects of the subject's speaking behavior—thereby reducing the necessity for the treatment conditions proposed in this chapter. Unfortunately, data collection in most of these studies is rarely pertinent to this issue.

Reports of therapy applications of response-contingent stimulation procedures have mainly described techniques for reinforcing fluency. Rickard and Mundy (1965) used verbal reinforcement and token reinforcement for periods of fluent oral reading and conversation by a 9-year-old boy who stuttered. When fluency was established, the child's parents administered reinforcemnt in a "generalization" phase. Fluency was not maintained in a six-month follow-up, which was assessed by listener reports and an oral-reading task.

Russell, Clark, and Van Sommers (1968) also reported establishing fluency during oral reading with four subjects. They used "unsolicited reports" as evidence of marked improvement and carry-over in conversational speech outside of treatment.

A similar method of outcome evaluation was used by Leach (1969) to evaluate results of another fluency reinforcement procedure. Leach used money as a reinforcer for 15-second periods of fluent speech during a twice weekly 15-minute interview with a 12-year-old boy who stuttered. "Mean block rate" decreased during 42 sessions from an unspecified number to less than one per minute. No data were provided on reliability of measurement, speech rate, or a two-month posttreatment follow-up when a partial return of dysfluent speech behavior was reported.

Shaw and Shrum (1972) token reinforced brief periods of fluent speech in three children (9–10 years) within an experimental treatment schedule. In a sequence of four 20-minute sessions on each of four days, changes in the number of 10-second fluent intervals were shown to increase with the introduction of reinforcement conditions and decrease when stuttering was reinforced during a reversal condition. After cessation of fluency reinforcement conditions in the last session, the authors gave listener reports of improved fluency in carry-over that were combined with a school speech therapy program.

Bar (1971) reported that 44 of 59 children (2–6 years) treated by verbal reinforcement of fluency became fluent speakers. But no data were provided in support of this claim.

Browning (1967) reported a reduced percent of words stuttered during a treatment program for a hospitalized 9-year-old schizophrenic boy. The treatment involved a combination of relaxation training, token and verbal reinforcement by the experimenter for fluency, and social reinforcement. There was also some evidence of response-contingent punishment because the subject was required to repeat statements that included a speech error. It is interesting to note that this program was conducted each day, in a relatively programmed environment, and with a final step which included social reinforcement. It is therefore regrettable that follow-up data were not reported.

Response-contingent punishment procedures have seen relatively little application in therapy in spite of many experimental demonstrations of their efficacy. McDermott (1971) reported a combination of time-out for moments of stuttering and token reinforcement for periods of fluency with a 9-year-old boy. Performance-contingent changes were also made in the number of listeners during 24-minute sessions conducted two and three times a week. Self-recording was also used to aid generalization. Follow-up, 15 weeks after termination of treatment, found a relapse to 3.4 percent of words stuttered, though this compared favorably with a pretreatment 13.9-percent mean base-rate. Details on reliability, rate of speech, and follow-up assessment procedures were not given.

Martin, Kuhl, and Haroldson (1972) also used a time-out procedure in the treatment of stuttering in two preschool boys (3.5 and 4.5 years old). Subjects coversed with a puppet that was situated within an illuminated stage room. The puppet ceased talking and the stage was darkened for 10 seconds following each moment of stuttering during once-a-week 20-minute sessions. Stuttering was reduced to near zero in both children from a base-rate of approximately 6.0 percent and 2.5 percent of words stuttered, respectively. Stuttering remained near zero during extinction sessions, while frequency of words spoken by both children did not decrease. Generalization was assessed by a probe measure which showed that the trend of scores was the same when subjects spoke with another person outside treatment. Carry-over was assessed from covert recordings made of subject's speech with family members: One subject emitted six stutters in over 2000 recorded words, while the other subject was stutter-free in nearly 1400 words. Follow-up recordings made a year after treatment showed less than 1 percent of words stuttered in the first subject and a slightly lower percentage in the other. These findings, coupled with a high level of reliability in measurement, make this one of the more promising demonstrations of the efficacy of a response-contingent punishment procedure in stuttering therapy. But in the absence of reversal conditions within the treatment design, it is still possible that the treatment procedure was not solely responsible for the improvements in fluency that occurred.

Ryan (1971a) has also provided results with a program in which fluency was verbally or token reinforced; in some subjects, stuttering was punished by repeating stuttered words, counting, or token penalties. After achieving a low stuttered-words-per-minute rate in conversation during 50-minute clinic sessions, various transfer and maintenance programs were scheduled for the home and school. Follow-up in four or five cases (ages 6–9) was reported 8–12 months after treatment, but no data were provided on word output or the procedure used for follow-up assessment.

Operant procedures have been applied to a variety of other types of behavior within stuttering therapy procedures. Shames (1969b) initiated one such experimental therapy program by integrating a combined reinforcement/punishment schedule with the procedures that clinicians used in a "Van Riper type" therapy program. Desirable and undesirable verbal responses by the subject to these procedures were accordingly reinforced by praise or punished by therapist silence. An adult subject was reported to increase desired responses and decrease undesirable responses over 17 50-minute sessions held twice weekly. Some stuttering behaviors were also reduced, although they were not included within the schedule. An 18-year-old subject was trained to identify his stuttering behaviors and use certain types of speech behaviors to reduce his stuttering behavior. Verbal rewards and penalties were delivered as a consequence of appropriate and inappropriate speech behaviors. The results showed that stuttering decreased to zero over approximately 20 sessions. Follow-up reports of fluency in various other situations were not supported by data.

Subsequently, Shames and his colleagues at the University of Pittsburgh reported therapy programs that have integrated response-contingent schedules for modifying both verbal responses and certain speech behaviors. These largely stem from a report by Shames, Egolf, and Rhodes (1969) on a reduced speech modification schedule and three Thematic Content Modification Programs (TCMP) designed to modify verbal behavior. Some examples of treatment with these programs were provided, along with intratherapy data. Egolf, Shames, and Blind (1971) described a variation on clinician-identified target behavior in a program for an adult female who stuttered. At first, poor eye contact during conversation was verbally punished; this was followed by a TCMP schedule and reinforcement for self-reports of reduced avoidance behavior. Stuttering frequency and severity decreased throughout treatment and were zero in a one-year follow-up session. Unfortunately, a continuing trend of reduced stuttering during and after treatment makes it difficult to ascribe changes in fluency to any aspect of the program.

Wahler et al. (1970) also reported a study in which contingency-management procedures were directed to nonspeech behavior. Secondary problem behaviors in two boys (aged 9 and 4) who stuttered were identified and response-contingently punished by the parents: These behaviors were "oppositional behaviors" in one and "activity shifts" in the other. These behaviors decreased during treatment and increased with the removal of treatment. But a parallel change was also found to occur in frequency of stuttering in both children. The schedules of punishment were continued in the home by the parents; stuttering was virtually reduced to zero, and word output was not reduced below baserate. Six-month follow-up sessions with one child showed zero stuttering and no decline in word output rate. In the other child, zero stuttering was maintained in follow-up sessions over an unspecified period.

There is obviously a great deal that is wanting in most of the foregoing therapy reports. But in some, particularly by Martin, Kuhl, and Haroldson (1972) and Wahler et al. (1970), there is promising evidence of the efficacy of response-contingent procedures in stuttering therapy. Perhaps there is also some indication in the findings that modifications to certain patterns of interaction have an associated effect on stuttering. In addition, it is probably significant that reported gains in therapy with older children, although culled from methodologically questionable studies, tend to be less stable and durable over time. Nevertheless, it is difficult to regard many of these therapy procedures as more than preliminary attempts at a serious application of operant methodology in therapy.

Rhythmic and prolonged-speech patterns have formed the foundation for a number of therapy programs that have used stimulus-control procedures in one way or another. Again there is a disappointing absence of data on the long-term durability and (of more relevance with this procedure) the quality of speech of subjects after treatment (Ingham and Andrews, 1973b). Some of these therapy programs have employed contingency-management procedures to maintain and shape speech patterns toward normal fluency. In the main, the sole concern in most reports of these therapies appears to have been to control and reduce stuttering behavior.

Reports on the therapeutic use of rhythmic stimulation to control stuttering can be divided into two parts: those that have used self-monitored rhythmic speech and those that report continuous or intermittent use of devices which deliver rhythmic stimulation. The former are mainly reports on the application of self-monitored rhythmic speech, such as S.T. speech (Andrews and Harris, 1964; Holgate and Andrews, 1966; Brandon and Harris, 1967). These have indicated that the procedure resulted in reduced frequency of stuttering. But no description has been given of a therapy schedule designed to either shape this speech pattern toward a target behavior or transfer improvements attained within the clinic setting. These programs generally prescribed "a method" for the subject, and its efficacy was determined by the amount of reduced stuttering on completion of a fixed-duration program. Wolpe (1969) and Wohl (1970) also reported unaided use of rhythmic speech within descriptions of therapy procedures. In none of these programs was mention made of how this ostensibly abnormal speech pattern is changed into the characteristics of normal speech. Nor is information given on how the subject is expected to use his speech pattern outside therapy (Does he use it all the time? Does he reserve it for difficult speech situations?).

Virtually the same questions arise in considering the contribution of rhythmic-stimulation devices to stuttering therapy. There have been a number of reports on hearing-aid-style metronomes designed to provide stutterers with continuous, audible rhythmic stimulation (Meyer and Mair, 1963; Wohl, 1968; Rothman, 1969). A portable tactile-stimulation unit has also been described (Azrin, Jones, and Flye, 1968) for delivering rhythmic pulses to the subject's wrist.

The main advantage these devices offer therapy is that the principal treatment condition can be constantly maintained and transferred to all speaking situations. One demonstration of this is found in Brady's (1971) Metronome-Conditioned Speech Retraining Therapy Program. This individualized program begins with slow, rhythmic speech practice (using a desk metronome) in clinic conditions. The subject is then taught to increase speech rate while maintaining a low nonfluency rate (no more than 20 percent of the nonfluency rate he exhibited before treatment without the metronome). At the same time the subject is taught "normal cadence and junctioning of speech" by varying pauses, number of words, and word lengths accompanying each stimulus beat. The desk metronome is then replaced by a small electronic metronome that is worn behind one ear. The subject then works through a hierarchy of difficult speech situations. If stuttering is not controlled, the subject slows his speech rate and uses a more exaggerated form of rhythmic speech. When fluency is attained in all situations, the subject removes the metronome and works through the difficult speech situations once more. The difficulty in evaluating this therapy program is that neither base-rate data nor details on the speech of subjects outside the clinic situation are provided. Data are also lacking on speech rate and the extent to which posttherapy speech approached normalcy. Also, only 12 of the 23 subjects who were assessed on follow-up were reported not wearing the electronic metronome. Nevertheless these subjects showed a mean percent reduction in "nonfluencies" of 73 percent when compared with their pretreatment level, although no subject (wearing or not wearing the electronic metronome) was reported free of non-fluency. Subsequently, Brady reported (Brady and Brady, 1972) that improvement in almost all subjects had been maintained after a 10-month follow-up. Solicited clinicians' reports have suggested that these improvements are achieved with several different clinicians and subjects (Berman and Brady, 1973).

The quality of speech behavior following rhythmic speech stuttering therapy is virtually an ignored issue in most therapy reports, though it is far from unrecognised. Jones and Azrin (1969) reported an experimental study on the effects of varying stimulus duration time (using a tactile rhythmic stimulus) on stuttering. They included a measure of the "naturalness" of speech and found a concomitant increase in observer ratings of naturalness as duration time of a rhythmic pulse was systematically increased by up to two seconds (with a fixed one-second interpulse time). Perhaps, therefore, by altering the duration of the rhythmic stimulus at an appropriate stage in a therapy schedule, a method may exist for shaping rhythmic speech into the cadence of normal speech. Even if this cannot be achieved, it could be that for some subjects, as Brady (1971) points out, the naturalness of speech is immaterial provided they can control their stuttering behavior. In fact they may choose to wear an aid to their speech with the same willingness that the hard-of-hearing wear a hearing aid. Some support for this notion is provided by Umberger (1971) and Adams and Hotchkiss (1973), who reported that some subjects found both the speech pattern and the earpiece metronome quite acceptable. Silverman and Trotter (1973) noted that listeners reported both adverse and less-than-adverse reactions to rhythmic speech according to pretreatment stuttering severity. Consequently, normal speech may not always be a desired or necessary target speech behavior for this therapy procedure. In general, however, there is a paucity of data from therapies using rhythmic speech. For example, there is no evidence within therapy reports on the extent to which therapists' instructions are involved in controlling the efficacy of this therapy procedure. There are also no reported speech performance data on the speech behavior of subjects in nonclinic speech situations. It would seem that the technology skill that has been devoted to developing the electric metronome could now be devoted to the development of a procedure for recording subjects' speech outside of therapy conditions, thereby providing the foundations of a more behaviorally based therapy program.

Since Goldiamond (1965) pointed to the appearance of a speech pattern he termed "prolonged speech," within the context of an operant-conditioning procedure using DAF, a large number of therapy programs have been reported utilizing various aspects of Goldiamond's procedure. Most have been concerned with establishing and shaping the prolonged-speech pattern toward normal speech. Few, if any, have actually employed the response-contingent schedule originally used to establish prolonged speech within Goldiamond's procedure. This is not surprising since Goldiamond (1967) noted that this speech pattern could be obtained without benefit of DAF. Nevertheless, this change in procedure also fundamentally changes therapy methodology. Prolonged speech is therefore no longer a consequence of a replicable procedure (regardless of whether or not the procedure was necessary), but is virtually a consequence of a therapist's instructions—and thereby subject to the vagaries of therapist judgments as to whether prolonged speech is being spoken by the subject. It might be argued that therapist judgment played a substantial part in Goldiamond's original procedure since, as he reported, other speech patterns also appeared during DAF conditions but were not as desirable as prolonged speech. Presumably these were either rare or controlled; Goldiamond (1965) has reported that 48 subjects (aged 8–56) have achieved fluency by this procedure. Regrettably, these preliminary findings have not been followed by posttherapy assessment.

Webster and Lubker (1968) reported that they achieved "marked improvements" in the fluency of 14 subjects from a program using continuous DAF conditions in an otherwise replicated version of Goldiamond's procedure. A subsequent program reported by Webster (1970) abandoned experimenter control over oral-reading rate and instructed subjects to make consonant sounds with decreased speed and amplitude as well as smooth transitions between speech sounds within a word. Very careful training in this procedure with oral reading and conversation has characterized later reports of this program (Webster, 1971, 1972a). These include the use of an on-line computer to signal to subjects the accuracy with which they achieve target behaviors. This goes some distance toward developing a procedure that reduces therapist judgment from the initial establishment of prolonged speech. Some results of this therapy procedure have been reported (Webster, 1971) with pretherapy and posttherapy (6–30 months) data on 16 subjects (8–52 years). Oral-reading assessments on both occasions indicated that stuttering was reduced to almost zero, but no information was provided on speech-rate performance across situations or on the normalcy of posttherapy speech.

Curlee and Perkins (1969) reported a therapy program that used conversation during continuous DAF conditions. The DAF schedule was essentially similar to Goldiamond's except that subjects established their own speech rate at each delay level. If the subject emitted more than two stutters in 5 minutes (within a 15-minute session), he returned to the preceding level. After completing the hierarchy, a response-contingent time-out procedure (Haroldson, Martin, and Starr, 1968) was used to control speech rate, phrasing, and stuttering. This step was followed by sessions in which "site and social complexity successive approximation procedures" were used with each individual to aid in the transfer of fluency to the individual's nonclinic environment. In this preliminary report, the authors claimed that 15 adults and adolescent achieved speech that "could be judged as within normal limits of rate, fluency and prosody" in the clinical laboratory. The subjects estimated their stuttering decreased 75–95 percent outside his setting. Subsequently, Perkins (1973a) reported further alterations to this therapy procedure that tend to shift the emphasis of therapy methodology even more toward the motor-linguistic apects of prolonged speech. Progress through a DAF schedule, including increase in speech rate, is contingent on "breath-stream management," fluency, prosody change, and subjects' self-confidence that they can maintain fluency. Breath-stream management is included because Perkins (1973b) assumes that "the smooth, easy flow of breath from the initial through the final syllables of each phrase will necessarily exclude abnormal dysfluency" (p. 287). To achieve this, subjects are instructed to use a "a soft vocal attack to initiate phrases, maintenance of continuous airflow through the phrase, and a style of vocal production conducive to airflow" (p. 287). Procedures for improving speech prosody involve concomitant increases in phrase length and speech rate during the DAF hierarchy. Self-confidence is determined by subjects' judgment that their speech feels easy to produce. In a companion paper (Perkins, 1973c), a description is given of therapy goals and procedures for a therapist to implement these techniques and generalize fluency. Of special interest in the treatment procedure was a concern to maintain subjects' speech pattern within the clinic, and *not* outside the clinic, until they reached the stage in treatment where fluency was to be transferred to outside situations. The report on therapy research (Perkins, 1973a) from which this program emerged indicated that 17 subjects (aged 19–51) were treated by generally similar procedures and approximately 53 percent achieved normal fluent speech six months after completion of treatment. This was according to a "stringent criterion of improvement" (85 percent below pretreatment %SS and above 225 SPM speech rate).

Among the many notable aspects in Perkins's (1973a) evaluation of this program is the finding that subjects treated on a three-hour-per-day program completed treatment in three-fifths the number of treatment hours required by a group treated on a three-hour-per-week schedule. Another is the methodology for outcome assessment: Speech-sample recordings of subjects treated by this procedure and another group treated by the Curlee and Perkins (1969) procedure were compared on a number of variables with a sample of normal speakers (the normal speakers were members of a college public-address course). It was found that listeners judged subjects treated by the Perkins (1973c) procedure as speaking as fluently and expressively as normal speakers, although the normal speakers were judged as speaking significantly faster. There was also evidence of a correlation between %SS scores obtained in the clinic situation and similar scores obtained in a range of easy-to-difficult situations in which subjects recorded themselves outside of the clinic.

There are many extremely interesting and attractive features in Perkins's report of this therapy program. Perhaps the most attractive is that it addresses itself to the problem of restoring normal fluency as well as removing stuttering. Nevertheless, there are some substantial problems with the program. The procedure used to establish the characteristics of normal fluency (e.g., breath-stream management, prosody, and self-confidence) are not described in ways that permit easy replication. Also, the method of judging soft vocal attack, continuous airflow, number of words in a phrase, and the like is not described. Presumably, as with judgments of stuttering, the methodology relies on observer skill and observer consistency in using the skill. Consequently, the reliability of these judgments should be established before the crucial features of the subject's speech behavior can be regarded as being more than capriciously managed within therapy. It should also be mentioned that there is little evidence in this program, or in the design of the program, that these behaviors are subjected to stimulus control; if anything, they can only be described as therapist-controlled procedures and similar to many nonbehaviorally oriented therapies. Indeed it is fair to add that Perkins (1973b) regards effective stuttering therapy as likely to be composed of many nonbehavioral features.

Among other reports of therapy procedures using DAF, Watts (1971) used continuous DAF to instate prolonged speech within an 11-day (two hours per day) group therapy program for eight subjects (ages not specified). Following brief DAF practice, subjects were instructed to maintain prolonged speech at all times and in all situations. No details on the treatment schedule were provided, and follow-up four months after treatment, using severity-of-stuttering assessments, indicated substantial relapse outside of clinic conditions. Ryan (1971a) established prolonged speech with continuous DAF in a schedule that incorporated verbal and token reinforcement for fluency at each delay level. No data were presented indicating that reinforcement modifies rate of passage through the schedule. But a transfer and maintenance schedule designed for each subject was reported (Ryan, 1971b) to result in maintained improvement when compared with outcome for subjects not treated by a complete transfer and maintenance schedule. The procedure for outcome evaluation was not described, nor was evidence presented on the resemblance between improved or maintained fluency and normal speech.

The foregoing studies clearly indicate that prolonged speech has slowly assumed the status of a therapy technique. It has shifted from a description of a speech pattern, which is a by-product of another set of procedures, to the position that it is now *the* procedure. Yet the necessary and sufficient features of this speech pattern that are associated with changes in stuttering behavior have been only vaguely defined. Some of the phonetic features of prolonged speech have been described in a general fashion or are alluded to within a number of studies. It seems that reduced speech rate is an important element initially, though there is no evidence (so far) of attempts to use this procedure without alteration in speech rate. "Gentle onset," "soft contacts," or reduced vocal effort at the beginning of vocalizing all imply some reduced initial vocal intensity on certain phonemes or, perhaps, a slower rate of increase in amplitude of the speech signal. If the latter is the case, perhaps variation in vocal intensity at crucial points in speech behavior should be more closely explored. "Continuous vocalization," or reduced pause intervals during vocal activity, is also mentioned, but as yet there is little evidence pointing to the extent of pause reduction necessary to reduce stuttering. Indeed all, any, or many other aspects of speech behavior may describe prolonged speech. In any event, in the absence of a more relevant description of the operations necessary to achieve this speech pattern, it is unfortunately possible that this procedure could fossilize into another therapy "method."

Nevertheless, even if the crucial features of prolonged speech were located, the problem that still remains is to devise a therapy schedule which will sustain appropriate changes in the subject's speech. It seems unlikely that intermittent therapy is sufficient to control and maintain these changes, as this type of procedure appears to require constant and accurate feedback to ensure that relevant features are being maintained. One solution is to employ portable speech-signal recording equipment that may be used to feed back departure from the target characteristics of prolonged speech. Holbrook and Bailey (1973) have suggested that a portable "voice intensity controller," which is used in therapy for voice disorders, may be suitable for instating and shaping prolonged speech. Webster (1972a) is also proceeding in this direction with exploratory investigations of a device that delivers an aversive stimulus (mild shock) consequent on cessation of voice signal within a voice-activated period of time: Ostensibly, this results in negative reinforcement of continuous vocalization. If this procedure results in a reduction or elimination of stuttering, shaping and weaning from the device would be the next appropriate step; this step could be contingent on maintained fluency verified by some method of speech monitoring. These are only some of the endless possibilities open to stuttering therapy from the spectacular developments in electronics in recent years. If nothing else, these developments offer one avenue for meeting the demanding requirements of operant methodology in a treatment setting.

One alternative approach this author is currently exploring is the use of telemetry in a therapy setting. Although this auditory-bound procedure is limited by absence of visual observation of the subject's behavior, it has the merit of enabling continuous monitoring of speech behavior and remote delivery of a stimulus to the subject contingent on the appearance of undesirable (or desirable) speech behavior. Telemetry technology has the additional benefit of permitting covert monitoring of the subject's behavior in various situations and over time. By this means it may be possible to shift away from the group approach, an inherent feature of the Token-Economy Stuttering Therapy Program, to more intensive study of the individual.

Summary and Conclusions

This chapter has considered the relevance, application, and general contribution of operant methodology to stuttering therapy. In doing so a general description and analysis were provided of the Token-Economy Stuttering Therapy Program, which was developed in an endeavor to fulfill the requirements of operant methodology in stuttering therapy.

In recent years operant methodology in laboratory studies on stuttering behavior has demonstrated that the frequency of these behaviors in oral reading and spontaneous speech can be brought under stimulus control. Under these conditions, most requirements of this methodology can be fulfilled. In therapy programs using operant methodology, the requirements are not as easily met. Honig's (1966) outline of the requirements of operant methodology was used to identify some of the areas of difficulty. Perhaps the most problematic is the requirement that the behavior be continuously observed and the environment rigorously controlled. This is especially true with therapies that seek to replace the pattern of speech behavior containing stuttering with a fluent speech pattern: Typical therapy conditions do not permit continuous control over a subject's speech behavior, or speaking environment, which is necessary to ensure that the new speech pattern is maintained across situations and over time. These difficulties are compounded by the problem involved in reliably identifying and measuring stuttering behavior. There is also a need to control for changes in stuttering behavior that result in an alteration to the contextual features of speech behavior, as well as alterations in the environmental context of the subject's speech behavior.

The rapidly accumulating reports on applications of operant methodology to stuttering therapy were also reviewed. They suggest that the contribution of operant methodology to the development of reliable and effective therapy procedures is far from satisfactory. Some reasons for this are highlighted in the conclusions that Martin and Ingham (1973) reached in their review of stuttering therapy reports on applications of response-contingent stimulation procedures:

> There is evidence that the procedures may affect changes within some therapy programs, but the data are difficult to evaluate. Most reports are premature and do not include carefully obtained carry-over or follow-up data. Most reports contain no information at all about the reliability of the observers. Many reports do not employ a carefully specified and unambiguous stuttering response class. Many reports do not make it clear that the treatment variable under study is in fact responsible for the change in stuttering. Most reports contain no data about the extent to which speech parameters other than fluency are modified. Hopefully, future clinical studies will take account of these shortcomings, even though it may be expensive. In the interim, there is little reliable evidence to support the use of response contingent treatment procedures in stuttering therapy. (pp. 126–127)

This conclusion can also be extended to include therapy programs that amalgamate speech-pattern procedures and operant methodology. An additional reason for the questionable status of these therapy reports may be that more often than not they have been unable to apply fully the requirements of operant methodology.

Consequently, at this point in time the potential of operant methodology in stuttering therapy, particularly with nonstuttered aspects of speech behavior and nonspeech behavior, has hardly begun to be realized. In fact, its major contribution may not be in demonstrations of the operant nature of aspects of speech behavior but in detecting the complex controls that motor-linguistic aspects of vocal behavior may have over stuttering behavior. In turn, this may lead to an expanding and fruitful contribution of yet another derivative of psychological theory to speech pathology.

References

Adams, M. R., and Hotchkiss, J. (1973) Some reactions and responses of stutterers to a miniaturized metronome and metronome conditioning therapy: Three case reports. *Behavior Therapy*, 4, 565–569.

Adams, M. R., and Moore, W. H., Jr. (1972) The effect of auditory masking on the anxiety level, frequency and dysfluency, and selected vocal characteristics of stutterers. *Journal of Speech and Hearing Research*, 15, 572–578.

Adams, M. R., and Popelka, G. (1971) The influence of "time-out" on stutterers and their dysfluency. *Behavior Therapy*, 2, 334–339.

Ainsworth, S. (1971) Methods for integrating theories of stuttering. In L. E. Travis, ed., *Handbook of speech pathology and audiology*. New York: Appleton.

Andrews, G., and Harris, M. (1964) *The syndrome of stuttering*. Clinics in Developmental Medicine, No. 17, London: Heinemann.

Andrews, G., and Ingham, R. J. (1972a) An approach to the evaluation of stuttering therapy. *Journal of Speech and Hearing Research*, 15, 296–302.

Andrews, G., and Ingham, R. J. (1972b) Stuttering: An evaluation of follow-up procedure for syllable-timed speech/token system therapy. *Journal of Communication Disorders*, 5, 307–310.

Atkinson, C. J. (1952) Vocal responses during controlled aural stimulation. *Journal of Speech and Hearing Disorders*, 17, 419–426.

Ayllon, T., and Azrin, N. H. (1965) The measurement and reinforcement of behavior of psychotics. *Journal of Experimental Analysis of Behavior*, 8, 357–383.

Ayllon, T., and Azrin, N. H. (1968) *The Token Economy*. New York: Appleton.

Azrin, N. H., Jones, R. J., and Flye, B. (1968) A synchronization effect and its application to stuttering by a portable apparatus. *Journal of Applied Behavior Analysis*, 1, 283–295.

Baer, D. M., Wolf, M. M., and Risley, T. R. (1968) Some current dimensions of applied behavior analysis. *Journal of Applied Behavior Analysis*, 1, 91–97.

Bar, A. (1971) The shaping of fluency, not the modification of stuttering. *Journal of Communication Disorders*, 4, 1–8.

Barber, V. (1939) Studies in the psychology of stuttering. XV. Chorus reading as a distraction in stuttering. *Journal of Speech Disorders*, 4, 371–383.

Barber, V. (1940) Studies in the psychology of stuttering. XVI. Rhythm as a distraction in stuttering. *Journal of Speech Disorders*, 5, 29–42.

Beech, H. R., and Fransella, F. (1968) *Research and experiment in stuttering.* London: Pergamon.

Berman, P. A., and Brady, J. P. (1973) Miniaturized metronomes in the treatment of stuttering: A survey of clinicians' experience. *Journal of Behavior Therapy and Experimental Psychiatry,* 4, 117–119.

Bernard, J. R. L. (1965) Rates of utterance in Australian dialectic groups. Occasional Paper No. 7. University of Sydney, Australian Language Research Centre.

Bird, K. (1970) Dimensions of driving performance. Paper read to Australian Psychological Society Annual Conference, Hobart.

Black, J. W. (1950) Some effects upon voice of hearing tones of varying intensity and frequency while reading. *Speech Monographs,* 17, 95–98.

Bloodstein, O. (1950) A rating scale study of conditions under which stuttering is reduced or absent. *Journal of Speech and Hearing Disorders,* 15, 29–36.

Bloodstein, O. (1972) The anticipatory struggle hypothesis: Implications of research on the variability of stuttering. *Journal of Speech and Hearing Research,* 15, 487–499.

Brady, J. P. (1969) Studies on the metronome effect on stuttering. *Behaviour Research and Therapy,* 7, 197–205.

Brady, J. P. (1971) Metronome-conditioned speech retraining for stuttering. *Behaviour Therapy,* 2, 129–150.

Brady, J. P., and Brady, C. N. (1972) Behaviour therapy of stuttering. *Folia Phoniatrica,* 24, 255–259.

Brandon, S., and Harris, M. (1967) Stammering—an experimental treatment programme using syllable-timed speech. *British Journal of Disorders of Communication,* 2, 64–86.

Browning, R. M. (1967) Behaviour therapy for stuttering in a schizophrenic child, *Behaviour Research and Therapy,* 5, 27–35.

Brutten, G. J. (1972) Behaviour assessment and the strategy of therapy. In Y. Lebrun and R. Hoops, eds., *Neurolinguistic approaches to stuttering.* Proceedings of the International Symposium on Stuttering, Brussels.

Brutten, G. J., and Shoemaker, D. J. (1967) *The Modification of Stuttering.* Englewood Cliffs, N.J.: Prentice-Hall.

Brutten, G., and Shoemaker, D. J. (1971) A two-factor learning theory of stuttering. In L. E. Travis, ed., *Handbook of Speech Pathology and Audiology.* New York: Appleton.

Burke, B. D. (1969) Reduced auditory feedback and stuttering. *Behaviour Research and Therapy,* 7, 303–308.

Cattell, R. B. (1963) *I.P.A.T. Self Analysis Scale.* Champagne, Ill.: Institute for Personality and Ability Testing.

Cautela, J. R. (1969) Behavior therapy and self control. In C. M. Franks, ed., *Behavior therapy: Appraisal and status.* New York: McGraw-Hill.

Chase, R. A., Sutton, S., and Rapin, I. (1961) Sensory feedback influences on motor performances. *Journal of Auditory Research,* 1, 212–223.

Cherry, C., and Sayers, B. McA. (1956) Experiments upon the total inhibition of stammering by external control, and some clinical results. *Journal of Psychosomatic Research,* 1, 233–246.

Cooper, E. B., Cady, B. B., and Robbins, C. J. (1970) The effect of the verbal stimulus words "wrong," "right" and "tree" on the disfluency rates of stutterers and nonstutterers. *Journal of Speech and Hearing Research*, 13, 239–244.

Curlee, R. F., and Perkins, W. H. (1969) Conversational rate control therapy for stuttering. *Journal of Speech and Hearing Disorders*, 34, 245–250.

Daly, D. A., and Cooper, E. B. (1967) Rate of stuttering adaptation under two electro-shock conditions. *Behaviour Research and Therapy*, 5, 49–54.

Dunlap, K. (1932) *Habits: Their making and unmaking.* New York: Liveright.

Egolf, D. B., Shames, G. H., and Blind, J. J. (1971) The combined use of operant procedures and theoretical concepts in the treatment of an adult female stutterer. *Journal of Speech and Hearing Disorders*, 36, 414–421.

Egolf, D. B., Shames, G. H., and Seltzer, H. N. (1971) The effects of time-out on the fluency of stutterers in group therapy. *Journal of Communication Disorders*, 4, 111–118.

Eysenck, H. J. (1960) *Behaviour therapy and the neuroses.* London: Pergamon.

Eysenck, H. J., and Eysenck, S. B. G. (1963) *Eysenck Personality Inventory.* London: University of London Press.

Ferster, C. B., and Skinner, B. F. (1957) *Schedules of reinforcement.* New York: Appleton.

Findley, J. D. (1966) Programmed environments for the experimental analysis of human behavior. In W. K. Honig, ed., *Operant behavior: Areas of research and application.* New York: Appleton.

Flanagan, B., Goldiamond, I., and Azrin, N. (1958) Operant stuttering: The control of stuttering behavior through response-contingent consequences. *Journal of Experimental Analysis of Behavior*, 1, 173–177.

Fransella, F. (1965) The effects of imposed rhythm and certain aspects of personality on the speech of stutterers. Ph.D. dissertation, University of London.

Fransella, F., and Beech, H. R. (1965) An experimental analysis of the effect of rhythm on the speech of stutterers. *Behaviour Research and Therapy.* 3, 195–201.

Goldiamond, I., (1965) Stuttering and fluency as manipulable operant response classes. In L. Krasner and L. P. Ullman, eds., *Research in behavior modification.* New York: Holt, Rinehart & Winston.

Goldiamond, I. (1967) Supplementary statement to operant analysis and control of fluent and non-fluent verbal behavior. Report to Department of Health, Education, and Welfare. Public Health Service. Application No. MH-8876-03.

Greenspoon, J. (1955) The reinforcing effect of two spoken sounds on the frequency of two responses. *American Journal of Psychology*, 68, 409–416.

Halvorson, J. (1971) The effects of stuttering frequency of pairing punishment (response cost) with reinforcement. *Journal of Speech and Hearing Research*, 14, 356–364.

Ham, R., and Steer, M. D. (1967) Certain effects of alterations in auditory feedback. *Folia Phoniatrica*, 19, 53–62.

Hanley, T. D., and Steer, M. D. (1949) Effect of level of distracting noise on speaking rate, duration and intensity. *Journal of Speech and Hearing Disorders*, 14, 363–368.

Haroldson, S. K., Martin, R. R., and Starr, C. D. (1968) Time-out as punishment for stuttering. *Journal of Speech and Hearing Research*, 11, 560–566.

Holbrook, A., and Bailey, C. W. (1973) Measurement of daily talking time with VIC (Voice Intensity Controller). Paper read to American Speech and Hearing Association Convention, Detroit.

Holgate, D., and Andrews, G. (1966) The use of syllable-timed speech and group psychotherapy in the treatment of adult stutterers. *Journal of the Australian College of Speech Therapists*, 16, 36–40.

Honig, W. K. (1966) *Operant behavior: Areas of research and application.* New York: Appleton.

Horan, M. C. (1968) An improved device for inducing rhythmic speech in stutterers. *Australian Psychologist*, 3, 19–25.

Hoshiko, M., and Holloway, G. (1968) Radio telemetry for the monitoring of verbal behavior. *Journal of Speech and Hearing Disorders*, 33, 48–50.

Ingham, R. J. (in press, 1975) A comparison of covert and overt assessment procedures in stuttering therapy outcome evaluation. *Journal of Speech and Hearing Research*.

Ingham, R., and Andrews, G. (1971a) Stuttering: The quality of fluency after treatment. *Journal of Communication Disorders*, 4, 279–288.

Ingham, R. J., and Andrews, G. (1971b) The relation between anxiety reduction and treatment. *Journal of Communication Disorders*, 4, 289–301.

Ingham, R. J., and Andrews, G. (1971c) Stuttering: A description and analysis of a token economy in an adult therapy programme. Paper read to American Speech and Hearing Association Conference, Chicago.

Ingham, R. J., and Andrews, G. (1973a) An analysis of a token economy in stuttering therapy. *Journal of Applied Behavior Analysis*, 6, 219–229.

Ingham, R. J., and Andrews, G. (1973b) Behavior therapy and stuttering: A review. *Journal of Speech and Hearing Disorders*, 38, 405–441.

Ingham, R. J., and Andrews, G. (1973c) Details of a token economy stuttering therapy programme for adults. *Australian Journal of Human Communication Disorders*, 1, 13–20.

Ingham, R. J., Andrews, G., and Winkler, R. (1972) Stuttering: A comparative evaluation of the short-term effectiveness of four treatment techniques. *Journal of Communication Disorders*, 5, 91–117.

Ingham, R. J., Martin, R. R., and Kuhl, P. (1974) Modification and control of rate of speaking by stutterers. *Journal of Speech and Hearing Research*, 17, 489–496.

Johnson, W. (1959) *The onset of stuttering*. Minneapolis: University of Minnesota Press.

Johnson, W., ed. (1955) *Stuttering in children and adults*. Minneapolis: University of Minnesota Press.

Johnson, W., Darley, F. L., and Spriestersbach, D. C. (1963) *Diagnostic methods in speech pathology*, New York: Harper & Row.

Johnson, W., and Rosen, L. (1937) Studies in the psychology of stuttering: VII. Effect of certain changes in speech pattern upon frequency of stuttering. *Journal of Speech Disorders*, 2, 105–109.

Jones, H. G. (1970) Stuttering. In C. G. Costello, eds., *Symptoms of psychopathology: A handbook*, New York: Wiley.

Jones, R. J., and Azrin, N. H. (1969) Behavioral engineering: Stuttering as a function of stimulus duration during speech synchronization. *Journal of Applied Behavior Analysis*, 2, 223–229.

Kanfer, F. H. (1968) Verbal conditioning: A review of its current status. In T. R. Dixon and D. L. Horton, eds., *Verbal behavior and general behavior theory*. Englewood Cliffs, N. J.: Prentice-Hall.

Kazdin, A. E. (1972) Nonresponsiveness of patients to token economies. *Behaviour Research and Therapy*, 10, 417–418.

Kazdin, A. E., and Bootzin, R. B. (1972) The token economy: An evaluative review. *Journal of Applied Behavior Analysis*, 5, 343–372.

Kern, A. (1932) Der einfluss des horens auf das stottern. *Archives of Psychiatry*, 97, 429–449.

Krasner, L. (1971) Behavior therapy. *Annual Review of Psychology*, 22, 483–532.

La Croix, Z. E. (1973) Management of disfluent speech through self-recording procedures. *Journal of Speech and Hearing Disorders*, 38, 272–274.

Leach, E. (1969) Stuttering: Clinical application of response-contingent procedures. In B. B. Gray and G. England, eds., *Stuttering and the conditioning therapies*. Monterey, Calif.: Monterey Institute of Speeach and Hearing.

Lee, B. (1951) Artificial stutter. *Journal of Speech and Hearing Disorders*, 16, 53–55.

Lotzman, G. (1961) Zur anwendung veriierter verzogerungszeiten bei balbuites. *Folia Phoniatrica*, 13, 276–312.

McDermott, L. D. (1971) Clinical management of stuttering behavior: A case study. *Feedback*, 1, 6–7.

Maraist, J. A., and Hutton, C. (1957) Effect of auditory masking upon the speech of stutterers. *Journals of Speeach and Hearing Disorders*, 22, 385–389.

Martin, R. R. (1965) Direct magnitude-estimation judgements of stuttering severity using audible and audible-visible speech samples. *Speech Monographs*, 32, 169–177.

Martin, R. R., and Berndt, L. A. (1970) The effects of time-out on stuttering in a 12 year old boy. *Exceptional Children*, 36, 303–304.

Martin, R. R., and Haroldson, S. K. (1967) The relationship between anticipation and consistency of stuttered words. *Journal of Speech and Hearing Research*, 10, 323–327.

Martin, R. R. and Haroldson, S. K. (1969) The effects of two treatment procedures on stuttering. *Journal of Communication Disorders*, 2, 115–125.

Martin, R. R., and Ingham, R. J. (1973) Stuttering. In B. Lahey, eds., *The modification of language behavior*. Springfield, Ill.: C. C Thomas.

Martin, R. R., Kuhl, P., and Haroldson, S. (1972) An experimental treatment with two preschool stuttering children. *Journal of Speech and Hearing Research*, 15, 743–752.

Martin, R. R., and Siegel, G. M. (1966a) The effects of response contingent shock on stuttering. *Journal of Speech and Hearing Research*, 9, 340–352.

Martin, R. R., and Siegel, G. M. (1966b) The effects of simultaneously punishing stuttering and rewarding fluency. *Journal of Speech and Hearing Research*, 9, 466–475.

May, A. E., and Hackwood, A. (1968) Some effects of masking and eliminating low frequency feedback on the speech of stammerers. *Behaviour Research and Therapy*, 6, 219–223.

Meyer, V., and Comley, J. (1969) A preliminary report on the treatment of stammer by the use of rhythmic stimulation. In B. B. Gray and G. England, eds., *Stuttering and the conditioning therapies*. Monterey, Calif.: Monterey Institute for Speech and Hearing.

Meyer, V., and Mair, J. M. M. (1963) A new technique to control stammering: a preliminary report. *Behaviour Research and Therapy*, 1, 251–254.

Moore, W. H., Jr., and Ritterman, S. I. (1973) The effects of response contingent reinforcement and response contingent punishment upon the frequency of stuttered verbal behaviour. *Behaviour Research and Therapy*, 11, 43–48.

Naylor, R. V. (1953) A comparative study of methods of estimating the severity of stuttering. *Journal of Speech and Hearing Disorders*, 18, 30–37.

Neelley, J. N. (1961) A study of the speech behavior of stutterers and non-stutterers under normal and delayed auditory feedback. *Journal of Speech and Hearing Disorders*, Monograph Supplement No. 7, 63–82.

Nessel, E. (1958) Die verzogerte sprachruckkopplung (Lee-effekt) bei stotterern. *Folia Phoniatrica*, 10, 199–204.

Pattie, F. A., and Knight, B. B. (1944) Why does the speech of stutterers improve in chorus reading? *Journal of Abnormal and Social Psychology*, 39, 362–367.

Paul, G. L. (1969) Behavior modification research: Design and tactics. In C. M. Franks, ed., *Behavior therapy: Appraisal and status*, New York: McGraw-Hill.

Perkins, W. H. (1973a) Behavioral management of stuttering. Final report. Social and Rehabilitation Service Research Grant No. 14-P-55281.

Perkins, W. H. (1973b) Replacement of stuttering with normal speech: I. Rationale. *Journal of Speech and Hearing Disorders*, 38, 283–294.

Perkins, W. H. (1973c) Replacement of stuttering with normal speech: II. Clinical procedures. *Journal of Speech and Hearing Disorders*, 38, 295–303.

Premack, D. (1959) Toward empirical behavior laws: I. Positive reinforcement. *Psychological Review*, 66, 219–233.

Prins, D., and Lohr, F. (1972) Behavioral dimensions of stuttered speech. *Journal of Speech and Hearing Research*, 15, 61–71.

Quist, R. W., and Martin, R. R. (1967) The effect of response contingent verbal punishment on stuttering. *Journal of Speech and Hearing Research*, 10, 795–800.

Rickard, H. C., and Mundy, M. B. (1965) Direct manipulation of stuttering behavior: An experimental clinical approach. In L. P. Ullmann and L. Krasner, eds., *Case Studies in behavior modification*. New York: Holt, Rinehart & Winston.

Rogers, C. R. (1951) *Client-centered therapy.* New York: Houghton Mifflin.

Rothman, I. (1969) Practical rhythmic desensitization for stuttering with description of a new electronic pacer used for stutterers' insomnia and anxiety. *Journal of American Osteopathic Association,* 68, 573–577.

Rousey, C. L. (1958) Stuttering severity during prolonged spontaneous speech. *Journal of Speech and Hearing Research,* 1, 40–47.

Russell, J. C., Clark, A. W., and Van Sommers, P. (1968) Treatment of stammering by reinforcement of fluent speech. *Behaviour Research and Therapy,* 6, 447–453.

Ryan, B. P. (1971a) Operant procedures applied to stuttering therapy for children. *Journal of Speech and Hearing Disorders,* 36, 264–280.

Ryan, B. P. (1971b) The transfer and maintenance of fluent speech in adult stutterers using operant technology. Paper read to the American Speech and Hearing Association Convention, Chicago.

Sander, E. K. (1961) Reliability of the Iowa Speech Disfluency Test. *Journal of Speech and Hearing Disorders,* Monograph Supplement No. 7, 21–30.

Sander, E. K. (1963) Frequency of syllable repetitions and "stutter" judgments. *Journal of Speech and Hearing Disorders,* 28, 19–30.

Scheier, I. H., and Cattell, R. B. (1961) *Neuroticism Scale Questionaire.* Champagne, Ill.: Institute for Personality and Ability Testing.

Shames, G. H. (1969a) Operant conditioning and stuttering. In B. B. Gray and G. England, eds., *Stuttering and the conditioning therapies.* Monterey, Calif.: Monterey Institute for Speech and Hearing.

Shames, G. H. (1969b) Verbal reinforcement during therapy interviews with stutterers. In B. B. Gray and G. England, eds., *Stuttering and the conditioning therapies.* Monterey, Calif.: Monterey Institute of Speech and Hearing.

Shames, G. H., Egolf, D. B., and Rhodes, R. C. (1969) Experimental programs in stuttering therapy. *Journal of Speech and Hearing. Disorders,* 34, 30–47.

Shames, G. H., and Sherrick, C. E. (1963) A discussion of nonfluency and stuttering operant behavior. *Journal of Speech and Hearing Disorders,* 28, 3–18.

Shane, M. L. (1955) Effect on stuttering of alteration in auditory feedback. In W. Johnson, ed., *Stuttering in children and adults.* Minneapolis: University of Minnesota Press.

Shaw, C. K., and Shrum, W. F. (1972) The effects of response-contingent reward on the connected speech of children who stutter. *Journal of Speech and Hearing Disorders,* 37, 75–88.

Siegel, G. M. (1970) Punishment, stuttering and disfluency. *Journal of Speech and Hearing Research,* 13, 677–714.

Silverman, F. H., and Trotter, W. D. (1973) Impact of pacing speech with a miniature electronic metronome upon the manner in which a stutterer is perceived. *Behavior Therapy,* 4, 414–419.

Skinner, B. F. (1953) *Science and human behavior.* New York: Macmillan.

Soderberg, G. (1959) A study of the effects of delayed auditory side-tone on four aspects of stutterers' speech during oral reading and spontaneous speaking. Ph.D. dissertation, Ohio State University.

Speech Foundation of America (1970) *Conditioning in stuttering therapy.* Publication No. 7, Memphis, Tenn.

Spielberger, C. D. (1966) Theory and research on anxiety. In C. D. Speilberger, ed., *Anxiety and behavior.* New York: Academic.

Starbuck, H. (1971) Personal communication.

Sutton, S., and Chase, R. A. (1961) White noise and stuttering. *Journal of Speech and Hearing Research,* 4, 72.

Trotter, W. D., and Brown, L. (1958) Speaking time behavior of the stutterer before and after speech therapy. *Journal of Speech and Hearing Research,* 1, 48–51.

Trotter, W. D., and Leach, M. M. (1967) Personal experiences with a stutter-aid. *Journal of Speech and Hearing Disorders,* 32, 270–272.

Tuthill, C. E. (1946) A quantitative study of extensional meaning with special reference to stuttering. *Speech Monographs,* 13, 81–98.

Ullmann, L. P., and Krasner, L. (1965) *Case studies in behavior modification.* New York: Holt, Rinehart & Winston.

Umberger, F. G. (1971) The effect of rhythmic auditory stimulation on selected parameters of the stuttering problem. Paper read to American Speech and Hearing Association Convention, Chicago.

Van Riper, C. (1958) Experiments in stuttering therapy. In J. Eisenson, ed., *Stuttering: A symposium.* New York: Harper & Row.

Van Riper, C. (1970) Historical approaches. In J. G. Sheehan, ed., *Stuttering: Research and therapy.* New York: Harper & Row.

Van Riper, C. (1971) *The nature of stuttering.* Englewood Cliffs, N.J.: Prentice-Hall.

Wahler, R. G., et al. (1970) The modification of childhood stuttering: Some response-response relationships. *Journal of Experimental Child Psychology,* 9, 411–428.

Watts, F. (1971) The treatment of stammering by the intensive practice of fluent speech. *British Journal of Disorders of Communication,* 6, 144–147.

Webster, L. M. (1968) A cinematic analysis of the effects of contingent stimulation on stuttering and associated behaviors. Ph.D. dissertation, Southern Illinois University.

Webster, R. L. (1970) Stuttering: A way to eliminate it and a way to explain it. In R. Ulrich, T. Stachnik, and J. Mabry, eds., *Control of human behavior, vol. 2.* Glenview, Ill.: Scott, Foresman.

Webster, R. L. (1971) Successive approximations to fluency: Operant response shaping procedures for use with stutterers. Paper read to Seventeenth International Congress of Applied Psychology, Liege, Belgium.

Webster, R. L. (1972a) New help for stutterers. *Newsweek,* June 5, 49–50.

Webster, R. L. (1972b) Personal communication.

Webster, R. L., and Dorman, M. F. (1970) Decreases in stuttering frequency as a function of continuous and contingent forms of auditory masking. *Journal of Speech and Hearing Research,* 13, 82–86.

Webster, R. L., and Lubker, B. B. (1968) Interrelationships among fluency producing variables in stuttered speech. *Journal of Speech and Hearing Research,* 11, 754–766.

Wingate, M. E. (1964) A standard definition of stuttering. *Journal of Speech and Hearing Disorders,* 29, 484–489.

Wingate, M. E. (1969) Sound and pattern in "artificial" fluency. *Journal of Speech and Hearing Disorders,* 12, 677–686.

Wingate, M. E. (1970) Effects on stuttering of changes in audition. *Journal of Speech and Hearing Research,* 13, 861–873.

Wingate, M. E. (1971) The fear of stuttering. *ASHA,* 13, 3–5.

Winkler, R. C. (1973) An experimental analysis of economic balance, savings and wages in a token economy. *Behavior Therapy,* 4, 22–40.

Wohl, M. T. (1968) The electronic metronome—an evaluative study. *British Journal of Disorders of Communication,* 3, 89–98.

Wohl, M. T. (1970) The treatment of nonfluent utterance: A behavioural approach. *British Journal of Disorders of Communication,* 5, 66–76.

Wolpe, J. (1969) Behavior therapy of stuttering: Deconditioning the emotional factor. In B. B. Gray and G. England, eds., *Stuttering and the conditioning therapies.* Monterey, Calif.: Monterey Institute for Speech and Hearing.

Yates, A. J. (1970) *Behavior therapy.* New York: Wiley.

Young, M. A. (1961) Predicting ratings of severity of stuttering. *Journal of Speech and Hearing Disorders,* Monograph Supplement No. 7, 31–54.

Young, M. A. (1969) Response-response agreement for marking moments of stuttering. Paper read to American Speech and Hearing Association Convention, Chicago.

VI
Stuttering as Perseverative Behavior

Jon Eisenson, Ph.D.

Professor of Special Education and Director of the Scottish Rite Institute for Childhood Aphasia, San Francisco State University Professor Emiritus, School of Medicine, Stanford University; formerly Professor and Director of the Speech and Hearing Clinic, Queens College of the City University of New York; Lecturer in Otolaryngology, College of Physicians and Surgeons, Columbia University. Fellow, American Psychological Association; Fellow, American Association for the Advancement of Science; Fellow, American Speech and Hearing Association. Author, *The Psychology of Speech, Examining for Aphasia, Aphasia in Children, Adult Aphasia, Voice and Diction;* coauthor of *Basic Speech* (with Paul Boase), *Speech Disorders* (with Mildred Berry), *Speech Correction in the Schools* (with Mardel Ogilvie), *The Psychology of the Physically Handicapped* (with Pintner and Stanton), *Psychology of Communication* (with Auer and Irwin); contributor to *Handbook of Speech Pathology and Audiology* (L. E. Travis, editor); editor and contributor to *Stuttering: A Symposium.*

Perseveration and Stuttering:
A Restatement of Position

In the first *Symposium*, (1958, pp. 225–269) we presented our hypothesis that most stutterers had a constitutional and abnormal predisposition to perseveration and that stuttering, when it occurred, was perseverative behavior manifest in speaking. Based on some of our own investigations and those of others during the period from 1930 to 1955, there seemed to be sufficient support for the basic hypothesis. However, subsequent studies (Martin, 1962 and Wingate, 1966a), perhaps more sophisticated and more carefully designed than the earlier ones, failed to support the hypothesis that stutterers had a general tendency toward perseveration in behavior other than speech. So, because theories die even more slowly than theorists, we will present a position that can still fit most of the facts about stuttering. Further, by definition of perseveration, stuttering is without a doubt linguistic perseverative behavior.

In this essay, we will try to establish (1) the constitutional (organic) differences between stutterers and nonstutterers, (2) the linguistic situations that are associated with an increase in perseveration, and (3) the therapeutic procedures that permit a stutterer to be perseverative according to his needs and yet speak so that his dysfluencies do not become frank stuttering.

Perseveration defined

Perseveration is a tendency for a mental or motor act to persist, either in overt expression or in drive, for a longer than normal time after the stimulus that evoked the behavior has ceased to be present. Spearman (1927, 165) considered perseveration to have several related aspects:

1. *Persistence or secondary function*—the persistent effect of a presentation beyond the period of conscious awareness.

2. *Recurrence*—the tendency for an act to occur when it is no longer appropriate to the situation.
3. *Hindrance*—"the degree of interference" or the degree of hindrance which the perseverating effect of past mental activity causes to a new one of the same kind.
4. *Inertia*—a generalized effect of resistance to change that is basic to perseveration in all its aspects. (p. 165)

Implicit in Spearman's concept of perseveration is a notion of "set" or a "central factor." Such a factor, in turn, implies that in order to establish attitudes and maintain a line of behavior, the organism must possess some sort of neural substrate that permits functioning relatively independent of immediate (ongoing) afferent (incoming) stimulation.

Perseveration and persistence

It should be apparent that "set," or "the central factor," is necessary for behavior—human or subhuman. Without a preparatory set, or an attitude to a situation, each event would have to be considered *de novo* and, in effect, there could be no learning. The persistence or maintenance of a set, *when and as long as* it is *appropriate*, makes for economy of intellectual functioning and behavior. However, the persistence of a set may become so strong that it interferes with new perceptions. A rigid set impairs an individual's potential for appropriate organization or reorganization of events. Perceptions become misperceptions when a set or attitude prevents awareness of differences between situations which may be only superficially alike. If this becomes the state of the responding individual, then we are dealing with perseveration rather than persistence. Perseveration interferes with, rather than enhances, learning and adjustment. We might note at this point that brain damage is associated with perseverative behavior in individuals who had no constitutional predisposition to perseveration.[1] Later we will return to this point and consider its implications for the understanding of stuttering.

Review of Studies
of Perseverative Tendencies
in Stutterers

Eisenson (1937) administered items from the Maller-Elkin Attention Test for the Measurement of Perseveration to a group of 30 male stutter-

---

[1] Perseveration is a frequent and frustrating involvement in aphasia. It is often manifest in the repetitive utterances and linguistic contaminations of aphasic patients. See Eisenson (1973, pp. 149–150) for a discussion of this subject.

ers and a matched group of 30 male nonstutterers ranging in age from 10 to 16. The test situations were arranged along the following lines: (1) A situation was presented (copying of letters, easy arithmetic calculation) in which the subject was required to perform as directed for a given period of time. (2) A variation of this situation was presented in which the subject was required to make a different response for an equal period of time. (3) A situation consisting of a combination in random order of the first two situations was then presented. The subject was then required to change his responses quickly and relatively frequently. Failure to make the required changes was interpreted as a failure to respond readily and appropriately to new and changing situations.

The results indicated that stutterers as a group made more errors (continued to respond to situations that were no longer present, such as adding when multiplying was required or writing uppercase letters when the situation called for lowercase) than did the nonstutterers. In addition, the stutterers slowed down more (completed fewer items) than the nonstutterers. Interestingly, when the experimental situation called for the continuation of the same response to a nonchanging situation, the stutterers worked more rapidly (completed more items) than the nonstutterers.

In a later study, Eisenson and Winslow (1938) experimented with a group of 15 Brooklyn College students who were in therapy at the college speech clinic and a control group of 15 nonstuttering students. The experimental situation called for the subjects to respond to (1) an original situation consisting of an arrangement of colored squares on a card exposed through the aperture of a tachistoscope and (2) variations of this situation in the form of new colors not presented on the first card and the elimination of colors shown on the first and subsequent cards. The subjects were required to respond to the color cards by noting the total number and different colors observed.

The results indicated that there was a significant difference between the stutterers and nonstutterers in their responses to color cards. The stutterers were influenced more than the nonstutterers by stimuli (colors) that were once present but were no longer physically present at the moment of the called-for response. Stutterers continued to respond to and "see" colors in new situations that had been presented only in previous situations.

In an experiment along similar lines, Goldsand (1944) measured perseveration by the reaction time for perception of a dim light after her subjects were exposed to a bright one. She concluded that stutterers as a group made higher scores (were more perseverative) than nonstutterers. She observed also that stutterers were more variable in their responses than nonstutterers.[2]

Falk (1956) investigated perseveration as one of several traits in a group of stutterers ranging in age from 5 to 59. Although he found no consistent pattern of behavior that might describe or characterize all stutterers, he did find that perseveration correlated positively with the tendency of stutterers to demonstrate tonic blocks.

An investigation of several areas of perseveration was undertaken by King (1953). Specifically, he set out to learn whether stutterers differed from nonstutterers in the areas of alternating motor perseveration, dispositional rigidity, and sensory area. He also compared male and female stutterers with one another as well as with nonstutterers. He employed a series of tests designed to measure (1) alternating motor perseveration, (2) dispositional rigidity in a motor task, and (3) sensory perseveration (maintenance of response to sensory stimulation). His subjects included 72 stuttering males, 8 stuttering females, 82 nonstuttering males, and 55 nonstuttering females.

King's main finding was that stutterers showed significantly more perseverative tendencies in general than nonstutterers. The tests that seemed to be most discriminative for the two groups were those which required a rapid and contiguous change of set. Some of King's other findings, especially those related to sex differences, are also worthy of note. Boy stutterers were significantly more perseverative than boy nonstutterers. While the same contrast was found between girl stutterers and girl nonstutterers, the differences were not as great as for the boys when the individual tests were considered. However, when the test results were pooled (the probabilities combined), the cumulative difference approached statistical significance.

On tests of dispositional rigidity, which measure the subject's ability to break away from old, well-established habits to perform according to the needs of the test situation, King found boy stutterers to be more perseverative than boy nonstutterers. Girl stutterers, however, were not more perseverative than girl nonstutterers. In general, though the results of the King experiments do not establish clear-cut sex differences in perseveration between boys and girls who do not stutter, some individual tests do show that such a difference exists.

---

[2] The factor of variability observed by Goldsand and others is consistent with the present writer's findings. Even when group differences between stutterers and nonstutterers are statistically significant, they should not alone become the basis for predicting how an individual stutterer, or a normal speaker for that matter, may behave. Variability in regard to perseveration, or of any factor that might be interpreted as "constitutional," should not be surprising.

We do not wish to leave an impression that King found uniform and consistent differences relative to perseveration between stutterers and nonstutterers. Like other investigators, he found considerable variability among stutterers. In some of the sensory tasks, there were no significant differences between stutterers and nonstutterers. Nor does King feel that his findings can support a contention, such as has been made by Spearman, that perseveration exists as a general behavioral factor. King did find, as indicated earlier, that stutterers are significantly more perseverative than nonstutterers in motor- and mental-test situations that call for a rapid and contiguous change of set.

From our point of view, the difficulty stutterers manifest in test situations calling for constant change of set is highly important. Conversational speaking, which calls for changing thought and linguistic content that cannot be readily anticipated and for which general but not specific preparation is possible, requires rapid and continuous change of set. Such speaking contrasts with the evocation of memorized content or the repetition of content previously evoked. Those speech situations, callng for relatively little change in set, are among the "easy" ones for most stutterers. We shall return to this point later. For the present we will report additional studies relevant to the thesis under discussion.

Doust and Coleman (1955), in an article supporting a neurogenic basis of stuttering, report the results of a flicker-fusion experiment with 46 adult stutterers and 131 adult nonstutterers. They found that the mean critical-flicker-fusion (CFF) threshold for the stutterers was significantly lower than for the nonstutterers. The stutterers' mean number of cycles per second for flicker-fusion was 37 compared with 41 for the fluent speakers. Stated otherwise, they found that on the average the color wheel had to be slowed down five cycles for stutterers to perceive flicker.

Although the experimenters were not primarily concerned with establishing differences in perseveration (differences in change of perception from constant color to flicker and vice versa), we think that their results may be so interpreted. On the basis of their findings, Doust and Coleman observe that "it is . . . interesting to speculate on the relationship of communication, consciousness, and the CFF and the nature of the dysplasia existing between these variables in the stutterer. If each is correlated with the other, and if discriminatory awareness is impaired outside the expressive end of the communicative spectrum, then it is probable that more than a single aspect of the process of thought may be affected" (p. 652).

We do not consider differences in flicker-fusion as presumptive evidence of neurogenic differences; such differences may also be a manifestation of anxiety. However, regardless of whether the CFF difference is neurogenic or psychogenic, it probably is related to perseverative lag in a visual-perceptual function.

Martin (1962) used tests similar to those of Eisenson with a population of 52 stutterers and 109 controls. He found no significant differences between the two populations. As an extension of his study, Martin found no relationship between the degree of perseveration in stutterers and the amount of observed stuttering. Thus, Martin found no support for a general perseveration factor in stutterers.

Wingate (1966a) used a list of general behavioral rigidity in a study involving 12 stutterers and 12 controls. His findings indicate that there were no significant differences between stutterers and control speakers.

The studies reported in this brief review employed a variety of tests and experimental designs and subjects ranging considerably in age. Thus, a firm conclusion may still not be in order. However, as we indicated earlier, the bulk of the evidence does not support a hypothesis that stuttering is a manifestation of a general tendency to perseveration. This does not, of course, obviate the assumption that stuttering in and of itself is perseveration behavior. What we shall now try to establish are the factors, organic (constitutional) and environmental, that are conducive to perseveration and, specifically, to that kind of perseveration in linguistic behavior we assess and identify as stuttering.

Psychogenic perseveration

We would be loath to leave the impression that excessive perseveration is invariably an organic component or a product of constitutional predisposition. Certainly, a temporary increase in perseverative behavior may be brought about by essentially psychological rather than organic conditions. Earlier we indicated that persons who are perseverating are attempting to make a response and perform in a manner they assume is required of them. In general, perseverative behavior is likely to occur when the motivating forces or determining tendencies for a given act are in some way interfered with (blocked, diverted, or overcome) by counterforces or inhibiting events or ideas. These inhibiting events or ideas may well have a psychogenic basis. They may arise, as Bloodstein and Sheehan point out in this *Symposium*, from competing forces to act and not to act in regard to a specific situation. The inhibiting events or ideas may arise as a result of recalled and/or anticipated penalties that may result from the expected performance. Inhibition may also arise out of a sense of insecurity as to the degree of appropriateness of the performance. Isolated or situational and infrequent episodes of perseveration are therefore not necessarily related to a chronically morbid condition or process or with any relatively constant trait of personality or character. Habitual or generalized perseveration is another matter, even if the perseverative behavior as a habitual approach to a situation had an original psychogenic onset.

Organic Differences
Among Stutterers

The search for organic differences between stutterers and nonstutterers would be more realistic as well as heuristic if we knew not only what but when particular findings may have significance and implications in the long-term history of individual stutterers. When does a given difference, if found, make for an ultimate difference in oral linguistic behavior? Organic differences that are present in one age stage may not be objectively evident at a later stage, but the effects of the difference may nevertheless impair normal development and expression of an expected function. Most developmental stages are organizational periods for a hierarchy of functions. There may be some children, so few as to be almost unique, who walk without ever having crept or crawled. Most children, however, do not stand up and take off upright without first having experience in moving about on all fours. So also, most children cry and babble and engage in echoic pseudospeech before they say their first words. Further, almost all children go through predictable stages in their phonological, morphemic, and syntactical acquisitions before they achieve a language system that, by age 3 or 4, enables them to behave linguistically in the manner of key speakers in their environment.

Unfortunately, the state of our present knowledge does not permit us to assert with confidence that a factor or a difference is causal to a function. Beyond this, we cannot or at least should not assume that all children necessarily go through particular developmental stages with the same constitutional equipment. Thus, one child may learn a function as complicated as speaking with what ordinarily is regarded as an impaired mechanism, such as a moderate-to-severe degree of hearing loss, while another, with the same objectively measured hearing loss, grows up deaf. Thus, in our review of the literature on organic difference, we should be cautious in overgeneralizing the implications of our findings. Human beings are not all alike and so we should not expect all stutterers to be alike, either in their stuttering or in factors that correlate with their atypical linguistic behavior. This observation is not intended to minimize the importance of investigations that look for differences that presumably have correlative if not frank causal implications for stuttering. We tend to overlook findings that a given percentage of stutterers in a given age group were found to manifest certain differences that distinguished them from other stutterers as well as nonstutterers. It would probably be considerably more fruitful and meaningful if our investigations compared subjects on the bases of motor, perceptual, and cognitive-developmental stages. If we were to become so oriented, we might then learn more about what makes a given child stutter even though we would not necessarily be able to account for all stuttering. With this attitude in mind, we will review some of the recent findings that suggest the possibility if not the likelihood that most stutterers have some constitutional (organic) differences that distinguish them from those of us who do not stutter.

In his review of organicity in stuttering, Van Riper (1971) observes that "throughout the centuries this belief in the organic nature of stuttering has persisted—probably because of . . . first intuitive impressions" (p. 335). Recorded organic theories go back as far as Aristotle, were prevalent and almost dominant in the nineteenth century, and have had waves of recurrence up to the present. Etiological emphases have varied from specific organ weakness—the tongue, the respiratory mechanism, the bile, the endocrine system (chemical imbalance), to the central nervous system, and particularly the brain as related to cerebral dominance for language and/or for motor functioning. Our own emphasis will be on evidence to support the hypothesis that the cerebral controls for language functioning are different for most stutterers when compared with nonstutterers. These differences, we believe, are usually constitutional but may be shown to be present for persons with acquired brain damage.

Heredity factors

In his review of heredity factors associated with stuttering, Van Riper (1971) notes: "Many of the early writings on the heredity causes of stuttering reported the family history in fairly general terms. Stutterers were interviewed to determine how many of their immediate ancestors or siblings stuttered. No control groups were used. Only the unanimity of these findings make them worth mentioning here" (p. 340). The research reported by Van Riper (pp. 340–344) is impressive in that the studies are cross-cultural; they include such countries as Russia, England, Japan, and the United States. The studies span a period of more than 50 years (1913–1966). Except for one by Sheehan and Martyn (1966), a questionnaire study on recovery from stuttering, the data all point to a hereditary and so, presumably, a constitutional factor in stuttering.

Some of the findings of the studies permit the following conclusions:

1. The sex ratio of stutterers consistently shows that more males than females stutter. The ratios range from 2 males to 1 female to 5 males to 1 female. Andrews and Harris (1964a) found a ratio of 2.5 males to 1 female in a survey of British schoolchildren. Eisenson (1966), in a study conducted in Israel, found a ratio of about 4 males to 1 female. The 4-to-1 ratio seems to be about the median for the studies reported by Van Riper (1971, p. 46).
2. There are more stutterers in families of stutterers than in families of nonstutterers.
3. There is a higher incidence of stuttering among twins than among single-born childen. The factor of twinning may be associated with premature birth and delay in onset and development of speech.
4. Stutterers as a total population have a higher incidence of delayed onset and development of speech than do normally fluent children.

In a summary of heredity factors in stuttering, Andrews and Harris (1964a), based on a long-term study in an English school system (Newcastle on Tyne), report findings of delayed onset of speech and of a higher incidence of language problems other than stuttering. They also observed the presence of neurological predisposing factors and birth traumas. However, ". . . by far the most important predisposing factor is the inheritance from either parent of the genetic predisposition to stammer" (p. 101).

Cerebral dominance and handedness

It is now clearly established that upward of 95 percent of right-handed persons have language control in the left cerebral hemisphere. In contrast, about 60 percent of left-handed persons are also left cerebral dominant for language, but about 40 percent are right cerebral dominant. Some left-handed persons and manifestly ambidextrous persons seem to have hemispheric ambilaterality for language control. This small population may then have language "equally represented" in both hemispheres.

Reviews of cerebral dominance and laterality may be found in *Adult Aphasia* (1973) by Eisenson, pp. 32–38; *Speech and Brain Mechanisms* (1959) by Penfield and Roberts, pp. 89–101; and *The Nature of Stuttering* (1971) by Van Riper, pp. 352–356. The Van Riper reference emphasizes the implications of the cerebral dominance and laterality studies for stutterers.

After reviewing the literature on handedness and cerebral dominance and studies from the early 1900s to the 1960s, Van Riper (1971) sagely concludes:

> In reviewing all this material with due regard to limitations of methodology it seems apparent that we cannot conclude that stutterers are generally left-handed or ambidextrous, at least insofar as peripheral sidedness is concerned. The question is still unresolved and will remain so until better measures of laterality preference are resolved. This does not mean that differences in *central* ambilaterality do not exist. (p. 356)

Handedness may not be a good measure of cerebral laterality because of a variety of conditions that make for change, usually in the direction of becoming right-handed. Certainly most cultures, perhaps Eastern more so than Western in current times, emphasize the desirability of being right-handed. Perhaps more important, as the data we referred to above indicate, is that handedness is not a good indicator of cerebral dominance for language. About 5 percent of right-handed persons may be right rather than left cerebral dominant for language. But a majority of left-handed persons have left cerebral dominance, and some left-handed persons and ambidextrous persons have bilateral (bicerebral) control of language function. Thus, if future studies using better indexes and measurements for hand preference were to show that stutterers are more like some left-handed persons or like most ambidextrous persons in regard to cerebral dominance for language, we might have a difference that makes a difference. A recent promising approach employs *ear preference* (auditory laterality) as an index of cerebral dominance for language.

Ear preference

Whether one has right- or left-ear preference is rarely as apparent as whether one has right- or left-hand preference in performing unimanual tasks. Ordinarily, we listen with both ears. We turn our heads with a "preferred" ear only when one ear is much better (or much worse) in receiving auditory signals than the other. Nevertheless, we do have ear preference when preference is measured by efficiency or accuracy in responding to auditory signals under special conditions. The conditions include (1) the nature of the auditory signals, (2) the presence of cerebral lesion in one hemisphere, and (3) the conditions under which the auditory signals are sent to the two ears. We will review a few studies relevant to the three special conditions.

The two cerebral hemispheres of man show differences related to the nature of the auditory signal. In general, the functional differences are along the line of whether the signal is verbal (language) or nonverbal. Milner (1962) reviewed a number of studies, including her own, and concluded that the perception of verbal material is normally a function of the left temporal lobe and that the perception of nonverbal material is normally a function of the right temporal lobe.

Kimura (1967), Bryden (1963), Carr (1969), and others, using dichotic-listening tasks, found that when verbal signals are sent simultaneously to the two ears, most persons report a right-ear preference.[3]

Dichotic-listening studies, though still relatively few in number, tend to show that the differences in auditory perception which hold for adult nonstutterers do not hold for adult stutterers. However, the findings indicate that stutterers are more variable in dichotic listening tasks than are nonstutterers. Curry and Gregory (1969) found that, out of a population of 20 stutterers, 11 had left-ear preference (more accurate reporting) compared to 5 of the normal-speaking control subjects. In addition, the size of the difference between the scores for the left and right ears was significantly smaller for stutterers than for nonstuttering control subjects. No differences were found for nonverbal tasks. If, as is assumed, cerebral dominance is related to ear preference, the results suggest that stutterers may have less clear-cut (less cerebral) asymmetry for auditory perception. This may imply that stutterers as a general population, and most individual stutterers, have a different cerebral organization—at least as hemispheric dominance for speech is concerned—than do non-stutterers. Further, these findings may suggest, as the study of Perrin (1969) with adults indicates, that the cerebral hemispheres of stutterers do not show the functional differences for speech and nonspeech, as is the situation with most nonstutterers. Specifically, Perrin found that in dichotic reception stutterers showed a *clear left-ear preference* for words and sentences. Nonstutterers, in contrast and in keeping with expected findings, showed a clear right-ear preference. Stutterers were not distinguished as a group from nonstutterers in regard to vowels and the reception of noises. Perrin concluded that "when a hemisphere exerts some control over speech functions in the stutterer, it is the right. This is the reverse of that found in most normals" (p. 117).

A study at variance with those findings is reported by Slorach and Noehr (1973). This investigation compared three groups of 15 primary-grade children who were identified as being stutterers, dyslalics, or nor-

---

[3] In dichotic listening, competing signals of the same type are sent simultaneously to the two ears. These competing signals may be verbal (digits, alphabet letters, words) or nonverbal (musical tones or balanced nonspeech signals). The subject reports what each ear hears. Thus, the accuracy of the "reporting ear" is determined. The difference in accuracy between the ears is accepted as an indication of ear preference. On the assumption that the contralateral hemisphere is the primary processor of the signals, cerebral dominance or lack of dominance is determined.

mal speakers; the children came from middle- and upper-socioeconomic background and attended primary schools in Brisbane, Australia. The dichotic-listening task consisted of 24 sets of three-digit pairs. The findings indicated that the stutterers fell between dyslalics and normal speakers relative to accuracy of right-ear reporting. All three groups showed a right-ear preference for digit reporting. Slorach and Noehr observed that certain sub-groups of stutterers showed special patterns of lateralization but did not infer that all stutterers have this factor in the etiology of their stuttering. Interestingly, the investigators also reported that of particular interest regarding the stutterers was the fact that none of them appeared to have any difficulty in reporting the digits even though all had been noted to be stuttering in general conversation prior to the test situation. They speculate: "This was probably due to the fact that the test responses were of a non-propositional nature and there was no communicative stress in the reporting of the digits" (p. 299).

The current findings on differences in cerebral asymmetry between stutterers and nonstutterers may justify a review of older theories of cerebral control that go back to the early nineteenth century in Europe and became prominent in the positions of Orton, Travis, and Bryngelson in the United States in the 1920s and 1930s. These studies are reviewed by Van Riper (1971, pp. 337–341). Basically, the theorists held that stuttering is either (1) a dysarthric involvement resulting from poor coordination of the focal, respiratory, and articulatory mechanism due to neuropathology (Kussmaul, 1877; Gutzmann, 1898) or (2) a form of aphasia, transient in nature, and associated with weakened imagery of the word that the stutterer was trying to evoke (Bluemel, 1913; Swift, 1932). A third position (Orton, 1927; Travis, 1934; Bryngelson, 1935) attributed stutterers' difficulties to a lack of cerebral (cortical) dominance between the hemispheres. Emphasis was on the motor aspect of speaking. The essential aspects of the "lack of cerebral dominance" theory included the following:

1. All muscles involved in speech production are paired and contralaterally controlled.[4]
2. The streams of impulses coming from the two cerebral hemispheres must be synchronized for the production of fluent speech.
3. Synchronization is accomplished if one cerebral hemisphere has a clear margin of dominance over the other so that its patterns, or synergies, are imposed on the articulatory utterance.
4. Stutterers have inadequate or insufficient margins of cerebral dominance compared with nonstutterers, hence the characteristic blocks, repetitions, and other manifestations of stuttering.

---

[4] Actually, some of the muscles receive impulses from the same side of the brain (homolateral); but most are contralateral.

We believe that the cerebral dominance theorists were on the right track, but possibly not in the right tract. Their error, possibly, was in the emphasis on articulation rather than the symbolic-linguistic aspect of speech. The appearance of stuttering, at least as characterized by dysfluencies and repetitions, has been noted as an accompaniment of aphasia by several observers, including Eisenson (1947) and Arend, Handzel, and Weiss (1962). Later we shall again consider the relationship between stuttering and aphasia and the parallel linguistic situations in which both stutterers and aphasics have greatest and least difficulty in speaking.

Delayed auditory feedback

The subject of delayed auditory feedback (DAF) and its implications in therapy are discussed by Ingham and Brutten in this *Symposium* and by others, including Soderberg (1969) and Van Riper (1971, pp. 382–398). Our concern for the present is with the significance of the finding that most stutterers differ from most nonstutterers in the effects of DAF on the fluency and productive output of their speech. Perhaps the DAF responses may also, in time, provide us with a critical basis for distinguishing organic from nonorganic stutterers.

Although considerably more research needs to be done before an unreserved statement should be made, we believe that in their DAF responses, most sutterers indicate they possess a defective monitoring system for propositional (intellectual-communicative) speech. Just how the monitoring system is defective is not yet clear. It may be that, except for nonpropositional speech (content that can continue on its own once triggered so that auditory feedback is not needed for the stutterer to check on what he says) the deficiency in auditory feedback is solely responsible for the distortion and resulting disruptions in speaking. A second possibility is that the integrative system is defective, so a breakdown in speech occurs when proprioceptive (motor-kinesthetic) feedback cannot be integrated (synchronized) with auditory feedback. Thus, two systems that should work cooperatively, as they do for most speakers, work competitively for most stutterers. When competition is reduced by the masking of the auditory flow so that only the motor-kinesthetic feedback system is used, most stutterers increase their fluency. (See Van Riper, 1971, pp. 391–392 for a review of studies.)

To summarize our position, stutterers for the most part show an increase in speech fluency as a DAF response whereas most nonstutterers show a breakdown in fluency and sound like stutterers. The critical DAF range and the difference in speech response occurs within 0.05 to 0.25 seconds. Black (1951) and Lee (1951) found that the critical disruptive delay for normal speakers was about one-fifth of a second.

We consider this difference to be a manifestation of a central nervous system that cannot integrate two feedback systems when oral-language output is not automatic. The result of delayed feedback for stutterers is a compensation for what the central nervous system cannot do regularly or reliably. The difference between stutterers and nonstutterers is one that organically distinguishes the two populations of speakers as a whole. It is a difference that makes for a difference.

Linguistic Conditions
Associated with Stuttering

In other contributions to this *Symposium,* notably in Bloodstein's essay, conditions associated with an increase and a decrease in stuttering are considered. Stuttering is by and large predictable, both on an individual basis and for stutterers as a special population. The overall conditions related to predictability are reviewed by Van Riper (1971, pp. 171–189). Our primary concern will be to review the linguistic conditions associated with changes in the severity of stuttering, with emphasis on utterances that require continuous formulations and involve the speaker in informative interchanges and communicative responsibility.

Hesitation as a phenomenon of speaking is not exclusive to stutterers. Persons who are regarded as normal speakers and generally fluent also hesitate (pause) in their utterances. Goldman-Eisler (1958) and McClay and Osgood (1959) found that hesitations occur normally before words that have high information value within an utterance. Soderberg (1967), in a study on linguistic factors related to stuttering, found that prolongations tended to occur on lexical items (information-carrying words) while repetitions occurred with about equal frequency on either lexical or function words (articles, conjunctions, prepositions). Thus, fairly recent studies on hesitation phenomena show parallel tendencies for nonstutterers and stutterers. The tendencies are predictable and are more severe in nature and occur more frequently for stutterers than for speakers regarded as essentially normal in regard to oral utterance. We shall now review some older studies that emphasize communicative responsibility as well as linguistic import.

In several studies, Brown (1945) found that stutterers tend to have verbal cues which are related to increased stuttering. These verbal cues include (1) initial words in sentences, (2) longer words in sentences, (3) accented syllables within sentences, and (4) nouns, verbs, adverbs, and adjectives as opposed to other parts of speech. He concluded that stutterers interpret these verbal cues as threatening and anxiety producing and, therefore, conducive to increased stuttering. But another evaluation of the findings may also be in order. Verbal cues related to stuttering—word position, word length, and parts of speech—are generally those that carry the burden of meaning in communicative speech. Longer words may be anxiety producing because of the stutterer's lack of familiarity with them. They may also be words that, because of lack of occurrence and practice, do not provide a basis for familiar or habitual articulatory set. They may also be the significant words in the sentence in terms of what the speaker is trying to communicate.

Eisenson and Horowitz (1945) found that stutterers experienced increased difficulty in oral reading as the intellectual significance or meaningfulness (propositionality) of the material was increased.[5] Three selections of varying propositional value were used: a simple list of 130 words, a nonsense selection of 130 words, and a meaningful paragraph taken from a letter written by Franklin Delano Roosevelt. Each of the three selections contained the same set of 20 adjectives, ranging in length from one to five syllables. The number of other parts of speech (nouns, verbs, prepositions, etc.) was determined for the propositional selection, and the same number was used for the first two selections. The subjects, 23 male and 3 female college students, were attending in college speech clinics.

Some of the specific findings of the study included the following: (1) An increase in the propositional value of an oral-reading selection was accompanied by an increase in stuttering on nouns, verbs, adverbs, and adjectives. (2) In contrast, there was a decrease in stuttering on words conventionally classified as pronouns, conjunctions, and articles. There was no significant difference with reference to prepositions. (3) There was a greater difference in total percentage of stuttering between a meaningful and a nonsense selection than between a nonsense selection and a list of words. In general, Eisenson and Horowitz observed that "the content of the reading selection determines whether an utterance is composed of a series of sounds or a series of semantic units. As meanings and the responsibility for communicating meanings become prominent, stuttering increases. . . . The stutterer has greatest difficulty in the utterance of propositional speech" (198).

The earlier mentioned studies by Brown and by Eisenson and Horowitz, and the observations of Bluemel (1957, chaps. 3, 9), suggest strongly that many if not most stutterers experience difficulty in communication, in saying something meaningful and expected in terms of the overall situation.

---

[5] A proposition is a unit of intellectually meaningful linguistic content. Nonsense material, oaths, and utterances expressive of strong feelings and emotions are non-propositional. Language that occurs in regular sequence, such as counting and reciting the alphabet, may be considered as having low propositional value.

From our point of view, stuttering will not be understood unless we evaluate the linguistic component in the speaking situation. Most stutterers can speak nonsense if they are not expected to make sense. When not suffering from stage fright, they can speak from memory better than impromptu. But memorized content does not call for intellectual organization and linguistic formulation, as does impromptu and conversational speech. Stutterers can speak alone, to themselves, because there is no challenge to what they have to say and no response from a listener that may call for a quickly formulated linguistic response from them. In this situation they are not engaged in meaningful, propositional language usage but in an exercise in the use of word-forms that resemble phonetically, but not semantically, real word usage. This is also the case when stutterers "talk" to nonunderstanding animals or to young children who have not arrived at the stage of wanting to know, or daring to ask, what the words to which they were exposed are supposed to mean.

In choral situations, when the stutterer shares the responsibility for this artificial and pseudocommunicative situation, most stutterers also speak with comparative fluency. Here again we are dealing with a situation in which, to say the least, the stutterer shares but does not carry the individual responsibility for what is said.

In contrast to these relatively easy situations, we can generalize the difficult situations along the following lines: The incidence of stuttering for most stutterers increases when the individual finds himself unequal to the demands of the speaking situation. In such a situation the stutterer suffers from a temporary breakdown or disorganization of propositional language usage. The linguistic disturbance becomes most apparent in situations which normally require that the speaker (1) formulate the language symbols (the propositional units), (2) evoke the proposition orally, audibly, and individually, and (3) anticipate an immediate specific response, oral or otherwise, appropriate to the situation and to his initial evocation. Under these conditions, the stutterer cannot maintain an established linguistic set. He must expect to make continuous changes consistent with the demands of the changing linguistic situation. He must anticipate that he will utter not just one linguistic unit, for which he may prepare, but also additional units for which specific preparation is possible. He may have difficulty with his first-formulated linguistic unit because of his anxiety in anticipating the need for not-yet-formulated linguistic units. Under this general condition, the stutterer who may also be a constitutional perseverator has his greatest difficulty in speaking. The difficulty may be aggravated by anxiety; but it originates because of the stutterer's basic difficulty in communicative interchanges and so his tendency to perseverate in situations not normally conducive to much perseveration for most speakers. We shall return to this point later.

Aphasic involvements and stuttering

We have made reference to the presence of speech that strongly resembles stuttering in persons who, after incurring brain damage, became aphasic. Beyond the presence of dysfluencies—hesitations, repetitions, and occasional blocks—there is another parallel feature between aphasia (language impairment associated with brain damage) and stuttering. The feature is in the nature of the language that is most difficult for aphasics to formulate and evoke and the nature of the language that is more easily retrievable for most aphasics. In *Adult Aphasia*, Eisenson (1973) states, "Aphasia is an impairment of language functioning of persons who have incurred localized cerebral damage that results in a reduced likelihood that an individual involved in a communicative situation will understand or produce appropriate verbal formulations" (p. 26). In general, the greater the degree of adjustment required of the brain-damaged individual to determine the adequacy and appropriateness of the verbal formulations in his communicative interchange, the greater the likelihood that he will experience difficulty. In contrast, set verbal formulations that express strong feelings, emotion, and established series such as the days of the week, months of the year, and counting are better retained, retrieved, and evoked than are formulations that call for specific formulation according to the particular needs of the communicative situation. We may generalize the differences by using the terms "creative language" for verbal formulations and productions that are specifically informative (communicative) and "preestablished language" for those that require no creative formulation. The terms "propositional" for creative formulations and "nonpropositional" for the set formulations have been used to designate the language of aphasic persons. Aphasia is often defined as an impairment of propositional language usage.

Although we can oversimplify and overgeneralize the similarities between aphasia and stuttering, several features are shared:

1. Many aphasics, especially in the early states of their recovery, manifest the hesitations and repetitions of stuttering.
2. Propositional (communicative, informative) utterances are most difficult for aphasics and stutterers; nonpropositional utterances are relatively easy.
3. Singing well-memorized songs or reciting well-memorized verse or prose selections (preformulated content) is considerably easier than language content that requires ongoing formulation.

Although stuttering, or speech resembling stuttering, may well be one of the associated impairments of aphasia, it does not necessarily follow that stuttering is a form of aphasia. Nevertheless, we can appreciate why several previously cited authorities consider stuttering to be a form of transient aphasia. We do, however, believe that it is consistent with what we know about stuttering and stutterers to refer to stuttering as *a transient disturbance in informative, communicative (propositional) language usage.* We shall return to this point later in a more complete statement of our position on the nature and likely etiology of stuttering.

Modification and reduction
of the incidence and severity of stuttering

Let us now review two types of studies relative to the reduction of the incidence and severity of stuttering. The first type deals with the nature of different speaking situations and the reaction of stutterers to these situations. The second deals with "controlled" speaking situations in which stutterers modify their speech with repeated responses to the "same" situation.

Bloodstein (1950) reported on a study in which he sought to determine the conditions under which stutterers report their stuttering to be reduced or absent. He presented a list of 115 conditions reported in the literature as being relatively easy for stutterers. Some of these conditions, such as speaking to an animal, speaking nonsense, and reciting from memory, have been discussed earlier. Bloodstein found that it was possible to specify 100 conditions under which a fairly large proportion of his subjects, 50 adult stutterers, reported a substantial reduction in stuttering. He classified these specific conditions into six general conditions: reduced communicative responsibility, reduced need to make a favorable impression, absence of unfavorable listener reaction, changes in speech pattern, associated activity (speaking while walking, speaking to a set rhythm), and intense or unusual stimulation.

Bloodstein noted that, despite the strong tendency for uniformity of conditions under which stuttering is reduced or absent, there was considerable variability: "In part, this variability is probably an artifact of the wording of the item. For example, it is obvious that 'ordinary conversation with your mother' involves very different objective stimulus conditions depending upon whether the behavior of the mother tends to be critical, distressed, sympathetic, indifferent, or understanding" (p. 35). In general, variability can probably be accounted for by differences in the subjects' evaluations of the speaking situation, whether it is a mother, stranger, policeman, or formal audience.

Among other studies of interest on the reactions of stutterers to speaking situations is one by Trotter and Bergmann (1957). They compared the ratings of a group of 50 stutterers (41 males and 9 females), having a mean age of 22, with the ratings of 100 nonstuttering members of a college psychology class. The Speech Situation Rating Sheet for Stutterers, developed by Johnson, was used to rate 40 speaking situations. A comparison of the findings for two groups indicated the following:

1. Stutterers tend to avoid speaking situations more and enjoy speaking less than nonstutterers. However, a considerable number of nonstutterers were more avoidant of speaking situations and reported that they enjoyed speaking in them less than did many stutterers.

2. Those nonstutterers who most avoid speaking situations also enjoy speaking in them the least. They are also the most nonfluent of the nonstuttering speakers.

3. There is a tendency for stutterers and nonstutterers to agree in a relative way in their reactions to different kinds of speaking situations. With the important exception of using the telephone, situations most avoided by nonstutterers tend also to be most avoided by stutterers; those least enjoyed by nonstutterers are also least enjoyed by stutterers; those in which nonstutterers are found to be most nonfluent are the ones in which stutterers have greatest difficulty. In regard to all situations involving the use of the telephone were ranked much higher in avoidance by stutterers than by nonstutterers. For instance, "telephoning to inquire about a price, train fare, etc." was ranked second in avoidance by stutterers and nineteenth by nonstutterers.

On the basis of these findings we may conclude that, in general, the difference between the reactions of stutterers and nonstutterers to many speaking situations is one of degree. Those situations that are difficult or not pleasant for nonstutterers are more so for stutterers. The interesting exception is the telephone situation, which appears to be considerably more disturbing for most stutterers than for most nonstutterers. This finding supports the impression most clinicians have that the telephone is a bugaboo for stutterers. The reason for this could be that when a person initiates a telephone call he is expected, at least at the outset, to say something, to reveal or communicate the purpose of his call. Moreover, he is expected to identify himself, to assume communicative responsibility.

Adaptation studies. A series of studies at the University of Iowa was concerned with the "adaptability" of the stutterer to recurring speaking situations. The general problem considered was the effect of repeated utterances of the "same" linguistic content in reading and in self-formulated speech. Johnson and Knott (1937) and Johnson (1955) demonstrated that when stutterers read a given passage several successive times there is a decrement in the incidence of stuttering between the first and fifth consecutive readings. As a rule, marked decrements are found as early as the second reading of the passage. Leutenegger's procedure (1957) varied from some of the earlier adaptation studies in that different time intervals (20 minutes, 1 hour, and 24 hours) took place between successive readings of the same passage. The subjects were 36 adolescent and adult stutterers (31 males and 5 females) ranging in age from 15 years 6 months to 37 years 5 months, with a mean of 22 years 2 months.

As indicated, Leutenegger found evidence of significant adaptation (reduced incidence of stuttering) as early as the second trial and continued evidence of adaptation with successive trials. Beyond this, he found that stutterers showed recovery from adaptation (tendency toward resumption of stuttering) to increase as the time interval between reading trials increased. He pointed out the analogy between the recovery from adaptation (recovery of the stuttering response) and the experimental extinction of a conditioned or learned response as a result of a weakening of reinforcement.

Wingate (1966b) rejects the implication of Johnson and his colleagues that the adaptation effect is evidence that stuttering is a learned form of behavior in that it responds to the extinction phenomenon of laboratory learning experiences. Wingate holds that the analysis of the data generated by adaptation studies provides several fundamental features of stuttering adaptation that are not analogous to accepted principles of experimental extinction and/or psychological recovery. One specific criticism is that adaptation does not generalize. Van Riper (1971), after reviewing several adaptation studies, concludes: "In our view the adaptation effect is merely a special case of stimulus habituation" (p. 320).

We would like, for the sake of our own theoretical position, to suggest related but alternate interpretations of the results. First, the amount of mental and motor set that has to be reestablished in the oral reading of a passage varies directly with the time interval between successive readings. Second, immediately repeated readings reduce the intellectual significance of what is read. By the time of a fifth or sixth successive reading, word-forms rather than semantic word-units are being uttered. Increasing the time intervals restores the intellectual significance of the material the subject has to read aloud. He is reading for meaning, or looking for meanings as he reads, rather than acting as a transformer of visible signs to audible signs. Later in our discussion we will return to this argument and its implications. For the present, let us consider evidence of the effect of repeated evocations of self-formulated speech rather than the effect of the readng of prepared written materials.

Newman (1954) compared the severity of stuttering of a group of 20 stutterers in an oral-reading and a communicative-speaking (self-formulated speech) situation. In the first situation, the subjects read prepared descriptions of a set of picture sketches; in the second, they formulated their own oral descriptions of the sketches. In the oral-reading situation the greatest decrement of stuttering took place on the second trial; in self-formulated speaking, the largest decrement took place on the third trial. Newman also found that the reduction in stuttering (adaptation effect) was always less in self-formulated speech than in oral reading.

We do not, at this time at least, care to take issue with any of the many experimenters and students who have studied the so-called adaptation effect. Whether subjects experience reduction in anxiety, get rid of their anxieties, or gain whatever satisfaction they need by stuttering in one trial so that the severity and/or incidence of stuttering is reduced in successive trials when the "same" content is involved may all be moot points. However, it is naive to overlook the extremely small likelihood that in a normal speaking situation anybody ever repeats the "same" content, even though the same word-forms may be used. Successive utterances of any linguistic word-form content, whether in reading aloud or in self-formulated speaking, modifies the intellectual significance or propositional value of the utterance. In reading aloud, unless we are directed to read for meaning and communication, as the subjects of Eisenson and Wells (1942) were, many of us are inclined merely to utter the sounds we have associated with the signs we call written words. Our responses are different when we are required to read to search out and communicate meanings. In essence, mere reading aloud is subpropositional; reading for meaning is propositional. But the reader, unless he happens also to be the writer, is not responsible for the intellectual content—only for the transmission of the content. Repeated or successive readings, especially when they are immediately successive, reduce the propositional value of the content. One reason for this is that, except for occasional school situations, we do not often have to read aloud successively. If we do, it is to commit content to memory and so, in effect, to establish an articulatory and vocal set that approaches the automatic in preparation for a special situation.

If we are not preparing to read aloud for a special situation, and if we can continue to listen to ourselves as we read a passage five or six times, we are likely to find that something along the following lines takes place: (1) We may begin to slur and to increase the rate of utterance with successive readings. (2) We may change the stress of words and actually modify word-forms so they are phonetically different in successive readings, especially by the time of the third or fourth reading. (3) We may, if our ability to memorize is good, begin to read from memory with only occasional cues from the written passage. (4) A combination of (1), (2), and (3) may occur. In any event, it should be apparent that, though the spellings of the words we read aloud in successive trials remain the same, the words we utter, their meanings and phonetic patterns, are modified from reading to reading.

Modifications in self-formulated speaking parallel those for oral reading. In a normal speaking stuation we rarely repeat what we have said exactly as we said it in the first instance. Even when we are asked to "say it again" by someone who did not quite hear or understand us, we usually change some of the words we use. Exact repetition of self-formulated content is an artificial speaking situation. It is a situation that may occur as part of an experimental design but is not likely to occur in real life. Repeated utterances of material not conventionally read occurs in acting, but it is of interest that actors refer to "the reading of their lines." If, then, we find experimental evidence that even in an artificially created situation repeated self-formulated speech shows reduced stuttering, we should not be at a loss for an explanation. To begin with, self-formulation takes place only on the first trial. On this trial the speech is propositional: The subject is saying something in the presence of somebody, if not to somebody, with words formulated and selected as appropriate to the situation. On the second trial, if the subject is directed to repeat what he has said, he is no longer formulating and selecting propositional units. He is instead recalling and evoking, as far as he can remember, what he previously uttered. The task has changed from formulation of linguistic units, as in normal communicative speech, to one of recalling and evoking what has been previously formulated. If the experimental subject has a good memory or, if for reasons inherent in his relationship to the experimental situation, he is not anxious or apprehensive or wanting to put on a good show, he begins to perform in a speaking situation that is nonpropositional and noncommunicative. In such general situations, we know, most stutterers can speak with comparative fluency. The situation calling for successive utterances of initially self-formulated speech proves to be no exception. It is significant that there is less reduction in stuttering in repeated self-formulated utterances than in repeated readings. This is probably because there is greater deviation in repeated utterance from trial to trial than there is in repeated readings. Both initially and in successive evocation, there is greater propositional value in self-formulated speaking than in oral reading. To be sure, "repetitions" reduce the propositional value for spoken utterances as they do for reading; but the process is slower and so, therefore, is the reduction in the severity of the stuttering.

Summary of results of stuttering relative to
changes in incidence and severity of stuttering

In the preceding pages, day-to-day speaking situations and experi-
mental-laboratory speaking situations have been reviewed for their varying effects and relationships to the incidence and severity of stuttering.
In spite of considerable individual variability, general tendencies could
nevertheless be observed for stutterers taken as a group or as a special
population. These tendencies may be generalized, according to our viewpoint, along the following lines:

1. Stuttering increases as the semantic significance (propositional)
    value) of the linguistic content increases.
2. Stuttering increases as the speaker is required to formulate the lin-
    guistic content.
3. Stuttering increases as the speaker becomes aware of and accepts
    responsibility for a communicative effort.
4. Stuttering increases as the speaker must modify his set—intellectual,
    linguistic-articulatory, and vocal—to immediate and changing speech
    situations.

The above generalizations could of course be written as converse
statements about circumstances associated with a decrease in stuttering.
We would like, instead, to add conditions that are associated with a
decrease in stuttering, as follows:

1. Stuttering decreases in situations in which the speaker feels little
    or no need to make a favorable impression.
2. Stuttering decreases in situations that permit the speaker to modify
    his usual speech pattern so that he no longer speaks as his usual
    self.
3. Stuttering decreases as the speaker assumes a role instead of speaking
    as his usually recognized self (reading, acting, and role playing
    in general).

Stuttering as a Perseverative Phenomenon:
Restatement of Position

The first three sections of this chapter discussed some concepts of
perseveration and its organic and psychogenic correlates as aspects of
human behavior in the population at large and the stuttering population
in particular. The fourth section discussed the relationship between the
nature and significance of oral linguistic content and its implications

for perseveration and stuttering. We shall now be concerned with perseveration as an etiological correlate of stuttering.

According to the viewpoint presented here, stuttering *is a transient disturbance in communicative, propositional language usage.* Speech, the medium for oral language usage, becomes involved because the symbol-tool of speech—language—is temporarily disturbed. The articulatory aspect of speech may show impairment as an associated involvement, especially if the speaker had defective articulation as part of his developmental speech history. The basic involvement, however, is in the linguistic component of speech.

Propositional language, as we have indicated, is language used meaningfully, intellectually, and intentionally. The term "proposition" is used here in the sense in which it was used by Jackson (1915). A proposition is a meaningful arrangement of *speaker-formulated words,* or a meaningful unit of speech. When we use words propositionally, we indicate that significance and relationship of the words within the unit, and of the unit for the speaking situation in general and for the listener or listeners in particular. When, as listeners, we comprehend a proposition, we perceive and understand word relationships and their meanings for us.

To appreciate the significance of a propositional unit—which may be a word, phrase, or sentence—we must understand the difference between words and word-forms. Human beings are unique in their ability not only to use words as symbols, but to use word-forms in nonsymbolic or nonpropositional ways. When, for example, we swear, say sweet nothings, or respond to a social gesture such as "How do you do?" with the very same "words," we are speaking either nonpropositionally or subpropositionally. The difference, from the point of view under discussion, is one of degree. Swear words, "coo" words, and the language of strong feeling and emotion in general we regard as nonpropositional. Its use has little relationship to the presumed listener. Often there is no listener, and the speaker evokes the affective expression to ventilate his feelings without any regard to the situation, the literal or figurative meanings of the individual words, or the outpouring of sounds that resemble words. Sometimes the speaker may direct a verbal outpouring at a listener, who may return in kind. It is highly unlikely that either party to this verbal interchange is at all concerned with the semantic and biological incompatabilities that would be involved were the word-forms to be evaluated as words and interpreted as if meaning rather than feeling were intended. The reader may determine for himself what he really means when he uses his favorite term of affective language, his invective if he is inclined to use invective, or his term of endearment if this is more consistent with his inclination. Such an exercise should help him understand the difference between words and word-forms and the difference between propositional and nonpropositional language usage. As an additional, immediate exercise the reader should distinguish between the meaning of "How are you today?" when these words are spoken by a passing acquaintance, a good friend, or a relative, and the family physician when visiting his office as a patient.

We recognize that most stutterers who have a vocabulary of affective terminology are usually fluent in its use. Fluency, however, should not be expected from stutterers who have relatively small and infrequently practiced affective vocabularies. We should now also be able to recognize that particular situations and the relationship of the speaker to the situation make for differences in the significance of the linguistic content for the speaker. The situations that are conducive to decreased difficulty for the stutterer, reviewed in the previous section, are in general situations in which propositionality is reduced or absent. Communicative responsibility is also reduced in these situations.

On the dual and related bases of reduced propositionality and reduced communicative responsibility, we are able to understand why few stutterers have difficulty in singing, especially in a group; in choral speaking; or in speaking to pets or children who do not understand or would not be inclined to ask what the speaker really meant by the words he used. These expressive but noncommunicative situations also helps us to understand why a change in the manner of speaking—such as speaking in a singsong manner, speaking with an imposed rhythm or to the rhythm of a metronome, altering the pitch or the rate, or whispering—helps to reduce temporarily the incidence and severity of stuttering. When speakers concentrate their attention on their manner of speaking rather than their communication of content, on sounds rather than words, they are less concerned with the meaning of the words and more concerned with sounds and word-forms. Linguistic content has been reduced in propositional value, and speaking tends to become easier and more fluent. Another possibility is that the multiple tasks of communicative speaking have been reduced. Prosody and appropriate word or syllable stress are not matters of immediate concern. The result is that speakers can concentrate on the remaining concerns. These, however, do not constitute normal communicative effort.

The etiology of stuttering

Our basic position is that a majority of stutterers, 55–60 percent, are predisposed to a manner of oral language behavior called "stuttering." Further, we believe that this proportion of the stuttering population, at least when linguistic formulations are involved, is constitutionally inclined to perseverate to an extent or degree greater than is the case for most speakers. A minority of the stuttering population includes persons who, at the moment of speaking, are confronted with psychological factors and influences that are conducive to perseveration. This point of view will now be elaborated. A distinction will be drawn between the organically predisposed and the functional, or nonorganic, stutterer, and the suggestion will be advanced that both are products of perseveration.

Organic stuttering

As indicated earlier, we believe that the tendency for constitutional perseveration, and its associated tendency for more than a normal amount of blocked and repetitive speech, has its etiology in differences in the neurological makeup of the speaker. The differences may arise because of peculiarities of cortical development, possible competition between the cortical centers for control of language function, or possible competition between the cortical and subcortical centers for such control. In some instances neurological damage before birth, during the act of birth, or at a later time—usually before language control is normally established—may be the underlying causal factor. We believe that more often, however, the difference is developmental and one that probably lasts through later adolescence and, in some instances, into adult life.

From perseveration to stuttering.   Whether a constitutional perseverator becomes a stutterer is probably determined by circumstances that permit perseveration and speaking efforts to become associated. Among very young children, for whom perseverative behavior is normal, speech is characterized by a considerable amount of repetition. The general tendency is for repetitive behavior, including repetition in speech, to decrease with age. Davis (1939) found that the average child between the ages of 24 and 62 months, a crucial period for the organization and integration of language function, repeats 45 times per 1000 words spoken in a free-play situation. Repetitions were found to be more frequent for phrases than for words and syllables. Interestingly, boys tended to repeat syllables more often than girls.

With presently available clinical techniques and scientific devices, it may not yet be possible to distinguish the potential stutterer from the normally fluent child in terms of repetitive speech behavior. It is possible, however, that among the vulnerable 1 percent or less of children who become stutterers there may be a majority who cannot prevent themselves from being and continuing to be perseverative speakers, but who try to do so. The reasons for their trying may lie, in part, within themselves and, in part, may be present as a result of their reactions to environmental pressures. It is possible that some of the children who become stutterers, who begin to be apprehensive and manifest anxiety and struggle behavior about their tendency to be repetitive in speaking, are among the more sensitive and have greater awareness about their behavior than other children who are merely repetitive or dysfluent. Beyond this, it is possible that children with greater sensitivity and awareness have the effects of these inclinations heightened by adults who, at a crucial time, respond to these reactions and thus strengthen them. It may well be that during the period of language development some children respond more intensely than others to adult reactions to their speech. The same children who are verbally encouraged to "speak up" may meet with considerable competition from the adults who "asked" them to do so. Despite the negative influence of many adults on the speech of their children, most children survive this untoward influence and become normal speakers. A few, however, are not equal to the pressures, demands, and rejections to which they are exposed.

Wyatt's developmental crisis theory.   Wyatt (1969, chap. 6) presents a theory of the genesis of stutterings, the developmental crisis theory, in which stuttering is interpreted as a disturbance in the learning (acquisition) of speech in early childhood. According to Wyatt, how and why children learn to stutter is "embedded in the normal learning of speech patterns, from which it begins to deviate at a certain point" (p. 105). Wyatt presents her theory in the form of six basic assumptions (pp. 105–106):

1. Although language acquisition is dependent on maturational factors in children, it is essentially a learning process. In this process the mother, or mother surrogate, serves as both a primary model and a provider of feedback for the child who is engaged in learning the language patterns of his culture.
2. The optimum condition for successful language acquisition is an affectionate relationship between mother and child in situations that provide frequent opportunity for appropriate verbal interaction.
3. The process of language acquisition includes a series of interrelated stages. At each stage the child organizes and integrates new features of language and also builds on features of previous levels. For some children, and according to circumstances, the need to move from the achievements of an earlier level to those of a higher and more differentiated level may produce a crisis in language acquisition.

4. With increasing mastery of the patterns and features of language, the child is able to sustain a relationship with the mother over greater and greater distance in place and time. Eventually, the child reaches a stage of capability of internalizing the basic linguistic patterns and features of the special model. At this stage he can "reproduce" the model despite absence or distance. The child now has achieved autonomy of function and can dispense with the original model. Increasingly, the child becomes able to modify his linguistic patterns according to his needs and circumstances. The child can also attend to different models (speakers) for additional language learning. A normal child's network of interpersonal communication changes gradually and continuously from one that is dualistic to one that is pluralistic.

5. The child's relationship with the original model, usually the mother or a mother surrogate, is of vital importance during the early periods when a new function of language or a new feature is being acquired. Any disturbance in the mother-child or surrogate-mother-child relationship during these "practicing" periods may disturb language behavior. Such disturbance may be expressed in effortful or compulsive repetition. It may also be expressed in a fixation at the stage of development at which the disturbance occurs. A third manifestation may be in hostile behavior at the child's general developmental level.

6. If the mother-child relationship is disturbed when the child is in the acquisition stage of grammatical (syntactical) speech, further language learning may be delayed or the child may regress to an earlier stage of language acquisition. Disturbance may be expressed in initial symptoms of stuttering. Wyatt believes that if the child becomes unable to maintain identification with his mother at a distance, he may direct his anxiety and anger at the mother. The feelings of anxiety and anger may bring about a change in how the child perceives his mother and further complicate and disturb the mother-child relationship. Ultimately, the consequence may be increased and chronic anxiety and depression and defensive mechanisms along with symptoms of advanced stuttering.

Even if we could accept Wyatt's theoretic position without reservation, we would still need to account for the vulnerability of some children to respond so severely and to maintain responses so chronically, as do many children identified as stutterers before they are 6 years old. Is it possible to distinguish the 1 child in 100 from the remaining 99%? Andrews and Harris (1964a), on the basis of a longitudinal study in which stuttering schoolchildren were compared with nonstuttering controls, came to the following conclusions:

> In this study a number of important differences did emerge on simple intergroup comparison. To recapitulate briefly, the stutterers were characterised by a degree of social deprivation in the home, by their mother's

poor ability to manage, by a positive family history of stuttering, by their own history of late and poor talking, and by their poor attainment on tests of intellectual ability. This picture of the way that the two groups differ was reinforced by the factor analysis, in which the first factor (compounded of the child's poor ability to think, talk and behave and the mother's inability to cope generally), correlated 0.59 with stuttering.

Given the total information, an individual could be identified as a stutterer or a control with some degree of reliability. When using only 3 items (family history, late talking, poor talking) it was possible to identify correctly 120 of the 160 children. Thus stutterers, apart from their stutter, do differ from non-stutterers in simple and obvious ways. This information is evident in early childhood and may be of considerable help in assessing the prognosis of the speech disorder.

As a group, then, the stutterers showed a "lack of capacity" when compared with the controls. Perhaps this expresses one set of conditions which predispose towards stuttering. This set of conditions may handicap the child's attainment of fluent speech long enough to make him run an increased risk of becoming a stutterer. It is not likely that this is the only set of conditions which increases the risk of stuttering, for a number of children of undoubted high ability who clearly have no "lack of capacity" have become stutterers. In these children, despite the protection offered by high intelligence, some other factor has apparently provoked the stutter. It is therefore essential to look closely at the group of stutterers themselves, in an attempt to discover whether they represent a single homogeneous group or the final common pathway of a number of aetiological factors. (pp. 108–109)

The conclusions of Andrews and Harris are considerably different from those of Johnson and his colleagues (1956, p. 233), who regarded children who stutter as essentially normal. They emphasized that the unrealistic expectations and perfectionism in their homes, especially in regard to speech proficiency (fluency), was the important differentiating factor. Perhaps perfectionism and unrealistic expectations in regard to some children is a manifestation of poor coping on the part of parents. Even highly intelligent adults are not always proficient at coping, especially when their own children are involved. Stuttering, however poor, may be a way of coping for vulnerable children of such parents!

Perseveration and stuttering: The constitutional stutterer

We shall now attempt to relate stuttering to perseveration, first on a constitutional (organic) basis and later on the basis of psychogenic and environmental influences. We shall first consider how the special symptoms—the behaviors associated with stuttering—become reinforced so that stutterers and members of their environment think of deficient speakers as stutterers rather than normal or somewhat dysfluent persons.

Part of the behavior of full-fledged stutterers, who until recently were referred to as "secondary stutterers," includes facial tics, contortions, tremors, tonic spasms, and associated signs of stress and struggle during some moments of speaking. Anxiety about these, apprehensions of speaking, and a wish to avoid speaking are internal reactions to some speaking situations. These overt and covert reactions probably become associated with some speaking situations along the following lines: Stutterers, because of their strong emotional reactions to their manner of speaking, are not in a position to judge objectively which part of what they do helps them get through their blocks or stop repeating. They tend to interpret two events of behavior as cause and effect merely because they are sequential. (Such confusion and error in judgment is not peculiar to stutterers; it happens, however, to be more costly for stutterers.) The sequence of events that becomes confused is usually the block in speech and the spasm, tremor, contortion, forcing, or struggle behavior which begins to take place just before or during the block. There is little likelihood that the associated overt behavior which apparently is the cause of so much annoyance and distress to stutterers has anything to do initially with the termination of the stuttering block. Unfortunately for the stutterer, these overt manifestaions are almost always terminated at the given moment of stuttering by the utterance of the blocked sound or word. So, as most of us have observed, eventually and almost without regard to what stutterers do, some words come out. When verbal flow is initiated or resumed, the panic and the fear associated with the particular evocation—the moment of stuttering—subsides. Because of the reduction of fear and anxiety and probably because of the disturbed state immediately preceding and accompanying the block, stutterers may mistakenly conclude that their struggle behavior was directly responsible for the evocation of the word and their release from anxiety. Thereafter they repeat a gross and complicated act to overcome a spasm and secure momentary release from anxiety. What they did worked, so they do it all again. This kind of behavior is generally found in animals. It is also found in emotionally disturbed human beings. At the moment of stuttering many, if not most, stutterers behave like disturbed human beings. In a sense, this is again a case of Charles Lamb's boy who burnt his entire house down to get the fire for roasting a pig. It took the boy a little time to learn that the fire can be confined and the pig roasted more effectively in something like a pit, a fireplace, or an oven.

There are, of course, alternative explanations for the significance and maintenance of the oral manifestations and associated mannerisms of stuttering. Some of them are considered elsewhere in this *Symposium*. In organic stutterers, at least, it is probable that oral satisfactions or the satisfaction derived from the realization of morbid expectations, if they exist, constitute secondary gains rather than primary causes of stuttering. Organic stutterers may have some secondary gains in common with nonorganic stutterers, and stuttering may be maintained by some organic stutterers because of these gains. Whether this is true probably depends on the stutterer and his needs as an individual. If, even as a young child, he needs to punish an adult, he may find his stuttering an excellent weapon for such punishment. The stuttering may also be used as self-punishment, if this answers the individual's need. It may also be used to keep listeners waiting and anxious, uncomfortable and yet reluctant to break away from the verbal clutch of the stutterer. In short, stuttering may take on values and meanings for the individual unrelated to its etiology or its onset, some of which may serve to maintain stuttering and intensify and complicate the therapeutic problems of the stutterer. This aspect of stuttering will be considered later in this discussion. For the present, let us review the steps that transform some constitutional linguistic perseverators to stutterers.

Stuttering as a perseverative manifestation may take place whenever speakers find themselves unequal to the demands of a speaking situation. For a young, normally perseverative child, and even more so for a child with a constitutional predisposition for excessive perseveration, an over-demanding speaking situation may be ever-present in the form of unrealistic parental expectations. Such expectations may arise either because the parents are perfectionistic and generally high-aspiring persons or because they are making comparisons that seem reasonable but are not. Parents whose first child is a girl may be comparing and expecting her younger brother to follow her schedule. Unless the boy is precocious, he is not likely to meet this schedule. If he is normally perseverative but is looked on as an excessive repeater or hesitator by his parents, who do not recall the sister having spoken in this manner at a particular age, the boy may suffer the results of parental memories and comparison. If he is excessively perseverative, the comparisons are likely to be even more damaging in their effects.

It is probably fortunate that not all children who are more-than-normal perseverators are equally sensitive to the reactions and expectations of their parents. If they were, the incidence of stuttering in the population would be considerably higher than it is. Some children, regardless of their degree of dysfluent repetitive speech, may pay little attention to the reactions of their parents. Perhaps, because of their early health histories, these children may assume that parents are anxious persons and so take them in stride. Other children may simply be unaware of their parents' attitudes and so develop according to their own inclinations and despite the anxieties and drives of their parents. We believe that the perseverative child who becomes a stutterer does so because of a constitutional predisposition which combines with intelligence, sensitivity, and awareness of environmental expectation. The combination of factors, operating at a crucial period, usually between the years 3 to 5, makes for the stuttering. In the absence of any of these factors, most speech-perseverative children are likely to grow up to be speech-perseverative adults—the hesitant, repetitive, "uh . . . uh" type of speakers. If they do not try to become more verbally facile than they are capable of being, they run little risk of becoming stutterers as adolescents or adults. If they make an attempt to increase their fluency, possibly because of the pressure of a teacher or a friend, and then decide that the effort is beyond them, they are also not likely to become stutterers. In all walks of life, teaching and speech pathology included, we have speakers who are repeaters and hesitators. Most of these persons do not consider themselves stutterers, and most of them are not. They would become stutterers if they responded to their hesitancies and repetitions with anxiety and apprehension rather than mild annoyance or a vague wish that they could speak better or differently. But most do not, and so most of our so-called dysfluent speakers are just that rather than stutterers. A few of these perseverator-speakers may feel the need to have something especially worth saying when they engage a listener, and so most of us are the gainers for this felt need. Unfortunately, a few others may try to compensate for their perseverative tendencies by entering fields that demand more than a normal amount of verbal facility and ready articulateness. They try to become politicians or lawyers or salesmen, who use language as the tool of their trade. Some, perhaps most of them, are destined to fail. In their attempts to achieve aspirations inconsistent with their native capacities, they may develop personalities and meet with problems that could have been avoided had their potentials been evaluated early enough and had guidance been given and accepted. In many respects these preseverator-speakers develop traits, attitudes, and problems similar to those of nonorganic stutterers.

We have presented an explanation, however conjectural, for how half or more of the stuttering population became stutterers rather than dysfluent speakers. This is an answer to "what kind of a child is it who has to become a stutterer in his attempts to relate to his home and to key persons in his extended environment?" We shall now attempt to present an answer for nonorganic stutterers.

Nonorganic stuttering

Stutterers who do not share the constitutional, organic backgrounds described earlier in this essay represent a heterogeneous population.

They may stutter for a variety of causes that explain either onset or maintenance of their anxious, repetitive, blocked way of speaking. They are probably less likely than constitutional perseverative speakers to show a difference in fluency between propositional and subpropositional or nonpropositional speech. In an important sense, they are more consistently committed to sounding like stutterers whenever they speak. One explanation of how some children became "committed" to stuttering was presented in our discussion of Wyatt's developmental crisis theory.

Members of the nonorganic group, we believe, include persons who begin to stutter, or at least maintain more than normal dysfluency, because dysfluency was reinforced by recognition and attention. Some, but probably only a very few, may begin their careers as stutterers by imitating another child or adult who stutters, and then continue their careers because of the psychological values and "secondary gains"—attention, sympathy, exemption from communicative obligations—associated with this manner of speaking. The nonorganic group also includes persons for whom stuttering is a manifestation of a basic emotional disturbance, usually having its origin in early childhood. This group may be termed "psychogenic stutterers." A psychoanalytic explanation for this subgroup was presented by Glauber (1958) in the first *Symposium*. Another explanation along this line is presented by Travis (1971) in the *Handbook of Speech Pathology and Audiology*.

Situational difficulties for psychogenic stutterers. Our impression is that psychogenic stutterers have their greatest difficulty in situations in which they are required to give verbally of themselves, to "speak themselves" without pretending or role playing or through the use of another person's language. On the surface, the situations appear to be the same as those presented earlier for organic stutterers. Propositional, communicative, self-formulated language usage is difficult for stutterers in general. The dynamics of the difficulty for psychogenic stutterers distinguish them from those with an organic predisposition to stuttering. Because of their inability to give of themselves, psychogenic stutterers cannot readily evoke words. Unfortunately, psychogenic stutterers cannot always escape the need to talk. Beyond this, they do not always wish to avoid talking. If, however, they are conditioned and their reactions generalized, they may experience anxiety and apprehension in many speech situations not logically related to early ones that may have been anxiety-producing or penalizing. Their need or drive to speak and their difficulty in giving verbally of themselves produce a state of ambivalence characterized by perseverative speaking.

Earlier in this paper it was indicated that perseveration may occur whenever the determining tendencies for a given task are overcome, blocked, or diverted in some manner by inhibiting events or ideas. Perseveration may occur whenever the usual means or avenues of access to a goal are blocked. The immediate goal of the psychogenic stutterer is to say something. The counterforces may be the conditioned habitual fears of the consequences of saying something or the inhibiting force of not wishing to give of oneself. It may be the fear that if the speaker gives a little he may be expected to continue to give more and still more to a point beyond his needs, wishes, or immediate capabilities.

Through the process of generalization, unsagacious and often irrational, psychogenic speakers may spread their anxieties from saying something to somebody to the act of talking as if they were saying something. Through this process, seriously disturbed psychogenic stutterers are likely to have considerably more difficulty with nonpropositional language than organic stutterers. Their difficulty may become generalized to include speaking to pets and nonunderstanding persons, to counting and reciting, and even to speaking and singing in chorus. In a sense, the difficulty becomes one of oral evocation, regardless of the significance of the evocation or the responsibility for communication. We may at this point have arrived at a difference between organic and nonorganic stutterers. *For organic stutterers the basic problem is one of linguistic formulation and production; for nonorganic stutterers the problem is one of evocation. For organic stutterers stuttering is primarily an intermittent disturbance of propositional language usage; for nonorganic stutterers it is a speech disturbance, a problem of the expression of the self.* For the nonorganic subgroup, we are able to accept Bloodstein's characterization of stuttering in this *Symposium* as *an anticipatory, struggle and avoidance reaction* in a speech situation.

Predisposing factors for nonorganic stutterers. Whether one assumes the position of Johnson, Travis, or Glauber relative to the origin and onset of stuttering, we still have to arrive at some explanation as to just what there is about approximately 1 percent of the population (one-half percent from our point of view) that predisposes it to stuttering. Is there any special trait in this group that causes its members to react to their environments with stuttering? We know that most members of this group begin their speech difficulties as children. We also know that more of them will be males than females. Are there any other significant common-denominator predisposing factors? In the first *Symposium,* Glauber described a neurotic, maternally dominated family constellation that accounted for the child's predisposition to stuttering. Johnson, as indicated earlier, emphasized that some normal children were subject to pressures by somewhat perfectionistic, unrealistic parents. These children, in attempting to relate and adjust to their parents, became victims of expectations they could not but nevertheless tried to meet. They accepted their parents' interpretations of their normal dysfluencies as deviant speech, accepted the aspirations of their parents, and began to think of themselves as stutterers. In doing so, or thinking so, they became stutterers.

Travis also attributes the essential fault to parents. In earlier writings, however, Travis held that children who became stutterers had somewhat different potentialities from nonstutterers and so were predisposed to their difficulties. In a 1946 writing, Travis held that there was a somatic variant that served as a pathological subsoil of stuttering. This variant presumably is a tendency for the brain hemispheres of the stuttering child to be more nearly equal in potential and control of speech functions than is true of nonstutterers. Given this deviant if not pathological sub-soil, stuttering itself develops because the child cannot quite cope with the demands of his (Western) culture in which ". . . an early, harsh, complete and uncushioned renunciation of infantile and childish behavior works in conjunction with the somatic variant possessed by a few infants and children to produce stuttering." Travis viewed stuttering as an expression of a child's failure to deal successfully with a given life demand, as well as a failure for the child to find socially acceptable gratification for his subjective needs according to particular circumstances.

In 1957 Travis spelled out some of the characteristics of stutterers and of the environment to which stutterers are maladapting: "These people, as children, had no tolerance for the delay of the satisfaction of their needs. They could not yet learn to wait, to reason, to hope, to plan. Rather, they were compelled by all-consuming drives, tensions, and discomforts to action—crying, twisting, flaying . . ." (p. 918).

Travis argued that such children developed possibly tumultuous relationships which furnished the subsoil for "unverbalized and hence unconscious emotional conflicts" (p. 918). Unfortunately, because the stutterers as children were treated with less rather than more indulgence than their needs and drives required, they became stutterers. "Their savage drives should have been kept at the lowest possible level by the attentiveness of their parents. Every supportively encouraging effort should have been made by the parents to teach the child to talk and to think in order that he might in turn learn to wait, hope, reason, and plan" (p. 919).

Instead of the indulgent treatment these children needed, they were, according to Travis (1957), treated as if they were emotional and intellectual adults. "Adult powers to control their drives and feelings were assumed. Incompatible demands were made and utterly impossible checks and tasks were set. Unlearned and at times unlearnable discriminations were expected. Heavy sanctions were applied for mistakes and failures" (p. 919).

More recently, Travis (1971) described and explained the nature of repression (inhibition) as follows:

Society takes a firm and consistent stand toward the responses of anger in inhibiting them by fear and pain and allowing them reign only in a few circumstances of play and self-defense. Parents resent and fear the anger and rage of a child; and the culture, since it is dominated by parents, accepts and even rewards the virtuous chastisement of the rebellious youngster. Possibly it would not be so harmful if anger and anger alone could be inhibited or extinguished by fear and pain. But universally anger is associated with toilet and cleanliness training, eating, sleeping, sex, and all the other learning situations in the home. So we come to have such combinations as anal and oral sadism, and sexualized aggression. The fear and pain that was meant for the anger and its responses became attached to all feelings, drives, thoughts, and words that were in the child's consciousness at the time. Too, those people and things and relationships that were present became connected to the fear and anxiety responses of the child. Thus fear and anxiety became attached not only to anger, but to all the other emotional responses which the child might have been making at the time, and to all the cues of the situation in which the responses were occurring. After this learning has occurred, the cues produced by any emotion of anger may set off anxiety responses which will outstrip not only the emotional responses of anger themselves but all the associated feelings and emotions. This produces conflict, and repression results to relieve the situation. When anger with its partners in pluralistic marriage is repressed, it is constantly exposed to reactivation, and as it stirs to subject the person to pain and humiliation, the counterforces of fear and guilt arise to hold it down. Among other evidences of this fear is stuttering, the inhibition of speaking for fear of revealing anger and its several associates. (p. 1019)

Regardless of what we believe the stutterer is repressing, the starting and stopping of words may be considered as specific oral manifestations of this tendency. Through the process of generalization, or overgeneralization, the stutterer may begin to repress words that have little direct relationship to the original drive or motivation which was associated with the repressed verbalism.

Underlying the positions of many theorists, as diverse as those who are psychoanalytically inclined and the semantogeneticists, is the common assumption that somehow key persons in the environment did not treat stutterers as they should have been or needed to be treated. Adults, particularly parents, were harsh, rejecting, perfectionistic, or misevaluating of the behavior of the children. To be sure, the adults were more conforming to the environment than the children they adversely influenced. The children, however, needed different treatment, more permissive and accepting adults, than our culture seems to provide. In this unfortunate relationship of stutterers or potential stutterers, to the adults in their environment, two tendencies become evident. One is that the children are unable to meet the needs of their environment;

the second is that the adults are unable, for a crucial period at least, to meet the needs of their children.

The tendencies and traits just considered are among those we consider predominant in the common background of nonorganic stutterers. We have made no attempt to be exhaustive. Emphasis has been on the presentation of factors and influences that many theorists consider important. The fact remains, however, that the same factors may be present for children who do not become stutterers. There is still a need to find out why stuttering, rather than some other deviant behavior, becomes the behavioral manifestation. We are not entirely satisfied that we have as yet arrived at a suitable answer unrelated to constitutional predisposition for stuttering as a symptom choice. In brief, we need more research and perhaps more soul-searching to arrive at the answer to the key question about stuttering: "What kind of a child is it who responds to his environment, and to himself with behavior identified as stuttering?"

Therapeutic Approaches and Their Implications for a Theory of Stuttering as Linguistic Perseveration

A rationale for therapy

Therapeutic approaches in stuttering have in recent years shifted from treating what, in theory at least, might be the underlying cause or causes of stuttering to the treatment or modifications of the symptoms of stuttering—to the behavior itself. This change may be a result of the failure of theorists and clinicians to arrive at a tenable theory for the genesis of stuttering. The change may also result from a realization that, although we can do little about the onset of stuttering, we can often do enough about modifying stuttering behavior regardless of possible cause to justify a "let's get on with it" approach. In part, of course, the influence of Skinnerian behaviorism and the application of Skinnerian principles as behavior modification are expressed in a variety of therapeutic approaches to stuttering. Behavior modification is included in several of the essays in this *Symposium*. Principles and practices of behavior modification are incorporated into many of the therapeutic approaches recommended by Van Riper (1973) in his treatment of stutterers and their stuttering.

Although we shall be discussing if not prescribing symptom treatment, our rationale will be one consistent, we hope, with our view about the nature of stuttering and the person who becomes a stutterer. Thus, we too shall be living up to Van Riper's (1973) observation that "many clinicians do the same things for different reasons and different things for the same reason" (p. 2). The basic rationale in our therapeutic procedures is to help stutterers to be as fluent as they can within the limitations of their constitutional predisposition and environmental imposition. Along this line stutterers should be encouraged to *express rather than repress* their overt speech "symptoms" and to be themselves. Techniques of behavior modification, if employed, should also help stutterers to be themselves; this includes, of course, speaking in a manner according to circumstances acceptable to them. Such attitudes, happily, are also usually acceptable to listeners.

Whenever possible the symptom treatment should be such as to help the stutterer evaluate himself and his symptoms and what they may mean for him. Still further, the clinician and the stutterer should, if at all possible, evaluate the therapeutic approaches and what the therapist and patient are trying to accomplish through their use. The "if at all possible" reservation is one that should be determined by the patient's intellectual capacity and emotional readiness. There is no point in verbalizing for a patient reasons or rationale that he cannot assimilate. On the other hand, there is little justification for a clinician competent and confident in his techniques and the overall objectives of his therapeutic procedures to hold back information and insights from his patient.

An additional point in regard to symptomatic treatment should be emphasized. The assumed reason for the efficacy of an approach is not necessarily the real reason, or it may be only part of the real reason, for its efficacy. For example, the therapist who directs his stutterer to chew his breath, or his words, to overcome his stuttering block may do so on the assumption that by "chewing" the patient returns to a basic biological use of his oral mechanism that has been "forgotten" by the stutterer when he tries to speak. Chewing, however, may have other values that may be more or less momentarily therapeutic. First, because in our culture it is not considered polite to chew as we speak or speak as we chew, the patient is permitted to do something conventionally tabooed. This may satisfy a need he dare not ordinarily express, and so it may be good for him. Second, the technique may serve as a distraction device. We know that any technique which shifts attention from what is said to a manner of speaking serves, temporarily, to reduce stuttering. Third, the patient who is busy "chewing his words" may actually be envisioning a person, possibly even the therapist, he is "chewing out." This too may satisfy a need and hence be therapeutic. Fourth, the kind of linguistic content a patient may be verbalizing while chewing may have little or no propositional value, and so the situation may become a relatively easy one for the stutterer. This listing by no means exhausts the possibilities of what goes on within the patient when a specific technique is employed, but it should suggest that whatever is going on may be very different in the thinking and feelings of the stutterer and those of the clinician. With this in mind, let us examine some of the current symptomatic approaches from the point of view of the perseverative theory of stuttering.

Negative practice. When clinicians direct stutterers to imitate their own stuttering, they probably do so on the assumption that this procedure enables clients to raise their level of awareness of a habitual mode of behavior and so to control the behavior. This, essentially, is the technique of negative practice formulated by Dunlap (1942). In general, the principle of negative practice is that the conscious and purposeful repetition of an error results in the control, decrease, and eventual elimination of the error. When applied to stuttering, the assumption is that the act or expression of stuttering is learned but erroneous behavior which has become habitual. To eliminate this behavior, or to modify it to be more acceptable, the stutterer must learn to control it. Self-imitation is the way toward conscious control and modification or elimination. This, of course, may well be true. It is also possible, however, that what might be taking place is that the stutterer is permitted to repeat as long as he needs to repeat, to perseverate according to his need, rather than avoid doing what he is inclined to do. In effect, the stutterer is given encouragement and approval to *be himself*. If the stutterer is a constitutional linguistic perseverator, this is excellent therapy. If, on the other hand, the stutterer is a neurotic individual who has become victimized by a habit, the approach may still be good therapy. Perhaps this kind of stutterer may become satiated with a particular mode of conduct and thus be ready to make the modifications suggested by his clinician.[6]

Voluntary stuttering. The foregoing comments on negative practice also hold for the technique of voluntary stuttering. The emphasis given by Bryngelson (1943, 1966) on the importance for stutterers to see themselves as well as their speech symptoms objectively points again to the therapeutic implications of not only permitting but approving the expression of an inclination. Bryngelson began to train stutterers to speak repetitively whenever they felt they might stutter. Through repetitive speech the stutterers were helped to face rather than avoid speaking situations. Struggle behavior became reduced. When the stutterers could not voluntarily repeat, they were encouraged to stutter without inhibition, to express rather than repress their inclinations. From our point

---

[6] Van Riper (1973) cautions about the use of pseudostuttering (a form of negative practice) with implications related to our observations: "We have found no utility in the indiscriminate use of pseudo-stuttering. It should be employed for a specific purpose, one well understood by the stutterer. We have found some stutterers using it to punish themselves masochistically or their listeners sadistically" (pp. 287–288).

of view, Bryngelson helped stutterers go a long way toward the goal of self-acceptance of the need for repetitive (perseverative) speech in certain situations. The situations generally are those calling for communicative responsibility and the use of propositional language.

Easy repetition. Johnson et al. (1956) recommended a form of voluntary, controlled, and easy repetition as a therapeutic goal for stutterers. Johnson observed that when a stutterer is working toward the reduction of tension and development of control over stuttering behavior and a sense of choice over how he is to stutter, "the result tends to be that the stutterer, in performing his stuttering behavior more and more simply and easily, either repeats or prolongs the initial sound or syllable of the stuttered word" (p. 291). It seems to us that, in this observation, Johnson recognized that dysfluency is an essential aspect of the speech of the stutterer. To be sure, so-called dysfluency (hesitation and repetition) is also an essential aspect of nonstutterers' speech. In any event, if an individual who cannot help repeating (perseverating) wins approval rather than penalty for his manner of speaking, he is in effect encouraged to perseverate in his speech according to his need. In further therapy, the stutterer may reduce the number of his repetitions according to his immediate situational needs. In this way the perseverative speaker who becomes a stutterer can be helped to resume his constitutional status as a linguistic perseverator rather than continue as a stutterer.

Prolongation. When we teach stutterers to prolong a sound rather than repeat, we are probably accomplishing the same result in terms of symptom treatment. If stutterers prolong a sound as they move from one articulatory position to the next, they are probably perseverating covertly rather than overtly. What we may be helping them do is to maintain a set until the neural lag is gone. Then, without struggle, they can move on to the next sound or the next word.

Cancellation. The technique of cancellation is used by Van Riper when the client demonstrates he is ready and able to stutter openly and without inhibition. Further, because the stutterer has insights about his psychodynamics, the clinician is satisfied that "any neurotic profit or secondary gains which have accrued to the stuttering no longer have their old value" (Van Riper, 1973, p. 318). Superficially, canceling consists of having the stutterer come to a deliberate and complete halt (pause) when he has stuttered in a word and then to say the word again in a prescribed manner. This manner is modifiable and more fluent, though still identifiable as stuttering. Says Van Riper (1973), "We are ready to teach him a new fluent way of stuttering, a new way of coping with the fear and experience of fluency disruption" (p. 319). During the "moment" of pause (Van Riper recommends that the minimum moment be three seconds), the stutterer is supposed to scrutinize the feelings he experienced on the stuttered word, achieve an attitude of relaxation and calm, and prepare for the modified-stutter evocation. This preparation—the filling of the pause—calls for the stutterer to undertake two specific behaviors. "First, he is to reduplicate in pantomime a foreshortened version of the stuttering behavior he has just experienced and, secondly, he is to rehearse, again in pantomime, a *modified* version of that behavor. Only when he has done both of these pantomimings is he free to continue talking" (p. 384).

Cancellation, we believe, is another instance of a therapeutic technique that permits a stutterer to become a perseverator without penalty, and so helps him overcome his reactions to stuttering.

Pseudostuttering. The technique of pseudostuttering, or the "faking" of stuttering—stuttering intentionally without regard to the speaker's moments of fears, blocks, and so on—may be considered a form of negative practice. Van Riper (1973, pp. 284–288) considers pseudostuttering a technique for desensitization and self-revelation. We appreciate that many things may go on in the mind of a stutterer when he is directed to speak with intentional repetition. Among other things, he has the approval of a clinician, an authority figure, to be himself instead of struggling to avoid being himself. He can improve his self-esteem and, in so doing, overcome some of the feelings that may aggravate his reactions and lower his self-esteem. He may even, if this happens to be the case, entertain some of the secondary gains of stuttering until he is ready to surrender them because they are no longer essential to his needs. He can have all this and perseverate too. This, unquestionably, is potent symptom therapy as well as psychotherapy. We recommend it!

Adaptation. The technique of adaptation, that of having stutterers repeat the linguistic content read aloud or self-formulated, has been evaluated earlier in this essay. One assumption that has been considered to explain the adaptation effect was that, when stutterers repeat what they have previously read or spoken, anxiety is reduced with successive utterances. As a result there is reduced stuttering. There is, of course, no argument with the assumption that anxiety is reduced with repeated utterances of the same material. However, as indicated earlier, repeated iteration of any linguistic content reduces the intellectual significance and the propositional value of that content and speech may become more fluent. Another result of repeated iteration is that, to a considerable degree, articulatory positions become practiced and are anticipated according to the established linguistic formulations. Thus formulation, phrasing, and motor production, with successive reiterations, are not novel acts. In effect, the stutterer is dealing with established content that requires no change of either intellectual or motor set. He is engaging in approved perseverative behavior.

Easy articulation. Some therapists teach stutterers new patterns of articulation that call for less articulatory tension and for less "sticking" on some sounds than most of us use in speaking. Perhaps what these therapists are helping their cases to accomplish is a manner of articulation that does not require a firm motor set. If the perseverative tendency is in part related to inertia, the less firm an articulatory position is the smaller the amount of energy that will be needed to modify or change the position. Speaking that is reduced in normal articulatory tension may be a way of avoiding the onset of a perseverative state.

Rate control. Most therapists who employ rate control usually direct their patients to speak more slowly rather than more rapidly. In this slower rate of speaking, we may be helping stutterers adjust to their capacity for linguistic formulations and articulatory expression. In effect, we may be teaching them how to avoid obvious perseverative behavior that would become evident if they were to speak at a rate more like most speakers. At the modified, slower rate, stutterers are afforded the time they need for changing their mental and motor sets according to their inclinations.

Symptomatic treatment: Summary

The symptomatic treatment of stuttering seems to have two goals: (1) the immediate goal of self-acceptance of stuttering symptoms and (2) fluent "stuttering." The second is an intermediate goal for some stutterers and a final one for others. From our point of view, whether fluent stuttering is an intermediate or a final goal depends on whether we are dealing with a constitutional linguistic perseverator or with a nonorganic psychogenic stutterer. For the constitutional perseverator, repetitive speaking relieved of associated anxiety, apprehension, struggle, and its inner and overt manifestations is all we can hope to accomplish. Individuals, with the help of as much insight and self-acceptance as they can gain through direct or indirect psychotherapy, learn to speak in a manner and with an attitude consistent with their constitutional predisposition. Constitutional perserverators can also be considerably helped through a recognition of situations, such as those discussed earlier, that are conducive to increased linguistic perseveration. Such recognition should help prepare speakers to adjust to situations without apprehension. If needed, they can get set for the use of techniques that enable them to continue their communication rather than block and struggle.

Psychogenic stutterers may possibly be helped beyond the point of voluntary repetition. They may be helped to speak with only a normal amount of so-called dysfluency—perhaps better described as speaking with normal fluency, which includes some repetitiveness and dysrhythmia suggestive of dysfluency and stuttering.

Although some symptomatic treatment may serve the same functions for psychogenic stutterers as for organic stutterers, much of the treatment may serve different purposes. What some of these may be was indicated in the first part of this section. Beyond symptomatic treatment, regardless of the significance of this therapy for psychogenic stutterers, avowed psychotherapy may be in order. In some instances this may be to determine the underlying cause and meaning of the symptoms for the stutterer. The goals, nature, and extent of psychotherapy are matters to be determined by the needs of the individual stutterer. The factors determining these objectives will be considered in the discussion that follows. For the moment, however, we wish to emphasize that not all psychogenic stutterers fall into a common category and stutter for the same reason and not all neurotics who stutter ought to become exposed to the same psychotherapeutic techniques.

Psychotherapy

Any good relationship between a patient and a therapist is in part psychotherapeutic.[7] This incidental psychotherapy takes place regardless of technique. Sometimes it takes place despite the symptomatic technique employed. For some stutterers who have not developed additional or associated maladaptive behavior, only incidental psychotherapy is necessary. This may well be the case with young stutterers. Of course, considerably more therapy may be necessary for the parents and other adults in the stutterer's environment. It is likely that the more effective therapy is for these adults, the less direct psychotherapy the child will need. If this is not possible, therapy for the child must in part include helping him to accept the adults as they are.

Adolescent and adult stutterers, regardless of the genesis of their stuttering, are likely to need more that just incidental psychotherapy. Any moderately intelligent individual who is aware that an important aspect of his behavior is significantly different from most others in his environment is likely to develop some reactions to this behavior that will need treatment. Our emphasis is that we cannot ignore the symptoms of stuttering, especially if the stutterer's history suggests a constitutional predisposition for his disturbance. Neither can we overlook the need many stutterers have for psychotherapy.

Adolescents and adults, especially intelligent ones, are likely to make some use of their handicaps. If the handicap is stuttering, it can be used to excuse them from social situations that may be unpleasant for reasons quite unrelated to their speech. As suggested earlier, stuttering can be used to make others uncomfortable, to punish persons deemed by the stutterer to be in need of such punishment. It can be a stand-by

---

[7] See Van Riper's chapter in this *Symposium* on the role of the therapist.

alibi for failure, for not trying because there may be a failure, and for a host of other purposes that only a resourceful human mind can anticipate. These uses make stuttering a way of life. They must be dealt with if therapy for the stutterer is to be successful.

Just how much psychotherapy the adolescent or adult stutterer needs depends upon the individual. Some adult stutterers may have worked through their problems themselves and be ready to give up—or have given up—the secondary gains when they come to a therapist. In such instances there may be a danger of too much rather than too little psychotherapy. Symptomatic treatment may be all that is indicated. Presumably, this is the position of behavior modifiers who see no need to treat anything but presented symptoms. Some adults may be reluctant or unable to accept the notion that stuttering is without value. They come to the therapist with the presenting symptoms of stuttering and "want no messing around" with their personal lives. For these adults, symptomatic treatment may be of some help, and incidental insight may be attained if the therapist is understanding and patient. Some patients begin to ask questions that suggest they have growing doubt and perhaps an inkling of insight about the values and their need to stutter as symptomatic treatment progresses.

Clinicians as well as stutterers reach a point in therapy when the question of the need for deeper psychotherapy must be faced. The clinician must then determine whether his training and inclination are sufficient to permit him to be of further help to the patient. If not, a referral is in order to a therapist with competence in psychotherapy, and if at all possible, one who has had successful experience with stutterers.

Review of therapeutic approaches for the organic stutterer

Earlier we evaluated some of the symptomatic and psychotherapeutic approaches for stutterers and indicated how these may have efficacy for stutterers with a constitutional predisposition toward their difficulty. At this point a more positive approach is in order, with an outline of a therapeutic program for stutterers whose difficulty is related to their tendency toward excessive perseverative behavior.

We believe it important to secure evidence that may establish the likelihood that we are in fact dealing with an essentially organic rather than functional speech disorder. Specifically, we ought to determine whether there is a basis for believing that the individual stutterer with whom we are dealing is inclined to excessive linguistic perseveration and so has become a stutterer, or whether he is stuttering and perseverating for psychogenic reasons. A clinical history and the criteria considered earlier for perseverative tendencies should be of help. Beyond this, specific and appropriate tests of perseveration may be administered. Some of these were described in the first part of this chapter. Medical information—especially information suggestive of either atypical neurological development or neuropathology in early childhood—should also be presumptive of a tendency for the existence of excessive perseveration.

Some words of caution are in order. We presented several organic factors that we believe to be associated with perseveration in general and others we believe to be associated with linguistic perseveration. However, our information is not "hard" and conclusions should still be considered tentative. We do know that persons with brain damage are strongly inclined to perseverate. Even these persons, however, reduce their perseverative inclinations as their general physical condition improves and as they adjust to the limitations imposed by the conditions. Excessive perseveration may be a temporary state; the physical correlates of perseveration should therefore be checked and reevaluated periodically. The excessively perseverative child need not be an excessively perseverative adult: The physical conditions may have changed for this individual. If this, indeed, turns out to be the case, we may be dealing with a habit of perseveration rather than constitutional perseveration. For such an individual new insights and a different set of objectives should be in order.

If we are satisfied that when the stutterer comes to us for therapy we are dealing with a constitutional linguistic perseverator, therapeutic approaches toward the following objectives are indicated:

1. To help the stutterer toward an acceptance of himself as a functioning organism.
2. To weaken the nonorganic causes that tend to increase conflict, ambivalence, and other attitudes associated with psychogenic perseveration.
3. To modify, control, and if possible eliminate stuttering blocks and the secondary symptoms of stuttering.
4. To help the stutterer to speak in a manner consistent with his constitutional predisposition, repeat as often as necessary, modify rate, and otherwise speak so that the effort is devoid of anxiety, conflict, struggle, and the covert and overt characteristics of stuttering.

Except for emphasis on organic or constitutional factors, these objectives are such as to be acceptable to any but strongly psychoanalytically inclined therapists. The reader will recognize that within this *Symposium* therapeutic programs toward these objectives have been presented by other contributors.

Self-acceptance. To an extent determined in part by the age and intelligence of the individual, the stutterer need to be helped toward an objective evaluation of himself, his stuttering, and his reactions to his stuttering. Many stutterers need to be helped to accept themselves as persons who will continue to be repetitive or hesitant to an extent greater than most of their associates. At the outset they must confront the realities of their stuttering. If they can pause to stop and look at themselves, literally as well as figuratively, at their moments of stuttering and ask "What is this about?" instead of "Why is this happening to me?" they will probably get better answers to both questions.

Many therapists stress the need for more rather than less speaking at the outset of therapy, regardless of how much stuttering takes place. By speaking more, the patient is presumably not trying to avoid situations that might betray him. Instead, he is going out of his way to reveal himself so that there will be no fear of being found out.

By speaking more and stuttering more, the individuals can make note of the situations conducive to his stuttering, as well as those associated with nonstuttering. Through such awareness the individual may begin to look upon himself as a stutterer under one set of conditions and a relatively fluent speaker under another set. He may, through such an evaluation, look forward to some situations while getting over apprehensions and anxieties about others. When the stutterer is enabled to make the distinction between stuttering and perseveration, he may be able to adopt an attitude of "sufficient unto the situation is the perseveration (hesitation and repetition) thereof."

In our therapy, when we feel we are dealing with a constitutional perseverator, we stress the point that repetitions and hesitancy constitute perseveration. The addition of anxiety, apprehension, and struggle behavior to repetitions and hesitancies transform perseveration into stuttering. Perhaps this is also what Johnson means when he has patients evaluate the "normal nonfluencies" of speech. We, of course, regard perseveration as excessive recourse to so-called nonfluencies. So we do not try to convince the stutterer that he too can be a perfectly normal speaker if he reevaluates his nonfluencies. Instead, we emphasize the need for objective evaluation and acceptance of the amount of perseverative oral language usage the stutterer seems to require in specific situations and types of situations. Through this approach, we help the stutterer to self-acceptance—to accept himself for what he cannot help being rather than to try to be somebody he is constitutionally unable to become.

Weakening of the nonorganic causes of perseveration. The therapeutic approaches considered under the headings of symptomatic treatment and psychotherapy all help toward the objective of weakening the nonorganic causes of perseveration. Any forces that help to reduce ambivalence and increase the drive toward speaking will serve this end. Acceptance of the stuttering and later of perseveration help to reduce the psychological overlays associated with avoidance and refusal to accept the reality of stuttering. A strengthened wish and willingness to speak may become too strong for any residual fear of speaking. So the determining tendencies for speaking become greater than the inhibiting force, and the requirements for perseveration on the basis of a volitional disturbance no longer pertain. With a reduction in struggle behavior, the amount of perseveration existing on an organic basis need no longer be reinforced by nonorganic perseveration. The result may be a marked decrease in repetitions and hesitations, with speech beginning to approximate the normal.

Modification and control of the secondary symptoms of stuttering. Several of the techniques considered in this discussion of symptomatic treatment of stuttering are recommended as entirely appropriate for the modification and control of secondary symptoms. The nonverbal mannerisms, the ticlike behavior that is superimposed on the oral blocks, require awareness and voluntary control for their modification and eventual elimination. The techniques of negative practice, of *voluntary reproduction of the whole act of stuttering,* and other procedures for the modification of stuttering behavior are pertinent for this objective.

Establishment of a Manner of Speaking Consistent with Constitutional Predisposition. When we help a stutterer to become aware of how much perseverative behavior he normally needs to exercise in a speaking situation, we are helping him to approach normal speech. There can, of course, be no prescription for all stutterers in terms of constitutional predisposition. The needs of A are not the needs of B because the constitutions of A and B are not the same. Even if they were, since their reactions are not the same the overall effects are different.

A stutterer must learn how slowly or how quickly he must speak in a given situation. He needs to learn with what appropriateness he can generalize from specific situation to situation. He must be helped to repeat only as often as he needs to repeat and then move on to the next utterance. He must learn not to yield to repetition for repetition's sake, yet not to regard a moment's pause as an unbearable hiatus. When a stutterer learns this and begins to speak in the light of this knowledge, he is beginning to leave stuttering behind and to be a perseverator. When the perseverative utterances are reduced to a minimum without discomfort and anxiety, the speaker is no longer a stutterer. In some situations there will be no need for perseveration. In others there may be comparatively little perseveration, little enough to be considered normal dysfluency. In a few situations there will be greater than normal perseveration. But this will be greater than normal only when a constitutional perseverator compares himself, or is compared with, so-called statistical norms. What we try to establish, however, is the norm or norms an individual is to observe for himself. When this objective is achieved, the speaker will have established a manner of speaking consistent with his constitutional predisposition for linguistic perseveration. The individual will no longer be a stutterer but a speaker who is an occasional perseverator. If he accepts himself as such, the battle over stuttering has been won.

References

Andrews, G., and Harris, M. (1964a) *The syndrome of stuttering*. London: Heinemann.

Andrews, G., and Harris, M. (1964b) Stammering. In C. Renfrew and K. Murphy, eds., *The child who does not talk*. London: Heinemann.

Arend, R., Handzel, L., and Weiss, B. (1962) Dysphatic stuttering. *Folia Phoniatrica*, 14, 55–66.

Beech, H. R., and Fransella, F. (1968) *Research and experiment in stuttering*. Elmsford, N.Y.: Pergamon.

Black, J. W. (1951) The effects of delayed sidetone upon vocal rate and intensity. *Journal of Speech and Hearing Disorders*, 16, 56–60.

Bloodstein, O. (1950) A rating scale of conditions under which stuttering is reduced or absent. *Journal of Speech and Hearing Disorders*, 15, 29–36.

Bluemel, C. S. (1913) *Stammering and cognate defects of speech*, vol. 1. New York: Stechert.

Bluemel, C. S. (1957) *The riddle of stuttering*. Danville, Ill.: Interstate Press.

Brown, S. F. (1945) The loci of stuttering in the speech sequence. *Journal of Speech Disorders*, 10, 181–192.

Bryden, M. P. (1963) Ear preference in auditory perception. *Journal of Experimental Psychology*, 65, 103–105.

Bryngelson, B. (1935) Sidedness as an etiological factor in stuttering. *Journal of Genetic Psychology*, 47, 204–217.

Bryngelson, B. (1943) Stuttering and personality development. *The Nervous Child*, 2, 162–171.

Bryngelson, B. (1966) *Clinical group therapy for problem people: A practical treatise for stutterers and normal speakers*. Minneapolis, Minn.: Denison.

Carr, B. M. (1969) Ear effect variables and order of report in dichotic listening. *Cortex*, 5, 63–68.

Curry, F. K., and Gregory, H. H. (1969) The performance of stutterers on dichotic listening tasks thought to reflect cerebral dominance. *Journal of Speech and Hearing Research*, 12, 73–82.

Davis, D. M. (1939) The relation of repetition in the speech of young children to certain measures of language maturity and situational factors. *Journal of Speech Disorders*, 4, 303–318.

Doust, J. W. L., and Coleman, L. I. M. (1955) The psychophysics of communication, *A.M.A. Archives of Neurology and Psychiatry*, 74, 650–652.

Dunlap, K. (1942) The technique of negative practice. *American Journal of Psychology*, 55, 270–273.

Eisenson, J. (1937) A note on the perseverating tendency in stutterers. *Journal of Genetic Psychology*, 50, 195–198.

Eisenson, J. (1947) Aphasia: Observations and tentative conclusions. *Journal of Speech Disorders*, 12, 290–292.

Eisenson, J. (1958) A perseverative theory of stuttering. In J. Eisenson, ed., *Stuttering: A symposium*. New York: Harper & Row.

Eisenson, J. (1966) Observations of the incidence of stuttering in a special culture. *ASHA*, 8, 391–394.

Eisenson, J. (1973) *Adult aphasia*. Englewood Cliffs, New Jersey. Prentice-Hall

Eisenson, J., and Horowitz, E. (1945) The influence of propositionality on stuttering. *Journal of Speech Disorders*, 10, 193–198.

Eisenson, J., and Wells, C. (1942) A study of the influence of communicative responsibility in a choral situation for stutterers. *Journal of Speech Disorders*, 7, 259–262.

Eisenson, J., and Winslow, C. N. (1938) The perseverating tendency in stutterers in a perceptual function. *Journal of Speech Disorders*, 3, 195–198.

Falk, F. J. (1956) Interrelationships among certain behavioral characteristics, age, sex, and duration of therapy in a group of stutterers. Ph.D. dissertation, Pennsylvania State University. (Reported in *Speech Monographs*, 23, 2, 141–142.

Glauber, I. P. (1958) The psychoanalysis of stuttering. In J. Eisenson, ed., *Stuttering: A symposium*. New York: Harper & Row.

Goldman-Eisler, F. (1958) The predictability of words in context and the length of pauses in speech. *Language and Speech*, 1, 226–231.

Goldsand, J. (1944) Sensory perseveration in stutterers and non-stutterers. *Speech Abstracts*, 4.

Gutzmann, H. (1898) *Das stottern*. Frankfurt: J. Rosenheim.

Jackson, J. H. (1915) Selected Writings of J. Hughlings Jackson. In H. Head, ed., *Brain*, 38, 1–25.

Johnson, W., ed. (1955) *Stuttering in children and adults*. Minneapolis: University of Minnesota Press.

Johnson, W. et al. (1956) *Speech handicapped school children*, rev. ed. New York: Harper & Row.

Johnson, W., and Knott, J. (1937) The distribution of moments of stuttering in successive readings of the same material. *Journal of Speech Disorders*, 2, 17–19.

Kimura, D. (1967) Functional asymmetry of the brain in dichotic listening. *Cortex*, 3, 163–178.

King, P. T. (1953) Perseverating factors in a stuttering and non-stuttering population. Ph.D. dissertation, Pennsylvania State University.

Kussmaul, A. (1877) Die Störungen der sprache. In H. V. Ziemssen, ed., *Cyclopaedia Medica*, 21–22.

Lee, B. S. (1951) Artificial stutter. *Journal of Speech and Hearing Disorders*, 16, 53–55.

Leutenegger, R. R. (1957) Adaptation and recovery in the oral reading of stutterers. *Journal of Speech and Hearing Disorders*, 22, 276–287.

McClay, H., and Osgood, E. I. (1959) Hesitation phenomena in spontaneous English speech. *Word,* 15, 19–44.

Martin, R. (1962) Stuttering and perseveration in children. *Journal of Speech and Hearing Research,* 5, 332–339.

Milner, B. (1962) Laterality effects in audition. In V. B. Mountcastle, ed., *Interhemispheric relations and cerebral dominance.* Baltimore, Md.: Johns Hopkins Press.

Newman, P. W. (1954) A study of the adaptation and recovery of the stuttering response in self-formulated speech. *Journal of Speech and Hearing Disorders,* 19, 312–321.

Orton, S. T. (1927) Studies in stuttering. *Archives of Neurology and Psychiatry,* 18, 671–672.

Penfield, W., and Roberts, L. (1959) *Speech and brain mechanisms.* Princeton, N.J.: Princeton University Press.

Perrin, K. (1969) An examination of ear preference for speech and non-speech in a stuttering population. Ph.D. dissertation, Stanford University.

Sheehan, J., and Martyn, M. M. (1966) Spontaneous recovery from stuttering, *Journal of Speech and Hearing Research,* 9, 121–135.

Slorach, N., and Noehr, B. (1973) Dichotic listening in stuttering and dyslalic children, *Cortex,* 9, 295–300.

Soderberg, G. A. (1967) Linguistic factors in stuttering. *Journal of Speech and Hearing Research,* 10, 801–810.

Soderberg, G. A. (1969) Delayed auditory feedback and the speech of stutterers. *Journal of Speech and Hearing Disorders,* 34, 20–29.

Spearman, C. (1927) *The abilities of man.* London: Macmillan.

Swift, W. B. (1932) Why visualization is the best method for stuttering. *Proceedings of the American Speech Correction Association,* 2, 89–91.

Travis, L. E. (1934) Dissociation of the homologous muscle functioning in stuttering. *Archives of Neurology and Psychiatry,* 31, 127–133.

Travis, L. E. (1946) My present thinking on stuttering. *Western Speech,* 10.

Travis, L. E. (1971) In L. E. Travis, ed., *Handbook of speech pathology and Audiology.* Englewood Cliffs, N.J.: Prentice-Hall.

Travis, L. E., ed. (1957) *Handbook of speech pathology.* Englewood Cliffs, N.J.: Prentice-Hall.

Trotter, W. D., and Bergmann, M. F. (1957) Stutterers' and non-stutterers, reactions to speech situations. *Journal of Speech and Hearing Disorders,* 22, 40–45.

Van Riper, C. (1971) *The nature of stuttering.* Englewood Cliffs, N.J.: Prentice-Hall.

Van Riper, C. (1973) *The treatment of stuttering.* Englewood Cliffs, N.J.: Prentice-Hall.

Wingate, M. E. (1966a) Behavioral rigidity in stutterers. *Journal of Speech and Hearing Research,* 19, 626–630.

Wingate, M. E. (1966b) Stuttering adaptation and learning. I. The relevance of adaptation studies as "learned behavior." *Journal of Speech and Hearing Disorders,* 31, 148–156.

Wyatt, G. L. (1969) *Language learning and communication disorders in children.* New York: Free Press.

VII

The Stutterer's Clinician

C. Van Riper, Ph.D.

Distinguished University Professor, Western Michigan University. Fellow and Honors of the American Speech and Hearing Association. Author of *Speech Correction: Principles and Methods, Voice and Articulation* (with John V. Irwin), *The Nature of Stuttering, The Treatment of Stuttering, Introduction to General American Phonetics* (with Dorothy E. Smith).

Millions of words have been written about stutterers, but only a few about the clinicians who have treated them. Surely it is time to examine stuttering therapy from this other perspective. No matter what kind of treatment is used and no matter what its rationale may be, the clinician is always a significant part of the therapeutic dyad. Carkhuff and Berenson (1969) insist that the therapist rather than the theory or technique is the most important factor in successful psychotherapy. Rosenzweig (1936) is even more emphatic:

> Given a therapist who has an effective personality and who consistently adheres in his treatment to a system of concepts which he has mastered and which is in one significant way or another adapted to the problems of the sick personality, it is of comparatively little consequence which particular method the therapist uses. (p. 412)

Few speech pathologists would hold such an extreme position, but all of us do recognize that the clinician's role is vital. To give only one example, consider this statement by Murphy and Fitzsimons (1960): "The most important single variable affecting success in the treatment of stutterers is—*the clinician*" (p. 27). Even if we wish this were not true and hope that eventually it will not be, at the present time and in the present state of the art the clinician's characteristics, roles, and competencies are determinative.

Perhaps there may come a time when the stutterer can be placed in a box and hooked up to a machine run by a computer, but in the present state of the art—or semiscience—of speech pathology, that day has not arrived. Even Goldiamond (1965), who used a booth rather than a box in the initial stages of his operant conditioning program, found it necessary to sketch the clinician's role during transfer in the following fashion:

> The weekly therapy sessions then become research conferences, as though between a professor and his research associate on what has to be done next to bring the organism's behavior into line. The S (Stutterer)

is the acknowledged expert in the content of the field—his own behavior
and its ecology—and E (Experimenter-clinician) brings to bear on the
problem his knowledge of procedures and past effects. Eventually, as
in a good professorial relationship, S may become an independent
investigator, capable of tending to things on his own. (p. 153)

A psychoanalytic clinician would doubtless prefer a different set of roles
and relationships. But the point we are making is that the clinician,
of whatever faith, is a very important part of the therapeutic problem
and hence should be scrutinized.

Clinicians come in a wide assortment of sizes, shapes, and colors;
but these differences are, of course, negligible as compared to the cos-
tumes they wear on the therapeutic stage where they play their parts.
For some, the preferred cloak is that of authoritarian controller, the
omniscient dispenser of punishment and reward. For others, the role
of priest in the confessional may be favored. For other clinicians, the
cap and gown of information giver seem to be worn most frequently.
Indeed, it is possible that not only our roles as clinicians but our basic
beliefs concerning the nature of stuttering as well as its treatment may
be determined largely by the sort of roles we prefer or have been conditioned to accept. One of our colleagues once made the pertinent (or
impertinent) observation that Wendell Johnson was doomed to devise
a semantic form of therapy because he loved to play with words; that
Robert West had to invent dysphemia because he always wanted to
be a physician; that Joseph Sheehan had to develop a therapy based
on approach-avoidance conflicts because he demonstrated so many of
his own; and that Van Riper, who had been whipped so often in his
childhood by his playmates, was destined to create a therapy demanding
that both clinician and client be excessively heroic. Be that as it may,
it seems reasonable to recognize that the self-concepts of clinicians will
tend to be reflected in their clinical behavior toward their clients and
that it would be wise of all of us to recognize our biases.

The Clinician's
Beliefs

It seems most probable that one of the most important determinants
of the stutterer's clinician's behavior is his concept of the nature of
the disorder. If he views stuttering as consisting of a set of instrumental
behaviors, that and nothing more, then he will inevitably structure his
therapy in terms of operant conditioning and his major role will be
that of competent reinforcer or punisher—in short, that of controller.
If, on the other hand, he believes that the stuttering behaviors have

their origin in and are maintained by classically conditioned negative emotion, the clinician will see his professional role as that of desensitizer and will use deconditioners and counterconditioning as basic tools. The clinician's prime function is to calm. If he is a psychoanalyst like Glauber (1958), who believes that stuttering is "a pregenital conversion neurosis," then the clinician's basic role would be quite different. If the stutterer's clinician is a psychiatrist like Freund (1966), whose position is that stuttering is an expectancy neurosis, then he would be more interested in the "symptoms" themselves and more willing to play an active, supportive role in therapy.

Anyone who has kept up with the current proliferation of psychotherapies must recognize that the Rogerian model (Rogers, 1957) of the clinician is only one of many. This situation undoubtedly poses some threat to uncertain student clinicians seeking unrealistically for one clear picture of what clinicians must be. But it may become more tolerable when they understand that, if they can attain their own set of beliefs and act in accordance with them, their clinical impact will be considerably greater than they had suspected. We have had to change our own beliefs about the nature of stuttering several times during the course of our professional life and have experienced successes and failures in each of these phases; the failures have led to revisions of our beliefs and practices. No one has any right to be completely certain of the complete validity of his beliefs, for there are still too many pieces of the ancient puzzle still missing. In Stevenson's *Treasure Island,* one old pirate growled, "I knows what's what!" whereupon the other pirate said, "Ah, it's a wise man as knows that." If we are presently denied the ultimate wisdom about stuttering, we certainly can learn enough about the disorder to give us a set of beliefs sufficiently reasonable to form a rationale for a therapy program that will help, if not cure, stutterers.

Indeed we know a lot about the nature of stuttering even though we may not know all. We know, for example, that many of the behaviors shown by stutterers are learned responses to the expectancy or the experience of fractured fluency. We know that stutterers have fears—reasonable fears, not phobias—and a good many other negative emotions that contribute to the frequency and abnormality of the disorder. We know that there is evidence of mistiming of the sequencing of motor speech. We recognize that stutterers' self-concepts have been affected by their stuttering. We see the impact of the disorder on their language, perception, thinking, and social relationships. We have clear evidence that the frequency, duration, and kinds of their stuttering behaviors are not only variable but that they can be decreased by a variety of clinical techniques. Certainly, then, no clinician need despair of ever having a dearth of available knowledge on which to base his beliefs or thera-peutic regime. What is necessary, however, is that he acquire that knowl-edge and then evaluate it. As Williams (1968) points out so cogently:

> Before a clinician can begin to do stuttering therapy meaningfully, he
> must assess his own beliefs about the nature of stuttering. Once he does
> this, he formulates a retraining program that is related to the basic concepts
> he holds about the nature of the problem. He adopts a language in talking
> about the problem. He devises procedures that he believes will achieve
> his goals of therapy. (p. 441)

We would also add that the clinician then assumes clinical roles that are appropriate and necessary to the administration of those procedures.

The Clinician's Needs

It also seems fairly obvious that the clinician's behavior in the therapy situation will tend to be shaped in some fashion by his personal needs. When these are unrecognized, they may affect his therapeutic roles very drastically for then he cannot take countermeasures to offset the bias they produce. It is for this reason that most psychoanalysts undergo a personal analysis before practicing professionally. A certain amount of distortion is always to be found in our clinical perceptions because the information we process must pass through the filters of our past experience. But if we know what those filters are and how they tend to alter that information, we can hopefully make the necessary correc-tions. Since few speech pathologists or stutterer's clinicians have the opportunity for an in-depth exploration of themselves, most of us come to recognize our biases in the mirrors of our failures. One excellent illustration of this is to be found in the remarkably honest account of a clinical failure reported by Robinson (1968):

> However, the friendly relationship was by no means the most important
> factor in this particular example of a clinical failure. Much more critical
> was the reason for the cultivation of Harry's friendship. We completely
> failed to recognize a personal need to identify with the class of people
> that Harry appeared to us to personify. Our lack of insight was an appalling
> truth. We had exploited this case for our personal benefit. And in so doing,
> we fostered a kind of relationship that permitted Harry to continue to
> use the facade of his social sophistication to cover a host of problems,
> and it was too late when we realized that the stuttering in this case
> was intricately interrelated with other personal problems. We shall not
> soon forget our experience with Harry. (p. 74)

Although failures in therapy may be therapeutic for clinicians, we feel that some self-scrutiny of one's own deficits, past and present, may help prevent them. We have trained many clinicians in the course of a lifetime, and it is our impression that those who became the most successful were able to undergo this self-scrutiny. All of us have suffered deprivations of one sort or another in our youth and childhood, and few of us are without currently unsatisfied hungers. Perhaps we were status-deprived; if so, we should beware of our tendency toward assuming the role of authority. Perhaps we were overcontrolled in our childhood; if so, we must guard against an excessive need to control others or its opposite, the compulsion to delegate all responsibility to the client. Certainly, few of us ever got enough love, for the need to be loved seems insatiable; we must therefore be alert to the problems presented by transference.

First in the list of the six characteristics of the competent stutterer's clinician as described by Barbara (1954) is this one: "He should have his own personal problems reasonably well resolved, or be sufficiently aware of them so they will not interfere with his working constructively with others" (p. 265). We like this statement's implication that all clinicians have personal problems, which need be only reasonably resolved. Far too often we hear professors reciting lists of qualifying adjectives that include all the Boy Scout virtues and a dozen more as prerequisite to success in this field; then we look at our colleagues and grin. And then we look at ourselves and the grin grows broader. Let us be reasonably healthy, of course, for one does not heal a wound by applying a dirty bandage. If you know what the imperfections of that tool are, you can still wield it effectively. The crucial criterion with respect to one's conflicts, then, is that they do not critically interfere with one's work.

As a special case, we might consider the question as to whether one stutterer should treat other stutterers. There are training institutions that routinely reject or discourage any stutterer from entering the speech pathology curriculum on the grounds that the blind should not be trained to lead the blind or that bald-headed barbers should not sell hair tonic. Had such a practice been universal in the early days of our profession, its development would have been markedly retarded, for stutterers have made major contributions. Perhaps the sanest view is one that recognizes both the advantages and disadvantages of such an experience. On the one hand, the clinician who has been a stutterer does not have to cope with the accusation by his clients that because he is a normal speaker he cannot comprehend their difficulties or distress. Though we do not at all accept the validity of such an accusation, we recognize that it often occurs. Brody and Harrison (1954) describe it well:

From the very beginning this group of stutterers formed a cohesive band that seemed to look upon the psychotherapist as an outsider who could not possibly understand their problem. The presenting picture was that of a long-suffering, persecuted minority group. Their concept of how the stuttering should be overcome by the individual was striking in its uniformity. They expressed the opinion that the symptom should be dealt with violently. . . .

The psychotherapist tried to encourage the group, but this seemed to cause the men to become even more resentful. The psychotherapist found himself fighting to extend a ray of hope to the group. He offered the interpretation that each of these individuals was prejudiced against himself, and perhaps, if as individuals each would accept and be proud of himself including his stuttering, that would be his first step in overcoming it. The group reacted as a unit, saying that this substantiated their feeling that the psychotherapist did not understand them at all. (p. 155)

Though this membership qualification may help the stuttering clinician initially, we find that it also creates other problems. The clients of a stuttering clinician will make exorbitant demands on that clinician for a perfection of fluency that reflects their own unreasonable picture of what normal speech should be. The same hesitancy in formulation of a thought, the same "ah" or clearing of the throat that stutterers would ignore in the clinician whom they consider a normal speaker, are immediately challenged as evidence of the clinician's phonemic fears. The stuttering clinician faces some real difficulties in the modeling role, but none that cannot be overcome.

There are also some advantages that accrue from the stuttering clinician's relative freedom from the kinds of fears that Wingate (1971) says are commonly felt by many normal-speaking clinicians who have to work with stutterers: that stuttering is so mysterious a disorder they cannot possibly be competent to work with it, that it demands a clinician who must be a highly trained psychotherapist, and that they should never deal with the symptoms or stuttering behaviors or even use the tabooed word. Stuttering clinicians, at least, are not afraid of stutterers. They know from their personal experience that they are tough animals, that they have endured and survived, and moreover that most stutterers respect a clinician who will not handle them gingerly.

In short, the problem resolves itself in terms of Barbara's criterion. Do stuttering clinicians live with their own stuttering problem in such a way that it does not interfere with their therapy? Certainly they must be reasonably fluent. Certainly, they must be aware enough of its dynamics so they will not perceive the problems of their clients too distortedly. As Murphy and Fitzsimons (1960) say, "The real criterion is personal adjustment, not the speech component. Some stutterers should not treat stutterers. Some nonstuttering workers should not treat sutterers" (p. 37).

The Clinician's
Characteristics

So far as we know, there is very little research in the field of speech pathology that deals specifically with the characteristics of the successful clinician, and there is even less that is concerned with the stutterer's clinician. Most of the information we do possess concerns the psychotherapist, and although stuttering therapy often involves some psychotherapy, few speech pathologists would feel it fair to be evaluated solely on this basis. Nevertheless, to the degree that the results of these studies are pertinent to stuttering therapy, they indicate that the competent clinician should at least possess the three characteristics that Truax and Carkhuff (1967) refer to as *accurate empathy, nonpossessive warmth,* and *genuineness.* We have reviewed a large number of these research studies and find this triad appearing over and over again.

Empathy

What is meant by "accurate empathy"? Blackman et al. (1958) use an analogy to describe it:

> One can say that empathy is the ability to step into another person's shoes and to step back just as easily into one's own shoes again. It is not projection, which implies that the wearer's shoes pinch him and that he wishes someone else in them; it is not identification, which involves stepping into another person's shoes and then being unable or unwilling to get out of them; and it is not sympathy, in which a person stands in his own shoes while observing another person's behavior, and while reacting to him in terms of what he tells you about shoes—if they pinch, one commiserates with him, if they are comfortable, one enjoys his comfort with him. (p. 547)

Certainly empathy involves clinicians' sensitivity to their clients. Smith (1966) says that "sensitivity is the ability to predict what a person will feel, say, and do about you, himself and others" (p. 93). We think that this emphasis on prediction may be unduly stringent. Clinicians may often be surprised at the same time that they clearly comprehend how a client is feeling; then later they may find evidence to indicate that they have indeed been truly tuned in. Empathy is the ability to imagine how it feels to be inside another person's skin. It is an assumption blended of observation and inference, an elusively vague concept at best. We would willingly reject it completely were it not that any clinician worth his salt knows there are moments in therapy when his assumptions concerning the thoughts and feelings of his client are corroborated. Even as each partner of a long and successful marriage knows what the other is thinking and feeling, we find a similar empathetic perceptiveness in a successful pairing of clinician and client. Perhaps it is all delusion, but most successful clinicians of stutterers seem to attribute much of that success to their ability to "understand" their stutterers, and they often blame their failures on their inability to empathize with particular clients.

At any rate, if empathy is to have any sembance of accuracy, it must be based on a solid foundation of careful observations. Most competent clinicians of all persuasions are careful observers. They know the need for distinguishing observation from inference. The know the common tendency to generalize from insufficient data, so they collect as large a sample as they can before setting up any hypotheses or inferences. It is necessary to get an adequate sample of observations, especially in stuttering therapy, because the disorder is so variable in its manifestations from one situation to another.

Competent clinicians also know that all observing is selective. No one can attend to all the behaviors being emitted by the stutterer even in a single minute of therapy, and there are always dangers that this selectivity may distort the picture. Wise clinicians therefore open the lenses of their scanners and sweep their client many, many times before formulating an hypothesis or making an inference. Habitually, their clinical judgments are tentative ones and they search for rejecting evidence even more than for corroboration before coming to any conclusions. It is not easy to operate in this way, but we can and must. As Darley (1966) writes:

> The continuing occupational hazard of the clinician is letting his biases and preconceptions do his thinking for him. Each of us is prone to ride certain hobbies, to see what he wants to see, to rationalize behavior in terms of a notion he is devoted to. The scientific method abhors such slanting; it insists, rather, that one observe dispassionately, hypothesize coldly, test hypothesis disinterestedly and accept inevitable conclusions unreservedly. (p. 9)

That at least is the ideal we seek.

A bit more should be said about what clinicians of stutterers should observe. Certainly they should do more than merely count those instances they define as stuttering, for some of the behaviors are as unlike as apples and onions. To give just two examples, they need to assemble their catalogs, sorting out, for example, the gasps that time the moment of speech attempt after a pause from those that terminate a prolonged phoneme or a recycled syllable. They need to observe those often overlooked behaviors that appear just prior to a lip tremor or precede its cessation. They need to elicit the verbalizations that reflect the feelings and evaluations characterstic of the stutterer's anticipation or experience of broken fluency—and these too need to be observed and categorized before inferences are made about their dynamics. There are many other behaviors to observe carefully.

Equally important, of course, are those components of the body language that can tell the clinician much. For years we personally have worked hard to read that body language of stutterers so we could gain the understanding we needed to help them, and perhaps we should share some of the self-training methods we have employed. Briefly, we learned to stutter as they did, duplicating with ever-increasing exactness what they were doing, first overtly then covertly. By using the shadowing technique, we trained ourselves to be able to pantomime unnoticeably all their speech, the normal as well as the abnormal. We practiced assuming their postures, their gestures, their inflections, and the tempo and patterning of their movements until we felt we could do so with fair fidelity. Using unfinished sentences as material, we sought to predict how a given stutterer would complete them and thus gained some acquaintance with the chaining of his associations. We recorded our interviews with stutterers and then, after they were cold and forgotten, played them back, stopping the tape whenever they began to talk and then trying to predict what they would say. We studied transcripts of some of our interviews to scrutinize our reflecting of the stutterers' verbalizations for evidence of congruence or dissonance.

Those are just a few of the things we did to improve our own clinical skills in the area of empathy. It has been our impression that this training was extremely valuable, that it paid off in many ways. Though the published research studies on the effectiveness of training in sensitivity and empathetic understanding have not been very impressive, and although Truax and Carkhuff (1967) state that evidence for the efficacy of existing training procedures is virtually nonexistent, we feel that those training procedures are faulty and that better ones can be devised. Each clinician must design his own.

This brings us to another important component of empathy: clinicians' awareness of themselves and their ability to observe themselves at the same time they are observing stutterers. No one can read another person's mind nor truly feel the squirting of his glands. All one can know is his own. Harrison and Carek (1966) describe the situation from a psychiatric point of view: "Some have talked of this mode of observation in terms of an 'evenly hovering' or 'suspended' or 'free floating' attention, since it is a divided attention in which the therapist simultaneously pays heed to the patient and himself." We personally have never been able to do both kinds of observation simultaneously, but instead seem to have to alternate back and forth very swiftly. However, we know that this comparing process is essential if we are to recognize bits of dissonance or incongruence, that is, when we are in or out of tune with our client. Perhaps Rogers's (1961) description can sum it up:

> To sense the client's private world as if it were your own, but without ever losing the "as if" quality—this is empathy, and this seems essential to therapy. To sense the client's anger, fear, or confusion as if it were your own, yet without your own anger, fear or confusion getting bound up in it, is the condition we are endeavoring to describe. (p. 284)

We conclude this section with a caution about overidentification. One's empathy should be used as a way of achieving understanding, not as a means for possessing stutterers or for being possessed by them. The clinicians' and clients' circles should intersect, but there must always be a clear area outside the intersection if clinicians are to maintain enough objectivity to be able to help stutterers. It is possible to get over-involved. Mandl (1964) makes the point clearly:

> While empathizing is a requisite in counseling, every counselor faces the question of how close, emotionally, he should get to his client. In effective counseling, it is important to stay close enough to the individual with whom we are working to remain in touch with how he feels and responds, but yet not so close as to lose perspective. There is a special danger in feeling just the way the client feels. You can get to know how sad his life is, how miserable his situation is, and reach the stage where client and counselor do nothing more than become articulate about the client's misery. The two, in a sense, peel back the onion together and cry. Instead, maintain enough distance so that your eyes may sting a little, but you do not cry as vigorously as the client does. You should not get as angry about situations as the client does. You must understand what he is saying and accept his feelings, but must not take on all of these feelings yourself. (p. 75)

The clinician's warmth

Another trait or characteristic of successful psychotherapists is what is termed "personal warmth," and we feel it is also found in successful clinicians of stutterers. Like "empathy," it is not a precise term; it seems to refer to a cluster of clinicians' behaviors that beget a favorable and reciprocal response from their clients. Rogers (1957) speaks of it as unconditional positive regard. Truax and Carkhuff (1967) preface it with an adjective and call it nonpossessive warmth to differentiate it

from love, among other things. Rotter (1964) insists that the good therapist is "warm" and communicates to his patients his concern and interest
in them. Even Wolpe (1958) says that "the therapist is permissive;
the therapist is interested and friendly, communicating in this way a
certain warmth that makes the relationship more personal than is ordinarily the case" (p. 106). Shoben (1953), who has been mainly concerned with learning theory, describes the relationship in psychotherapy
in these words: "The attributes of the relationship are, first, friendliness,
warmth, and a comfortable closeness" (p. 126). Indeed we even find
Schofield (1964) entitling his book on psychotherapy *The Purchase of
Friendship*. In speech pathology, a similar point of view has been expressed by most of the writers who have discussed the characteristics
of the stutterer's clinician. Thus Barbara (1954) states that "the therapist
should be, in every aspect of his personality, a human being. He should
have a feeling for struggle and suffering in humans, and use every constructive asset in himself toward expressing warmth, understanding,
sincerity and respect for the patient's own wishes and rights" (p. 52).
Murphy and Fitzsimons (1960) boil it down to this: "The successful
clinician is the worker who is able to establish the warm relationship
on which new learning is dependent" (p. 28).

Consider the alternative: therapists who are cold, who do not show
they care for their clients. How many stutterers would be willing to
place themselves in such impassive arms? Consider this brief excerpt
from a "therapeutic" conversation between a computer and a live human
subject:

> Computer: "How can I help you?"
> Person: "I don't know."
> Computer: "What don't you understand?"
> Person: "No."
> Computer: "Can you elaborate?"
> Person: "I am sick and tired today."
> Computer: "Do you have any idea why?"
> Person: "Yes, I'm old."
> Computer: "Please go on." (Colby, Watt, and Gilbert, 1967)

Many beginning clinicians do try to make the right responses to the
stutterer's verbal offerings, but if those responses are not couched in
the inflections and prosody that signify warm acceptance and concern,
their impact will be negative or nil.

Basic to clinicians' warmth is their acceptance of clients as persons
in their own right even though they are persons in trouble. To accept
them is to accept their anger as well as their unfolding potential for
self-realization. Acceptance need not mean indiscriminate agreement or

approval. Clinicians will often have to help stutterers to discriminate between behaviors that facilitate fluency from those that do not. As Shames (1970) has illustrated, clinicians may approve stutterers' positive statements and disapprove or fail to respond positively to negative ones; but this does not mean at all that clinicians thereby reject their clients as persons.

But acceptance is at best a meager word for what the competent clinician really feels. There is also a deep commitment to the stutterer's welfare. When we accept a stutterer for therapy, we do not do so lightly, casually. Instead we sign what Menninger (1958) calls "the invisible contract" that always exists between the client and the therapist. Moreover, we sign it first, knowing that the stutterer cannot and dare not sign until he has come to sense our dedication and competence. The basic content of this contract is that we will do our utmost to help him lose his deviance and become an adequate human being. Our utmost!

Yet acceptance and commitment, necessary as they are, encompass only a small portion of clinicians' warmth. The major part lies in clinicians' regard. Stutterers must feel very vividly that we like, respect, and care for them as persons. In our many years of practice we have had to work with a large number of severe stutterers, some of whom were most unattractive, unlikable, even nasty human beings. No, we cannot say, as did Will Rogers, that we have never met a man we didn't like. Nevertheless, *in the therapeutic relationship,* with only a few exceptions, we discovered in ourselves a profound regard for each client once our lives became intertwined in the course of therapy. (May we say, in passing, that when we could not really like a stutterer we always failed.[1]) In that liking, there may be compassion but no pity; there may be a kind of love but never lust. If there is any possessiveness, it is not that we possess them but they us. We are companions together as we make our way out of the dismal swamp of stuttering, and having suffered together, we find that special kind of close relationship that battle survivors know. At times it is the sort of painful affection that can only be expressed with profanity. How can one find words to describe this deep caring of clinician for their clients? Perhaps there are no words, but it is certain that clinicians feel this warmth and so do stutterers.

Lest we give a false impression, we hasten to state that no emotional attitude can ever be sustained at a peak level. It is not necessary for clinicians to die of a rose in aromatic pain or to feel unworthy of their calling when they find that their "unconditional positive regard" for

---

[1] A detailed account of one of these failures, which ends with the words "Damn her hide!" may be found in Van Riper, 1968, p. 124.

their clients ebbs as well as crests. We have personally never been able to care deeply about any stutterer 100 percent of the therapy time. For that matter we cannot even care deeply about ourselves very long, as we have had to tell student clinicians who became upset when they found these fluctuations. Indeed, there are times when too constant or too high a level of regard on the clinician's part may be viewed by the stutterer as either threatening or too demanding. A study by Mills and Zytowski (1968) found that when the clinician's demonstrated regard for his client was too high and too constant, his empathy became less accurate and his genuineness more suspect. Such a finding is not too hard to understand because stutterers have often been hurt by those who professed to love them. The important thing is not that one's level of caring varies but that it exists. The pilot light of love must always be burning.

The clinician's genuineness

Love, alone, is not enough. Stutterers seek clinicians not for warmth nor for understanding, but for relief from their fractured fluency. They want to overcome their stuttering. They want to be able to speak without fear or frustration. When clinicians do not recognize that this terrible urgency is the stutterers' prime concern, they are certain to fail. Stutterers want clinicians who can help them gain this relief.

We should recognize, however, that few stutterers come to their clinicians without having some real doubts and reservations about their clinicians' competence or commitment. Many of them have had previous experiences in therapy that provided no satisfactory resolution of their problems. All of them have received therapeutic suggestions from a host of untrained persons, friends, parents, even from strangers—suggestions that were absurd or ineffective. How can stutterers be sure that their new clinicians are any different from all the others? There have been many pseudotherapists in their lives.

It is equally important to the success of therapy that clinicians recognize that stutterers may be reluctant to enter into close relationships with them. Starved as stutterers are for such closeness and companionship, they often come to us with long histories of social rejection. Abnormal speech is not conducive to social relationships; it interferes with both their establishment and maintenance. Stutterers have often had to be content with fringe membership in the few groups they have managed to pump up enough courage to enter. In the few dyadic friendships they have been able to create, they often found themselves being parasitical or being exploited. In short, they often come to clinicians not only with doubts but with suspicion. They will therefore have to test clinicians time after time before they are willing to sign that invisible contract, and even then they will do it hesitantly and with some hidden reservations.

Of course, some of this initial distrust occurs in the establishment of any close interpersonal relationship—even in marriage. It certainly is to be found in psychotherapy, as the following quotation from Bone (1960) illustrates:

> Why should a person trust his innermost privacy to an untested stranger? Of course, the therapist may say, "It's for your own good; you can trust me; I'm your therapist, and therapists are by definition trustworthy." The person has heard that before: "It's for your own good, you can trust me, I'm your mother, and mothers are by definition trustworthy." The fact is that generally an important part of the person's difficulty is a distrust born of an early, naive trusting outgoingness to an untrustworthy person.

Only when clinicians are able to recognize and accept the fact that stutterers' testing is both natural and necessary will they be able to do the things that have to be done to prove their dependability. Many beginning clinicians are appalled when they first meet this testing. They cannot understand why some stutterers seem to do their utmost to sabotage the therapy; they cannot understand why they may lie and cheat and refuse to work, or why they attack and challenge the person who is trying so hard to help them. More experienced clinicians would hear the stutterer's silent cry and know that these behaviors beg for evidence of his trustworthiness. No stutterer wants to put himself in the arms of a person who might drop him.

It is therefore necessary for clinicians to be able to disclose themselves as real persons, persons without facades. In his book *The Transparent Self,* Jourard (1964) clearly shows the folly of distortion and its contribution to all sorts of unhealthiness. Clinicians soon discover how much time and energy stutterers devote to pretending they do not stutter, how often they go to extreme lengths to protect their temporary masquerade. They invent a hundred tricks and strategies to prevent exposure. Though their masks usually fail them, they continually put them on in a desperate attempt to escape the disclosure of their stigma. Any clinician who also puts on a false face will be hard put to get stutterers to confront their stuttering.

Rogers (1961) speaks of therapists' "congruence" as the core of their integrity and influence. He says that a therapist who shows congruence is freely, deeply, and acceptingly, *himself*. That therapist has himself all together, flaws and all; he neither parades his favorable facets nor hides the unfavorable ones. Like Popeye, he says, "I am what I am!" flaws, fleas, and all. Kramer (1970) writes:

> There are two closely related aspects to this reality and honesty of the therapist: one, he is accurately aware of his own experiences, and two, he lets those experiences be seen by the patient. Perhaps a better wording for the second aspect is that the therapist does not hide parts of himself from the patient. He may, however, ignore some of his own experiences during the therapy hour. He may try to ignore those experiences that intrude on meeting the patient's needs. (p. 62)

The last point is well made. The stutterers' needs come first, not the clinicians'. The latter certainly should not use the therapy session for narcissistic display nor for their own need for ventilation. Clients come first, second, third, and always.

One of the best clinicians of stutterers that we have known was Bryngelson. His therapy was based on honest self-confrontation of the problem, as evidenced by the title of one of his books: *Personality Development Through Speech: Getting Next to Yourself* (1964). What is pertinent here is that this particular clinician offered himself to his stutterers without defenses; he let them see him as he was—prejudices, hang-ups, and all. Stutterers do not seem to mind seeing a clinician's frailty if he seems to accept it instead of being defensive about it. What stutterers cannot bear is the smell of fraudulence. In this connection, Brammer and Shostrom (1960) state that "clients seem to have a remarkable tolerance for counselor error providing other aspects of the relationship are adequate and that this attitude of alertness to error serves as a useful antidote to counselor complacency, the 'pedestal syndrome' or the 'Jehova complex'" (p 166). Competent clinicians, therefore, can be characterized by what psychotherapists call "openness"—the willingness to provide a nondefensive disclosure of their unique humanness. To experience a close relationship with another human being who can openly disclose his warmth and understanding is one of the better spin-offs of living. When that person can also reveal that he has wrestled with his own personal demons and has won the battle for genuine self-acceptance, we are fortunate indeed: We have then found someone we may be able to trust. Certainly the bedeviled stutterer needs such an experience. And every clinician has had his demons.

Yet there is still another barrier to be surmounted before stutterers can trust their clinicians. They must also become convinced that the clinicians are competent, that they know their professional stuff. This competency cannot be assumed or taken for granted. It must be present and it must be disclosed and demonstrated. Again, we will find stutterers probing and testing us, searching for evidence that we understand the nature of their difficulties and how they can be resolved. No matter how warm and understanding and genuine we may be, they also want something more in their clinicians. They want competence. Too many amateurs have had their dirty fingers in the stutterer's pie. Stutterers demand guides who know the terrain, who know where the stutterers are in the swamp and which way they must go to get out of it. They want guides who will not abandon them, who are strong, warm, and understanding; but above all, they want their guides to be experienced and skillful and to have some kind of a map.

How do beginning clinicians gain this competence? First of all, they must acquire a solid foundation of information about the nature of stuttering. Second, they must come to know an adequate sample of stutterers personally. Third, they should assume the role of a severe stutterer long enough, and in enough situations, to enable them to experience the frustrations, anxiety, shame, and other negative emotions that constitute the context of the stutterer's daily life. Mulder (1961) in his article "The Student of Stuttering as a Stutterer," offers an outline of this vicarious experiencing, and Sheehan (1970) is even more emphatic:

> The role experiences of a stutterer have a certain uniqueness which can only be tapped by role taking. Speech clinicians who would qualify themselves to work with the stutterer could best begin by entering the role, not once as a gesture but many times. Instead of merely "faking" stuttering to a few people as part of an introductory speech pathology course, or superficially during his clinical training, the clinician should have shared the stuttering experience over a significant period of time. If he has not done so, he is depriving himself and his stutterers. Taking the role of the stutterer, finding out what it is the stutterer experiences, is the principal way the clinician can overcome the handicap of being a normal speaker." (p. 283)

These three prerequisites to competence—empathy, warmth, and genuineness—might seem to be sufficient, but they are not. It is also necessary that the clinician, the guide, has that map. Of course, there are many routes to the Rome of fluency for stutterer, and at the present time no one of them may be said to be the best one for all stutterers or for all clinicians. But if the clinician is to hope for the stutterer's trust in his guidance, he must have organized his beliefs so that they present a fairly clear picture of the route that he intends to take in leading the stutterer to his goal. As a guide, he must be able to point out the landmarks in between. No stutterer will put his trust in a guide who, too, is lost.

Finally, we should recognize that the stutterer needs a strong clinician, not a weak one. There will be many times during the course of therapy when the stutterer will not only desire, but really need, some temporary support. This does not mean that he can expect the clinician-guide to carry him out of the swamp on his back; rather, it means that he needs a guide strong enough to stay by him when the going gets tough. The weak clinician would find it too hard to share the stutterer's distress in confronting the unpleasant aspects of his disorder. Such a clinician could not tolerate the necessary testing of his competence. His faith in the stutterer's potential ability to solve his problem would fade when progress is delayed or uneven. If the stutterer is to put his trust in the clinician, he must sense the clinician's strength.

That strength is disclosed in many ways. It is demonstrated in the sureness with which clinicians carry out the diagnostic examination. It is found in the decisiveness of their evaluations, in the structuring and programming of the therapy, in the acceptance of their responsibilities. Competence clinicians write their name on the invisible contracts with firm hands. Evidence of their strength is revealed by their physical energy and enthusiasm, by the way they accept themselves, and, let us not forget, by the gaiety of their spirit. It is difficult to describe the many ways in which clinicians discloses their strength; but you can be sure that if it is there, the stutterers will feel it.

Other characteristics of the clinician

We have presented at some length what we feel are the three most important characteristics of the stutterer's clinician: empathy, warmth, and genuineness. Let us say, however, that in the actual work of therapy even the best of clinicians may show many other traits as well—some of them useful and appropriate, some not. What is most unfortunate is that we often find it difficult to know how we are behaving when the interaction is hot. We need some kind of feedback if we are to improve our clinical skills.

If, for a time I may escape from the constraints of the editorial "we," I would like to recount some of my personal efforts to improve myself as a clinician through self-scrutiny. I have long sought in vain to find some instrument that might yield a fairly comprehensive evaluation of my own traits as a clinician and one that I might also use in evaluating the student clinicians I supervise. Far too often I just did not know how I had behaved when interacting with a client. Far too often I made my judgments of my students on insufficient data. Far too often judgments were distorted by the prominence of only a few interactions. Since, so far as I can ascertain, no one has assembled a universe of items that would encompass all the kinds of clinical interactions or all the clinician's traits from which such an instrument could be created, I had to devise one of my own. "A poor thing," as Shakespeare wrote, "but mine own." I view it as only a crude beginning.

It consists essentially of paired bipolar adjectives, culled from a wide reading of the literature in speech pathology and psychotherapy, that refer to the behavior of a clinician as judged by an observer. This observer simply makes a mark on the line between the two adjectives, a mark that represents his evaluation of the clinician's characteristics at a given time. There are three sets of these bipolar adjectives; the three categories represent judgments that deal with evaluation, activity, and strength, respectively. These categories are based on Osgood's (1957) finding that his 50 adjective pairs fell into these three dimensions. I have no idea whatsoever concerning the reliability of these items. Others will have to apply Osgood's semantic differential or some other treatment to these items to determine this checklist's adequacy, which at present is admittedly suspect. I provide it merely as an illustration of how one clinician tried to scrutinize his clinical behavior.

Bipolar Adjective Checklist

Evaluative

1. Enthusiastic _____ Phlegmatic
2. Likable _____ Detestable
3. Cold _____ Warm
4. Organized _____ Disorganized
5. Unconcerned _____ Concerned
6. Tolerant _____ Intolerant
7. Boring _____ Interesting
8. Negative _____ Positive
9. Accepting _____ Rejecting
10. Genuine _____ Fraudulent
11. Authoritarian _____ Nonauthoritarian
12. Open _____ Defensive
13. Interesting _____ Boring
14. Insensitive _____ Sensitive
15. Critical _____ Nonjudgmental
16. Clear _____ Confused
17. Antagonistic _____ Friendly
18. Self-concerned _____ Client-concerned
19. Abrasive _____ Kind
20. Pleasant _____ Unpleasant
21. Sad _____ Joyous
22. Close _____ Distant
23. Organized _____ Disorganized
24. Humorous _____ Stolid
25. Attractive _____ Unattractive
26. Accurate empathy _____ Inaccurate empathy
27. Depressed _____ Cheerful
28. Sympathetic _____ Unsympathetic
29. Self-disclosing _____ Aloof; reticent

30. Disagreeable _____ Agreeable
31. Pessimistic _____ Hopeful
32. Tactful _____ Blunt
33. Cruel _____ Kind
34. Trustworthy _____ Unsafe
35. Goal-centered _____ Technique-centered

Activity oriented

36. Uncomprehending _____ Insightful
37. Controlling _____ Permissive
38. Active _____ Passive
39. Rigid _____ Flexible
40. Calm _____ Nervous
41. Encouraging _____ Discouraging
42. Uncooperative _____ Cooperative
43. Enthusiastic _____ Apathetic
44. Patient _____ Impatient
45. Unpredictable _____ Predictable
46. Well-coordinated _____ Awkward
47. Repressed _____ Spontaneous
48. Unhurried _____ Hurried
49. Uninhibited _____ Inhibited
50. Effective _____ Ineffective
51. Persistent _____ Gives up easily
52. Disapproving _____ Approving
53. Highly mobile _____ Restrained motorically
54. Quick _____ Slow
55. Challenging _____ Accepting
56. Energetic _____ Low energy expenditure
57. Extravertive _____ Introvertive

Strength

58. Weak _____ Strong
59. Secure _____ Insecure
60. Dignified _____ Undignified
61. Threatening _____ Supportive
62. Competent _____ Incompetent
63. Self-punitive _____ Self-accepting
64. Convincing _____ Unconvincing
65. Cautious _____ Assured
66. Possessive _____ Nonpossessive
67. Committed _____ Uncommitted

I have used this checklist in several ways. First, I used it in evaluating my own therapeutic roles. It is very illuminating to watch or hear yourself on videotape and to make these judgments, a few at a time, but—over a series of client contacts—to cover all of them. I have found it convenient to type the adjective pairs on cards, pick about 10 of them at random, and then do my ratings. It was often difficult to make the mark on the line at the place that I thought was accurately representative of what I had been observing; but usually I could place it to one side or the other of the midpoint. There were some therapy sessions and interactions that provided no pertinent material, and then the card was left unmarked. Some cards got marked many times and not always similarly, though usually the scatter was not great.

Clinician's behaviors vary widely at times. There were instances, for example, when I marked myself near both borders of *likable* and *detestable, accepting* and *rejecting, controlling* and *permissive,* depending on what the client and I were doing or not doing. No clinician should be always *active* or always *passive.* No clinician should be always anything. But this does not mean that the instrument has no value. There were enough times when I checked the same point on the same set of adjectives (not always to my credit, either!), which provided a clear picture of how I was behaving and how I must appear to my client or to others. There were enough cards where there was very little scatter in my self-ratings of different therapy sessions to indicate some fairly basic traits. In short, this self-confrontation taught me a good deal about myself in my clinician's role. I offer the list without illusions as to its validity or reliability mainly because I feel all clinicians need to examine their clinical behaviors and impressions.

The Clinician's Role
in Motivation

No matter how many favorable traits the clinician possesses, much of his success will depend on his awareness of the importance of the stutterer's motivation or apparent lack of it. How hard and consistently the stutterer works to overcome his communicative disability can almost be said to be the yardstick by which the clinician's competence is measured. There are many factors that determine the influence of the clinician in motivating the stutterer to do the work of therapy and that determine its success. We shall consider three of them: the clinician's ability to arouse hope; the clinician's role in goal-setting; and the clinician's use of reinforcement and punishment.

The clinician's ability to arouse hope

Because of their many daily failures in speaking and previous failures in therapy, many stutterers come to the clinician with only a small fund of hope. They come more out of desperation than from expectation of relief. Any clinician who does not recognize this situation or respond to it appropriately will find difficulties. The quack practitioners of the old commercial schools for stutterers knew this well. The walls of their schools were covered with testimonial letters from the stutterers they claimed as cures. The sentences of confidence in "The Method" that we chanted as we swung our arms or recited in unison while relaxing on the floor were almost hypnotic in their suggestion. Modern clinicians rarely use these blatant devices to achieve favorable expectations in their clients, but we find other ways of accomplishing the same result.

The placebo effect is found in all therapy, and it is not merely the clinical procedure but clinicians themselves that constitute the pink pill. This is not bad or necessarily fraudulent. Placebos may help and do help certain patients. Indeed, as Frank (1961) has shown clearly, much of the healing that occurs in modern medicine may in part depend on them. In a pill-consuming culture such as ours, this should not seem strange. Nor should we be surprised to find, with Goldstein (1962), that patients who received psychotherapy did no better than a control group who merely had an equal amount of intimate association with the therapist. Hope is not evil, however is engendered. Indeed, as Mowrer (1960) has shown, hope is absolutely necessary if any learning or unlearning is to be accomplished. Truax and Carkhuff (1967) phrase it in this way: ". . . the patient's initial hope for improvement is a major factor contributing to the likelihood of its actual occurring" (p. 175).

In arousing hope, much has been made of the importance of the clinician's charisma, whatever that word really means. West (1958) calls it

> that subtle, difficult-to-define thing called personal magnetism. This is
> a complex of impressions made upon the patient. The therapist possessed
> of this ability to impress the patient seems to be frank but tactful; penetrat-
> ing but understanding; confident but humble. In my professional lifetime
> I have seen several supreme examples of therapists so equipped. Some
> of them have succeeded in spite of the fact that such magnetism is almost
> the entire equipment of their therapeutic armamentarium. Personalities
> that are long on magnetism and short on knowledge are, however, undesir-
> able members of our profession. (p. 220)

If such charisma or personal magnetism exists, we suspect that its clinical effectiveness is due to its ability to arouse the stutterers' latent hopes.

We also suspect that clinicians' ability to arouse hope in their stuttering clients stems from the amount of confidence they hold for their own beliefs, from their past history of successful therapy with stutterers, and perhaps from their basic optimism. Like fishermen, clinicians had better be optimists! If they have no faith in their procedures, they will certainly fail to inspire any faith or hope in their clients, for stutterers seem to have an uncanny ability to detect self-doubts in their clinicians. Having spent much time and energy in devising strategies for the disguising or concealment of their disorder, they are not easily deluded. They will soon ask the test question: "Can you cure me?" How the clinician responds will be crucial to the outcome of therapy.[2]

To drop the editorial "we" again: I have often wondered why I have had this capacity for hope arousal in the stutterers with whom I have worked. Being a small-potatoes-and-few-in-a-hill sort of nondescript person, I cannot possibly attribute it to personal magnetism of the kind mentioned by West. Moreover, my confidence in my own theories and therapy procedures has never been at an extremely high level of self-delusion. The only explanation that seems to make sense is that, whenever I see a new stutterer, I find in him so much more strength and potential than I remember having at that age that I immediately expect a favorable outcome. The feeling is this: "Lord, if that weak, miserable mess that once inhabited my skin could solve his problems and become reasonably fluent, then surely this potential client can!" Moreover, I have known other stutterers for whom the prognosis looked pretty poor but who were also able to master their tangled tongues and selves with my help. Perhaps other clinicians who create hope in their clients have similar perceptions.

Motivation is not a fluid that can be injected. No one motivates a stutterer or any other kind of client. What a clinician can do is create conditions so that the motivations already present in the client can be mobilized in the interests of therapy. A successful clinician is one who constantly plays the role of diagnostician, continuously identifying the motives that seem to influence the stutterer's behavior and continuously finding ways for using them to achieve the goals of treatment.

Though some of these motives are easily ascertained, others are not; it is then that the clinician's ability to empathize accurately with the stutterer finds its greatest challenge. Moreover, the clinician must recognize that the strength of the stutterer's various drives must be continually assessed since they vary widely from time to time and from situation to situation. What is equally important is that we rarely find single drives existing alone. Some of the stutterer's needs may actually be antagonistic to other ones, so the clinician has the difficult task of determining the resultant of this array of forces. Though this assessment may seem almost impossible to accomplish, this is what the clinician must do to be successful. What happens, of course, is that the clinician's

---

[2] A presentation of how we respond to this question can be found in Van Riper, 1973, pp. 229–230.

errors in judgment show their effects very quickly in the stutterer's behavior and thus revision and correction take place. No one does any therapy without making mistakes. Competent clinicians are those who know they will make errors in judgment and are alert to their occurrence, so they can make the necessary changes in their approach to the problems encountered. Passivity, resistance, and emotional upheavals of many kinds are the signals that tell clinicians they must reassess the stutterers' needs.

If I can again speak in the first person singular, some useful questions I have asked myself in this connection are these: (1) What major deprivations and frustrations has this stutterer encountered in the past or which ones are present now? (2) What have been and what are his present major satisfactions? (3) What are his hopes and fears for the future and how aware of them is he? (4) What expectations have others held out for him and how do they jibe with his own? (5) What characteristic signaling behaviors indicate that I am not recognizing his needs? The answer to these questions usually have given me some awareness of the stutterer's basic needs and some hints as to how to exploit them. And there are, of course, other questions equally significant.

When progress in therapy zooms or when it falters, clinicians again and again ask themselves why. This "Why?" is probably the most important tool any therapist possesses. In all the years that I have been treating stutterers, I do not think there has ever been a single time that I entered a therapy session without asking myself: "What does he need? What does he need from me? What does he need from me right now? And why?" Often no satisfactory answers were immediately forthcoming; but when they did come, they always came from my perception of the stutterer's drives and motivations. And when, in the course of therapy, I have found repeated frustration and failure, again I learned to ask myself the question "Why?" and to formulate a hypothesis or two. It was always apparent that I had not been tuned in, that I had failed to recognize certain needs of the stutterer which were more important than those I thought should have been present. Or, worse yet, my own personal needs had supervened. When student clinicians complain to me that their cases are lazy or unmotivated, I tell them I have never known a lazy or unmotivated stutterer. When I find one who appears to justify such a description, it merely means that his values at the moment differ from mine.

The clinician's role in goal-setting

Nothing is so important in therapy as the setting of goals in terms of the stutterer's motivations. There are long-range goals as well as the short-range ones (subgoals) to be defined. We use the plurals because we do not view successful stuttering therapy in terms of fluency alone. Any clinician worth his salt can make any stutterer fluent in five minutes, though the fluency thereby produced might not last much longer than another five minutes. Adult stutterers have many other facets to their problem, and all of them require consideration and planning if we desire to have more than temporary fluency. We need to change the stutterer as well as his speech.

The specification of target goals is so vital that we have come to believe that almost every therapy session should include some reference to goals directly or indirectly. Stutterers are persons, not pigeons. They were not hatched from laboratory eggs. Their history of reinforcement is tremendously complex. People are goal-seeking animals, and they work harder when they have goals they believe they can attain. At the same time, we must realize that most adult stutterers have suffered many defeats daily over the course of years. Accordingly, many of them covertly or overtly resist goal-structuring of any kind. How this resistance is handled by the clinician is of the utmost importance. We must understand that hope makes us vulnerable to the hurt of failure. Many stutterers have become afraid to hope. Yet we have found that in the depths of the saddest stutterer there reside some embers of hope that only need the breath of the therapist's faith and expectation to begin to glow. How do we show that faith? How often? At what times? All clinicians have their own ways of conveying their belief that the treatment will be successful. And all stutterers have their own ways of armoring themselves against that belief. They will test and retest, always probing the validity of the clinicians' faith. Much of the clinicians' skill can be measured by how they cope with this probing and the other defenses erected by the stutterers.

In replaying audiotapes and videotapes of my own therapy sessions, I have found the answers to the following questions to be illuminating: (1) How did I structure the goals of this particular therapy session and show their pertinence to the final goals of therapy? (2) How well were both the long- and short-range goals defined? (3) How and why did the stutterer respond to the goal-setting? (4) How else might I have accomplished the same ends? (5) How clearly does he perceive my expectancies with respect to eventual goal achievement? (6) What, at the present time, are his expectations? How clearly does he visualize the final target goals? (7) How is he defending himself against hope? (8) How should I cope with these defenses? (9) What have I done to help him discern the *route* that must be taken to attain those final goals? How clearly does he see the map of the territory that must be traversed? And does he know where he is *now*? (10) Is his concept of goal distance realistic? If not, what can I do to help him regard it objectively—and without discouraging him? (11) Is he convinced that I am a competent guide for such a journey?

Goal-setting poses many problems, not the least of which is the consideration of the possibility of achievement. The realistic appraisal of the probabilities that the stutterer will succeed in a certain task should be the joint concern of both the clinician and the stutterer. We have found that, in general, it is unwise to impose the goal upon the stutterer without having him participate in the decision process and, if possible, in the formulation of the therapeutic activity. Often, the clinician must explain the purposes to be served by the task and the manner in which it can be carried out; but the criteria of success versus failure need mutual discussion. Since the prediction of success versus failure involves the estimation of probabilities, the views of the stutterer certainly have some importance.

Most clinicians learn that things work out better if goal-setting is structured in terms of maximum and minimum goals. The maximum goal should tax the stutterer's resources and strength to the limit and yet be possible of attainment, while the minimum goal should almost certainly be expected to be achieved. Goal-setting should usually be done by both the clinician and the client, with the end result being something of a compromise. What is most important in this procedure is that it immediately involves stutterers in confronting themselves, in taking an active part in therapy, in commitment. It provides an opportunity for clinicians to check their expectancies against those of the stutterers so that more congruence can be obtained. It makes therapy a mutual process rather than one administered by clinicians and experienced by their captive guinea pigs. In the give-and-take of assessing aspiration and performance levels and probabilities of achievement, many of the important interpersonal conflicts between clinician and client will become obvious enough to be resolved. A good amount of psychotherapy often takes place in these encounters.

Finally, by participating in the decision process, stutterers make a commitment and this often makes all the difference in determining whether they will or will not be successful. There are, however, certain clients with whom, and certain times with any client when, goal-setting in terms of maxima and minima is unnecessary or unwise. Sometimes the task is simply one in which stutterers explore a new technique or undergo a new experience or test their ability to operate adaptively under stress. There are also times when it is even good for the stutterer to fail because it is possible to learn much from one's failures, and all of us must learn how to fall forward. We should recognize, too, that there are some clients, especially at the beginning of therapy, who are unready for the responsibility of decision. But if we can structure our goals so that stutterers will exceed their minimum subgoals, even if they cannot achieve their maximum subgoals, they will make faster progress. Also, we recognize that there are some therapists who cannot operate in this way and yet are very successful, especially with stutterers having strong dependency needs and when a strong transference has taken place.

In the light of these remarks you will understand why, when I review one of my therapy sessions, I ask myself these questions: (1) Who really set the goals for the tasks? (2) Were they stated in terms of maximum and minimum achievements? (3) Were either of the latter unrealistic and, if so, why? (4) What difficulties were encountered in setting up the goals and why did they occur? (5) What have I learned about the stutterer as the result of this goal-setting?

The clinician's use of reinforcement and punishment

One of the hallmarks of successful clinicians is their ability to handle reinforcement. Though they have done much to understand its importance, the Law of Effect was not first discovered by the operant conditioners. Clinicians and therapists of all disciplines have long known that to be effective, they must identify the behaviors, overt or covert, that are to be weakened and decreased and those other behaviors which are to be strengthened and increased. All of us use positive reinforcement and reward in one form or another. All of us employ at times the powerful force inherent in the escape from unpleasantness (negative reinforcement) to shape the behaviors of our clients. And all of us, whether we know it or not, have used punishment. We know the importance of contingencies. We realize that the consistent use of reinforcement is very helpful in the early stages of creating a desired response, but that later on in therapy it should be administered intermittently if we hope to prevent satiation or rapid extinction. We know that our clients will not always be in the therapy room or subject to our controls. Therefore, we seek to build self-reinforcement.

Experienced clinicians also know that if their approvals are to have any reinforcing value, they must create a relationship that is valuable to the clients, that somehow they must earn and deserve that approval value. Moreover, they rarely rely on verbal approvals and disapprovals alone. They study their clients to ascertain their deprivations, hungers, and needs; then the clinicians find ways of relieving and gratifying those that can be used as reinforcing consequences. Experienced clinicians are always alert to the possibility of satiation, shifting from one form of reinforcement to another when signs of this satiation appear. They are conservative in their dosages of that reinforcement for the same

reasons, making the punishments fit the crimes and designing consequences appropriate to the amount of achievement. They learn to reinforce change in the desired direction, to reward progress as well as goal
attainment. At times they withold reinforcement so that new behaviors
can be created and, in turn, be reinforced. They find ways of combining
several reinforcers to create greater impact. They program positive reinforcement for a desired response in combination with mild punishment
for an undesired, but competing, response to obtain counterconditioning.
They are careful about their disapprovals and punishments. They know
that strong punishment rarely weakens a response, even though it temporarily suppresses or represses it. They may use punishment at times
as a jolting stimulus or to suppress an old response long enough to
permit replacement by a more desirable one. More often, they use mild
and even humorous penalties as alerting devices, as methods for confrontation and identification of behaviors.

Finally, experienced clinicians measure the value of a given reinforcement by its effects. They do not assume that the "reward" they administer
is really reward until they discern that the behavior for which it was
the consequence has indeed increased in frequency or strength. They
know, for example, that praise for some clients can be punishing and
that others hunger to be punished. They know that the proof is in
the pudding, not in the recipe, that all assumptions concerning reinforcement must be tested before their effects can be predicted. Few of us
who must work long hours in the vineyard daily will be willing to
undergo the laboratory labor of interminable counting, baselining, or
graphing so enthusiastically recommended by the operant-conditioning
people; but most of us make comparable assessments with reasonable
accuracy.

In reviewing my own tapes of therapy sessions, I have found it extremely valuable to scan them in terms of these reinforcement strategies.
In doing so I have discovered many clinical mistakes and misjudgments,
many more than I had anticipated. And I continue to make these mistakes—though not as many as before I underwent the confrontation—and
I feel I have improved my competence as a therapist. To satisfy my
own hunger to improve myself, and also to aid me in supervising student
clinicians, I compiled a set of guideline questions that seem to have
some value. Here they are:

(1) What behaviors (or what verbal statements) did I try to reinforce positively? (2) Were there some of these that I should have reinforced and didn't? (3) Was the client aware of the contingency? Did
he know why he was rewarded? (4) What kinds of positive or negative
reinforcement did I use? Which appeared to be most effective? Least
effective? What are the possible reasons for the difference? (5) In terms

of his needs and drives and deprivations as I know them, what other kinds of reinforcers could I use in the future? (6) Did I handle the contingencies effectively? What sort of scheduling did I use? How soon were the consequences delivered? Did I reinforce for change or progress? (7) For what behaviors or verbal statements did I show disapproval or did I punish in some way? Did I withold positive reinforcement when I should have provided it? Did the witholding of positive reinforcement act as a punisher? For example, did it reduce the frequency or strength of the behavior being emitted? (8) Were the disapprovals or punishments ever noncontingent? In my eyes? In those of the client perhaps? (9) How did he react to the punishment or disapproval and how did I react to his reaction? Did he feel that *he* rather than the specified behavior was being punished? (10) With this client, does mild punishment have any effectiveness as an alerter? (11) What other punishers might be appropriately used in the future and under what conditions? (12) Does he have some hidden need to be punished? For that matter, do I?[3]

The Clinician's Language

Anyone who works professionally with stutterers has only one real tool he can use—his language. There are, of course, the audiotape and videotape recorders, the delayed auditory feedback (DAF) apparatus, the metronome, or perhaps a packet of M & M's, but even these are useful adjuncts only when they become activated by a speaking clinician. Our "Medication" is the spoken word. It would be well, therefore, to examine the language of clinicians as they do their work.

Wendell Johnson (1961) and others of the so-called Iowa school of stutterer's clinicians did much to make the members of our profession highly aware of the importance of the language factor as it relates to stuttering. They described the onset of the disorder and its maintenance as being due to semantic distortions, not only on the part of stutterer but also in the speech and language of those who sought to help them. They insisted that the main thrust of treatment should be toward the revision of this language. This well-known quotation from Williams (1957) is illustrative:

> The person who we say "stutters" demonstrates a similar point of view when he begins talking about "my stuttering." To him, it represents

---

[3] For an expanded discussion of the role of the clinician in motivation, see chap. 9 in C. Van Riper, 1971.

something that just happens because he is a "stutterer." He reports that when he gets a particular feeling in his stomach or in his chest this is a sign that "it is about to happen." Therefore, his attempt to talk is combined with an attempt either to "hold the stuttering back" or to "get the words out without the stuttering coming out too." In his sense, his stuttering is an entity, an animistic "thing" that lies inside him. This is fundamentally a belief in magic. He talks and acts as though he believes either that there exists a little man inside him eager to grab certain words, or that certain words are possessed of physical properties such that they get "stuck" in his throat. "When I talk, I try to hide 'it'!" I "feel like 'it' is going to happen." " 'It' stops me from talking." These statements, and more, are quite common in the clinical situation. The word "it" has been placed within quotations because of its frequent use as a referent to nothing more than an undefinable "thing" inside him. As long as one functions as though an "it" makes things happen, he is not motivated to observe cause and effect relationships in his behavior, for "it" is both cause and effect. (p. 391)

But Williams (1957) also points out that the clinician also falls into the same erroneous way of thinking and talking about stuttering:

It should be pointed out that not only the so-called "stutterer," but oftentimes the therapist operates with the kind of orientation described above. It is obvious that when a therapist begins working with a person who stutters, he trains that person to think the way he, the therapist, thinks. That is, he tries (consciously or unconsciously), in some degree, to train the speaker to approach his problem in the way in which he, the therapist, approaches it, to use the language he uses, and to make the assumptions he makes. (p. 393)

As might be expected, the basic method of semantically oriented clinicians is therefore a probing and modeling approach with an emphasis on questioning. In another article describing some of his successful therapy with a stutterer, Williams (1968) writes:

I adopted the role of a person who would attempt to help him become the kind of person who could solve his own problems. We began by taking some of his problems other than speech and began to discuss how one adopts or one begins to employ a problem-solving approach to problems. This included such things as (1) the difference between describing and evaluating, (2) trying to find the "right" solutions to problems versus attempting to first clearly define the questions, then (3) thinking of all the different alternatives that one has; then thinking of the consequences of each; and then arriving at the best solution—with a willingness to pay the consequences for that decision. This involved a discussion of what is meant by a question. That is, the kinds of questions that could never be answered versus the kinds of questions that could be answered by discussion, reading, and experimentation.

Finally, we discussed within the problem-solving attitude the necessity of acting upon obtained information as opposed to an intellectual "game playing" with the information obtained.

The clinician adopted a role of helping him define the questions. To help him learn the difference between a meaningful question and a "nonsense" question, he helped him define the different alternatives and then discussed with him the possible consequences. This was followed then by adopting a role of providing emotional support for him as he cautiously adopted one course of action in relation to a problem and fearfully proceeded on it. Perhaps emphasized more than anything else was a role of asking the client questions, the most important of which was, how can you find out? Do you need to read some and obtain information, do you need to discuss it with me, or can you go out and experiment by behaving in different ways and observing the consequences? (p. 126)

We hasten to say that the preceding discussion has been presented only to illustrate the point that clinicians should know how they talk while doing stuttering therapy. It is not a confession of our belated conversion to the semantic view of the nature of stuttering and its treatment. Though we recognize the real contribution the semanticists have made, we fear we'll never be able to join Korzybski, the "father" of the school of general semantics.

But we do feel that all clinicians should be aware of the kind of talking they do with their clients. In order to improve our own skills, we have recorded many therapy sessions with the tape recorder and through the use of videotapes, and we have done the same thing with the students we have supervised in their work with stutterers. The confrontation is always very revealing, even though we have often winced to have to see and hear our errors. We found, however, that merely listening to these recordings was not sufficient. We needed to analyze them in terms of certain categories of utterance. Those that we have found most useful are the following: (1) The total time spent by the clinician and the stutterer in talking—and the ratio between these times. (2) The number of utterances exceeding three consecutive sentences. (3) The number of self-references made by the clinician. (How many perpendicular pronouns or "I"'s were used, etc.) (4) The number of questions asked by the clinician or the stutterer and the ratio between them. (5) The times that the clinician made other demands (requests, directions). (6) How often the clinician reflected the feelings being expressed by the stutterer. (7) The number of times the clinician's utterance showed approval or disapproval and the ratio between them. (8) The number of times the clinician interrupted the stutterer. We also checked other categories, but these eight seemed to be most correlated with our overall impression of the adequacy of the therapy session.

In addition to this survey of the utterances involved in the interaction, we also scrutinized features that were harder to measure objectively but which we felt provided valuable information. These were: (1) The appropriateness of the clinician's voice quality and inflections. (2) His rate of speaking. (3) The number of times the interpersonal distance seemed inappropriate (physically withdrawing from the client, etc.). (4) A rating of the mobility of the clinician and client (e.g., how fixated or stiff were their postures?). (5) The ratio between smiles and frowns. (6) The number of mirrorings shown by the clinician (e.g., when the stutterer smiles, the clinician does too, etc.). We also counted the number of verbal or nonverbal tics ("What I mean is . . ." "My point is . . ." or clearings of the throat, head scratching, sniffing, or the shaking of a finger). Sometimes the confrontation of one's behavior on videotape is almost appalling, but it certainly helps one change.

Some comments on our own experiences in this self-scrutiny may be of interest. To investigate the total talking time, we simply used a stopwatch in each hand while viewing the replay. We found, generally, that the more the ratio favored the client, the more often we had previously rated the session as an effective one. Much, however, depended on the activities being performed and the interaction desired. For example, there were times when we needed to clarify the nature of the rationale of an experience we hoped the stutterer would explore, and then it seemed appropriate that we should have done most of the talking. Nevertheless, even at these times, there was often too much redundancy; so we learned to be more succinct. Moreover, it became clear that when we dominated the interaction too long at a stretch, we tended to be less concerned with the stutterer than we should have been. He usually responded to these minimonologues perfunctorily if at all. After one of them, his response would be reciprocally abbreviated. Rarely would he respond to one of our multiple-sentence utterances with a long one of his own, and what he did say then usually had little real significance. As a result of this scanning, whenever we find ourselves saying four or five sentences in a row, invisible warning lights appear and we know we've got to be careful. Another similar warning signal we've come to recognize occurs when the stutterer responds with brief, even one-word, sentences or merely grunts.

We have also come to recognize the significance of too much self-reference on the part of the clinician. It is an open trap for any clinician, and the beginning clinician's speech is peppered with "I's" and "me's." Over and over again, our previous estimate of a therapy session's success was shown to be negatively correlated with the number of these self-references.

It is also a sobering experience to have to count how many times we make demands on our clients. Even when reasonable, their number seems exorbitant. Demands come in many forms besides the obvious ones of command or request, and sometimes they are couched in subtle ways; but always one could hear the inflection of demand in the clinician's voice. Until we heard the replay, we have often had the impression we were highly permissive and accepting when actually we were not. This does not mean, of course, that such demand speech is always inappropriate. We are not doing the client-centered kind of Rogerian psychotherapy (Rogers, 1951). We are working with stutterers on a lot of behaviors that need modification, and some direction is inescapable in an activity-oriented therapy. Yet far too many clinicians of stutterers make far too many demands and do not know they do. In this connection, we should recognize that every question (except the rhetorical kind) is itself a demand and will be felt by the client as such. As a result of this self-scrutiny, we have learned to hear the upward inflection in our voice as a clear warning signal that cautions us to be sure the demand is really necessary. Most stutterers have had many miserable experiences when being questioned, and that upward inflection is a cue that can trigger a lot of conditioned negative emotion—no matter how good the clinician-client relationship may be. Finally, the opening phrase "I want you to . . ." has come to be, for us, the loudest signal of all. The frequency with which it is emitted by clinicians is incredibly large. We train our own student clinicians to recognize it by having them shout it 50 times in succession whenever it is heard in the replay.

With regard to interruptions, we found a remarkably high positive correlation between the number of times the stutterers would interrupt us and how well the session as a whole seemed to go. In contrast, when we did the interrupting too frequently, the opposite result occurred—which, of course, makes sense. Although our students interrupt often, we fortunately did not seem to do so. Yet, in watching ourselves on videotape, we noticed little behaviors (e.g., averting the eyes) that the stutterer could well have interpreted as a listener loss equivalent to an interruption. Such information is extremely illuminating and valuable to the clinician who seeks to become a better one.

We also became highly aware of the importance of bodily behaviors as punishers or reinforcers. It is fairly easy to evaluate one's verbal utterances as being reinforcing, punishing, or neutral (if we do not use these adjectives in the strict operant sense in terms of their immediate consequences); but the kinesic body language emitted by the clinician may not always be concordant with his statements of approval or disapproval. Often that kinesic language is far more eloquent than the verbal language. Many a little movement or posture has a meaning of its own, a meaning the client often recognizes instantly. We may not know that one of our unconscious little fidgets is telling the stutterer that we are becoming impatient with his performance, but he may know it all too well. Messages coded in body language are hard for the clinician to recognize, much less count or graph; but we should recognize their impact in therapy.

If the objection is raised that such self-scrutiny of their verbal and body language would render clinicians so self-conscious they would lose all spontaneity in their interaction with stutterers, all we can say is that we have not found it so—nor have the students we have trained. As characteristic errors are recognized, they just seem to decrease automatically, gradually, and without conscious correction. But they never totally disappear.

The Clinician's Satisfactions

As we contemplate what we have written about the stutterer's clinician and when we recall the many stutterers we served over the years, we sometimes wonder why any clinician would ever want to work with a stutterer. The therapy can be incredibly demanding; the investment of time and energy seems excessive; one's successes are soon forgotten; one's failures continue to haunt the remote corners of the cranium. And yet we would not have traded this experience for any other. It might be appropriate, therefore, to examine the motives and rewards for doing stuttering therapy.

We suspect there are many motives, often mixed, that lead any of us to enter the general field of speech pathology—curiosity, altruism, perhaps even narcissism. According to Sheehan, Hadley, and Lechleidner (1964), who surveyed a large number of speech pathologists, the "best liked features [of their profession] included the challenging nature of their work, the opportunity to work with people, and the opportunity to help people" (p. 279). Then, too, there are some persons who doubtlessly enter speech pathology in the hope of vicariously solving their own interpersonal communication problems. Those few who find a special attraction in doing stuttering therapy may even be impelled by other motives less laudatory. Indeed, we have known times when we wondered whether our own involvement in helping stutterers stemmed from masochism. In over 40 years we've taken quite a beating from our clients. So we find some comfort in what two psychiatrists, Harrison and Carek (1966), have to say:

> An awareness of the unconscious reasons for wanting to be a therapist need not invalidate the desire to be one. Rather, an increased knowledge

of self that includes unconscious motivations leads to greater choice. . . . Another example can be taken from those dealing with children. Many have been attracted to this field because of their tendency to want to allay their own anxiety by becoming surrogate parents. This desire to identify with the aggressor is most obvious in almost all people who work with children—child psycho-analysts, child psychiatrists, child psychologists, social workers, pediatricians, teachers, pediatric nurses, child care workers, camp counselors. Many of them illustrate this attitude by stating at one time or another that their work would be a "snap" or a "breeze" were it not for the parents. (pp. 16–17)

They should have included stutterers' clinicians.

So let us move away from the unconscious motives that infest our psyches and concentrate instead on our consciously sensed satisfactions. A review of the literature unfortunately reveals more about clinicians' complaints than about their felt rewards. Witness this over 100-year-old wail from Klencke (1862): "Stutterers have certain characteristics which are associated with an inclination towards secrecy, indolence, suspicion, passive opposition to any inconvenience required by the treatment, and a sanguine devotion to anything that points toward and easy and rapid cure." Nevertheless, most of us who have worked with a number of stutterers are able to echo the statement by Murphy and Fitzsimons (1960) that speech therapy with stutterers is exciting, challenging and rewarding.

We have often been frustrated by the stutterers we sought to help, but we have certainly never been bored. The challenge to our competence has demanded that we constantly continue to learn and grow. Each new stutterer presents a different picture, a new puzzle, an intricate patterning of behaviors and emotions that cannot help but fascinate. One almost has to know everything about everything to serve stutterers well. To cite but one example, we once had to steep ourselves in the history, culture, and art of Japan before we were able to make any progress with a stutterer who came to us from that country. We have had to tailor our therapy to a special needs of stutterers who were mentally retarded and to those who were far more intelligent than we were. We have had to cope with the problems of clients who were millionaires as well as those who never had enough to eat. Often, our therapy had to be spread out to include whole families—even a vicious grandmother. We have worked with priests and with murderers in prison. We have lived not one but a thousand lives.

But even the most ordinary stutterer, if there are any, seems to be able to arouse the same consuming interest in us and we think we know why. Often it seems as though stuttering is the dark mirror of man. In his distress we see not just the poor helpless devil before us, but all the anxiety, frustration, and shame that has been the lot of humanity since Eden. Certainly, we find in stuttering the ancient cruelty of man toward man. But as the therapy proceeds, we glimpse also the unfolding power for growth and triumph that man has shown no matter what the obstacles. To be a participant-observer in the struggle of another person who was denied his birthright because he could not talk normally, to see him hold his head high and become able finally to rejoin the verbal human race—this is rewarding beyond measure. Vicariously, the clinician will share that triumph and that sharing is enough since it is the triumph of "becoming," of self-actualization.

The clinician therefore feels no urgent need for gratitude, for the thank-you. Indeed, we often have felt that the gratefulness should have been ours. Often, in seeing a stutterer find himself, we've felt the sort of grateful feeling one has when a flower thrusts itself up through the rocks and then blooms. Though there are plenty of costs in stuttering therapy, some that clinicians find hard to pay at times, surely there is no credit involved. Who can take all the credit for a blooming? Though their impact has assuredly been felt, clinicians know that much of their efforts have been spent in uncovering the potential for self-healing that lies latent in every stutterer. The credit, if any, belongs mainly to the client.

There is also the satisfaction of craftsmanship. The clinician deals with the most complicated stuff on earth—perhaps with God stuff, certainly not with clay. The constant necessity to diagnose with skill, to create conditions and experiences that will help the stutterer progress, to formulate appropriate hypotheses and find ways of testing them—these and a thousand other facets of the therapeutic interaction constitute a craft of the first order. As he becomes more skillful, more sure of his clinical judgments because he finds they have been corroborated, the clinician shares some of the intense satisfactions of the artist.

All these satisfactions should be enough, but there is still another one: the sense of meaningfulness that stuttering therapy gives the clinician. In an age and culture in which tremendous social forces thrust vivid feelings of helplessness and unimportance upon the individual, one hungers for meaningfulness. One rebels against the computer that turns one into a number punched on a card. The material possessions we labor so hard for seem to enslave and to add to the pollution in which we exist. Though accelerated, one's life span—in a era when the characteristics of the furthest galaxies are explored in terms of light years—seems as short as a flicker of flame. At a time when strangers are feared and close relationships are entered into with caution, there is a sense of alienation that is profoundly disturbing. In such a land and in such a time, an awareness of the meaningfulness of one's own existence can be tremendously satisfying.

We at least have been able to attain that particular satisfaction by doing stuttering therapy. Some years ago (Van Riper, 1966) we had the temerity to describe the personal philosophy on which this sense of meaningfulness is based:

> What is the meaning of my existence and function? How can I feel impor-
> tant—a tiny speck in the immensities of time and space? Suppose I have
> helped a thousand of my fellows to have a better life—so what? Am
> I not doomed thereby to the meaninglessness of profound personal failure?
> I do not think so. The two infinities of time and space intersect at point,
> the infinitesimally tiny point at which I stand, but I can and must erect
> a perpendicular at that point, the perpendicular of my impact on others.
> This is my measure! I grin thinking that in a whimsical sense I somehow
> play pool with eternity, bumping this ball so that it bumps that, and
> that bumps that forever. I know my original force will decline inevitably
> as its effects spread but still I will have had my impact and my meaning
> and I know that with each impact new forces are released. That I will
> be anonymous soon does not distress me. Not for me are the illusory
> possessions of property or the fruit-fly's life of fame. I will not be bound
> by time or space. Let me have impact! Only when I do not, do I fail.
> (p. 279)

References

Barbara, D. A. (1954) *Stuttering: A psychodynamic approach to its under-standing and treatment.* New York: Julian.

Barbara, D. A., ed. (1962) *The psychotherapy of stuttering.* Springfield, Ill.: C. C Thomas.

Blackman, N., et al. (1958) The development of empathy in male schizophrenics. *Psychiatric Quarterly,* 32, 546–553.

Bone, H. (1960) Purpose of psychotherapy and preparation. In N. P. Dellis and H. K. Stone, eds., *The training of psychologists.* Baton Rouge, La.: University of Louisiana Press.

Brammer, L. M., and Shostrom, E. L. (1960) *Therapeutic psychology.* Englewood Cliffs, N.J.: Prentice-Hall.

Brody, M. W., and Harrison, S. I. (1954) Group therapy with male stutterers. *International Journal of Psychiatry* 4, 154–162.

Bryngelson, B. (1964) *Personality development through speech: Getting next to yourself.* Minneapolis, Minn.: Denison.

Carkhuff, R. R., and Berenson, B. (1969) The nature, structure and function of counselor commitment to client. *Journal of Rehabilitation,* 36, 13–14.

Colby, K. M., Watt, J. B., and Gilbert, J. P. (1967) A computer program which conducts psychotherapy. In E. R. Hilgard and R. C. Atkinson, eds., *Introduction to Psychology.* New York: Harcourt Brace Jovanovich.

Cooper, E. B. (1965) An inquiry into the use of interpersonal communication as a source for therapy with stutterers. In D. A. Barbara, ed., *New directions in stuttering:* Theory and practice. Springfield, Ill.: C. C Thomas.

Darley, F. L. (1966) *Diagnosis and appraisal of communication disorders.* Englewood Cliffs, N.J.: Prentice-Hall.

Diehl, C. F. (1962) Patient-therapist relationship. In D. A. Barbara, ed., *The Psychotherapy of stuttering.* Springfield, Ill.: C. C Thomas.

Frank, J. D. (1961) *Persuasion and healing.* Baltimore: Johns Hopkins Press.

Freund, H. (1966) *Psychopathology and the problems of stuttering.* Springfield, Ill.: C. C Thomas.

Glauber, I. P. (1958) The psychoanalysis of stuttering. In J. Eisenson, ed., *Stuttering: A symposium.* New York: Harper & Row.

Goldiamond, I. (1965) Stuttering and fluency as manipulable operant response classes. In L. Krasner and L. P. Ullman, eds., *Research in behavior modification: New developments and their clinical applications.* New York: Holt, Rinehart & Winston.

Goldstein, A. P. (1962) *Therapist-patient expectancies in psychotherapy.* New York: Macmillan.

Harrison, S. I., and Carek, D. J. (1966) *Psychotherapy.* Boston: Little, Brown.

Johnson, W. (1961) *Stuttering and what you can do about it.* Minneapolis, Minn.: University of Minnesota Press.

Jourard, S. M. (1964) *The transparent self.* New York: Van Nostrand Reinhold.

Klencke, H. (1862) Die Heilung des Stotterns. Leipsig, Kiel.

Kramer, E. (1970) *A beginning manual for psychotherapists.* New York: Grune & Stratton.

Mandl, H. J. (1964) Interpersonal aspects of the rehabilitation process. In H. J. Mandl, ed., *Psychological aspects of disability and rehabilitation.* Washington, D.C.: U.S. Department of Health, Education, and Welfare.

Menninger, K. (1958) *Theory of psychoanalytic technique.* New York: Basic Books.

Mills, H., and Zytowski, D. G. (1968) Helping relationship: A structural analysis. *Journal of Consulting Psychology,* 37, 710–715.

Mowrer, O. H. (1960) *Learning theory and behavior.* New York: Wiley.

Mulder, R. L. (1961) The student of stuttering as a stutterer. *Journal of Speech and Hearing Disorders,* 26, 178–179.

Murphy, A. T., and Fitzsimons, R. M. (1960) *Stuttering and personality dynamics.* New York: Ronald.

Osgood, C. E., Suci, G., and Tannenbaum, P. (1957) *The measurement of meaning.* Urbana, Ill.: University of Illinois Press.

Robinson, F. B. (1966) *An introduction to stuttering.* Englewood Cliffs, N.J.: Prentice-Hall.

Robinson, F. B. (1968) A clinical failure: Harry. In H. L. Luper, ed., *Stuttering: Successes and failures in therapy.* Memphis, Tenn.: Speech Foundation of America.

Rogers, C. R. (1951) *Client-centered therapy.* Boston: Houghton Mifflin.

Rogers, C. R. (1957) The necessary and sufficient conditions o therapeutic personality change. *Journal of Consulting Psychology,* 21, 95–103.

Rogers, C. R. (1961) *On becoming a person.* Boston: Houghton Mifflin.

Rosenzweig, S. (1936) Some implicit common factors in diverse methods of psychotherapy. *American Journal of Orthopsychiatry,* 6, 410–413.

Rotter, J. B. (1964) *Clinical psychology.* New York: Harper and Row.

Schofield, W. (1964) *Psychotherapy: The purchase of friendship.* Englewood Cliffs, N.J.: Prentice-Hall.

Shames, G. H. (1970) Operant conditioning and therapy for stuttering. In C. W. Strakweather, ed., *Conditioning in stuttering therapy: Applications and limitations.* Memphis: Speech Foundation of America.

Sheehan, J. G. (1954) An integration of psychotherapy and speech therapy through a conflict theory of stuttering. *Journal Speech and Hearing Disorders,* 19, 474–482.

Sheehan, J. G. (1970) *Stuttering: Research and therapy.* New York: Harper & Row.

Sheehan, J. G., Hadley, R. G., and L. Lechleidner (1964) Career satisfaction and recruitment in speech pathology and audiology. *Journal of American Speech and Hearing Association,* 6, 277–283.

Shoben, E. J. (1953) Some observations on psychotherapy and the learning process. In O. H. Mowrer, ed., *Psychotheapy: Theory and research.* New York: Ronald.

Smith, H. C. (1966) *Sensitivity to people.* New York: McGraw-Hill.

Truax, C. B., and Carkhuff, R. R. (1967) *Toward effective counseling and psychotherapy: Training and practice.* Chicago: Aldine.

Van Riper, C. (1966) Success and failure in speech therapy. *Journal of Speech and Hearing Disorders,* 31, 276–279.

Van Riper, C. (1968) A clinical failure: Melinda. In H. L. Luper, ed., *Stuttering: Successes and failures in therapy.* Memphis, Tenn.: Speech Foundation of America.

Van Riper, C. (1971) *The nature of stuttering.* Englewood Cliffs, N.J.: Prentice-Hall.

Van Riper, C. (1973) *The treatment of stuttering.* Englewood Cliffs, N.J.: Prentice-Hall.

West, R. (1958) An agnostic's speculations about stuttering. In J. Eisenson, eds., *Stuttering: A symposium.* Harper & Row.

Williams, D. E. (1957) A point of view about stuttering. *Journal of Speech and Hearing Disorders,* 22, 390–397.

Williams, D. E. (1968) A clinical success: John. In H. L. Luper, ed., *Stuttering: Successes and failures in therapy.* Memphis, Tenn.: Speech Foundation of America.

Williams, J. E. (1962) Acceptance by others and its relationship to acceptance of self and others. *Journal of Abnormal and Social Psychology,* 65, 438–442.

Wingate, M. E. (1971) The fear of stuttering. *Journal of the American Speech and Hearing Association,* 13, 3–5.

Wolpe, J. (1958) *Psychotherapy by reciprocal inhibition.* Stanford, Calif.: Stanford University Press.

Index

Adams, M., 25, 203, 205, 206, 226, 346, 352, 384
Adaptation effect, 19–22, 127, 421–424
Adjacency effect, 8–13
  normal dysfluencies, 54n.
Adjustive responses, 102–103, 125–126, 205–208. *See also* Stuttering, second-ary symptoms
  instrumental conditioning and, 226–234
  modifiability of, 228–233, 240
Alcoholism, 120, 241, 247–248
Andrews, G., 26n., 54, 136, 293, 355, 357, 411, 430–431
Anger
  fluency resulting from, 125, 131–132
  repression of, as a cause of stuttering, 285, 438
Anticipation
  defined, 13, 30–34
  of fluency, 61–62
  physical manifestations, 31, 220–224

of stuttering, 30–34, 219–220. *See also* Anticipatory struggle hypothesis; Prediction ability
Anticipatory struggle hypothesis, 3, 7–10. *See also* Anticipation
  anxiety and, 24–25, 29
  in early stutterers, 57–58
  evidence for, 10–24
  motor plan difficulty and, 21, 33
  normal dysfluencies, 50–51
Anxiety. *See also* Emotional responses; Fear
  anticipatory struggle theory and, 24–25, 29
  autonomic arousal, 25–26, 29, 31
  Freud's definition, 133
  momentary fear vs., 128–129
  operational definitions, 25–29
  parental, 44–45, 59–60
  performance, effect on, 130
  potential, and conflict theory, 115

493